FILM
AN INTRODUCTION

FILM

AN INTRODUCTION

William H. Phillips

University of Wisconsin—Eau Claire

BEDFORD/ST. MARTIN'S   Boston ◆ New York

FOR BEDFORD/ST. MARTIN'S
Developmental Editor: Jane Betz
Production Editor: Bridget Leahy
Associate Editor: Maura Shea
Production Supervisor: Catherine Hetmansky
Marketing Manager: Charles Cavaliere
Production Assistant: Arthur Johnson
Copyeditor: Barbara G. Flanagan
Indexer: Steve Csipke
Text Design: Wanda Kossak
Cover Design: Donna Lee Dennison
Cover Art: (Front cover, left to right) *Like Water for Chocolate*, Miramax Films/Shooting Star; *Do the Right Thing*, Photofest; *The Truman Show*, Paramount Pictures/Shooting Star; (back cover, left to right) *The Cabinet of Dr. Caligari*, Photofest; *Fast, Cheap & Out of Control*, Fourth Floor Productions; *The Seven Samurai*, Photofest
Composition and Layout: DeNee Reiton Skipper
Printing and Binding: R. R. Donnelley and Sons

President: Charles H. Christensen
Editorial Director: Joan E. Feinberg
Director of Editing, Design, and Production: Marcia Cohen
Managing Editor: Elizabeth M. Schaaf
Executive Editor: Karen S. Henry

Library of Congress Catalog Card Number: 98–87541

Manufactured in the United States of America.

3 2 1 0 9
f e d c

For information, write: Bedford/St. Martin's, 75 Arlington Street, Boston, MA 02116 (617-426-7440)

ISBN: 0–312–17818–2

ACKNOWLEDGMENTS
Brown, Royal S. "Film Composers Talk about Their Work" from *Overtones and Undertones: Reading Film Music*, by Royal S. Brown. Reprinted by permission of University of California Press.
Glassman, Arnold, Todd McCarthy, and Stuart Samuels. "Observations about Cinematography in the Documentary Film *Visions of Light* (1992)." Reprinted by permission of the American Film Institute.

Acknowledgments and copyrights are continued at the back of the book on page 583, which constitutes an extension of the copyright page. For additional acknowledgments, see individual captions.

Preface

IN TEACHING INTRODUCTORY COLLEGE FILM courses since the 1970s, I have developed extensive materials to supplement existing college texts and to substitute for parts of them. The culmination of more than twenty years of research, experimentation in teaching, and writing is the book before you. *Film: An Introduction* aims to achieve a middle ground between film texts that are not very challenging for today's introductory students and texts that are too advanced. I wrote this book in the hope that its readers will better understand and appreciate individual films and gain a fuller understanding of the film medium's variety, achievements, and possibilities.

THE BOOK'S STRUCTURE   Part One of *Film* considers many of the techniques used in making a film and the consequences for viewers of the filmmakers' choices. The second and third parts of the book are more theoretical. Part Two considers the sources, kinds, and characteristics of the main types of films—fictional, documentary, and avant-garde. Part Three examines how viewers respond to a film: how they can better understand a film when they consider its contexts, how viewers formulate meanings, and how the book's concepts can be used to understand and appreciate any film. Many instructors should find that the arrangement of chapters reflects the order of the topics they cover in class, and these instructors will assign chapters or parts of them in order. Others might want to read or teach the book's chapters in a different order. I have made the book flexible to fit the different ways introductory material can be approached. In fact, the chapters can be read in any order because each is largely self-sufficient.

USEFUL APPENDICES   The book concludes with four appendices that offer some of its most distinctive features. (1) "Studying Films" includes a concise discussion of writing strategies; advice on improving reading comprehension; exercises for examining films; questions for thought, discussion, and writing; and an annotated list of film resources available in print, on videodisc, on CD-ROM, in database, and on the World Wide Web. (2) "A Chronology: Film in Context (1895–1998)" is a four-column chronology that places key films in their historical, artistic, and technological contexts. The chronology is also a place for students to find a date, check a spelling, and, I hope, be enticed into reading histories. (Other uses of the chronology are explained in its introduction.) (3) "How to Read Film Credits" reprints the end credits from *The Player* and explains what they mean. This feature encourages students to examine a film's credits and helps them appreciate the work and creativity involved in making a film. (4) The illustrated glossary defines terms used in the text, gives examples, and refers students to the in-text discussion. Photographs illustrate some of the terms defined. Students can use this glossary as a reference long after the course is over.

CAREFUL ATTENTION TO FILM LANGUAGE   In addition to providing the illustrated glossary, *Film: An Introduction* goes to great lengths to help students learn the terms and concepts essential to a critical understanding of film. Key terms for each chapter are defined in the text, so students never have to consult the glossary to understand a concept that is crucial to the chapter's topic. Additional film terms that students might not know are glossed in the margins, so students are not tempted to interrupt their reading to flip to the glossary. These marginal glosses also reinforce key concepts from other chapters and allow instructors to assign chapters in any sequence.

A BROAD RANGE OF FILMS   The book discusses films that students know (right up to the movies of 1998) and films that instructors believe students should know (including European and third world films, historical films, documentaries, avant-garde films, and short films). While a wide variety of films are cited in the text to illustrate aspects of the film medium, the primary focus is on the fictional films most often seen either in theaters or on video because most beginning film students will more likely be drawn into the study of film if they begin with something familiar and enjoyable. Then too, in our video age, if readers so like, they can check many of the clips cited for themselves. Films cited in the text were also drawn from a list of films that instructors who responded to a Bedford/St. Martin's questionnaire indicated they use most often in introductory film courses.

EXTENSIVE ART PROGRAM   The book's photographs consist of frame enlargements, publicity stills, and a few photographs of models. Both publicity stills and frame enlargements have advantages and disadvantages. Publicity stills are usually clear and readily available, but they are rarely a photograph of a frame from the film (Figure 2.17 on p. 84 illustrates how different a frame enlargement may be from a publicity still of the same scene). Publicity stills may even be photographs of material that doesn't appear in the finished film. Then, too, publicity stills may be cropped (as in Figure 1.39 on p. 45), so that we cannot see the intended setting and composition of the image. For color films, the colors are often unlike those of the projected film (too dark, too much contrast, or too saturated, for example).

Frame enlargements may be extremely useful for discussing mise en scène, cinematography, editing, and other aspects of a film. (The frame enlargements are uncropped and in the same aspect ratio in which the frames appear on the film prints to which I had access.) However, they too have drawbacks: they often lack the luster of a film in good condition projected correctly. Frame enlargements are difficult to acquire and are very time-consuming and costly to make. At times, only a 16 mm print is available from which to make the enlargement, and the enlarged frame lacks the clarity and detail of the projected film. (The increased availability of laser discs and DVDs and certain computer cards make it possible to copy frames, but the process distorts resolution and color.) Still, in spite of their limitations, frame enlargements are the best way to capture what is going on in a particular shot.

Throughout the book, short films (those less than sixty minutes long) are set off by quotation marks, feature films (sixty or more minutes) by italics.

ABUNDANT EDITORIAL APPARATUS   This book was designed as a teaching tool, to help students learn, study, write, and answer their own questions when their instructor cannot be with them. Chapter summaries highlight each chapter's key concepts. Sidebars—a unique feature of the text—include interviews with filmmakers, detailed analyses of particular aspects of a film (such as the use of sound in the shower scene of *Psycho*), and examples of student writing that provide models for students. Annotated lists at the end of each chapter include a wide variety of useful sources for undergraduates to consult for more information or for research projects.

INSTRUCTOR'S MANUAL   The Instructor's Manual includes suggested teaching strategies, test questions to accompany each chapter, a sample syllabus, sample essay and other assignments, a section written expressly for teachers on how to help students write more effectively about film, information on how to locate many of the major film clips discussed in the chapters, and useful sources for film teachers: film and video distributors, books, and articles. The test questions to accompany each chapter are also available on a computer disk. The Web site for this book includes supplementary material, updates, e-mail access to the author, and many links to useful film sites.

Acknowledgments

The following libraries and archives have aided me in my research: McIntyre Library, University of Wisconsin–Eau Claire; Library, California State University, Stanislaus; Pacific Film Archive, Berkeley; Library and Film Center,

Museum of Modern Art; and Motion Pictures, Broadcasting, and Recorded Sound Division, U.S. Library of Congress. The following film distributors have also cooperated: Anthology Film Archives, California Newsreel, Canyon Cinema, Chicago Filmmakers, Creative Thinking International, Film-makers' Cooperative, Flower Films, International Film Bureau, Kino International, Michael Wiese Productions, National Film Board of Canada, New Line Productions, New Video Group, and Pyramid Film and Video.

REVIEWERS   Over the many years as I wrote and rewrote this book, I consulted scores of professional filmmakers and film scholars about the accuracy and clarity of various sections of the book. The following people, generous professionals all, gave of their precious allotment of time and gave feedback appropriate for my introductory audience: Les Blank, Flower Films, El Cerrito, California; Rose Bond, Gaea Graphics, Portland, Oregon; Stan Brakhage, University of Colorado, Boulder; Jim Gardner, Sound One, New York; Cecelia Hall, executive sound director, Paramount Pictures; Michael B. Hoggan, past president, American Cinema Editors and now adjunct professor of filmmaking at University of Southern California and California State University, Northridge; Ken Jacobs, Independent Filmmakers, New York; George Kuchar, independent filmmaker, San Francisco, California; Tak Miyagishima, Panavision International, L.P.; Errol Morris, Fourth Floor Productions, Cambridge, Massachusetts; J. J. Murphy, University of Wisconsin, Madison; Robert Orlando, Coppola Pictures, New York; Lee Parker, Daedalus Corporation, Turlock, California; Colin Pringle, Solid State Logic, Oxford, England; Ferenc Rofusz, RF Fly Films, Inc., Oakville, Ontario; Jeff Wall, University of British Columbia; and technical representatives of the Imax Corporation, Toronto. These professional filmmakers supplied information or photographs (or both) or corrections, suggestions, and encouragement about different sections of the manuscript.

Many people have read the entire manuscript or parts of it and made helpful suggestions and corrections: Bob Baron, Mesa Community College; Frank Beaver, University of Michigan; Peter Bondanella, Indiana University; Christine Catanzarite, Illinois State University; Jeffrey Chown, Northern Illinois State University; Marshall Deutelbaum, Purdue University; Carol Dole, Ursinus College; Charles Eidsvik, University of Georgia; Jack Ellis, Northwestern University; Douglas Gomery, University of Maryland; Charles Harpole, University of Central Florida; Ken Harrow, Michigan State University; William H. Hayes, professor emeritus of philosophy, California State University, Stanislaus; Ron Heiss, Spokane Community College; Tim Hirsch, University of Wisconsin–Eau Claire; Deborah Holdstein, Governors State University; Barbara Klinger, Indiana University; Ira Konigsberg, University of Michigan; Don Kunz, University of Rhode Island; Bret E. Lampman, a former student of mine; Karen Mann, Western Illinois University; Mike McBrine, Amherst College; Scott MacDonald, Utica College;

Dale Melgaard, University of Nevada, Las Vegas, and a former student of mine; Avis Meyer, St. Louis University; Wayne Miller, Franklin University; James Naremore, Indiana University; Kevin O'Brien, University of Nevada, Las Vegas; Samuel Oppenheim, California State University, Stanislaus; August Rubrecht, University of Wisconsin–Eau Claire; Eva L. Santos-Phillips, University of Wisconsin–Eau Claire; Paul Scherer, Indiana University, South Bend; Carol Schrepfer, Waubonsee Community College; John Schultheiss, California State University, Northridge; John W. Spalding, Wayne State University; Terry Steiner, Spokane Falls Community College; Kristin Thompson, University of Wisconsin–Madison; Frank Tomasulo, Georgia State University; Tricia Welsch, Bowdoin College; and Vicki Whitaker, a former student of mine.

QUESTIONNAIRE RESPONDENTS   The following instructors of an introduction to film course responded to a Bedford/St. Martin's questionnaire, sharing strategies for teaching the course and their requirements in a textbook: Richard Abel, Drake University; Marilyn K. Ackerman, Foothill College; Dr. Robert Adubato, Essex County College; William A. Allman, Baldwin-Wallace College; Ann Alter, Humboldt State University; Bob Alto, University of San Francisco; Victoria Amador, Western New Mexico University; Lauri Anderson, Suomi College; Robert Arnett, Mississippi State University; Bob Arnold, University of Toledo; Paul Arthur, Montclair State University; Dr. Maureen Asten, Worcester State College; Ray Barcia, Goucher College; Dr. Bob Baron, Mesa Community College; Karen Becker, Richland Community College; Edward I. Benintende, County College of Morris; John Bernstein, Macalester College; Robin Blaetz, Emory University; James Bozan, University of Missouri, Rolla; Bruce C. Browne, University of Wisconsin, Sheboygan; Carolyn R. Bruder, University of Southwestern Louisiana; Lawrence Budner, Rhode Island College; Ken Burke, Mills College; George Butte, Colorado College; Jim Carmody, University of California, San Diego; Ray Carney, Boston University; Harold Case, Allan Hancock College; Lisa Cartwright, University of Rochester; Dr. Christine J. Catanzarite, Illinois State University; Rick Chapman, Des Moines Area Community College; Rick Clemons, Western Illinois University; Lois Cole, Mt. San Antonio College; David Crosby, Alcorn State University; Rita Csapó Sweete, University of Missouri–St. Louis; Ramona Curry, University of Illinois; Joan Dagle, Rhode Island College; Dr. Kathryn D'Alessandro, Jersey City State College; Mary Jayne Davis, Salt Lake Community College; Margarita De la Vega-Hurtado, University of Michigan, Ann Arbor; Larry R. Dennis, Clarion University; Carol M. Dole, Ursinus College; Gus Edwards, Arizona State University; John Ernst, Heartland College; Thomas L. Erskine, Salisbury State University; Jim Everett, Mississippi College; Patty Felkner, Cosumnes River College; Peter Feng, University of Delaware; Jody Flynn, Owensboro Community College; Mike Frank, Bentley College; Arthur M.

Fried, Plymouth State College; Don Fredericksen, Cornell University; Keya Ganguly, Carnegie Mellon University; Dr. Joseph E. Gelsi, Central Methodist College; Jerry Girton, Riverland Community College; Joseph A. Gomez, North Carolina State University; John M. Gourlie, Quinnipiac College; William J. Hagerty, Xavier University; Mickey Hall, Volunteer State Community College; James Hallemann, Oakland Community College; Ken Harrow, Michigan State University; Rolland L. Heiss, Spokane Community College; Thomas Hemmetier, Beaver College; Bruce Hinricks, Century College; Tim Hirsch, University of Wisconsin–Eau Claire; Allan Hirsch, Central Connecticut State University; Rosemary Horowitz, Appalachian State University; Sandra Hybels, Lock Haven University; Frank E. Jackson, Lander University; Susan Jhirad, North Shore Community College; Kimberlie A. Johnson, Seminole Community College; Edward T. Jones, York College of Pennsylvania; Leandro Katz, William Paterson College; Thomas K. Kegel, Oakland Community College; Harry Keyishian, Fairleigh Dickinson University; Les Keyser, College of Staten Island; Helmut Kremling, Ohio Wesleyan University; Al LaValley, Dartmouth College; Don S. Lawson, Lander University; Carol S. Layne, Jefferson Community College; Paul Lazarus, University of Miami; Peter Lev, Towson State University; Susan E. Linville, University of Colorado, Denver; Dr. Cathleen Londino, Keans College of New Jersey; Frances Lozano, Gavilan College; Jean D. Lynch, Villanova University; Karen B. Mann, Western Illinois University; Walter McCallum, Santa Rosa Junior College; James McGonigle, Madison Area Technical College; Marilyn Middendorf, Embry Riddle Aeronautical University; Joseph Milicia, University of Wisconsin, Sheboygan; Mark S. Miller, Pikes Peak Community College; Mary Alice Molgard, College of Saint Rose; James Morrison, North Carolina State University; Charles Musser, Yale University; Barry H. Novick, College of New Jersey; Kevin O'Brien, University of Nevada, Las Vegas; Jan Ostrow, College of the Redwoods; Richard Peacock, Palomar College; Richard Pearce, Wheaton College; Ruth Perlmutter, University of the Arts; David Popowski, Mankato State University; Joyce Porter, Moraine Valley Community College; Maria Pramaggiore, North Carolina State University; Cynthia Prochaska, Mt. San Antonio College; Leonard Quart, College of Staten Island; Clay Randolph, Oklahoma City Community College; Maurice Rapf, Dartmouth College; Jere Real, Lynchburg College; Gary Reynolds, Minneapolis Community & Technical College; David Robinson, Winona State University; James Rupport, University of Alaska, Fairbanks; Jaime Sanchez, Volunteer State Community College; Kristine Samuelson, Stanford University; Richard Schwartz, Florida International University; Richard Sears, Berea College; Eli Segal, Governors State University; Dr. Rick Shale, Youngstown State University; Craig Shurtleff, Illinois Central College; Charles L. P. Silev, Iowa State University; Joseph Evans Slate, University of Texas, Austin; Thomas J. Slater, Indiana University of Pennsylvania; Claude Smith, Florida

Community College at Jacksonville; Terry J. Steiner, Spokane Falls Community College; Kevin M. Stemmler, Clarion University; Ellen Strain, Georgia Institute of Technology; Judith A. Switzer, Bucks County Community College; Julie Tharp, University of Wisconsin, Marshfield; John Tibbetts, University of Kansas; Marie Travis, George Washington University; Robert Vales, Gannon University; Jonathan Walters, Norwich University; Shujen Wang, Westfield State College; Dr. Rosanne Wasserman, U.S. Merchant Marine Academy; J. R. Welsch, Western Illinois University; Tricia Welsch, Bowdoin College; Bernard Welt, the Corcoran School of Art; Robert D. West, Kent State University; Mary Beth Wilk, Des Moines Area Community College; Gerald C. Wood, Carson-Newman College.

To Chapter 11, Vicki Whitaker—one of my former students and now a teacher for the Farmington, New Mexico, schools—contributed considerable enthusiasm, humor, style, information, and insights.

Dennis DeNitto (professor of cinema, City College of New York) provided advice and encouragement and generously made available the following frame enlargements: 1.47, 1.58, 2.46, 2.51, 2.53 a, 3.11, 3.20, 3.24, 4.4, 6.3, 6.15, 6.27, 6.29, and 9.9. He has been a valued source.

The two photographs of Rey Phillips in Chapter 2 were taken by Noble Dinse. All other photographs of models in Chapter 2 were taken by Jon Michael Terry of Jon Michael Terry Photography, Turlock, California. Prints for most of the frame enlargements were done by Steve Allingham, Chris Melville, Kim Hyde, and Mindy Nyseth at the Snap Shot, Eau Claire, Wisconsin. At the Museum of Modern Art/Film Stills Archive, Terry Geesken again helped me secure many photographs used in the book. Alice Donham of Corpus Christi, Texas, generously gave of her time to gather information on the history of what is now called Corpus Christi Beach and of what was always called the Beach Theatre, and author Bill Walraven, also of Corpus Christi, graciously made available a negative of the theater.

Finally, I want to thank the many dedicated, hardworking people at Bedford/St. Martin's. It has been my good fortune to work with a publisher dedicated to quality, not quantity. First and foremost, I wish to thank my editor Jane Betz, early and continued champion of the book and a tireless worker in its behalf. Her advice on ways to make the book clearer and more useful for its intended audience has been uncommonly sound. Associate editor Maura Shea cheerfully, promptly, and expertly helped in a variety of tasks too numerous to list. J. Greenberg provided research assistance, Becky Anderson cleared permissions, and Karen Henry oversaw final stages of development. Barbara Flanagan, copyeditor, helped clean up and clarify many details in the manuscript. Bridget Leahy, production editor, kept us all on schedule yet was vigilant about details; she was assisted by Arthur Johnson. Donna Dennison succeeded in the difficult task of selecting from myriad proposed cover images then arranging them. Charles Christensen, publisher, and Joan Feinberg, general manager, have been involved in the evolution of the book from the beginning of my association with Bedford and have committed many company resources to the project. Their dedication to high-quality books produced by high-quality staff is rarer than ever today and all the more commendable in the current publishing environment.

ABOUT THE AUTHOR

William H. Phillips received his B.A. from Purdue University, his M.A. from Rutgers University, and his Ph.D. (in dramatic literature and film studies) from Indiana University. His postdoctoral studies in film include three sabbaticals to write and to do research at major film archives, libraries, and film distributors in the United States and Europe; participation in an eight-week National Endowment for the Humanities Summer Seminar for College Teachers on the history of film at Northwestern University; and attendance at the first (two-week) American Film Institute Center for Advanced Film Studies Symposium for College Film Teachers. He has also served as producer of readings of original short film scripts for live performance then rebroadcast on cable TV.

Phillips has taught introductory film courses at the University of Illinois, Urbana; Indiana University, South Bend; California State University, Stanislaus; and the University of Wisconsin–Eau Claire. His publications include the books *Analyzing Films* (1985) and *Writing Short Scripts* (2nd ed., 1999).

Updates of this book, supplements to it, information on accessing the author, and links to Web sites of interest to film students may be accessed through the home page of Bedford/St. Martin's: <http://www.bedfordstmartins .com/phillips-film>.

Brief Contents

Contents

APPENDICES   483

AUTHOR'S NOTE

This book began in the dancing lights
of my last picture show,
a *cinema paradiso,*
now gone with the wind,
the Beach Theatre, Corpus Christi,
where I met my first girlfriend
to hold hands in the dark,
as we watched heroes weekly elude death,
where in the light that did not dance
I too pasted up Rita Hayworth,
swept the lobby, stoked the candy machine,
and helped rope off the front rows
when the tide was up.

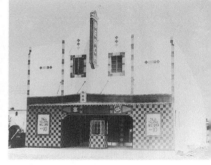

Above left: The movie theater featured in the 1988 Italian film *Cinema Paradiso.*
Above right: The Beach Theatre, Corpus Christi, Texas, shortly before its opening in 1940. *Courtesy of Bill Walraven, Corpus Christi, Texas.*

This book is dedicated to my first film teachers, at Indiana University, and some special recent film students.

For Harry Geduld, who taught me about narrative meanings; Charlie Eckert, who introduced me to avant-garde films and film theory; and the Indiana University Film Society, which introduced me to a wide variety of films.

And for some dedicated film students I have taught while working on this book at Indiana University, South Bend; California State University, Stanislaus; and the University of Wisconsin–Eau Claire. They made learning mutual, and their enthusiasm, intelligence, and diligence helped inspire me to write this book for them and those to come.

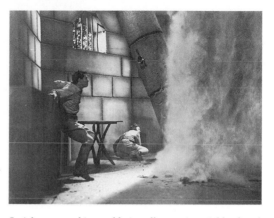

Serials appeared in weekly installments in neighborhood movie theaters and featured extensive action, danger, and romance often in exotic settings, most of which is evident in this publicity still for one of the fifteen chapters of the Republic serial *Nyoka and the Tigermen* (1942).

Ricci, the main character, at work in *The Bicycle Thief* (a.k.a. *Bicycle Thieves*, 1948). *PDS-ENIC; The Museum of Modern Art/Film Stills Archive.*

Catherine R. Atkins
Daniel Barrious
Rebecca Kay Crist
Wallace (Bud) Davis
Joan(ie) C. Duncan
Aaron Ellenbarger
Kirstin J. Forer
Lillaana Fortier
Sandra A. Garcia-Sanborn
Owen Hablutzel III
Marna Harlan
Sonya Kay Harrington
The Brothers Holliday,
    Mike and Tom
Debbie Houck
Kaye Kolkmann
Bret E. Lampman
Tara Lewis
Brook Marcks
Dale Melgaard

William V. Meyer
Bruce Miller
Marion Miller
Cherie L. Miranda
Jose Morales
Marilyn Ohlsson
David J. O'Leary
Kevin Pottorff
Joshua Puetz
Kirk Reynolds
Steve Reynolds
the late Estin G. Scearce
Virginia Silva
Mary Fatima Silveira
Karen E. Thibodeaux
Gary D. Tindle
Tammy VandenBosch
Andrew West
Vicki Whitaker
Lisa Wilson

Introduction

THE LINES AT THE MOVIE THEATER stretch down the block. At the neighborhood video store, all the copies of the latest hit movie are rented out. As a group of people in a remote Cuban village see their first film, their faces radiate joy and wonder, and a short Cuban film, "For the First Time," records the event. Immigrant children watch a movie and are captivated by it and united in pleasure (Figure I.1). A young American film-maker born in Vietnam returns there to make a documentary and interviews former Vietnamese leaders, who ask her "a lot of questions about American film stars." In a scene from the 1988 Senegalese film *Saaraba* (meaning

FIGURE I.1 The joy of movies
Immigrant children from different countries and ethnic groups are mesmerized by "The Immigrant," a 1917 film starring Charlie Chaplin. *Courtesy of Rebecca Cooney and New York Times Pictures*

FIGURE I.2 Photographs of movie stars
Anne Frank—a girl who with her family hid in a secret apartment
in an Amsterdam house during the Nazi occupation—is the subject of the documentary film *Anne Frank Remembered* (1995). At
several points in the film audiences see her bedroom wall, on which
are hung photographs of movie stars (at the top of the image shown
here)—yet another indication of the widespread influence of movies
on modern lives. *Sony Pictures Classics*

"Utopia") alienated youths in Dakar are seen in the
foreground smoking drugs; in the background can
be glimpsed a poster for *Apocalypse Now*. Audiences
watching the 1995 Academy-award winning documentary *Anne Frank Remembered* glimpse photos
of movie stars on Anne Frank's bedroom walls (Figure I.2). At various times in history, Mickey Mouse,
Charlie Chaplin, Rudolph Valentino, Marilyn
Monroe, John Wayne, Arnold Schwarzenegger,
and other stars have been more widely known
throughout the world than presidents, popes, and
pole vaulters. These examples attest to the power
and pervasiveness of film, especially American
commercial cinema.

No one questions the entertainment value of
movies: the proof is in the huge number of people
who watch them. Many people, though, disagree
about whether films have any additional value.
Movies' preeminent ability and commercial proclivity to show sex and violence have sometimes
made them seem beyond reasonable consideration. Movies have been dismissed as "ribbons of
dreams" and Hollywood as a "dream factory."
Nonetheless films can be more than commercial
entertainment, and studying them and the film
medium has many benefits.

STUDYING FILMS

Some people fear that studying films and other
imaginative creations will spoil their enjoyment of
them. But with guidance and a chance to reach
their own conclusions, most viewers find that studying films increases their
enjoyment of them and often their appreciation of the effort and creativity
involved in making them. Many people find, too, that they enjoy a wider variety of films for more different reasons than before studying films.

Film study helps viewers understand how different filmmakers have used
the medium. It also reveals the medium's possibilities and limitations. For
example, examination of *Unforgiven* reveals major variations from most commercial films. Though generations of western movies have shown otherwise,
Unforgiven shows that killing a person can be difficult for the killer—and
messy.

Film study also helps viewers understand and appreciate the wide variety of films, including short films, documentary films, avant-garde films, and hybrid films, not to mention various groupings of fictional films, such as Italian neo-realism and French new wave. Film study also helps viewers understand the various genres or types of fictional films, such as western and science fiction; mixtures of genres, such as horror and western; and the indebtedness of later films to earlier ones.

Viewers trained in film studies tend to notice more significant detail while viewing a film. They are more likely to appreciate or question choices the filmmakers made, such as the lighting, composition, camera angles, and camera distances from the subjects.

People who have studied films, their contexts, and the responses they bring forth tend to understand more meanings and to be more aware of how and why others might interpret the same film differently. They are also more likely to be aware of how the viewer's situation—where and when the viewer lives, for example—influences his or her responses to a film.

Studying films can make you more aware of contexts that influence how a film turns out. As illustrated in this book, when and where a film is made and the sources it draws on influence what the film will be like. A film made in a dictatorial third world country, for example, will differ fundamentally from any film made in modern Japan. A science fiction film will be influenced by earlier science fiction films: it will accept many of the conventions or traditions of sci-fi films; it may reject others.

Finally, films can help us understand different places, people, and cultures—whether in a foreign country or in an obscure region of one's own country. However, films, even documentary films, can never be accepted as completely reliable accounts. The subjects presented must be considered in light of the filmmakers' motives, methods, and skills. In the case of avant-garde films, the worlds glimpsed often exist only in the filmmakers' imaginations.

ABOUT THIS BOOK

To help readers understand unfamiliar terminology, many terms are explained within the text or in the margin. That way readers may read any chapter out of order without interruptions for trips to the glossary.

This book includes many other features for the beginning film student: sidebars consisting of examples of student writing or other interesting supplementary information; a summary of the major points of each chapter; annotated suggestions for further reading; an appendix on reading, thinking, researching, and writing about films; and an extensive chronology that can help readers see when certain events happened in relation to other events. The chronology may also be used to find a date, check a spelling, and double-check one's memory. More than four hundred and fifty frame enlargements and other photographs, most with extensive and informative captions, are also included.

Many readers of film books complain that they do not understand the concepts being explained when they have not seen the films used as illustrations. To try to minimize that problem, I have often supplied a photograph, drawing, table, or detailed description before explaining a point. In several places a brief description of an entire film is set off in a sidebar, again so that readers may understand the concepts discussed without having seen the film. If readers know those films well, they can skip the summaries and go right to the discussions that follow.

Throughout the text, the titles of short films (those less than sixty minutes) are set off by quotation marks, those of long films (sixty or more minutes) by italics.

CREDIT WHERE CREDIT IS DUE

As we discuss a film and our responses to it, to whom should we give credit? If the film is short and required only modest resources to make it—as is the case with many avant-garde films—often one person deserves most of the credit. But what of full-length movies? What one person could create one? To write, costume, direct, light, perform, film, edit, score, finance, and promote a movie is beyond the powers of one mortal. Nonetheless, many film reviewers and critics credit and blame a single person, usually the director.

In the case of a novel or painting, assigning responsibility to one person is reasonable enough. With films made by many people, however, it is often difficult to know which filmmaker contributed which aspect to the finished product, and in most cases it is difficult to believe that the director is responsible for the creativity of *every* aspect. For instance, did the writers, director, actors, or someone else rewrite crucial lines of dialogue? Did the writers, director, editors, actors, or studio head insist that certain scenes be dropped? Examining the film usually yields no answers to these and many other questions about creative contributions, and reliable publications about such information are rare. To compound the problem, screen credits often inaccurately report who did what. Many questions about specific contributions to the finished film remain unanswerable.

For compactness and ease of identification, films are often identified by director in this book, but readers should remember that such usage does not automatically mean the director alone is responsible for all the film's creativity. Consider the making of *Psycho*. A reading of the source novel and the script that describes the finished film reveals that author Robert Bloch and scriptwriter Joseph Stefano deserve partial credit for the shape and texture of the finished film. Many of the performers—especially Anthony Perkins, Vera

Miles, and Martin Balsam—do more than adequate work. Bernard Herrmann's music contributes to every scene in which it is employed: view any section without it and its absence is pronounced. The title work by Saul Bass at the beginning and the end of the film is unusually imaginative and appropriate. Doubtless, Hitchcock deserves much credit for supervising and coordinating all those and other efforts and for his own creativity. Various filmmaking strategies also suggest that *Psycho* is a film directed by Hitchcock. Nonetheless, to think of *Psycho* as "Hitchcock's *Psycho*" glosses over the contributions of many others. (For details on the creation of this film, see Stephen Rebello's *Alfred Hitchcock and the Making of* Psycho.)

Sometimes when I see someone giving the director full credit for a film that many people helped make, I am reminded of an account, apocryphal though it may be, of the director Frank Capra and his frequent collaborator, scriptwriter Robert Riskin. In Richard Walter's version of the story, in a lengthy interview Capra expounded on "the Capra touch" but not once mentioned Riskin. After the interview appeared, Riskin sent Capra a manuscript with the note "Frank, let's see you put the Capra touch on this." Inside were all blank pages (4).

WORKS CITED

Rebello, Stephen. *Alfred Hitchcock and the Making of* Psycho. New York: Dembner, 1990. Harper, 1991.

Walter, Richard. *Screenwriting: The Art, Craft and Business of Film and Television Writing*. New York: NAL, 1988.

Part One
THE EXPRESSIVENESS OF FILM TECHNIQUES

WHAT ARE THE CONSEQUENCES for viewers of the innumerable decisions filmmakers make while creating films? Some answers will be explored in this, the first and largest, part of the book.

Part One discusses what the settings, subjects, and composition may contribute to a film; how the film, lighting, and camera can be used to create certain effects; how the resulting footage might be edited and with what consequences; and what the sound track can contribute to viewers' experience of a film.

"Film techniques," the topic of Chapters 1–4, refers to the handling of everything used in making a film, such as the objects that make up the settings, composition or arrangement of everything within the image, lighting, camera distances from the subjects, camera angles, editing, and recording and manipulation of sound.

◄ In *Secrets & Lies* (1996), a woman (on the right) realizes that the woman on the left is her daughter, the result of a brief liaison. The entire scene consists of only two shots, the second one more than seven-and-a-half minutes long. In this publicity still, which closely approximates a frame from the second shot, the two subjects are centered and are the same height in the image: they are the main objects of interest and are of equal importance. The camera distance and lens make the subjects large enough that viewers can see the many shifting, complex feelings suggested by the actors' expressive faces. The background, a restaurant, is slightly out of focus and empty. The subjects and setting are clearly and evenly illuminated. The scene conveys many contrasts: the two women are of different races, social classes, and temperaments. The woman on the left is dressed professionally, holds briefcase and papers, and does not smoke. The woman on the right is casually dressed, disheveled, and smokes. The woman on the left has an enunciation and accent of an educated person; the woman on the right does not. The woman on the left largely reins in her emotions; the woman on the right gets extremely emotional. Although the two subjects are quite unlike, they share and help communicate a complicated, difficult emotional situation. Change the arrangement of the subjects within the frame, background, camera distance, camera lens, clothing, lighting, editing, or actors, and the scene and the audience's response to it would be altered. *October Films*

7

To create a desired effect, a technique, such as lighting, may be changed as the film progresses. In his book *Making Movies*, director Sidney Lumet gives several such examples. In *12 Angry Men*, which shows a jury deliberating extensively, Lumet changes both camera lenses and angles as the film progresses:

> As the picture unfolded, I wanted the room to seem smaller and smaller. That meant that I would slowly shift to longer lenses as the picture continued. Starting with the normal range . . . we progressed to . . . [longer and longer lenses that seem to make any background appear closer]. In addition, I shot the first third of the movie above eye level, and then, by lowering the camera, shot the second third at eye level, and the last third from below eye level. In that way, toward the end, the ceiling began to appear. Not only were the walls closing in, the ceiling was as well. The sense of increasing claustrophobia did a lot to raise the tension of the last part of the movie. (81)

Usually such changes are gradual and imperceptible, especially in mainstream movies.

A particular technique, such as a camera angle, may have one effect in one part of a film and a different effect elsewhere in the same film or in a different film. Often a low angle reinforces the sense that the subject is large or dominant or imposing or powerful, but not always. Sometimes, for example, the filmmakers simply want viewers to notice the relationship of the subject in the foreground to a tall object in the background. Similarly, as Figure 2.41 (on p. 101) illustrates, a high angle does not always make the subject(s) seem small, vulnerable, or weak, though in many contexts it does. It depends on the contexts and on other techniques used at the same time.

Finally, several techniques used together can create a particular effect. For example, in some shots in *Lawrence of Arabia*, such as the one illustrated in Plate 7 in Chapter 2, viewers may be struck by how much the characters are engulfed by an inhospitable environment, but it's not just the camera distance and smallness of the subjects in the image that create that effect; it's also the high angle that diminishes the size of the subjects, the unvarying and inhospitable (hot) color, and the shallow focus, as if even close by there is nothing worth seeing. To illustrate the expressiveness of various cinematic techniques, the following chapters focus on them one at a time, but in films they never function in isolation.

CHAPTER 1

Mise en Scène

M ISE EN SCÈNE—pronounced "meez ahn sen," with a nasalized second syllable—originally meant a director's staging of a play. Often in film studies the term refers to everything put before the camera in preparation for filming. As used in this book, mise en scène consists of the major aspects of filmmaking that are also components of staging a play: settings; the subject(s) being filmed, usually actors or people; and composition, the arrangement of the settings and subjects. In French *mise en scène* means "staging." The phrase is used in the opening credits for some French films where English-language films would use "direction," as in "*Mise en scène de Luis Buñuel*," meaning "Direction by Luis Buñuel." Although the designer and **cinematographer** are often deeply involved in matters of mise en scène , in large productions of fictional films, the director usually makes the final decisions about it.

So expressive can mise en scène be that sometimes entire major scenes use only visuals to convey moods, characterizations, and meanings or implications. The opening scene of the western *Rio Bravo* (1959), for example, introduces the main character (the sheriff), an alcoholic who later proves to be his deputy, and a murdering antagonist—all in a wordless scene of two minutes and thirty-two seconds. Mise en scène can be so expressive that sometimes only a few carefully selected images can convey much of a film's story, moods, and meanings. In *Woman in the Dunes* (1964), a family man trapped in a large pit with a young woman tries to escape, but villagers above

cinematographer: Person responsible for the photography during the making of a film.

Terms in **boldface** are defined in the Illustrated Glossary beginning on page 562.

FIGURE 1.1 Mise en scène conveying a story
The settings, subjects, and compositions of carefully selected frame enlargements reveal much of the story of *Woman in the Dunes* (1964). (a, top left) The man, an insect collector from a city, is seen first meeting the woman in her shack in a large sand pit. He's weighed down by equipment and wears a forced smile. (b, top right) The man wakes one morning and sees the woman's naked body. (c, above left) Eventually, they become lovers. (d, above right) Near the end of the story, he has found a project to work on and has resigned himself to a life with the woman in the dunes. He's now in traditional Japanese clothes; his hair is longer; he has a mustache. He is relaxed and at peace with himself. Frame enlargements. *Pathe Contemporary Films Release*

the pit prevent him from doing so; eventually the man resigns himself to a life with the woman. Much of the film's story is conveyed by only the four images shown in Figure 1.1.

SETTINGS

The **setting** is the place where filmed action occurs—either on a **set**, a constructed place used for filming (Figure 1.2), or on **location**, a real place that is not built expressly for the filmmakers (Figure 1.3).

FIGURE 1.2 **Early film studio**
Georges Méliès's glassed-in film studio, one of the world's first film studios, was built in France in 1897. Many windows were necessary because early films were made without artificial light. The studio was used for preparations for filming, for instance to paint scenery and to enclose small sets where Méliès's early, very short films were made. *The Museum of Modern Art/Film Stills Archive*

FIGURE 1.3 **Filming on location**
For "Feeding (the) Baby" (1895) the Lumière Brothers of France took a camera outside and recorded brief actions as separate films, such as a train arriving at a station, workers leaving a factory, and a family having a meal. The film illustrated here is one of the earliest home movies. Frame enlargement. *The Museum of Modern Art/Film Stills Archive*

FIGURE 1.4 Filming on a set
Filming on a set gives filmmakers maximum control of all aspects of shooting a film and recording sound. Here Alfred Hitchcock prepares to direct a shot for *Marnie* (1964). Since the set was located in a large enclosed room built for filming and recording sound, the filmmakers were free to work without the distractions of unwanted sounds or changes in lighting. If they had filmed the shot in a real office, all sorts of distractions might occur, such as an unexpected phone call or someone banging around in the next room. *Universal*

Types of Settings

Filmmakers have many options in selecting and creating settings. In recent years, settings for certain movies, especially science fiction and action films, have been made using a computer. Usually, though, a film is shot on a set or on location. Many films combine **shots** made on a set with those made on location.

Filming on a full-scale or nearly full-scale set has many advantages. It can be less costly than filming on location, and it allows the filmmakers greater control over sound, lighting, and climate (Figure 1.4).

To save money, time, or both, parts of films may be made using miniature settings, rear projection, or matte paintings. A miniature is a model of the original object that is painstakingly made to scale then photographed and included in the finished film. An example is the space station in *Outland* (1981), which has been built on a moon of a distant planet (see Figure 6.22 on p. 258).

shot: An uninterrupted strip of exposed motion-picture film or videotape. A shot presents a subject, perhaps even a blank screen, during an uninterrupted segment of time.

FIGURE 1.5 Matte shot
A matte is a partial covering placed in front of a camera lens to obscure part of the image. For a shot for *Citizen Kane* (1941) (a, above left) a matte was used to block out much of the setting as cars were filmed driving along a California beach. (b, above) A matte painting was made that more closely resembles a Florida coast, where the scene takes place, than a California coast. (c, left) The live action of the cars was combined with the painting. The setting of the shot was changed from California to Florida without sending the film crew across the country to film the shot. Frame enlargements. *From the collection of Linwood Dunn*

Rear projection has been used in films since the 1920s. In that process, live action in the foreground is combined with projected images on a screen in the background. The **technique** was often used to make a stationary vehicle appear to be moving. Still another way to create authentic-looking settings relatively inexpensively is to use matte paintings as part of the image (Figure 1.5).

Filming on location has its own advantages: generally it is not very time-consuming or costly to modify a few details in the setting, and nearly always the film gains authenticity in detail (Figure 1.6). To modern viewers, many of whom have been to New York City or seen it on TV news, a shot filmed on location in New York looks more authentic than one filmed on a set. *Schindler's List* (1993) was filmed on location in Krakow, Poland, not on a **sound stage**, a permanent enclosed set for shooting film and recording sound. When director Steven Spielberg was asked why, he was quoted as saying, "'Filming . . . in Europe contributed everything to the truth of the

technique: Any aspect of film-making, such as the choices of sets, lighting, and editing.

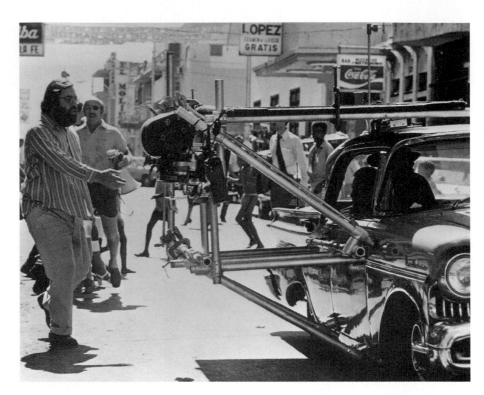

FIGURE 1.6 Filming on a substitute location
In this publicity still for *The Godfather Part II* (1974), Francis Coppola (left) is shown directing in Santo Domingo in the Dominican Republic. The Dominican Republic was used for the scenes set in Cuba. It was politically impossible for Americans to film in Cuba when the film was being made, and the Dominican Republic looked a lot like Cuba.
The Coppola Company; Paramount

FIGURE 1.7 The setting as subject
This set of Babylon for *Intolerance* (1916), directed by D. W. Griffith, is the largest, most elaborate set ever built for a U.S. movie—the towers were 165 feet high. The set serves as the main subject of this shot, filmed from the gondola of a balloon. Because *Intolerance* was a box office disaster, there was not enough money to tear down the set after filming, and for years its remains stood on the corner of Sunset and Hollywood Boulevards.
The Museum of Modern Art/Film Stills Archive

FIGURE 1.8 **Limbo set**
A nondescript background, sometimes called a limbo or limbo set, sets off the actors engaging in the first known screen kiss in the short film "The Kiss" (1896). With such a background, viewers have no choice but to give full attention to the two osculating subjects. Frame enlargement. *Edison; The Museum of Modern Art/Film Stills Archive*

FIGURE 1.9 **Imaginary set**
An imaginative, playful, childlike setting for "Triplets," a whimsical and satirical song and dance in *The Band Wagon* (1953). As in many musical numbers, the set is imaginary; the designers made no attempt to re-create a true-to-life background. None is needed. *Loew's Incorporated*

film'" (Wood). Filming on location, however, does not always make the **footage** seem more true-to-life. Curiously, the real sometimes does not look (or sound) realistic enough, so filmmakers modify a location to make viewers believe they are seeing and hearing the genuine article. Jack Lemmon has spoken of a director he worked for who preferred to make his own rain, because "'real rain is too rainy'" (Amory 4).

A setting may be the main subject of the **scene**, as in the famous shot from *Intolerance* (1916, Figure 1.7). At the opposite extreme, the setting may draw no attention to itself—for example, it may be blank (**limbo**) or out of focus (Figure 1.8). When limbo backgrounds are used and the subjects filmed close up, viewers have no choice but to examine the subjects' nuances.

Finally, sometimes settings are not meant to be true-to-life. Such settings may be enjoyed for their creativity or whimsy, as in such musicals as *The Band Wagon* (1953, Figure 1.9), *Gold Diggers of 1933* (1933, Figure 9.8a on p. 384), and *Gold Diggers of 1937* (1936, Figure 9.8b on p. 384). Imaginary settings also appear in many animated films, as in *Tim Burton's The Nightmare before Christmas* (1993), and in symbolic or allegorical stories, such as "Neighbours" (1952, Figure 8.37 on p. 364). In "Neighbours," a detailed, true-to-life setting would serve no purpose: the film focuses not on setting or the characters' relationship to it but on the significance of two neighbors' actions.

footage: A length of exposed motion-picture film.

scene: A section of a narrative film that gives the impression of continuous action taking place in continuous time and space.

Functions of Settings

Above all, settings indicate place and time. When the action shifts to Cuba in *The Godfather Part II* (1974), we can see that the location is a warm, humid climate (a long shoreline, palm trees, men dressed in short-sleeve shirts and lightweight hats, most people dressed in white or light-colored clothes). From the variety of skin tones of the many people on the sidewalks and from the style of the uniforms of the police or military authorities, we can infer that the story has shifted to a country with a tropical climate, probably somewhere in the Caribbean. From the car Michael is riding in (see Figure 1.6), a 1950s Chevrolet we had seen earlier, another 1950s car parked by the curb, and the ankle-length skirts on the women, many viewers can infer that it is the late 1950s or so. We scarcely need the sound track to reveal that the action shifts to Cuba.

In action movies set in nature or outer space, the filmmakers may dwell on the settings by using frequent shots of settings without people or with people seen only from a distance. They may use shots of the setting that do not advance the story or that last longer than necessary for narrative purposes. Such shots often stress the beauty, wonder, and vastness of nature (Plate 8 in Chapter 2). When a shot presents the subject with abundant space around it, the framing is called **loose framing**. At the opposite extreme, **tight framing** leaves little space around the subject. Such settings often convey confinement and stress (Figure 1.10).

FIGURE 1.10 **Tight framing** The stress suffered by the submarine crew is one of the main subjects of *Das Boot*, or *The Boat* (1981), and the tight framing increases the sense of the stress the men must endure. *Bavaria Atelier; Columbia*

FIGURE 1.11 Expressionism
In *The Cabinet of Dr. Caligari* (1919), viewers see a story told by an insane narrator, and the sets
of his story are done in an expressionistic style complete with many irregular, unexpected shapes.
Throughout the brief scene represented here, as in many scenes in this film, part of the image
was deliberately blocked out, or masked. Frame enlargement. *Decla-Bioscop; The Museum of
Modern Art/Circulating Film Library*

Expressionistic settings are often used to help reveal what a character is
like or to create or intensify moods. In *The Cabinet of Dr. Caligari* (1919), the
settings reflect the insanity of the character recounting the story that takes
up most of the film (Figure 1.11). Many a horror film is scarier and many a
comedy more amusing because of the settings. And movies such as *The Red
Desert* (1964) and *Little Vera* (1988) are more depressing because of the industrial, polluted environment in which the characters are mired. Near the
end of the Japanese film *Gate of Hell* (1953), the agitated setting mirrors the
feelings of the samurai who intends to kill the husband of the woman with
whom he has become obsessed. The first, brief shot of the samurai's approach
to the couple's house is of plants agitated by wind. The next shot is of plants in
the foreground blowing in a strong wind then the appearance of the samurai
far in the background, waist-high in vegetation. As he approaches the house
(and camera), the wind agitates the plants that surround him. Toward the

FIGURE 1.12 Setting reflecting character
With its shadows, barren surfaces, odd angles, and irregularly shaped windows sometimes rendered in the expressionistic style, the castle of *Frankenstein* (1931) is appropriate for the scientist who has twisted out of line in daring to play God. *Carl Laemmle; Universal*

end of the shot he disappears off to the right of the frame; only the plants and the sky remain briefly in the background. In the next, very brief shot, a few plants blow in the wind. The message conveyed by the setting is that the samurai is like the wind: his presence powerfully affects what is around him.

Where characters live or work, the objects that surround them, and how they arrange those objects can also tell us much about the characters. The castle of Dr. Frankenstein in *Frankenstein* (1931) seems appropriate for its occupant (Figure 1.12). In the opening scene of *Back to the Future* (1985), we see Dr. Brown's laboratory before we see Dr. Brown. The many types of clocks suggest that he is preoccupied with time. Photos of Edison, Franklin, and Einstein; various equipment; and contraptions to turn on a coffeemaker, TV, and toaster and to open and dump out dog food convey the sense that the occupant is messy, creative, brilliant, eccentric, and obsessive. And he is.

SUBJECTS

The subject of a shot may be the setting itself, as in shots of terrain or outer space. In a fictional film, the subject is usually the film's characters. In a documentary film, real people are often a shot's main concern.

Action and Appearance

We learn about people by observing their actions: dancing, marrying and divorcing, writing a novel. In movies, actions are usually the primary means of revealing characterization. Perhaps this is because films are superbly suited to single out actions, focus attention on them, and show them vividly and memorably. No one in *High Noon* (1952) tells viewers that the town marshal lives by his principles and that his integrity and willpower are mightier than his fear. Those characteristics are shown by his actions, by his movements, body language, and expressive face. No one in *The Remains of the Day* (1993) says that the butler was excessive in

FIGURE 1.13 Expressive mise en scène
In *The Remains of the Day* (1993), a man and a woman are servants of a wealthy master, and the man
feels so duty-bound to his master that he rejects the woman's romantic overtures. The mise en scène
of this publicity still with the two main characters conveys much about the early events of the story.
The setting is a large, wealthy interior. The subjects are a resolute-looking man and a woman
looking vaguely dejected. The composition has the man turned away from the woman and some
distance from her in a loosely framed shot (the two characters in a large room within a large residence). All the components of the mise en scène help convey the film's initial setting, characters,
and story. *Columbia*

his past devotion to a misguided master, and no one needs to point out how
the butler resists the attention of the housekeeper (Figure 1.13). His actions
—including his traveling to see the housekeeper after many years—reveal
the story's emotional core.

Often a character's cherished possessions suggest something about the
owner. Cars are a favorite vehicle for characterization: station wagons for
family members, sports cars for independent singles, VWs for the unassum-
ing, and Volvos for the cautious and middle-aged. As in the choice of actors,

the choice of vehicle may surprise and amuse audiences because characters may drive vehicles audiences would not expect. An example is the Oldsmobile minivan that the John Travolta character, a Miami loan shark, drives and promotes in *Get Shorty* (1995).

We also learn about characters by their appearances, including physical characteristics, posture and gestures, clothing, makeup, and hairstyle. The appearance of the self-appointed crime fighter of *Blankman* (1994, Figure 1.14) reveals much of his personality. Costume is often used to contrast characters, as in the appearances of Obi-Wan Kenobi and Darth Vader (Figure 1.15), and even to hide a character's identity, as Darth Vader illustrates. Costume and makeup can also obscure an actor's identity. Who is that actor in Figure 1.16? (Answer: the same one featured in Figure 1.26.)

Often a character's changing appearance reveals a change in situation and personality. As *Rocky* (1976) progresses, Rocky and especially Adrian become more attractive (Figure 1.17). In *Reversal of Fortune* (1990), clothing mirrors Sunny's decline into misery and illness (Figure 1.18).

Appearance reveals character, and it can also *create* character. As film scholar James Naremore explains:

> Costumes serve as indicators of gender and social status, but they also shape bodies and behavior. . . . Who shall say how much the lumbering walk of Frankenstein's monster was created by Karloff and how much by a pair of weighted boots? We even have Chaplin's word that the Tramp grew out of the costume, not *vice versa*: "I had no idea of the character. But the moment I was dressed, the clothes and make-up made me feel the person he was." (88–89)

Appearance can be so expressive that a single image sometimes conveys the essence of a story. In *Star Wars* (1977), much of the story is conveyed by the contending forces, dressed radically differently and facing each other from opposing sides of the frame against a backdrop of high-tech danger (see Figure 1.15).

FIGURE 1.14 Costume revealing character
In *Blankman* (1994), the character played by Damon Wayans is a self-appointed crime fighter who dons a homemade crime-fighting outfit. As critic Stephen Holden describes it, "His cape looks like a tacky, patterned bedspread, his red mask a swatch of old bath towel. Around his waist he wears an absurdly unwieldy belt, which is equipped with everything from a crude two-way radio to a homemade stink bomb." Blankman's costume reveals his inventiveness (varied gadgets), limited budget, inelegance, and untraditional fighting skills (a boxing pose but an unusual stance). We can see his determination, but his getup amusingly reveals his inadequacy as a Batman-type superhero. *Columbia*

FIGURE 1.15 Contending costumes, contending characters
Opposing costumes reveal opposing characteristics in *Star Wars* (1977). The softness of Obi-Wan Kenobi's robe and hood (left) contrast with the heavier fabric and metallic helmet of Darth Vader. Obi-Wan Kenobi looks like a monk; Darth Vader looks militaristic, his helmet a blending of German World War II helmets and the thirteenth-century Russian helmets worn in the film *Alexander Nevsky* (1938). Take away the light sabers and setting and one can almost imagine a monk confronting an armored knight. It looks as if Obi-Wan is unprotected and at a disadvantage, but then the force is with him. *Lucasfilm Ltd.*

FIGURE 1.16 Some functions of makeup
Makeup can obscure the identity of an actor, even a very famous one. As illustrated here in *The Man Who Understood Women* (1959), it can also help express mood (the downturn in the lip makeup) and age (the dark spots and wrinkles around the eyes). In this image, the makeup and costume send conflicting messages: melancholy and mirth. *20th Century-Fox*

FIGURE 1.17 Personality and appearance
(a, top) Early in *Rocky* (1976), Adrian's appearance fits her personality: she is shy, insecure, and rather plain. (b, right) Late in the movie, Adrian is attractive, poised, and unafraid of getting close to Rocky. Her hair has some curls and sheen, and she has gotten rid of the glasses and the plain sweater. During the movie Rocky's appearance improves, too, though less dramatically than Adrian's. At least he is better groomed. *United Artists*

FIGURE 1.18 Appearance reflecting changes in health and happiness
(a, above) When Claus and Sunny first meet in *Reversal of Fortune* (1990), Sunny is wearing a revealing dress that enhances her beauty and conveys her vitality. Frame enlargement. (b, left) After Sunny and her husband have lost their ardor for each other and her health is failing, she is miserable. She never again wears revealing clothes or dresses in vibrant colors: no ruffles, no glamour, only plain, sexless, functional clothing. *Warner Bros.*

Characters and Acting

Characters are imaginary personages in a fictional story. They are often based in part on real people—as the main character in *Ed Wood* (1994) is based on the real movie director Ed Wood—or on a combination of traits from several people; but characters may be entirely imaginary, as are the characters in most action movies. In a fictional film, humans usually function as characters, but characters can be anything with some human features, such as a talking animal or visitors from outer space. Characters' actions and language—and sometimes their thoughts, dreams, and fantasies—are the main ways we come to understand them and to get involved in the story. Depending on the needs of the story, characters may be round or flat. Round characters are complex, lifelike, multidimensional, sometimes surprising, and changeable. They tend to be the most important characters in a story. Flat characters are simple (stereotypical or minor), one-dimensional, and unchanging. They tend to play minor roles in a story, appearing in few scenes and rarely affecting the most significant actions. Narrative films tend to have only a few round characters because there is time to develop only a few characters in depth, and it is confusing for most viewers to keep track of more than a few major characters. In any case, characters are enacted by actors.

TYPES OF ACTORS

> Far from the movies not being an actor's medium, there's probably been no other artistic medium in this century whose appeal rests so strongly on the human presence, and in which the human image has occupied a place of such primacy and centrality. (Pechter 69)

In the earliest years of cinema, film acting was considered so disreputable that in the United States and elsewhere, stage actors who appeared in movies would not let their names be publicized. How different things are today. Now American movie actors generally have more prestige, power, and wealth than anyone else involved in making a movie. The most popular actors can command many millions of dollars per movie. And by agreeing to do a particular film, a famous actor often ensures that it will get funded and made. Critics and theorists have divided actors into various types, including stars, Method actors, character actors, and nonprofessional.

Some film industries—such as those of India, Brazil, France, and the United States—have film stars, famous performers who usually play a major if not *the* major role in an entertainment. Some American stars—such as Arnold Schwarzenegger, Sylvester Stallone, and Julia Roberts—tend to play a narrow range of characters but often generate widespread interest, command enormous salaries, and usually guarantee a large box office, both in the United States and abroad. Their power may extend to the choice of the director and even to the script. Stars and their previous roles may be so well known that sometimes scripts are written with them in mind or, once they are

FIGURE 1.19 Versatile acting
In *Tootsie* (1982), Dustin Hoffman plays a character who is sometimes himself and at other times another character. Here Hoffman is seen as (a, top) Michael Dorsey, an actor, and (b, left) Dorothy Michaels, who is in fact Michael Dorsey made up to look like a woman. With this film, Hoffman proved he was versatile enough to play two quite different roles within the same film. Frame enlargements. *Mirage; Columbia*

signed up for a movie, the script is rewritten to suit them better. Writer John Gregory Dunne explains how an early draft of *Up Close and Personal* (1996) included a scene with a dwarf-tossing competition in a bar, but once Robert Redford agreed to do the movie, the scene was dropped because no one could imagine Redford doing such a thing.

Dustin Hoffman (Figure 1.19), Robert De Niro, Tom Hanks, Marlon Brando, Al Pacino, Jack Nicholson, Peter Sellers, Alec Guinness, and others have been regarded as stars yet played a wide range of roles, sometimes within the same film. In *Kind Hearts and Coronets* (1949), Alec Guinness plays eight brief roles, including a woman; and in *The Nutty Professor* (1996), Eddie Murphy plays seven roles, including all five overweight members of the Klump family (Figure 1.20). Women stars—such as Glenn Close, Vanessa

FIGURE 1.20 One actor, one film, multiple roles
In *The Nutty Professor* (1996), Eddie Murphy plays (a, left) exercise guru Lance Perkins and all five members of the Klump family: (b, below) Grandma Klump, (c, bottom left) Papa Klump, (d, right) Mama Klump, (e, far right) Ernie Klump, and (f, bottom right) Professor Sherman Klump. On the right in (f) is Rick Baker, a special-effects makeup artist who won the first ever Academy Award for makeup for *An American Werewolf in London* (1981) and has done work in *The Exorcist* (1973), the 1976 *King Kong*, *Star Wars* (1977), *Starman* (1984), *Gremlins 2: The New Batch* (1990), and *Men in Black* (1997). *Universal City Studios*

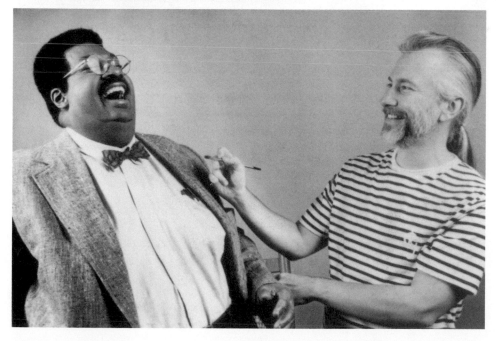

FIGURE 1.21 The versatile Anjelica Huston
(a, top) Anjelica Huston (right) as an Irish wife in 1904 Dublin in *The Dead* (1987); (b, middle) as a hardened con artist and aloof mother in *The Grifters* (1990); and (c, bottom) as Morticia in *The Addams Family* (1991). Huston has also played a Mafia princess in *Prizzi's Honor* (1985); Calamity Jane—the legendary army scout, mule skinner, and Wild West performer—in the TV movie *Buffalo Girls* (1995); and a Cuban American in *The Perez Family* (1995). *(a) Vestron Pictures; (b) Palace; Miramax; (c) Columbia TriStar; Paramount*

FIGURE 1.22 Chinese star Gong Li in two roles
(a, above) Gong Li as an abused wife who takes a lover, has a son by him,
then years later suffers misery from her own son in *Ju Dou* (1990);
(b, right) as a golden-hearted prostitute in *Farewell My Concubine* (1993).
Gong Li has also played such diverse roles as an innocent woman trapped
into becoming the fourth concubine of a wealthy man in *Raise the Red
Lantern* (1991) and, as Berenice Reynaud wrote in the film journal *Sight
and Sound*, "an unglamorous, heavily pregnant, touchingly obstinate
heroine" (12) in *The Story of Qui Ju* (1992). She has also appeared in
a comedy. *Miramax*

Redgrave, Anjelica Huston (Figure 1.21), Jessica Lange, Meryl Streep, Maggie
Smith, and Faye Dunaway—have been no less versatile and accomplished
though they rarely get a chance to play multiple roles in the same film. Versatile foreign stars include the French actor Gérard Depardieu and Gong Li
of China (Figure 1.22).

Some actors (for stage and screen), such as Marlon Brando, Al Pacino,
and Joanne Woodward, are **Method actors**. These performers were trained
at the Actors Studio in New York, which was founded by Elia Kazan and two
others in 1947 and later brought to prominence by Lee Strasberg. When
taking on a role, Method actors study the background of their character, immerse themselves in the role, and create emotion by remembering situations
from their own lives that evoke much the same emotion. Some Method actors,
such as Robert De Niro, may also change their bodies to look and feel the
part (Figure 1.23).

FIGURE 1.23 **Method acting**
(a, left) Robert De Niro as Jake La Motta in his fighting days and (b, right) as Jake La Motta
after his fighting days are over. To play the role of the aging prizefighter turned nightclub owner,
Method actor De Niro put on more than fifty pounds. *United Artists*

Character actors specialize in more or less the same type of secondary
roles. Recent examples of character actors are Lois Smith, Dan Hedaya, and
Dennis Hopper. Hopper has often played antisocial or deranged characters
from at least as early as *The Glory Stompers* (1967, Figure 1.24). Actors such
as Sydney Greenstreet, Peter Lorre, Harrison Ford, Gene Hackman, Morgan Freeman, and Kathy Bates began as character actors then with talent
and luck became stars; but most character actors do not.

And then there are nonprofessional actors, people with no training or
experience before the camera or theatrical audiences. Famed Soviet director
Sergei Eisenstein used nonprofessional actors for ideological reasons: the
Communist masses, not individuals, were the most important component in
his films; Eisenstein also believed that nonprofessional actors could best represent the types of working-class men and women and their oppressors, such
as capitalists, priests, and tsarist military forces. With nonprofessional actors,

FIGURE 1.24 The character actor
(a, top) Dennis Hopper as a motorcycle gang leader in *The Glory Stompers* (1967); (b, middle) as a freelance photographer involved in drugs and lost in his own mental world in *Apocalypse Now* (1979); (c, bottom) in *Waterworld* (1995) as the witty aquatic gang leader with a shaved head, piratelike eye patch, and codpiece. He is ironically called Deacon. In addition to the roles illustrated here, Hopper has played a drug-dealing and drug-consuming hippie in *Easy Rider* (1969), the sadistic drug-snorting boyfriend in *Blue Velvet* (1986), the town drunk in *Hoosiers* (1986), a drug-crazed recluse in *River's Edge* (1987), a Vietnam marine veteran turned double-crossing hit man in *Red Rock West* (1994), and a vengeful terrorist in *Speed* (1994). In all these and other roles he is so compelling that many viewers automatically expect his characters to be unstable, unreliable, menacing, and perhaps involved in drugs or alcohol. *(a) American International Pictures; (b) Omni Zoetrope Studios, United Artists; (c) Universal*

directors do not have to worry about audiences being distracted by the actors' previous roles or their activities in their private lives. For reasons of novelty and greater authenticity, some filmmakers use at least some nonprofessional actors. Sometimes they have no choice. Films such as *Salt of the Earth* (1954) and many films made in third world countries may use few or no trained actors because none are available locally and the production lacks the money to bring them in. Sometimes nonprofessional actors are so awkward and self-conscious, as in the low-budget *Night of the Living Dead* (1968), that they are distracting, even unintentionally laughable. But some directors, such as Vittorio De Sica of Italy, are especially adroit at casting nonprofessional actors and eliciting effective performances (see Figure 6.26 on p. 262).

Cameos are small parts usually limited to one scene and are often un-billed. Though cameos are usually played by famous actors, they may be played by any famous person. Perhaps the best-known cameos in cinema were done by film director Alfred Hitchcock, who put himself in *The Lodger*

FIGURE 1.25 **Hitchcock cameo**
In *Blackmail* (1929), a boy in a subway car annoys a fellow passenger, played by Alfred Hitchcock in one of his early cameos. Here, as in most of the other films he directed, early in the film Hitchcock makes a brief, silent appearance that has no impact on the story. Frame enlargement. *British International Pictures; The Museum of Modern Art/Circulating Film Library*

(1926) and every other film he directed after it. As an actor who appears for only seconds and says nothing, Hitchcock contributed little to the movies he made (Figure 1.25). But his cameos are playful and enjoyable tests of viewers' powers of observation and a challenge to Hitchcock's inventiveness, since he did not want to make the same type of appearance twice.

CASTING

Once an actor becomes strongly associated with certain behavior outside the movies, for many viewers the actor becomes larger than the character in a film. Sometimes those extra qualities supplement a role. Thus John Wayne, who was well known for his conservative political beliefs, was cast in many conservative and patriotic roles. And Jane Fonda, who was well known for her liberal political views, has often played liberal characters. To make a character even more unappealing than the script does, filmmakers sometimes choose an actor who is well known for playing offensive roles. In *Contempt* (*Le Mépris*, 1963) the part of the arrogant and pushy American film **producer** is played by Jack Palance, who was well known for his portrayal of unsavory characters in such earlier films as *Shane*.

> **producer:** The person in charge of the business and administrative aspects of making a film, typically including acquiring rights to the script and hiring the personnel to make the film.

Filmmakers sometimes cast against type to catch viewers off guard. One of the best examples is the casting of Henry Fonda in a 1969 Italian ("spaghetti") western:

> In Sergio Leone's *Once Upon a Time in the West* [1969], a homesteader and his two children are spreading a picnic in their front yard. This frontier idyll is shattered by the materialization of five menacing figures, who kill the family in cold blood. The sense of violation is exacerbated by the familiar, reassuring smile on the face of the leader of these merciless specters [Figure 1.26a]. It's the smile of young Abe Lincoln [Figure 1.26b], Tom Joad [Figure 1.26c], Wyatt Earp, and Mister Roberts, a smile which for four decades in American movies has reflected the honesty, moral integrity, and egalitarian values synonymous with its owner—Henry Fonda.
>
> By casting him as an almost abstract personification of evil . . . , Leone dramatically reversed the prevailing image of Fonda, at once complicating and commenting on our responses to that image. (Morris 220)

Casting against type is chancy. Some viewers want an actor to play the same type of role repeatedly and may reject the actor in the new role. But as is illustrated by the casting of Fonda in *Once upon a Time in the West*, casting against type can be effective. It can make viewers entertain new ideas: in this case, perhaps to be jolted into the realization that someone who looks virtuous and has a good reputation may in fact be evil. Casting against type may intrigue viewers into checking out a film or video, to see if the actors can succeed in the challenge they have taken on (Figure 1.27).

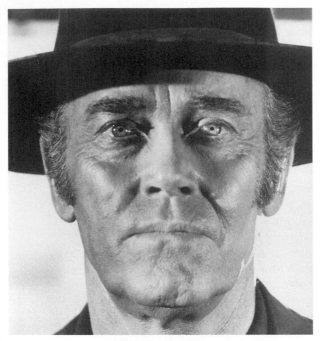

FIGURE 1.26 Casting against type
(a, left) Henry Fonda plays a child killer in *Once upon a Time in the West* (1968), a striking example of casting against type. Before this film, Fonda had played admirable characters, such as (b, below left) Lincoln in *Young Mr. Lincoln* (1939) and (c, below right) the sympathetic and kind Tom Joad in *The Grapes of Wrath* (1940).
(a) Paramount; Rafran; San Marco; The Museum of Modern Art/Film Stills Archive; (b) and (c) 20th Century-Fox

FIGURE 1.27 **Two stars cast against type**
Before *Mad Dog and Glory* (1992), Bill Murray (left) had played various amusing laid-back characters and Robert De Niro had played an assortment of urban criminals. In *Mad Dog and Glory*, they switch roles. Murray plays a Chicago hood who goes to a psychoanalyst and wants to be a stand-up comedian, but who also enslaves others and sanctions murders. De Niro plays a sensitive, mild-mannered police photographer ironically called "Mad Dog" by his co-workers. *Universal City Studios*

In some animated films and some documentaries, only actors' voices are used. In those cases, actors may also be cast against type. Usually, though, actors' voices are used as one might expect. The voice of Robin Williams, who usually plays comic parts in movies, is used in amusing ways in various animated films, such as *Aladdin* (1992). In *Toy Story* (1995), Don Rickles, who is known for his insulting grouchiness, supplies the voice of the caustic, cynical Mr. Potato Head, and Wallace Shawn, who has played uncertain and insecure characters, supplies the voice of the untyrannical (Tyrannosaurus) Rex. In Ken Burns's nine-part documentary film *Baseball* (1994), off-screen Gregory Peck—who has played a variety of well-known movie heroes—reads letters or statements by admirable men, such the 1919 Chicago White Sox manager, who was unaware that eight of his players were involved in throwing the World Series; elsewhere in the baseball documentary, Peck reads a passage from the Old Testament. In contrast, other actors were chosen to read the statements of "Shoeless" Joe Jackson, who was involved in the 1919 scandal, and the parts of other men the film depicts partially negatively, such as Ty Cobb.

PROCESS AND PERFORMANCE

A good part for an actor begins with an effective script and shrewd casting. Without a well-written part, usually an actor can achieve little. Often a successful screen performance also owes much to the casting. Many film directors, such as Martin Scorsese, say that if a movie is cast well, the acting will largely take care of itself.

Unlike stage actors, movie actors in big productions do their scenes piecemeal, usually out of order, and with extensive waiting between shots. Because filming is so time-consuming and costly, usually all the scenes at one setting are filmed together; then the crew moves to another setting and films all the scenes that take place there. Over many days, actors enact snippets here and snippets there. Unlike stage actors, film actors must be able to focus and deliver an appropriate performance after much waiting for the right weather, the right lighting, the right something or other. Often they have to maintain energy and focus through many versions of a shot.

Sometimes actors must improvise—say spontaneously what they think their characters would say under the circumstances. Although many directors allow no improvisation, in some films directed by Robert Altman, Mike Leigh, Rainer Werner Fassbinder, John Cassavetes, and Martin Scorsese, improvisation plays a major role. Those directors believe that what is improvised by an actor who is immersed in the character and the scene is likely to be truer to the character and situation than what has been imagined by the writer beforehand.

The actor's best allies are usually a skillful scriptwriter and a director who sets the contexts and establishes the moods for each scene. As is discussed in Chapter 3, the film actor can also be helped by an editor who selects the best version of each shot, shortens an ineffective shot, or **cuts** to a **reaction shot** during a brief lapse in the performance. During such lapses, music can also enhance the performance. In films with many action scenes and frequent brief shots, the writer, director, and editor—not the actor—may be the main creators of a performance.

Usually an effective performance compels viewers to believe in the character and helps keep them involved in the story. However, there is no one type of effective performance: what works depends on the film's **style** and to some extent on the viewers' culture. Droll, understated comedy—such as that found in *Mr. and Mrs. Bridge* (1990, Figure 1.28)—calls for restrained acting. Many films, including many comic films, work best if the acting is exaggerated. Film acting should be judged not by one absolute standard (such as "realism") but in light of the type of film it is in.

Judging a performance is difficult after only one viewing. A second viewing, comparison of a script and the performance, or a viewing of other films with the same actors can help viewers see the successes and failures of what is usually meant to be inconspicuous—the actor's art.

cut: To edit, as in "they cut the movie in four months."

reaction shot: A shot that shows someone reacting to an event.

style: The manner of presenting a subject in a creative work. In film studies, style also includes a consideration of the filmmakers' techniques.

FIGURE 1.28 **Understated comic acting**
Understated comic acting by Joanne Woodward and Paul Newman in *Mr. and Mrs. Bridge* (1990).
Note how Newman's and Woodward's body language and facial expressions convey their doubts
about the painting before them. *Miramax*

COMPOSITION: THE USES OF SPACE

Composition refers to how subjects are arranged in relation to each other
and to the sides of the frame. Before filming each shot, filmmakers may consider the following questions: What is the shape of the image to be? When
should empty space be used? Should the arrangement of subjects on the
sides of the frame or in the foreground and background be used to convey
some meaning or mood? Should the width and depth of the image be used
expressively within the same shot? Should the objects of main interest within
the frame balance each other or not? In this section we will examine some of
the consequences of answers to those and related questions.

Shape of Projected Image

The **aspect ratio** indicates the shape of an image; it refers to the relationship
of the image's width to its height. Thus an aspect ratio of 4:3 means that the
image is wider than it is tall by a factor of 4 to 3. Throughout film history the

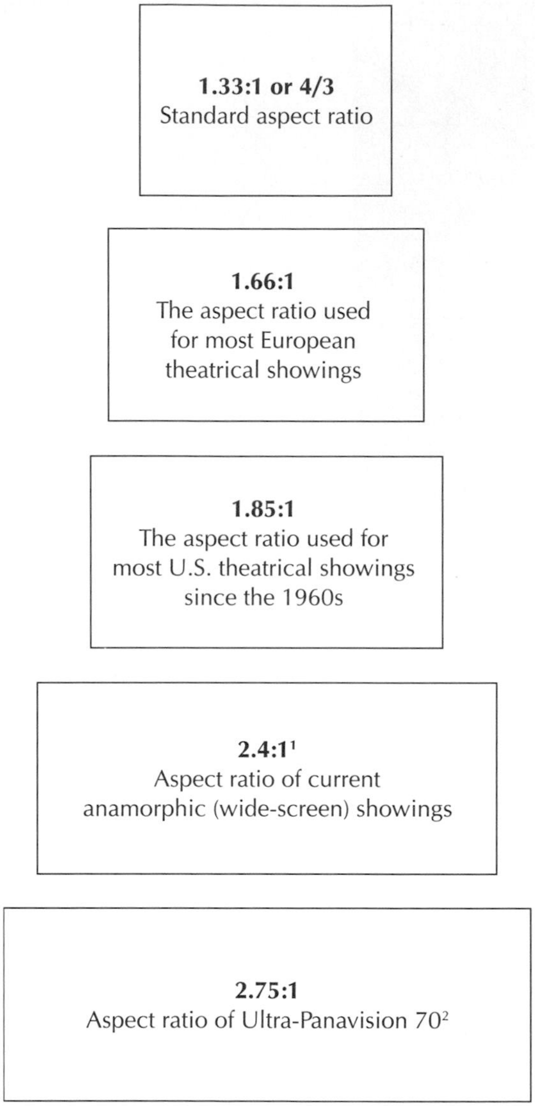

1.33:1 or 4/3
Standard aspect ratio

1.66:1
The aspect ratio used
for most European
theatrical showings

1.85:1
The aspect ratio used for
most U.S. theatrical showings
since the 1960s

2.4:1[1]
Aspect ratio of current
anamorphic (wide-screen) showings

2.75:1
Aspect ratio of Ultra-Panavision 70[2]

[1]Since about 1970, anamorphic showings of 35 mm films should be at 2.4:1, not, as is usually reported, 2.35:1.

[2]Anamorphic process used off and on in the 1950s and 1960s in such films as *Ben-Hur* (1959), *It's a Mad Mad Mad Mad World* (1963), and *The Greatest Story Ever Told* (1965).

FIGURE 1.29 **Five frequently used aspect ratios**
Movies have been shown in different rectangular shapes. Here are five of the most often used ones. They are drawn to scale; they are all the same height.

screen has nearly always been rectangular, but at different times the projected image has been wider than at other times. From about 1910 to the early 1950s, most films were shown in the **standard aspect ratio**: approximately 4:3 or 1.33:1. Since the 1950s, wider formats have dominated in theatrical showings. Figure 1.29 shows five frequently used aspect ratios. And Figure 1.30 illustrates how **wide-screen** films can be made and projected by using an **anamorphic lens**, which compresses the image onto the film during filming and then expands the image back to its original width during projection.

As wide-screen formats became commonplace in the 1950s to counter the growing popularity of TV, many filmmakers worried that the wider images would be suitable only for wide subjects. But filmmakers learned how to use the wide space effectively, as in *The Graduate* (1967) and in the Italian film *The Red Desert* (1964). At various points in *The Red Desert*, loose framing is used and the characters are appropriately scattered across the wide frame at various distances from one another and from the camera (Figure 1.31).

Though few filmmakers change the aspect ratio or shape of the image *during* filming, they can do so; more filmmakers did it in the silent era than since. A frame enlargement from *The Cabinet of Dr. Caligari* (Figure 1.32) illustrates another way to change the shape of an image: the sides, especially near the top, have been obscured by a process called **masking** to create an **iris shot**, here a triangular image. Other filmmakers change the shape of the image by simply illuminating only part of the frame. As the frame enlargement from *Caligari* shows, obscuring part of the image directs viewers' attention: there's nothing else to look at.

Because films have been made in a variety of rectangular shapes and the TV screen is a fixed shape, in videotape versions of movies and in films shown on analog TV, often the sides of the original image are lopped off (Figure 1.33c). In extreme cases—those films originally intended for theatrical presentation in a 2.75:1 aspect ratio, such as *Ben-Hur* (1959) and *It's a Mad Mad Mad Mad World* (1963)—less than half of the original image remains when the film is viewed in the standard aspect ratio.

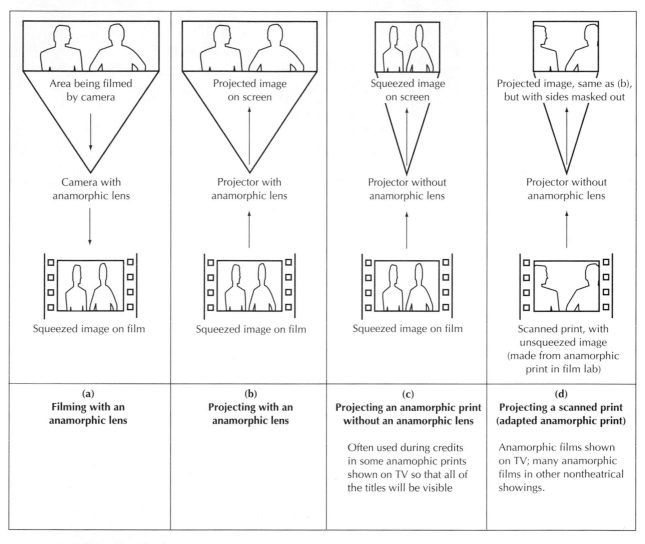

FIGURE 1.30 **The anamorphic lens**
An anamorphic lens is used to compress a wide filmed image onto the film in the camera.
Another anamorphic lens is attached to a movie projector to expand the image during projection.
(Not to scale.)

A "scanned print," or adapted anamorphic print, is a version made in the standard aspect ratio from an original wide-screen film. In making a scanned print, a technician—not the film's editor or director—decides which part of the complete anamorphic image to show at each moment of the film or video. Often in scanned prints the camera *seems* to glide sideways during a

FIGURE 1.31 Composition and meaning
Composition can convey major meanings in a story. With the characters at different distances from the camera and spread across the frame, this composition from *The Red Desert* (1964), reinforces the sense of the characters' alienation from one another, which is one of the film's main meanings. Frame enlargement. *Film Duemila; Cinematografica; The Museum of Modern Art/Film Stills Archive*

FIGURE 1.32 Masking to create an iris shot
An iris shot is made by placing a mask or covering over part of the lens while filming. An iris shot may be used to obscure background and to focus viewers' attention on the subject. It can also be used, as in this frame from *The Cabinet of Dr. Caligari* (1919), to suggest that something is not right in the film's world. Frame enlargement. *Decla-Bioscop; The Museum of Modern Art/ Circulating Film Library*

40

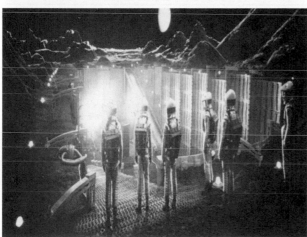

FIGURE 1.33 Three versions of an anamorphic film
(a, top) Theatrical showings of *2001: A Space Odyssey* (1968) in the 2.2:1 aspect ratio illustrate the advantages of the wide-screen image when the subject is vast. (b, above left) A squeezed frame (not projected through an anamorphic lens) elongates everything in the image. (c, above right) When the film is shown unsqueezed but in the standard aspect ratio on a television set, only about half of the original image is visible—not necessarily the center portion. In this case, the astronaut on the right has been cut from the image and the vastness of the setting is lost. Frame enlargements. *Metro-Goldwyn-Mayer*

FIGURE 1.34 Showing wide-screen films since the 1960s
Many theatrical films since the 1960s have been shot without an anamorphic lens with theaters *and* television in mind and can be shown in 1.85:1 in U.S. theaters (inner rectangle) or 1.33:1 elsewhere (outer rectangle). As illustrated by this frame from *Clueless* (1995), the visual information blocked out at the top and bottom of the wide-screen version is of little or no importance. Frame enlargement. *Paramount*

FIGURE 1.35 The letterbox format
The letterbox format is used to retain the original wide-screen aspect ratio (or a close approximation of it) of an anamorphic film shown on TV or a video monitor, here *2001: A Space Odyssey* (1968). Letterbox images are more or less in the shape of a business envelope (hence the name). Usually, the blacked-out bottom and top parts of the image are the same size, though occasionally only the bottom part of the screen is blacked out so that there is even more space for subtitles. Frame enlargement. *Metro-Goldwyn-Mayer*

shot. To trained viewers, however, these horizontal movements are distracting, since they do not usually occur when and how camera movements do during filming.

For some years now, filmmakers have known that their films will also be shown on television and have composed their images so that no important details are beyond the standard aspect ratio frame. Such films can be shown in theaters at 1.85:1 or on analog television at 1.33:1 with similar results (Figure 1.34).

Some videotapes include a message that the image has been "formatted to fit your screen," or some similar message. But for a film originally released in an anamorphic format (for example, a film in CinemaScope or any other process with *scope* as part of its name), the full image will be visible only in a videotape, laser disc, or DVD in the **letterbox format** (Figure 1.35). In a letterbox version, the film's original theatrical aspect ratio is retained by not using a portion of the top and bottom of the TV or monitor screen. Some videotapes of foreign-language films in the letterbox format include subtitles in the darkened area under the image so that viewers can see the original images in their entirety and read distinct subtitles.

When considering the shape of an image on the screen, consider whether you are seeing the whole picture. If not, what you say about composition may not be true to the film as it was intended to be seen.

Empty Space

Empty space is often used to convey a sense of loss as in *Tokyo Story* (1953, Figure 1.36). Another film that uses empty space to suggest the feeling of loss is *Fargo* (1996), in which a husband arrives home and finds that his wife has been kidnapped, as he had arranged. The reality of what the husband has set in motion, however, is quickly and visually conveyed largely by empty space (things being badly out of order also contributes to the effect) (Figure 1.37).

FIGURE 1.36 **Empty space to convey loss**
(a, top) Early in *Tokyo Story* (1953), the mother and father prepare to go visit their grown children. The mother is on the left side of the frame, the father on the right, and a neighbor outside a window chats with them. (b, above) In two shots near the end of the film, the same neighbor stops briefly at the same window, and the same camera placement is used. But now the mother has died and the left side of the frame is empty. Frame enlargements. *Shochiku; New Yorker Films*

FIGURE 1.37 Empty space suggesting disruption of order
Four shots from a scene in *Fargo* (1996) convey a sense of emptiness and loss, as the husband returns home and discovers that his wife is missing and their home a mess. (a, top left) A shot of the husband entering the front door parallels an earlier happier scene. (b, top right) The second shot, taken from inside a bathroom in which one of the kidnappers had found the wife, shows no one, no life, no movement, just a mess. (c, above left) The fifth shot of the scene focuses on an empty shower curtain rod from the husband's point of view. (d, above right) The sixth shot shows the TV that the wife had been watching when the kidnappers broke into the house. Even the TV, also "empty," contributes to the lifeless feeling of the scene: it's a dramatically right detail. Frame enlargements. *PolyGram Film Productions*

Like everything else in a film, the use of empty space has no inherent meaning. Empty space is not always used in a negative context. It can reinforce a sense of power and freedom, as in countless scenes of flying airplanes, or a sense of energy and free-spiritedness (Figure 1.38).

If we see largely empty space in a shot, followed by something intruding abruptly, the results can be startling. For example, in *The Shining* (1980) we see a locked bathroom door, then an ax cutting through it, then the Jack Nicholson character who is trying to get to his wife to murder her (Figure 1.39). Suddenly, he is intruding into his wife's space—and the viewer's world.

FIGURE 1.38 **Empty space to convey freedom**
A subject surrounded by empty space (loose framing) can seem to enjoy a maximum of freedom, as in this shot from *Black Stallion* (1979). *United Artists*

FIGURE 1.39 **Violating space**
In *The Shining* (1980), the Jack Nicholson character's sudden breakthrough into his wife's and the viewer's space is startling and threatening. *Stanley Kubrick; Warner Bros.*

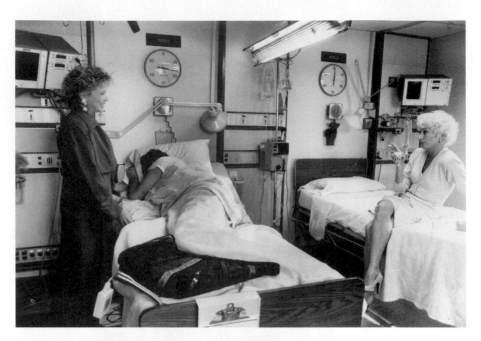

FIGURE 1.40 Framing to display contending forces

An often-used composition, illustrated by a shot from *The Grifters* (1990): (a, above) Two opposing forces on opposite sides of the frame, with the object of contention between them. (b, left) In many photographs advertising *The Grifters* (but not taken from the movie), the same composition is used: the man is between the two warring women. *Cineplex Odeon Films Production; Miramax*

Taking Sides

The width of the film image may be used expressively. Films often show two people alienated from each other on opposite sides of the frame. Late in *Raging Bull* (1980), the Jake La Motta character spots his brother Joey, from whom he has been estranged for years. Joey glances at Jake and walks away without a word. As Jake follows Joey, the camera moves parallel to them, and all the while we see Joey near the left edge of the frame and Jake near the right edge. The composition—the two on opposite sides of the frame, Joey keeping his back to his brother—conveys the emotional distance Joey wants to maintain. As in many films and staged plays, *The Grifters* (1990, Figure 1.40) often shows two opposing forces on opposite sides of the frame, with the subject of their conflict between them.

Occasionally filmmakers use split-screen techniques to show two or more images simultaneously on the same screen. *Napoléon* (1927) occasionally divides one screen image into three tall rectangles and early in the film divides the screen space into nine equal small rectangles, each one showing a different action. A split-screen effect may also be achieved by using separate films projected onto separate screens placed side by side, as in the ending of *Napoléon* (Figure 1.41). Often in *Napoléon*, multiple images on one screen or on all three screens allow the simultaneous viewing of events that are presumably happening at the same time.

FIGURE 1.41 **Split screen serving different functions**
Until near the end of Abel Gance's *Napoléon* (1927), only the middle screen of three side-by-side screens is used. During the concluding eighteen minutes, three projectors and all three screens are used. (a, top) Viewers sometimes see one vast subject spilling over into all three screens. Here Napoleon looks at his encamped troops. (b, above) At occasional points late in *Napoléon*, one subject is projected on the center screen and a different subject is projected on the right and left screens. Sometimes the outer screens are mirror images of each other, as here. At other times, the outer screens are identical. Frame enlargements. *Images Film Archive; The Museum of Modern Art/Film Stills Archive*

FIGURE 1.42 Split screen to show contrasts
This split-screen image from *Annie Hall* (1977) shows Annie with her therapist and Alvy with his. Viewers can quickly see the contrasting settings and postures of each patient without the film cutting back and forth between the two scenes. *Jack Rollins-Charles H. Joffe Productions; United Artists*

FIGURE 1.43 Screen split to show similarities and competition
Early in *The Grifters* (1990), we see the main characters, who are all grifters or con artists, on the same screen split vertically into three areas: mother, son, and son's lover. The three characters stop almost simultaneously, turn, and look around carefully before turning back and continuing with their work: the mother to enter a racetrack and cheat her mob boss out of some winnings, the son to enter a bar where he cons two men, and the son's lover to enter a jewelry store where she tries to con the jeweler. Filming the three characters in the same position (and having all three wear sunglasses) suggests that they have much in common. Here the split screen also communicates to viewers for the first time that the young man, placed between the two women, will soon be the object of their fierce competition. *Cineplex Odeon Films Production; Miramax*

A split screen may also be used to emphasize a contrast or similarity. In *Annie Hall* (Figure 1.42) the split screen emphasizes a contrast of settings and behavior. In *The Grifters* the split screen emphasizes fundamental similarities (Figure 1.43).

The split-screen technique may be used for many different purposes within the same film. The documentary film *Woodstock* (1970) uses many variations of split screen—for example, to show action and simultaneous reactions; to show actions and someone commenting on them; to show different actions occurring simultaneously; and to show simultaneous views (different distances and angles) of the same subject, usually musical performers. In *Woodstock* the extensive use of two or three simultaneous images also suggests that although the film runs nearly four hours, the events were too widespread and significant to be conveyed by one mere image at a time, even wide-screen images.

An effect similar to split screen, but without using multiple films or editing, can be achieved by showing a reflection of someone looking through a window on one side of the frame and, on the other side, what that person is looking at (Figure 1.44). Such a shot is also used briefly in *The Magnificent Ambersons* (1942): as George Amberson Minafer looks through a window at the departing Eugene Morgan, viewers see the reflection of George's face and through another part of the window the retreating Eugene Morgan.

FIGURE 1.44 Window and reflected looker
A window, a carefully chosen camera angle, and lighting are used in this shot from *Schindler's List* (1993) to show simultaneously Schindler looking at a scene and the subject he is looking at. If the filmmakers had instead used two shots to convey the same information—a shot of Schindler looking and a shot of what he sees—they would have had to determine how much time to give to each shot—and the effect would have been much different. *Steven Spielberg, Gerald R. Molen, and Branko Lustig; Universal*

Mise en Scène or Editing?

For each scene, filmmakers decide how much to rely on mise en scène—settings, subjects, and composition—and how much to rely on edited shots, connected pieces of film each of which shows a fragment of time and space.

In one scene in *Citizen Kane*, Charles Foster Kane, a wealthy newspaper publisher, and his wife, Emily, have gone to the residence of Kane's mistress, Susan, where they are met by Susan and a crooked politician (Gettys). During the scene Gettys tries to pressure Kane into withdrawing from the governor's race against him or face public exposure of Kane's affair with Susan. Early in the scene, one shot lasting 117 seconds contains the following compositions and major movements:

1. At the beginning of the shot, Kane is near the left of the frame facing Emily, who is on the right of the frame.

2. Susan joins Kane on the left (the camera pivots slightly to the left to accommodate her), and the three characters are positioned much as they are in the figure, although in the film Kane is closer to Susan than to Emily.

3. Kane turns away from the two women and starts to walk toward the background. As he walks, the camera pivots slightly to the right to follow him, excluding Susan from the frame, and Emily pivots and looks toward the background, where Kane joins Gettys. Emily is in the left foreground; the two men are in the background.

4. Gettys walks forward while staying on the right of the frame. Kane remains in the background, in the center of the frame between Emily on the left and Gettys on the right. For the rest of the shot Gettys and Emily remain in the foreground and on opposite sides of the frame.

5. Susan rushes into the frame from the left and joins Kane in the background, center.

6. Susan steps forward a few steps; Kane remains in the background.

7. Susan takes another step forward; Kane remains in the background.

8. Toward the end of the shot, Emily, Susan, and Gettys, all in the foreground, turn their heads and look toward Kane, who remains in the background (they await his response to Gettys's blackmail attempt).

Much is going on in this lengthy shot, both in groupings of characters (shifting alignments and confrontations) and in dramatic impact (who commands attention, who has power, who does not). For example, the shot begins with Kane between his wife and mistress, though closer to his mistress than his wife, and with the blackmailer out of the frame, in fact waiting in a dark part of the room. The shot ends with Kane in the center of the frame, facing his wife, mistress, and blackmailer in the foreground. By his own choice he is physically and emotionally alone. In spite of his wife's practical advice and his mistress's emotional appeals, he is determined that only he will make the decision he is about to announce.

Instead of using one shot and various movements and shifting compositions within it, director Orson Welles could have used a series of shots, edited after filming. With apologies to the memory of Orson Welles and to editor Robert Wise, here is one way the action could have been filmed as five shots:

Shot 1. Kane is near the left of the frame facing Emily, who is on the right of the frame. Susan joins Kane on the left (the camera pivots slightly to the left

Citizen Kane, 1941
Publicity still closely approximating the composition of a few frames of *Citizen Kane*. *RKO General Pictures*

to accommodate her), and the three characters are positioned much as they are in the figure, with Kane closer to Susan than to Emily. Kane turns away from the two women and starts to walk toward the background.

Shot 2. Kane arrives in the background where he joins Gettys. Emily is positioned on the left side of the frame in the foreground. After a while, Gettys begins walking toward Emily (and the camera).

Shot 3. Gettys joins Emily in the foreground, but on the opposite side of the frame. Kane can be seen in the background in the center of the frame.

Shot 4. Kane is seen in medium long shot as Susan rushes into the frame from the left and joins him. Later Susan begins to step forward.

Shot 5. As Susan finishes stepping forward, Emily can be seen in the left foreground and Gettys in the right foreground; Kane remains in the background. Susan takes another step forward. Toward the end of the shot, Emily, Susan, and Gettys turn their heads and look toward Kane, who remains in the background (they await his decision).

Many directors and editors would also include at least one reaction shot, a shot showing someone reacting to what is being said or done. The hypothetical edited version breaks up the continuity of space and time, gives less emphasis to the compositions, and in consequence gives somewhat more weight to the dialogue.

Mise en scène or editing? Anyone shooting and editing film or videotape faces the choice repeatedly.

51

FIGURE 1.45 Window and reflected subject looked at
In this publicity still from *The Godfather Part II* (1974), viewers see the subject through the window and, elsewhere on the window, a reflection of what the subject sees. *The Coppola Company, Paramount*

FIGURE 1.46 Window and reflected subject behind the looker
This publicity still for *The Silence of the Lambs* (1991) shows the person at the right looking, and what she is looking at (the person on the left) reflected off a glass or plastic barrier separating them. *Orion*

FIGURE 1.47 Reflection of looker superimposed on subject looked at
This frame enlargement from *My Darling Clementine* (1946) illustrates a reflection used to show the looker's face superimposed on what he sees. Doc Holliday, who is seriously ill and getting worse, drinks a shot of whiskey, looks at his medical certificate, says his own name scornfully ("Doctor John Holliday"), then throws the whiskey glass and breaks the glass protecting the certificate. Frame enlargement. *Samuel G. Engel; 20th Century-Fox*

Shots involving a window, a looker, and a subject looked at are also used in *The Godfather Part II* (1974) and *The Silence of the Lambs* (1991); in those films, however, the reflection is not of the looker but of what he or she sees (Figures 1.45 and 1.46). It's also possible to show the looker and what is looked at in the same position within the frame (Figure 1.47).

In using a shot of a reflection off glass, filmmakers show simultaneously a person and what he or she looks at. They maintain continuity of time and space rather than divide the information into a shot of the person looking and a shot of what is looked at. In other words, they choose to communicate the information by the composition of a single shot, not the editing of two shots.

Foreground and Background

How filmmakers position people and objects in the background and how they place people and objects in the foreground are options that much effect what the images communicate. The background of an action may go unnoticed because it is obscurely lit or out of focus or because the actions of the characters draw the viewers' attention. However, in some contexts, such as when a dangerous character is lurking nearby, a dark or out-of-focus background may command viewers' attention. Often the background is in focus, and details there affect how viewers respond to something in the foreground, or details in the foreground may influence how viewers react to some aspect of the background.

A filmmaker may use **rack focus**: changing the focus during a shot (usually rapidly) from foreground to background or vice versa. Rack focus directs viewers' attention to the relationship of foreground and background or to the action of a different subject. Often this shift in focus is done during a dramatic moment or while the primary

FIGURE 1.48 **Rack focus**
During a shot from *Apollo 13* (1995) rack focus is used to shift the focus from the foreground subject to a background subject. (a, top) Early in the shot the ground controller in the foreground is in focus; the ground controller in the background is not. (b, above) Less than a second later, rack focus has been used to shift the focus from the foreground subject to the background subject. Frame enlargements. *Universal*

subject of the shot is moving, or both, so that viewers do not notice the change in focus (Figure 1.48). In *Fatal Attraction* (1987), the Michael Douglas character, who is being stalked by a former lover, has driven into his driveway.

For a few moments he listens to part of a taped message from his stalker. He gets out of the car and reaches across the driver's side to get his briefcase. Then, as he reaches in the car for a rabbit cage and the cage momentarily crosses the screen, rack focus is used quickly and unobtrusively, and the previously out-of-focus background is replaced with a focused image of the stalker's black car. Like the use of reflections on glass discussed in the previous section, rack focus maintains continuity of space and time and is an alternative to editing.

Foreground and background elements can show the importance of something in the background to the subject in the foreground, as in *The General* (1926, Figure 1.49). Another example of background elements revealing the values of a subject in the foreground is seen in a publicity still for *Do the Right Thing* (1989, Figure 1.50).

Sometimes viewers can see something significant in the background that a character in the foreground is unaware of. Such is the case in a scene in *Local Hero* (1983). The citizens of a small Scottish village have been meeting in a church but do not want the main character in the foreground to know about it.

FIGURE 1.49 Background to convey something about subject in foreground
This photograph is Johnnie's gift to his sweetheart early in *The General* (1926). Overemphasizing the background at the expense of the human subject effectively—and amusingly—demonstrates the importance of the train to Johnnie. Frame enlargement. *United Artists*

FIGURE 1.50 Expressiveness of background elements
Part of a setting seen several times in the background is often significant, as in *Do the Right Thing*
(1989). Viewers never get to see the photos on the wall of Sal's Pizzeria clearly, but they are
referred to in the dialogue several times and an observant viewer can discern some of the Italian
American people and characters on the wall, including Joe DiMaggio and the celluloid Rocky.
Forty Acres and a Mule Filmworks; Universal

As the main character talks to his assistant, in the distant background viewers
can see the villagers scampering out of the church.

The foreground may subtly comment on the background (Figure 1.51).
Sometimes filmmakers film through a foreground object, but viewers are so
interested in the main subject in the background that they may not notice
the object in the foreground or consider how it relates to the subject in the
background. For example, when filmmakers impose something with bars (a
door, a window, a headboard) in the foreground, often the suggestion is of
entrapment or imprisonment for the subject in the background (Figure
1.52). Another example occurs in *Wish You Were Here* (1987). Lynda—an insecure teenage girl involved with Eric, a much older man—goes to live with
Eric after her father learns of the affair. Eric calls her to his bed where he has
stretched out. As she approaches the bed and sits on the edge of it, the camera
moves so that it looks through the bars of the headboard at the two figures.
The image suggests that being there with Eric is or will be a prison for Lynda.

FIGURE 1.51 Foreground affecting a shot's mood

Early in the last shot of *Annie Hall* (1977), the foreground contains empty tables and hard surfaces: no people, no plants, no soft textures. In the background, Alvy and Annie kiss goodbye for the last time, ending their relationship. The filmmakers could easily have filmed outside, with no objects between subjects and camera, but the mood of the shot is more effective—conveying a lonely or empty feeling—with Alvy and Annie's parting framed by a barren foreground. Frame enlargement. *United Artists*

FIGURE 1.52 Foreground suggesting entrapment
Bars or a wire cage in the foreground may suggest entrapment of the subject in the background. With the subject's hands on the cage, as in *The Pawnbroker* (1965), viewers may think of the subject as a caged zoo animal. *Allied Artists*

FIGURE 1.53 **Width and depth used expressively**
After the father slaps his son in a shot from *The Bicycle Thief* (1948), the sulking boy keeps his
physical and emotional distance. Their estrangement is suggested by the framing: they are on
opposite sides of the frame and the boy is deep in the background. Frame enlargement. *PDS-ENIC*

Occasionally, both width and depth are used expressively within the
same shot. In *The Bicycle Thief* (1948; also known as *Bicycle Thieves*), when a
boy is angry at his father, he is seen in the background and on the opposite
side of the frame from the father (Figure 1.53).

Symmetrical and Asymmetrical Compositions

In symmetrical compositions with only one major subject, the subject is seen in
the approximate center of the frame (Figure 1.54). In symmetrical compositions with two subjects, both may be in the center of the frame (Figure 1.55),
though typically they are on the opposite sides of the frame, or both may be
near the center (Figure 1.56). Even an extremely complicated composition
may still be symmetrical (Figure 1.57).

In asymmetrical compositions, major subjects are not offset by other
subjects elsewhere in the frame. An expressive asymmetrical composition
occurs at the end of *Shoot the Piano Player* (1960). By the penultimate scene,
Charlie, the main character, has lost the woman he loves. In the last shot of

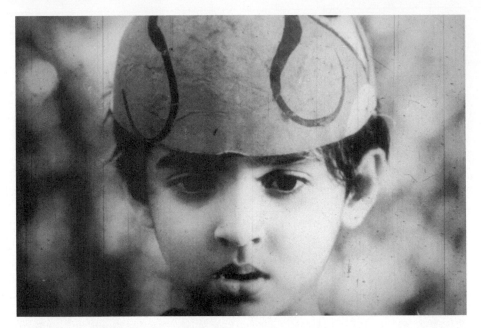

FIGURE 1.54 Symmetrical composition with one subject
In a symmetrical composition from *The World of Apu* (1959), the single subject appears in the middle of the frame with nothing in focus around his head to draw viewers' attention. Frame enlargement.
Edward Harrison

FIGURE 1.55 Symmetrical composition with one subject on another
This symmetrical composition from *Blowup* (1966) shows two subjects, one on top of the other, in the center of the frame, in which a fashion photographer photographs a model. Frame enlargement.
Carlo Ponti; Metro-Goldwyn-Mayer

FIGURE 1.56 Symmetrical composition with two subjects near each other
A symmetrical composition from *Personal Best* (1982) places two subjects side by side near the
center of the frame. *Warner Bros.*

the last scene, Charlie is on the extreme left side of the wide-screen frame;
on the right side is a plain wall. Charlie appears alone and out of balance—
and he is. (This effect is lost if the film is not seen in its original wide-screen
aspect ratio.) A film may use asymmetrical compositions more than only occasionally. *L'avventura* (1960) uses them repeatedly, including in the film's
last shot, an image of the two main characters off to the left of the wide-
screen frame (Figure 1.58). In *L'avventura*, typically the setting on one side
of the frame offsets the character(s) on the opposite side; this composition

suggests the importance of the film's settings—which have little movement, vegetation, or life—and reinforces the sense that something is missing in the characters' lives.

Occasionally tight framing is used until someone abruptly intrudes into the image. For example, a hand may quickly emerge from offscreen and grab a character, as often happens in eerie, frightening scenes (memorably in *Night of the Living Dead*). Sometimes this technique is used to frighten a character and viewers, but then both quickly learn that the intruder is not a threat. In *Fatal Attraction*, the Michael Douglas character is seen near an edge of the

FIGURE 1.57 Symmetrical composition with multiple subjects
In this image from *Cabaret* (1972), characters on the right balance characters on the left, and characters in the foreground are offset by characters in the background. The image could scarcely be more symmetrical. *Allied Artists–ABC Pictures*

FIGURE 1.58 **Asymmetrical composition**
The director of *L'avventura* (1959), Michelangelo Antonioni, often positioned human subjects on one side of the wide frame without corresponding human subjects on the opposite side. The resultant feeling is that things are out of balance. Frame enlargement. *Produzione Cinematografiche Europee and Société Cinématographique Lyre*

frame, listening to a menacing tape from his former lover; then his wife's hands quickly enter the frame to give his shoulders a massage. He and the viewers jump then are relieved; and perhaps viewers are a little amused.

MISE EN SCÈNE AND THE WORLD OUTSIDE THE FRAME

Sometimes filmmakers use settings, subjects, and composition to comment on the world outside the frame, for example to express a political viewpoint or promote a product. Mise en scène can also be used to parody something outside the film, including another film, or it can be used to pay tribute to another film.

Filmmakers may use an image to express political ideas that relate to the story yet promote the filmmakers' political views (Figure 1.59).

As music is used in some films to promote the sale of sound tracks on CDs and tapes, so mise en scène can be used to promote products. Moviemakers often make agreements with companies to display their products in

FIGURE 1.59 **Using mise en scène to promote a political viewpoint**
In more than one shot of *Do the Right Thing* (1989), the graffiti in the background includes the
slogan "Dump Koch." At the time of the film's making, Ed Koch was running for reelection as
mayor of New York City. The graffiti is credible in the story because many New York African
Americans believed that Koch had failed to deal with racial strife effectively. The graffiti also
allows director Spike Lee to express his own political views, at least indirectly: before and during
the making of *Do the Right Thing*, Lee openly opposed Koch's reelection. *Forty Acres and a Mule
Filmworks; Universal*

exchange for money, goods, services, or promotion of the movie. Sometimes
the products shown are cited in the end credits ("The Producers Wish to
Thank Stanley Furniture, . . . Coca-Cola, . . . Black Death Vodka, Folgers
Coffee, . . . American Tobacco"), but often they are not. So widespread has
product placement become that some large companies pay specialists to
arrange for placements in movies. An example of a film using mise en scène to
promote a product is *Silkwood* (1983, Figure 1.60). In *Stand by Me*—released
by Columbia Pictures in 1986 when Coca-Cola still owned controlling
shares of Columbia—an early scene includes an empty Coke bottle in the
background of sixteen shots. After a brief flashback to a different location,
the scene resumes, and that Coke bottle can be seen in twenty-three more

shots; in a few shots, the bottle on the left of the frame balances the human subject on the right. Paul Martin Lester describes other examples of product promotion in movies:

> Seagram's, the parent company for Mumm's champagne, paid $50,000 for Cher to drink that brand in the movie *Moonstruck*. General Motors paid to have Tom Cruise drive Chevrolet Luminas in *Days of Thunder*. Disney offered a sliding scale to advertisers for [its] little-seen film *Mr. Destiny*. Simply showing the product on the screen cost $20,000. But if a main character actually used the product, a $60,000 fee was demanded and received. (85)

FIGURE 1.60 **Using mise en scène to promote a product** Mise en scène is used throughout *Silkwood* (1983) to promote Coca-Cola, as shown in this publicity still. In many shots in the film, Coke bottles, cups, or machines (a lot of Coors beer cans, too) are visible. In the scene represented in this still, three men sit at a counter or table, each with a partially full bottle of Coke; the Meryl Streep character (right) joins the Kurt Russell character (left) briefly, and between them and in the background is a Coke machine. As she walks away from him and goes to a nearby table, the camera keeps the Coke machine visible in the background; on the table where she pauses are three empty Coke bottles. Perhaps Coca-Cola is so prominent in this film because at the time the film was made, Coca-Cola owned Columbia Pictures, the studio that produced *Silkwood*. *ABC Motion Pictures; Columbia; The Museum of Modern Art/Film Stills Archive*

FIGURE 1.61 Using mise en scène to promote a product humorously
In *The Flintstones* (1994), various products are adapted to prehistoric times in amusing ways yet promoted. For example, at one point, characters appear before a Liz Claybone store, a parody, or amusing imitation, of today's Liz Claiborne stores that sell women's clothing. Here, viewers see that sales are climbing at an early Roc Donald's. Frame enlargement. *Universal City Studios and Amblin Entertainment*

Movies may also plug a business. *Contact* (1997), released by Warner Bros., features Cable News Network (CNN) repeatedly. That's no accident. At the time *Contact* was being made, both Warner Bros. and CNN were owned by Time Warner. In multicorporate businesses, one branch often promotes another.

Product placement can be subtle, creative, and amusing as in *The Flintstones* (1994, Figure 1.61). Increasingly, though, product placements are heavy-handed. One scene in *Wayne's World* (1992) amusingly shows five name-brand products in a row, including Garth suddenly dressed in Reebok shoes, Reebok jogging suit, and a hat with "Reebok" emblazoned under the brim and above it. Product placement also can be obvious, unimaginative, and unamusing. Roger Ebert noticed that *Happy Gilmore* (1996) includes "one Subway sandwich eaten outside a store, one date in a Subway store, one Subway soft drink container, two verbal mentions of Subway, one Subway commercial starring Happy, a Subway T-shirt, and a Subway golf bag. Halfway through the movie, I didn't know what I wanted more: laughs, or mustard."

Some filmmakers consciously conceal product identity to avoid possible lawsuits. If a movie shows someone committing a crime, filmmakers are usually careful not to associate the crime with a commercial product. That is why viewers will not see a character listen to a particular heavy metal number or drink a famous whiskey then go out and murder someone.

Mise en scène can also be used to parody something or someone. A **parody** is an amusing imitation of serious human behavior, such as a famous story, part of a story, or type of film. For example, the mise en scène of Dr. Franken-stein's laboratory in the 1931 movie classic (Figure 5.8a on p. 224) is amus-ingly re-created in *Young Frankenstein* (1974, Figure 5.8b). Mise en scène can also be used to pay an **homage**, a complimentary reference to or re-creation of an earlier film or part of one. For instance, some shots of the main character in the French film *Breathless* (1959) re-create mannerisms that Humphrey Bogart used in his films.

SUMMARY

In this book mise en scène, which is originally a theatrical term, signifies the major aspects filmmaking shares with staging a play. It refers to the selection of setting, subjects, and composition of each shot. Normally in complex film productions, the director makes final decisions about mise en scène.

Settings

■ A setting is the place where filmed action occurs. It is either a set, which has been built for use in the film, or a location, which is any place other than one built for use in the movie.

■ Settings can reveal the time and place of a scene, create or intensify moods, and reveal what people or characters are like.

Subjects

■ In films, fictional characters or real people are the usual subjects, and their actions and appearances help reveal their nature.

■ Performers may be stars, Method actors, character actors, or nonprofes-sional actors. Depending on the desired results, actors may be cast with type or against type.

■ Usually film actors must perform in brief segments, and often after long waits.

■ Effective performances may depend on the script, casting, direction, edit-ing, and music. There is no one type of effective performance: what is judged effective depends on the viewers' culture and the film's style, its manner of presenting its subject.

Composition

- Filmmakers, especially cinematographers and directors, can use the space within an image expressively. They decide the shape of the overall image, when and how to use empty space, and what meanings will be conveyed by the arrangement of significant objects on the sides of the frame, in the foreground, or in the background. Filmmakers also decide if compositions are to be symmetrical or asymmetrical.

- Composition can be used to influence viewers' responses, for example by what they see around the subject and how the subject is positioned within the frame; to reveal information to viewers that the characters do not know; and to help reveal a characters' personalities or situations.

- Many films are seen in an aspect ratio other than the one the filmmakers intended, and the compositions are thus altered, sometimes severely.

Uses of Mise en Scène to Comment on Something Outside the Frame

- Mise en scène can be used to promote a political viewpoint or commercial product (the latter practice is called "product placement").

- Mise en scène can also be used to parody earlier work or to pay homage to an earlier film.

WORKS CITED

Amory, Cleveland. "When Jack Lemmon Refused to Change His Name." *Parade* 17 Mar. 1985: 4–8. Interview.

Ebert, Roger. Rev. of *Happy Gilmore*. *Chicago Sun-Times* 16 Feb. 1996. 27 Mar. 1998 <http://www.suntimes.com/ebert/ebert_reviews/1996/02/1020768.html>.

Lester, Paul Martin. *Visual Communication: Images with Messages*. Belmont, CA: Wadsworth, 1995.

Morris, George. "Henry Fonda." *The National Society of Film Critics on the Movie Star*. Ed. Elisabeth Weis. New York: Penguin, 1981.

Naremore, James. *Acting in the Cinema*. Berkeley: U of California P, 1988.

Pechter, William S. "Cagney vs. Allen vs. Brooks: On the Indispensability of the Performer." *The National Society of Film Critics on the Movie Star*. Ed. Elisabeth Weis. New York: Penguin, 1981.

Reynaud, Berenice. "Gong Li and the Glamour of the Chinese Star." *Sight and Sound* Aug. 1993: 12–15.

Wood, Daniel B. "Solemn Themes Won Praise on Oscar Night." *Christian Science Monitor* 23 Mar. 1994: 16+.

FOR FURTHER READING

Barsacq, Léon. *Caligari's Cabinet and Other Grand Illusions: A History of Film Design*. Rev. and ed. Elliott Stein. Boston: New York Graphic Soc., 1976. A history of film designers, movements, and techniques. Includes 160 black-and-white illustrations and filmographies for many art directors and production designers.

Bruzzi, Stella. *Undressing Cinema: Clothing and Identity in the Movies*. London: Routledge, 1997. Citing detailed examples from a variety of popular films, Bruzzi demonstrates how clothes are key elements in the construction of cinematic gender, identity, sexuality, and desire. The chapters are divided into three groups: Dressing Up, Gender, and Beyond Gender.

By Design: Interviews with Film Production Designers. Ed. Vincent LoBrutto. Westport, CT: Praeger, 1992. Interviews with twenty film production designers; the book includes a glossary and a bibliography with many annotated entries.

Carringer, Robert L. *The Making of* Citizen Kane. Rev. and updated. Berkeley: U of California P, 1996. An in-depth examination that includes a chapter on the art director. Many black-and-white illustrations.

Garnett, Tay. *Directing: Learn from the Masters*. Lanham, MD: Scarecrow, 1996. Directors such as Scorsese, Spielberg, Malle, Fellini, and Truffaut discuss their decisions in making films.

Haskell, Molly. *From Reverence to Rape: The Treatment of Women in the Movies*. 2nd ed. Chicago: U of Chicago P, 1987. An examination of female actors and the types of roles they have played, especially in American movies.

Leese, Elizabeth. *Costume Design in the Movies: An Illustrated Guide to the Work of 157 Great Designers*. Rev. ed. New York: Dover, 1991. Brief biographical information, screen credits, and a listing of major nominations for 157 costume designers. Includes 177 black-and-white photographs and design renderings.

Lumet, Sidney. *Making Movies*. New York: Knopf, 1995. On filmmaking by a famous American director. Chapter 6 is on art direction and clothes.

Making Visible the Invisible: An Anthology of Original Essays on Film Acting. Ed. Carole Zucker. Metuchen, NJ: Scarecrow, 1990. The essays in Part 1 deal "with film acting in a historical and generic context." The articles in Part 2 "concentrate on case studies of individual actors, or on a director's work with actors."

Miller, Mark Crispin. "Advertising: End of Story." *Seeing through Movies*. Ed. Mark Crispin Miller. New York: Pantheon, 1990. 186–246. A detailed discussion of product placement, sometimes called "product plugging."

Sennett, Robert S. *Setting the Scene: The Great Hollywood Art Directors*. New York: Abrams, 1994. Includes chapters on art direction in the silent film, the Hollywood musical, classic horror films, science fiction, and the western. Each chapter focuses on a few (usually famous) movies. Many photographs and sketches.

Thomson, David. *A Biographical Dictionary of Film*. 3rd ed. New York: Knopf, 1994. Short essays on directors, producers, and especially actors.

CHAPTER 2

Cinematography

WHAT MOVIES DO IS MAKE PERCEPTION EASIER. The darkened theater cuts out the claims of peripheral vision. The large images on the screen open up the perceived world for analysis . . . and allow [viewers] to see details simply not available in ordinary experience. Because film makers can further assist perception by careful lighting, lens choice, and camera placement, and can guide expectations and discriminations in a thousand more subtle ways, they can radically enhance the efficiency of seeing. . . . And, in a sense, the film maker can make the viewer more intelligent perceptually, at least while the film is running. Movies use perception in ways that make being "perceptive" remarkably easy. That is one reason why they are so involving. (Eidsvik 21, 23)

composition: The arrangement of settings and subjects (usually people and objects) within the frame.

In the previous chapter we saw how setting, subjects, and **composition**— all key components of staged plays—can function in a film. In this closely related chapter, we will explore some of the distinctly cinematic aspects of filming, such as some of the many ways the film, lighting, camera lenses, camera distances and angles, and camera movement affect the finished image. We will take up these topics in a temporal order: the film that is put into the camera; some of the ways the camera itself may be manipulated during filming; and, after filming is completed, how the cinematography may be corrected or supplemented digitally. Cinematography strongly influences how viewers respond to the finished film: it helps convey the subject matter, and it powerfully shapes the viewers' emotional responses and the meanings viewers detect in films.

FILM STOCK

Film stock is unexposed and unprocessed motion-picture film. It is made up of two basic components (Figure 2.1). The clear, flexible base resembles the **leader** on microfilm—the clear or opaque piece of film that is threaded into a projector. On top of the base is a very thin gelatin coating called the **emulsion**, which contains millions of tiny light-sensitive grains. When exposed to light then chemically developed, the emulsion is the part of the film that holds the image. (It is also what has gotten scratched when you see continuous un-

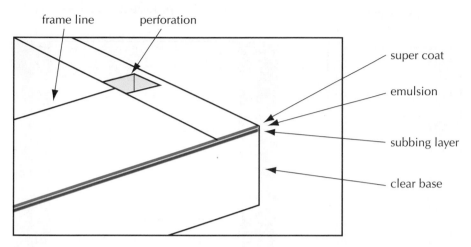

frame line   perforation

super coat

emulsion

subbing layer

clear base

FIGURE 2.1 Film's components (not to scale)
A piece of film consists of two basic parts: a clear base, which constitutes most of the film's overall thickness, and the emulsion, which consists of a very thin layer of gelatin in which are suspended the tiny light-sensitive crystals that make up the image after exposure to light. The emulsion is attached to the base by a clear adhesive called the subbing layer. A super coat on top of the emulsion protects it against scratching. Most film also has an antihalation backing (not shown) to prevent light reflection back through the base that would cause a blurred effect (halation) around the bright part of an image, as with oncoming headlights. (Adapted from Malkiewicz 50.)

wanted vertical lines in a projected movie.) The selection of a film stock influences the film's finished look, including its sharpness of detail, range of light and shadow, and quality of color.

Gauge and Grain

Film stocks are available in various **gauges** or widths (see Figure 2.2). The most common width used for filming and projecting movies in commercial theaters is 35 millimeter (mm), though occasionally movies are filmed in 16 mm then blown up and copied onto 35 mm film. Occasionally movies are shot on 65 mm stock then copied to 70 mm film for showings, though few movie theaters have the equipment to show 70 mm films. Generally, the wider the film gauge, the sharper the projected images (the laboratory work is also a determinant) because a wider gauge permits a larger frame, which requires less magnification to fill up a screen. So a 35 mm print of a movie is less grainy than a 16 mm print of the same film (if both are seen on the same screen and projected from the same distance). Although both prints have the same density of particles or grain in the film emulsion, the area of the 35 mm frame is much greater than that of the 16 mm frame (Figure 2.2), and to fill up the screen the 16 mm film needs to be magnified much more than the 35 mm

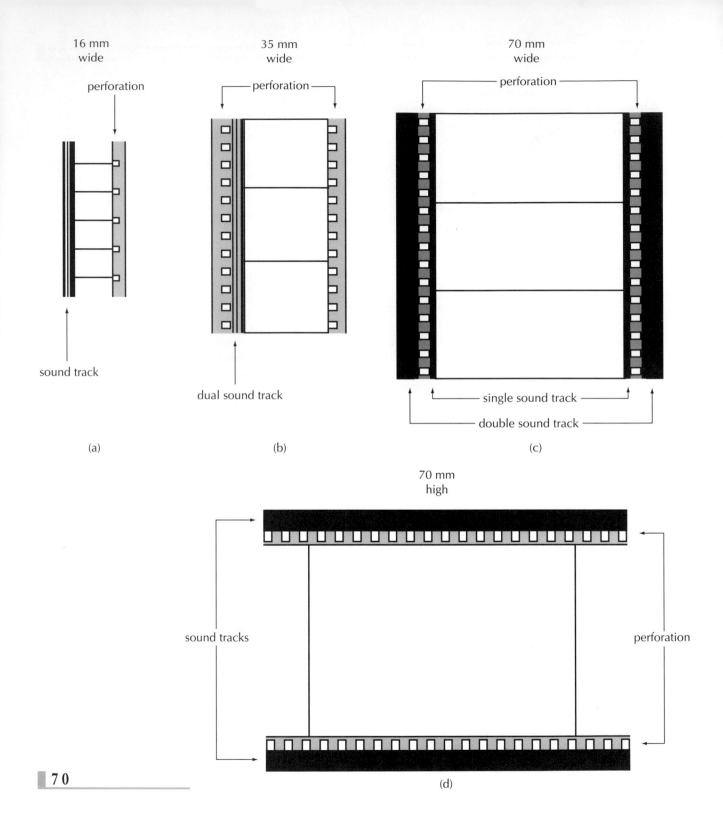

16 mm
wide

perforation

sound track

(a)

35 mm
wide

perforation

dual sound track

(b)

70 mm
wide

perforation

single sound track

double sound track

(c)

70 mm
high

sound tracks

perforation

(d)

◄ FIGURE 2.2 **Four film formats (actual size)**
(a) 16 mm wide. Occasionally used by small commercial theaters, TV stations, industry, military, and schools and universities. Usually the aspect ratio of the projected image is 1.33:1. Other formats in 16 mm include anamorphic (squeezed) prints with aspect ratio of 2.4:1 when projected with an anamorphic lens. (b) 35 mm wide. Used in most commercial theaters, sometimes for major TV showings, and showings at some large universities. When projected, the screen image may have an aspect ratio of 1.33:1; 1.66:1 for many European theatrical showings; 1.85:1 for most U.S. nonanamorphic theatrical showings; or 2.4:1 for anamorphic showings. (c) 70 mm wide, nonanamorphic (un-squeezed) image. Used only in selected large theaters. Aspect ratio: 2.2:1. In the United States and western Europe, films shown in 70 mm usually are shot on 35 mm and blown up or are filmed in 65 mm and printed on 70 mm stock. Here six sound tracks are included, depicted by the four dark stripes. (d) 15 perforation/70 mm format. Used by Imax. Filmed and projected by running the film horizontally through the camera and projector. The space for each frame is about ten times larger than the area of the 35 mm frame. The projector aspect ratio is 1.43:1.

FIGURE 2.3 **Fine-grained image**
In *Amadeus* (1984), fine-grained images were achieved with studio-controlled lighting and slow film stock, which tends to be associated with controlled (perhaps studio) conditions, recent work, and professional quality. *Saul Zaentz, Orion*

print. With the increased magnification comes increased graininess, just as when you hold a piece of processed film up to a light and look at it through a magnifying glass, you will see more of the grain than if you look at it with the naked eye.

Sometimes filmmakers *want* their film, or part of it, to look grainy. For example, before combining grainy footage of President Nixon with new footage of Tom Hanks as Forrest Gump, the filmmakers could have shot footage of Hanks on a small-gauge film stock, then enlarged and printed it on larger-gauge film, then copied the copy a few more times until the graininess of the recent footage of Hanks matched the graininess of the Nixon clip (Figure 9.15 on p. 400).

Speed

The graininess of an image also depends on the speed of the film stock, its sensitivity to light. **Slow film stock**, which often requires considerably more light than **fast film stock**, produces fine grain and a detailed, nuanced image. Often slow film stocks are used for musicals filmed on **sets** and for other films in which detailed images are important and the lighting can be carefully controlled during filming (Figure 2.3).

set: A constructed setting where action is filmed; it can be indoors or outdoors.

Filmmakers Talk about Cinematography

The documentary film *Visions of Light* (1992) includes excerpts from interviews of many cinematographers and other filmmakers. All of the following quotations are from cinematographers, except for Robert Wise.

In the beginning all there was was a guy with a camera. There were no directors. . . . There was a guy and a camera, and he would shoot these subjects, and the subject may be twenty seconds long of a train coming at you, whatever it is. Then actors were brought in and because the cameramen were basically photographers and weren't that facile with performers, usually one of the performers directed the performers, so right in the very beginning you saw that there was the division of duties. —Stephen H. Burum

A great DP [director of photography] adds to the material that already exists and really works to understand the subject matter and the language of the director they're working with. —Lisa Rinzler

I think visually. I think of how if you turned off the sound track, anybody would stick around and figure out what was going on. —Conrad Hall

Notice the beautiful jobs that were done on [actress] Marlene Dietrich where . . . if you light a set at 100 foot candles, she would be at 110, 15 foot candles. She would have just a little bit more light on her than anybody else so she would pop out amongst the crowd. —William A. Fraker

By having the deep focus, he [cinematographer Gregg Toland] was able to give Orson [Welles] a lot more leeway on how he moved his actors and staged the scenes and freed him up. I think that was a tremendous contribution that Gregg gave to the film [Citizen Kane]. —Robert Wise

With [cinematographer John] Alton and the people in film noir they were not afraid of the dark, and in fact they were willing to sketch things just very very very slightly to see how you could use dark, not as negative space, but as the most important element in the scene. —Allen Daviau

You see some of the scenes [from *Touch of Evil*, 1958], and you realize how much hand-holding [camera work] was done in the film, but it's extremely seamless. That film in particular was an inspiration to all of us because it was a textbook of what you could do. It was shot on a small budget in a short time, mostly on locations, and . . . you had almost simultaneously the breakout in France of the new wave. You had Orson Welles doing a new wave film in a Hollywood studio. And I think it has continued to be an inspiration to a lot of filmmakers. —Allen Daviau

The films of the French new wave . . . captured a sense of the life . . . by loosening up the camera and moving with it. . . . They would not think anything about picking up the camera and running with it. It had almost a documentary feel, and so that sort of quality about it would draw you into the film in the way that I think a more static camera would not. —Caleb Deschanel

Suddenly you're aware of the fact that things are not exactly as they seem. In other words, you create a representation of it, and lots of times that representation is more emotional than it is real. —Caleb Deschanel

PLATE 1 **Saturated colors**
In this scene from *Glengarry Glen Ross* (1992) two real estate salesmen sit at a bar as one of them broaches the subject of robbing their company of its cards on potential customers then selling them to the competition. As in so many scenes in the film, this scene includes saturated color, here the background greens and reds. In this movie the many saturated colors—especially reds, blues, and greens—contribute to the sense that the story's urban environment is unnatural and unhealthy. Frame enlargement. *Rank; Zupnik Enterprises; New Line Cinema*

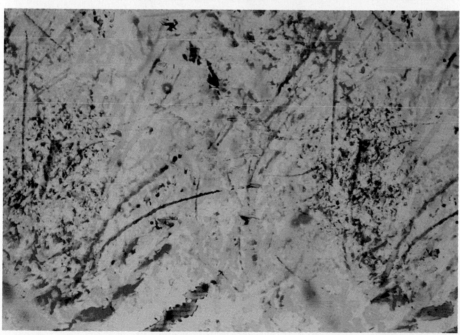

PLATE 2 **Largely desaturated colors**
In this frame from the abstract avant-garde film "Begone Dull Care" (1949), the traditional warm colors, such as the reds, are not intense or vivid, and there's much neutral color within the composition. Frame enlargement. *National Film Board of Canada*

PLATE 3 **Limited color range**
Late 1940s Hollywood is in part evoked by the colors in *Who Framed Roger Rabbit* (1988). The dominant browns are reminiscent of older movies. The animation, which was drawn and painted onto thin sheets of clear plastic (cels), is in saturated colors reminiscent of the short cartoons that were part of post–World War II movie theater programs. In the film, the color—for example, of Baby Herman's hair and ribbon—is not quite as saturated as in this publicity still. The sepia tones in the setting and in the live-action subjects are used throughout the film. *Warner Bros.; Touchstone Pictures; Amblin*

PLATE 4 **Wide range of colors**
Compared with the colors of Plate 3, the colors in this still for *Dangerous Liaisons* (1988) are much more varied and lifelike. *Lorimar Film Entertainment; NFH Limited Production; Warner Bros.*

PLATE 5 Selective use of color
In *Schindler's List* (1993), the little girl in the red coat is seen briefly in only two sequences during more than three hours of the black-and-white part of the film. Of all the characters, she alone is seen in color—and the color often associated with blood, which to Jews is seen as central to life and sacred. And since she is seen in color, viewers notice her and are moved by her fate. *MCA/Universal*

PLATE 6 Bright color in a drab image
The bright colors of the woman's dress plus her girth and gesture draw attention to her, even though she is at the extreme right side of the frame. (The colors in this still are close to those of the film, but in the film the woman's dress and the standing man's white clothing are not quite as bright.) This is an outtake or, more likely, a posed publicity still for *La Vie est belle* (Zaire [now Congo], 1987). *Courtesy of California Newsreel, San Francisco*

PLATE 7 **Color emphasizing an inhospitable environment**

In this image from *Lawrence of Arabia* (1962, restored and rereleased 1989), Lawrence (in white) and two followers are shown making the trek across the Sinai. (The color here is more saturated than in the corresponding scene in the film.) Much of the scene's hue derives from the golden light of the late afternoon or early morning sun (note the long shadows behind the camels). In the context of the film, the warm colors and barren setting show what a hot, unfriendly environment Lawrence and his two followers are up against. *Horizon; Columbia Pictures*

PLATE 8 **The wondrous colors of nature**

Many narrative films include striking views of nature—not to develop the story, but to allow viewers to pause briefly and savor the colors (and forms) of nature itself, as in this sunset in the Australian outback in *Walkabout* (1971, direction and cinematography by Nicolas Roeg). In the comparable shot in the film, the image is seen from a greater distance and the Aborigine subject is positioned farther on the left, so the natural vista is even more prominent. *Max L. Raab*

PLATE 9 Subdued lovers in cool colors
In this scene from *Betrayal* (1983), the lovers are only recently re-united, but their conversation during this part of the scene is void of passion, so the subdued and mostly cool colors seem appropriate. In the film, high-key lighting or bright illumination is used, and the film's comparable image is much lighter and less shadowed than in this publicity still. *Horizon Pictures Ltd., 20th Century-Fox*

PLATE 10 Passionate couple in warm colors
In this publicity still for *Top Gun* (1986), the golden light of the late afternoon reflects the characters' warmth for each other and their vitality. Similar lighting is used in many other exterior scenes in the movie. *Paramount*

PLATE 11 Black-and-white original of *It's a Wonderful Life* (1946)
Seen here are James Stewart, Donna Reed, and three child actors in the original black-and-white version of the popular Christmas-time movie. *RKO Radio Pictures*

Plate 11

PLATE 12 Colorized version (1986) of *It's a Wonderful Life*
Compared with recent color films, such as the one represented in Plate 4, colorized versions
of black-and-white films lack variety of color, subtlety, and detail. This one also draws too much
attention to the chair and the younger boy's legs. *Hal Roach Studios*

Plate 12

PLATE 13 **Extensive use of white**
THX 1138 (1971), the first feature film directed by George Lucas, is set in a futuristic society that attempts to suppress emotion. Except for the robot police that are dressed in black and have rigid silvery metallic faces, people are dressed entirely in white and all the interiors are white. People are not individualized by the colors they wear, and all the feelings that colors suggest and evoke are absent. *Warner Bros.*

PLATE 14 **Expressive use of black**
Most of the last scenes of *The War of the Roses* (1989) take place at night. The black out of which Oliver Rose emerges here represents destructive forces he can no longer suppress as the war between himself and his estranged wife escalates and nears an end. Frame enlargement. *20th Century-Fox*

FIGURE 2.4 **Grainy image**
Grainy images may be achieved by the use of older fast film stock, which tends to be associated with amateur filmmaking, newsreels, old footage, and old documentary films. Sometimes, as in parts of *Citizen Kane* and *Forrest Gump* (Figure 9.15 on p. 400), grainy images are deliberately made to support the illusion of old footage. Grainy images may also result from other causes and have other functions. In *The Killing Fields* (1983), many of the exterior scenes representing Cambodia are grainy because of the widespread smoke or dust, as seen here where helicopter blades have churned up dust. In this film the frequent grainy images caused by smoke or dust reinforce the sense of how chaotic and unhealthy Cambodia was during the time of severe political upheaval and genocide depicted in the film. *Warner Bros.*

Fast film stock requires less light. Often it is used in documentaries, especially when lighting options are limited, and in fictional films hoping to capture a documentary look, as in many war movies. Fast film stock is also used in fictional film **scenes** with little available lighting, such as night scenes. In older films, fast film stock produces graininess. The graininess may be created by other means as well, including fog, dust, or smoke (Figure 2.4). Today's fast film stocks, however, can produce remarkably detailed results even when shot with low lighting.

scene: A section of a narrative film that gives the impression of continuous action taking place in continuous time and space.

Film processing can also affect graininess. Some filmmakers ask the laboratory to make the processed film grainier to create or enhance certain effects, such as to depict harsh living conditions.

Color and Colorization

> It's funny how the colours of the real world only seem really real when you viddy [see] them on a [movie] screen.　　　　—Narrator of *A Clockwork Orange*
> (1971 film)

As early as 1896, some films had color. Some black-and-white films were hand-colored (each frame was painted with different colors using small brushes, sometimes in assembly-line fashion). Other early films, especially feature films of the 1920s, were **tinted**: whole scenes or groups of related scenes were dyed a color, and the same color was used for similar scenes or sequences throughout the film. Thus battle scenes might be tinted red and night scenes blue. Different tints could also be used to indicate flashbacks or fantasies, as in *The Outlaw and His Wife* (1918) and *Napoléon* (1927). By 1932, Technicolor combined three **negatives**, each sensitive to red, green, or blue. In 1935, the first three-color Technicolor feature film, *Becky Sharp*, was produced. Hollywood "in the 1930s and 1940s . . . decreed that colour should be reserved for certain genres that in themselves were not particularly realistic—stylized and spectacle genres (musicals, fantasy, epics)" (Hayward 52). But by the early 1950s, to counter the growing popularity of black-and-white television, more and more movies were made in color, and color was well on its way to becoming the usual way of showing celluloid lives.

Unfortunately, when you study film color, you cannot be certain you are seeing the colors that the filmmakers intended. Most prints of color films, including those for theatrical release, vary in quality because most are mass-produced. Eastman color films, especially those made for many years after 1949, usually turn reddish with age. And nearly all color photographs available for study are not directly from the finished film and do not convey the film's exact colors.

There are also dangers in discussing the significance of color. Color may be used in so many ways that it is important not to overgeneralize. As with discussions of all cinematic **techniques**, discussion of color is most useful when it is considered in context. Similarly, it is important to remember that color associations vary from culture to culture. For example, in pre-Communist China, yellow is often associated with the emperor, and saffron (orange-yellow) with Buddhist robes.

Saturated color is intense and vivid; it has been used in countless contexts, such as to render the heat and tension of an urban setting in *Do the Right Thing* (1989); to reveal garish tastes in interior decorating, as in the parents' residence in *A Clockwork Orange* (1971); and to help convey the

negative: Unexposed film to be used to record negative images. It is normally exposed, processed, then used to make (positive) prints for projection.

technique: Any aspect of filmmaking, such as the choices of sets, lighting, and editing.

pressure and other discomforts characters experience. In many scenes in the first half of *Glengarry Glen Ross* (1992), saturated colors suggest the intense, inhospitable environment in which the salesmen try to survive (Plate 1).

Desaturated color is muted, dull, and pale. Plate 2 illustrates desaturated (and neutral) colors: the colors do not command all of the viewer's attention. Desaturated color has been used to suggest a lack of energy or the draining of life, as throughout Werner Herzog's *Nosferatu, the Vampyre* (1979) and in the late scenes of *Terms of Endearment* (1983), in which the Debra Winger character is losing her bout with cancer. In *The Conformist* (1971), desaturated color helps convey both the main character's lack of vitality and resolve and the austerity of Italian fascism. Desaturated color is used throughout nearly all of *The Red Desert* (1964), which focuses on an emotionally tormented woman's struggle to find some connection, comfort, and reassurance in most of the film's major settings: a run-down shack on a pier, plain contemporary interiors void of plant life, and especially polluted, life-suffocating industrial exteriors rendered in muted colors and grays (some parts of exteriors were painted gray). The desaturated color in *McCabe and Mrs. Miller* (1971) has two purposes: director Robert Altman wanted the film to have the look of old, faded color photographs, and the desaturated color is appropriate to the story, which is set in a damp, cold environment and ends in death for one of the main characters.

A color image may have a limited spectrum of color, as in the live action parts of *Who Framed Roger Rabbit* (1988, Plate 3). Conversely and more typically, a wide range of color is used in films, as in *Dangerous Liaisons* (1988, Plate 4).

One color may be used selectively, as for the girl in the red coat in *Schindler's List* (1993, Plate 5). Similarly, bright colors in an otherwise drab image can help draw attention to a subject (Plate 6).

Colors can be classified as "warm" or "cool." In most western societies, warm colors (reds, oranges, and yellows) tend to be thought of as hot, dangerous, lively, and assertive and tend to stand forward in paintings and photographs. People trying to be sexy or feeling sexy may drive red sports cars and wear red clothing. And women who want to emphasize their sex appeal (or sexual availability) have long been known to use red to draw attention to themselves. In western cultures, the association of red with sexuality is at least as old as the "scarlet women" of the Bible.

Colors on the other side of the spectrum (greens, blues, and violets) are generally thought of as "cool." In Europe and the United States, these colors tend to be associated with safety, reason, control, relaxation, and sometimes sadness or melancholy. Green traffic lights and blue or green hospital interiors are supposed to calm and reassure. In *Reversal of Fortune* (1990), blue light is used in all the scenes with Sunny von Bulow in a coma. The room, her bedding, and her skin are all bluish. In those scenes, the blue suggests cold and lack of vitality, the opposite of a lively, passionate red. In the scenes in which windows are open and it's zero degrees outside, and in a night scene in the von Bulows' bedroom after they have argued and turned out the light, blue adds to the sense of coldness. Blue is used in many other ways in our lives. In the United States, for example, dark blue has long been used in business suits, perhaps to downplay the clothing and body and to suggest restrained emotions.

Color can be used in countless creative ways, such as to show nature's inhospitality (Plate 7) or its beauty and wonder (Plate 8) or to suggest mood and personal relationships. In Plate 9, the blues, greens, and muted red and rust create a predominantly cool look and seem appropriate for the reflective moment shown. In Plate 10, the intense, warm golden light on the two main characters suggests the subjects' vitality and their warmth for each other; in this case it also draws attention to Kelly McGillis's golden hair and, to many viewers, enhances its attractiveness. Like music, color can be especially effective in establishing a mood or revealing characters' feelings or personalities.

In western cultures, white—which is not, strictly speaking, a color but the presence of all colors—is often associated with innocence and purity, as in white wedding dresses. White may also imply lack of emotion or subdued emotions, as in men's white dress shirts and the white interiors and clothing used extensively in *THX 1138* (1971, Plate 13). The effect is similar in the scenes in the futuristic bar in *A Clockwork Orange* (1971), where the extensive use of white and the immobile patrons suggest lethargy.

Black, which is, strictly speaking, not a color but the absence of light, is often associated with death or evil, as in black hats on countless cowboy gunslingers; the black charioteer costume and black horses of the Roman tribune in *Ben-Hur* (1959); the black bra Janet Leigh has changed into when she decides to steal $40,000 in *Psycho* (1960); black capes on all those movie Draculas; Darth Vader's helmet, face piece, and clothing; and shadows surrounding various dangerous characters (Plate 14). Black is used in many situations, so it is important not to overgeneralize. For example, in Europe, the United States, Latin America, and Japan, though not in China, black is the preferred color for mourning. But for some women with an appropriate skin tone and hair color and for men who want to look formal, black can seem stately and elegant, at least to those raised in western societies.

From the early days of cinema, filmmakers have occasionally combined color shots and black-and-white shots in the same film. Probably the most famous example is *The Wizard of Oz* (1939), which renders Dorothy's ordinary life in Kansas in black and white and her adventures in Oz in color. *Schindler's List* reverses the situation: its opening and closing are in color and are set in the present, and, with one exception (Plate 5), the body of the film is in black and white and is set in a tragic past. Alternating between color and black and white throughout a film tends to draw attention to the practice—as in the documentary *Madonna Truth or Dare* (1991), in which most of the concert footage is in color and the off-stage action in black and white; and in

JFK (1991), where most of the flashbacks are in black and white. But such alternating may be less distracting when scenes from a character's imagination
are involved, as in *Heavenly Creatures* (1994), in which the images in the two
young women's imaginations are rendered in black and white, and *Wild Bill*
(1995), in which the memories and dreams of the title character are in black
and white.

As in many aspects of filmmaking, filmmakers use colors intuitively, simply
because they seem right. As cinematographer Allen Daviau has said of cinematographers in general, "We do some things that we don't even realize
we're doing until we see the film put together. And we did them out of instinct. . . ." And, as in other aspects of moviemaking, colors in films are often
more true-to-movies than true-to-life. Many viewers know, for example,
that real blood doesn't look real enough (or exciting enough?), so various
substitutes have been used in filming.

In recent years, new developments in technology and the search for
maximum profits are changing the images we see. With the aid of computers,
many black-and-white films on videotape (Plate 11) are being **colorized**:
years after the films were made, the blacks, whites, and grays are replaced
with colors (Plate 12). Color film is an approximation of the color we see in
life, and so far colorized images are only crude desaturated approximations
of color film. Furthermore, the colorized colors are not chosen by directors,
costumers, or set designers but by video technicians whose judgment in
choosing colors is often questionable, especially for films made many years
ago and perhaps in a different culture. As a consequence, they may choose a
color that draws undue attention to an unimportant part of the image or that
underplays the importance of its subject. To people who tend to dislike
black-and-white films, colorization has appeal. But to film scholars, film
teachers, and filmmakers, perhaps especially directors, the process is offensive. Gilbert Cates, a former president of the Directors Guild of America,
said that colorization "removes shadow and substance. . . . It really is neuter-
ing the picture" (Linfield 32). Director John Huston, after watching seven
minutes of the colorized version of his own *The Maltese Falcon* (1941)—he
could stand no more—said, "It's not color any more than pouring table-
spoons of sugar water over a roast constitutes flavoring."

LIGHTING

Light [is] the paintbrush of the cinematographer. (Turner 96)

Filmmakers often spend an enormous amount of time and money lighting their subjects. They do so because lighting can convey meaning and
mood in subtle yet significant ways. The importance of lighting is evident in
our lives: on sunny days, people are more likely to be cheerful; on cloudy

days, people tend to feel subdued. Studies show that some people in northern climates are subject to severe depression in winter if they receive too little light. The importance of lighting in filming is suggested by the word *photography*, which literally means "writing with light."

Hard or **harsh light** (Figure 2.5) tends to show people in unflattering ways—for example, by creating shadows in the eye sockets—so it may be used to depict characters or people as plain or even unattractive. Two excellent sources of hard light are a focused spotlight and bright (midday) sunlight, when the sun functions as an intense spotlight.

Soft light reflects off at least one object before it illuminates the subject. An excellent (and free) source of soft lighting is available during the so-called magic hour of each day. According to cinematographer Nestor Almendros, the best of the magic hour light is available for only twenty to twenty-five minutes after sunset (in the middle latitudes, with fewer minutes near the equator and more minutes near earth's poles). Sunlight at dawn is an equally

FIGURE 2.5 Hard or harsh lighting
The subject is illuminated by one direct, bright (spot) light. Hard light produces bright illumination; reveals many details, including imperfections in the subject; and creates shadows with sharp edges. *Model: Kimberlee Stewart; photographer: Jon Michael Terry*

FIGURE 2.6 Soft lighting
Soft light produces the appearance of smooth surfaces by softening the border between light and shadow. If there are shadows, they will be faint. *Model: Kimberlee Stewart; photographer: Jon Michael Terry*

FIGURE 2.7 Backlighting
The model was illuminated by one light from behind. Often backlighting makes the subject seem threatening because viewers cannot interpret the subject's mood or perhaps identity. *Model: Kimberlee Stewart; photographer: Jon Michael Terry*

useful source of soft light. Before dawn and after sunset, the sky itself becomes a broad source of soft light. Soft lighting tends to have the opposite effects of hard lighting. It fills facial wrinkles and makes people look younger; it makes young people look even more attractive (Figure 2.6). Typically, photographers use soft light to present subjects in an appealing way, as in romantic films, or to make actors look their most youthful or most attractive, as in many films produced in Hollywood studios in the 1930s and 1940s.

The direction of light on a subject is another expressive option for filmmakers. Some ways to light a subject by using sources from different directions are illustrated in Figures 2.7–2.12. In all these examples, the model is the same and so is her makeup. The camera distance, lens, and angle are unchanged. But notice what different images a change in direction produces, what different moods and meanings. (You can usually detect the directions and intensities of the light sources by looking at the subject's eyes. **Catchlight**, a reflection of the light sources, is visible for all bright light that reaches the eyes.)

FIGURE 2.8 **Top lighting**
The model was illuminated by a single light from above. Top lighting used by itself is not flattering. Here the hair looks lighter than it is; a slight imperfection on the model's right cheek is visible; and she has shadows under her eyes. *Model: Kimberlee Stewart; photographer: Jon Michael Terry*

FIGURE 2.9 **Bottom lighting**
The model was illuminated by a single light from below. Like top lighting, bottom lighting is unflattering to the skin. Often bottom lighting also adds a touch of menace; it is often used to enhance a frightening mood, as in many horror films. *Model: Kimberlee Stewart; photographer: Jon Michael Terry*

FIGURE 2.10 **Side lighting**
Here the model is lit by one light from the side. Side lighting creates many shadows on the face, including prominent shadows under the eyes. It may be used to suggest someone with a divided personality or someone feeling contradictory emotions. *Model: Kimberlee Stewart; photographer: Jon Michael Terry*

FIGURE 2.11 Main, frontal lighting
The model was lit by a single light in front of her and a little to the right of the camera. This lighting presents the subject in an attractive way, though not quite as much so as main or key and fill lighting together. *Model: Kimberlee Stewart; photographer: Jon Michael Terry*

FIGURE 2.12 Key light and fill light
A combination of key light and fill light presents the subject's skin in the most appealing way. Here the slight imperfection on the model's cheek is less noticeable and the right side of her face appears to be a little smoother than the photo made with only main, frontal lighting (Figure 2.11). *Model: Kimberlee Stewart; photographer: Jon Michael Terry*

For filming on a set, often at least three lights are used for each major subject: the **key light**, or main light; **fill light**, a soft light used to fill in unlit areas of the subject; and a **backlight** (Figure 2.13). For filming, the key light is usually the first light set, or it may be handheld and moved around during a shot to keep the main subject well illuminated. A key light and a fill light ensure adequate and fairly even illumination with few or no shadows on the subject. The backlight, often from above or below the subject, highlights at least some of its edges, such as the hair or shoulders, and helps set the subject off from the background, to give a sense of depth. Lighting the main subjects and parts of a set is complicated and often requires more than three light sources.

It's not unusual to light different characters differently within the same scene, as director Leni Riefenstahl did: "I always made sure the men, actors or not, were lit differently from the women. They [the men] were lit from the side so their features stood out, whereas what's important with women is to make them look young and lovely. . . . With a young woman, who must look beautiful, you need a very soft light from the front. No side-lighting at all, so no facial lines or flaws are visible."

Lighting can support the type of character an actor plays. As film scholar Richard Dyer points out, in *Butch Cassidy and the Sundance Kid* (1969) the lighting tends to glamorize the tongue-in-cheek, romantic character played by Robert Redford (Figure 2.14a). Conversely, in *All the President's Men*

FIGURE 2.13 Three-point lighting
From the catchlight in Joel Grey's eyes in this publicity still for *Cabaret* (1972), we can see that the key light is to the right of the camera; a small fill light comes from slightly to the left and a little lower than the key light. Soft backlight is reflected off the back wall, but there is enough of it to highlight Grey's left shoulder a little and to set him off from the neutral background. *Allied Artists–ABC Pictures*

FIGURE 2.14 **Soft and high-key lighting on a star**
(a, left) Soft lighting softens lines around the eyes and enhances Robert
Redford's looks in *Butch Cassidy and the Sundance Kid* (1969). (b, above)
The bright, hard lighting used on Redford in *All the President's Men* (1976)
does not soften his facial lines and enhance his looks. In this movie he
plays an investigative reporter, and lighting that glamorizes him would be
inappropriate. *(a) 20th Century-Fox; (b) Wildwood Enterprises; Warner Bros.*

(1976) Redford plays a no-nonsense investigative reporter and is often lit by
high-key lighting, a high level of illumination: the lighting on his face does
not hide skin imperfections (Figure 2.14b).

Figure 2.15, from *Citizen Kane* (1941), illustrates how light and shadows
can emphasize and de-emphasize parts of an image and thereby create
moods and meanings. Light and shadows are also used expressively in a
scene late in *Schindler's List*. Oskar Schindler has arrived at the Auschwitz
concentration camp to save a large group of Jewish women from extermina-
tion. For much of one scene in which he bribes a Nazi officer, the top half of
the officer's face is in shadows. It's as if he wears a mask, which is appropriate
because he is like an outlaw hiding in the dark. The *shape* of shadows can also
be used expressively, as in *Blackmail* (1929, Figure 2.16).

In cinematography, shadows may be as expressive as light (Figure 2.17).
Shadows may also be used effectively in animation, as in *The Little Mermaid*
(1989) when King Triton's eyes glow while his face remains in shadows after
he has learned of his daughter's love for a human.

Shadows and other areas of darkness can be central to an entire film or
even series of films. Cinematographer Gordon Willis lit the *Godfather* films

FIGURE 2.15 **Expressive use of shadows**
In *Citizen Kane* (1941), Charles Foster Kane signs his "Declaration of Principles" for a newspaper he has recently taken over, as Jed Leland (left) and Mr. Bernstein (right) look on. Kane's face is in shadows, which undercuts this supposedly noble moment. Indeed, later in the film we learn that Kane abandons these principles. The lighting on and the position of Bernstein remind us that Bernstein was a witness to the event, too. (This scene is part of Bernstein's version of events.) Frame enlargement. *RKO General Pictures*

FIGURE 2.16 **Shapes of shadows**
In *Blackmail* (1929), the main character has killed a man in self-defense. Late in the film, she has decided to surrender to the police. In this frame, the shadows of prison bars on and behind her suggest her possible fate. Frame enlargement. *BIP; The Museum of Modern Art/ Circulating Film Library*

FIGURE 2.17 Shadows vs. light
(a, top) A frame enlargement
from *The Third Man* (1949) shows
the Orson Welles character, Harry
Lime, as a desperate fugitive
trapped and in danger of being
captured. Note that only Welles's
face and the hand holding the gun
are illuminated; he is surrounded
by darkness and in this case im-
minent death. Frame enlargement.
(b, right) In a publicity still of
the same subject, Welles is so
brightly and evenly illuminated
that we can see more of him more
clearly, and the effect is to "lighten"
the mood. Note that for this
posed photograph Welles does
not recapture the intensity of the
film scene (perhaps in part because
the lighting did not help get him
into the appropriate mood).
*London Film Productions; Academy
of Motion Picture Arts and Sciences*

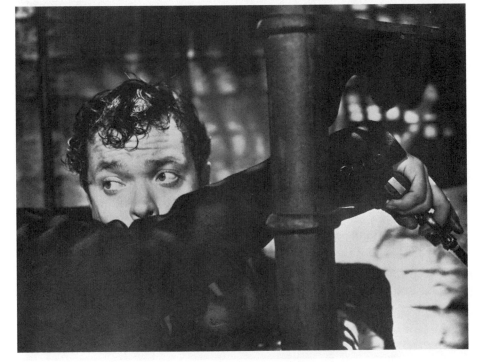

as darkly as he dared—and darker than most other cinematographers would have dared. In *The Godfather*, Marlon Brando and many other actors playing criminals are often lit from above, and frequently we cannot see their eyes, only dark sockets. That makes them hard to "read" or interpret, unnatural, and a little frightening. Given the dark and evil doings, the many dark scenes throughout the three *Godfather* films are appropriate.

In *Psycho*, shadows are used to heighten the mystery and suspense (Figure 2.18). When used in combination with other lighting, however, shadows can have a different effect (Figure 2.19).

The lighting may be changed during the course of a film to create or reinforce particular effects. Sidney Lumet explains how and why he changed the lighting throughout *Prince of the City* (1981):

> In the first third of the movie, we tried to have the light on the background brighter than on the actors in the foreground. For the second third, the foreground light and the background light were more or less balanced. For the last third, we cut the light off the background. Only the foreground, occupied by the

FIGURE 2.18 **Backlighting to obscure the identity of a subject**
The lighting in this scene of *Psycho* (1960) helps hide the identity of the attacker and make the attacker seem even more frightening. This effect is intensified by the low angle of the shot and the knife that seems as long as the attacker's forearm. Frame enlargement. *Universal*

FIGURE 2.19 Dramatic lighting for a special situation
Near the end of the Senegalese film *Saaraba* (1988), the subject shown here believes that he has reached *saaraba* (a mythical place without life's misery and uncertainties, or utopia). In the eleven-second shot represented here, the subject is driving a motorcycle at night, but the image was made indoors with the subject lit by three carefully positioned spotlights—one from each side and one from the back—and by one faint fill light. *Courtesy of California Newsreel, San Francisco*

actors, was lit. By the end of the movie, only the relationships that were about to be betrayed mattered. People emerged from the background. *Where* something took place no longer mattered. What mattered was *what* took place and to whom. (88)

Some films begin in the dark and end in the dark (*Citizen Kane*). Some films begin in the light until the mood and scenes tend to turn dark, and the films end in darkness (*I Am a Fugitive from a Chain Gang*, 1932). And some films begin in the dark but end in the light (*Jaws*, 1975).

THE CAMERA

To film, cinematographers need film stock, light, and a camera. What lens or lenses are used on the camera and the location of the camera relative to the subject are crucial determinants of the final images and thus the final effects.

Lenses and Focus

Images are filmed with three types of lenses; often all three are used at different times within the same film. The **wide-angle** lens shows more of the sides of the image than the normal lens; the **normal** lens most closely approximates the perceptions of the human eye; and the **telephoto** lens makes the subject appear closer. Each type of lens has different properties and creates different images (Figures 2.20–2.22).

FIGURE 2.20 Wide-angle lens (here a 28 mm lens on a 35 mm camera)

▪ The wide-angle lens may be used to emphasize distances between subjects or between subjects and setting because it causes all planes to appear farther away from the camera and from each other than is the case with a normal lens.

▪ Deep focus: sharp focus in all planes.

▪ Compared to a normal lens, as in Figure 2.21, more of all four sides of the image are visible.

▪ With very wide-angle lenses or with the subject close to the camera, there is much distortion or curvature of objects, especially near the edges of the image, as in Figure 2.24. This is sometimes called *wide-angle distortion*.

▪ Movements toward or away from the camera seem speeded up. *Models: Kimberlee Stewart and Carlos Espinola; photographer: Jon Michael Terry*

FIGURE 2.21 Normal lens (approximately 50 mm lens for a 35 mm camera)

At most distances, this lens causes minimal distortion of image and movement. As its name implies, the normal lens creates images close to what the normal human eye would see in the same circumstances. *Models: Kimberlee Stewart and Carlos Espinola; photographer: Jon Michael Terry*

FIGURE 2.22 Telephoto lens (in this case, 200 mm)

▪ All planes appear closer to the camera and to each other than is the case with a normal lens (Figure 2.21).

▪ Shallow focus: only planes very close to each other are in focus.

▪ Less of the sides of the image is visible than is the case with a normal lens.

▪ Movements toward or away from the camera seem slowed down. *Models: Kimberlee Stewart and Carlos Espinola; photographer: Jon Michael Terry*

FIGURE 2.23 **A normal lens for close-ups and extreme close-ups** (a, right) This lens creates images closest to human perceptions, and at nearly all distances, including close-ups, no distortion is noticeable. (b, bottom) In an extreme close-up, the 50 mm lens distorts the subject a little. When this is an unwanted result, a longer lens, such as 80 mm, could be used. *Model: Rey Phillips; photographer: Noble Dinse*

Figure 2.23 illustrates that even a slight wide-angle lens used at a very close range distorts the image somewhat. Striking uses of the wide-angle lens and the extreme wide-angle or **fisheye lens** occur near the end of *Seconds* (1966, Figure 2.24). In other films, the wide-angle lens has also been used to suggest that something is not right. Near the end of *Murder on the Orient*

fisheye lens: A lens that captures nearly 180° of the area before the camera but causes much curvature of the image, especially near the frame's edges.

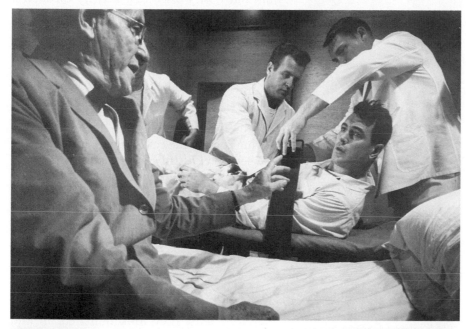

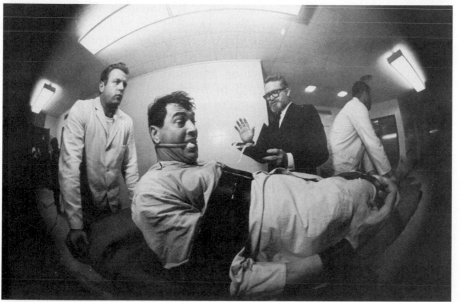

FIGURE 2.24 Wide-angle and extreme wide-angle lenses (a, top) In *Seconds* (1966), the Rock Hudson character is seen through a wide-angle lens as he is unexpectedly being strapped onto a gurney to be wheeled into an operating room and surgically killed. (b, left) When the character realizes what is happening to him but it is too late to do anything about it, he is shot through an extreme wide-angle, or fisheye, lens. The effect is chilling and unforgettable. *Paramount*

FIGURE 2.25 **A telephoto shot made with a telescope and camera**
For filming the documentary *The Man Who Skied down Everest* (1975),
a telescope was attached to a motion picture camera to show a subject in
the extreme distance. In this case, the telescope and camera were used
to record a two-minute, twenty-second shot of a Japanese skier's extraordinary attempt to ski down part of Mt. Everest's upper slopes. Telephoto
shots are rarely made with a lens even remotely this long. *Crawley Films;
Pleasant Pastures*

Express (1974), the detective tells the assem-
bled suspects about parts of earlier testimony;
as he does so, snippets of interviews with the
same suspects and a brief shot of a woman
walking away are repeated from earlier in the
film, but now we see that activity through a
wide-angle lens.

The normal lens is used most often in
films because it most closely approximates the
reality people see with their own eyes, and
most films attempt to present the illusion of
reality.

The telephoto lens (Figure 2.25) has
been used in many films to depict someone
moving toward the camera laboriously slowly,
as when the Dustin Hoffman character runs
to prevent a wedding late in *The Graduate*
(1967). Or it can be used to compress a long
row of signs, to seemingly crowd them together, as if to say, "Look at the dense forest
of signs in modern life." The telephoto lens is
used similarly in several opening shots in
Short Cuts (1993). Helicopters flying toward
the camera are spraying Los Angeles with in-
secticide, but because they are shot with a
telephoto lens, they look bunched up and
slowed down. It's one of the film's first views
of life in Los Angeles and a striking image
that viewers are unlikely to ignore.

Choice of lens, the lens **aperture** or
opening, and film stock largely determine the
depth of field, or the distance from foreground to background in which all objects are
in focus. In **deep focus**,[1] which is achieved by
using a wide-angle lens or small lens aperture
or both, much or all of the depth of the image is in sharp focus. In low illumination, **fast lenses**—lenses that transmit light efficiently—and fast film
stock also help achieve deep focus. Some film theorists, including André
Bazin, believe that deep-focus scenes are closer to life as we live it than are

[1]*Deep focus* is a term used by many film critics and scholars. For the same situation, filmmakers
are more likely to use the phrase *great depth of field*. *Deep focus* can be confused with *depth of
focus*, which refers to the distances between the camera lens and the film in the camera in which
the image remains in acceptable focus.

edited scenes (33). Certainly deep focus can be used to let viewers experience clear images for lengthy segments of uninterrupted time. Deep-focus scenes may be less manipulative than edited footage: viewers may be freer to look at the details in the frame and select those that seem significant, though filmmakers can guide viewers' attention through lighting, focus, camera placement, and composition. Unarguably, deep focus does give filmmakers more opportunities to use foreground-background interplay expressively (see Figure 1.49 on p. 54).

When filmmakers use **shallow focus**—for example, by using a telephoto lens or a large lens aperture in low light—usually either the foreground or the background will be in sharp focus, and viewers' attention is directed to the subject(s) in sharp focus (see Figure 2.22 on p. 87). Unfocused subjects may be ambiguous, disturbing, threatening (see Figure 1.46 on p. 52), or some other effect. Unfocused subjects may be out of focus because the director chose to focus on something else within the frame or because the type of lighting, film stock, and lenses available when the film was made precluded deeper focus.

The resolution and mood of the image may also be changed by using a **diffuser**—material such as a nylon stocking, frosted glass, spun glass, wire mesh, gelatin, or silk—placed in front of the camera lens or a light source to soften the image's resolution. Figure 2.26 illustrates how diffusers soften facial lines, sometimes to obscure aging and to glamorize, sometimes to lend a more

FIGURE 2.26 **Some functions of diffusers**
A diffuser is a material placed over a light source or camera lens to soften the image. (a, far left) The diffuser used here softens the image. Depending on the context, such a diffuser may glamorize, lend a more spiritual or ethereal look, obscure aging, or result in a combination of these consequences. (b, left) Heavy diffusion creates an even softer look. *Model: Eva L. Santos-Phillips; photographer: Jon Michael Terry*

FIGURE 2.27 **Diffusers to help obscure an action**
In this shot from *Vampyr* (1932), viewers glimpse an old woman near a supine young woman.
The very grainy image was probably achieved by placing a diffuser in front of the camera lens.
The subject and setting are much obscured. That foggy look along with the long camera distance
and brevity of the shot prevent viewers from seeing if the old woman is a vampire. Viewers will
find out later in the film. Frame enlargement. *Filmproduktion Paris-Berlin*

spiritual or ethereal, less material look; Figure 2.27 shows how a diffused
look can be used in a film to help obscure what is happening in a scene.

Camera Distances

Camera distance helps determine what details will be noticeable in the
frame, what details will be excluded, and how large the subject will appear.

Figures 2.28–2.33 illustrate six camera distances and the terms usually
used to describe them. (In the last three photographs, a longer lens was used
so the photographer would not be intruding into the model's space.)

When a film begins or when it shifts to a new setting, filmmakers often
use an extreme long shot to present an **establishing shot**, a view of the surroundings. Once viewers are oriented, the camera normally moves in closer
to the subject.

An extreme long shot or a long shot may be used to create or enhance a
humorous situation, perhaps because at that distance viewers can see the

FIGURE 2.28 Extreme long shot
If a person is the subject, the entire body is visible (if not obstructed by some intervening object) but very small in the frame, and much of the surroundings are visible. This camera distance is often used to show the layout and expanse of a setting. *Model: Carlos Espinola; photographer: Jon Michael Terry*

FIGURE 2.29 Long shot
Usually the subject is seen in its entirety, and much of the surroundings is visible. This camera distance has many possible uses, for example to stress how small a human subject is in relation to the environment. *Model: Carlos Espinola; photographer: Jon Michael Terry*

FIGURE 2.30 Medium shot
This camera distance tends to give about equal importance to the subject and the surroundings. When the subject is a person, he or she is usually seen from the knees or waist up. *Model: Carlos Espinola; photographer: Jon Michael Terry*

FIGURE 2.31 Medium close-up
The subject fills most of the height of the frame. When the subject is a person, the medium close-up usually reveals the head and shoulders. *Model: Kimberlee Stewart; photographer: Jon Michael Terry*

FIGURE 2.32 Close-up
The subject fills the height of the frame and the shot reveals little of the surroundings. When the subject is a person, the close-up normally reveals all of the head. *Model: Kimberlee Stewart; photographer: Jon Michael Terry*

FIGURE 2.33 Extreme close-up
The subject or, frequently, part of the subject completely fills up the frame and thus looks very large to the viewer. If the subject is a person's face, only part of it is visible. This camera distance is used to show the texture of a subject or part of a subject; with this camera distance, typically none of the background is visible. *Model: Kimberlee Stewart; photographer: Jon Michael Terry*

FIGURE 2.34 **Extreme long shot to create humor**
A publicity still approximating a shot of three hominids in a tree in *Quest for Fire* (1981). In three of the four shots taken from a distance, the hominids are seen in silhouette and thus seem remote. In these shots they look small and pitiful—not so much endangered as silly—and some viewers chuckle at their plight. *ICC; Cine Trail; 20th Century-Fox*

pain, discomfort, awkwardness, or embarrassment involved but not in so much detail that they are troubled by it. Charlie Chaplin reputedly said, in effect, close-up for tragedy, long shot for comedy, and his own movies repeatedly illustrate that practice. A sequence from *Quest for Fire* (1981) illustrates how long shots are used for comedy and closer shots for serious moods. Eighty thousand years ago, three hominids are treed by saber-toothed tigers. Early in the sequence many close-ups and medium shots are used, such as of the hominids scampering up the tree, tigers at the base of the tree, and the hominids' faces registering panic. These shots thrust viewers up close to the actions and reactions and involve them in the danger and fear. The sequence also contains three long shots and one amusing extreme long shot showing the three creatures in a rather small tree (Figure 2.34).

At other times, an extreme long shot or a long shot can distance viewers from a painful sight. In *Wish You Were Here* (1987), a teenage girl, Lynda, feels unloved, so she seeks male attention in various ways, including displaying her legs publicly and accepting as a sex partner her father's friend Eric, a man in his fifties who often belittles her. After her father discovers that Lynda has been having sex with Eric and evidently kicks her out of the house, she goes to Eric's. Soon in a medium shot we see Eric start to unbutton her blouse; then she starts crying. He responds, "Come on. . . . What's all the fuss." She says, "Hold me, please; just hold me," but he doesn't. He keeps undressing her during most of the rest of the shot and the following medium close-up shot. In a second medium close-up shot, he talks to her briefly. Then in a long shot, we see him over her and still undressing her. Here the long shot prevents the viewer from spying too long or too closely at Lynda's emotional pain. The long shot also discourages viewers who find her sexually attractive from enjoying seeing her being further exposed. To some extent, it protects her from further intrusion.

The long shot or extreme long shot requires viewers to be especially attentive to see exactly what is happening. Such a shot may also have emotional rewards. For instance, a long shot or extreme long shot may contribute a melancholy tinge to a scene because it shows the subjects as small and alone (Figure 2.35).

FIGURE 2.35 Extreme long shot to support a melancholy mood In *Tokyo Story* (1953), a grandfather and grandmother have gone to the suburbs of Tokyo to visit their children and grandchildren, who all seem too busy to take much interest in their elders. In the scene depicted here, the grandmother has taken her unwilling grandson on a walk and tries to get his attention, to connect with him. Instead the boy keeps his back to her and is preoccupied with playing. He keeps his distance, in two senses. The scene concludes with the two seen in an extreme long shot, the image consisting largely of the two characters and a lot of empty space. For some viewers this scene has resonance near the end of the film, after the grandmother has died unexpectedly and left an empty space (see Figure 1.36b on p. 43). Frame enlargement. *Shochiku; New Yorker Films*

FIGURE 2.36 Nuances of feeling revealed in a medium close-up
In *Guarding Tess* (1994), Shirley MacLaine plays Tess, a strong-willed widowed First Lady protected by a Secret Service contingent. In this scene, the agent in charge has told her not to sit behind the car's driver. In refusing, she reacts as shown here in a publicity still. Her mouth and eyes and the direction of her gaze, all clearly visible in this medium close-up shot, hint at her resolve and mostly suppressed anger. *TriStar Pictures*

For close-ups, the camera can be positioned near a performer's face, or, much more often, a telephoto lens can be used so the camera does not have to get so close to the performer. Close-ups and medium close-ups may be used to show the many nuances and complexities of human feeling (Figure 2.36); the usefulness of close shots to reveal emotions and character or personality cannot be overestimated. In his book *Kinesics and Context*, Ray Birdwhistell claims that the human face is capable of "some 250,000 different expressions" (8).

Perspective

By changing the camera lens and the distance at the same time, filmmakers can change **perspective**: the relative size and apparent depth of objects in the image. Figures 2.37–2.39 illustrate three ways that filmmakers can use perspective.

In these three photographs the main subjects are approximately the same size in the frame and appear in about the same position within the frame. But everything else changes when camera distance and lens are modified together. By changing the lens and the distance together, cinematographers can emphasize or de-emphasize certain areas of the image; they can change the relationships of people and objects in the frame, to convey the information and the moods they intend. Often viewers cannot tell the distance of the camera from the subject or the type of lens used unless they know the subject and its setting well and detect distortion in their presentation.

Filmmakers often change perspective from shot to shot, but occasionally they change perspective *within* a shot by moving the camera forward or backward as they simultaneously use a **zoom lens**—a

zoom: To use a zoom lens to cause the image of the subject to either increase in size as the area being filmed seems to decrease (zoom in) or to decrease in size as the area being filmed seems to increase (zoom out).

lens that can be changed smoothly toward the wide-angle range or telephoto range while the camera is filming. A striking example occurs in a two-second shot from *Jaws* (1975). As Chief Brody, who is sitting on the beach, sees someone being attacked by a shark, the camera **dollies**, or moves on a wheeled platform, forward as the camera **zooms** from normal to wide angle. The dollying forward more than offsets the effect of zooming out and increases the size of the subject in the foreground a little while the zooming out makes the background recede and exposes more and more of the sides.

FIGURE 2.37 Wide-angle lens (28 mm) at 8 feet 10 inches
This photograph was made by positioning the camera closer to the human subjects than in the comparable photograph made with a normal lens (Figure 2.38). Here the camera angle seems to be a slight high angle, and the bench seat on the left seems elongated. This camera distance and lens could be used to stress the depth of the background, to show more of the sides, or to emphasize the distance of the subjects from the background. *Models: Kimberlee Stewart and Carlos Espinola; photographer: Jon Michael Terry*

FIGURE 2.38 Normal lens (50 mm) at 15 feet 6 inches
This photograph closely mirrors the distances and relationships human eyes see. *Models: Kimberlee Steward and Carlos Espinola; photographer: Jon Michael Terry*

FIGURE 2.39 Telephoto lens (200 mm) at 62 feet
This photograph was made by moving the camera back from its position for Figure 2.38 and using a telephoto lens. Here the background seems much closer and more out of focus. The camera angle is not as high as in Figures 2.37 and 2.38, and the bench on the left now seems somewhat shorter. (To see how the camera angle changes, look again at the three photographs and note the angles from which the camera seems to view the cement area under the picnic table.) *Models: Kimberlee Stewart and Carlos Espinola; photographer: Jon Michael Terry*

99

The changing image seems to pull Brody forward from the receding background, suggest his growing concern, and intensify the viewer's momentary confusion. The same technique is used in *Raging Bull* (1980). The Jake La Motta character is taking a beating from the Sugar Ray Robinson character. Before Robinson's final hurricane of punches concludes the fight and Jake's boxing career, viewers see Robinson in a medium close-up (from about his knees up). Robinson does not move his feet, and he remains in the center of the frame and seemingly at the same camera distance. But as he stands there, for about six seconds the background seems to recede from him and from Jake and from the camera. Soon much more of the sides of the image in the background is visible, and the audience in the background seems much farther away. As in the shot from *Jaws*, this effect was achieved by moving the camera forward as it simultaneously zoomed from normal to wide angle. The effect is highly disorienting for viewers. (The sound track also contributes to the disturbing effect: while the background seems to recede, the sound fades to near silence.)

Another change in perspective during a shot occurs in *GoodFellas* (1990), but with the opposite camera movement and opposite simultaneous type of zooming. Late in the film Jimmy, an older gangster who for years has been Henry's unofficial mentor, is meeting Henry in a restaurant. Jimmy is about to try to betray Henry and send him to his death. They sit on opposite sides of the frame, with a large window between them. As they talk, the camera **tracks** backward as it zooms in, going from normal to telephoto. The two men stay the same size and in the same positions, but the background becomes larger and its planes become more compressed: for example, the car parked across the street seems progressively closer to the large sign advertising sandwiches behind it. Viewers may not notice the change in the composition, but it is eerie, unsettling, and effective. Perhaps the shot suggests that Jimmy's attempt to betray his friend is unnatural and unexpected.

These rapid but fluid changes in perspective within shots from *Jaws*, *Raging Bull*, and *GoodFellas* affect the subjects and their relation to the setting in disturbing ways. They also briefly disorient viewers, in part because the changes are unexpected and even unnatural. Although these changes in perspective last only a few seconds, they are so rarely used in films that they may stand out, momentarily drawing viewers' awareness.

Angles and Point-of-View Shots

Another important technique that filmmakers can use to determine the expressiveness of images is the angle from which they film the subject. Figures 2.40–2.43 illustrate four basic camera positions: bird's-eye view, high angle, eye-level angle, and low angle. The camera may be placed at any angle above or below those indicated in the figures.

In the highest of the high angles, the **bird's-eye view**, the camera is directly above the subject, often mounted on a device called a crane. The

track: To film while the camera is moving.

FIGURE 2.40 Bird's-eye view
This camera angle in *Psycho* (1960) obscures the identity of the attacker and disorients viewers.
Frame enlargement. *Universal*

FIGURE 2.41 High angle
High angles make the subject appear smaller, as in this publicity still from *Sister Act* (1992). They
also can make the subject seem shut off from the surroundings (sometimes all that is visible of the
background is a floor or the ground) and in some contexts vulnerable. *Touchstone Pictures*

FIGURE 2.42 Eye-level shots
(a, right) An eye-level angle, such as this one from *Dangerous Liaisons* (1988), approximates the angle at which we usually meet and interact with people, so viewers tend not to notice its use. (b, below) The height of the camera may depend on the filmmaker and the culture in which the film is made. In films directed by Yasujiro Ozu, such as *Tokyo Story* (1953), eye-level shots are often taken with the camera approximately two feet above the ground when the subjects are sitting on the ground. In eye-level shots for films from western societies, the camera is normally positioned five to six feet above the floor for standing subjects and three to four feet for sitting subjects. If Ozu had followed that practice, the results would have been a high angle, with the camera tilted down toward the subjects sitting on the floor.
(a) Lorimar; NFH; Warner Bros.; (b) Shochiku; The Museum of Modern Art/Film Stills Archive

FIGURE 2.43 **Low angle**
In low angles, as in this publicity still for *Himatsuri*, or *Fire Festival* (1984), the surroundings are often minimized, with a lot of sky or ceiling in the background. The subject seems more prominent and, in some contexts, dominating or intimidating. Low angles are often used in shots emphasizing a person's physique. *Courtesy of Kino International, New York City*

bird's-eye view is used during the first shot of *The Untouchables* (1987) and later after the Al Capone character has clubbed a man to death with a baseball bat; it is used several times in *Barton Fink* (1991), for example to look down on the writer in his hotel bed; and it is used at the conclusion of a moving camera shot from *Psycho* (Figure 2.40). In each case the effect is a little disorienting, perhaps even dizzying, since viewers look straight down on the subject. A moving bird's-eye view is also used memorably late in *Taxi Driver* (1976) when viewers look down on the aftermath of a violent scene; the camera movement makes the shot even more disorienting than the usual bird's-eye view. Many films never use the bird's-eye view. It can attract attention to itself and be distracting.

Figures 2.41–2.43 illustrate high angles, eye-level angles, and low angles.

In a **Dutch angle** shot the subject appears to be on a slanted surface. It is often used to disorient viewers or make them ill at ease. In a point-of-view shot the Dutch angle may suggest a character's confused state of mind. The Dutch angle is used in many scenes in *The Third Man* (1949), *Fatal Attraction* (1987), *Do the Right Thing*, and *Natural Born Killers* (1994). It is also used in the early scenes of *Bagdad Café* (1988, Figure 2.44) to suggest unhappy personal relationships.

In **point-of-view** shots (often called p.o.v. shots), the camera films a subject from the approximate position of a character, a real person, or an animal in the film. Such camera placements contribute to the viewer's sense of identification with the subject and of participation in the action. In *Vampyr* (1932), the main character hallucinates that he is in a coffin with a small glass window. He thinks he looks up and sees (and viewers feel as if they are seeing) what it looks

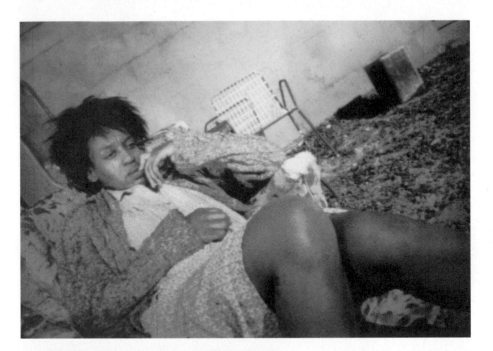

FIGURE 2.44 Dutch angles
Dutch angles are used early in *Bagdad Café* (1988) after a woman quarrels with her man and he leaves her. These two consecutive frame enlargements reinforce the sense that things are now out of order in the woman's life. Frame enlargements. *New Yorker Films*

FIGURE 2.45 Point-of-view shot
In this point-of-view shot from within a coffin in *Vampyr* (1932), viewers see a vampire with a lighted candle looking down into the coffin. Later the coffin is carried outside, and viewers see the outside surroundings from within the coffin. Frame enlargement. *Filmproduktion Paris-Berlin*

FIGURE 2.46 Sustained point of view
Lady in the Lake (1946) was an experiment with sustained point of view: viewers see events from the main character's point of view, except for an occasional shot of a mirror showing the main character, detective Philip Marlowe. Here Marlowe is about to get slugged and knocked out. This frame is somewhat blurred because the subject is moving so rapidly. Frame enlargement. *George Haight; MGM*

like from inside a coffin (Figure 2.45). In parts of more modern films, such as the two murders in *Psycho*, the beginning of *Halloween* (1978), and late in *The Silence of the Lambs* (1991), viewers are frequently put into the uncomfortable position of seeing horrendous events through the eyes of a killer. On a tamer note, in *Toy Story* (1995), viewers are often allowed to see impending dangers, such as a large menacing dog, from the same point of view as one of the toy characters. In *Lady in the Lake* (1946), a rare attempt was made to present the entire film from the point of view of a single character (Figure 2.46).

Student Writing

Bret Lampman's essay was written in response to this assignment: Choose either *Reversal of Fortune* or *The War of the Roses*; then select a scene that consists of at least a few shots but not more than twenty. View the scene repeatedly, and make a table that includes the shot number, a brief description of the major action of each shot, and the camera distance(s) and angle(s). Next write a 750-to-1,000-word analysis on two to four major points about the expressiveness of *camera distances and angles* in the scene: what do they contribute to the film? Before beginning your essay, review Chapter 2 carefully.

Camera Distances and Angles in a Scene from Reversal of Fortune
by Bret Lampman

In this flashback/vignette (see the table), the camera views a bedroom doorway (interior) in the first shot and shortly thereafter takes up the point-of-view shots of Claus and Sunny Von Bulow: one representing Sunny's seated point of view from the settee (slightly low angle of Claus), the other Claus's standing point of view from near the window (slightly high angle of Sunny). The slightly high and low camera angles give the viewer a nearly point-of-view aspect at first, while about halfway through the scene we see Sunny and Claus closer to eye level. This technique seems appropriate for two reasons. First, the high and low angles at the beginning are conventional: since Claus is standing we get a high angle from his point of view, and likewise for Sunny. Also, as the confrontation heats up, seeing the characters more at eye level helps involve the viewer in the action.

This is an uncomfortable and emotional scene in which the two maintain a total physical separation. At no time in the scene do Sunny and Claus appear in the same frame. Two people casually chatting in a hotel lobby, keeping a respectful social distance, might have stood closer together than this man and his wife, who are in the privacy of their own bedroom. Even though Sunny eventually starts to fall apart emotionally, Claus does not approach to console or confront her. He does not even speak, despite her stinging barbs and her demand "Say something!" Their emotional distance is exquisitely portrayed as she remains on the settee, eventually beating her hands in her lap and sobbing, while he remains rooted in place. These two characters do not move; the camera moves instead, bringing viewers closer to each of them as the confrontation unfolds.

This is the closest we viewers come to either Claus or Sunny in the entire film spatially or emotionally. By this point, two-thirds of the way through the film, the background (their bedroom) is familiar to us, so the initial long shots do less to reveal mise en scène than to convey the characters' emotional distance. We find that Sunny is not so drugged up that she is beyond thinking or caring about her relationship with Claus; in fact, she is terribly upset that her marriage might be ending, that Claus might be leaving her or at least slipping from her control. Her plaintive emotional agony, honestly if angrily voiced, should have been enough to bring Claus to her side (there was plenty of room for two on the love seat), but he appears totally unprepared for her reaction; he does not move or even speak. His mostly passive face, even in medium close-up, is a stark contrast to Sunny's expressive face: she pleads, shouts, and sobs like a desperate child, for once holding nothing back.

As the emotional intensity builds, the camera brings us increasingly closer to Sunny and Claus (note particularly shots 8-14), while its eye-level angle involves us almost naturally in the confrontation. The predominant use of long shots earlier in this film leaves the viewer unprepared for the relative nearness of the camera here, making the viewer feel uncomfortably close, yet not so close. It is revealing that even a medium close-up should have the power to draw us into this exchange, presumably the last real communication Sunny and Claus ever had.

Of course, the flashback is Claus's, and we might believe that this is as near as Claus ever got to anyone, especially during an emotional display (except perhaps when making love). Were the memory related by Sunny, we may very well have found closer, higher, or lower camera distances and angles to reflect her feelings at the moment. But since this is Claus's narration, there is even here a feeling of distance which cannot quite bring us face to face with this sad couple.

They are separated by more than their physical distance. The emotional distance between them is equally noticeable. The camera brings us closer to Sunny, closer to Claus, than they are to each other. The scene is the film's most successful at helping us understand the relationship Claus and Sunny shared: even when they are together, they are somehow apart. Whether separated by a dinner table, a backgammon board, an affair, alcohol or night blinders and earplugs or by this emotional vacuum that not even Sunny's tearful collapse can bridge, the two are never close. We may believe that if only Claus had come as near to Sunny as this scene allows us viewers to, if only he had come down to her eye level as we do, rather than looking impassively down on her, she may have been reassured or encouraged. She may have lived.

But as we see in this scene, Claus keeps his social and emotional distance. In the end, so does Sunny.

A Scene from Reversal of Fortune

Shot	Dist.*	Angle	Shot Description
1	LS	eye level	Alexander and Claus enter through open bedroom door.
2	LS	sl. high	Cosima on settee, looking toward Alexander and Claus (off frame). Bathroom door in background opens and Sunny emerges, leans on door frame. Cosima looks over her shoulder, gets up, and walks to her mother.
3	MS	sl. low	As Sunny had requested, Alexander opens the window.
4	MS-MCU	POV** eye level	Sunny leans unsteadily on Cosima as they walk toward the settee. Sunny stands on her own, smiles kindly, and kisses her daughter, who leaves her side (walks off frame). Sunny leans heavily on the settee.
5	LS	eye level	Claus kisses Cosima and walks her to the door. She and Alexander leave; Claus closes the door.
6	LS	sl. high	Sunny sinks onto the settee, leaning her head back.
7	LS	sl. low	Claus adjusts fluttering drapes over the open window. He takes a few steps toward Sunny, then stops suddenly, looking toward her.
8	LS	sl. high	Sunny is speaking to Claus. With effort, she sits up.
9	MS	sl. low	Claus is listening, standing still. He is silent.
10	MCU	eye level	Sunny continues speaking but remains seated. She looks arrogant but frightened, then angry.
11	MCU	sl. low	Claus reacts, looking injured, curious, or cautious (hard to read).
12	MCU	eye level	Sunny shouts angrily.
13	CU	sl. low	Claus remains still and silent, quietly controlled, stunned or uncertain (still hard to read).
14	MCU	eye level	Sunny begins to sob and beat her hands in her lap, seemingly at her wit's end.

*LS = long shot; MS = medium shot; MCU = medium close-up; CU = close-up.
**All following shots are point of view (POV).

FIGURE 2.47 Panning
For this shot for *Little Fauss and Big Halsy* (1970), two camera operators (left) pivot their cameras sideways on top of a tripod to follow the speeding motorcycles. At the same time, a camera operator on the crane films on-rushing action. *Paramount*

Much more often in films, the camera is placed outside the action, in an **objective camera** shot, and the audience is more spectator than participant.[2]

Moving Camera

A motion-picture camera can **tilt** up and down on its base and pan from side to side. Tilting is an effect achieved when a camera on a stationary base pivots vertically, down to up or up to down, during filming. It is often used to reveal a subject by degrees, frequently with a surprising or humorous conclusion. In **panning**, the camera is handheld or mounted on a tripod and pivoted sideways, as the two camera operators on the ground are doing in Figure 2.47. Panning is often used to show the vastness of a location, such as a sea, plain, mountain range, or outer space. As film scholar Ira Konigsberg points out, it may also be used to "guide the audience's attention to a significant action or point of interest, . . . follow the movement across the landscape of a character or vehicle, and . . . convey a subjective view of what a character sees

[2]For helpful explanations of lighting, color, camera angles, and camera lenses selected to support the films he directed, see Sidney Lumet's discussion in Chapter 5, "The Camera: Your Best Friend," in his *Making Movies* (1995).

when turning his or her head to follow an action" (284). Rarely, as in *Husbands and Wives* (1992), a 360-degree (circular) panning shot is used to show the surroundings on all sides of the camera, though that practice usually draws attention from the subject to the technique itself.

Panning too quickly causes blurred footage; such a result is called a **swish pan**. It is seldom used in commercial films, though it occurs in parts of *Napoléon* (1927) and in the breakfast **montage** of *Citizen Kane*. In *Schindler's List*, swish pans done with an unsteady handheld camera intensify the chaos when Nazis roughly sort naked prisoners. Swish pans may also be point-of-view shots. Late in *The Wild Bunch* (1969), Angel, a member of the wild bunch, realizes he is now under the control of a Mexican general and is upset. From Angel's point of view, we see some laughing Mexicans, then after a swish pan other people laughing at him. After a very brief shot of Angel, we see another point-of-view swish pan in the opposite direction and more laughter at his expense. The point-of-view swish pans convey some of his frustration and disorientation.

montage: A series of shots used to present a condensation of time and events.

The earliest motion pictures were seldom made while moving the camera through space. The filmmakers simply plopped a camera before the subject and started filming. But by the 1920s, moving the camera while filming was commonplace. In the early years of synchronized sound on phonograph records or on the film itself (late 1920s), moving the camera during filming largely halted because the sound from the projectors was being picked up by the sound recording equipment (Figure 9.16 on p. 401). But gradually inventors developed camera shields (blimps and barneys) to muffle sound, and filmmakers learned how to record sound effectively while moving the camera. Since the early 1930s, camera movement has been common during shots.

Camera movement during filming usually changes the distances and angles from the subject and thus changes the impact of images. In the early years of filming, the camera was so bulky it had to be mounted on a sturdy tripod (Figure 2.48) and could be moved only by placing it in some type of moving vehicle, such as the back of a flatbed. By the 1920s, however, various filmmakers had learned how to film while moving the camera. In a striking shot from *Napoléon*, the camera was

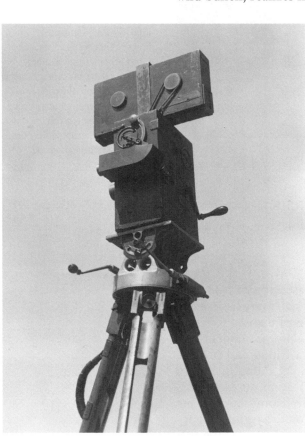

FIGURE 2.48 Early motion-picture camera
This camera was used to film a very lengthy early film classic, *The Birth of a Nation* (1916). In time, cameras became smaller, more portable, and thus more versatile. On the right of the camera seen here is the hand crank that camera operators turned continuously during filming. *The Museum of Modern Art/Film Stills Archive*

FIGURE 2.49 **Dolly shots**
(a, left) Two dollies used in filming *Boomerang* (1992). The dolly on the left supports a seated Steadicam operator; the one on the right, a light source, power pack, and reflective screen used to soften the effects of hard outdoor light. (b, below) Dollies can be used on any smooth supporting surface, even on ice, as here for *Slap Shot* (1977). *(a) Paramount; (b) Universal*

mounted at the base of a huge swing device suspended from a very high ceiling, and the camera filmed a crowded room below as it swung back and forth over the room. Almost as striking are the concluding two shots of *The Crowd* (1928), which were taken from a camera above the film's central family and receding from it, showing the family more and more engulfed by a crowd at a theater. More recently, as the camera is filming, it may glide about by dollying (Figure 2.49) or **tracking**, moving on tracks (Figure 2.50). Such camera

FIGURE 2.50 Tracking shot
Tracking allows the camera to glide along smoothly to follow
an action or recede from it. Seen here is director James Ivory (left)
and a camera crew on location for filming *Slaves of New York* (1989).
Tri-Star

shots should not be confused with shots made
with a stationary camera with a zoom lens. In
zooming, the camera appears to move in or away
from a flat surface, whereas in dollying or tracking,
viewers get some sense of contour and depth.

With a **crane**, a camera may be positioned
at a particular location in the air or moved
smoothly through space (see Figure 2.47). A crane
makes possible otherwise impossible camera
angles and distances. Crane shots may be unobtrusively slow, gracefully slow, or rapid and disorienting; depending on the contexts, the effect
can be soothing, exhilarating, or threatening. They
may be used to create or heighten many different
effects (Figure 2.51).

The **Steadicam**—a device consisting of a lightweight frame, torsion arm, movie camera, and
small TV monitor—allows the camera operator
to move around smoothly while filming (Figure
2.52). Using a Steadicam has many advantages:

Visually, the Steadicam duplicates many benefits of
handheld shooting without the lack of stability inherent in the latter practice; indeed, to the crew, it can
provide speed, flexibility, mobility, and responsive-
ness. And, of course, it can also energize the film with
visual dynamism. (Geuens 12)

The Steadicam can be used in long, continuous shots, such as in a virtuoso three-minute four-
second shot in *GoodFellas*. In this shot, Henry
gives money to a car attendant across the street
from the Copacabana nightclub; then Henry and
Karen walk across the street, cut through a line of
people waiting to get into the club, go in a side
entrance and down some stairs, and walk through
corridors and the kitchen to the nightclub itself.
There a special table is set up for them, and
Henry is greeted by men at nearby tables. Henry and Karen sit; they receive
a complimentary bottle of wine from men at another table and talk a little;
then Henry and Karen watch the beginning of a comedian's routine. For
more than three uninterrupted minutes, the use of a Steadicam allows viewers
to see and to some extent experience the deference, attention, and favors
that Henry enjoys as a mobster.

FIGURE 2.51 **Filming from a crane**

In *High Noon* (1952), the town marshal—who knows he is soon to confront four armed men intent on killing him—is seen in a close-up revealing his worry and fear. The next shot begins as a medium shot showing him from the waist up; then immediately (a, top) the camera begins moving backward and (b) continues moving backward and upward, stopping when it shows him in an extreme long shot even more distant from him than the image seen in (b, above). During this crane shot, viewers see the marshal wipe sweat from his brow then turn away from the camera and walk away alone toward a deadly showdown. Rather than show the action of this thirty-second crane shot in two or more shots—for example, a medium shot followed by a high-angle, extreme long shot—the director chose to preserve continuity of space and time. (Perhaps because of this shot's expressiveness, much of it was chosen to begin the trailer promoting *High Noon* as it was released in 1952.) Frame enlargements. *United Artists*

FIGURE 2.52 The Steadicam
This device for stabilizing moving handheld camera shots was first
used in feature film production in the mid-1970s. Depicted here is a
Steadicam Video SK with video monitor and Sony Hi-8 video camera
below. A 35 mm movie camera is even larger and heavier than the video
camera shown here. Operating a Steadicam expertly takes training
and practice because it initially upsets the operator's sense of balance,
especially when moving. *"Steadicam" is a registered trademark of Cinema
Products Corp., Los Angeles*

A Steadicam is also used effectively near the
end of *The Shining* (1980). As the ax-wielding
main character chases his son through a large,
snow-covered outdoor maze, hoping to catch
him and murder him, the Steadicam follows the
pursued then the pursuer without making viewers seasick. In *Reversal of Fortune* (1990), a
Steadicam is used in the scenes narrated by the
comatose Sunny. As the director of the film explains, the Steadicam "has a floating quality; it
doesn't go straight from one point to another.
It's not shaky, but it's floating. I said . . . that
quality . . . can turn to my advantage here—
whenever Sunny is narrating, having the camera
float around the room like the soul of Sunny, or
Sunny having an out of body experience"
(Schroeder 6).

Camera movement may be used in countless ways. It can allow viewers to follow along
with a moving subject, as in the Steadicam shot
from *GoodFellas* described earlier. Sometimes
camera movement is used to show the subject
from a very different angle, as when the camera
moves to below Norman Bates's chin as the detective in *Psycho* questions him. Occasionally, camera movement is used to prevent the audience
from learning information, as when the camera
moves overhead in *Psycho* immediately before
Norman carries his mother down the stairs.

Camera movement may allow viewers to
see a subject more clearly. Moving the camera
forward may create or intensify tension (what
will we see next?) or slowly introduce viewers to
the setting of the story, as in the beginnings of
West Side Story (1961), *The Remains of the Day*
(1993), and countless other films. Conversely,
camera movement away from the subject can be
used to reveal more and more of a setting, as in
the concluding two shots of *The Crowd* mentioned earlier and the opening shot of *A Clockwork Orange*. During this ninety-two-second
shot, the camera reveals the main character in
close-up (Figure 2.53a), then pulls back to show his collaborators in crime
(Figure 2.53b), then a major setting, where the patrons are all drugged into
immobility and where women are seen as sex objects to display and demean

(Figures 2.53c and 2.53d). Sometimes camera movement backward reveals someone watching what viewers have been watching (Figure 2.54). Moving the camera back may give a sense of release or conclusion, as in the helicopter shots used for the endings of *The Remains of the Day* and *The Shawshank Redemption* (1994). A similar effect results when film stories end with the main character(s) walking away from a stationary camera.

FIGURE 2.53 Camera movement to reveal subjects, setting, and mood
Four photographs approximating the opening tracking shot of *A Clockwork Orange* (1971). (a, top left) The film begins with a close-up of the main character, Alex. Frame enlargement. (b, top right) After a few moments the camera begins to dolly backward slowly, revealing Alex and the other drugged gang members, with Alex's feet propped atop one of two interlocking tables in the form of nude women. (c, above left) As the camera continues tracking backward, viewers can see an attendant in the background to the far right and the first of the nude statues on pedestals. As the camera continues its backward movement, viewers see more and more of the setting, including more of the women tables, more statues on pedestals, other immobile (and drugged) patrons on the sides of this futuristic bar, and the names of the liquid drugs available: Moloko (Milk) Plus and three others. (d, above right) Toward the end of the shot, in the foreground viewers can see two more immobile attendants. Finally the camera stops moving, and during the last second or two of the shot the image looks much like this one, except a longer lens was used for this publicity still than in the movie so everything here looks slightly more compressed. *Polaris; Warner Bros.*

FIGURE 2.54 Tracking backward to reveal surprising information
Sometimes a shot shows viewers its subject, then the camera moves backward and viewers see on the side of the frame someone watching the action they had recently seen, as is done in *Reservoir Dogs* (1992) seconds after the action depicted here. *Lawrence Bender; Miramax*

Camera movement without a Steadicam can disorient or confuse viewers, as in *Dr. Strangelove: Or, How I Learned to Stop Worrying and Love the Bomb* (1963). Immediately after a guided missile hits a bomber, the camera jars around vigorously and erratically, and viewers feel momentarily at a loss. Filming with a handheld camera while moving through a crowd results in footage that might make viewers feel the movement and perhaps excitement of crowd scenes.

And camera movement can help control *when* during a shot viewers learn certain information. In *National Lampoon's Vacation* (1983), a shot begins with children asleep in the backseat of a moving car at night. The shot continues with the camera panning to the front seat, where the mother is also asleep; then the camera continues its movement and we learn that the driver, the father, is also deep in sleep! It's a surprising and hilarious moment.

DIGITAL CINEMATOGRAPHY

In postproduction—that is, after a film has been shot—computers are increasingly being used to create or manipulate film images. Any image, just as any written language, can be scanned into a computer then changed in many

FIGURE 2.55 Morphing

In morphing, the filmed frames are scanned into a computer. Then the parts of the image that are to change are marked manually and transformed in stages by a sophisticated computer program. The images are then transferred to film stock and incorporated into the finished film. Morphing was used in many shots during postproduction of *The Mask* (1994). It was used for the shot represented here to make the lower half of a man's body incredibly elastic so that the character can evade bullets fired at him. (a, top left) This frame has not been morphed. (b, top right) The following frame, shown here, begins the morphing process. (c, above left) The man has succeeded in evading the bullets. (d, above right) Approximately two seconds after the morphing process was begun, the film resumes live action. Frame enlargements. *New Line Cinema*

ways. Computers can be used to composite (or combine) two or more images. They can be used to **morph** images—to change their shape—so that we can see Eddie Murphy briefly become other characters in *Vampire in Brooklyn* (1995) or a character change shape to avoid harm (Figure 2.55). Later the computer frames of the transformation are transferred to film and incorporated in the final version of the film.

Computers can also be used to remove or cover up objects from images. An article in a major journal on cinematography cites several specific examples:

> They can eliminate scratches and remove objects which don't belong in period films. In one recent Western, bloodstains were removed from a character's shirt to make it acceptable for use in a trailer. In another PG-rated film, a brief bathing suit bottom was extended to cover some of an actress' exposed body . . . with the aid of 'electronic paint.' In *Wrestling with Ernest Hemingway* [1993], an actor was clearly breathing after he was supposed to be dead. The image was fixed by scanning the film into digital format, literally erasing parts of frames where the actor's shirt was moving or breathing, and replacing it with cloned images from frames where the shirt was still. (Fisher 101)

After Brandon Lee was killed in an accident with three days of filming left in making *The Crow* (1994), for a few scenes a computer was used to move the image of his character to new settings. Now filmmakers with a large budget can use special effects during filming, as in *True Lies* (1994), then clean up the images in the computer—for example, remove wires that supported actors as they were moved through the air.

Digital work allows filmmakers to correct mistakes that would be even more costly or impossible to correct (for example, perhaps the actor has moved on to another job and cannot return to reshoot an indispensable botched shot). Like animation, computer work makes possible manipulation of the film's images and makes visible what was previously impossible to show. For example, for one scene in *In the Line of Fire* (1993), footage of President and Mrs. Bush getting out of the presidential airplane was scanned into a computer and their faces were replaced with the faces of the movie's characters. Digital cinematography, however, is not without its limitations. Some people think it still too often looks a little fake; then, too, it is still enormously costly and time-consuming. Even films known for their digital creativity—such as *Jurassic Park* (1993) and *The Lost World: Jurassic Park* (1997)—continue to combine digital visual effects with shots made by filming models (life-size or miniature), robots, **animatronics**, and the like.

animatronic: A puppet likeness of a human, creature, or animal, whose movements are directed by electronic, mechanical, or radio-controlled devices.

Because of costs and visual quality, filming and projecting theatrical film as film, not video, seems likely for years to come. It also seems likely that transferring parts of a film to a computer, manipulating the digitized visuals, then transferring the visuals back to film will grow in importance. Perhaps some combination of video and computers will eventually replace traditional cinematography, but the history of film technology shows that technological advances alone do not bring about radical changes in filmmaking and film exhibition. At least for big-budget movies, profits for those involved in the production and distribution of moving images and sounds and the tastes of the viewing and paying public are also potent determinants.

SUMMARY

Cinematographers are responsible for the choice and manipulation of film stock, lighting, and cameras. Some of their main concerns are film grain, color, lenses, camera distance and angle from the subject, and camera movement.

Film Stock

- Generally, the wider the film gauge, the sharper the projected images. Slow film stock, which requires more light than fast film stock, produces a more detailed, more nuanced image. In older films, fast film stock usually produces more graininess.

- Color associations vary from culture to culture, and a color's impact depends on the context—where and how it is used.

- Color may be saturated (intense, vivid) or desaturated (muted, dull, pale). In most western societies, warm colors (reds, oranges, and yellows) tend to be thought of as hot, dangerous, lively, and assertive. Greens, blues, and violets are generally thought of as cool. In Europe and the United States, these colors tend to be associated with safety, reason, control, relaxation, and sometimes sadness or melancholy.

- Colorized videos are made with colors that were not chosen by directors, costumers, or set designers but by video technicians whose judgment in choosing colors is often questionable, especially for films made many years ago and perhaps in a different culture.

Lighting

- Hard lighting comes from a direct source while soft light comes from an indirect source. Hard lighting is harsh and unflattering; soft lighting is flattering.

- The direction of light can change an image's moods and meanings.

- Like light, shadows can be used expressively in countless ways.

The Camera

- During filming, one of three types of lenses is used: wide-angle, normal, or telephoto. Often all three are used at different times within the same film. Each type of lens has different properties and creates different images.

- Choice of lens, aperture (or opening), and film stock largely determine the depth of field, or distance in front of the camera in which all objects are in focus.

- Diffusers may be placed in front of a light source or in front of a lens to soften facial lines, to glamorize, or to lend a more spiritual or ethereal look.

- Camera distance helps determine what details will be noticeable, what details will be excluded from the frame, and how large the subject will appear within the frame.

- By changing the camera lens and the camera distance between shots or during a shot, filmmakers can change perspective: the relative size and apparent depth of objects in the photographic image.

- The angle from which the subject is filmed influences the expressiveness of the images. There are basically four camera angles: bird's-eye view, high angle, eye-level angle, and low angle.

- In point-of-view (p.o.v.) shots, the camera films a subject from the approximate position of someone in the film. Such camera placements contribute to the viewer's identification with the subject and participation in the action.

- A motion-picture camera may remain in one position as it is pivoted up or down on its base (tilting) or rotated sideways on a stationary base (panning), or it may be moved through space as it is filming.

- Panning too quickly causes blurred footage: such a result is called a swish pan.

- Ways to move the camera around during filming include dollying, tracking, using a crane, and employing a Steadicam.

Digital Cinematography

- Film images can be scanned into a computer, changed, then transferred back to film. Such computer manipulation can correct errors or change the images in ways impossible or more troublesome and costly to do with film alone.

WORKS CITED

Almendros, Nestor (cinematographer). Interview. *Visions of Light* (documentary film). 1992.

Bazin, André. "The Evolution of the Language of Cinema." *What Is Cinema? Essays Selected and Translated by Hugh Gray.* Vol. 1. Berkeley: U of California P, 1967.

Birdwhistell, Ray. *Kinesics and Context: Essays on Body Motion Communication*. Philadelphia: U of Pennsylvania P, 1970.

Daviau, Allen (cinematographer). Interview. *Visions of Light* (documentary film). 1992.

Dyer, Richard. *Stars*. 2nd ed. London: British Film Inst., 1998.

Eidsvik, Charles. *Cineliteracy: Film among the Arts*. New York: Random, 1978.

Fisher, Bob. "Looking Forward to the Future of Film." *American Cinematographer* Aug. 1994: 98–104.

Geuens, Jean-Pierre. "Visuality and Power: The Work of the Steadicam." *Film Quarterly* Winter 1993–94: 8–17.

Hayward, Susan. *Key Concepts in Cinema Studies*. London: Routledge, 1996.

Konigsberg, Ira. *The Complete Film Dictionary*. 2nd ed. New York: Penguin Reference, 1997.

Linfield, Susan. "The Color of Money." *American Film* Jan.–Feb. 1987: 29+.

Lumet, Sidney. *Making Movies*. New York: Knopf, 1995.

Malkiewicz, Kris. *Cinematography: A Guide for Film Makers and Film Teachers*. 2nd ed. Englewood Cliffs: Prentice, 1989.

Riefenstahl, Leni (filmmaker). Interview. *The Wonderful, Horrible Life of Leni Riefenstahl* (documentary film). 1993.

Schroeder, Barbet. "Justice, Irony, and *Reversal of Fortune*: An Interview with Barbet Schroeder." By Robert Sklar. *Cineaste* 18.2 (1991): 4+.

Turner, George. "A Tradition of Innovation." *American Cinematographer* Aug. 1994: 93–96.

FOR FURTHER READING

Alton, John. *Painting with Light*. 1949. Berkeley: U of California P, 1995. Alton, an accomplished cinematographer, explains the duties of the cinematographer and how lighting, camera techniques, and choice of location determine the visual mood of films. This edition includes new introductory material and a filmography.

Coe, Brian. *The History of Movie Photography*. New York: Zoetrope; London: Ash and Grant, 1981. A short history of evolving filmmaking equipment and processes. Many photographs, some in color.

Eyman, Scott. *Five American Cinematographers*. Metuchen, NJ: Scarecrow, 1987. Interviews with Karl Struss, Joseph Ruttenberg, James Wong Howe, Linwood Dunn, and William H. Clothier.

Rogers, Pauline. *Contemporary Cinematographers on Their Art*. Boston: Focal, 1998. Thirteen interviews cover such topics as pre-production, special effects, aerial photography, and second unit. Often the cinematographers tell how popular shots were lit and filmed.

Schaefer, Dennis, and Larry Salvato. *Masters of Light: Conversations with Contemporary Cinematographers*. Berkeley: U of California P, 1984. Cinematographers interviewed include Nestor Almendros, John Alonzo, Conrad Hall, Laszlo Kovacs, Vittorio Storaro, Haskell Wexler, Gordon Willis, and Vilmos Zsigmond.

CHAPTER 3
Editing

THE CLICHÉ ABOUT SCULPTURE, that the sculptor finds the statue which is waiting in the stone, applies equally to editing; the editor finds the film which is waiting hidden in the material. (Priestly 273)

How do film editors work? After the many labeled strips of film have been developed, the film editor or editors—often in the later stages of the work, in cooperation with the director—select the best version, or **take**, of each shot for the finished film. Often the editor shortens the shot; sometimes the editor divides a shot and inserts another shot or part of it (a **cutaway**) into the middle of the split shot. Often the editor consults a **master shot**, which records an entire scene. Sometimes parts of the master shot are used in the **final cut** of the scene; occasionally the master shot is used in its entirety. All of this work is usually done on an editing machine (Figures 3.1 and 3.2).

It's often said that an impressive performance is made in the cutting (or editing) room. The editor can make an actor look effective by selecting only the best takes and by cutting to **reaction shots** if an actor even momentarily lapses out of character. The editor can also make the writer or writers look better, especially by dropping weak dialogue and by ensuring an appropriate **pace** to the dialogue and action. Editors can make everyone involved in the film look better by cutting the tedious and extraneous. In a movie, viewers never see, for example, all the filmed reactions of someone in the film watching some important action. We should be grateful. As Hitchcock is reputed to have said, "Drama is life with the dull parts left out."

For a **feature film,** the editing process, which is often called "cutting the film," may take months and may require the efforts of two or more editors or an editor and assistants. Editing is so time-consuming that it's no wonder that for a feature film the job usually consumes months and can consume years. Although they faced extreme situations, the editors of *Crimson Tide* (1995) fashioned a 113-minute film out of 148 hours of footage, and Leni Riefenstahl had so much **footage** while making the **documentary film** *Olympia* (1936) that it took her ten weeks of ten-hour days just to view all the **dailies** (the prints made from a day's filming) then nearly two years to edit the film into its final version of more than 3½ hours (Riefenstahl).

---

final cut: The last version of an edited film.

reaction shot: A shot that shows someone reacting to an event.

pace: A person's sense of a subject (such as narrative developments or factual information) being presented rapidly or slowly.

feature film: Usually, a film that is at least sixty minutes long.

footage: A length of exposed motion-picture film.

documentary film: A film that presents a version of events that viewers are intended to accept not primarily as the product of someone's imagination but primarily as fact.

FIGURE 3.1 An early flatbed editing table
Acclaimed Soviet filmmaker Sergei Eisenstein works at an editing table with takes of 35 mm film. In the background, light behind frosted glass illuminates the film strips that hang before it. *Courtesy Herbert Marshall Archives, Center for Soviet and East European Studies, Southern Illinois University*

FIGURE 3.2 The two basic types of editing machines
An upright editing machine, a 16 mm Moviola (back and center), and a 16 mm flatbed editing table (right) as seen in *Boogie Nights* (1997). With these machines a film editor can compare different takes of the same shot, select the take, then splice it to another shot and another and another. . . . The editor can then play the edited footage to see how effective it is. The Moviola company made many of the upright editing machines, and that brand name is widely used for all such machines. With upright editing machines, editors control the speed and direction of the shots by means of a pedal. With flatbed editing tables, all the work is done by hand. *Lawrence Gordon; New Line Cinema*

In large productions editors typically work within the boundaries set by the script and the footage the director has shot. Nonetheless, by selecting shots and arranging, doubling, and shortening them, editors can expand or compress an action, promote continuity or lack of it, affect the film's pace and moods, and intensify viewer reactions. Editing can even sometimes salvage an otherwise mediocre film.

In this chapter, we will examine the components available to editors, how they use them, and how they consequently determine a film's handling of pace and time. The chapter concludes with a brief discussion of how computers may help in editing.

EARLY FILM EDITING

In the first decades of this century, the film editor simply projected the uncut film, made notes, and then returned to a room equipped only with a bench, a pair of scissors, a magnifying glass, and the knowledge that the distance from the tip of his nose to the fingers of his outstretched arm represented about three seconds. (Murch 75)

reel: A spool to hold film.

In the first motion pictures, from the 1890s, filmmakers positioned the camera and filmed until the short **reel** of film ran out (see Figure 1.3 on p. 11). That was it: one shot. Other than deciding which shots to include in the finished film and their order, there was no editing to be done. Georges Méliès's early films, such as "Cinderella" (1900) and "A Trip to the Moon" (1902, Figure 3.3), were longer than those of the Lumière Brothers and consisted of a succession of scenes, each made up of one shot and showing continuous limited action in one place.

In "The Life of an American Fireman" (1902) and "The Great Train Robbery" (1903), Edwin S. Porter tried more daring editing strategies, such as suggesting actions occurring at two places at the same time and combining others' footage with footage he filmed. But in D. W. Griffith's short films from 1908 to 1913 and his first features, Griffith proved to be one of cinema's most innovative and adept editors. Griffith's *The Birth of a Nation* (1915) has more than 1,300 shots of widely varying length, and much of the film—such as the Civil War battles and the assassination of President Lincoln—is still highly engaging cinema.

Some later Russian filmmakers—especially Lev Kuleshov, Dziga Vertov, Vsevolod I. Pudovkin, and Sergei Eisenstein—were much impressed with Griffith's editing (it is said that Pudovkin had planned to become a chemist until he saw Griffith's 1916 film *Intolerance*). These filmmakers studied some of Griffith's films closely and discussed or wrote about the art, craft, and theory of film editing. The four of them and other Soviet filmmakers also experimented with editing, and though they developed somewhat different editing

FIGURE 3.3 Consecutive one-shot scenes
In "A Trip to the Moon" (1902), explorers from earth have been captured by moon creatures but escape. (a, left) In this frame enlargement, the leader of the earth expedition (with an umbrella) holds a moon creature (right) at bay. (b, below) In the next shot/scene, the earthlings' rocket is perched on the edge of a precipice. The leader hits a moon creature, which disappears in a puff of smoke, closes the hatch, and climbs down a suspended rope attached to the rocket. A moon creature clings to the base of the rocket as it starts to fall. As in other early fictional films, in every scene the camera is unmoving; the action plays itself out before the camera then a new shot and scene begins. Frame enlargements. *The Museum of Modern Art/Circulating Film Library*

FIGURE 3.4 **Editing to suggest ideas**
In (*Battleship*) *Potemkin* (1925), the editing of three consecutive shots makes an inanimate object, a stone lion, appear to come to life. The editing is used both to suggest a reaction to an event (the battleship's beginning to fire shells) and to express an idea (the *Potemkin* is so powerful that it brings stone to life). Frame enlargements. *Goskino; The Museum of Modern Art/Circulating Film Library*

styles, they promoted what came to be called "Soviet montage" or simply **montage**. Such editing aims not so much to promote the invisible continuity of a story, strongly favored in **classical Hollywood cinema**, as to suggest **meanings** from the dynamic juxtaposition of many carefully selected details. As film theorist and scholar Dudley Andrew explains, Eisenstein

> was appalled at how inefficient and dull most cinema was, especially cinema which sought to give its audience the impression of reality. Reality, he felt, speaks very obscurely, if at all. It is up to the filmmaker to rip reality apart and rebuild it into a system capable of generating the greatest possible emotional effects. (69)

Soviet montage is illustrated in *Strike* (1924), in which Eisenstein uses a visual metaphor to express the terrible situation of strikers in a capitalist society by cutting from shots of the striking workers and their families being attacked by police to shots of farm animals being slaughtered. In (*Battleship*) *Potemkin* (1925), the tsar's troops and mounted Cossacks have viciously attacked unarmed civilians in 1905 Odessa, Russia. In retaliation, the guns on the *Potemkin* have fired at the headquarters of the generals and shells are starting to land. Then a sleeping stone lion seems to spring to life (Figure 3.4). The three consecutive shots suggest that the *Potemkin*'s guns are so powerful that they rouse even a stone lion, or perhaps suggest that the Russian civilians (represented by the lion) are coming to life and will fight back; or perhaps these three shots suggest both meanings. The three shots do not help develop the story; they do not even show any damage from the bombardment. Instead, they express an idea somewhat obtrusively (probably many viewers will be impressed and distracted by the editing of the three shots). Ever since the films of Griffith and those of the later Soviet masters Pudovkin and Eisenstein, the expressiveness and power of editing have been beyond dispute.

style: The manner of presenting a subject in a creative work.

classical Hollywood cinema: A term used by some film scholars to describe the type of narrative film dominant throughout most of world movie history. Classical Hollywood cinema shows one or more distinct characters with clear goals who overcome many problems in reaching them. The films tend to use unobtrusive filmmaking techniques and to stress continuity of action.

meaning: An observation or generalization about a subject.

BUILDING BLOCKS

In constructing films that show stories, editors select shots to fabricate scenes and sequences. They connect shots in various ways, and most often they edit to create maximum continuity, an unobtrusive style of editing that helps viewers to follow the characters and action.

Shots, Scenes, Sequences

A **shot** is an uninterrupted strip of exposed motion-picture film made up of at least one **frame**, an individual image on the strip of film (Figure 3.5). A shot presents a subject, perhaps even a blank screen, during an uninterrupted segment of time. Typically, a feature film consists of hundreds of

avant-garde film: A film that rejects the conventions of popular movies and explores the possibilities of the film medium itself.

narrative: A series of unified consecutive events situated in one or more settings.

shots, sometimes more than a thousand. For example, *Toy Story* (1995), which is 77½ minutes long, has 1,623 shots (Grignon). At the opposite extreme, some **avant-garde films**, such as some films made by Andy Warhol, consist of a single, often very lengthy, shot.

A **scene** is a section of a **narrative** film that gives the impression of continuous action taking place during continuous time and in continuous space. A scene seems to have unity, but editors often delete tedious or unnecessary footage in such a way that viewers will not notice. For example, we may not see every step a character presumably takes in moving within a scene. A scene may consist of one shot and usually consists of two or more related shots, but on rare occasions a shot is used to convey multiple scenes, as in the more than eight-minute opening shot of *The Player* (1992). At various times during that first shot, the camera moves closer to certain groups of characters so we can see them interact (Table 3.1). In the opening of *The Player*, as in the opening of *Touch of Evil*, there is not a scene consisting of the usual shot or shots, but a shot consisting of scenes.

The term *sequence* lacks a universal meaning. Filmmakers, critics, and scholars often assign it different meanings. And comparison of several published outlines of sequences for the same film reveals different "sequences." It is most useful to think of a **sequence** as a group of related scenes, though what unifies the scenes is not universally agreed upon.

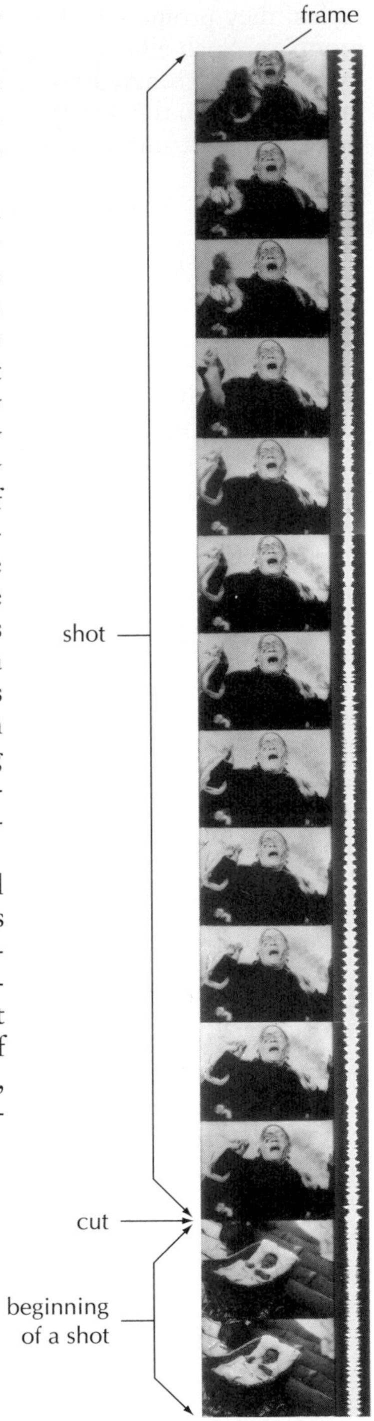

FIGURE 3.5 **Frames, shot, and cut**
The top twelve frames constitute a complete shot, and the bottom two the beginning of a new shot. They were spliced together in (*Battleship*) *Potemkin* (1925). When the film is projected at twenty-four frames per second, the top shot will last a half-second. Frame enlargements. *Goskino; The Museum of Modern Art/Circulating Film Library*

TABLE 3.1
The Opening Shot of *The Player*

SCENE NUMBER AND ACTION

1. A woman in Joel Levison's office takes a brief call from Larry Levy then hangs up. Another woman scolds her then sends her hurrying off for the day's trade papers.

2. Griffin drives into a parking space and gets out of his Range Rover. He is accosted by Adam Simon, who begins pitching a story for a possible movie. Griffin tells him to run the idea by Bonnie Sherow.

3. A man in a suit and another man who makes deliveries on a bicycle discuss tracking shots in movies.

4. Outside Griffin's office, we see through a window a man in a cap (Buck Henry) make a pitch for *The Graduate, Part Two*.

5. Adam Simon and Bonnie Sherow emerge from the same building; he is pitching his story to her. The delivery man on a bike has had an accident. Bonnie tries to help him.

6. A man in a Porsche briefly flirts with a young woman then asks where Joel Levison's office is. We learn that Levison is the studio head.

7. Another man is giving a studio tour to a group of Japanese people.

8. Bonnie, still pursued by Adam Simon, tells him to write down his story for her.

9. Joel Levison arrives in a large Mercedes immediately after the young woman of scene 1 arrives back and gives the papers to the other secretary.

10. Two men and a woman emerge from the building and talk about rumored upcoming changes at the studio, including the possibility that Griffin may be replaced.

11. In his office, Griffin hears two women make a story pitch.

12. The delivery man of scenes 3 and 5 mistakenly thinks that a man looking for Griffin Mill is the director Martin Scorsese.

13. The man in the suit from scene 3 and the man who made the pitch for *The Graduate, Part Two* discuss editing and tracking shots in movies.

14. While crossing the parking lot, Bonnie scolds her assistant for meeting with a writer.

15. The man from scene 12 makes a movie pitch to Griffin.

To illustrate *shot*, *scene*, and *sequence*, I will describe the first two shots of the restored 1989 version of *Lawrence of Arabia*, which constitute the first scene, then the rest of the scenes in the first sequence.

Sequence 1 (in England):

Scene 1:

Shot 1: On the left side of the frame Lawrence fusses with a motorcycle as the opening credits roll in the center and on the right of the frame.

Shot 2: Lawrence starts the motorcycle, gets on it, and drives away until he is out of sight.

Scene 2 (consisting of 23 shots): As he rides quickly, even recklessly, up a hill, two bicyclists appear on his side of the road. He swerves and rides off the road.

Scene 3 (consisting of 2 shots): After Lawrence's funeral in St. Paul's Cathedral and before a bust of Lawrence, Colonel Brighton and a cleric exchange brief and somewhat opposing views of Lawrence.

Scene 4 (consisting of 4 shots): Outside St. Paul's Cathedral, four people are questioned about who Lawrence was; they are evasive, or claim to have not known him well, or point out contradictory qualities.

The first sequence of *Lawrence of Arabia* thus is made up of four scenes, and those four scenes consist of thirty-one shots.

Narrative films stitch scenes together; if a film follows the traditions of classical Hollywood cinema, the scenes are usually combined in an unnoticeable manner. Feature narrative films vary enormously in the number of scenes, but a hundred or more is common.

Transitions: From Here to There

Shots may be joined in many ways. The most common method is to splice, or connect, the end of one shot to the beginning of the next. This transition is called a **cut** (or **straight cut**) (see Figure 3.5) because pieces of film are cut and spliced together. In narrative films, normally only cuts are used *within* a scene.

A **match cut** (sometimes called a form cut) maintains continuity between two shots by matching objects with similar or identical shapes or similar movements or both similar shapes and similar movements. One of the best-known examples of a match cut is from *2001: A Space Odyssey* (1968), in which a bone slowly tumbling end-over-end in the air is replaced by an orbiting spacecraft with a similar shape (Figure 3.6). A match cut in which the second shot continues a movement begun in the previous shot is found in *M* (1931, Figure 3.7). A match cut can convey much information quickly. In

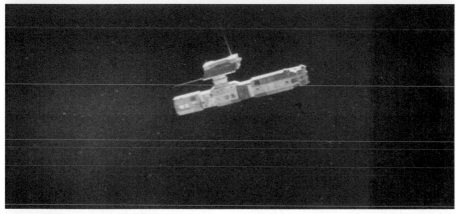

FIGURE 3.6 Match cut of similar forms
In *2001: A Space Odyssey* (1968), a shot of a bone is followed by a shot of an orbiting spacecraft. The transition suggests that both bone and orbiting spacecraft are weapons. When projected, the film gives the appearance of the bone becoming the orbiting spacecraft, and viewers do not notice that the angles of the two objects do not match. Frame enlargements. *Metro-Goldwyn-Mayer*

I Am a Fugitive from a Chain Gang (1932), one scene ends with a judge banging down his gavel while sentencing a man; after a brief transition, the next scene begins with a hammer striking a leg iron then the camera pulls back to reveal that the person being imprisoned is the same man. In little more than the blink of an eye, two similarly shaped objects used in two similar movements convey a change of time, **setting**, and situation but also a correspondence between the banging of the judge's gavel and the banging of a prison hammer.

A **jump cut** is a discontinuous transition between shots. For example, one shot shows a woman running on a beach toward the water and the next shot shows her running away from the water. A jump cut is sometimes used

setting: The place where filmed action occurs; a location or set.

FIGURE 3.7 Match cut of form and movement
In the German film *M* (1931), (a, right) the head of Berlin's underworld begins a sweeping motion with his arm, and (b, below) the movement is picked up and completed by a match cut to the chief of police at a different meeting. The suggestion is continuity and similarity between the groups: both have the same goal—to catch a child murderer so as to restore order to their disrupted routines. Frame enlargements. *Nero Films*

to surprise or disorient viewers. But it may also occur if the film print or video has missing footage.

The **fade-out**, **fade-in** can provide a short but meaningful pause between scenes or sequences. Normally in a fade-out, fade-in, an image is gradually transformed into a darkened frame; then the next shot changes from a darkened frame into an illuminated one. But variations are possible. Early in *The Discreet Charm of the Bourgeoisie* (1972), a shot (and scene) ends

FIGURE 3.8 Lap dissolve between scenes of a trailer
Lap dissolves are often used to convey what someone is thinking or remembering. (a, top left)
The main character in *Amistad* (1997), a slave who led a rebellion on an 1839 slave ship, looks at
a gift his wife back in Africa had given him. (b, top right) and (c, above left) By degrees the image of
the African wife emerges and gradually replaces the image of the man. (d, above right) The transition
is complete. In little more than a second the lap dissolve allows the filmmakers to change subjects
and locations. Frame enlargements. *DreamWorks*

with the camera **zooming in** as the image goes out of focus; the next shot
(and scene) begins out of focus, then quickly comes into focus. The transition functions much like the more traditional fade-out, fade-in. If a fade-out,
fade-in is done slowly, it can serve as a leisurely transition; if done rapidly, it
is less noticeable, or not noticeable at all. Perhaps because of the current
popularity of fast pacing in films, in recent movies this transition is used less
often than it used to be.

A **lap dissolve** or dissolve blends the end of one shot and the beginning of
the next: one shot fades from view as the next shot fades into view and replaces
it (Figure 3.8). It has been used in many ways, for example to introduce and

zoom in: During filming, to
adjust a zoom lens so that the
size of the subject appears to
increase as the area being
filmed seems to decrease.

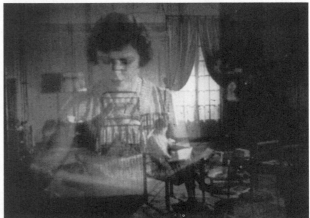

FIGURE 3.9 Lap dissolve within a scene
Although lap dissolves are now rarely used within scenes, in earlier films—as in this example from "Un Chien Andalou" (1928)—they occasionally were. Frame enlargements. *The Museum of Modern Art/ Circulating Film Library*

cutaway (shot): A shot that briefly interrupts the visual presentation of a subject to show something else.

serial: From the 1910s until the early 1950s, an action film divided into chapters or installments, one of which was shown each week in movie theaters.

conclude a **cutaway** that shows what a character is thinking. In Buster Keaton's *Our Hospitality* (1923), the Keaton character looks straight ahead then a rapid lap dissolve introduces a brief shot showing what he is thinking about followed by a rapid lap dissolve that returns to the shot of him looking straight ahead. Usually filmmakers have used the lap dissolve to suggest a change of setting, the passage of time, or both. Lap dissolves may be rapid and nearly imperceptible or slow and quite noticeable, creating a momentary superimposition of two images (see p. 140). Dissolves between scenes have long been commonplace but now are rare within scenes (Figure 3.9).

A **wipe** seems to push one shot off the screen as it replaces it with the next shot (Figure 3.10). This transition, which comes in many variations, has been popular in science fiction, **serials**, and action movies, but it has also been used in such diverse films as *It Happened One Night* (1934), *The Maltese*

Falcon (1941), *The Seven Samurai* (1954), *Ed Wood* (1994), and *The First Wives Club* (1996). For yet other examples, see the opening and closing credits of some Pink Panther movies, in which an animated pink panther seems to help push off one shot as it is replaced with the next shot.

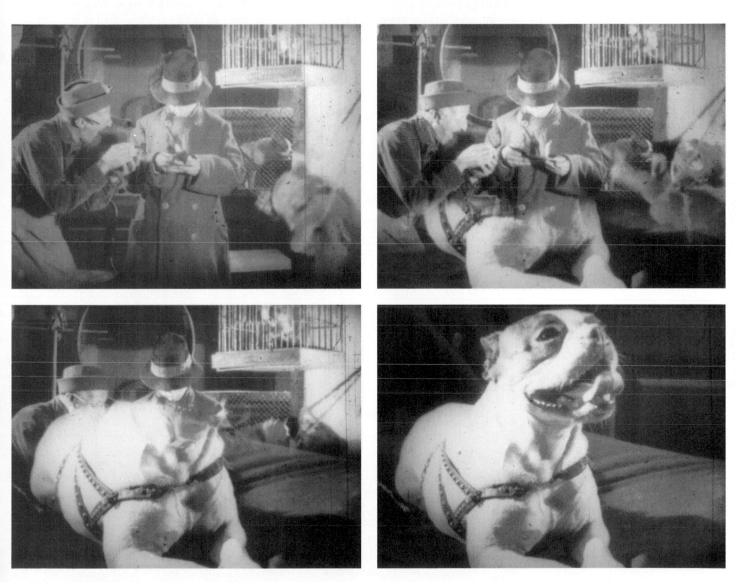

FIGURE 3.10 A wipe
In *Strike* (1924), a wipe is used between two scenes when (a–b, top) the image of two men is replaced with (c–d, above) the image of a dog. Wipes may move across the frame from any direction: from below (as here), from above, from one of the sides, even on a diagonal. Frame enlargements.
The Museum of Modern Art/Circulating Film Library

The six transitions discussed thus far are summarized in Table 3.2.

Many other transitions are used less often than these six. The others can be thought of as combination transitions. In many films from the silent era, some sound films set in the past, and some films that imitate filmmaking **techniques** of older films, an iris-in or iris-out may connect scenes. In the **iris-in**, a widening opening reveals more and more of the next shot until it is

technique: Any aspect of film-making, such as the choices of sets, lighting, and editing.

TABLE 3.2
Six Frequently Used Transitions between Shots

Cut	The end of the first shot is attached to the beginning of the second shot. The most often used of all transitions, it creates an instantaneous change in one or more of the following: angle, distance, subject. See Figure 3.5.
Match or form cut	The shape or movement of a subject in the beginning of the second shot matches or is very similar to a subject's form or movement at the end of the previous shot. See Figures 3.6 and 3.7.
Jump cut	A transition in which the viewer perceives the second shot as abruptly discontinuous with the first shot. See Figures 3.15b and c.
Fade-out, fade-in	The first shot fades to darkness (normally black); then the second shot fades in (by degrees goes from darkness to illuminated image).
Lap dissolve or dissolve	The first shot fades out as the second shot fades in, overlaps the first, then replaces it entirely. See Figures 3.8 and 3.9.
Wipe	The first shot seems to be pushed off the screen by the next shot. Not a common transition, but not rare either. For a "wipe chart" illustrating 120 types of wipes, see Roy Huss and Norman Silverstein, *The Film Experience* (New York: Dell, 1968), 60. Examples they give include beginning with a small part of the second shot in one area of the frame then expanding the smaller area until it displaces the original, larger one. As Huss and Silverstein also explain, "a second image 'wipes' . . . a first from the screen . . . in several directional and formal ways: horizontally, vertically, diagonally, in the shape of a fan, like the movement of the hands of a clock, with a 'flip' (the frame revolves 360 degrees)" (59). See Figure 3.10.

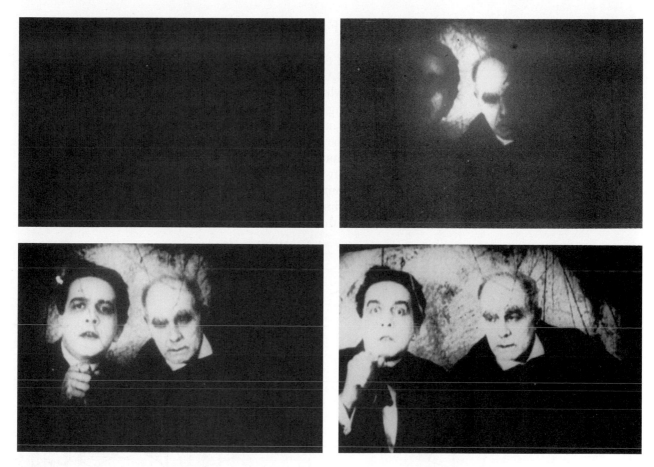

FIGURE 3.11 Iris-in

Four frame enlargements from early in *The Cabinet of Dr. Caligari* (1919) illustrate an iris-in: a transition between shots in which the image is gradually exposed by a widening opening, usually a circle. (a, top left) The shot begins with four black frames then (b, top right; c, above left) reveals more and more of the image by means of an irregularly shaped opening. (d, above right) As is common in *Caligari*, part of the image remains in the dark. Frame enlargements. *Decla-Bioscop*

more visible (Figure 3.11). In an **iris-out**, the image is closed out by a constricting shape, usually a circle.

A more complicated transition is used in *Wish You Were Here* (1987): a shot (and scene) end with a view of a seated woman's back. After a brief fade-out, fade-in, viewers see the back of the same seated person but at a different period of her life. This transition might be called a match cut with fade-out, fade-in.

CONTINUITY EDITING

In narrative films and certainly in classical Hollywood cinema, **continuity editing** is normally used. Shots seem to follow one another unobtrusively, and viewers always know where characters are in relation to other characters and in relation to the setting. Continuity editing allows the omission of minor details within scenes yet maintains the illusion of completeness.

Continuity may be achieved in several ways. Primarily, it is maintained within scenes if all shots show the subjects from one side of an imaginary straight line drawn between them. This is sometimes referred to as the 180° system (Figure 3.12). Similarly, shot/reverse shot editing promotes continuity. A shot from over the first person's shoulder or to the side of it shows the face of a second person; in the next shot the camera is behind or to the side of the

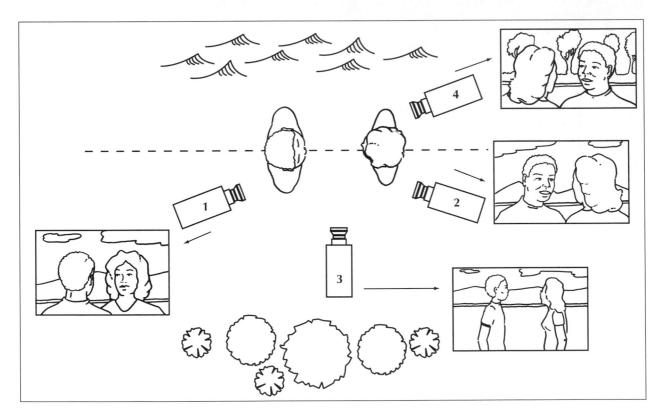

FIGURE 3.12 Using the 180° system to support continuity editing
Usually each scene in a narrative film is filmed and edited so that all camera angles of the subjects are from one side of an imaginary line, as in 1, 2, and 3. If shots are filmed from the other side of that imaginary line, as in 4, the relation of the subjects to each other and to the setting shifts abruptly and perhaps confusingly.

FIGURE 3.13 **Eyeline match**
In *The White Balloon* (1995), an Iranian film, (a, left) the main character points off-frame. (b, below) Then from her point of view, the camera sees what she sees: a fish she is eager to buy. Such eyeline matches are one way filmmakers maintain continuity from shot to shot within a scene. Frame enlargements. *C.M.I.*

second person, and we now see the first person's face. See camera placements 1 and 2 in Figure 3.12. Shot/reverse shot is often used for scenes with dialogue.

Continuity editing is often achieved by cutting on action: one shot ends during a subject's movement, and the next shot, usually from a different distance or angle, continues or concludes the action. In such instances, dead time (the middle part of the movement) may be omitted, yet continuity is maintained because the same subject moves in a consistent way.

Continuity is also maintained by **eyeline matches**: a subject looks at something **offscreen**, and the next shot shows what was being looked at from approximately the point of view of the subject (Figure 3.13). Continuity

offscreen: Area beyond the frame line.

editing is the usual way narrative films are edited, though some filmmakers choose to ignore continuity from time to time, and other filmmakers—such as Jacques Tati and Yasujiro Ozu—largely reject the conventions of continuity editing.

IMAGE ON IMAGE AND IMAGE AFTER IMAGE

Editors can combine two or more images into the same image—although it's usually hard for viewers to distinguish more than two images at the same time—or they can juxtapose images in expressive ways.

FIGURE 3.14 **Superimposition of three images**
In a few frames near the conclusion of *Psycho* (1960), viewers may notice that three images are superimposed briefly: Norman from the shoulders up, a skull, and Marion's car being pulled from the swamp by a chain. In a 35 mm version of the film that is in good condition or a laser disc or DVD version viewed on a high-resolution monitor, viewers may notice the images and consider their significance. (Viewers are unlikely to see them on a videotape version.) The triple superimposition suggests that Norman is his mother or that underneath Norman is his mother and that Norman is, in at least one sense, already dead. The superimposed images also suggest that Norman, his mother, and death are a swamp and that Norman has within him death and destruction. A psychoanalytic critic might see the swamp as the vast, untamed id near the human heart. Frame enlargement. *Universal*

Superimpositions

Occasionally editors **superimpose** images during a lap dissolve. The lap dissolve near the end of *Psycho* (1960) fleetingly juxtaposes three images (Figure 3.14). If a dissolve is slow enough—or even halts briefly midway, as is done on rare occasions—viewers are more likely to notice the superimposed images.

Near the beginning of *The Wild Bunch* (1969) occurs a complex example of combined images within a lap dissolve. Children in a western town are burning scorpions and ants. A slow lap dissolve combines images of the burning insects with images of many townspeople and railroad employees who had recently been shot in the cross fire between bounty hunters hired by the railroad and the wild bunch, who had robbed the railroad office. During the dissolve from the children to the scene of carnage, viewers hear the giggles of the children burning the insects mingled with the moans of the injured people and some crying. The combination of images and sounds suggests that people can be like helpless scorpions and ants, painfully destroyed by powerful forces indifferent to their well-being. The blending of images also undercuts any notion of youthful innocence: the children who enjoy destroying insect life may grow up and destroy human life, as did the bounty hunters and the wild bunch.

superimposition: Two or more images photographed or printed on top of each other.

Expressive Juxtapositions

Even in films that use continuity editing extensively, filmmakers sometimes want to surprise, amuse, or confuse viewers, so they may follow a shot with one viewers don't expect. In *The War of the Roses* (1989), the Michael Douglas character has met the Kathleen Turner character for the first time and finds her attractive, but she's rushing off to catch a ferry. He runs after her and shouts, "Barbara, wait a second. I've got a great idea." In the next shot, they are in bed having sex. The juxtaposition is unexpected and to many viewers amusing.

Occasionally the unexpected shot appears after a brief lap dissolve. In *Citizen Kane* (1941), immediately after Kane marries Susan, his second wife, he has decided she'll have a career as an opera singer. As the newlyweds are about to be driven off, Susan tells the reporters around the car that if necessary, Kane will build her an opera house. Kane shouts, "That won't be necessary." After a rapid lap dissolve, the next shot is a large newspaper headline reading "Kane Builds Opera House." The effect is surprising and amusing; the combination of shots also shows that Kane's judgment can be faulty.

Occasionally filmmakers use jump cuts to confuse or disorient viewers, as in several places in the classic **French new wave** film *Breathless* (1959, Figure 3.15). Sometimes two shots simply show contradictory aspects of a subject, as in consecutive shots from near the beginning of *The Third Man* (1949, Figure 3.16).

French new wave (cinema): A diverse group of French fictional films made in the late 1950s and early 1960s marked by the independent spirit of their directors. Often new wave films include unconventional editing, homages, and surprising or whimsical moments.

FIGURE 3.15 Jump cuts to create discontinuity

In one scene in Jean-Luc Godard's *Breathless* (1959), a man driving a car pulls off a country road to elude two pursuing motorcycle police officers, then one officer pulls off the same road, and the man shoots the officer and runs away. To viewers reared on continuity editing, the scene seems discontinuous or jerky, as if the camera were sometimes in the wrong position or as if shots or parts of shots had been left out. The last seven shots of the scene (top, from left to right; bottom from left to right), represented here, illustrate three areas of confusion for viewers. Shots (a) and (b) are taken from one side of an imaginary line between the two subjects, with the man facing left;

Don't move or I'll shoot.

but shots (c–e) are inexplicably filmed from the other side of the line, and the man is now facing right. Godard is not editing by the 180° system. Where the police officer is when he gets shot is also puzzling: he is certainly not on the path leading from the road, shown in shots (a) and (f). Finally, the relation of the last shot (g) to the preceding shots is unclear: where and how far the man is now from the shot police officer viewers cannot know. Perhaps (g) is a separate scene consisting of one shot. Although the seven shots are elliptical and confusing in some of their details, one could make a case that the main action is clear and that the discontinuous editing is appropriate for the action shown: a sudden, unplanned murder. Frame enlargements. *SNC; New Yorker Films*

FIGURE 3.16 Consecutive shots revealing contradictory aspects of a setting
These two shots early in *The Third Man* (1949) suggest the contradictory aspects of Vienna
shortly after World War II: (a, above left) a statue of Beethoven and (b, above right) two black
marketeers. The consecutive, discontinuous images quickly convey that the story will be set in
a city of both culture and crime. Frame enlargements. *London Film Productions*

filmic: That which is characteristic of the film medium or appropriate to it, such as parallel editing or the combination of editing and a full range of vocals, silence, and music.

Editors often join two shots to illustrate similarities. Near the end of *The Wild Bunch*, after the final shoot-out, we see a shot of perched vultures; then two shots later gleeful bounty hunters swooping down on the dead to strip them of valuables, as birds—vultures?—fly across the frame in the foreground and a vulture is visible briefly in the background, then a shot of a vulture perched on a dead man. The juxtaposition of shots constitutes a none-too-subtle **filmic** metaphor suggesting that the bounty hunters are vultures.

Less obvious yet still damning by association are some of the accompanying shots of Miss Michigan in the satirical documentary *Roger & Me* (1989). We first see Miss Michigan riding in a car on which is affixed a sign for a Chevrolet dealer during a parade in Flint, Michigan, immediately after a shot of a man scooping up horse dung from the parade route. Later a man speaking of the poor labor conditions in Flint concludes that some people know what is going on and some don't; the next shot is of Miss Michigan. Later still, we see brief footage of the 1988 Miss USA pageant and learn that Miss Michigan won the national title; the next shot is a match cut of a man in Flint knocking on a door to evict people from their housing, presumably because they are out of work and behind in the rent. Because of the selection and arrangement of the shots (and because of how Miss Michigan responds

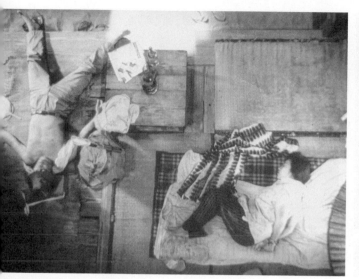

FIGURE 3.17 Consecutive shots suggesting characters' situation
Woman in the Dunes (1964) begins with a city man collecting samples of insects in a remote setting near a sea. Some local men tell him that he has missed the last bus back into town and invite him to stay overnight with a woman in a shack in a sand pit. Soon the man realizes that the villagers and the woman intend for him to live with her and help her. The man manages to catch the woman off guard and tie up her hands and feet, but he fails to escape from the pit. The three shots represented here come from the beginning of a scene. (a, above left) A bird's-eye view shows the two of them sleeping (she is still bound hand and foot). (b, above) The next shot shows a trapped insect trying to escape its glass prison. (c, left) The third shot is of sand falling down cliffs of sand, presumably nearby. Shot (a) shows that the couple is exhausted (they are motionless and she sleeps even though her hands and feet are bound). Shot (b) suggests that though the man has tied up the woman, they are trapped, as is the insect the man had collected. Shot (c), of falling sand, reminds viewers that sand continues to fall and endanger the shack (viewers earlier had learned that the woman has to shovel sand, which the villages sell, or it will overwhelm her shack). In short, in a mere seventeen seconds, the three shots convey that the man and woman are tired, trapped, and in danger. Frame enlargements. *Pathe Contemporary Films Release*

to director Michael Moore's unexpected questions), Miss Michigan comes across as someone who cares not about labor and living conditions in Flint but about winning the national title. Consecutive shots may serve yet other purposes. Consecutive wordless shots may, for example, subtly suggest the predicament that characters are in (Figure 3.17).

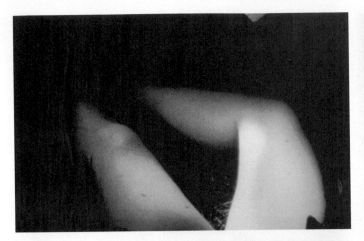

FIGURE 3.18 Consecutive shots creating meaning
Three consecutive images from the nonnarrative documentary film "The Match That Started My Fire" (1991) illustrate how the selection and arrangement of shots can create meaning beyond what the shots convey individually. Various women describe their first awareness of their sexual feelings as viewers see a wide variety of images, some created for this film (a, above left, and b, left), some selected from existing footage (c, above). The three consecutive images shown here—of a woman's bare legs illuminated in the dark, an open flower, and a mechanism shoving a load of metal into a blazing furnace—suggest various facets of a woman's sexuality, including opening, blossoming, and being penetrated. Frame enlargements. *Cathy C. Cook; Women Make Movies, New York*

In nonnarrative films, the juxtaposition of shots may also be as expressive as in fictional films (Figures 3.18 and 3.19).

Action and Reaction

How viewers react to a movie is often intensified by how subjects in the film react. In virtually all narrative films (fictional and documentary), many scenes show actions *and* other people's reactions, and those reaction shots tend to intensify viewer's responses. Humorous scenes are usually funnier because someone is shown to be bewildered or stunned or in some way made uncomfortable. Horrifying scenes can be more frightening because of shots

FIGURE 3.19 Consecutive shots to create a visual poem
In a shot from the avant-garde film "Un Chien Andalou" (1928), (a, above left) a man begins to fall forward, presumably mortally wounded. (b, above, and c, left) In the next shot, now in the countryside, as he continues to fall, his hands brush the bare back of a seated woman. The woman's image then fades away. The two shots show that dying can be like momentarily brushing the bare back of a woman who quickly fades away and leaves the beauty of nature. The juxtaposition of shots suggests the fragility and beauty of life as human life ebbs away. Frame enlargements. *The Museum of Modern Art/Circulating Film Library*

of characters reacting to scary sights or sounds. Suspenseful athletic contests, as in the **narrative documentary** *Hoop Dreams* (1994), are even more involving because of how individuals in the crowd are shown reacting to them. Scenes of anguish can be more gripping if interspersed with reaction shots, as in *The Bicycle Thief* (1948, Figure 3.20). Reaction shots that follow action shots can be used in a limitless variety of situations (Figure 3.21).

Reaction shots can also be used in untraditional ways, as in the Cocteau version of *Beauty and the Beast* (1946). In one scene, Beauty's father plucks a rose; then a strong wind blasts him and the plant. He turns and sees (as do viewers) the angry beast for whom the roses have special importance. In a later shot we see that the father is only ten feet or so from the beast, but in later

narrative documentary: A film that presents mainly a factual narrative or story.

FIGURE 3.20 **Reaction shot intensifying emotional pain**

Two consecutive shots show an action and reaction in the last scene of *The Bicycle Thief* (1948). The boy has recently seen a crowd chasing, catching, and reviling his father, who in desperation was trying to steal a bicycle so he would not lose his job. (a, top) First viewers see the father's emotional pain then (b, middle, and c, bottom) the boy looking up to see his father's anguish and taking his hand. The reaction shot of the boy shows his anguish and empathy and intensifies viewers' response to his and his father's plight. Frame enlargements. *PDS-ENIC*

FIGURE 3.21 **Reaction shots intensifying varied situations** ▶

(a, top) In this shot from *Fargo* (1996), Jerry Lundegaard, a Minneapolis car salesman, sees the bloody body of a parking garage attendant, for whose death Jerry is partially to blame. The camera lingers on Jerry's face for five seconds as he drives by slowly while continuing to look at the dead man whom he and viewers saw briefly in the previous shot. Five seconds is a long time for a reaction shot. This relatively lengthy shot allows the shock and horror Jerry is feeling at this bloody turn of events to sink in, for him and viewers. (b, bottom) In this shot from late in *Toy Story* (1995), the toy characters Buzz and Woody are trying to catch up with the moving van carrying their fellow toys to a new home. In the seconds preceding this shot, Slinky Dog had been leaning out of the van trying to lend two helping paws but had become overextended and had gone hurtling back into the van. The looks of anguish on the two heroes' faces in this reaction shot intensify the tension in their situation and perhaps its humor. Frame enlargement. *(a) Gramercy Pictures; (b) Pixar; Walt Disney*

FIGURE 3.22 Reaction shot to an unseen action
Near the end of *The Seventh Seal* (1957), the personification of death has come to claim the four subjects shown here. In the scene, viewers see Death in only one brief shot then see at length the other characters' reactions. The filmmakers chose to include this lengthy reaction shot rather than shots alternating between Death and his victims or shots of Death in the same frame as his victims. Frame enlargement. *Svensk Filmindustri*

shots of the father alone, he is always wind-blown; in the shots of the beast, the beast is not. The reaction shots of the father are intensified by the addition of a strong wind, as if to suggest that the beast, when angry, is so powerful that he has the force of a small gale and can cause mere men to quake.

Sometimes filmmakers dwell on reaction shots rather than on the subject being reacted to and let viewers' imaginations supply the rest. An example occurs in *The Seventh Seal* (1957, Figure 3.22).

Here and There Now: Parallel Editing

In **parallel editing**, or **cross-cutting**, the film shifts back and forth between two or more lines of action, often suggesting that the actions are occurring simultaneously and are related to each other, but sometimes depicting events from different times. Parallel editing that suggests simultaneous events is used in an early sequence in the classic German film *M* (Figure 3.23).

Parallel editing is occasionally used throughout a movie to suggest two or more simultaneous **plotlines** and to generate suspense, as in *Dr. Strangelove:*

plotline: A series of related events usually involving only a few characters or people and capable of functioning on its own as an entire story.

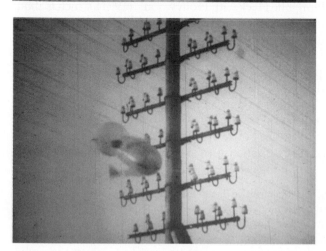

FIGURE 3.23 Parallel editing to suggest simultaneous events
In the German film *M* (1931), before the shots shown here, a young
girl, Elsie, leaves school and plays with a ball. Viewers learn that a
child murderer is on the loose and see Elsie being greeted by a stranger
who buys her a balloon. Elsie's mother waits for her daughter and
frets that she is late. (a, top left) As the mother calls out Elsie's name,
we see a view of an empty stairwell in the building where Elsie and
her mother live, (b, top right) an empty attic, presumably in their
building, and (c, above left) Elsie's empty chair and table setting. The
three parallel shots suggest concisely, even eloquently, that at that
moment Elsie is not on the stairs, in the attic, or at the table. (The
three shots being void of life and tinged with darkness are disquieting, too.) The next two shots resume the flow of action and confirm
our suspicion that Elsie has come to harm: (d, above right) the ball
she played with earlier rolls into view and stops, and (e, left) the
balloon the man had bought her floats up and briefly gets caught in
wires before being carried away by the wind. The little movement
in the last two shots ends in disturbing stillness. Frame enlargements.
Nero Films; The Museum of Modern Art/Circulating Film Library

Or, How I Learned to Stop Worrying and Love the Bomb (1963). Except for that film's expository prologue, its doomsday device finale, and its third sequence, which is located in undisclosed residential quarters, all the film's sequences occur at one of three locations: a U.S. air force base where General Jack D. Ripper takes it upon himself to order a group of U.S. bombers to attack Soviet targets; an American bomber in which the crew is trying to reach a target in the Soviet Union; and the Pentagon War Room, where the U.S. president and his advisers, the Soviet ambassador, and, via phone, the Soviet premier try to avert catastrophe. Although viewers get the sense of time moving forward as the film progresses, the parallel editing gives the impression that some of the events happen simultaneously.

Often parallel editing shows someone being menaced while someone else is on the way to help. Early in the twentieth century, D. W. Griffith perfected this technique and often used it in his films. It is still commonplace in movies, as in the ending of *Tom Jones* (1963), where Tom is being taken to the gallows to be hanged as Squire Allworthy and Squire Western rush to try to save him. Parallel editing may also be used to show one subject trying to achieve a goal as another subject tries to overcome various problems and prevent the first subject from achieving the goal. A memorable example occurs near the end of Hitchcock's *Strangers on a Train* (1951), where extensive and suspenseful parallel editing shows one character on his way to plant incriminating evidence at a spot where a murder had been committed as another character tries to overcome various problems and arrive there before him.

Parallel editing can show a contrast. In *A Fish Called Wanda* (1988), it is used amusingly to contrast a bored married couple getting ready for bed with a young unmarried couple fully attending to each other as they undress then have sex. In the documentary film "The Heck with Hollywood!" (1991), which is about the difficulties of marketing one's own low-budget film, parallel editing is used to contrast the views of an independent filmmaker with those of her distributor.

Parallel editing can also highlight a similarity. Throughout *M*, parallel editing shows that the police, organized beggars, and organized crime in a German city of the early 1930s are all trying to capture a child murderer. Griffith also used parallel editing throughout *Intolerance* to present four stories supposedly illustrating intolerance in four eras and places.

As we see so many times in this book, a technique is not restricted to a certain type of film. Parallel editing can also be used in films that tell no story, as in the nonnarrative documentary *Titicut Follies* (1967, Figure 3.24).

FIGURE 3.24 Parallel editing in a nonnarrative documentary ▶
Parallel editing is not restricted to narrative films. It may be used to compare and contrast any two subjects or events from different places or different times. In *Titicut Follies* (1967), Frederick Wiseman's first film, shots of a man being force-fed by a psychologist in a mental hospital (left column, top to bottom) are alternated with shots of the corpse of the same man being prepared for display before his burial (right column). In his later films, Wiseman is much more likely to present long, uninterrupted takes of events and let viewers interpret relationships and meaning. Frame enlargements. *Zipporah Films*

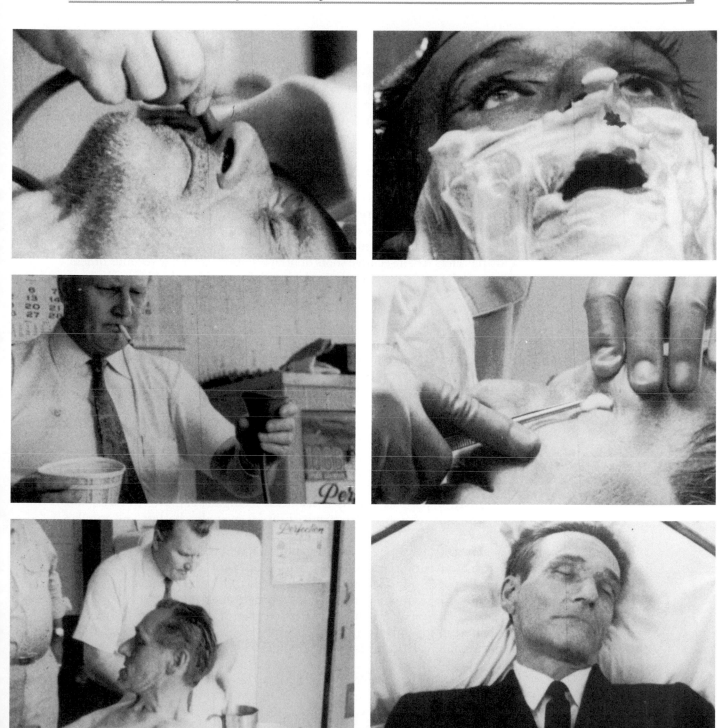

PACE AND TIME

Pace is the viewer's sense of a film's material (such as succeeding events in a narrative film or information in a documentary film) being presented rapidly or slowly. Although it is a highly subjective experience and is influenced by many aspects of the film, a film's pace can help keep viewers involved or alienate them.

Fast and Slow Cutting

A shot may be as brief as one frame, but when it is, few viewers see its content. At the opposite extreme, as Hitchcock demonstrated in *Rope* (1948), a shot may run for as long as the reel of film in the camera. Shots in feature films typically range from several seconds to about twenty seconds. **Fast cutting** refers to consecutive shots of brief duration, say a few seconds or less. **Slow cutting** refers to consecutive **long takes** or editing dominated by long takes. It's difficult to set a number here, but an average shot length (ASL) of fifteen or more seconds will seem slow to many viewers in western cultures.

long take: A shot of long duration.

trailer: A brief compilation film that advertises a movie or video release.

Fast cutting may impart energy to its subjects. It is also an effective way to convey a lot of information in a brief time, as in many **trailers** shown on TV, in movie theaters, and at the beginning of many videotaped movies. Makers of music videos and other filmmakers often use fast cutting to intensify a sense of confusion or loss of control or to add urgency or energy. It's no accident, for example, that the opera montage in *Citizen Kane* (see pp. 156–57) uses fast cutting throughout. During that section of the story, Susan is under unbearable pressure, and the fast cutting reflects the fact that events seem to gallop out of her control. Fast cutting is sometimes used to show images flashing through someone's mind during a crisis, as when late in *Spanking the Monkey* (1994) the main character has jumped from a high cliff and is plunging toward water. Fast cutting is also used for fights, climaxes to races, and montages summarizing past events. Editing may also be fast and regular (Figure 3.25).

Slow cutting can be used to establish a mood before fast cutting injects energy. Slow cutting may also be used in scenes of calm or reflection. And filmmakers can use slow cutting to slow down the pace, just as the second movement of a symphony or concerto typically does.

Too much of any technique—fast cutting or slow—causes viewers to lose interest, so editing can be used to vary a film's pace. Like poets writing in meter, filmmakers can establish a regular rhythm then maintain it or work expressive variations on it. In the last sequence of the classic Soviet film (*Battleship*) *Potemkin*, for example, the battleship *Potemkin* is steaming along. The cutting is brisk but by no means hurried or frantic. After possible rival ships are spotted and the men called to their battle stations, the cutting becomes faster and faster until it is clear there will be no battle after all; then the pace of the editing slows. Technique reinforces mood.

FIGURE 3.25 Editing to create a regular rhythm

Early in *October* (1928), which was codirected and edited by Sergei Eisenstein, two frames of a soldier firing a machine gun are alternated with two frames of the gun being fired. This extremely rapid alternation between the soldier and gun, soldier and gun, soldier and gun, sets up a regular rhythm, as if the man is relentless, as if he is a machine or part of one, or as if the weapon consists of the man plus the gun. Through editing, the man and the gun become one. To recapture some of the experience of seeing these two alternating images in the film, look at frame (a, top) only long enough to see its subject (surely less than a second); then do the same with frame (b, above); then allotting the same fraction of a second to each image, look back and forth, back and forth, and so on. Frame enlargements. *The Museum of Modern Art/Circulating Film Library*

Student Writing

Most edited film scenes illustrate how film saves time and keeps viewers involved. Perhaps few sequences in cinematic history convey more information in less time (are more compressed) than the forty-two-second montage of Susan's opera tours to five cities in *Citizen Kane*. The sequence is so complicated—using rapid lap dissolves and multiple superimpositions—that it is impossible to describe it adequately. But the following notes from students made after viewing and reviewing the sequence convey some of its visual wealth. In the previous scene, Kane dominated Susan, standing over her and putting her into his shadow. The opera montage includes the following:

The Opera Montage

in Citizen Kane

-- Susan is desperate, unlike her image in Kane's newspapers.

-- Susan is competing with both her picture in the paper and the music.

-- Susan is lifting her hands as if in supplication.

-- Often Susan looks tired and listless.

-- Susan appears small and pathetic in the frame, though in later scenes she is seen closer up.

-- She often seems alone in the frame.

-- She's isolated on the stage, without contact or encouragement.

-- She's "under the spotlight," almost like a lab specimen, subject to the cold and unfeeling examination of the audience.

-- The roses she receives after one performance are too heavy for her, and she drops them--like Kane's burden.

-- The light is harsh, flashing, irritating--the visual counterpart of the music.

-- Newspapers are ever present; it's as if Kane's newspapers are behind this whole sad affair.

-- Newspapers and audiences are often superimposed; newspapers bring out the audiences.

-- The Washington audience is restless and unresponsive.

-- Audiences are unresponsive, though newspaper headlines say they are enthusiastic.

-- Never do we see anyone smile or enjoy Susan's performance.

-- Susan's opera coach tries to help her but fails.

-- The San Francisco newspaper's proclamation "Conquers World of Song" is superimposed on her frustrated voice coach.

-- As montage goes on, Kane is large, larger, always grim and determined.

-- Kane is demanding, controlling, disappointed.

-- Kane's press campaign brings out the audiences and misery for Susan, audiences, and viewers--a jumble of images and a cacophony of sounds.

-- In the last few cities, the voice coach and Kane are seen, suggesting the pressure they put on Susan. Few other individuals are singled out by the editing.

-- The montage gives the feeling that the tour happened quickly and is a jumble of images and sounds. This part of the narrative is told by Susan to Thompson.

-- Confusion and fast pace are conveyed.

-- The pace is relentless. . . . The quick shots make the viewer nervous.

-- Urgency increases until the strain is too much for both Susan . . . and the viewer. The end is a relief for both of us. It is also a relief for her coach, and probably for Kane, though he would never admit to being weak enough to feel relief.

-- The moods are frenzy, chaos, burnout, exhaustion, nervousness, tenseness.

-- Some meanings: you can burn a light only so long; people burn out as do lights.

-- The last scene has the most shots, and the faster cutting suggests that Susan is finally broken.

-- At the end, image and sound die out, come to a screeching halt.

The next scene is in darkness and quiet except for Susan's heavy breathing (she has attempted suicide). Without this montage, the film could neither provide this information overload in a mere forty-two seconds nor make us feel as much of the stress Susan endures.

Studies of editing show that since the mid-1970s, movies have had a much shorter average shot length than in earlier decades. Film scholar Barry Salt reports that from 1976 to 1987, the average shot length of a large sample of movies was about 8.4 seconds (296). Of course, some shots are 25 or even many more seconds, but there are also many stretches of fast cutting. Why there is so much fast cutting in recent movies, TV, and music videos in western cultures is not easy to determine. Perhaps it's because we modern viewers absorb the meaning of a shot more quickly. Perhaps we are visually jaded and need more of a kick. Michael Hoggan, during his tenure as president of American Cinema Editors, said that if the narrative is poor, editors may dazzle viewers with exciting editing techniques. Or perhaps the fast cutting reflects the fast pace most people feel is an inescapable part of their lives. Maybe it's a combination of these or other causes. Music videos with their fast cutting and jump cuts bombard viewers with such an overload of information that it is often impossible to discern in them any coherence or meaning, and for many viewers this lack of coherence and meaning is characteristic of contemporary life.

Condensing Time and Stretching It: Montage and Other Editing Techniques

In classical Hollywood cinema—but not in the films of some directors, such as Yasujiro Ozu and Carl Theodor Dreyer; some avant-garde films; and some documentary films—one of the main goals of editing is to eliminate dead time, any footage that does not contribute to the desired effects. One of the most effective means of showing viewers much information quickly is a montage, or a "quick impressionistic sequence of . . . images, usually linked by dissolves, superimpositions or wipes, and used to convey passages of time, changes of place, or any other scenes of transition" (Reisz and Millar 112). One of the most famous montages in cinema is from *Citizen Kane*, the montage of breakfasts experienced by Kane and his first wife. In twenty-seven brief shots plus brief blurry transitions lasting altogether only 133 seconds, the filmmakers show the couple's deteriorating marriage (Figure 3.26).[1]

Another use of a montage—this one without lap dissolves—occurs in *Raging Bull* (1980). One scene ends with the boxer Jake La Motta soaking his fist in a bucket of ice water. Then we see a **title card** announcing a La Motta fight, a few brief stills from the fight, then snippets from home movies. The same pattern is repeated during which six fights are accounted for and Jake and Vicki date, marry, indulge in horseplay beside and in a swimming pool, and begin a family and Jake's brother Joey marries and begins a family. In two minutes thirty-five seconds, the story jumps ahead more than three

title card: A card or thin sheet of clear plastic that supplies information in a film.

---

[1]For a detailed description of the breakfast montage in *Citizen Kane*, including ten frame enlargements and an analysis of the sequence, see Reisz and Millar 115–21.

FIGURE 3.26 The breakfast montage in *Citizen Kane* (1941)
(a, top) At the beginning of the sequence Charles Kane and his first wife, Emily, are close to and attentive to each other; by stages they become alienated; (b, above) at the end they are far apart, reading rival papers. In slightly more than two minutes, this montage shows their growing alienation and failing marriage. Frame enlargements. *RKO General Pictures*

years, from January 14, 1944, to sometime after a March 14, 1947, fight. This montage shows Jake's work and personal life and Joey's personal life all going well, but the filmmakers chose to skim through those events.

Montages usually consist of many brief shots, often connected by lap dissolves, but a montage can be as simple as a few shots without lap dissolves. In *Hook* (1991), we see three consecutive shots from behind a seated Wendy. Each shot ends with Wendy turning around, and each time we can see that she is older; this simple montage represents an expanse of forty or so years in a matter of seconds.

Montages are not the only way editors have of condensing time. Sometimes editors provide much information by a rapid succession of relatively brief shots, as in the ending of *Breaking Away* (1979). The film presents the story of four unemployed young men living in a university town; they have graduated from high school but have not yet found their places in life. The most important of the four is Dave Stoller, whose father runs a used car lot and disapproves of Dave's zealous imitation of professional Italian bicycle racers and his attempts to emulate everything Italian. The four young men are harassed by university students and decide to prove themselves by entering the annual university team bicycle race, which they manage to win in a close race against thirty-three fraternity teams.

After the race, the film has three more scenes, which seem to take place at the beginning of the following fall semester:

Scene (two shots, twelve seconds)

1. Used car lot, Mr. Stoller leaving on a bike; his pregnant wife is talking about a car to an interested couple, though we do not hear her.
2. On a bike, Mr. Stoller leaves the Cutter Cars lot and rides into street.

Scene (three shots, nineteen seconds)

3. On campus: a young French woman asks Dave where the "office of the bursar" is.
4. After hesitating, he replies, "You must mean the Bursar's Office."
5. She agrees and smiles.

Scene (three shots, twenty-two seconds)

6. Dave and the French woman biking; Dave tells her he was thinking about studying French and talks to her about the major French bicycle race.
7. Dave continues to talk to the French woman; then Mr. Stoller, riding a bike from the opposite direction, passes Dave and the woman and calls out to Dave. Dave replies hello in French.
8. Mr. Stoller's startled reaction.

Without these last three scenes, the film would end after the bicycle race as a working-class success story, with four sons of limestone cutters as victors, working-class brothers united (one of the four young men and his police officer brother), and Dave and his parents reconciled. But the last three scenes quickly shift emphasis from social class to individual psychology.

The last scene suggests that Dave may be about to take on a new role—that of would-be cosmopolitan student studying French, rather than Italian. He's still an adolescent trying out different roles. The Stollers also assume new roles, probably too many in too short a time to be believable if we think about the situation. Mr. Stoller has changed the name of the car lot from Campus Cars to Cutter Cars, suggesting that he will henceforth seek the town market and that the victory by the four young men has renewed his social class pride; the father has imitated the son and taken up bicycle riding; for the first time in the film he allows his wife to help with the work at the car lot; and the Stollers are going to start a new family. Mr. Stoller is more relaxed, more accepting of his son, more willing to accept his own limitations (his wife helping at the car lot). His calling out to Dave in the last scene reminds viewers of an earlier scene in which he snubbed Dave in public—when Dave was deep into his Italian period. The last two shots being of Dave (and the French woman) and Mr. Stoller is as it should be: throughout the film, Dave acts; Mr. Stoller reacts. In these last eight shots, viewers are swept along on a rapid river of images until the final one without noticing that all these changes in the lives of the Stollers are depicted in so brief a time. All this and more is conveyed by only eight shots, in fifty-three seconds of carefully edited film.

Editors nearly always try to condense time. But a few films—for the most part outside the classical Hollywood cinema—occasionally and briefly expand time, allowing more time to show an action than the action itself would take. Eisenstein used this technique in several of his films. In *October* (1928), he often stretched out an action slightly by including shots that repeat part of a movement, as in the toppling of a statue of a former tsar: one shot ends with the statue well on its way to the ground; the next shot begins with the statue not as far from the ground; the shot after that does the same thing. Three somewhat overlapping shots are used to show one brief action. Later in the film we see parts of the raising of a drawbridge more than once. Two other famous examples of expanded time are from Eisenstein's (*Battleship*) *Potemkin*. In one scene, an angry sailor breaks a plate, but the footage has been so edited that we see parts of the sailor's arm movement twice, first from above his left shoulder then his right.[2] Parts of the famous massacre of civilians on the Odessa steps is edited so that the running time is longer than

---

[2]For enlargements for each of the sixty-one frames making up the eight key shots in this scene, see David Mayer, *Eisenstein's* Potemkin: *A Shot-by-Shot Presentation* (New York: Grossman, 1972), 23–30. For Mayer's analysis of these shots, see 13–14, 15.

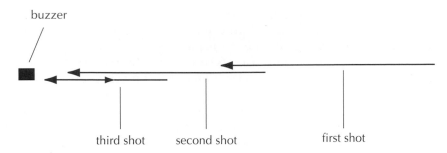

buzzer

third shot   second shot   first shot

FIGURE 3.27 Expanding film time
Three shots from *Shoot the Piano Player* (1960) overlap slightly and thus expand time a little. The shots show a character raise an arm and reach out toward a doorbell but hesitate briefly right before touching it then begin to withdraw his hand. The filmmakers could have shown this movement in one shot. Instead, they chose to present it in three shots that overlap slightly: at the beginning of the second and third shots the finger is slightly farther away from the doorbell than it was at the end of the preceding shot. By expanding time, the filmmakers emphasize the character's hesitancy.

story time: The amount of time covered in a film's narrative or story. For example, if a film's earliest scene occurs on a Sunday and its latest scene takes place on the following Friday, then the story time is six days.

the **story time**. Because of the surprising structure of the classic film "Occurrence at Owl Creek Bridge" (1962), the film's running time (twenty-eight minutes) is longer than its story time (slightly more than ten minutes).

Occasionally other films include brief uses of expanded time, as in three shots from *Shoot the Piano Player* (1960, Figure 3.27). A much more obvious example of expanded time occurs near the ending of *Living in Oblivion* (1995) when a thirty-second test recording of "room tone" takes more than four minutes of running time as viewers see the fantasies of six characters. (Although it is not a matter of editing, time can also be expanded when the camera films at a faster rate than the film is projected, as when an explosion is filmed at 300 frames per second but is projected at 24: an explosion that would normally last approximately a quarter of a second will last about three seconds.)

DIGITAL EDITING

producer: The person in charge of the business and administrative aspects of making a film, typically including acquiring rights to the script and hiring the personnel to make the film.

As with other aspects of filmmaking, increasingly computers are being used in editing. Shots may be scanned into a computer, where they can be edited more easily than when working with film. Once film footage has been transferred to digital format, the digital version may also more easily be integrated with special effects or even sent long distances electronically, for example via satellite to an anxious **producer**. When the computer editing is finished, the digital information is transferred back to film. Digital editing is now used for many national TV commercials, music videos, and TV shows, but not yet for an entire movie that was shot on film. One of the major problems: the film image is so rich in detail that to store the many takes of the many shots of the typical movie would require enormous hard disk space. The advantages and limitations of digital editing are explained in the Afterword of Walter Murch's book *In the Blink of an Eye*.

SUMMARY

Editing involves decisions about which shots to include, the most effective take of each shot, the arrangement and duration of shots, and the transitions between them. Editors of narrative films work in terms of shots, scenes, and sequences. Editors often shorten shots, repeat parts of a shot, insert a cutaway, consult master shots, and sometimes include master shots or part of them in scenes.

Early Film Editing

- The first films of the 1890s consisted of one shot or multiple one-shot scenes.

- By the time of *The Birth of a Nation* (1915), editing was used to maintain continuity while telling complex stories.

- In the 1920s, the editing of some Soviet filmmakers conveyed a story and promoted ideas by the juxtaposition of shots.

Building Blocks

- The shot is the most basic unit of editing. It is a piece of continuous film that depicts an uninterrupted action or an immobile subject during an uninterrupted passage of time.

- A scene is a section of a narrative film that gives the impression of continuous action taking place during one continuous time and in one continuous space. A scene usually consists of one or more shots.

- A sequence is a series of related consecutive scenes that are perceived as being a major unit of a narrative film.

- Editors can use one of many possible transitions between shots, such as a cut, lap dissolve, or wipe.

Continuity Editing

- Continuity editing, which is used in most narrative films, maintains a sense of clear and continuous action and continuous setting within each scene. It is achieved in filming and editing by making sure viewers will instantly see the connection between the end of one shot and the beginning of the next.

Image on Image and Image after Image

- A momentary superimposition of two or more images is possible in a lap dissolve, as in the ending of *Psycho*.

- Consecutive shots can stress differences or similarities.

- Reaction shots intensify viewers' response. Usually a reaction shot follows an action shot, but it may precede one, or it may occur alone with the action not shown to the audience.

- Parallel editing can give a sense of simultaneous events, contrast two or more actions or viewpoints, or create suspense about whether one subject will achieve a goal before another subject does.

Pace and Time

- Usually fast cutting is used to impart energy and excitement; slow cutting may be used to slow the pace or reinforce a sense of calm.

- A succession of shots of equal length may suggest inevitability, relentlessness, boredom, or some other condition.

- Shifting the rhythm of the editing can change viewers' emotional responses, as in the excerpt analyzed from near the end of (*Battleship*) *Potemkin*.

- Montage compresses an enormous amount of information into a short time, as in the montage of Susan's opera career in *Citizen Kane*.

- Editing often condenses time (for example, by cutting dead time), but it can expand time, for instance, by showing fragments of an action more than once.

Digital Editing

- Increasingly computers are being used as part of the editing process. Images are scanned into computers, edited there, then transferred back to film.

WORKS CITED

Andrew, J. Dudley. *The Major Film Theories: An Introduction*. New York: Oxford UP, 1976.

Grignon, Rex. Address. "The Making of *Toy Story*." Monterey, CA, Conf. Center. 10 Apr. 1996.

Hoggan, Michael, president, American Cinema Editors. Telephone interview. July 1994.

Huss, Roy, and Norman Silverstein. *The Film Experience: Elements of Motion Picture Art.* New York: Dell, 1968.

Leff, Leonard. *Film Plots: Scene-by-Scene Narrative Outlines for Feature Film Study*. Vol. 1. Ann Arbor: Pierian, 1983.

Murch, Walter. *In the Blink of an Eye: A Perspective on Film Editing*. Los Angeles: Silman-James, 1995.

Priestly, Tom, film editor. Quoted in Ralph Rosenblum and Robert Karen, *When the Shooting Stops . . . the Cutting Begins: A Film Editor's Story.* New York: Viking, 1979.

Reisz, Karel, and Gavin Millar. *The Technique of Film Editing*. Enlarged ed. New York: Hastings, 1968.

Riefenstahl, Leni, filmmaker. Interview. *The Wonderful, Horrible Life of Leni Riefenstahl* (documentary film). 1993.

Salt, Barry. *Film Style and Technology: History and Analysis*. 2nd ed. London: Starword, 1992.

FOR FURTHER READING

Balmuth, Bernard. *Introduction to Film Editing*. Boston: Focal, 1989. An introduction for someone who wants to edit film.

Oldham, Gabriella. *First Cut: Conversations with Film Editors*. Berkeley: U of California P, 1992. Interviews with twenty-three award-winning editors, including editors of documentary films.

Selected Takes: Film Editors on Editing. Ed. Vincent LoBrutto. Westport, CT: Praeger, 1991. Interviews with twenty-one film editors plus a glossary and bibliography.

CHAPTER 4
Sound

DURING THE 1986 ACADEMY AWARDS CEREMONY, a clip from *Chariots of Fire* (1981) was shown in which young men ran on a beach accompanied by the sounds of feet splashing in water. Although the sound track may have been true-to-life, it was uneventful. Then the same **footage** was shown with the film's famous title music, not the sounds of splashing feet. The effect was so different that viewers felt as if they were seeing different footage. Somehow the runners gained the grace of dancers and the action became special, more than life. It was vibrant cinema.

During the making of big-budget movies, sounds are recorded, often created, then **mixed**. The steps followed in recording, creating, and mixing sound vary from movie to movie, so the following summary is only an approximation of the process.

The dialogue is usually recorded during filming. If the filming is done on **location**, the sound personnel may also unavoidably record some **ambient sound**, the ordinary sounds of a place that people tend not to notice in real life. If the filming is done on a **sound stage**—an enclosed area for shooting film and recording sound—ambient sound is rarely a problem. After the filming and the initial recording of dialogue are completed, various sounds may be modified, created, or eliminated.

Sometimes dialogue must be redone through **ADR** (automated dialogue replacement): actors rerecord dialogue by means of a projector interlocked with a machine for playback of sound on either magnetic film or a computer. Much of the dialogue for *The Hunt for Red October* (1990) had to be redone using ADR because during filming the equipment picked up inappropriate sounds from the wooden submarine **set**.

A **sound effect** is any sound in a film other than a sound made by a human voice or music, such as a dog's bark or thunder. For commercial movies, most sound effects are added after filming is completed. Sometimes sound effects inadvertently picked up during filming must be replaced. During the making of *The Hunt for Red October*, the sounds from the wooden submarine set were replaced with metallic sounds. Unwanted ambient sound can also be reduced by digitizing the sound then erasing the ambient sound.

---

footage: A length of exposed motion-picture film.

mix: To select sound tracks of one or more of the following: music, dialogue, sound effects; adjust their volumes; and combine them into a composite sound track.

location: Any place other than a constructed setting that is used for filming.

set: Constructed setting where action is filmed.

FIGURE 4.1 **Three-position mixing console**
This equipment is used to mix dialogue, sound effects, and music for commercial feature films. Most of the levers are for adjusting the volume on a sound track. For a simplified example of sound mixing, see a brief scene before the opening credits of *Blow Out* (1981). *Courtesy of Solid State Logic, Begbroke, Oxford, UK*

Usually after filming has been completed, a composer is hired and brought in, often with little time to complete the score. During the final mixing, the mixers and often the director blend the various sound tracks and synchronize them with the final edited version of the film (Figure 4.1). Figure 4.2 summarizes the usual steps in recording and mixing sound.

Sounds usually seem lifelike in movies. As with visuals, though, what seems true-to-life is an illusion. If you study sound in movies, you will notice that sounds we would normally hear are omitted or replaced by music. Listen carefully and repeatedly to the sound that accompanies one character slugging another, and you will notice that it is not entirely true-to-life. In movies we accept such sounds (yet another movie **convention**). How are film sounds

convention: In films and other creative works, a frequently used technique or content that audiences tend to accept without question.

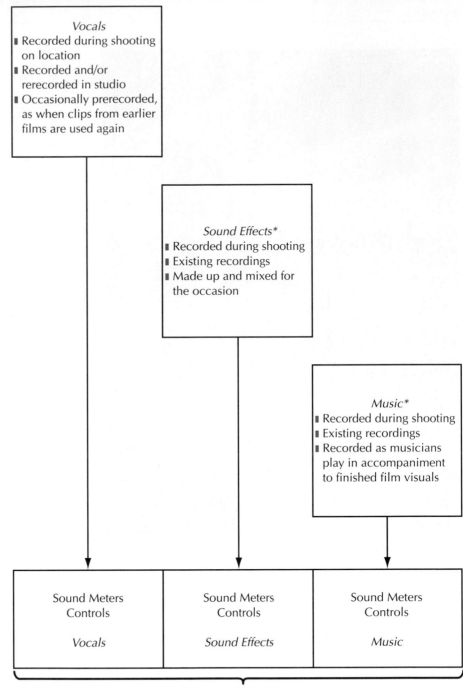

*During the filming of many big-budget movies, every attempt is made to exclude sound effects and music and to record only the vocals.

FIGURE 4.2 **Recording and mixing sound**

created, how are they used, and how do they affect audiences? This chapter gives some answers to those questions by examining uses of the four major components of a sound track, possible sound transitions, and some general uses of sound in **narrative** films.

narrative: A series of unified consecutive events situated in one or more settings.

EARLY FILM SOUND

Sound has always been a part of film viewing. Even during showings of the first short films in the 1890s, music was usually played to cover the sounds of the audiences and projectors and to reinforce mood and support **continuity**. Later in film history, the theater management also supplied sound effects. As is demonstrated repeatedly in *Monty Python and the Holy Grail* (1975), people could beat half coconut shells against a hard surface or against each other to make sounds like horses' hooves. Large pieces of sandpaper might be rubbed together to sound like a running river; a flexible strip could be stuck into spinning bicycle spokes to simulate the sound of an early airplane engine. Some large theaters even had a sound effects machine with a whistle, bell, horn, chains, drum, and sheet metal for thunder (Figure 4.3). "Silent" films were rarely silent.

continuity: The editing of a narrative film's visuals and sounds so that viewers can easily understand the relationship of shot to shot and scene to scene.

FIGURE 4.3 Allefex sound effects machine
This machine was first marketed in Britain in 1909. Film historian David Robinson writes that the Allefex "was capable of producing upwards of fifty sound effects from storm noises, bird-song, and barking dogs to gun-fire, escaping steam and the rattle of pots and pans" (159). Historian Brian Coe includes a quotation that explains how some of the sounds were made: "The shot of a gun is imitated by striking a drum on the top of the machine, on which a chain mat has been placed. . . . Running water, rain, hail and the sound of rolling waves are obtained by turning a handle, which rotates a ribbed wooden cylinder against a board set at an angle from the top of which hang a number of chains. . . . The puffing of an engine is made by revolving a cylinder with projections against a steel brush. . . . Pendant tubes serve to produce the effects of church bells, fire alarm, ship's bell, and similar noises; the sound of trotting horses is caused by revolving a shaft carrying three tappets which lift up inverted cups . . . ; the cry of the baby is emitted by the dexterous manipulation of plug-hole and bellows" (91–92). *British Film Institute Stills, Posters and Designs*

In the late 1920s, some sound films used the Vitaphone system, a large phonograph disc synchronized with the projector. Warner Bros. created a sensation with this system in *The Jazz Singer* (1927), which was basically a silent film with synchronized musical numbers and a little ad-libbed dialogue. In 1928, Warner Bros. used the system in *The Lights of New York*, the first all-dialogue motion picture. In the same year, two rival and not entirely compatible sound-on-film systems were used on feature films, and the days of Vitaphone were numbered. With the sound-on-film systems, as the projector displays the image on the screen, it simultaneously converts the optical information in the sound track to electrical information that it amplifies and sends to speakers in the theater. (Figure 2.2 on p. 70 illustrates where optical or the later magnetic sound tracks may be located on film.) Since 1928, if theaters have adequate sound equipment—and many do not—audiences can hear the **vocals** (dialogue and other sounds made by the human voice), sound effects, music, and silence the way the filmmakers intended.

In the late 1920s and early 1930s, such directors as René Clair, Ernst Lubitsch, Rouben Mamoulian, Alfred Hitchcock, and Walt Disney experimented with film sound and discovered some new uses for it. In later years, Orson Welles, Robert Altman, George Lucas, and others experimented with film sound and made major advances in its use. Today, with sophisticated filmmakers and advanced equipment including computer programs to store, manipulate, and blend sounds, sound is more varied and more expressive than ever.

COMPONENTS OF THE SOUND TRACK AND THEIR USES

Dialogue is usually dominant and intellectual, music is usually supportive and emotional, sound effects are usually information. Their uses, however, are not inflexible. Sometimes dialogue is nonintellectual and aesthetic, sometimes music is symbolic, and on occasion sound effects may serve any of those functions. Any of these elements may be dominant or recessive according to the sharpness or softness of the sound and the relationship of the sound to the image. (Murch 298)

Filmmakers can include vocals, sound effects, music, and silence in the sound track. In this section, we will see some of their choices and the consequences.

Vocals

Most sound films since 1930 include dialogue and other vocals. Some movies—such as *Swimming to Cambodia* (1987), *When Harry Met Sally* (1989), *Vanya on 42nd Street* (1994), and *The Designated Mourner* (1997)—have a dense mix of words, and dialogue or monologues cascade and swirl throughout them. These and other films may use overlapping dialogue. Viewers cannot make out all the words, but they hear most of them and sense the busy, chaotic atmosphere that overlapping dialogue can help create. Many films directed by Howard Hawks—such as *Bringing Up Baby* (1938) and *His Girl Friday* (1940)—and several films directed by Orson Welles—perhaps most notably *The Magnificent Ambersons* (1942) and *Touch of Evil* (1958)—use extensive overlapping dialogue, as do some films directed by Robert Altman, such as *McCabe and Mrs. Miller* (1971), *California Split* (1974), *Nashville* (1975), and *The Player* (1992). In some films directed by Altman, characters speak without being entirely heard by those they speak at, and flash floods of words are symptomatic of the characters' nervousness, isolation, or unconscious attempts to mask their painful situations.

Overlapping dialogue may also be used in a brief section of a film, as in the **documentary** *Madonna Truth or Dare* (1991) where in one part many offscreen people give their opinions about Madonna. At one point in the documentary "Personal Belongings" (1996), viewers hear many different fragments of news reports about anti-Semitism and ethnic fighting in Central and Eastern Europe. During approximately thirty-two seconds, seven or eight **sound dissolves** and extensive overlapping dialogue convey the rapidly escalating strife. At the beginning of *Contact* (1997), as we see the receding earth, then planets, then galaxies, we hear overlapping snippets of speech from U.S. TV and radio, generally representing earlier and earlier moments in time and suggesting that the earth has been proclaiming its life to the universe ever since the first radio transmission.

Often in a theater or in our home video environment we hear dialogue more distinctly than we could in a similar situation in real life (another movie convention). Usually dialogue in movies is louder than it would be in life. In a scene from *A Fish Called Wanda* (1988), for instance, viewers hear a couple arguing but not shouting even though they at first seem to be at least a city block away from the camera; as they approach, their voices become only slightly louder.

Vocals may also be deliberately distorted. In several scenes in *Nick of Time* (1995), what is being said to the main character is distorted. The effect is analogous to a visual **point-of-view shot:** viewers hear as the distracted character presumably does.

Dialogue is invaluable for revealing a character's ideas, goals, and dreams, though often it does so more concisely, obliquely, and revealingly than conversation in life. Sometimes word choices and accents provide clues about a character's background: country or region of origin, ethnic group, occupation. The tone of voice, volume, and speed and rhythm of speech also reveal what a character is like. So infinitely expressive is the human voice that the words "You had better go" can be threatening, pleading, sad, indifferent, questioning, ironic, amusing, matter-of-fact, or something else. Perhaps second only to an expressive face, a trained voice can convey countless shades of emotion.

documentary film: A film that presents a version of actions that viewers are intended to accept not primarily as the product of someone's imagination but primarily as fact.

sound dissolve: A transition in which the first sound begins to fade out as the next sound fades in and overlaps the first sound before replacing it.

point-of-view shot: Camera placement at the approximate position of a character or person that gives a view similar to what that creature would see.

Many movies, however, use limited or no vocals. *Quest for Fire* (1981) uses an assortment of grunts, pants, screams, and so forth but has neither narration nor intelligible dialogue, only imaginary prehistoric languages that are not translated and are only vaguely understandable. The first and fourth parts of *2001: A Space Odyssey* (1968) are without intelligible dialogue, and only 43 of the film's 141 minutes contain dialogue. Other feature films employing little dialogue are *Blood Wedding* (1981), which consists of backstage preparations, a brief warm-up session, and a flamenco version of most of Federico Garcia Lorca's famous play of the same title, and *Sidewalk Stories* (1989), which has no dialogue during its 97 minutes except for a few lines near the end—and those are not integral to the story. Short films also sometimes use little or no dialogue. The films' images, music, and perhaps sound effects convey story, meanings, and moods. "The String Bean" (1962) and "The Other Side" (1966) use no vocals, and they are used only occasionally and briefly in "The Red Balloon" (1955).

Often films begin without words, though music is often used: the opening scenes reveal the **setting**, major character(s), and mood without the help of the human voice. Many movie scenes with sound are without the human voice, and most movies now use dialogue less than half the time. As scriptwriting books and scriptwriting teachers often advocate, many filmmakers use dialogue only to reveal important information that cannot be conveyed visually.

setting: The place where filmed action occurs, either a location or set.

Sound Effects

Sound effects specialists tend to use sound effects selectively. In life we hear, but usually ignore, insignificant and potentially distracting sounds, such as an airplane overhead or a beeping digital watch. In cinema, such sounds are usually omitted from a sound track, and the sound effects that are included tend to be unnoticeable because usually they are played at low volume and along with music or dialogue or both.

Sound effects are often used to help create a location; they can make a place—for example, a studio set—seem more lifelike than it looks (Figure 4.4). Offscreen sound can also make the area viewers see on the screen seem larger. Effects can make viewers *feel* more involved. In *Das Boot*, or *The Boat* (1981; expanded and reissued with 8 channel digital sound in 1997), when the submarine is trying to evade detection deep below the surface, viewers hear the sheet metal groaning then the bolts popping from pressure they were not designed to withstand. Frank Serafine—who did sound effects for *Star Trek: The Motion Picture* (1979), *Tron* (1982), the 1983 TV movie *The Day After*, *Star Trek III: The Search for Spock* (1984), and *The Hunt for Red October*—said that the director of *The Day After* originally wanted silence after a nuclear explosion but eventually agreed to a more dramatic and more involving blend of animal screams processed so viewers would not recognize the sources.

FIGURE 4.4 Sound used to fill out a set

In *Citizen Kane* (1941), sound sometimes makes a set seem more appropriate. The budget for *Citizen Kane* was limited, and the set shown here was flimsy and incomplete (that's also an important reason shadows were used). The set alone could not have nurtured the right sounds for the scene, but the reverberations in the sound track help mightily to convey the size, emptiness, and sterility of Kane's and Susan's lives in Xanadu. Frame enlargement. *RKO General Pictures*

Effects may be used to intensify a mood. At one point in *The Conversation* (1974), the assistant of Harry's client threatens Harry (Gene Hackman), so he leaves. The elevator he gets on makes sounds like wind in a tunnel. They are loud, fluctuating, eerie, unsettling—like those in a horror film. The sounds add tension to the scene and along with Gene Hackman's expressive face show how upset and frightened Harry is. Sometimes a sound effect, such as a beating heart, intensifies the mood of the moment even though we wouldn't hear such a sound in life outside the movies (yet another movie convention).

In the theater or out, a sound from an unknown source—the basement, the attic, outside the window, under the bed—may frighten us. We are rattled by the unknown, so films often use sound from beyond the lighted **frame**, in the darkness. Even if we know the source of the sound, such as tree limbs brushing against a window, hearing a sound and not seeing its source leaves much to the imagination. We have paid money to be frightened, and filmmakers try to oblige us.

frame: The borders of the projected film or TV set or monitor.

Another example of sound effects used to support a mood comes from *The Godfather* (1972). After Michael prevents an attack on his hospitalized father, a corrupt police captain and his men arrive at the hospital entrance. During the men's arrival and their confrontation with Michael, we hear thunder three times. The first time occurs as Michael pushes another man away (presumably so he will not become involved with the police) and as police officers grab Michael. The thunder occurs a second time as the police captain gets out of his car and approaches Michael. It occurs a third time as we see the police captain's reaction after slugging Michael. We *hear* this thunder, though we may not much notice it, as we *see* the police in action. The thunder underscores the power of the police, especially the captain. In *Shane* (1953), *Unforgiven* (1992), and many other films, thunder often accompanies danger and violence.

Sound effects are often used to enhance humorous or light moments. In *Mr. Hulot's Holiday* (1953), Hulot is so clumsy and disruptive that he amuses viewers but not most of his fellow vacationers. On the tennis court, Hulot hits a shot that bounces high in the air then hits a girl on the head as she curtsies off court. The sound is louder than it would be in life and more amusing. In an earlier example from this same film, the sputtering and backfiring viewers hear as Hulot drives his shaky, thirty-year-old car, which is not much bigger than a bathtub, are amusing in themselves, and the scenes in which they appear are funnier because of them.

Another use of sound effects is to conceal an action. In *Chinatown* (1974), Jake goes to the hall of records to investigate recent land sales. After he finds the page he wants, he lines up a ruler against the page and coughs as he rips out part of the page. When Jake coughs, the clerk looks up, does not hear the ripping sound, and resumes his work. Near the end of *Fatal Attraction* (1987), Alex has somehow slipped into the home of the married man with whom she had a brief affair. Alex attacks the man's wife with a knife in the upstairs bathroom while downstairs the whistling tea kettle masks the wife's screams—and prolongs and intensifies the suspense: will the husband learn of the danger soon enough to save his wife? The moment the husband takes the kettle off the stove and it quits whistling, he hears the screams and springs into action.

Like light and shadow, sound effects often add to a film in significant yet inconspicuous ways. In many of the examples just discussed, the effects are not true-to-life: the too-loud elevator sound in *The Conversation*, the timely confluence of thunder and police in *The Godfather*, and the amusing sound of the tennis ball hitting the girl on top of the head in *Mr. Hulot's Holiday*. Except for the example of the loud tennis ball, however, the effects are not so untrue-to-life as to draw attention to themselves, especially during a first, or even second, listening.

Sound effects may be recorded during filming; may be added later from a library of sound clips; may be recorded on location for later use (Figure 4.5);

or may be created by a **Foley artist**. As the Foley artist watches the action in a film projected on a screen, he or she creates and records corresponding sound effects. For example, to simulate the sounds of walking in grass, a Foley artist may take tape from a cassette, crumple it, then walk on it in synchronization with the film's action (Figure 4.6).

Ironically, sounds that are faithful to their sources sometimes do not seem "real," so moviemakers substitute other sounds. If the Foley artist decides that the sounds of footsteps on dirt don't sound right, he or she may walk on coffee grounds on cement. If an effects specialist isn't satisfied with the sound of someone being hit, he or she creates a new sound. During the making of *The Texas Chainsaw Massacre* (1974), the sound of a man getting

FIGURE 4.5 **Recording sounds in nature**
In *Blow Out* (1981), the John Travolta character is a sound effects specialist who records and mixes sounds for movie sound tracks. Here he is shown with a microphone recording sounds of the night for storage on magnetic tape. *George Litto; Filmways Pictures*

FIGURE 4.6 A Foley artist at work
(a) The Foley artist clomps around in high heels on a hard surface in synchronization with the image projected before him (partially visible in the background).
(b) The Foley artist is about to break a bottle in synchronization with the projected footage he is watching.
Brian Vancho, Foley artist; Sound One Corp., New York

his head bashed in was made by blending "sounds of smashing a cantaloupe, beating a dead chicken, stepping on a pecan shell, and snapping a piece of wood" (Simpson 28). In a fleeting second or so, this smashing-beating-breaking-snapping sound intensifies viewers' response to the action.

A sound specialist may speed up or slow down the original recorded sound in digital format. At least as early as 1938, sounds were played backward to create new sounds. In that year Loren L. Ryder—the eventual winner of six Academy Awards in sound—recorded a pig's squeal and played it backward as the sound of an ice avalanche. A suction sound may be made by running an explosion sound backward.

Sometimes completely synthetic sounds are created and blended. Other times, especially in action movies, animal sounds—such as a monkey screaming, a pig squealing, a lion roaring, or an elephant trumpeting—are distorted or used as is and blended with other sounds because many sound experts believe that animal sounds or variations of them can affect listeners more powerfully than human-made sounds. *Top Gun* (1986) includes many sounds of jet airplanes, but the recording of their sounds could not capture the excitement of the original noise, so animal sounds and human screams were blended in. In this and other uses of sound, the effect can be subliminal: viewers are unaware of why they respond as they do.

Music

> Music can extend the emotional and psychological range of characters and envelop and involve audiences in ways nothing else in movies can.   —Cecelia Hall

Music is infinitely flexible. It can be played in different keys, at different volumes, at different tempos, by different instruments, and by different combinations of instruments.

Music can also serve countless functions, such as to mirror a film's central conflict while intensifying it, as in *The Omen* (1976). That film shows the story of an American family, the Thorns: Robert, an ambassador (played by Gregory Peck), his wife Kathy (Lee Remick), and their son, Damien. They make a lovely family, except for one problem: Damien is the son of the devil. The movie shows what happens as the parents come to realize the nature of their son. In brief, the story is another variation of the battle of evil versus good. Jerry Goldsmith created two types of music for the movie: what I call "demonic music" and "Kathy and Robert's music," mirroring the evil versus good theme. The demonic music is sometimes dissonant and electronic. More often, it is represented by many low male voices accompanied by relentless and pronounced rhythms. The low male voices are effective because masculine voices are usually felt to be more threatening than feminine ones. (When people—especially males?—feel hostile, they often automatically use their lowest, most threatening voice, and young children are more often frightened

Film Composers Talk about Their Work

Film musicologist Royal S. Brown has interviewed various film composers about many topics, including their background, working methods, professional philosophy, and experiences working on different films and with various filmmakers. The following excerpts come from his book *Overtones and Undertones: Reading Film Music*.

From the interview with David Raksin (*Laura* [1944], *Will Penny* [1968], many others):

R.S.B.: What exactly do you feel should be the relationship between the musical score and its film?

D.R.: . . . You should try to find what the film is really about, and what it is doing. Which means that at certain times the music will have to be at odds with the subject. At the end of *Force of Evil* [1948] they thought I was nuts. John Garfield [the actor playing the main character] was running like crazy, and I'm playing slow music. I feel it was the right thing to do, and so do a number of others. . . . You try and figure out, with help from your innards, "What's going on here?" And you listen for what-

ever your subconscious is telling you. My music was communicating the fact that this was the first time that the Garfield character had ever come down to earth. . . . (285–86)

From the interview with Maurice Jarre (*Lawrence of Arabia* [1962], *Doctor Zhivago* [1965], *Ryan's Daughter* [1970], *A Passage to India* [1984], *Witness* [1985], *Fatal Attraction* [1987], *Jacob's Ladder* [1990], many others):

R.S.B.: Have you ever worked with a director during the shooting, or has it always been afterwards?

M.J.: I tried an experiment with Peter Weir for a film called *The Mosquito Coast* [1986]. . . . He gave me the screenplay and said, "Here. I want you to write me three pieces, three sequences lasting three, four, five minutes, as you wish, and I'm going to use them to create the mood for my actors while we're shooting." And so I composed those three pieces. He used them during the shooting, thinking that he would keep them for the music track. But when

by a low male voice than by a more high-pitched female voice.) Kathy and Robert's music is much more melodic and more varied to fit different moods. Unlike the demonic music, Kathy and Robert's music is never loud and threatening, never persistently rhythmical, and never electronic. It is usually played on a piano or stringed instruments. As Kathy and Robert's prospects grow more gloomy, though, their motif is played briefly and in minor keys: it's still beautiful but less prominent and sadder.

Throughout the film the two kinds of music war with each other. Sometimes they battle within the same scene. By the end of the film, the demonic music triumphs over Kathy and Robert's music—within the scene and in the film as a whole—just as Damien and evil triumph over Kathy and Robert and those who tried to help them.[1]

---

[1]Another movie with two competing types of music that reinforce the film's central conflict is *The Pawnbroker* (1965), whose score by Quincy Jones and the making of it are described by the film's director Sidney Lumet in *Making Movies* (175–77).

he finished the film, we realized that this music didn't work. And so I had to write electronic music that was entirely different. . . . His conception of the music had changed while he was shooting. The music that he played for the actors and for the scenes was interesting for creating a certain ambience. But after the film was edited, dramatically we needed something else. I have read that certain directors have asked their composers to write the music before the film is shot. But that's rare; it's purely intellectual, and it's all but impossible to make it work. If the director has to plan his shots along the lines of the music, it isn't necessarily good for the rhythm of the film or for the film itself. . . .

When you compose music for a film, you have the same problems as an actor: some of your musical sequences will completely disappear, because during the final cut the director decided that he didn't need music for a particular sequence—or else the sequence was entirely eliminated. That's never very good for your ego, but it's all part of professionalism. What matters is whether the film is good and whether the music works well with the film. (309–11)

From the interview with John Barry (*Goldfinger* [1964], *The Ipcress File* [1965], *The Lion in Winter* [1968], *Midnight Cowboy* [1969], *Superman II* [1980], *Body Heat* [1981], *Out of Africa* [1985], *Dances with Wolves* [1990], many others):

J.B.: [The composer's involvement in the film] varies a great deal. . . . I worked on *Body Heat* right from the beginning. With *Dances*, everything had been shot. . . . It goes both ways, and frankly I don't know which is best. I like as much thinking time as I can get, but sometimes the pressure can work for you. (330)

From the interview with Howard Shore (*After Hours* [1985], *The Fly* [1986], *Dead Ringers* [1988], *The Silence of the Lambs* [1991], many others):

R.S.B.: Did you go to electronics in *Scanners* [1981] because of the movie's theme?
H.S.: Yes, I guess. Maybe. A lot of this is intuitive. I don't really think about it so much. Why I did this, or why I did that. If you're lucky enough to have an idea, it's best not to analyze it too much. (340)

Music can also direct viewers' attention. It can be used, for example, to draw attention to something presumably occurring off-frame, as when we hear party music beyond the bedroom door near the ending of *Betrayal* (1983).

Film music can help establish the place or time period of the story. In *The Godfather Part II* (1974) the Latin music helps orient viewers right away when the movie shifts from New York to Cuba. In *Tom Jones* (1963), the lively harpsichord music helps establish the time of the narrative, because the harpsichord was popular in the eighteenth century. In many movies, such as *American Graffiti* (1973) and *Stand by Me* (1986), the popular music played at dances, on juke boxes, and on radios suggests when the story takes place.

Often music suggests what a character feels. In *My Life as a Dog* (1985), as a girl plays a recorder with other students in front of a class, she sees another girl pass a note to the boy they both like then unintentionally starts playing badly. Music also helps reveal what a character is feeling in the first scene of *The Purple Rose of Cairo* (1984). In one shot a young woman looks at a poster for a romantic adventure movie as viewers hear Fred Astaire singing. The woman's expression and the music show that she is thinking romantic thoughts, until her daydreaming and the music are abruptly cut off by the sound of a letter from the marquee crashing onto the sidewalk behind her. As in many films, music and an expressive face convey emotional nuances that words cannot.

As in *The Omen*, a musical motif may be played in different ways at different times to help convey something about a character. In *Citizen Kane* (1941), Bernard Herrmann's music suggests how Kane feels at the six times his own song is heard. The first time it is played, Kane is near the height of his power and happiness. He has recently bought the staff of a rival newspaper, and a party has been arranged to celebrate the occasion. During the party a band plays Kane's song loudly, briskly, and in a major key. After his affair with a young woman comes to light and he loses the election for governor, his song is played softly, slowly, and in a minor key. It is so subdued that many viewers do not notice it, though it adds to the melancholy of the scene. (The visuals of these two scenes also reinforce this contrast: at the party the screen is alive with movement. The scene after the election defeat contains only two people: Leland and a man who is sweeping the sidewalk outside Kane's election headquarters, and their movements are lethargic, as if Leland and the worker were sapped of energy.)

Another example of music played different ways at different times to reveal a character or situation occurs in *The War of the Roses* (1989). The song "Only You" is heard three times. The first time, we hear it largely as it was meant to be heard: at the beginning of a scene Barbara Rose watches and listens to the Platters sing the song on TV, but it is accompanied by her husband's snoring; love has flown. Later in the scene Barbara tells Oliver she wants a divorce. The second playing occurs after Barbara has led Oliver to believe that she has killed his beloved dog and used it to make the pâté Oliver has been savoring. In a fury, Oliver spits out the remaining pâté, overturns the table, and chases Barbara up the stairs. As he grabs at her and she kicks him down the stairs, "Only You" is played briefly, faintly, and in a minor key, accompanied by a sustained bass note. The song is distorted and used ironically: it accompanies Oliver's attempts to hurt Barbara and her forceful rejection of him. The song is an appropriate choice because Oliver is obsessed with Barbara and wants only her, although she has declared she wants out of the marriage. The third time we hear the song, a drunken Oliver sings the first three notes as he tries to accompany himself with music he makes by dipping a finger in wine and running it along the rims of partially full wineglasses (Figure 4.7). Again, how the music is played is appropriate. Oliver's mood is no longer loving and he's no longer entirely in control of himself, so the song is crudely rendered: he sings somewhat drunkenly and off-key, and the wineglass notes

FIGURE 4.7 **Music to express a changed situation**
Michael Douglas as Oliver Rose uses a collection of partially full wineglasses to play part of
"Only You" to his very estranged wife in *The War of the Roses* (1989). "Only You" is heard three
times in the film, each time more discordant than the last. *James L. Brooks and Arnon Milchan;
20th Century-Fox*

are only crude approximations. Partway through his serenade, Barbara asks
herself, "What fresh hell is this?"

Sometimes a musical motif is associated with a character or group of
characters, and the music is played the same way every time it accompanies
the character or group. In *The Seven Samurai* (1954), the samurai who is an
outsider has his own (jazzy) melody, and the other six samurai have their own
group melody.

Music is often used for emotional effect. In *Jaws* (1975), a relentless,
strongly rhythmical, and accelerating bass melody accompanies the shark
attack on a boy. As the shark approaches its victim, the music is played more

loudly and more quickly, suggesting the shark's power and acceleration. Once viewers have heard the shark's theme and associated it with the shark, the mere melody sets their nerves on edge because music and viewers' imagination are a powerful combination.

Filmmakers sometimes use music—knowingly or not—to distract viewers from a weak part of the script or to enhance a performance. *The Omen* illustrates both uses. Certain details about the film's story may trouble viewers, but the music is so effective it helps involve viewers and keep them from dwelling on narrative weaknesses. Though the acting in *The Omen* is generally convincing, as in many films the music enhances the performances. Billie Whitelaw is exactly right as the frightening, evil governess, but she often has an accomplished assistant, the demonic music. Gregory Peck is also well cast and is convincing as the American ambassador, but in the scene where he learns of his wife's death, he is convincing only up to a point. As Peck buries his head in his hands in grief, the slow, melancholy strings and woodwinds increase in volume and build on the emotion he began.

In other films, the music is not as integral as in *The Omen*. Inappropriate or intrusive music can distract viewers. As one critic wrote of a movie, "The film's score is outstandingly intrusive, wringing emotion at every possible moment with weepy laments and ominous choral flourishes; few events in the film occur without the kind of musical accompaniment that preempts the viewer's emotional response. Television routinely treats its audiences this way. Feature films of real gravity don't have to" (Maslin 6). Films may use music to disguise shortcomings. The saying that cooks cover their mistakes with mayonnaise and physicians bury theirs should perhaps be joined by this: filmmakers drown out weaknesses with (loud, insistent, overwrought) music.

More than ever, movies help sell recorded music. *The Bodyguard* (1992), *Dazed and Confused* (1993), *The Crow* (1994), *Waiting to Exhale* (1995), *Batman Forever* (1995), *Evita* (1996), and *Space Jam* (1996) are examples of movies that helped make their music into huge successes. The music sales in turn plus music videos—sometimes with clips from the films—created more interest in the movies. As never before, movies have a symbiotic relationship with musical tapes and CDs. The president of CBS Records said, "What is critical to selling a sound track album from . . . [a] dramatic movie is that several of the film's emotional high points be reinforced by music that makes a strong enough impact so that viewers exit the theater remembering the music" (Holden 19). The composer or performer may also be a factor in selecting music for a movie. Names such as Elton John and Whitney Houston generate interest not only in the movie but also in future music sales. In other words, in some movies, the music may be emphasized so that another division of the corporate conglomerate that made the film can sell tapes and CDs based on it.

At its most effective, music—which draws from the same creative well as poetry—helps elicit feelings and moods, but it is impossible to capture precisely in words its meanings and moods. As Irwin Edman has written:

> But just because music cannot be specific it can render with voluminousness and depths the general atmosphere or aura of emotion. It can suggest love, though no love in particular; worship or despair, though it does not say who is worshiped or what is the cause of the despair. Into the same music, therefore, a hundred different listeners will pour their own specific histories and desires. . . . Words are too brittle and chiseled, life too rigid and conventional to exhaust all the infinity of human emotional response. The infinite sinuousness, nuance, and complexity of music enable it to speak in a thousand different accents to a thousand different listeners, and to say with noncommittal and moving intimacy what no language would acknowledge or express and what no situations in life could completely exhaust or make possible. (116–17)

Silence

Occasionally, filmmakers use no sound, not even the background or ambient sound we experience during waking hours.

Silence has been employed during dream scenes in sound films, as in *My Life as a Dog*. The effect is unsettling and, if carried on for long, distancing.

Filmmakers have utilized silence to suggest dying or death. In *2001*, as astronaut Frank Poole goes outside the spaceship, we hear Poole's breathing and the hiss of pressurized air; then after the space pod has presumably cut Poole's air line, all sounds stop. As Poole struggles with his air line then tumbles lifelessly through space, we hear no sound. Nothing. These deadly silent scenes outside the spacecraft are alternated with scenes containing ambient sound as the other astronaut, Dave Bowman, tries to help. Later when Bowman explodes the pod door of the spacecraft and is catapulted into the vacuum of the emergency air lock, at first we hear nothing. Then he pulls a switch that starts to close the spaceship's outer door and send air surging into the entry chamber, returning him and us listeners to the normal world of glorious sound.

A similar use of silence occurs in *The Body Snatcher* (1945). A woman walks into the darkness in the background of the frame as she sings loudly. She is followed into the darkness by a slow-moving horse-drawn carriage. Eight to ten seconds after the woman and carriage disappear into the darkness, her voice remains strong and clear; then her singing stops abruptly in mid-song. The rest is silence. The suggestion created by the interruption of the sound—and the engulfing darkness of much of the frame—is that she has been murdered.

More generally, silence can function as a pause in music or poetry does: as a break in the natural rhythm of life, a change that can be unsettling and

Vocals, Sound Effects, and Music in an Excerpt from *Psycho* (1960)

An excerpt from *Psycho* illustrates some major ways filmmakers can use the sound track.

In a motel where she is staying Marion Crane steps into a shower bath. Viewers hear the shower curtain being pulled, Marion sighing, the soap being unwrapped, and the water running. At first, there is no music (see Figure). The sound of the water continues as we see through the shower curtain the indistinct image of someone coming toward Marion (and seemingly toward the audience). As that person pulls the shower curtain aside and begins to attack Marion with a large knife, the sound of the water disappears from the sound track. At the beginning of the attack, we hear Marion's screams and, more loudly, a slashing sound and Bernard Herrmann's pulsating music. During the attack the loudest sounds are the pulsating extreme high notes played by an orchestra of string instruments. After the attack is well under way, the sound of the running water gradually reemerges, and briefly and simultaneously we hear screams, slashing sounds, music, and running water. (When the film was first released in 1960, some viewers also heard the audience's screams.)

 After the attacker leaves and Marion is losing consciousness, the screams stop and bass strings play loudly and slowly but still rhythmically. As she reaches for the shower curtain then holds on to it momentarily, the music slows and decreases in volume, while the sound of the water gets louder. The music then stops, and, while popping the shower curtain hooks in succession, Marion falls forward in death.

As is usually the case in films, in this scene from *Psycho* sound effects are used selectively—only six

Sound in *Psycho*, before, during, and after Marion's shower
From the time Marion steps into the shower until she half falls out of it, about 106 seconds elapse. During this time, what happens is so riveting and upsetting that few viewers notice the sound track. However, this chart, created after replaying this section of the film many times and listening carefully, shows that it is not only the visuals and editing that make this part of *Psycho* effective and memorable.

Visuals	Vocals
Marion steps into shower tub.	
	Marion sighs.
Marion begins shower.	
Approaching person seen indistinctly through shower curtain.	
Shower curtain pulled aside.	
Person stabbing Marion.	
	Marion's screams and panting.
Attacker seen going out bathroom door.	
Marion slowly slipping downward.	
Marion holding on to shower curtain.	
Marion falls forward over edge of tub to the floor.	

in all. The first sounds are neither unusual nor particularly expressive. The soft tone and regular rhythm of the running water, for example, seem uneventful: all sounds normal. Once the attack begins, however, the sound of splashing water is not dramatic enough; instead we hear the sounds of Marion screaming and panting, music, and a knife supposedly slashing flesh. After the attacker leaves and Marion falls, the sounds of the shower curtain being pulled free and of her falling forcefully to the floor suggest life rushing from her body.

If we listen to this part of the film several times, we begin to notice that some of the sound effects don't sound as they would in life. When Marion unwraps the new bar of soap, for example, the paper sounds more crinkly and louder than any actual soap wrapper. And the running water in the shower doesn't sound like water running in a shower. It sounds nearly the same as the heavy rain when Marion arrived at the motel. But the sound of the water in the shower also includes a sound like that of a liquid being sloshed around in a large container. The sound of the knife stabbing Marion is probably different from and more noticeable than that sound in life. One of my students said it sounded as if someone were slicing cabbage with a knife. Another said it sounded as if someone were chipping away on a block of ice with an ice pick.

The sound effects in this 106-second excerpt illustrate a commonplace in movies: what we see and hear normally seems true-to-life—that can be a source of cinema's enormous power—but under close examination we learn that it is not. In most popular movies such deceptions are to be expected. Audiences are meant to believe in what they see and hear, to stay caught up in what happens before them, but the techniques used are often truer of movies than of life.

Notice two sound effects *not* supplied in this section of *Psycho*: when the attacker pulls the shower curtain aside, we do not hear it slide on the rod, though we did earlier when Marion got into the tub. What is more effective is the loud, pulsating music that accom-

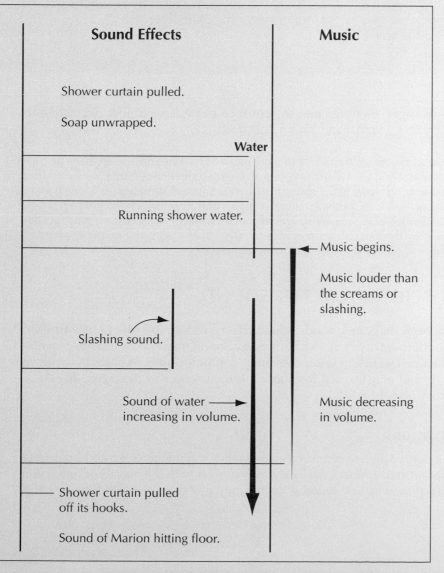

Sound Effects	Music
Shower curtain pulled.	
Soap unwrapped.	
Water	
Running shower water.	
	Music begins.
	Music louder than the screams or slashing.
Slashing sound.	
Sound of water increasing in volume.	Music decreasing in volume.
Shower curtain pulled off its hooks.	
Sound of Marion hitting floor.	

185

panies the shower curtain being pulled aside. The other significant sound not supplied is noise coming from the attacker, but the high-pitched music during the attack suggests both the attacker's violent and sexual frenzy and Marion's (and the viewers') panic.

Music is not used before the attack. Unlike countless film scenes, this excerpt lacks music to establish a mood or create suspense. But as the attack begins, Bernard Herrmann's music intensifies the audience's shock. During the attack, the music is louder than any other sound. The people mixing the sounds could have relied more on the screams or the slashing sounds, or both, but they chose to emphasize the music. During the attack, the loud, piercing string music sounds like bird cries (perhaps many viewers hear bird cries in the music because images of birds and references to them appear earlier in the film). The music also suggests Marion's heartbeat. When the attack begins, the music is rapid and frantic, as Marion's heartbeat would be. As the attacker leaves and Marion slips toward death, the music slows but retains a regular rhythm. And as Marion loses her grip on life, the music loses its jagged up and down melody and its volume or force then comes to a halt. The melodies and rhythms of life fade out. What remain are only a silent body and the sound of water streaming on indifferently.

make us eager, even nervous, to return to the sounds of life. According to film scholars Thomas and Vivian Sobchack,

> Just as the freeze frame in a moving picture frustrates the expectations of continuous, lifelike movement, so does the sudden absence of sound in a sound film frustrate our sense of the reality of a given situation. Continued for a long period, cinematic silence becomes almost tangible and extremely discomforting. Thus, an absence of sound over images of activity tends to distance the viewer, pushes us away from our absorption with the illusion of reality and makes us aware of the artificial nature of sound in the cinema. (198)

ADDITIONAL USES OF SOUND

As has been suggested, vocals, sound effects, music, and silence may be used in countless creative ways within scenes. Sound may also be used as a transition between scenes, to foster continuity or promote discontinuity. In narrative films, sound may be used from an on-screen source or offscreen, as part of the story or not.

Transitions

Sound may be used to connect scenes in many ways. Figures 4.8–4.12 illustrate five sound transitions. Usually the sound ends with the visuals of one scene and is replaced by new sound at the beginning of the next scene (Figure 4.10).

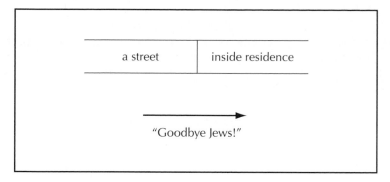

FIGURE 4.8 The sound from one scene continues into the next scene
In *Schindler's List* (1993), a girl's hateful shouts of "Goodbye Jews!" in a scene in the street are heard three times at lower volume at the beginning of the next scene, which takes place inside a well-furnished residence that a Jewish family had occupied but that Schindler is taking over.

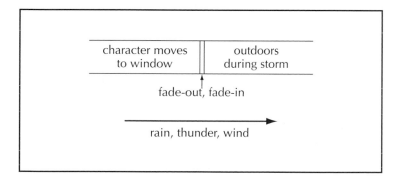

FIGURE 4.9 The sound for the second scene begins before the scene does
Near the beginning of *The War of the Roses* (1989), as the character played by Danny DeVito moves toward an office window, the sounds of rain, thunder, and wind can be heard more clearly. The wind sounds continue loudly during a brief visual fade-out, fade-in. In the next scene, which takes place in a different setting, it is a stormy day and the sounds of rain and thunder can be heard. Similar sounds are used at the end of one scene, during the brief transition, and at the beginning of the next scene to promote continuity, the smooth transition from shot to shot and scene to scene.

But the sound ending one scene may be similar to the sound beginning the next scene (this transition is comparable to a visual **match cut**). An example of a similar, linking sound occurs in *Local Hero* (1983). A scene at an office ends with a woman office worker responding to the main character's request for a date: she simply says "no." The next scene, in the main character's apartment, begins with him on the phone saying, "No, it's not. It's Mac." Although the

match cut: Transition between two shots in which an object or movement at the end of one shot closely resembles an object or movement at the beginning of the next shot.

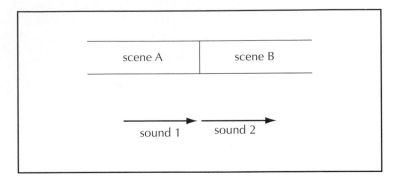

FIGURE 4.10 Sound ends with the scene
If the sound of the earlier scene is even vaguely like the sound in the following scene, the transition seems continuous. But if the sound of the earlier scene does not match the sound of the next scene, the transition is discontinuous, even startling.

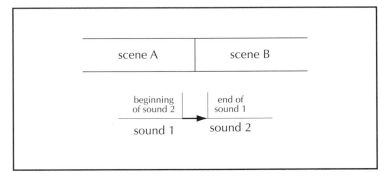

FIGURE 4.11 A sound dissolve
The sound from the first scene fades out as the sound from the following scene fades in, momentarily overlapping it then replacing it. The sound near the end of a scene dissolves into the new sound of the new scene.

speaker and tone of voice are different, the linking word "no" is the same. Another example of a similar sound linking scenes occurs in *Mr. Hulot's Holiday*. At the end of a scene near a tennis court, we hear a distant ringing bell signifying that a meal is about to be served at the hotel. In the next scene, outside the hotel, we see the bell ringing then see a worker ringing it, but now it sounds much louder.

Sometimes the sound of the first scene is quite unlike the sound beginning the next scene (something like a **jump cut**). One scene late in *Citizen*

jump cut: A discontinuous transition between shots.

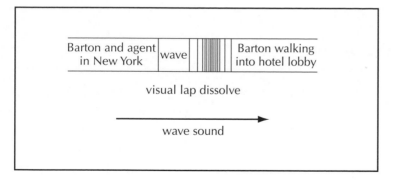

FIGURE 4.12 A sound used to connect multiple scenes
In *Barton Fink* (1991), sound is used to connect three scenes: from near the end of one scene, throughout a second brief scene, and into the beginning of a third scene. Slightly before the end of a scene in New York between Barton and his agent, viewers can hear the sound of an ocean wave. In the next scene, viewers see and hear a large wave hitting a large rock close to the shoreline. As the shot fades out visually and the next shot fades in, overlapping it then replacing it, the sound of the ocean decreases but continues briefly into the beginning of the following scene, in which Barton is walking in a deserted Los Angeles hotel lobby. Here sound—presumably the sound of a Pacific Ocean wave—helps viewers quickly understand the change from New York theatrical life to Hollywood.

Kane ends with the butler, Raymond, saying that he knew how to handle Kane, "like that time his wife left him." The next scene begins with a cockatoo shrieking and flying away. The result: surprise and discontinuity.

During a sound dissolve (Figure 4.11), the first sound begins to fade out as the next sound fades in and overlaps the first sound before replacing it. Sound dissolves may be used to shift sound and mood gradually from one scene to the next and to promote continuity. Continuity is also achieved when a sound is used between many scenes (Figure 4.12). If only music is used between scenes, the transition is often called a **bridge** or **sound bridge**.

Depending on their similarity or difference, the sounds between scenes will contribute to continuity or disruption. Usually, in **classical Hollywood cinema** the new sound in the new scene is different but not noticeably so, and continuity is supported.

classical Hollywood cinema: A term used by some film scholars to describe the type of narrative film dominant throughout most of world movie history.

Uses of Sound in Narrative Films

Table 4.1 illustrates sources and functions of sound for narrative films. In most films, vocals, occasional sound effects, and music that someone hums, whistles, sings, or plays all come from sources seen on the screen. On-screen sound in narrative films can also include a person's thoughts, memories,

TABLE 4.1
Some Sources of Sound in Narrative Films

	ON-SCREEN SOUND	OFFSCREEN SOUND
	A	B
▪ PART OF THE STORY (Sound derives from someone or something that is part of the story)	▪ INTERNAL: Vocals to convey thoughts, memories, dreams, or fantasies ▪ EXTERNAL: Vocals Sound effects Music	▪ Vocals Sound effects Music
	C	D
	EXAMPLES	EXAMPLES
▪ NOT PART OF THE STORY (Sound derives from a source outside the story)	▪ Someone looks at the camera and says something that is not part of the story or something that comments on the story ▪ The source of background music is visible, as in a scene in *Blazing Saddles* (Figure 4.13)	▪ Music that is not part of the story but serves some function in conveying it, for example, by heightening a mood ▪ Vocals, often narration, by someone who is not a character or person in the story

narrator: A character, person, or unidentifiable voice that provides commentary before, during, or after the main body of the film, or a combination of these options.

dreams, or fantasies, conveyed by the character's voice played over the action while the person is not directly speaking (Table 4.1, column A).

Sometimes sounds that are part of the story come from offscreen (Table 4.1). In a few films, a **narrator** who is also a character in the film says something about a scene he or she is not in, as in *Double Indemnity* (1944) and *Citizen Kane*, or makes a few introductory comments in some scenes, as in *Menace II Society* (1993) and *GoodFellas* (1990). Often, offscreen sound effects, such as ambient sound, are part of the story's environment. They may function as more than mere background noise. In *American Graffiti*, Curt and John Milner are talking when a car revving its engine is heard offscreen. Curt says, "Hey, John. Someone new in town." We need not see the

FIGURE 4.13 Visible source of background music
As in many movies directed by Mel Brooks, *Blazing Saddles* (1974) sometimes makes viewers aware
of movie conventions by presenting something unconventionally. Immediately before this point of
Blazing Saddles, the main character, on the horse, is riding along with orchestral music in the background. Then the man rides up to the music's source: Count Basie and his orchestra! *Warner Bros.*

car; hearing it is enough. Occasionally we hear vocals and music that are
part of the narrative though we do not see their sources. It's even possible to
hear the sounds of one scene as we see a later scene. Late in *Nelly and Mon-
sieur Arnaud* (1995), we hear Arnaud's voice on a telephone imploring Nelly
to come to him as we see her hurrying along a sidewalk in response to his
call.

Occasionally—as in *Tom Jones*, *Ferris Bueller's Day Off* (1986), *Wayne's
World* (1992), *Just Another Girl on the I.R.T.* (1992), and *Double Happiness*
(1995)—a character looks at the camera and says something that is not part
of the story. Another example of a sound that is not integral to the story yet
whose source is visible on-screen occurs in *Blazing Saddles* (1974, Figure 4.13).

FIGURE 4.14 **A sound with a surprising source** In *The 39 Steps* (1935), directed by Alfred Hitchcock, (a, top) a cleaning woman has discovered a body with a knife sticking out its back and opens her mouth to scream. (b, right) In the next shot, viewers see and hear a loud on-rushing train. (a) is a frame enlargement of the last frame of the shot; (b) is a frame enlargement from a half-second or so into the next shot. *Gaumont British; the Museum of Modern Art/Film Stills Archive*

In classical Hollywood cinema, however, viewers rarely hear a sound that is not part of the story as they see its source.

Sounds that are not part of the narrative are more typically used off-screen. An example of this film convention is music to create or reinforce a mood. For example, the screeching violins in *Psycho* tend to frighten viewers. Of course, the string section of an orchestra is not part of the narrative: viewers have no sense of a string orchestra holding a timely rehearsal in the

Bates Motel. Another example of offscreen sound that is not part of the story is **narration** by someone outside the story, as in *Tom Jones*, *The Age of Innocence* (1993), and the opening of *Dr. Strangelove: Or, How I Learned to Stop Worrying and Love the Bomb* (1963).

Most often sounds are synchronized with their sources, as when spoken words match lip movements. But filmmakers may use **asynchronous sound** —a sound from a source on-screen that precedes or follows its source. And movie sounds usually sound like what we expect from their sources: a scream, for example, usually emanates from a frightened or an upset person. In *The 39 Steps* (1935), though, the sound of a loud, onrushing train seems to emanate from a woman's mouth (Figure 4.14).

Today surround sound, or 360° sound, is available in theaters equipped with both projectors capable of reading multiple sound tracks on the film and speakers in front of, on the sides of, and behind the audience. For such showings, sound can be used in new, more flexible ways. For example, it is possible to see something seemingly approaching the audience then seemingly going over or beside it as viewers hear the corresponding sounds. An airplane can be shown firing a machine gun as it approaches viewers then flies over them, and a split second after it is beyond the viewers' peripheral vision a booming explosion can be heard behind them. Nobody is going to sleep through that.

No aspect of film is so taken for granted as the sound track. Perhaps part of the reason we disregard sound is that even if we want to discuss it, we have a paltry vocabulary to do so. English and many other languages have many more words for visuals than for sounds, and to describe a sound we must often compare it to other, well-known sounds.

Viewers are seldom meant to notice the shadings of a trained voice, sound effects, music, and silence, but an effective sound track helps involve us in the film and amplifies our responses to it. Like **designers** and directors, cinematographers, and editors, sound specialists can direct viewers' attention and powerfully influence how audiences respond. In movies usually the results seem true-to-life—and they are in spirit—but they are also true to cinema, its illusions and its artistry.

> **narration:** Comments or commentary about some aspect of the film or a subject in the film, often from someone offscreen.

> **designer:** Person responsible for the visuals of a film, including architecture, locations, sets, costumes, makeup, and hairstyles.

SUMMARY

Vocals

- Vocals consist of dialogue and other sounds of the human voice.

- Overlapping dialogue can reinforce a sense of nervousness, stress, and isolation.

- Vocals are usually rendered as true-to-life as possible but may be distorted for effect.

- Although vocals can be extremely expressive, many films rely heavily on visuals and use only limited vocals.

Sound Effects

- Sound effects are sounds other than vocals and music.

- Sound effects may be used to help create a location, intensify a mood, enhance a humorous situation, or conceal an action.

- Sound effects specialists have many options in manipulating sounds, such as playing them backward, playing them faster or slower than they were recorded, constructing them, and blending them.

Music

- Music can be played in countless ways, including in different keys, at different volumes, in varying tempos, and by different instruments.

- Film music may be used to mirror a film's central conflict, direct viewers' attention, establish place and time, suggest what a character feels or an animal is like, and cover weak acting.

- In large-budget movies, sometimes the film music is selected with an eye to future recorded music sales.

Silence

- Silence can be used in films during dreams, to suggest dying or death, or to interrupt the regular rhythm of life's sounds.

Transitions

- Sound transitions between scenes are used to reinforce continuity or cause discontinuity.

Sources of Sound

- Sound in narrative films may come from on-screen or offscreen and may derive from a source in the story or outside the story.

WORKS CITED

Coe, Brian. *The History of Movie Photography*. New York: Zoetrope, 1981.

Edman, Irwin. *Arts and the Man: A Short Introduction to Aesthetics*. New York: Norton, 1939.

Hall, Cecelia (executive sound director, Paramount Pictures). Telephone interview. 5 Aug. 1994.

Holden, Stephen. "The Pop Life: Movie Soundtracks Score in Top 10." *New York Times* 6 Aug. 1986, late ed.: C19.

Lumet, Sidney. *Making Movies*. New York: Knopf, 1995.

Maslin, Janet. Rev. of *Triumph of the Spirit. New York Times* 8 Dec. 1989, natl. ed.: B6.

Murch, Walter. "The Sound Designer." *Working Cinema: Learning from the Masters*. Ed. Roy Paul Madsen. Belmont, CA: Wadsworth, 1990.

Robinson, David. *The History of World Cinema*. New York: Stein, 1973.

Serafine, Frank. Lecture. "Audio Cinemagic." Art Institute of Chicago. 27 Apr. 1985.

Simpson, Mike. "Texas Chainsaw Massacre." *Filmmakers Newsletter* Aug. 1975: 24–28.

Sobchack, Thomas, and Vivian C. Sobchack. *An Introduction to Film*. 2nd ed. New York: Harper, 1987.

FOR FURTHER READING

Brown, Royal S. *Overtones and Undertones: Reading Film Music*. Berkeley: U of California P, 1994. The book focuses "on how the interaction between a film and its score influences our response to cinematic situations." Includes interviews with eight major film composers, including Miklós Rózsa, Bernard Herrmann, and Maurice Jarre. An appendix contains an outline of what to listen for and consider about a film score.

Film Score: The Art and Craft of Movie Music. Ed. Tony Thomas. Burbank, CA: Riverwood P, 1991. Includes a list of film scores for each composer featured.

Film Sound: Theory and Practice. Ed. Elisabeth Weis and John Belton. New York: Columbia UP, 1985. Part I: History, Technology, and Aesthetics; Part II: Theory; Part III: Practice.

Gorbman, Claudia. *Unheard Melodies: Narrative Film Music*. Bloomington: Indiana UP, 1987. A work of theory and analysis to account for the possible functions of music in fictional films.

Kalinak, Kathryn. *Settling the Score: Music and the Classical Hollywood Film*. Madison: U of Wisconsin P, 1992. History, theory, and analysis of music in classical Hollywood cinema plus an extensive bibliography.

Manvell, Roger, and John Huntley. *The Technique of Film Music*. Rev. and enlarged ed. New York: Hastings, 1975. Includes chapters on music in silent films, early sound films, and later sound films plus a chapter on music in four films since 1955.

Sound-on-Film: Interviews with Creators of Film Sound. Ed. Vincent LoBrutto. Westport: Praeger, 1994. Includes glossary, filmographies, and bibliography.

TYPES OF FILMS

N OW THAT WE HAVE CONSIDERED the expressiveness of film techniques, we will consider completed films. Part Two discusses the sources, types, and characteristics of the live-action fictional film and the alternatives to it: documentary, avant-garde, hybrid, and animated.

Considering the sources, type, and characteristics of a film can help us relate it to other films and understand it more clearly. Examining a variety of films also helps us understand the film medium more fully: the properties, techniques, forms, and purposes of different films. Understanding that the film medium is far more inclusive and diverse than what is found on the screens of the nearest multiplex, in the neighboring video store, on TV movie channels, and even in music videos helps us avoid simplifying and overgeneralizing about the film medium. A film, for example, does not always last 80 to 180 minutes, tell a story, and reassure viewers in their values; indeed, a film does not even necessarily aspire to coherence, completeness, and popularity. As the following chapters demonstrate, film is and has been much more.

◀ Jean Cocteau's *Beauty and the Beast* (1946) illustrates how varied films can be, both in subject matter and style. The beast is complex, both animalistic and credibly human. The film mixes elements of historical fiction, satire, and magic, with flashes of magic realism (Beauty's tears turning to diamonds as she praises the goodness of the Beast is an example of a highly improbable or impossible event that is used symbolically). *Jean Cocteau; Anthology Film Archives, New York*

CHAPTER 5

Sources for Fictional Films

U SUALLY, A FICTIONAL FILM is based on a script, and normally the script is based on history, fiction (usually a novel), a play, or other films. In this chapter we will focus on some of the most frequent sources for fictional films and on the process of transforming sources into films. In doing so, we will come to understand the film medium more completely—to understand, for example, some strengths and limitations of a film and its sources.

GENERAL SOURCE: SCRIPTS

Each script, regardless of its source, may appear in different versions. The **screenplay** is the earliest version, written before filming begins. A **shooting script** is the version of the script used during filming. It includes changes made in the screenplay; it usually breaks the scenes into shots; and it usually includes instructions on camera placement and use. The third general type of script, the **cutting continuity script**, is not a *source* for a film but a description of the finished film.[1]

The Scriptwriter's Territory

As Table 5.1 illustrates, for movies the scriptwriter largely determines the **settings**, dialogue and action, structure, and the **meanings** the story states and suggests. Usually all other aspects of a film—such as camera angles and

setting: The place where filmed action occurs, either a location or set.

meaning: An observation or general statement about a subject.

---

[1]The cutting continuity script can refresh a viewer's memory of a film and reveal details and patterns not noticed while seeing the film. For a foreign-language film, usually more complete and more accurate translations are given than in the film's subtitles.

  Most viewers find that reading any kind of script before seeing a film is tedious, because the script itself is neither literary nor cinematic. Many scripts, too, are carelessly published and abound in errors and questionable interpretations. Nonetheless, a script usually reveals some of the intermediate stages in the development of a film.

TABLE 5.1
Creative Territories for Making Fictional Films[1]

THE WRITER'S TERRITORY	TERRITORY OF PRODUCTION PERSONNEL
SETTINGS: where and when the action takes place and something about what the settings look like	**CASTING AND PERFORMANCE:** people, animals, or creatures selected to play the roles; behavior, gestures, tone of voice
CHARACTERS: what the characters do and say	**CINEMATOGRAPHY AND MISE EN SCÈNE:** camera distances, angles, lenses, lighting, composition, and so forth
STRUCTURE: selection and arrangement of actions and dialogue (if any)	**EDITING:** length and arrangement of shots; transitions between scenes[2]
MEANINGS: stated in the story or more often implied by it; what the film explains about its subjects in general terms or shows about them	**MUSIC AND MOST SOUND EFFECTS[2]**

[1]Adapted from Phillips.

[2]Occasionally editing transitions, music, and sound effects that were indicated by the writer are followed by the production personnel.

transitions between shots—are the domain of the other filmmakers such as the cinematographer and editor, under the guidance of the director. We cannot know the scriptwriters' exact contributions to a film with a large production company because so many people involved—especially the producer, director, actors, and editors—may all edit and rewrite parts of the script. In elaborate productions, "script doctors" may be hired to rewrite the script, sometimes again and again, and they often go uncredited.

The Script and the Finished Film

Comparison of a screenplay or shooting script with the finished film sometimes reveals some of the contributions of the writer(s) and director. We can see these relative contributions by comparing a scene from a script for *The Third Man* (1949) with the comparable section of the finished film. In the film Holly Martins has come to Vienna to work for an old friend, Harry Lime. Martins learns that Lime has been involved in stealing penicillin, diluting it, and selling it at an enormous profit. Late in the film Calloway, a British officer trying to enlist Martins's aid in trapping Lime, has brought Martins to a children's hospital. Here is what the shooting script says of that scene:

123. CHILDREN'S HOSPITAL (NIGHT):

As they [Calloway and Martins] *come through the doors, a nurse passes and Martins realizes he has been shanghai-ed, but it is too late to do anything.*

CALLOWAY: I want to take a look in No. 3 Ward.

NURSE: That's all right, Colonel Calloway.

CALLOWAY (*to Martins*): You've been in on this story so much, you ought to see the end of it.

124. CHILDREN'S WARD (NIGHT):

He pushes open a door and, with a friendly hand, propels Martins down the ward, talking as he goes in a cheerful, professional, apparently heartless way. We take a rapid view of the six small beds, but we do not see the occupants, only the effect of horror on Martins's face.

CALLOWAY: This is the biggest children's hospital in Vienna—very efficient place. In this ward we have six examples—you can't really call them children now, can you?—of the use of the Lime penicillin in meningitis. . . . Here in this bed is a particularly fascinating—example, if you are interested in the medical history of morons . . . now here. . . .

Martins has seen as much as he can stand.

MARTINS: For pete's [*sic*] sake, stop talking. Will you do me a favour and turn it off?

As they continue their walk past the small beds, dissolve. (123–24)

This version of the script is written in scenes, the **master-scene format**, which indicates the scene number, setting, and the segment of the day (such as day, night, dawn, noon, late afternoon). The scriptwriter describes the action briefly and supplies all the dialogue but does not indicate *how* the dialogue is to be delivered. The writer knew that well-written dialogue usually suggests its delivery and that the director and actors would probably have ignored overly specific directives.

Now here is my description, including all the dialogue, of the comparable part of the finished film. It's only one scene, which runs about fifty-eight seconds.

Martins and Calloway enter a large ward of a hospital. As they walk past beds and Martins looks into them, Calloway tells Martins, "This is the biggest children's hospital in Vienna. All the kids in here are the result of Lime's penicillin racket." Calloway moves away from Martins and talks to a nurse (unheard) as Martins walks on slowly, still looking into each bed. Martins stops at the foot of one bed and looks into it; Calloway joins him (Figure 5.1) and says, "It had meningitis. They gave it some of Lime's penicillin. Terrible pity, isn't it?" Calloway then walks away from Martins, and Martins turns away and walks a few steps (we do

FIGURE 5.1 Frame from *The Third Man* (1949)
Martins (right), accompanied by Calloway, sees the results of Lime's diluted penicillin in a Viennese children's hospital. Throughout the scene, viewers see shots of Martins's reactions to the children in the hospital beds but never see what he sees. Those horrors are left to the viewers' imaginations. Frame enlargement. *London Film Productions*

not see Calloway and Martins together again during the scene). Nurses tend the offscreen children: taking temperatures, giving oxygen, marking a chart, tossing aside a teddy bear (presumably the child who had it won't need it anymore).

The scene in the film is generally true to the script and takes its cue from the script not to show the children, but to show only Martins's reactions to them. But the film has many differences from the script. Two scenes in the shooting script have become one scene in the film—a wise decision because the earlier of the two scenes adds little to the story. The film also has far less dialogue (34 words versus 103) and relies more on the visuals, especially the expressions on Martins's face, which we see in six of the scene's fifteen shots, including the part of the shot depicted in Figure 5.1. In the film scene, Martins says nothing. In the film, too, Calloway is more subtle. He does not push Martins along and talk so much; instead he brings Martins into the ward and lets the sights of the place work on Martins, while the director lets the images of Martins work on viewers. In the film viewers can infer how extensive is the evil that Lime's actions have spawned. The film also portrays a large ward full of Lime's victims; the script indicates victims in only six beds.

The film shows many nurses busy tending the children; the script says nothing about the nurses. When we compare screenplays or shooting scripts with the corresponding films, we find that, as in the case of *The Third Man*, the film is often more concise, less reliant on dialogue, and more visual.

Although we cannot say with certainty who is responsible for all the changes in this part of *The Third Man*, we can see roughly what the scriptwriter, Graham Greene, wrote and the final filmed product. Director Carol Reed probably deserves much credit for the changes from the script, which compress the action and present the information and moods more visually and more subtly.

SPECIFIC SOURCES

Possible but infrequent sources for fictional films are nonfiction magazine articles (*The Peacemaker*, 1997), video games (*Mortal Kombat*, 1995), comic books (various *Batman* movies), comic strips (the Peanuts films), series of short animated movies (*Casper*, 1995), TV series (*The Brady Bunch*, 1995), musical albums (*Pink Floyd the Wall*, 1982), and operas (*The Magic Flute*, 1974). Sometimes there is a chain of sources, as is the case with the Teenage Mutant Ninja Turtles, which was first a comic book, then a TV cartoon, then a series of movies. Fictional films can have other possible sources, but four of the most frequent ones are history, fiction, plays, and other films.

The filmmakers' adaptations of their sources may be loose (perhaps the adaptation retains only a few major aspects of the original, for example only the title and a character or a few scenes). An adaptation may be faithful (it follows the story of the original and captures its mood or spirit but with some changes). An adaptation may be literal (as nearly as possibly a translation from one medium to the other, which is rare but most likely to happen with plays). Which type of adaptation is "best" is subject to debate. Some advocate literal adaptations, arguing or assuming that what is most important is that the original be presented as closely as possible. At the opposite extreme, those who support loose adaptations argue or assume that what is important are effective films, whatever their sources.

History

Many films, such as *Amistad* (1997) and *Titanic* (1997), are based on historical events. For many viewers a key issue about such films is how faithfully they comply with written histories of the same events. Filmmakers, however, have additional concerns. Historian Robert Brent Toplin argues:

> If we hold cinematic historians strictly to the standards of most written history, we are almost certain to be disappointed, for filmmakers must attend to the demands of drama and the challenges of working with incomplete evidence. In

creating historical dramas they almost always need to collapse several historical figures into a few central characters to make a story understandable. Often they are pressed to simplify complex causes so that audiences will comprehend their movies' principal messages and not lose interest, and the dramatic medium often leads them to attribute changes in history to the actions of dynamic individuals rather than to impersonal forces. Cinematic historians often lack detailed evidence about situations in the past, so they invent dialogue and suggest impressions about the emotions and motivations of historic figures. Also, they suggest **closure** on a story, revealing few doubts, questions, or considerations of alternative possibilities. (10)

closure: The consequences of previous major actions in a story are shown or implied by the end of the narrative.

Usually movies must attract large audiences to recoup the fortunes needed to make and market them. Consequently, filmmakers do not typically aim to teach their audiences traditional historical accounts because that tends to be unprofitable. When a film deals with news or history, filmmakers usually omit or change details to make the film more entertaining or to give it different meanings, or both. For centuries novelists and playwrights, including Shakespeare, have done the same.

The subjects and often the titles of films based on news or history suggest factuality. Their publicity normally does too. So impressive and mesmerizing are large, bright, moving images presented without interruption that often a film looks like what viewers believe does or did exist. But commercial films are posed life. They usually look and sound like what we think we experience in the world, but the look and sound are artificially achieved. In feature films sounds are selected, usually amplified or diminished, and normally blended with other sounds. Crowds are carefully rehearsed beforehand and coached to move casually. Lights and colors are carefully selected. Products, such as Coca-Cola or Pepsi, are sometimes placed in conspicuous positions (Figure 1.60). On first glance a movie may look true-to-life; during a second or third viewing, we might sense that a similar situation in life would look and sound different. The events depicted may seem like life, but some are imaginary and the story leaves out many boring, insignificant actions; for example, it rarely gives every moment of a trip or of a long conversation.

Sometimes a movie indicates near its beginning that it is factual or historical when it is not. *Fargo* (1996) has a subtitle claiming to be factual, but some reviewers of the film were skeptical, and an investigation by the *Minneapolis Star Tribune* failed to unearth any case like the one the movie depicts. A film may imply at its conclusion that it has been factual though it has not. The 1994 Russian-French film *Burnt by the Sun* has an epilogue explaining the fates of the main characters, but the film's director and co-writer, Nikita Mikhalkov, said "he added the epilogue for dramatic effect and invented the characters himself" (Stanley B1).

Typically fictional films based on history blend fiction and fact throughout. One example is *Stand and Deliver* (1987), the story of a real Latino high school math teacher, Jaime Escalante, and one of his largely Latino classes.

The film shows various barriers to learning in the students' lives, the methods the teacher used, and the students' hard work. All this is presented in such a way that viewers are led to believe the account is factual. In spirit, yes; in some significant details, no. For example, in the film the entire class seems to have to retake a test because authorities at a national testing service suspected cheating, but in fact only fourteen of the eighteen students had to take the test again. The film shows the students having only one day to review for the second test. In actuality, the second test was administered several months later. Yet another example: as in nearly all fictional films, the movie character is more lively and more engaging than **documentary film** of the real person (Figure 5.2).

documentary film: A film that presents a version of actions that viewers are intended to accept not primarily as the product of someone's imagination but primarily as fact.

FIGURE 5.2 Actor and subject
Actor Edward James Olmos (left) as Jaime Escalante in *Stand and Deliver* (1987), with the real high school math teacher Jaime Escalante. Comparison of clips of the celluloid Escalante teaching with documentary footage of the real Escalante teaching illustrates that, as in most movies based on real people, the movie character seems more lively and engaging than the actual person. *American Playhouse; Warner Bros.*

FIGURE 5.3 The look and manner of a famous subject re-created by an actor
Occasionally a famous person is portrayed by an actor who bears an amazingly close resemblance, as was the case when (a, left) Malcolm X was portrayed by (b, right) Denzel Washington in Spike Lee's *Malcolm X* (1992). The glasses, suit, placement of the hand, and concentration all help complete the illusion that viewers of the movie are seeing the famous man. *Warner Bros.*

Malcolm X (1992) blends fiction and written accounts (including *The Autobiography of Malcolm X*). The film captures much of Malcolm's experiences and ideas but takes some creative liberties. For instance, the cause of the death of Malcolm's father, which the film shows in gruesome detail, is not known with certainty, and Malcolm was converted to Islam by his family, especially his brothers, not as in the film by a fellow prisoner. In various ways the film slights the contributions of Malcolm's siblings. For example, his half-sister Ella underwrote Malcolm's lengthy pilgrimage to Mecca, oversaw his two new organizations while he was abroad, and continued to lead them after his death (Painter). More generally, the movie "conveys neither the complexity nor the self-critical aspects of the *Autobiography*. . . . As source documents, [director Spike] Lee used Malcolm's memoirs and public statements rather than the testimony of those who knew him" (Carson 278). Unlike the situation in *Stand and Deliver*, in *Malcolm X* it's debatable whether the source person or actor is the more engaging since Malcolm X was so focused and charismatic (Figure 5.3).

Popular movies are rarely consistent with accepted written histories. However, in extreme cases, such as *Mississippi Burning* (1988) and *JFK* (1991), they vary so widely from orthodox interpretations that many historians and social commentators argue that viewers who know no other sources on the subjects will be profoundly misled. Historian Robert Brent Toplin urges, "It is worthwhile to observe errors of fact and to point out misleading representations that serve no important dramatic purpose" (11–12).

In recent years, some historians have stressed how subjective histories are. They remind us that all historians are unavoidably influenced by their own backgrounds and that all history is a "construction, not a reflection" (Rosenstone 11). Some historians, such as Robert A. Rosenstone, contend that films of historical subjects can be alternative histories, other ways of creating (or "doing") history: language "itself is only a convention for doing history—one that privileges certain elements: fact, analysis, linearity. . . . History need not be done on the page. It can be a mode of thinking that utilizes elements other than the written word: sound, vision, feeling, and montage" (11).

Many historical sources for films are cited in the first column of the chronology for 1895–1998 (pp. 513–54).

Fiction

According to critic and theorist Dudley Andrew, "well over half of all commercial films have come from literary originals" (98). To see some of the changes made when fiction is adapted into a film and to see what each medium is capable of, we will look at a passage of fiction then the corresponding section of a film based on the fiction. The passage is from the end of Chapter 12 of *Woman in the Dunes* (1964), Kobo Abe's Japanese novel about a man trapped in a large sand pit with a woman who lives there in a shack:

> The woman sidled up to him. Her knees pressed against his hips. A stagnant smell of sun-heated water, coming from her mouth, nose, ears, armpits, her whole body, began to pervade the room around him. Slowly, hesitantly, she began to run her searing fingers up and down his spine. His body stiffened.
> Suddenly the fingers circled around to his side. The man let out a shriek. "You're tickling!"

Student Writing

The following essay was written in response to this assignment: Review the section on history as a source for films in Chapter 5. Next, choose either *High Noon*, *The Ballad of Little Jo*, *West Side Story*, or *Apocalypse Now* and write a 750-to-1,000-word essay that has one of the following theses:

a. The film is largely consistent with written historical accounts of the times and places depicted in the film.

b. The film is largely inconsistent with written historical accounts of the times and places depicted in the film.

c. In some major ways, the film is largely consistent with written historical accounts of the times and places depicted in the film, but in some other major ways it is inconsistent with them.

Be sure to select only a few *major* points, to arrange them in a significant order, and to explain and illustrate each one carefully.

Understanding the History of the 1870s West
with The Ballad of Little Jo
by Brook Marcks

In general, traditional western films have ignored women or portrayed them in a stereotypical manner. However, in recent years, with a new perspective being taken regarding women's history, some filmmakers have begun to focus on women in the West. One such production is The Ballad of Little Jo, a film that was written and directed by a woman, Maggie Greenwald. The Ballad of Little Jo helps the viewer understand the history of the times and place which it depicts. This western revisionist film allows the viewer to see some of the characteristics of life in the West during the 1870s, what women's roles were in this society, and how some women, like Josephine Monaghan, broke away from the traditional gender roles for women of this time period.

This film shows how the American West was a frontier that promised a life of opportunities during the 1870s. To begin with, this untamed land offered homesteading, mining, and ranching to anyone who dared to take it on (Riley 2). Throughout this film, the viewer sees how the West offered new lives for many people, like the Russian family who homesteaded near Ruby City. However, these opportunities weren't without a cost. The West was also violent, uncivilized, and cursed with alcoholism and prostitution, as shown in The Ballad of Little Jo. For instance, when Josephine begins her journey in the West, she accepts a ride from a stranger who soon intends to sell her into bondage. After being pursued by two armed lecherous men, she realizes that surviving as a single woman would be impossible. Furthermore, it becomes painfully obvious how large a role alcohol and prostitution had on the people of the West (Griswold 22). For instance, the citizens of Ruby City focused their lives around the saloon, thus around alcohol and prostitution. Greenwald's film shows how such an environment had no place for a contemporary woman, unless she was willing to change her identity.

The gender roles for women of the 1870s were shown in The Ballad of Little Jo. Glenda Riley, author of The Female Frontier, states that women of this time were expected to partake wholly in domestic tasks, whether for their parents, their husbands, or other families, and if they wished to seek employment outside their homes, opportunities were severely limited. Furthermore, in the West, the only job opportunities for women were schoolteachers, cooks, storekeepers, or prostitutes (2-3). For instance, in this film, the only occupations held by women, besides Josephine, are that of a storekeeper, cook, and prostitute. Also, prostitution was the largest single source of income for women in one mining community in Montana during the 1870s (Griswold 22). The Ballad of Little Jo illustrates the restricted gender roles for women of that time and place.

The townspeople's reaction to Jo's true identity reflects their attitudes regarding women's gender roles. Since simply dressing or acting as the opposite sex was a crime in the United States in the nineteenth century, after Jo's death Ruby City was shocked and agitated by Josephine's actions. Their reactions illustrate how strongly many Americans felt about the boundaries of traditional gender roles for women. Julie Jeffrey, author of Frontier Women, contends that at that time, women who crossed gender role boundaries could expect a disaster (23). For example, when Percy, the man whom Jo lives with, discovers Jo's gender, he threatens to tell everyone. Percy goes on to say that this kind of news spreads quickly and that no matter where she would go in the West, she would be persecuted for her deception. Luckily, Josephine's gender wasn't widely known until after her death.

In the 1870s, not all women stuck to the traditional gender roles in the West. A woman by the name of Willie Matthews, a nineteen-year-old from New Mexico, broke traditional gender roles of that time. After seeing her own father be a drover, she decided that she wanted to experience what it would be like. Thus, when a man by the name of Samuel Houston came into town looking for trail hands, Willie Matthews borrowed her brother's clothing and joined the drive. After four months of hard work,

Willie decided that she was ready to head back home, so she notified Houston. Later that day, Houston met up with a "well-dressed" woman in the city, who just so happened to be Willie Matthews. Of course Houston was shocked to find out Willie's true gender and demanded an explanation. However, despite the fact that she had deceived him, he was quite impressed that she made a "good hand with the horses and cattle," and what a hard worker she had been (Roach 14).

Another such woman was Josephine Monaghan, the subject of The Ballad of Little Jo. Quite surprisingly, the film stuck faithfully to Josephine's real-life story. James Horan recounts the history of "Little Jo" in his book Desperate Women. Josephine, being from a wealthy family in New York, had a baby out of wedlock. After strong disapproval from her parents, Josephine attempted to support the baby herself. However, in much financial strain, she was forced to leave the baby to her younger sister. After such an experience, Josephine decided to go West. In her westward move, she stated that she would have rather worn men's attire than to travel the West "as a woman alone." In the spring of 1868, Jo, a slim young man, arrived in Ruby City, Idaho. After a month of unsuccessful mining, Jo took a job herding sheep in seclusion for nearly three years. Then, after returning to Ruby City, she purchased some cattle and a homestead. The real-life "Little Jo" even employed a Chinese man as a cook. In addition, after Jo died, the undertaker entered the town saloon and informed the townspeople of Jo's true identity (305-10).

The woman laughed. She seemed to be teasing him, or else she was shy. It was too sudden; he could not pass judgment on the spur of the moment. What, really, was her intention? Had she done it on purpose or had her fingers slipped unintentionally? Until just a few minutes ago she had been blinking her eyes with all her might, trying to wake up. On the first night, too, he recalled, she had laughed in that strange voice when she had jabbed him in the side as she passed by. He wondered whether she meant anything in particular by such conduct.

Perhaps she did not really believe in his pretended illness and was testing her suspicions. That was a possibility. He couldn't relax his guard. Her charms were like some meat-eating plant, purposely equipped with the smell of sweet honey. First she would sow the seeds of scandal by bringing him to an act of passion, and then the chains of blackmail would bind him hand and foot. (90–91)

The comparable section of the film version runs about forty-five seconds and consists of the conclusion of one **shot** and three additional shots. The following is my description; dialogue is from the subtitles of a print, not the published script.

shot: An uninterrupted strip of exposed motion-picture film or videotape made up of at least one frame.

By exposing us to the western lifestyle of the time, the roles that women played, and how some daring women broke away from traditional gender roles, The Ballad of Little Jo helps us to understand the history of the West during the 1870s. Maggie Greenwald's film counterbalances the long-held traditions of the western film and gives the viewer a new historical perspective on women. In the future, I hope that filmmakers will continue to challenge traditional treatments of subjects, as Maggie Greenwald did in The Ballad of Little Jo.

Works Cited

Griswold, Robert L. "Anglo Women and Domestic Ideology in the American West in the Nineteenth and Early Twentieth Centuries." Western Women: Their Land, Their Lives. Ed. Lillian Schlissel, Vicki Ruiz, and Janice Monk. Albuquerque: U of New Mexico P, 1988.

Horan, James D. Desperate Women. New York: Putnam's, 1952.

Jeffrey, Julie Roy. Frontier Women: The Trans-Mississippi West, 1840-1880. New York: Hill, 1979.

Riley, Glenda. The Female Frontier: A Comparative View of Women of the Prairie and the Plains. Lawrence: UP of Kansas, 1988.

Roach, Joyce Gibson. The Cowgirls. 2nd ed. Denton: U of North Texas P, 1990.

Shot 1. . . . *At the end of this lengthy shot, the woman, carrying a pan of water and a rag, approaches the man—who is lying on his back, naked from the waist up—and kneels beside him.*

WOMAN: "How do you feel?"

Shot 2. *The man turns his head slightly away from her and groans.*

MAN: "Not too bad."

WOMAN: "I'll wipe you down."

As she turns him on his side, he lets out more groans. The camera moves slightly to the left, and we see and hear her rinse and wring the rag in the metal pan; the camera moves right and we see her begin to wipe the man's back with the damp rag (Figure 5.4). She turns the rag over.

Shot 3. *We see part of the man's back and side. The camera follows the woman's hand as she slowly wipes near his side. With a finger, she thumps or tickles his side.*

Shot 4. *As we see the man's head and shoulders, he giggles then quickly turns his head back toward the woman.*

MAN (*angry and loud*): "Stop it!"

With a serious look on his face, he lowers his head and faces forward again.

WOMAN (*unseen*): "It hurts?"

MAN (*still serious*): "Yes!"

Obviously, there are many differences between the experience of reading the passage and seeing and hearing the corresponding section of the film. Some of the differences result from choices of the filmmakers. For example, the filmmakers chose to have the man laugh, then catch himself and become brusque, whereas in the book the man shrieks and the woman laughs. Although filmmakers typically prune the dialogue they adapt from fiction, the filmmakers of *Woman in the Dunes* chose to supply slightly more dialogue than is in the novel.

Many differences between the passage in the novel and the corresponding section of the film, however, result from differences in the two media. The novel gives many of the man's thoughts, including a memory, but to

FIGURE 5.4 Fiction into film
In *Woman in the Dunes* (1964), the woman wipes down the injured man. Unlike fiction, films allow viewers to quickly see such actions in all their subtlety and complexity. *Pathe Contemporary Films Release*

render these mental states in a film might confuse viewers. Look again at the last two paragraphs reprinted from the book. How can film accurately convey what those words do? Without *words*, how can a filmmaker convey the simile and the two implied metaphors in the sentences "Her charms were like some meat-eating plant, purposely equipped with the smell of sweet honey. First she would sow the seeds of scandal by bringing him to an act of passion, and then the chains of blackmail would bind him hand and foot"? The figurative language cannot be entirely converted into visual images and sounds and music. Similarly, neither images nor sounds can convey well the experiences of smell, taste, and feeling. Thus, "A stagnant smell of sunheated water, coming from her mouth, nose, ears, armpits, her whole body, began to pervade the room around him" cannot be translated into film.

Other differences between the passage and the film result from the capabilities of film. In forty-five seconds, the film gives viewers an excellent sense of place, shape, volume, textures, and sounds. For example, we can see the forms and sizes of the man and woman; we can see the texture of the man's skin; we hear his groans and the tone of voice of the man and woman. Most of these details are not rendered in the comparable passage of fiction. To do so would require enormous space and slow the story to a crawl, and even then the images in the reader's mind would be less precise than the images and sounds of the film. The movie camera can select actions and render them with clarity and force (as in the second shot where the camera moves left, then right); it can capture movements and gestures and their significance (such as the man's spontaneous laugh, followed by a quick suppression of it). Film can convincingly show places, real and imaginary. It can juxtapose objects more quickly than the blink of an eye. It can present visual details such as faces, the viewing of which, as scientist and educator David Attenborough has said, is itself extremely expressive:

> Letting others know how you feel is a basic part of communication. No creature in the world does so more eloquently than man, and no organ is more visually expressive than his face. Even in repose the human face sends a message and one that we tend to take for granted. Each face proclaims individual identity. In teams, recognition of other members is of great importance. A hunting dog in a pack proclaims its identity by its own personal smell. Primates, with their reduced sense of smell but their very acute vision, do it by the infinite variety of their faces. We have more separate muscles in our faces than any other animal. So we can move it in a variety of ways that no other animal can equal, and not only convey mood but send precise signals. By the expression on our face we can call people and send them away, ask questions and return answers without a word being spoken.

Film can also capture well the nuances of sound and music. Prose is hard pressed to compete with cinema in presenting what can be seen and heard and in making us feel that we are at a particular place.

"In the book she dies."

JOHN JONIK

FIGURE 5.5
Copyright 1989 by John Jonik, from *Movies Movies Movies: An Entertainment of Great Film Cartoons*, edited by S. Gross.

Fictional films that are based on novels or short stories rarely re-create the source fiction faithfully. Passages of characters' thoughts, descriptions of characters' backgrounds, analysis by the author, and a more or less consistent point of view or means of perception are uncommon in film stories. The order of scenes may also be changed. Especially in popular movies, the ending of the source novel is often changed to a happier, more crowd-pleasing conclusion (Figure 5.5). Nor does the fictional film usually re-create all the characters and action of a novel. *Greed*—the 1925 American film classic, which is a literal adaptation of the novel *McTeague*—attempted to do so, but the initial version reportedly ran 9½ hours. Such a length was quickly judged too long to be marketable because it could be shown only in two or three lengthy sessions, whereas a two-hour film can be shown several times a day and thus can generate more revenue. Soon *Greed* was edited down to about two hours. Even *Tom Jones* (1963), which critics have praised for re-creating the structure and events of the very long novel, omits characters and events.

Reading fiction and seeing a film are quite different, because each medium has its own techniques, potential, and limitations. Perhaps the basic difference between fiction and film is that fiction requires its audience to visualize and subvocalize from words printed on the page, whereas film presents images and sounds directly. People who enjoyed a novel are rarely satisfied with a film made from it because, in part, they visualize as they read. They mentally create complex experiences that films often do not approximate because the films present different visuals and different details. Then, too, sometimes readers are disappointed that film adaptations do not include all of the novel's plot.

Fiction and film are distinct media, with their own strengths and weaknesses. It is misleading to judge a film by how closely it re-creates the novel one visualized as one read. Instead, the film is something related yet new and separate, a creative expression in a different medium with its own resources and techniques. Likewise, whenever a novel or play is based on a film, it is unfair and misleading to evaluate the later work in another medium by how well it re-creates the source film. If one takes the view that a derivative creative fictional work should be judged by its fidelity to its source(s), then many of Shakespeare's plays, such as *Macbeth* and *Richard III*, would be judged deficient: they are not reliable history but make for effective theater.

Instead of evaluating a film by comparing it to its source, it is more helpful to compare the film version to other, similar films (and to compare the fiction with other, similar fiction). However, a close comparison of a film and its fictional source can be instructive, revealing what the two forms share and what is distinct to each.

Plays

In the early years of cinema, many fictional films imitated plays closely. After all, plays had been around the western world for more than two thousand years, and in the 1890s people on both sides of the footlights had a good sense of what a play was and wasn't. Thus many early films look like awkwardly filmed theater (Figure 5.6). Gradually, though, film found what *it* could be, and that was not filmed theater. Today, the two forms are still cousins, but not as close as they were in film's first decade.

Basically, plays are the more verbal medium. If you listen to a recording of a play, you will notice that much of its moods and meanings comes through from the words and their delivery. So expressive is the human voice that a trained actor can convey a world by pauses, volume, timbre, timing, and pronunciation.

Films, in contrast, tend to be more visual. Several times I have begun a film course by turning off the volume of the projector or TV monitors and showing students the beginning of a British film few of them have seen. Before I show the clip, I give the students a list of questions to consider, such as

Student Writing

The following student essay was written in response to this assignment: Choose either *The Dead*, *Dangerous Liaisons*, *Like Water for Chocolate*, or *Woman in the Dunes* and write a 750-to-1,000-word essay that has one of the following theses:

a. In several major ways the film is like its literary source.

b. In several major ways the film is unlike its literary source.

c. In some major ways the film is like its literary source, but in other major ways they are different.

Be sure to select only three to five *major* similarities or differences, to arrange them in a significant order, and to explain and illustrate each major point carefully.

The Dead: Novella to Film

by William Meyer

Contemporary film critics praise Tony Huston's adaptation of "The Dead" for its faithfulness to James Joyce's original text. Tim Pulleine calls the film "a close literary adaptation" (67). Richard Blake asserts that the adaptation is "extremely faithful to the text" (194-95). And Vincent Canby simply calls the film a "magnificent adaptation." However, despite its reputation for faithfulness, a careful analysis reveals that the film is unlike Joyce's novella in three major ways. First, the adaptation expands the scope of the original narrative by adding new scenes. Second, the adaptation deletes important contextual elements from its literary source. Finally, the adaptation modifies significant dramatic elements in the literary source.

Perhaps the most apparent difference between the film and its source is the addition of new scenes not found in the novella. For example, the opening scene of the film is shot from the exterior of the Morkans' home. It includes images of snow falling, carriages stopping, guests arriving, and people dancing. While the scene effectively establishes the social context and physical setting of the film, it does not appear in Joyce's novella. A second example is a scene in which Freddy Malins walks into a bathroom, washes his face, combs his hair, and relieves himself. The elements of this scene clearly reinforce Joyce's depiction of Malins as a disheveled drunkard, but the scene itself fails to appear in the literary source. While Huston's new scenes extend

216

elements of the narrative introduced by Joyce, they are still invented. It seems clear that Tony Huston's addition of scenes to the screenplay supports Michael Klein's observation that the brevity of short stories provides scriptwriters with room for "imaginative expansion" (10).

A second major difference between the film and its literary source is the deletion of important contextual elements from the novella. For example, in the original text, we learn the context of Molly Ivors's relationship with Gabriel. "They were friends of many years' standing and their careers had been parallel, first at the University and then as teachers" (Joyce 204). This background information is deleted from the screenplay. Consequently, the audience never fully understands the professional and academic nature of their relationship. Another contextual element which is deleted from the film is a scene in which Gabriel becomes discontent with the party and wishes to leave the Morkans' home. In the novella, we learn that he walks to a window, taps his fingers on a windowpane, and stares outside (Joyce 208). Moreover, we learn that he wonders "how much more pleasant it would be there than at the supper-table" (Joyce 208). Because this scene is cut from the screenplay, viewers of the film cannot accurately gauge the depth of Gabriel's discontent. Therefore, they can never fully appreciate the emotional context in which his words and actions are expressed.

A third major difference between the film and the short story is the modification of significant dramatic elements in the original novella. For example, Molly Ivors's exit from the party is modified to clarify her political significance for contemporary audiences. In the novella, "Joyce allows his patriot to depart quietly, offering only that she does not choose to join the party for dinner" (Blake 194). However, in the film, Molly's exit is modified to include the lines "I'm off to a union meeting at Liberty Hall. A Republican meeting." Film critic Richard Blake argues that in the novella, "Her farewell is shot through with irony: 'Beannacht libh' (a blessing upon you all). The point would not be lost on the original readers, but for film audiences Huston must underline Molly's political function in the story" (194). In this case, Huston's modification of the literary source effectively clarifies the political significance of an important dramatic element in the film.

By addition, deletion, and modification, Tony Huston created a screenplay adaptation which is different from its literary source. However, commentary by professional film critics seems to indicate that different does not necessarily mean unfaithful (Blake 194-95; Canby; Pulleine 67). Perhaps this is why Huston's adaptation of "The Dead" received so much critical praise. Such praise clearly underscores Huston's skill at weaving his way through what film critic Gabriel Miller calls the filmmaker's "dilemma of remaining faithful to the novel's spirit while realizing the necessity of altering its design" (xi).

Works Cited

Blake, Richard A. "The Living and the Dead." America 20 Feb. 1988: 194-95.

Canby, Vincent. "The Party's Over." New York Times 17 Dec. 1987, natl. ed.: C19.

Joyce, James. "The Dead." The Portable James Joyce. Ed. Harry Levin. New York: Viking, 1966. 190-242.

Klein, Michael. "Introduction: Film and Literature." The English Novel and the Movies. Ed. Michael Klein and Gillian Parker. New York: Ungar, 1981. 1-13.

Miller, Gabriel. Screening the Novel. New York: Ungar, 1980.

Pulleine, Tim. "A Memory of Galway." Sight & Sound Winter 1987/88: 67-68.

scene: A section of a narrative film that gives the impression of continuous action taking place during one continuous time and in one continuous space.

Who is the main character? What does he or she seem to want? What does that character's personality seem to be like? Where and when does the story take place? I show the film clip twice; after each showing, I ask students to jot notes in answer to my questions and about anything else they noticed in the clip. Then I collect and read the responses aloud. The results: students generally come close to what the film is showing—and without the sounds of the film, with only its moving pictures. So visual can films be that the highly acclaimed 1924 silent German film *The Last Laugh* includes readable words only four times and then briefly at that. If you examine many movies—for example, *2001: A Space Odyssey* (1968) and *The Piano* (1993)—you will notice that many **scenes** have little or no dialogue or sign language. If you watch a foreign-language film with inadequate subtitles—and do not allow yourself to be distracted with thoughts about how annoying it is not to know all that is being said—you will notice how much you understand from the film's visuals.

Some would argue that in essence a play consists of at least one live actor who interacts with whatever other actors are involved. The actors also interact with the audience. Experienced theater actors attest to how much an alert, responsive, and supportive audience contributes to their performance. Live acting differs markedly from the rehearsed, edited, larger-than-life performances we see from different distances and angles on the movie screen. The live actor is more nearly what we see in our lives outside the theater, someone who might even occasionally look *us* in the eye, someone who makes imperfect delivery or has all-too-human movements. In small theaters where the audience is close up, live acting also seems more intimate.

Because of these basic differences between plays and films, certain changes tend to be made when a play is transformed into a film. Most film-makers want to make a film, not simply record a performance of a play. A film version of a play tends to locate some of the scenes outdoors. This process is called "opening up" the play. With more scenes, it's not unusual for a film to have more characters than its source. The film derived from a play often prunes the play's dialogue and relies more on the visuals and music and sound effects. And as we watch a film, in a sense, we get to sit in many seats, to view the action from many distances and angles.

To see some of the differences between a play and its film version, consider *Betrayal*, which was first a play (1978), then a film (1983). (That is the usual but not inevitable order of creation.) The play has nine scenes; the film has approximately forty-five. The play has four characters. The film has at least double that number, although, as in the play, only three are major.

FIGURE 5.6 **Film actors with theatrical backgrounds** In the 1912 film "Queen Elizabeth" Sarah Bernhardt, one of the most famous actors of her era, played the part with broad gestures because actors of the day had been trained to use such gestures extensively to be seen in large theaters. Actors with a background in theater had not yet learned to restrain their acting style for the movies. Frame enlargement. *The Museum of Modern Art/Film Stills Archive*

The play begins:

SCENE ONE

Pub. 1977. Spring.
Noon.

EMMA *is sitting at a corner table.* JERRY *approaches with drinks, a pint of bitter for him, a glass of wine for her.*
He sits. They smile, toast each other silently, drink.
He sits back and looks at her.

JERRY: Well . . .
EMMA: How are you?
JERRY: All right.
EMMA: You look well.
JERRY: Well, I'm not all that well, really.
EMMA: Why? What's the matter?
JERRY: Hangover.

He raises his glass.

Cheers.

He drinks.

How are you?
EMMA: I'm fine.

She looks round the bar, back at him.

Just like old times.
JERRY: Mmm. It's been a long time.
EMMA: Yes.

Pause

I thought of you the other day. (Pinter 11–12)

And they sit and drink and talk for eighteen more pages.

The film shows four wordless scenes before we see and hear the man and woman in the pub. The following is my description of the film's opening.

Scene 1. Outdoors. Seen in long shot, guests are leaving a wealthy residence, evidently after a party, as opening credits are superimposed and music is played. After all the guests have left, the camera glides forward then stops outside a window. We see a man and a woman talk but do not hear what they say. She slaps him; he slaps her back. She sits and cries. A boy enters the room. The woman gets up, goes to him, and comforts him.

Scene 2. Outdoors. Junkyard and nearby buildings in an industrial section of a city.

Scene 3. Indoors. Briefly we see the woman of scene 1 waiting at a table, presumably in a pub.

Scene 4. Outdoors. A man (not the one in scene 1) is walking toward the pub. Before entering it, he looks around.

Scene 5. Indoors. At the bar, the man from scene 4 picks up a glass of wine and
a tall glass of something else and takes them to the waiting woman. He
sits. She looks at him.

MAN: Well . . .

He toasts her.

Cheers. How are you?
WOMAN: I'm fine.

(*pause*) *She looks round the bar and back at him.*

Just like old times.
MAN: Hmmmp. It's been a long time.
WOMAN: Yes.

(*pause*)

I thought of you the other day.

The film has more scenes, more settings (indoors and out), and more details about the settings. In the film, for example, we see that the woman is
wealthy and evidently unhappy in her relationship with the man of scene 1 and
that she meets another man, who looks around before entering the pub, in an
industrial section of a city. The film, then, suggests visually that the two are
seeing each other surreptitiously. The film also has less dialogue (up to this
point, the play uses forty-five words of dialogue; the film, twenty-five). Some
of the lines in the play are reassigned to the other character. For example, in the
play Emma asks, "How are you?" and Jerry responds, "All right." In the film, the
man asks, "How are you?" and the woman replies, "I'm fine." These and other
differences show what can happen when a play is transformed into a film.

There are exceptions to these generalizations about films and plays. The
film *My Dinner with André* (1981), for example, has much in common with
traditional plays: few scenes, much dialogue, and limited visuals. Some recent
plays have much in common with films: scores of short scenes, many (minimal)
settings, and sparse dialogue.[2]

---

[2]In recent decades films increasingly influence plays, both in the writing and the staging. Sometimes films are discussed or alluded to, as in *The Baltimore Waltz* (1990), a play that refers to
the films *The Third Man* (1949); *Dr. Strangelove: Or, How I Learned to Stop Worrying and Love
the Bomb* (1963); and *Wuthering Heights* (1939). Plays may also be structured as a film typically
is. In general, more and more recent plays consist of many more brief scenes than before the
arrival of cinema. *The Baltimore Waltz*, for example has thirty scenes during its approximately
eighty minutes of playing time. A. R. Gurney's *The Dining Room* (1982) has eighteen scenes
(and nearly sixty characters) and a playing time of about ninety minutes. Often, staging is influenced by films. A 1996 production of *Four Dogs and a Bone* added video versions of imaginary
film footage made during a day's work.

Films have also been modified and staged as musical plays. Examples are *Little Shop of Horrors*,
which was a 1960 film then musical play (then a more lavish 1986 film); *Sunset Boulevard*; *Big*;
Victor/Victoria; the MGM musicals *Singin' in the Rain*, *Meet Me in St. Louis*, and *Seven Brides for
Seven Brothers*; and the Disney hits *The Little Mermaid*, *Beauty and the Beast*, and *The Lion King*.

Other Films

Some theorists refer to the relationship of a human work to other forms of human expression as **intertextual**. Films are intertextual—that is, they evoke or use other films and other forms of human expression—in a variety of ways. For example, in *What's Up, Tiger Lily?* (1966) Woody Allen took a Japanese movie and gave it a different story by adding a changed sound track in English. Some films may be doubly intertextual (Figure 5.7). Much more commonly, intertextuality in films takes the form of a remake, parody, homage (or tribute), sequel, or **prequel**.

In a remake, the original film is re-created but updated: some changes are made in the hope that the remake will seem more appealing to current audiences. Remakes are attractive to **producers** because the original film usually made a lot of money and some of the public will remember it favorably and be curious to see a more modern version of it. For economic reasons,

prequel: A narrative film made after the original film that tells a story that happens before the original.

producer: The person in charge of the business and administrative aspects of making a film, typically including acquiring rights to the script and hiring the personnel to make the film.

FIGURE 5.7 Intertextuality in a movie
Mystery Science Theater 3000: The Movie (1996) consists mainly of two robots and a man making wisecracks as they and viewers see much of the opening credits to an earlier sci-fi movie, much of the earlier sci-fi movie, and the ending credits for *Mystery Science Theater 3000*. The movie is also intextual in that many of its wisecracks refer to other creative works, such as various TV shows and such movies as *My Own Private Idaho* (1991), *Fearless* (1993), *Citizen Kane* (1941), *Harvey* (1950), *The Invisible Man* (1933), and *Casablanca* (1942). *Best Brains, Inc.; Gramercy*

then, remakes have been plentiful in Hollywood; examples with the same title are *Miracle on 34th Street* (1947 and 1994) and *Little Women* (1933, 1949, and 1994). Remakes with title changes include *The Wizard of Oz* (1939), remade as *The Wiz* (1978), and *Les Compères* (1984), remade as *Fathers' Day* (1997). It is not rare for a remake to be based on a successful foreign film; American producers seem to favor popular French originals. *Cousin, Cousine* (1975) became *Cousins* (1989); *Trois Hommes et un Couffin* (1985) became *Three Men and a Baby* (1987); and *La Cage aux Folles* (1978) was remade as *The Birdcage* (1996). In recent years, American studios have been buying remake rights to many French films, remaking them with American stars, including more action, and, as part of the original agreement, preventing the French originals from being shown in the United States. American films sometimes are remade abroad, too. The classic comedy *It Happened One Night* (1934) has twice been remade in India as *Chori Chori* (1956) and *Dil Hai Ke Manta Nahin* (1991) but with changes:

> Whenever a Hollywood film is remade in India it has to be recast in the Indian mould, that is, emotions have to be overstated, song, dances and spectacle have to be added, family relationships have to be introduced if they do not exist in the original, traditional moral values such as dharma (duty) must be reiterated and female chastity must be eulogised. (Kasbekar 389)

If you examine one of the reference books or CD-ROMs that describes and evaluates thousands of films, you may be surprised by how many hundreds and hundreds of films are remakes. A later film with the same title, however, does not guarantee that it is a remake, because many titles are reused for a quite different story (both film stories and titles get recycled, but not necessarily together).

A film may remake an earlier film or part of it, either as a parody or homage. A **parody** is an amusing imitation of unamusing human behavior, often in the form of a creative work, part of a work, or various works. In a parody viewers who know the subject being parodied recognize similarities to it yet see amusing differences. Re-creating the approximate look of a film or part of it is not the only way to parody earlier films. Parody may also result from highly selected excerpts from the original story, as in "The Fifteen Minute Hamlet" (1996), which reenacts snippets of the original play (and delivers the lines at maximum speed). For example, as Laertes is dying, he is cut off in midsentence and instead of the original "Exchange forgiveness with me noble Hamlet" we hear "Exchange forgiveness with me noble Ham."

A **feature film** may consist of parodies of a basic film type plus parts of films, as in *Fatal Instinct* (1993), a parody of **film noir** and parts from *Fatal Attraction* (1987), *Basic Instinct* (1992), *Chinatown* (1974), *Body Heat* (1981), *Double Indemnity* (1944), *Cape Fear* (1991), *Sleeping with the Enemy* (1991),

feature film: A film usually regarded as being at least sixty minutes long.

film noir: A type of film characterized by frequent scenes with dark, shadowy lighting; urban settings; and characters motivated by selfishness, greed, cruelty, ambition, and lust and characters willing to lie, frame, double-cross, and kill or have others killed.

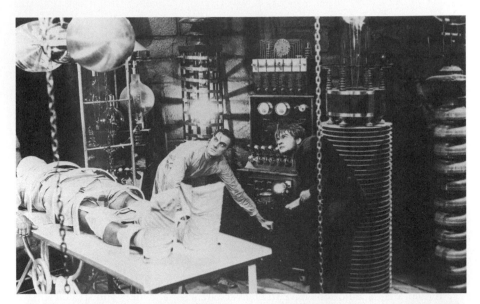

FIGURE 5.8 **A parody of a film**

(a, top) Dr. Frankenstein with his assistant, Fritz, and the body Frankenstein is attempting to bring back to life in *Frankenstein* (1931). (b, above) In a setting similar to that of the 1931 *Frankenstein*, Dr. Frankenstein (he insists that his name is pronounced "FRAHNK en steen") with his attentive laboratory assistant Inga and the body he is about to bring back to life in Mel Brooks's parody *Young Frankenstein* (1974). In many details the parody imitates the action and look of the original, but with amusing differences. The assistant, for example, is an attractive woman with makeup and long flowing hair who holds the "doctor's" hand, and Dr. Frankenstein wears a stethoscope and has a lot of bad hair days. Then, too, he is played by Gene Wilder, an actor well known for playing comic roles. *(a) Carl Laemmle; Universal; (b) 20th Century-Fox*

FIGURE 5.9 **A parody of a film genre**
The Rocky Horror Picture Show (1975) is a parody of horror films, especially various Frankenstein movies. (a, above) The Dr. Frankenstein-type character (center) is the "scientist" Dr. Frank N. Furter, a bisexual transvestite from the distant planet of Transylvania. His assistant, Riff Raff (left), at first looks and acts like Dr. Frankenstein's hunchback assistant of the 1931 Frankenstein (see Figure 5.8a). (b, left) Near the end of the movie, Riff Raff dresses (at least from the hips up) and acts as if he stepped out of a 1930s Flash Gordon movie. *20th Century-Fox*

and probably others, and as in *Spy Hard* (1996), a parody of James Bond movies and sections of *Speed* (1994), *True Lies* (1994), *Pulp Fiction* (1994), *Sister Act* (1992), *Home Alone* (1990), and other movies. A movie is rarely parodied in its entirety, though most of *Frankenstein* (1931, Figure 5.8a) is parodied by Mel Brooks's *Young Frankenstein* (1974, Figure 5.8b).

Films that parody earlier groups of movies include *The Rocky Horror Picture Show* (1975, Figure 5.9), a musical parody of mostly horror movies; *Blazing*

FIGURE 5.10 A parody of a group of films by the same director
"The Dove" (1968) parodies three films—*Wild Strawberries* (1957),
The Seventh Seal (1957), and *The Silence* (1963)—which were all
directed by Ingmar Bergman. (a, above) In Bergman's *The Seventh
Seal* the personification of death and a knight are about to begin a
game of chess that the knight hopes will allow him to escape death's
clutches. The subjects of this Bergman film are grim: plague, death,
and a crisis of faith. (b, right) In "The Dove" Death favors not chess
but badminton. This short film illustrates that the more serious the
source (a), the more amusing a parody might be. *(a) Svensk Filmindustri; The Museum of Modern Art/Film Stills Archive (b) Photo
courtesy of Liberty Studios Inc., New York*

Saddles (1974, Figure 6.21 on p. 257), a parody of western films; and "The Dove" (or "De Duva"), a 1968 film parody of some earnest films directed by Ingmar Bergman. The more unamusing the original subject and the better the viewer knows it, the more amusing the parody might be. Thus, to those who know well the early films directed by Bergman, "The Dove" is especially amusing (Figure 5.10). The Swedish of films directed by Bergman becomes the mock Swedish of "The Dove," as when Death says, "All dem peoples bin feelin my presenska zooner or latska," the English subtitle reads, "Yes, all mankind feels my presence eventually." And "He must've morten in da blacka" is translated as "He must have died at night."

Other films are parodies of the documentary film. At first, these mock documentary films seem to be factual and to follow the conventions of documentary filmmaking—interviews and subtitles, handheld camera shots, and other techniques of **cinéma vérité**—but they are amusing fictional imitations of documentary films. Examples are Albert Brooks's *Real Life* (1979), supposedly a documentary film about trying to make a documentary film about a typical American family and *This Is Spinal Tap* (1984), purportedly a documentary about an inept, aging heavy-metal band. Another example of a mock documentary is *Fear of a Black Hat* (1994)—supposedly a documentary film about the endless problems confronted by a rap group, including troubles with various recording companies, rivalry with other rap groups, and losing their managers to gunfire (six of them in a row!).

Unlike a parody, an **homage** is a tribute to an earlier film. It may be a brief reference to or an affectionate re-creation of parts of the earlier film. Examples of brief references in films to earlier films are plentiful. Filmmakers may even pay an homage to their own earlier films. In two scenes in *The Sure Thing* (1985), directed by Rob Reiner, a poster for *This Is Spinal Tap*, also directed by Reiner, is visible briefly in the background. In a scene in *Spaceballs* (1987), which was produced and directed by Mel Brooks, various videotapes are seen on a spaceship's shelf. All of them are of films directed by Brooks! In *American Graffiti* (1973) director George Lucas pays an homage to his student film and his first feature film (Figure 5.11).

Examples of homages to parts of earlier works by other (often famous) filmmakers occur in *Darby O'Gill and the Little People* (1959, Figure 5.12); near the end of *Play It Again, Sam* (1972); and in various scenes in *Ed Wood* (1994). *Play It Again, Sam* more or less re-creates part of the ending of *Casablanca* (1942); *Ed Wood* re-creates scenes from movies directed by Ed Wood, such as *Glen or Glenda* (1953) and *Plan 9 from Outer Space* (1959). *The Sure Thing* borrows so heavily from *It Happened One Night* (1934), as does *The Pallbearer* (1996) from *The Graduate* (1967), that the later films can be said to be homages to the earlier ones. Homages are usually visual, but not necessarily. In *The Long Day Closes* (1992), a boy growing up in working-class Liverpool in the 1950s raptly watches movies that viewers do not see but only hear. As viewers hear the excerpts, they can conjure up the corresponding visuals.

cinéma vérité: A style of documentary filmmaking developed in France during the early 1960s, the aim of which was to capture events as they happen with minimal interference from the filmmakers.

FIGURE 5.11 An homage to one's own work
Like a number of other directors, George Lucas has paid tribute to his own earlier work. Here the reigning speedster in *American Graffiti* (1973) drives a sporty coupe with the license plate THX 138, an homage to Lucas's 1965 USC student film and his first feature film *THX 1138* (1971). *Universal*

satire: A creative work or part of one that includes language or depictions of behavior that have as their aim the humorous criticism of individual or group behavior.

Another source for a movie is a sequel or prequel. If a film is popular and contains enough unresolved issues as it concludes and if later filmmakers see ways to continue the story and develop it, they may make a sequel. On rare occasions, a film may be a sequel to a remake; such was the case with *Father of the Bride Part II* (1995). Normally sequels are for fictional films, but a documentary film may also have one, as in "Pets or Meat: The Return to Flint" (1993)—Michael Moore's follow-up to *Roger & Me* (1989)—which shows what happened to some of the people featured in the earlier film and even more sharply **satirizes** its subjects. Another sequel to a documentary is *Best Man* (1998); this follow-up to the Academy Award-winning *Best Boy* (1979) shows how the gentle, mentally retarded subject of the earlier film fares nearly twenty years later. If the ending of a popular fictional film seems too final

FIGURE 5.12 **An homage to others' work**
This negative image of a horse-drawn coach driven by a headless coachman from *Darby O'Gill and the Little People* (1959) is an homage to the classic German vampire film *Nosferatu* (1922). In several major aspects the shot represented here imitates a striking similar shot from the earlier film. In both shots viewers see the negative image of the same subject, setting, and composition: a horse-drawn coach races along in the countryside, moving diagonally across the frame. *Walt Disney Productions*

(the main character dies, for example), a sequel based on one of the main characters' offspring may be made, as in *Son of Kong* (1933), which was made and released in the same year as *King Kong* and is a sequel to it. Since 1997, the death of a protagonist no longer precludes a sequel. Thanks to cloning, the main character of the *Alien* movies was reconstructed from leftovers before the plot of *Alien Resurrection* (1997) begins. Occasionally a **prequel** is made: a popular movie is followed by a movie depicting some of the characters from the original film at earlier stages of their lives. *Butch Cassidy and the Sundance Kid* appeared in 1969; in 1979, *Butch and Sundance: The Early Days* came out (Figure 5.13). It's also possible but rare for a film to be both a prequel and a sequel, as in the case of *The Godfather Part II* (1974), which has related events involving the same characters that precede and follow the story of *The*

FIGURE 5.13 A film and its prequel
(a, top) Robert Redford (left) as the Sundance Kid and Paul Newman as Butch Cassidy in *Butch Cassidy and the Sundance Kid* (1969). (b, above) William Katt (left) as the Sundance Kid and Tom Berenger as Butch Cassidy in the prequel *Butch and Sundance: The Early Days* (1979). *20th Century-Fox*

FIGURE 5.14 **A film's complicated ancestry**
Sometimes a film, such as *Cabaret*, has a complicated genealogy. A story—"Sally Bowles" in the 1939 book *Goodbye to Berlin* by Christopher Isherwood—was the basis for the play *I Am a Camera*, which was filmed in 1955 then made into a Broadway musical, called *Cabaret*, in 1966. The film version of *Cabaret*, with Liza Minnelli and Joel Grey (shown here), appeared in 1975. In 1998, a revamped stage musical hit Broadway, to much critical acclaim. *Allied Artists–ABC Pictures*

Godfather (1972). It's also possible to make chronologically related films in succession—such as *Star Wars* (1977), *The Empire Strikes Back* (1980), and *Return of the Jedi* (1983)—then chronologically related prequels.[3]

Although many fictional films derive from history, a novel, novella, short story, play, or previous films, some films have a more complicated ancestry. The film *Dangerous Liaisons* (1988), with a screenplay by Christopher Hampton, is based on Hampton's 1985 play *Les Liaisons Dangereuses*, but his play was based on the 1782 French novel of the same title. The 1931 film version of *Dracula* has similar sources, being based on a play, which in turn was based on the 1897 novel. Sometimes the creative family tree gets even more tangled (Figure 5.14).

---

[3]Sometimes art is an important source for films. At various times in film history, painters and other visual artists have been especially prominent in making films. Two such periods were the 1920s in Europe and the 1950s and 1960s in the United States (pop art). Filmmakers have also long learned from painters, especially in the use of lighting, composition, color, and grain. Such filmmakers as Martin Scorsese in *The Last Temptation of Christ* (1988), Stanley Kubrick in *Barry Lyndon* (1975), Tony Richardson in *Tom Jones* (1963), and Derek Jarman in *Caravaggio* (1986) have all imitated particular painters and sometimes specific paintings. In recent years, some filmmakers have made artworks, including temporary museum exhibitions involving two or more arts (installation art), and increasingly museums of modern art include video art and mixed media, such as video and sculpture.

SUMMARY

General Source: Scripts

- Typically the scriptwriter indicates the settings, dialogue, action, and structure of a fictional film and therefore by implication many of its meanings.

- Comparing a screenplay or shooting script with the finished film seldom reveals who contributed exactly what, but typically the film is more concise, less reliant on dialogue, and more visual than the script.

History

- Fictional films based on history often capture the spirit and look of the times and occurrences they represent but, for dramatic effects, usually omit, change, or fabricate events.

- Some historians contend that films of historical subjects can be alternative histories, other ways of creating (or "doing") history, though some critics fault parts of historical fictional films for making changes that serve no dramatic purpose.

Fiction

- Novels, short stories, and novellas are well suited to render a character's mental activity. Other strengths of fiction include descriptions of characters' backgrounds, analysis by the author, figurative language, and a more or less consistent point of view or means of perception.

- Film is adept at presenting sights and sounds. It can also show the nuances of faces and the infinite flexibility and expressiveness of movement. It can render the human voice and music in much of their fullness. And through editing, it can condense the time needed to present significant events and transport viewers through time and space instantaneously.

- People who admire a novel are usually disappointed with a film adaptation of it because as they read the novel, they visualized it and later usually find someone else's visualization inadequate. Then, too, a novel is usually too long and involved for a complete rendition on the screen; consequently much of it is omitted.

- A film based on a fictional source should be understood and evaluated as a film, not as adapted fiction.

Plays

▪ Plays, in general, are a verbal medium; films, a visual one. Plays filmed with minimal variations in the camera work and editing tend to be disappointing as films because they do not take advantage of film's capabilities.

▪ Fundamentally, plays rely on the give-and-take of audience and live performers, whereas films rely on the audience's responses to controlled moving images and usually a sound track.

Other Films

▪ A movie may be a remake, an amusing remake (parody), or a respectful remake of parts of an earlier film (homage).

▪ A movie may also be a sequel or, far less commonly, a prequel.

WORKS CITED

Abe, Kobo. *The Woman in the Dunes*. Trans. E. Dale Saunders. New York: Knopf, 1964.

Andrew, Dudley. *Concepts in Film Theory*. New York: Oxford UP, 1984.

Attenborough, David. "The Compulsive Communicators." *Life on Earth*. Program 13. BBC Bristol. 1979. (The wording is from the television program, not the book based on the series.)

Carson, Clayborne. "Malcolm X." *Past Imperfect: History according to the Movies*. Ed. Mark C. Carnes. New York: Holt, 1995. 278–83.

Kasbekar, Asha. "An Introduction to Indian Cinema." *An Introduction to Film Studies*. Ed. Jill Nelmes. London: Routledge, 1996. 365–91.

Painter, Nell Irvin. "Malcolm X across the Genres." *American Historical Review* 98 (1993): 432–39.

Phillips, William H. *Writing Short Scripts*, 2nd ed. Syracuse: Syracuse UP, 1999.

Pinter, Harold. *Betrayal*. New York: Grove, 1979.

Rosenstone, Robert A. *Visions of the Past: The Challenge of Film to Our Idea of History*. Cambridge: Harvard UP, 1995.

Stanley, Alessandra. "Surviving and Disturbing in Moscow." *New York Times* 21 Mar. 1995, natl. ed.: B1+.

Toplin, Robert Brent. *History by Hollywood: The Use and Abuse of the American Past*. Urbana: U of Illinois P, 1996.

The Third Man: A Film by Graham Greene and Carol Reed. New York: Simon, 1968.

FOR FURTHER READING

Armes, Roy. *Action and Image: Dramatic Structure in Cinema*. Manchester, Eng.: Manchester UP, 1994. The first of the book's three parts, "Film as Drama," consists of four chapters: "Readings and Viewings," "Showing and Telling," "Text and Performance," and "Stage and Screen."

Atkins, Robert. *ArtSpeak: A Guide to Contemporary Ideas, Movements, and Buzzwords*. New York: Abbeville, 1990. Short entries on terms used in art, including some terms used in film studies.

Bluestone, George. *Novels into Film: The Metamorphosis of Fiction into Cinema*. Baltimore: Johns Hopkins UP, 1957. Includes chapter titled "The Limits of the Novel and the Limits of the Film" plus chapters on six films adapted from famous novels.

McFarland, Brian. *Novel to Film: An Introduction to the Theory of Adaptation*. New York: Oxford UP, 1996. An examination of fiction and film with examples from such book and film versions as *The Scarlet Letter* and *Cape Fear*.

Manvell, Roger. *Theater and Film: A Comparative Study of the Two Forms of Dramatic Art, and of the Problems of Adaptation of Stage Plays into Films*. Rutherford, NJ: Fairleigh Dickinson UP, 1979. "Part I: Stage Play and Screenplay: Forms and Principles"; "Part II: Examples of Adaptation from Stage to Screen." Appendix C: "Select List of Dramatists Whose Plays Have Been Filmed."

Revisioning History: Film and the Construction of a New Past. Ed. Robert A. Rosenstone. Princeton: Princeton UP, 1995. Theoretical issues about films based on history.

CHAPTER 6

Types of Fictional Films

FICTIONAL FILMS ARE ENORMOUSLY POPULAR, numerous, and enduring. Perhaps that is why critics and scholars often try to classify them. Seeing similarities and patterns helps viewers place a film in context and understand it more completely. Considering some of the types of fictional films also helps viewers understand the properties and potentials of the film medium.

    Documentary, **avant-garde**, and **hybrid films** are major alternatives to fictional films, but those groupings of films are so large that they are treated in a separate chapter. In this chapter we will examine some ways to group fictional films: classical Hollywood cinema—the most popular and influential type of fictional film—Italian neorealist cinema, French new wave cinema, and independent films. Although various groupings of films are discussed in this chapter and Chapter 8, it is important to remember that filmmakers are not ruled by formulas or textbooks; they may be influenced by such matters as intuition, creativity, cinematic traditions, demographic patterns (such as the percentage of teens who attend movies), and box office potential. As a consequence, some films are not exclusively one type.

CLASSICAL HOLLYWOOD CINEMA

> The film experience resembles a fun house attraction, a wild ride, the itinerary of which has been calculated in advance but is unknown to the spectator. By spurts and stops, twists and roller coaster plunges, we are taken through a dark passage, alert and anxious, yet confident we shall return satisfied and unharmed. (Andrew 144)

Film scholars have explored many ways of grouping fictional films. David Bordwell, Janet Staiger, and Kristin Thompson studied representative American films across the years to see if they could discover recurrent stylistic

documentary film: A film that presents a version of actions and happenings that viewers are intended to accept not primarily as the product of someone's imagination but primarily as fact.

avant-garde film: A film that rejects the conventions of popular movies and explores the possibilities of the film medium itself.

hybrid film: A film that is not simply fictional or documentary or avant-garde, but instead shares characteristics of two or all three of the major types of films.

convention: In films and other creative works, a frequently used technique or content that audiences tend to accept without question.

conventions (3). In their influential book *The Classical Hollywood Cinema: Film Style and Mode of Production to 1960* and elsewhere, Bordwell, Staiger, and Thompson argue that most American feature films have shared certain qualities that will be explained in this section.

Characteristics of Classical Hollywood Cinema

According to Bordwell, Staiger, and Thompson (1–84), **classical Hollywood cinema** tends to have the following characteristics:

1. The story is mainly set in a present, external world and is largely seen from outside the action, although **point-of-view shots**, memories, fantasies, dreams, or other mental states are sometimes included.

2. The film focuses on one character or a few distinct individuals.

3. The main characters have a goal or a few goals.

4. In trying to attain their goals, the main characters must confront various antagonists or problems.

5. The film has **closure**: the plot has no "loose ends," and usually in American movies the main characters succeed in reaching the goals (happy endings).

6. The emphasis is on clear causes and effects of actions: what events happen and why are clear and unambiguous.

7. The film uses **continuity editing** and other unobtrusive filmmaking **techniques**.

point-of-view shot: Camera placement at the approximate position of a character or person that gives a view similar to what that creature would see.

continuity editing: Film editing that maintains a sense of continuous action and continuous setting within each scene of a narrative film.

technique: Any aspect of filmmaking, such as the choices of sets, lighting, and editing.

The First Wives Club (1996) can serve as an example of classical Hollywood cinema (Figure 6.1).

Bordwell, Staiger, and Thompson argue that in American films of recent decades, "the classical paradigm continues to flourish, partly by absorbing current topics of interest and partly by perpetuating seventy-year-old assumptions about what a film is and does" (372). They also point out that many foreign films exemplify the traits of classical Hollywood cinema.

So widely seen is classical Hollywood cinema that it has influenced virtually all **narrative films**: filmmakers either imitate characteristics of classical Hollywood cinema or decide not to.

narrative: A series of unified consecutive events situated in one or more settings.

Film Genres: Related Films

Action, war, western, comedy, science fiction, horror, mystery/suspense, drama, family, and children. Sound familiar? These divisions are commonly used in video stores. They are attempts to divide films into major types, in this case for ease of marketing. Many other films are seen as part of a group,

FIGURE 6.1 Classical Hollywood cinema

The First Wives Club (1996) is about how three middle-aged women, discarded by their husbands for younger women, bond and get revenge, or, some would say, justice. Like most popular movies, it exhibits all the characteristics of classical Hollywood cinema. The story is set in the present world and is largely seen from outside the action, although occasional point-of-view shots are included. The movie focuses on three distinct characters that soon share the same goal. In pursuing that goal, they confront a variety of problems, including resistance from their husbands and at one point a major falling-out among themselves. The film has closure: by the end viewers have no major unanswered questions, and there is no uncertainty as to what happens and why. Like most movies of classical Hollywood cinema, the ending is happy for those in the audience it intends to please. Finally, the film never uses distracting techniques; most viewers watch it without noticing, for example, anything about the film's compositions, camera work, or editing. Frame enlargement. *Scott Rudin; Paramount*

such as adaptations of literature (movies based on the novels of Jane Austen or the plays of Shakespeare), road movies, urban comedies, and ethnic films. Filmmakers, film critics, film scholars, and film viewers all think of films in terms of categories, though for different reasons.

Most films of the classical Hollywood cinema are genre films or members of a widely recognized group of films. Exactly what constitutes a film genre (or type) and which films belong to it is subject to much debate. For our purposes

setting: The place where filmed action occurs.

we can think of film **genres** as commonly recognized groups of films—such as the western, musical, romantic comedy, detective, gangster, science fiction, horror, and war—that share characteristics and evolve, but the criteria for one genre differ from those for another genre and different critics and scholars define particular genres in somewhat different ways. Westerns, for example, tend to share the same basic conflict and usually the same **setting**: civilization versus the wilderness west of the Mississippi River, in northern Mexico, or in the Canadian Rockies. Detective films all share the same basic story: the uncovering of causes (who did what when). In musicals, singing and usually dancing are more prominent than they would be in similar situations in life and in other films.

Since filmmakers and experienced film viewers share a sense of what constitutes a particular genre, filmmakers can follow the traditions of the genre and thus reassure audiences; or reject the genre's conventions and thereby amuse, shock, or disturb viewers; or in some ways reassure audiences but in other ways reject some of the genre conventions. Sometimes genres evolve because social attitudes change. Many westerns before World War II depicted Native Americans in negative ways that encouraged European Americans to continue to think of themselves as superior. An example can be seen in the comedy western *My Little Chickadee* (1940), which consistently depicts Native Americans in stereotypical ways and as the butt of tired jokes. But later westerns such as *Little Big Man* (1970) and *Dances with Wolves* (1990) show American Indians in a far more sympathetic light, in fact sometimes more favorably than they do the European American settlers. Makers of genre films also cannot help being influenced by previous films of the same genre. They may not set out to imitate earlier films, or to reject the genre's fundamentals, or to follow the genre in some ways and change it in others, but inevitably they do. Let's consider two genres: the western and film noir.

THE WESTERN   Since at least as early as "The Great Train Robbery" (1903, Figure 6.2) and throughout most of the twentieth century, audiences have enjoyed western films. Westerns have proven so popular and enduring that they have been made in many countries, including Italy, Mexico, Spain, and East Germany. "Between 1965 and 1983, the East German studio . . . produced 14 westerns. Shot on location in Yugoslavia, Czechoslovakia, Romania, Bulgaria, the Soviet Union and Cuba, and usually starring a hulking former physical-education instructor . . . , these so-called *Indianerfilme* are as clumsy and predictable as many of Hollywood's cowboy films. There is one notable distinction: in East German westerns, the American Indians are always the good guys" (Shulman).

Typically the setting of a western film is the United States plains, Rockies, the Northwest, the Southwest, northern Mexico, or perhaps the Canadian Rockies, and usually some shots linger on the vastness, openness, beauty, and occasionally menace of the terrain. The usual focus of westerns is people who

FIGURE 6.2 **An early western**
"The Great Train Robbery"
(1903), which was an enormously
popular film in its time, includes
what was to become the basic story
of many western films: a threat
to civilization in the West (outlaws enacting a crime) and the
eventual re-establishment of order
(outlaws getting killed). Frame
enlargement. *Edison*

stand for law and order, for settling and taming the West (often territories before they become states), for bringing to the wild the civilization of the eastern
United States or Europe (often women serve this last role). Symptomatic of the
transformations celebrated in westerns are lines from two westerns: in *Bend
of the River* (1952) a settler says, "We'll use the trees that nature has given us.
Cut a clearing in the wilderness. We'll put in roads. . . . Then we'll build our
homes. . . . There'll be a meeting house, a church. We'll have a school. Then
we'll put down seedlings . . ." and near the end of *The Man Who Shot Liberty
Valance* (1962), the main woman character says of the area now settled, "It
was once a wilderness. Now it's a garden." To achieve the western's goals,
those who represent civilization usually have showdowns and shootouts with
one or more of the following: Native Americans, Mexicans, and the men who
wear black hats. Makers of westerns work variations, slight or major, on the
generic western.

A good example of a film that fits into the parameters of the generic
western is *Shane* (1953). The film is situated in the western United States
and focuses on the attempts of a small community of settlers—families that
grow gardens and raise pigs, chickens, and dairy cows—to resist a greedy and
powerful cattle baron who finally hires one of those lean, mean men wearing
a black hat. Ultimately the forces of civilization prevail: the hired gun and

his employer are killed in the final showdown and shootout and the unhired gun who defends the community (Shane) is self-exiled presumably because he knows that henceforth he will be in the way of family and community.

Most westerns directed by John Ford are generic but not without complexities, subtleties, and surprises, including music, dancing, and humor. In many respects Ford's *My Darling Clementine* (1946) reenacts the generic western story. The film's basic conflict involves the attempt of Wyatt Earp and his brothers to establish order in a town (which includes reining in the ill, troubled, and dangerous Doc Holliday) and bringing the murderers of their eighteen-year-old brother to justice. Another important conflict is between Chihuahua—the sensual, emotional Mexican saloon singer—and Clementine, the less sensual, more emotionally restrained Boston nurse. By the end of the film, the drunken, unruly Native American has been silenced and disappears from the movie screen; the crooked professional gambler has been run out of town; a traveling actor has recited Shakespeare, the quintessence of British culture. The town's first church has been dedicated, and an outdoor dance held as American flags blow in the breeze; Chihuahua, the dishonest and unfaithful Mexican beauty, has died; and Clementine—the re-

FIGURE 6.3 Generic western
Although *My Darling Clementine* (1946) surprises viewers with its low-key Marshal Earp, a complex Doc Holliday, and the lack of closure to the budding Wyatt Earp–Clementine Carter romance, the film is a generic western. In this frame enlargement from the film's last shot, Earp is seen riding away from Clementine toward the wilderness, Monument Valley. Most of the basics of westerns such as *Shane* and *The Searchers* are contained within this image: the wilderness and the promise of domesticity, and a tug of allegiance for a man between them. Frame enlargement. *Samuel G. Engel; 20th Century-Fox*

FIGURE 6.4 **Skill and power protecting law and order from violence and disorder**
The mise en scène of this publicity still for *The Man Who Shot Liberty Valance* (1962) summarizes much of the film: between the gunslinger on the left, Liberty Valance, and the civil man skillful in the use of force is the new and evidently only lawyer in town, who's been robbed and reduced temporarily to working in a saloon. The men in the background are uninvolved because Liberty has already intimidated them. *John Ford Productions and Paramount*

strained, churchgoing easterner—plans to stay and teach school. Most significantly, two of the four Earp brothers survive. They are leaving, although Wyatt may return to Clementine. He has achieved what he set out to do: see that the evil ones are brought to justice (though at the cost of brothers and sons killed) and order established in the town. Civilization as many European Americans might think of it is coming to the dusty desert community of 1882 Tombstone, Arizona (Figure 6.3).

Sometimes viewers enjoy having their expectations gratified by a conventional genre film. Other times, viewers enjoy seeing how a group of filmmakers takes a genre and makes major variations on it. John Ford's *Two Rode Together* (1961) may at first look generic, but the town lacks community; the settlers seeking their relatives long lost to Comanches are largely misguided or delusional; the soldiers lack the camaraderie of earlier Ford westerns; the soldiers and their wives are intolerant of an outsider; and the two central figures, a civilian and a military man, fall short of the usual western heroes, the civilian (a marshal preoccupied with money) especially so. In short, the "civilization" the European Americans are trying to bring to the wilderness is more than a little suspect. *The Man Who Shot Liberty Valance* also exhibits major creative variations of the western. Here the agent of civilization is a man of the law, in this case a lawyer, who doubles as a teacher of English and civics, but, like *Shane*, the film shows that without the power conferred by skill in using a gun, the agent of law and order is helpless in the face of a bullying murderer (Figure 6.4). *The Man Who Shot Liberty Valance* also shows that legend masks the truth, in this case of the real hero's bravery and integrity.

In more recent years, most westerns have been so atypical as to be called revisionist: they revise or challenge long-held views, the long-standing and

FIGURE 6.5 A 1950s revisionist western

The Searchers (1956), directed by John Ford from a script by Frank Nugent, begins in 1868 with Ethan Edwards (on the right) arriving at his brother's ranch in Texas. Here we see Ethan shortly after the reunion with his brother, nephew, two nieces, and sister-in-law, Martha. Ethan proves to be a complex hero, unlike any seen in westerns before and few since. He has many of the typical western hero's qualities—including knowledge of a Native Indian culture, skill with guns and horses, bravery, self-sacrifice, and perseverance. It is also hinted through such details as the tender way Martha hangs up Ethan's coat that the two share deep though undefined feelings: he seems worthy of an admirable woman's love. However, Ethan is also consumed by vengeance and doomed to remain an outsider. The film's memorable last shot shows him with his mission finally accomplished but ignored by a family and outside the door leading into a home from which he turns and walks away. Then that door closes on his image in the windy wilderness, and darkness fills the screen. In *The Searchers* the main agent of European American civilization is flawed and without a place in an enclave in the wild, without a place to hang his coat or have it hung. *Warner Bros.*

---

fundamental traditions of the western film. *Unforgiven* (1992) is an example. Its subject and setting make it instantly recognizable as a western, but for those who have seen many westerns, the film has many big surprises. The major antagonist is not a Native American, Mexican, or an evil cowboy but the sheriff himself; he's so brutal the townspeople are both embarrassed and afraid when he starts (literally) kicking someone around. The film's killings, which are committed in the name of justice, are based on rumor and soft moral grounds and are not easily executed; they're messy, excruciating, and in one instance protracted. Perhaps most surprisingly, the hero is not a macho cowboy. He is an aging pig farmer aching to forget his past and to be left alone and longing for his deceased wife, who helped him give up alcohol and helped civilize him. Furthermore, the hero has a nagging conscience: he regrets murders he committed years before.

Most westerns since about 1950 have been revisionist, though few as strikingly so as *Unforgiven*. Fifties revisionist westerns include *Broken Arrow* (1950), which depicts Native Americans at least as sympathetically as the European settlers; *High Noon* (1952), which attacks the cowardly group behavior of townspeople afraid of or sympathetic to those in black hats; and *The Searchers* (1956), which shows the human cost of pursuing vengeance long-term (Figure 6.5).

Later revisionist westerns include the 1960s "spaghetti westerns" directed by Sergio Leone in Italy, which show the characters as more gross and brutal than in the 1950s westerns; *The Wild Bunch* (1969), which features violent outlaw heroes that many disillusioned viewers of the late 1960s could relate to; and *Little Big Man*, which castigates the western settlers and sympathizes with Native Americans. *McCabe and Mrs. Miller* (1971) has a disorganized setting (Figure 6.6) and two central characters who are not settlers bringing

FIGURE 6.6 Revisionist depiction of western settings
Unlike most earlier western movies, *McCabe and Mrs. Miller* (1971), which was filmed on location, teems with the messiness of life. Even the film's weather is untraditional for westerns: except for a few shots, it is persistently gloomy and the color is desaturated throughout. At the beginning of the story, the air is so cold and drizzly that McCabe wears a huge animal coat to try to stay warm and dry. Later there is lots of mud, rain, gray skies, and fallen snow, light snowing, then near the end heavy snowing. Throughout most of the exterior scenes, there is also an unfriendly howling wind, which is loudest at the film's end. *David Foster & Mitchell Brower; Warner Bros.*

FIGURE 6.7 A 1990s revisionist western
Tombstone (1993) is yet another western featuring a Wyatt Earp (right), but in this movie Earp tries to retire from law enforcement and remain faithful to a temperamental wife addicted to opium. The film also features Earp's two brothers (center) and his close friend Doc Holliday (left), who quotes Latin, plays Chopin, speaks sardonically, draws a gun even more quickly than Earp, drinks heavily, and overexerts himself although he is dying from TB. So revisionist is the film that the good guys wear black, stylishly at that. Frame enlargement. *Buena Vista Pictures*

socially acceptable goods or services but a practical, opium-smoking prostitute and madam and "an enterprising, nonheroic type" (Lenihan 164) of businessman pimp who is too naive and proud to see when to cut a deal with those with power.

In recent years, revisionist westerns include *Tombstone* (1993), which, like *My Darling Clementine*, is set in the Arizona territory and focuses on Wyatt Earp. In *Tombstone*, Earp wants to put his law enforcement days behind him, go into business, and enjoy his extended family, but widespread lawlessness makes that impossible until he, his two brothers, and Doc Holliday use force to establish law and order (Figure 6.7). *The Ballad of Little Jo* (1993) shows the trials, triumphs, and civilizing effects (such as compassion) of a woman in the man's world of 1870s Montana territory (Figure 6.8). Another recent western that focuses on a group usually on the periphery of

FIGURE 6.8 A feminist revisionist western

In *The Ballad of Little Jo* (1993), (a, left) Josephine Monaghan is first seen dressed much as she is here, carrying a suitcase and protecting her head from the sun with a parasol. Viewers eventually learn that she has had a baby out of wedlock and been exiled by her family. (b, right) In the West, men menace her—she is nearly raped—so to avoid further danger and abuse, Josephine becomes Jo by inflicting a scar on her cheek, dressing as a man, and gradually learning how to act as one. Unlike most westerns, *The Ballad of Little Jo* stresses both the limited options available to nineteenth-century American women and the civilizing influences that a woman doing men's work could bring to the wild West. *Fine Line Features*

FIGURE 6.9 An African American revisionist western

Posse (1993)—which focuses on five African Americans and one European American (four of the group are shown here)—gives a contemporary African American perspective on a group rarely seen in mainstream westerns, even in recent years. In *Posse*, blacks do not face opposition from the usual western antagonists, such as native American Indians, Mexicans, or an assortment of obvious outlaws. Instead, they have to contend with the white power structure. The posse's major antagonists are two European Americans: a cruel, corrupt army officer and his motley band of Spanish-American War veterans eager to steal war booty from the "posse" and to exact revenge and a racist, greedy, power-hungry sheriff and his followers who years earlier had killed blacks with impunity. It is not clear if the white sheriff and his followers constitute the local version of the KKK or if that is a separate group, but the KKK is also a threat. Another problem for the African American community is that the black marshal of an all-black town has naively struck an illegal business deal with the racist white sheriff then fails to oppose him when the sheriff treats blacks unjustly. Frame enlargement. *Gramercy Pictures*

westerns, if included at all, is *Posse* (1993); most of its main characters are African American (Figure 6.9). *Bad Girls* (1994) also focuses on characters normally peripheral in the conventional western, prostitutes (Figure 6.10). *Wild Bill* (1995, Figure 6.11) is set in the wild West, but unlike most westerns is not so much about the bringing of civilization to the West as the powers of celebrity and problems a man may face: VD, glaucoma, lack of emotional intimacy, a poor sex life, and depression.

FIGURE 6.10 Taming the wild West
Throughout *Bad Girls* (1994) the four major women characters fight back against any injustice. Initially, they are prostitutes wronged by men's laws but when provoked they outsmart, outride, and outshoot the men. Early in the film one of them catches up with a runaway horse-drawn carriage, jumps into it, and reins it to a halt. Among their many accomplishments as a group are rescuing one of their own from being hanged, killing four armed outlaws, and evading two detectives on their trail. While they are at it, two of them also win the love of two attractive young men. In their own fashion, they help tame the West. Frame enlargement. *20th Century-Fox*

FIGURE 6.11 A love life in a revisionist western
Most of *Wild Bill* (1995) shows events from the last days of Wild Bill Hickok's life in 1876, with flashbacks to crucial events in 1861. By the last months in his thirty-ninth year, Wild Bill has become a "drifter" suffering from impending blindness, doubts, and disquieting dreams and passing time with poker, drink, and opium. Calamity Jane, with whom he formerly enjoyed a healthy love life, continues to show her love and desire for him. For his part, Bill is undemonstrative and only once "in the mood." The film's narrator, Bill's best friend, says, "Typical for a man of action, Bill found romance the most perplexing aspect of his life." Frame enlargement. *United Artists Pictures*

FILM NOIR

> This large body of films, flourishing in America in the period 1941–58 [from *The Maltese Falcon* to *Touch of Evil*], generally focuses on urban crime and corruption, and on sudden upwellings of violence in a culture whose fabric seems to be unraveling. Because of these typical concerns, the *film noir* seems fundamentally *about* violations: vice, corruption, unrestrained desire, and, most fundamental of all, abrogation of the American dream's most basic promises—of hope, prosperity, and safety from persecution. (Telotte 2)

style: The manner of presenting a subject in a creative work.

Another major genre is **film noir**. As critic and scholar R. Barton Palmer has written, "Of all the studio **styles**—including such favorites as westerns and musicals—the film noir has received the most attention from critics since film study became a respectable discipline within the American academy [even though its] . . . complex history . . . has made its definition somewhat elusive" (ix). *Film noir* is a partial translation of *cinéma noir* (black or dark cinema), a term first used by some French critics to describe a group of American films made during and after World War II. Different critics and scholars define the term differently, as a genre, "sub-genre of the crime thriller or gangster movie," movement, "quasigeneric category," "fluid concept," mode, mood, style, visual style, or "stylistic and narrative tendency." But here and in other sources, film noir stands for a film genre whose films tend to have frequent **scenes** with dark, shadowy (**low-key**) **lighting** (often including shots with shadows made by open venetian blinds, as in Figures 6.16 and 6.20) and many night scenes (Figure 6.12). Other characteristics of film noir are urban settings and characters who are motivated by selfishness, greed, cruelty, and ambition and are willing to lie, frame, double-cross, and kill or have killed (Figure 6.13). Often films noirs are fatalistic, and the main characters seem doomed to fail. In *Detour* (1945), for example, we hear such lines as "Until then, I'd done things my way, but from then on something else stepped in and shunted me off to a different destination than the one I had picked for myself" and "That's life. Whichever way you turn, Fate sticks out a foot to trip you." Films noirs tend to exhibit embittered or cynical moods and to be compressed and convoluted, as in *Double Indemnity* (1944), which begins and ends in the present and has five flashbacks, and *Out of the Past* (1947), which also includes flashbacks.

scene: A section of a narrative film that gives the impression of continuous action taking place during one continuous time and space.

low-key lighting: Lighting with predominant dark tones, often deep dark tones.

Because these films were made when the American production code was strongly enforced (see pp. 384–89), characters who go astray are eventually punished. By the end of *Murder, My Sweet* (1944), for example, the three who commit murder have murdered each other; by the end of *The Lady from Shanghai* (1948), the three lethal characters have also killed each other. Near the end of *Force of Evil* (1948), the three major criminal characters confront one another in a dark room; two get shot; then the third calls the police and says he'll be turning himself in.

FIGURE 6.12 Film noir lighting and darkness
This still closely approximates the last shot of *The Big Combo* (1955), cinematography by John Alton, who later wrote a book on cinematography, *Painting with Light*. In Todd McCarthy's introduction to a reprinting of that book, McCarthy writes, "In fashioning the nocturnal world inhabited by noir's desperate characters, Alton was ever consistent and imaginative in forging his signature, illuminating scenes with single lamps, slanted and fragmented beams and pools of light, all separated by intense darkness in which the source of all fear could fester and finally thrive.... Often, the light would just manage to catch the rim of a hat, the edge of a gun, the smoke from a cigarette. Actors' faces, normally the object of any cameraman's most ardent attention, were often invisible or obscured, with characters from *T-Men* to, perhaps most memorably, *The Big Combo* playing out their fates in silhouette against a witheringly blank, impassive background.... [In *The Big Combo*] Alton pushed his impulse toward severe black-and-white contrasts and silhouetting of characters to the limit.... And the final shot, with the figures of a man and woman outlined ... against a foggy nightscape and illuminated by a single beacon [beyond the fog and midway between the man's head and the woman's], makes one of the quintessentially anti-sentimental noir statements about the place of humanity in the existential void" (x, xxix). *Sidney Harmon; Allied Artists*

Often films noirs feature a femme fatale, invariably an attractive, young, worldly woman who thinks and acts quickly and is verbally adroit, manipulative, evasive, sexy, dangerous, perhaps even lethal, especially to men who succumb to her wiles and charms—and many do (Figure 6.14). In *The Lady from Shanghai* she is a Circe who figuratively enchains her husband's business

FIGURE 6.13 Film noir classic
Touch of Evil (1958), which some critics regard as the last of the classic films noirs, has all the characteristics of film noir, including many scenes with dark, shadowy (low-key) lighting and as the central character a police detective (shown here) who's shrewd, driven, complex, and flawed. (The horns behind the actor's head are probably not accidental in this posed publicity still.) *Albert Zugsmith; Universal*

partner and nearly lures the film's central character to his doom (Figure 6.15). In *Criss Cross* (1949) the self-centered and monetary motives of the femme fatale are hidden from both the viewers and the main character—a naive young man who has had trouble living with her but cannot live without her—until it is too late. In *Out of the Past*, the femme fatale is so dangerous that when another woman character says of her, "She can't be all bad. No one is," the Robert Mitchum character, who is no innocent yet succumbs to her more than once, replies, "Well, she comes the closest."

The changing role of women in American society has influenced film noir. During World War II women were urged to take over factory jobs traditionally held by men, and millions did. After the war, the men returned and displaced the women workers, often unceremoniously. The self-sufficiency many women showed during the war doubtless threatened many men, perhaps including those involved in making films noirs. "A large number of the postwar *noir* thrillers are concerned to some degree with the problems represented by women who seek satisfaction and self-definition outside the traditional contexts of marriage and family" (Krutnik 61). Preeminent in this group of women characters are those femmes fatales.

Other influences on films noirs were a reaction to both the brightly lit studio entertainment films of the 1930s and the nationalistic films of World War II and German and Austrian immigrant filmmakers attuned to **expressionistic** lighting and **mise en scène**. The detective fiction of such writers as Raymond Chandler, Dashiell Hammett, and James M. Cain was a major influence and provided sources for some major film noir scripts. Yet another influence was the unsettled times, the disorientation and lack of clear identity many experienced after surviving the severe economic depression of the 1930s then the massive casualties, genocide, torture, and atomic clouds of World War II. Symptomatic of the lack of purpose in films noirs is the following exchange between a young woman and detective Philip Marlowe in *Murder, My Sweet*:

> ANN GRAYLE: You go barging around without a very clear idea what you're doing. Everybody bats you down, smacks you over the head, fills you full of stuff, and you keep right on hitting between tackle and end. I don't think you even know which side you're on.
>
> MARLOWE: I don't know which side anybody's on. I don't even know who's playing today.

Many film scholars see the 1941 version of *The Maltese Falcon* as the first film noir, and though that film has most of the characteristics outlined here, it is not nearly as dark and shadowed as many later films noirs. Other members of this group of films are *Double Indemnity* (Figure 6.16); *Murder, My Sweet*; *Detour*; *The Big Sleep* (1946); *Out of the Past*; *The Lady from Shanghai*; *Force of Evil*; *Criss Cross*; *The Big Combo* (1955); and *Touch of Evil* (1958).

Some later American color films are film noir or have been influenced by it—such as *Chinatown* (1974, Figure 6.17); *Body Heat* (1981, Figure 6.18); *Pulp Fiction* (1994); *Fargo* (1996, Figure 6.19); *Devil in a Blue Dress*

expressionism: A style of art, literature, drama, and film used early in the twentieth century the primary goal of which is not to depict external realities but to convey the artists' imaginations and their feelings about themselves and their subjects or to convey the characters' states of mind.

mise en scène ("meez ahn sen"): The setting, subject (usually people or characters), and composition (the arrangement of setting and subjects within the frame).

FIGURE 6.14 A femme fatale
Like most femmes fatales in films noirs, the Jane Greer character in *Out of the Past* (1947) is young, worldly, attractive, calculating, resourceful, and charming when need be and gets her way with men, including the Robert Mitchum character. *RKO General Pictures*

FIGURE 6.15 **Various faces of a femme fatale**
Rita Hayworth as the femme fatale in *The Lady from Shanghai* (1948). (a, top) She is on the deck of a boat singing, and her song lures the main male character up to the deck; she's a Circe. (b, middle) The background reminds viewers she doesn't obey laws. (c, bottom) By the end of the film, she has pulled a gun on her husband and is ready to kill him in a fun house full of mirrors. She does, but the film was released in 1948 and was subject to the production code, so she does not go unpunished. Frame enlargements. *Columbia*

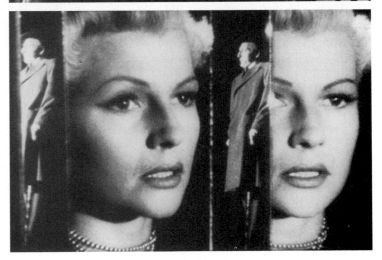

FIGURE 6.16 Femme fatale and the male animal
The Barbara Stanwyck character, who proves to be a poised femme fatale, and the gullible Fred MacMurray character leaning forward eagerly in the classic film noir *Double Indemnity* (1944). As in so many film noir scenes, the background shadows are made presumably by sunlight through open venetian blinds. *Joseph Sistrom; Paramount*

FIGURE 6.17 A night scene in a modern film noir
Detective Jake Gittes gets his nose cut by two thugs hired to help guard secrets in the night. In its night scenes filled with mystery, danger, and violence and in its lying, duplicitous, and murderous antagonists, *Chinatown* (1974) is a film noir in color. Like so many films noirs, it also includes interiors with the shadows of venetian blinds against the walls. *Long Road Productions, Paramount*

FIGURE 6.18 **A femme fatale in a post–production code film noir**
Body Heat (1981) was made after the production code was abolished in 1968 and a ratings system instituted. In *Body Heat* the woman uses the gullible male and goes unpunished. *The Ladd Company; Warner Bros.*

FIGURE 6.19 **Noirish aspects of a 1990s movie**
In its many dark scenes and malevolent characters, as illustrated here, and in a plot whose events spin unexpectedly out of control, *Fargo* (1996) has been labeled film noir, or at least influenced by it. *Gramercy Pictures*

A Femme Fatale in Action

The following excerpt is from the screenplay for the classic film noir, *Double Indemnity* (1944), screenplay by Billy Wilder and Raymond Chandler, which in turn is based on the novel by James M. Cain. (The following screenplay excerpt is reprinted in Raymond Chandler's *Later Novels and Other Writings*, 1995.) The movie follows the excerpt closely but not slavishly, pruning words and lines and changing a few words. Nonetheless, the situation of the excerpt and corresponding section of the film is classic film noir: a man, who is eager and gullible, is outmatched by an attractive, dangerous woman unhappy in her marriage. She is a *femme* who in more than one sense is *fatale*.

The doorbell rings. Neff goes to the door and opens it, revealing Phyllis standing there.

PHYLLIS: Hello. (*As Neff just looks at her in amazement.*) You forgot your hat this afternoon. (*She has nothing in her hands but her bag.*)
NEFF: Did I? (*He looks down at her hands.*)
PHYLLIS: Don't you want me to bring it in?
NEFF: Sure. Put it on the chair. (*She comes in. He closes the door.*) How did you know where I live?
PHYLLIS: It's in the phone book. (*Neff switches on the standing lamp.*) It's raining.
NEFF: So it is. Peel off your coat and sit down. (*She starts to take off her coat.*) Your husband out?
PHYLLIS: Long Beach. They're spudding in a new well. He phoned he'd be late. About nine-thirty. (*He takes her coat and lays it across the back of a chair.*) It's about time you said you're glad to see me.
NEFF: I knew you wouldn't leave it like that.
PHYLLIS: Like what?
NEFF: Like it was this afternoon.
PHYLLIS: I must have said something that gave you a terribly wrong impression. You must surely see that. You must never think anything like that about me, Walter.

NEFF: Okay.
PHYLLIS: It's not okay. Not if you don't believe me.
NEFF: What do you want me to do?
PHYLLIS: I want you to be nice to me. Like the first time you came to the house.
NEFF: It can't be like the first time. Something has happened.
PHYLLIS: I know it has. It's happened to us.
NEFF: That's what I mean.

Phyllis has moved over to the window. She stares out through the wet windowpane.

NEFF: What's the matter now?
PHYLLIS: I feel as if he was watching me. Not that he cares about me. Not any more. But he keeps me on a leash. So tight I can't breathe. I'm scared.
NEFF: What of? He's in Long Beach, isn't he?
PHYLLIS: I oughtn't to have come.
NEFF: Maybe you oughtn't.
PHYLLIS: You want me to go?
NEFF: If you want to.
PHYLLIS: Right now?
NEFF: Sure. Right now.

By this time, he has hold of her wrists. He draws her to him slowly and kisses her. Her arms tighten around him. After a moment he pulls his head back, still holding her close.—Then they break away from each other, and she puts her head on his shoulder.

NEFF: I'm crazy about you, baby.
PHYLLIS: I'm crazy about you, Walter.
NEFF: That perfume on your hair. What's the name of it?
PHYLLIS: I don't know. I bought it down at Ensenada.
NEFF: We ought to have some of that pink wine to go with it. The kind that bubbles. But all I have is bourbon.
PHYLLIS: Bourbon is fine, Walter.

255

FIGURE 6.20 Continuing popularity of film noir
Well into the 1990s, many films noirs continued to be made. By anyone's definition of the term, *L.A. Confidential* (1997) is film noir or, more precisely, film noir in color. (a, right) As in many films noirs, in *L.A. Confidential* light and shadows from partially opened venetian blinds illuminate several interior scenes. Here a meeting of Los Angeles police detectives has been called to announce the discovery of multiple murders, including the killing of a recently discharged police detective, the partner of Bud White, seen here in the frame's center. (b, below) As in all films noirs, the main characters tend to be flawed, dangerous, and hard to figure out. A good example is the police captain, Dudley Smith, seen here looking toward a car that Bud White had abruptly driven away in after seeing Captain Smith supervising the beating of yet another out-of-town hoodlum hoping to set up in Los Angeles. Part of the continuing appeal of films noirs in the 1990s is that they reinforce the widespread public perception that those in authority, perhaps especially the police, are not to be trusted because they act as if they are above the law. Frame enlargements. *Warner Bros./Regency*

FIGURE 6.21 A parody of westerns
The bad (and dense) guys rein up to pay a toll for the Gov. William J. Le Petomane Thruway. Here, as elsewhere in *Blazing Saddles* (1974), the subjects (cowboys) and settings (wild West) are those of the traditional western, but such actions as building a railroad, saving a town from corruption, and brawling in a saloon are exaggerated and mocked. As illustrated here, often *Blazing Saddles* also includes details from twentieth-century life. *Crossbow; Warner Bros.*

(1995); and *L.A. Confidential* (1997, Figure 6.20). Some French films—such as *Breathless* (1959); *Shoot the Piano Player* (1960); and *Alphaville* (1965)—have also been labeled film noir or influenced by it. Film noir, then, is not restricted to one period (1941–1958) or to one country (the United States). It is not a movement but a genre, and one with continuing appeal.

Occasionally a film is a **parody** of a genre: an amusing imitation of traditional films in the genre. Examples of parodies of westerns are *Lust in the Dust* (1985) and Mel Brooks's *Blazing Saddles* (1974, Figure 6.21). Westerns have been parodied elsewhere. In one, a supremely poised ("cool") fighter for hire arrives in a town torn by two greedy, violent, warring groups. Amused by the shortcomings of both groups, he plays one group off against the other. In fact, he partially orchestrates their eventual mutual destruction (though greatly outnumbered, he also kills some on his own) then strides away. The story re-creates many elements of the western, such as *High Noon*

FIGURE 6.22 Sci-fi western: science fiction setting, western story
Outland (1981) is set in the future on a moon of Jupiter, but the basic story closely mirrors that of the classic western *High Noon*. *The Ladd Company; Warner Bros.*

FIGURE 6.23 A vampire western
In this publicity still for *Billy the Kid vs. Dracula* (1965), a vampire in western clothes and in a western setting menaces a beautiful woman. *Embassy Pictures*

FIGURE 6.24 A musical gangster film—featuring children
The offbeat movie *Bugsy Malone* (1976) is a parody that combines elements of (a, above left) the gangster film and (b, above right) the musical. It is acted out on slightly scaled-down sets by a cast composed entirely of children. The "violent" action in (a) and elsewhere is something like a paint-gun war; the guns shoot soft white blobs. *Rank; Paramount*

and *Shane*, but much of its characterization and action is rendered humorously, even **satirically**. The country and film: Japan and *Yojimbo* (*The Bodyguard*) (1961).[1]

Many filmmakers combine elements of two or more genres. *Westworld* (1973) and *Outland* (1981, Figure 6.22) combine science fiction and the western. Elements of horror films are combined with those of westerns in *Curse of the Undead* (1959) and *Billy the Kid vs. Dracula* (1965, Figure 6.23). *Bugsy Malone* (1976, Figure 6.24) combines elements of the gangster film and the musical. *Some Like It Hot* (1959) blends elements of gangster films, musicals, and farcical comedies; *Shoot the Piano Player* mixes crime, romance, and slapstick comedy. *The Relic* (1997) combines aspects of the horror film and disaster movies. *Alien* (1979) and its sequels set horror stories in science fiction settings (Figure 6.25). As is partially suggested by the title of a recent book, *Future Noir: The Making of Blade Runner*, the 1982 movie *Blade Runner* (revised and rereleased in 1991) combines visual and story elements of film

satire: Depiction of behavior through language or visuals or other means that has as its aim the humorous criticism of individual or group behavior.

[1]For a comparison and contrast of *Yojimbo* and *High Noon*, see Alan P. Barr, "Exquisite Comedy and the Dimensions of Heroism, Akira Kurosawa's *Yojimbo*." *Massachusetts Review* 16 (1975): 158–68.

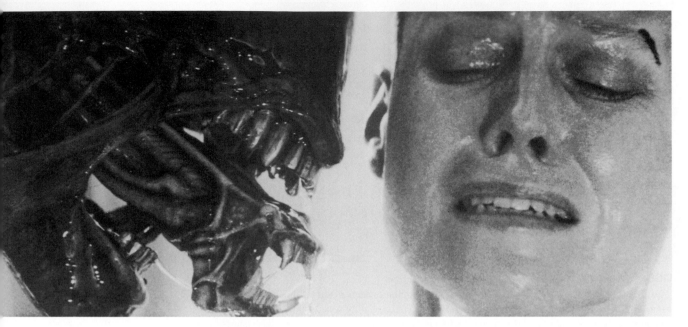

FIGURE 6.25 Sci-fi horror

As so often happens in the *Alien* movies, in *Alien³* (1992) people cut off from others are destroyed by a swift, voracious, and unrelenting monster. Here the Sigourney Weaver character is once again in mortal danger from an alien, but she survives this encounter halfway into *Alien³* because of a surprising condition viewers learn about later. Like the other *Alien* movies, *Alien³* combines the horror film components of shadows, disturbing sounds, unsettling music, and a lurking monster with a futuristic science-fiction setting. *20th Century-Fox*

noir with horror (a Dr. Frankenstein type and his dangerous yet finally pitiable creation) in a decayed futuristic science fiction world. Sometimes these combined genre films have outrageous results, as in *Plan 9 from Outer Space* (1959), which mixes "science fiction" and "horror" with its story of aliens resurrecting the dead.

Genres are subject to waxing and waning popularity. The western, for example, was out of favor in the 1980s and not a few film critics proclaimed the "death of the western." Since *Unforgiven* appeared in the early 1990s and was a critical and commercial success, the genre has revived vigorously. Another genre subject to changing fortunes is the musical. Since the 1960s, movie musicals have been scarce, and some critics have lamented the "death of the musical." Well, for a while. If one counts the Disney animated musicals of recent years and music videos, one could say the genre, though not in the pink of health, is far from pallid.

OTHER CINEMAS

There are many influential groups of fictional films other than classical Hollywood cinema, but space allows us to consider only a few of them: the two movements of Italian neorealist cinema and French new wave cinema plus independent European cinema and American independent cinema.

Critics and scholars sometimes group films into movements—related films, typically from the same country and usually made during a period of a few years—although different critics and scholars define and explain a movement somewhat differently. Two influential film movements are neorealist cinema and new wave cinema.

Italian Neorealist Cinema

Along with [Luchino] Visconti, such other directors as Roberto Rossellini and Vittorio De Sica strove to create a film art of authenticity. . . . Feeling that reality could better be conveyed through created situations than through the direct recording of actual events, they employed a synthesis of documentary and studio techniques, merging actual situations with a scripted story line. The essentials of neorealist films were the use of nonprofessional actors, authentic settings, naturalistic lighting, simple direction, and natural dialogue. (Phillips 686)

In *The Bicycle Thief* (1948, Figure 6.26), a long-term unemployed family man finally gets a job pasting up movie posters (see p. xxiii) but soon loses his bicycle to a thief and accomplices then faces the loss of his job if he cannot retrieve it. Most of the film is devoted to showing the man and his young son searching for the bicycle in various parts of Rome and the conditions under which different people live. *The Bicycle Thief* exhibits all the characteristics of **Italian neorealist films**: nonprofessional actors (in the three major roles), unaltered **location** settings (for the most part), and a chronological story. The film uses mostly available lighting (see Figure 6.26a), few **close-ups**, straightforward camera angles, and other unobtrusive filmmaking techniques (even its **wipes** are about as unnoticeable as an editor could make them). Its dialogue is natural, not rhetorical, and includes a range of dialects.

In addition to *The Bicycle Thief*, other important neorealist films include *Open City* (1945), *Shoeshine* (1946), and *Umberto D* (1952). *Open City* shows Catholics (especially a humane and compassionate priest), Communists, and others working together to resist the brutal Nazi occupation of Rome and exposes the myth of German superiority. A year later, *Shoeshine* showed two boys trying to survive in the streets of Rome but getting into trouble and suffering arrest, prison, reform school, then mutual betrayal. *Umberto D* is the story of an old pensioner distraught because he is behind in his payments to his wealthy, uncaring landlady; he is comforted only by his dog and to a lesser extent by his landlady's young, pregnant, unmarried servant. The characters

location: Any place other than a constructed set that is used for filming.

close-up: An image in which the subject fills most of the frame and shows little of the surroundings.

wipe: A transition in which it appears that a shot is pushed off the screen by the next shot.

FIGURE 6.26 **The Italian neorealist film** *The Bicycle Thief* **(1948)**
(a, top) The photograph illustrates two aspects of neorealistic films: filming on location and using available lighting while filming. The man on the left in the hat is the director, Vittorio De Sica.
(b, above) Like other neorealist films, *The Bicycle Thief* deals with ordinary, believable characters caught up in difficult social and economic conditions. The main character, Ricci, is despondent here because a thief and two accomplices have stolen his bicycle. If Ricci cannot get his bicycle back soon, he will lose his job. Frame enlargement. *(a) PDS-ENIC; The Museum of Modern Art/Film Stills Archive (b) PDS-ENIC*

in neorealist films are ordinary and believable and are caught up in difficult social and economic conditions. Generally these films failed to make money in Italy because audiences found them depressing and not diverting enough.

The movement began in Italy during World War II and largely died out there by the early 1950s. It is a product of the economic and social conditions of its times. In part, neorealism was also a reaction to the established ways of prewar and wartime Italian cinema that often presented idealized images of fascist Italy, studio-made comedies, and costume histories.

Neorealism did not set out mainly to be an alternative to classical Hollywood cinema; indeed, in its clear linear plots and unobtrusive filmmaking techniques, neorealism imitates it. However, in its use of nonprofessional actors, unadorned settings, natural lighting, colloquial dialogue, concern for the social and economic problems of everyday people, and unhappy endings, neorealism is an alternative to the classical Hollywood cinema of its time. Neorealist films were also a strong influence on some later films—such as the early films directed by Federico Fellini, Michelangelo Antonioni, and the Bengali filmmaker Satyajit Ray. Since the 1950s, students of neorealist films have come to see their artifice more clearly. Nonetheless, the characters, stories, and contexts of neorealist films continue to fascinate, involve, and move film students and film scholars.

French New Wave Cinema

New wave films were a diverse group of French fictional films made in the late 1950s and early 1960s that are marked by the independent spirit of their directors and were sometimes shot on location with portable, handheld equipment and film that required little additional lighting.

> The New Wave—however we define it—captures the surface texture of French life in a fresh way, if only because the low budgets with which most young directors work initially necessitate a certain contemporary flavour lacking in the 1951–57 period, when the characteristic works were . . . period reconstructions. The newcomers had no money to build elaborate **sets**, pay for costumes or employ star names: they shot on location, with reduced crews and fresh young performers. But this contemporary flavour was not accompanied by any real social or political concern. . . . The post-1958 feature film industry . . . remains essentially a Parisian cinema, dealing with middle-class problems in middle-class terms, and above all concerned with the "eternal" issues of human emotions and relationships. (Armes 169, 170)

set: Constructed setting where action is filmed; it can be indoors or outside.

The films of the new wave were made by such directors as François Truffaut, Jean-Luc Godard, Claude Chabrol, and, to a lesser extent, Eric Rohmer and Jacques Rivette.[2] Most new wave directors had watched many

---

[2]As Susan Hayward points out in her *Key Concepts in Cinema Studies*, in its location shooting, avoidance of stars, "subversion of genres," and in other ways, Agnès Varda's 1954 film *La Pointe courte* is a forerunner of French new wave cinema (137).

films at the Cinémathèque Française (French national film archive) and various film clubs and had written about films and the film medium in the journal *Cahiers du cinéma*. In their writings they advocated that directors should have control over all creative stages of production and criticized traditional French films, especially those of the preceding decade. Before the new wave, French movies—as typified by the famous 1945 film *Children of Paradise* (Figure 6.27)—tended to be costume films, period pieces, and more literary than **filmic**. New wave directors argued that such films gave too much control to writers at the expense of directors.

New wave films are often imbued with a knowledge of earlier films, especially American genre films, and even more so are marked by unpredictable plot developments and the independent spirit of their directors. Jeanne Moreau, whose independent and openly sexual characters embody quintessential qualities of new wave films, said that the new wave way of making films freed up actors:

> In other films I made . . . the lighting was so complicated. There were shadows on one side and another light on the other side, so, really, when you are in close-ups you are in a corset. It was impossible to move. That's what the new wave was about, that absolute freedom. The light was made in such a way that you could move and do whatever you wanted, like in real life.

Like a type of documentary filmmaking evolving in France at about the same time (**cinéma vérité**), new wave films were set in the present or recent past and were often **shot** on location with portable, handheld equipment, **faster film stock**, and new lighting equipment. Sometimes they include

filmic: That which is characteristic of the film medium or appropriate to it.

cinéma vérité: A style of documentary filmmaking developed in France during the early 1960s the aim of which was to capture events as they happen with minimal interference from the filmmakers.

shot: Filmed.

fast film stock: Film stock that requires relatively little light for re-creation of images.

FIGURE 6.27 French film before the new wave
In the theatrical and literate *Children of Paradise (Les Enfants du paradis)* (1945), one of the main characters is a mime. As a costume film and period piece that was shaped more by the script than the direction, *Children of Paradise* was the type of film the filmmakers of the French new wave rebelled against in their publications and their filmmaking. Frame enlargement. *S. N. Pathé Cinéma*

FIGURE 6.28 A source and a French new wave homage
(a, above left) The two main characters in *The Kid* (1921): Charlie Chaplin as the tramp and Jackie Coogan as the abandoned boy the tramp has taken upon himself to raise. (b, above right) An homage from one filmmaker (François Truffaut) to another (Chaplin): in this publicity still we see Jeanne Moreau as she is dressed and made up for a brief section of Truffaut's *Jules and Jim* (1961): her shoes and mustache are reminiscent of Charlie Chaplin's in *The Kid*; her cap and sweater are like the boy's. *(a) Charlie Chaplin, First National (b) Marcel Berbert; Les Films du Carrosse*

surprising or whimsical moments, perhaps the product of improvisation while filming.

New wave cinema may also include **homages** or tributes to earlier films or parts of them. In *Breathless*, the main character, Michel, sometimes pays homage to Humphrey Bogart. In various scenes Michel runs his thumb across his lips and back as Bogart did in many films; in one scene he does this while looking at lobby cards (photographs advertising a movie), especially a close-up photo of Bogart. Another homage results when visual details from the two main characters in Charlie Chaplin's *The Kid* (1921, Figure 6.28a) are seen briefly in the appearance of the main woman character of *Jules and Jim* (1961, Figure 6.28b).

cutaway (shot): A brief interruption in the visual presentation of a subject.

jump cut: A discontinuous transition between shots.

New wave films abound in editing rarely used in classical Hollywood cinema. Sometimes the results are surprising and whimsical. In *Shoot the Piano Player*, a gangster says to a boy being kidnapped, "I swear it on my old lady's head. May she die if I lie." In a **cutaway**, a woman old enough to be his mother moves her hand toward her chest, falls down backward, then briefly kicks her legs straight up in the air. In the next scene, the boy being kidnapped says, "Then I believe you," and the gangster replies, "Didn't I tell you so?" And the film resumes its story. *Breathless* sometimes uses **jump cuts**, as in the scene where Michel shoots the motorcycle police officer; as edited, the scene is a little disorienting and confusing (Figure 3.15 on pp. 142–43). Jump cuts are also used in a later scene where Michel and Patricia are talking in a moving car and the background changes in inexplicable ways between shots. There is continuity in the conversation in the foreground (continuity of time) but discontinuity of settings in the background. In *The 400 Blows* (1959), two boys emerge from a movie theater and start running; then their movement blends into a blurred horizontal image (**swish pan**) that ends by blending with the boys arriving at another movie theater (Figure 6.29). In one brief scene of *Shoot the Piano Player*, Charlie and Léna are in bed; as she talks to him, five times the scene alternates with even briefer shots of them together in bed at some other time. Quite unconventionally, each of these five cutaway shots is preceded and followed by a rapid **lap dissolve**: as the first shot fades out, the next shot fades in, momentarily overlapping it.

New wave films influenced European and American cinema—for example, the British film *Tom Jones* (1963), the French film *A Single Girl* (1996), and even one scene in *Pulp Fiction*. In *Pulp Fiction* when the Uma Thurman character and the John Travolta character arrive at a restaurant in a car, she says to him, "Don't be a" then finishes her sentence by fashioning a temporary square (more or less) consisting of small white dots in front of her face. New wave films had "an impact which was to help free the cinema in the United States and Germany, for example, from conventionality and tradition and contribute to the movement toward **auteur** filmmaking in these nations" (Konigsberg 268).

auteur ("oh TOUR") **theory:** A critical approach for analyzing films and filmmakers. Auteur (French for "author") critics usually examine the recurrent meanings and techniques of filmmakers who have left a strong imprint on films they have worked on.

European Independent Films

Neorealism and new wave cinema are not the only European alternatives to classical Hollywood cinema. Various post–World War II films directed by European directors working outside of the commercial mainstream—such as Jean-Luc Godard and Francois Truffaut (throughout their careers, not merely during their earlier new wave years), Ingmar Bergman, Federico Fellini, Michelangelo Antonioni, and Luis Buñuel—are also alternatives to classical Hollywood cinema. Sometimes these films are called "art cinema," but it is more descriptive to refer to them as "European independent films."

FIGURE 6.29 Untraditional editing in a French new wave film

In *The 400 Blows* (1959), two boys are playing hooky. (a, top) They emerge from a movie theater then move off to the left along the sidewalk. (b, middle) As they do so, the camera begins to pan from right to left then moves so rapidly that the image becomes blurred, a swish pan. (c, bottom) The swish pan ends, and we see the two boys approaching another movie theater, where they buy tickets. Frame enlargements. *Les Films du Carrosse*

Perhaps the easiest way to consider the main features of these films is to begin by comparing and contrasting them characteristic by characteristic with those of classical Hollywood cinema listed on page 236:

1. Memories, fantasies, dreams, and other mental states are rendered much more often than in classical Hollywood cinema. Such films are more likely fragmented, more likely to shift quickly and without explanation between different states of consciousness.

2. As in classical Hollywood cinema, the films focus on one character or on a few distinct characters.

3. Often the main characters' goals are unclear or shifting. Often the characters are ambivalent and hard to figure out (as in most films directed by Antonioni).

4. The main characters confront various antagonists or problems, but the antagonists and problems are not always so clear-cut, for example, so obviously evil.

5. Often the films lack closure and have unresolved **plotlines**, and the protagonists do not succeed in reaching a goal (the endings are more likely to be true-to-life than the typical happy endings of most commercial American movies).

6. The emphasis is not as emphatically on clear causes and effects of actions; ambiguity may be widespread; and sometimes the narratives are **episodic**: scenes could be shifted without changing the film substantially, as in films directed and co-written by Jacques Tati.

7. As in classical Hollywood cinema, filmmaking techniques tend to be unobtrusive, but European independent films are more likely to have authorial **narration**, as in some films directed by Truffaut or Godard, and they are more likely to be **self-reflexive**. They are more likely to be in part about the film medium or filmmaking or to interrupt the viewers' involvement to draw attention to themselves as films. *Tom Jones* is full of amusing self-reflexive touches, as when Tom breaks out of his character, looks directly into the camera, and talks to the audience or when he takes off his hat and places it in front of the camera so viewers cannot gawk at a woman who has lost most of her blouse. In *Shirley Valentine* (1989), the title character sometimes interrupts what she is doing and looks at the camera and speaks her thoughts (Figure 6.30). *Persona* (1966) is another highly self-reflexive film: on one level, it is about the nature of film and film presentation. At one point, for example, the story is interrupted with a **title card** reading "One moment please while we change **reels**," and indeed after a **fade-out**, we see briefly only blackness and hear silence before a rapid **fade-in** introduces the next scene.

plotline: A brief narrative; a series of related events usually involving only a few characters or people and capable of functioning on its own as a story.

narration: Commentary about some aspect of the film or a subject in the film, often from someone offscreen.

self-reflexive: The characteristic of a creative work to make reference to or comment on itself.

title card: A card or cel that supplies printed information in a film.

reel: 1,000 feet of 35 mm motion-picture film stored on a spool.

fade-out, fade-in: A transition between shots in which a shot changes by degrees from illumination to darkness; then, after a pause, the image changes from darkness to illumination.

Additionally, European independent films are likely to stress relationships between people and to have a **pace** and intensity that approximate those of normal human experience, whereas the films of classical Hollywood cinema are more likely to emphasize physical action and to have a pace and intensity beyond normal experience. The independent European cinema is more likely to be explicit about sexuality, whereas classical Hollywood cinema is more likely to be explicit about violence. Finally, films directed by independent European directors are much less likely to be genre films than are films of classical Hollywood cinema. *The Crying Game* (1992), for example, is not recognizable as a western, musical, science-fiction film, horror film, or any other genre, though it perhaps comes closest to a mystery film.

Although few films have all the characteristics cited here, all independent European films have many of them.

American Independent Cinema since the 1960s

American **independent films** are made without Hollywood studio support or creative control. Such films are made all over the United States, not only in southern California. An example is *Just Another Girl on the I.R.T.* (1992), which is a candid film about a bright seventeen-year-old African American living in Brooklyn who plans to go to college but gets pregnant. The movie concludes with a title card reading "A Film Hollywood Dared Not Do." In recent years some American independent films have later been distributed by a major studio, such as Warner Bros., MCA/Universal, Paramount, MGM/United Artists, Buena Vista (Disney), and TriStar/Columbia. Some independent films—such as *Pulp Fiction* and *Four Weddings and a Funeral* (1994)— may be distributed by and sometimes partially financed by "such quasi-independents as Miramax, Gramercy and Fine Line, which are owned by large companies but operate with a high degree of freedom and flexibility" (Weinraub B2).

pace: A person's sense of a subject (such as narrative developments or factual information) being presented rapidly or slowly.

FIGURE 6.30 Self-reflexiveness

In *Shirley Valentine* (1989), the title character sometimes interrupts the story to look at the camera and tell viewers what is on her mind. As she looks toward the camera, she may speak out loud, or, if someone else is present, viewers may hear what she is thinking. Her comments to the audience are usually about the characters and situations in the film's story, but they may be about a filmic convention. At one point as she and a man are having sex on a sailboat and orchestral music plays loudly, she looks at the camera and says, "Oh, my God. Where did that orchestra come from?" Self-reflexiveness is sometimes used in films that are alternatives to the classical Hollywood cinema. *Paramount*

So varied are American independent films that it is extremely difficult to generalize about their subjects and styles, as we can about neorealist films, new wave cinema, and independent European films. Usually American independent films are made without costly directors, writers, and stars (or with stars willing to work for a relatively small salary or a percentage of the profits, or both). "Most directors have had to scrabble together the financing—for their early projects, anyway—from family or friends or savings or a mosaic of grants" (Lyons xiii). With lower budgets, the films need not draw huge crowds to turn a profit, and the filmmakers are freer to take on a controversial subject or a subject of limited interest, so independent films tend to be more varied, less formulaic, and more individualistic than films of the classical Hollywood cinema. They are more likely, for instance, to deal with a controversial subject without showing audiences what they want to see and to include an unhappy ending if the story has been building toward it.

Such independent films as *Night of the Living Dead* (1968), *Eraserhead* (1978), *Blood Simple* (1983), *She's Gotta Have It* (1985), *Daughters of the Dust* (1991), *Reservoir Dogs* (1992), and *El Mariachi* (1993) have usually won awards and often secured a distributor at one of the major film festivals such as Cannes, New York, and Sundance. Many independent films garner excellent reviews then critics' awards, as those given by the National Society of Film Critics, a group of critics who write for major U.S. newspapers and magazines.

Independent filmmakers have two major cooperating organizations: the Association of Independent Video and Filmmakers (AIVF) and Independent Feature Project (IFP). Both groups foster independent filmmakers and promote the independent film. Each organization also publishes a magazine: AIVF publishes *The Independent Film & Video Monthly* and IFP publishes *Filmmaker*. Each March since 1986, members of Independent Feature Project/West, one of four branches of IFP, have gained publicity for independent films by giving Independent Spirit Awards. Best feature awards for 1990–97 have gone (in order) to *The Grifters*, *Rambling Rose*, *The Player*, *Short Cuts*, *Pulp Fiction*, *Leaving Las Vegas*, *Fargo*, and *The Apostle*.

Two cable channels devoted solely to the independent film—Independent Film Channel (since 1995) and the Sundance Channel (since 1996)—also promote independent films, including fictional shorts and documentaries, from countries throughout the world.

Classical Hollywood cinema is so much a part of the world most of us were born into and grew up in that many viewers do not easily adapt to other cinemas; initially other films seem odd and perhaps too demanding. But in seeing more of these films and learning about them, many viewers come to enjoy and appreciate them and to broaden their understanding of the film medium, its many possibilities, its countless achievements.

SUMMARY

Classical Hollywood Cinema

- Classical Hollywood cinema has been the most influential group of fictional films in history.

- Such films show one or more individualized characters with clear goals who face many problems in reaching them; these films stress continuity and the clear causes and effects of actions; and they tend to use unobtrusive filmmaking techniques.

- A film genre is a commonly recognized group of fictional films. Two popular film genres are the western and film noir. Traditionally the western features civilization versus the wilderness west of the Mississippi River, in northern Mexico, or in the Canadian Rockies. Films noirs include scenes with low illumination, convoluted plots, and complex, flawed characters caught up in crime.

- A genre film may be traditional or revisionist. Most westerns made since about 1950 are revisionist and vary widely from the traditional western.

- Occasionally a film is a parody of a genre. A film may be a combination of two or more genres, such as horror and science fiction or, far less frequently, western and horror.

Other Cinemas

- Other fictional films—such as those of (Italian) neorealism, (French) new wave cinema, the independent European cinema after World War II, and many American independent films since the 1960s—offer alternatives to classical Hollywood cinema.

- Neorealism was a film movement in Italy during and after World War II. Neorealist films, which are a mixture of scripted and actual situations, are located for the most part in real settings and show ordinary and believable characters caught up in difficult social and economic conditions. The endings of neorealist films tend to be unhappy. Other characteristics are the heavy reliance on nonprofessional actors and the use of available lighting and colloquial dialogue.

- New wave cinema was a movement in late 1950s and early 1960s France. This diverse group of films, which were sometimes shot on location with portable, handheld equipment, is marked by the independent spirit of the directors. Compared to classical Hollywood cinema, new wave films are more likely to include homages and untraditional editing.

- The post–World War II films directed by such Europeans as Ingmar Bergman, Federico Fellini, Michelangelo Antonioni, and Luis Buñuel have also been alternatives to classical Hollywood cinema. These films are likely to have a pace and intensity that approximate those of normal human experience. Compared to the films of the classical Hollywood cinema, they are more likely to be explicit about sexuality than violence, are less likely to belong to a genre, and are more likely to be self-reflexive.

- American independent fictional films since the late 1960s have lower budgets than their Hollywood counterparts and are free of Hollywood studio creative control, so they tend to be more varied and less formulaic than the movies of classical Hollywood cinema.

WORKS CITED

Andrew, Dudley. *Concepts in Film Theory*. New York: Oxford UP, 1984.

Armes, Roy. *French Cinema*. New York: Oxford UP, 1985.

Bordwell, David, Janet Staiger, and Kristin Thompson. *The Classical Hollywood Cinema: Film Style and Mode of Production to 1960*. New York: Columbia UP, 1985.

Konigsberg, Ira. *The Complete Film Dictionary*. 2nd ed. New York: Penguin, 1997.

Krutnik, Frank. *In a Lonely Street: Film Noir, Genre, Masculinity*. New York: Routledge, 1991.

Lenihan, John H. *Showdown: Confronting Modern America in the Western Film*. Urbana: U of Illinois P, 1980.

Lyons, Donald. *Independent Visions: A Critical Introduction to Recent Independent American Film*. New York: Ballantine, 1994.

McCarthy, Todd. Introduction. *Painting with Light*. By John Alton. Berkeley: U of California P, 1995.

Moreau, Jeanne. Interview. *Morning Edition*. Natl. Public Radio. 11 Mar. 1994.

Palmer, R. Barton. *Hollywood's Dark Cinema: The American Film Noir*. New York: Twayne, 1994.

Phillips, William H. "Neorealist Cinema." *Benét's Reader's Encyclopedia*. 3rd ed. Ed. Katherine Baker Siepmann. New York: Harper, 1987.

Shulman, Ken. "From a Vanished Country, a Viewable Cold War Archive." *New York Times on the Web* 26 Oct. 1997. <http://www.nytimes.com>.

Telotte, J. P. *Voices in the Dark: The Narrative Patterns of Film Noir*. Urbana: U of Illinois P, 1989.

Thompson, Kristin, and David Bordwell. *Film History: An Introduction*. New York: McGraw, 1994.

Weinraub, Bernard. "In Sheer Quality, TV Is Elbowing Hollywood Aside." *New York Times* 14 Feb. 1995, natl. ed.: B1+.

Wilder, Billy, and Raymond Chandler. "Double Indemnity." In Raymond Chandler, *Later Novels and Other Writings*. New York: Library of America, 1995.

FOR FURTHER READING

Armes, Roy. *Patterns of Realism: A Study of Italian Neo-Realist Cinema*. Cranbury, NJ: Barnes, 1971. Includes contextual information and descriptions, photographs, and analyses of major Italian neorealist films.

Film Genre Reader. Ed. Barry Keith Grant. Austin: U of Texas P, 1986. Twenty-four essays on issues related to film genres.

Film Genre Reader II. Ed. Barry Keith Grant. Austin: U of Texas P, 1995. A wide variety of essays by a variety of film scholars. Includes bibliographic references.

Mintz, Steven. "Western Films: A Bibliography." *Film & History* 26 (1996): 78–80. Recent and wide-ranging bibliography.

Phillips, Patrick. "*Genre, Star, and Auteur: An Approach to Hollywood Cinema*." *An Introduction to Film Studies*. Ed. Jill Nelmes. London: Routledge, 1996. 121–63. Uses Martin Scorsese's film *New York, New York* to explore issues in genre, star, and auteur.

Pierson, John. *Spike, Mike, Slackers & Dykes: A Guided Tour across a Decade of American Independent Cinema*. New York: Miramax/Hyperion, 1995. An introduction to American independent films from 1984 to 1994 by someone involved in their making and marketing. Appendix I lists all American independent features from late 1984 to 1993.

They Went Thataway: Redefining Film Genres. Ed. Richard T. Jameson. San Francisco: Mercury, 1994. Introductory essays on thirteen film genres (including directors and stars) each followed by essays by members of the National Society of Film Critics.

CHAPTER 7

Characteristics of Fictional Films

feature film: A film that is at least sixty minutes long.

A FEW YEARS AFTER THE FIRST MOTION PICTURES were created in the 1890s, the new medium was used to present short, entertaining fictional stories. Fictional films became so popular that during the 1910s, **feature**-length fictional films became commonplace, drew large audiences, came to serve as an evening's or afternoon's major pastime, and supported a large and growing filmmaking industry. Since then, people have remained fascinated by fictional films, perhaps especially because they are endlessly captivated by the possible motivations and consequences of human behavior. The consequences may be unanticipated and have considerable impact. In *Fargo* (1996), for example, a car salesman has gotten into debt, has arranged for two men to kidnap his wife, and has plans to pay the kidnappers part of the ransom to be extracted from his wealthy father-in-law. As a consequence of the car salesman's initial actions, eventually seven characters get killed, one is apprehended and presumably will face multiple felony charges, and by implication one is left without parents and his grandfather.

Most people are so drawn to narratives or stories that when they are confronted by a creative work with no obvious story, they still try to find one. As film archivist and critic Robert Rosen wrote,

> Film and painting . . . display intriguing points of convergence, among them the inescapability of narrativizing spectators. Even in the face of totally nonrepresentational works, viewers have a powerful urge to uncover or invent narrative—a basic need to normalize the challenge of the unfamiliar by situating it in a comfortably recognizable sequence of events. (252)

In this chapter we will briefly consider what a narrative is then examine the fictional narrative, the fictional film.

NARRATIVES

> Unlike ordinary experience, which mixes the meaningful with the amorphous and random, a story's ingredients are selected for appropriateness to the story's intended effects, meanings, and structures. A story can therefore be almost free from redundancy, meaninglessness, and, especially, inexpressiveness. Stories have what electronics technicians call a high signal-to-noise ratio. Thus a story promises comprehensibility in a way that ordinary experience does not. (Eidsvik 61)

"Narratives" or stories are commonplace in every society. All of us produce them, enjoy them, and often learn from them, yet explanation of what precisely constitutes a narrative is a complex, contentious issue in contemporary critical theory. For our purposes **narrative** can be defined as a series of unified **events** situated in one or more **settings**. The events may be arranged chronologically or nonchronologically and may be factual, fictional, or a blend of the two. Consider the main events of the seventeen-minute wordless film "The String Bean" (1962):

1. An old woman finds a discarded potted plant near her apartment building.

2. In her apartment, she discards the dead plant and takes a seed she had taken from a package and plants it in the pot.

3. In her apartment, the plant grows to only a certain size.

4. The woman transplants the plant in a park, where it thrives.

5. One day, she sees park caretakers pull out the plant and discard it. The woman takes pods from the discarded plant.

6. In her apartment she takes seeds from a pod, plants them, places the pot outside on the sill, and looks on as rain begins to fall on the pot.

This narrative shows selected chronologically arranged events in the life of one character. Viewers can usually figure out the relationship of later events to earlier ones. To illustrate: between the major units of the narrative (or **sequences**) numbered 3 and 4, viewers can infer that the woman transplants the plant in the park because she hopes it will grow even larger and healthier outdoors.

If the film showed only sequences 1–5, it would still be a narrative, though one with a disappointing ending, both for the woman and for those in the audience who identify with her. If the film showed only sequences 1–3, there would still be a narrative, though to many viewers the narrative would be unsatisfactory because it would be too short to include complications and resolution of them.

event: In a narrative either an action by a character or person (such as Darth Vader and Obi-Wan Kenobi dueling with light sabers) or a happening (such as it raining on the streets in *Blade Runner*).

setting: The place where filmed action occurs.

sequence: A series of related consecutive scenes, perceived as a major unit of a narrative film.

A narrative's events are unified in some manner. The following describes three events presented without interruption, but they are not clearly related and thus constitute no narrative:

6. In her apartment an old woman takes seeds from a pod, plants them, places the pot outside on the sill, and looks on as rain begins to fall on the pot.

5. One day, she sees park caretakers pull out a plant and discard it. The woman takes pods from the discarded plant.

1. The woman finds a discarded potted plant near her apartment building.

If a film showed only these sequences, viewers could detect no unity to the events and could make no sense of them. The film would have no narrative.

Some films—such as many films directed by the French directors Jean-Luc Godard and Alain Resnais—make it difficult or impossible for viewers to perceive the unity of depicted events. Other films—such as *Mr. Hulot's Holiday* (1953), *Playtime* (1968), *Nashville* (1975), *Short Cuts* (1993), and *Clerks* (1994)—are only loosely unified overall. Although individual **scenes** are unified and easy to follow, some scenes could be located elsewhere in the story with little noticeable consequence. Such films are said to have an **episodic plot**.

A fictional film is a narrative that is not factual. It shows mostly or entirely selected imaginary events arranged in a unified and meaningful order. The events are presented over time (chronologically or not chronologically), and they are presented in a certain **style** or manner. The rest of this chapter considers structure, time, and style.

scene: A section of a narrative film that gives the impression of continuous action taking place during one continuous time and in one continuous space.

STRUCTURE

Structure refers to the parts of something and their arrangement. In a fictional film, the selection and order of events help viewers comprehend the story and strongly influence how they respond to the film. This section discusses the basic fictional structure (characters, goals, and conflicts); some functions of beginnings, middles, and endings; and the combination of different brief stories into a larger, more complex story.

Fictional films include at least one character (imaginary person in a narrative) that is often based in part on characteristics of actual people. Occasionally other subjects with some human qualities—such as extraterrestrials, robots, zombies, animals, even geometrical shapes, such as a dot and a line—function as characters. Fictional films show mostly imaginary events, though fictional filmmakers often re-create some actual events, film them, and combine them with the fiction. It is even possible, though rare, to combine fictional action with footage of actual (not re-created) action, as in some scenes late in *Medium Cool* (1969) where one character gets into the 1968 Chicago Democratic National Convention and another character is threatened by tear gas and rioting outside the convention hall. The fictional *Chinese Box* (1998) also includes actual action, parts of the ceremony of Hong Kong's transition from British to Chinese rule. The settings of narratives may be fictional, as in most science fiction stories, or they may be essentially factual, as in the Italian **neorealist films** made in the 1940s or other movies filmed on largely unaltered **locations**.

Characters, Goals, Conflicts

Some generalizations about characters, goals, and conflicts apply to all fictional films regardless of length, but feature films and short films also have some major differences. In this section we will consider the qualities of fictional films regardless of length then how characters, goals, and conflicts tend to be handled in the short film.

FEATURE FILMS AND SHORT FILMS   A fictional narrative nearly always includes at least one character who wants something but has problems trying to get it. People are fascinated with characters who have trouble reaching their goals, in part because in such circumstances they learn about human nature or think they learn about how they might handle a similar situation or perhaps in part because they sometimes enjoy seeing *others* have trouble. Whatever the motivations of viewers, they tend to be fascinated by how others try to overcome problems and how their efforts affect them and others around them.

Typically the main character's goals are not immediately apparent, though one major goal becomes clear early in the film or viewers lose interest. As a story progresses, sometimes a second goal emerges. In the French film *Ridicule* (1996), viewers soon learn that the main character, an engineer, wants the king's support for draining a swamp that breeds disease and kills the engineer's peasants. In pursuing that goal, the man goes to Versailles, where he meets two women: one young, attractive, and intelligent, the other older, more worldly, and more calculating. The story illustrates that pursuing a second goal (the young woman) may preclude achieving the first (Figure 7.1).

In films with two or more major characters, usually the characters have different goals, at least initially; the result is conflict, with or without humor. Conflict largely without humor is prominent in many movies, including war movies. Conflict with humor abounds in most romantic comedies, such as *It Happened One Night* (1934), *Bringing Up Baby* (1938), *Four Weddings and a Funeral* (1994), and *My Best Friend's Wedding* (1997).

In pursuing goals, conflict or problems are inevitable, in fiction as in life. In *Jaws* (1975), a huge killer shark is menacing people who venture into the waters off an island that caters to summer tourists. Throughout *Jaws* a major

neorealism: A film movement in Italy at the end of and after World War II, whose films were a mixture of imaginary and factual occurrences usually located in real settings and showing ordinary and believable characters caught up in difficult social and economic conditions.

location: Any place other than a constructed setting that is used for filming.

FIGURE 7.1 Character, goals, conflicts
Nearly all of *Ridicule* (1996) takes place in 1783 France at a time when wit was king and ridicule could kill. (a, top) The main character is an engineer who seeks royal support to clear swamps and thus eradicate a fatal disease. (b, middle) In pursuing his goal, he meets and becomes entangled with a calculating, worldly woman of the king's court, who helps him gain the king's ear. (c, bottom) At about the same time, the engineer becomes attracted to Mathilde, an intelligent, individualistic woman. After many complications, the man abandons the woman of the court, so she arranges his downfall and thus failure to attain his initial goal. A title card that concludes the story informs viewers that twelve years later the engineer and Mathilde succeed in draining the swamps. Frame enlargements. *Miramax Zoë*

conflict is between people and the shark (people versus nature). But the film also shows many conflicts between people (Figure 7.2). There are conflicts between some townspeople and Chief Brody; the mayor and Brody; and Mrs. Kintner, whose young son was killed by a shark, and Chief Brody. Also Brody is in conflict with himself: early in the film he allows his better judgment to be overruled and he's feeling guilty about the consequences. At the film's end, however, presumably all the conflicts are resolved. The veteran fisherman Quint is destroyed by his shark adversary; soon afterward the shark is destroyed. Hooper and Brody paddle back to the beach. The townspeople and tourists will no longer be in danger. *Jaws* exemplifies the three traditional types of conflict: people versus nature (for example, Quint and Hooper versus the shark); people versus people (the chief versus the mayor); and conflict within a character (Brody wants to accommodate the political

FIGURE 7.2 **The three types of conflict**
The three main human subjects of *Jaws* (1975) are (left to right) the chief of police (Brody), a veteran fisherman (Quint), and a marine-life specialist (Hooper). During the film each comes into conflict with each of the others. All three come into conflict with a great white shark. Early in the film Brody comes into conflict with townspeople and the mayor and is in conflict with himself. In short, the film illustrates the three basic types of conflict in stories: people versus people, people versus nature, and one aspect of a character versus another aspect. *Universal*

FIGURE 7.3 Two opposing forces in a fictional film
As in many fictional tales, in Disney's animated feature *The Lion King* (1994) there are two contending forces. The king of the animals, Mufasa (center), and his son Simba are opposed by Mufasa's discontented brother Scar (on the left and turned away from Mufasa) and the three vicious hyenas near him. During the story, power shifts from Mufasa to Scar and his henchmen hyenas then to Simba: from a benevolent monarchy to an evil one then back to a benevolent absolute ruler. *Walt Disney; Buena Vista*

classical Hollywood cinema:
A type of narrative film dominant in world cinema. Classical Hollywood cinema shows one or more distinct characters with clear goals who overcome many problems in reaching them. The films tend to use unobtrusive filmmaking techniques and to stress continuity of action.

leaders and businesspeople yet wants to protect townspeople and tourists against shark attacks). Often fictional stories take the form of two opposing characters or two opposing forces (Figure 7.3).

In films of **classical Hollywood cinema**, regardless of their length, typically the main character achieves all his or her major goals. If a feature film has only one major character, that character normally has more than one major goal. For example, in countless movies—such as *Rocky* (1976), *Top Gun* (1986), *The Mask* (1994), and *Outbreak* (1995, Figure 7.4)—the central male character tries to succeed in love *and* work or some other major goal—and does. In many musicals, the main male character eventually wins the woman of his dreams and is instrumental in the successful staging of a show

FIGURE 7.4 **Major character with two goals: success in love and work**
In *Outbreak* (1995), the Dustin Hoffman character not only (a, top) saves the life of his ex-wife and wins back her love but also (b, above) overcomes *many* other obstacles—including his military superiors—to save the United States from an airborne virus that spreads as rapidly as rumors. Stories about a character struggling to succeed in work and love then doing so have often been commercially successful in American movies. Frame enlargements. *Warner Bros.*

or making of a movie. In most movies, especially the popular ones, the major characters don't just succeed; they succeed against enormous odds. Not only in *Outbreak*. In *Pretty Woman* (1990), a glamorous streetwalker manages to thaw the heart of an aloof wealthy businessman. In *Stand and Deliver* (1985), an overworked high school teacher in an L.A. barrio wins the respect of his math students; they overcome their various problems at home and work so diligently that they all pass the math advanced placement test twice, the second time after only a few days to study.

SHORT FICTIONAL FILMS   From 1895 to about 1906, all fictional films were less than sixty minutes, the usual definition of the **short film**. Until the 1960s, short fictional films often accompanied a feature film in movie theater showings. Today, short films are seldom shown in theaters and are rarely available in video stores. They are shown at film festivals; by film societies, museums, and libraries; on some cable channels, especially the Sundance Channel and the Independent Film Channel; and in various high school and college courses. Making a short film is usually required of filmmaking students. Sometimes their short films attract attention at film festivals and lead to funding for feature productions. At its best, a short fictional film is not a truncated feature, but a flexible and expressive form in its own right. Like a short story, its brevity can be an advantage: for example, compared with a feature film, it may be more compressed, demanding, and subtle. And since its budget is far less than that for a feature, even for an **independent film**, typically its makers are under fewer financial pressures to conform to the generic Hollywood movie and are freer to be true to their vision. Let's examine a sample short film.

independent film: Film made without support or input from the dominant, established film industry.

"Leon's Case" (1982), which is twenty-five minutes long, shows the often amusing story of the idealistic Leon Bernstein, who as "the last fugitive member of the Village 8" still thinks and acts as he did in the 1960s. He attempts to rally people to protest the social injustices and militarism of the 1980s. If you have not seen the film, take a moment to read the plot summary on pages 284–85.

Like "Leon's Case," most short fictional films exhibit the characteristics of classical Hollywood cinema but have fewer major characters and fewer events. Most short fictional films have

story time: The amount of time covered in a film's narrative or story.

1. one or two major characters who usually do not change goals or personality during a brief **story time**, usually a few days or less;

2. one goal: the main character usually does not say explicitly what he or she wants, but viewers can figure it out early in the film;

3. one or more obstacles or conflicts in trying to reach the goal but none of them very time-consuming;

4. success or failure in reaching the goal.

A minority of short fictional films reject the conventions of the classical Hollywood cinema. A good example is "The Other Side," a ten-minute 1966 black-and-white film from Belgium. The film has no dialogue, no narration, and no music except during the opening credits and the final moments. The only sound effect is occasional machine-gun fire. "The Other Side" is a brief, complex, and somewhat ambiguous film that calls for multiple viewings, which are easier to manage with short films than with features. If you have not seen the film, take a moment to read the **cutting continuity script** on page 286.

cutting continuity script: A written description of a finished film.

Conflict between characters is used in stories of classical Hollywood cinema to show what individual characters are like and to initiate and develop the plot. In "The Other Side" we see only one side of the conflict: we never learn about those suppressing the people in the street, nor do we know why they do so. The oppressors kill people one at a time and evidently kill no more than necessary to keep the others in line (literally and figuratively). The film shows that the authorities shoot rebels. At the beginning of the film we cannot be sure, but they may also shoot nonrebels at random.

Unlike classical Hollywood cinema, "The Other Side" reveals little about individual characters. Certainly we learn nothing about the oppressed characters from dialogue—the film has none—and the film has no written language except the final "1966." "The Other Side" also lacks **close-ups** of faces, so viewers cannot infer what the characters are feeling. No one looks happy, yet no one looks angry either. In nearly all of the film, people move lethargically, like drugged inmates in institutions and animals in zoos. The lack of emotion and interaction between characters are two of the film's most prominent features. The main character is not an individual or a few distinct characters, as in classical Hollywood cinema, but a group. The film focuses on political issues—force and conformity—not individual psychology.

close-up: Image in which the subject fills most of the frame and which shows little of the surroundings.

As in most short films of classical Hollywood cinema, the main characters—here a mass of people—have a single goal: freedom from oppression and conformity. Failing at that, they want to survive, even if that requires conformity, lack of interaction, and the absence of vitality. Unlike most films of classical Hollywood cinema, the characters fail to achieve their main goal, and the film ends as it began—except more bodies fill the street than in the beginning.

"The Other Side" demonstrates that even a very short film may be rich in **meanings**. In the face of death, people can be forced to suppress their desires for freedom and to disregard evil—even though their actions result in conformity and depersonalization. Sympathy for fallen companions can be quickly subdued, and people can be forced to live without meaning, having no interaction with others. The characters in the film move sideways, not forward, with their backs to suppression and death, and to each other. Presumably, most characters move in a basically circular way, returning evidently again and again to the same locations, as if in an endless, repetitive

meaning: An observation or generalization about a subject. Meaning in films may be explicit, implicit, or symptomatic.

Plot Summary for "Leon's Case"

In trying to publicize his opposition to the U.S. military-industrial complex, Leon Bernstein goes through the following steps:

1. In his basement apartment Leon, who is dressed as a priest, puts on a false mustache and leaves (see figure, part a).

2. At the house of his two friends, Keith and Karen, Leon tells them of his plans and hides his manuscript about his life in the resistance. His two friends offer no direct support and sometimes ignore him.

3. At a duplicating shop, Leon gets copies made of a press release and of a flyer announcing a demonstration he plans to stage. The worker in the store, a former hippie, does not give Leon a "discount for the movement."

4. At the *Los Angeles Times* building, Leon is unable to see his friend Keith, who writes a real estate column, to give him a copy of a news release.

A short film in the classical Hollywood cinema tradition
(a, right) In "Leon's Case" (1982), the "fugitive" Leon, disguised as a priest, is about to begin another day for the cause, his resistance to the military-political establishment. Early in the film viewers learn of Leon's goal; the bulk of the film shows him confronting various problems in trying to attain it. (b, far right) Leon disguised in jacket and baseball hat trying and failing to promote his cause. He thinks he needs to wear costumes to avoid detection by the FBI. *Daniel Attias*

5. At a university, wary students accept Leon's flyers then quickly discard them (see figure, part b). Leon finds the discarded flyers.

6. Leon has trouble getting in to see a lawyer, and when he does, he learns the lawyer doesn't do resistance work anymore "'cause there's no resistance."

7. At a telephone booth, Leon calls the FBI to announce the demonstration the next day, but he learns that President Carter pardoned war resisters years ago.

8. Back at his apartment, Leon's friends give him a surprise party. He is uncomfortable and uncharacteristically speechless; his friends do not entirely support him in his cause.

9. The next day, Leon cuts his hair and wears conventional clothing, goes to the Los Angeles Airport, presumably chains himself to a bomber on display there, gets arrested, and gets coverage on the local television news. Mission accomplished.

Cutting Continuity Script for "The Other Side"

What follows is a written description of the finished film. How much time passes between the film's shots is unclear; therefore, I have not attempted to divide the film into scenes.

The opening credits, accompanied by music.

EXT. CITY STREET—DAY

The image fades-in from white to a narrow city street and sidewalks. In the street is the body of a person. On the sidewalks men and women face walls and slowly shuffle sideways in the same direction as they keep both hands raised and touching the walls. They do not speak; they do not touch. One man runs away from the wall and is machine-gunned down from an unseen source. The others continue moving sideways along the walls. We hear machine-gun shots. Another body is seen in the street. In close-up we see a man's hand moving along a wall near a woman's hand. Machine-gun fire drops another person to the pavement.

One man stares at the most recently shot person; then he moves slowly toward him. The others stop, slowly turn around, and look at the man approaching the body. The man who had walked toward the body is himself shot. Others walk slowly toward the two fallen bodies. One at a time, some are shot and collapse. All mass together, then stop and turn around slowly. We see the faces of people in the crowd. The mass of people walks forward slowly (see figure, part a). Some are felled by machine-gun fire.

As the sporadic machine-gun fire continues, some move toward the walls; then the rest of the survivors scatter and run to the walls. The machine gun is heard no more. The film's last image, like its first, is of the dead in the street and people moving slowly sideways with hands raised touching the walls (see figure, part b). Fade-out to white, then "1966" is shown against the white background and is accompanied by brief, loud music; then the image fades out to black.

loop of humanity. The people feel their way, as if blind, to nowhere. Like the mythical Sisyphus doomed to push that rock up the hill only to see it tumble down again and again, the characters in "The Other Side" exist without vitality, pleasure, or variety. The film gives a distinctive view of crowd psychology in modern urban life. It might be interpreted as an urban nightmare. Today, with many urban dwellers plagued with apathy and loss of purpose and with people trapped in their homes after dark because it is dangerous to go out, cut off from direct contact with others, out of its silence "The Other Side" speaks loudly and clearly.[1]

---

[1]Both the description and analysis of "The Other Side" are adapted from the first edition of William H. Phillips, *Writing Short Scripts* (Syracuse: Syracuse UP, 1991).

A short film outside the classical Hollywood cinema tradition
(a, above left) For a while the masses in an unidentified town in "The Other Side" (1966) are
unified in opposition to an unseen enslaving force. Unlike in classical Hollywood cinema, in
"The Other Side" no character is distinct or shown in any depth. (b, above right) Unlike films
of classical Hollywood cinema, "The Other Side" ends with little change in the initial situation:
the mass is subdued—except that more people have been murdered. Frame enlargements.
Herman Wuyts, Belgium

Beginnings, Middles, and Endings

The beginning of a fictional film tends both to establish where and when the
story starts and to involve viewers. It usually gets viewers to start anticipating
and readjusting to developments as they unfold before their eyes. Many fictional films start with one or more shots of the setting before introducing
the subjects. Usually soon after that, the story begins.

Typically, a fictional film's beginning uses minimal **exposition** (information about events that supposedly transpired before the beginning of the plot):
more than a little of it, especially at the beginning of a story, tends to be un-
involving. Tellers of tales—whether in print, on the stage, or on the screen—
typically use as little initial exposition as possible but feed us tidbits of it when
needed as the story progresses.

Beginnings typically introduce the major characters and allow viewers to infer their goals. The events of fictional films are so intertwined that often something missing in a character's life at the story's beginning largely determines the story's ending. In *Finzan* (*A Dance for the Heroes*) (1990), from Mali, the narrative begins with the death of a man and his brother's desire to force the man's widow to marry him (Figure 7.5). *Women on the Verge of a Nervous Breakdown* (1988) begins with the main character wanting to talk to her lover. Much of the film shows her trying to connect with him, but only in the penultimate scene does she succeed.

The middle section of fictional feature films typically includes a series of obstacles that deter or delay the main characters from achieving their goals. In the long central section of *Schindler's List* (1993), for example, Schindler tries to thwart the Nazis and help save as many Jews as possible, but in pursuing his goals, he faces setbacks, dangers, and delays. In dealing with the impediments to reaching their goals, the central characters reveal their natures and the consequences of their actions for them and others. Consider the structure of *Unforgiven* (1992). The film begins with acts of injustice both by a cowboy

FIGURE 7.5 A character's initial lack causing story consequences
Nanyuma (right) is the main character in *Finzan* (Mali, 1990). Early in the film Nanyuma's husband dies; soon her husband's brother, the village idiot, wants to marry her. In pursuing that goal, he sets in motion most of the film's complications. The story ends with the man not getting what he wants: the widow evades the consummation of her forced marriage but only by exiling herself and her young son from her village and chancing an uncertain future. *Courtesy of California Newsreel, San Francisco*

who assaults a woman and by the sheriff who acts as law officer, jury, and judge. The large middle section of the film shows who will avenge the injustice against the woman, how they will do so, and the consequences of their actions, for both themselves and others. The middle section of a fictional film also tests the filmmakers' inventiveness and skill in creating satisfying surprise and suspense and in other ways keeping the audience involved with the story.

Film endings show the consequences of the major previous events. Filmmakers, however, sometimes tack on an ending that is exciting, moving, or simply reassuring (and commercially appealing) but doesn't dovetail with the rest of the story. An example is the final scenes of *Schindler's List*. After Schindler has retrieved the Jewish women from the Auschwitz concentration camp, he seeks out his wife to be reconciled with her and presumably strays no more. Viewers learn that the armaments his factory builds are deliberately flawed to sabotage the German war effort. He urges the rabbi who works for him to prepare for the Sabbath. Viewers learn that Schindler spent a lot of money sustaining his workers and bribing Reich officials. At the war's end, he credits his Jewish workers with saving themselves and persuades the armed camp guards to leave without harming the workers. Later, as the music swells, he breaks down as he says that he squandered money and should have saved even more Jews; then he is quietly and lovingly enfolded by many of those he did save. Earlier, the film showed Schindler as a complex, fascinating man—exploitative, philandering, and callous, yet shrewd, self-confident, powerful, and somewhat inexplicable. The movie ends not with chords but a single note, hero worship. The ending may be emotionally satisfying for many viewers—and understandable given the filmmakers' desire to honor Schindler—but it does not tie in with the film's earlier restraint and complexity, and as the film draws to an end, it tries too hard to make sure no one could miss Schindler's admirable qualities.

Films with **closure** show the consequences of events viewers have become curious about. Films may also lack closure, that is, be open-ended: the fate of a significant character or person is uncertain or the consequences of an important action unknowable. Generally, films of classical Hollywood cinema have closure, because mainstream audiences tend to dislike inconclusive or puzzling endings. The endings of independent films, however, are more likely to be open. Examples are *The Crying Game* (1992) and *L.A. Confidential* (1997). At the end of *The Crying Game* viewers cannot know what Fergus and Dil's relationship will be. They can only review relevant events from the film and make an informed guess. By the end of *L.A. Confidential* viewers cannot know Ed Exley's fate. He has survived an attempt on his life and been awarded honors again. For now, the police chief and district attorney are using Exley to repair damage done to the image of the LAPD—and Exley knows it—but in the long run can he trust the police chief and the DA, especially now that colleague Bud White, a powerful ally, is leaving for Arizona?

closure: The consequences of previous major actions in a story are shown or implied by the end of the narrative.

FIGURE 7.6 Consecutive plotlines but with gaps of time between them
In one plotline of *Being Human* (1994), humans live in caves; (a, top) in another, in ancient Rome; and (b, above) in the fifth one, in modern-day New York. The film is unified in various ways: all five major characters are called Hector and are played by Robin Williams, and all five plotlines show a male's strong desire for family yet the difficulty of holding on to one's family or returning to it. *The Bountiful Company; Warner Bros.*

Plotlines

A **plotline** is a brief narrative—a series of related events, perhaps continuous, perhaps interrupted—usually involving a few characters or people. A plotline can function as a complete short narrative, as it typically does in a short film. A feature film, however, often has two or more plotlines. When a film consists of two or more, the plotlines may be combined in countless creative ways and, as we will see, serve many different functions.

To compress a wide-ranging story into an endurable movie, plotlines can be consecutive yet with large gaps of story time between them. *2001: A Space Odyssey* (1968) contains the consecutive but not continuous plotlines of four groups: man-apes, scientists, a computer and two astronauts, and the star-child. *Being Human* (1994) has five plotlines, but with vast gaps of time between them (Figure 7.6).

Multiple alternating plotlines can be used to show relationships between different time periods. *The Godfather Part II* (1974) and *Heat and Dust* (1983) alternate between plotlines: a narrative primarily about one character and a story set years earlier about a relative. *The Remains of the Day* (1993) also alternates two plotlines to show in what ways the times and a relationship have changed: one in the 1930s, the other in the late 1950s (the two plotlines focus on the same two characters but at different stages in their lives) (Figure 7.7). *Intolerance* (1916), directed by D. W. Griffith, alternates four stories, each set at a different place and historical period: Babylon in 539 B.C., Judea toward the end of Christ's life, France in 1572, and America early in the twentieth century. As might be expected from a film with so complicated a structure, many viewers see little unity in the film and are confused about what it adds up to.

A film can alternate between simultaneous plotlines to heighten suspense. *Dr. Strangelove: Or, How I Learned to Stop Worrying and Love the Bomb* (1963)

FIGURE 7.7 Two characters, two plotlines set at different times (a, above left) The main subjects of *The Remains of the Day* (1993) are Stevens, a devoted British servant, and Miss Kenton, a house-keeper who tries to get close to him. He rejects her overtures then (b, above right) years later travels to see her in hopes of enticing her back into her old job and rekindling the romantic spark. *The Remains of the Day* alternates between the plotline of Stevens and Miss Kenton in service and the plotline years later of Stevens traveling to and briefly visiting with her. *Columbia*

FIGURE 7.8 A plotline that is an offshoot of another plotline
Short Cuts (1993) shows the stories of nine pairs of characters. In addition, one member of one of the nine pairs (center) leaves his wife and goes on a fishing trip with two male friends: they have breakfast at a diner; they drive to a site, park, and hike; they set up camp, find a woman's body in the water, and decide what to do with the rest of their weekend. That is one plotline. Frame enlargement. *Cary Brokaw; Fine Line Features*

has three major simultaneous plotlines: at a U.S. air force base where the paranoid General Jack D. Ripper has ordered U.S. bombers to attack the U.S.S.R.; on a U.S. bomber on its way to bomb a target in the Soviet Union; and in the Pentagon war room, where the U.S. president, military commanders, and the top scientist try to prevent the catastrophe.

To show many aspects of a large group, plotlines may also be numerous, chronological, simultaneous, and intersecting. *Short Cuts*, which was adapted from various short stories by Raymond Carver, includes nine pairs of major characters plus six other important characters, but the film has so many groupings of characters that one cannot say there are *nine* plotlines. Different critics of the film have detected "nine interlocking narratives," "approximately ten stories," or "a dozen stories." There are at least ten (Figure 7.8). The film's multiple plotlines are arranged chronologically or simultaneously—the film is unclear about that—and each couple interacts with at least one other major character. With so many characters and intersecting plotlines in something as fleeting and onrushing as a film, however, a viewer may sometimes lose track of who is who or may not see any character long enough to identify with or be intrigued by or even believe in (one murder seems insufficiently motivated and its "cover-up" highly unlikely). Nonetheless, a story consisting of many intersecting plotlines can effectively present a panoramic view of a society. In *Short Cuts* as in *Nashville* (1975), *A Wedding* (1978), and *The Player* (1992), director Robert Altman and his collaborators are exploring how inclusive a narrative can be—both in terms of the number of characters and the various combinations of plotlines—yet remain unified. (See Figure 7.9.)

FIGURE 7.9 Multiple, simultaneous, and intersecting plotlines ▶
Short Cuts (1993) has twenty-four major characters and many different groupings of them. For example, (near right, top to bottom) (a) Howard Finnigan (a TV news commentator) and his wife, Ann, have a son Casey who is hit by a car, walks home, falls asleep, lapses into a coma, and is treated in a hospital. Two other characters are seen in the film only in relation to the Finnigans: (b) Mr. Bitkower, a baker who as requested has made a special birthday cake for Casey, and (c) Howard's father, Paul, who unexpectedly appears at the hospital after years of alienation from his son. Other characters have lives in the film beyond their interactions with the Finnigans: (far right, top to bottom) (d) Doreen, a waitress, drives the car that Casey darted in front of; (e) Ralph Wyman is the physician in charge of Casey's care; and (f) Zoe is a disturbed cellist who lives next door to the Finnigans with her mother and is upset by news of the boy's fate. Frame enlargements. *Cary Brokaw; Fine Line Features*

FIGURE 7.10 Multiple simultaneous plotlines

Night on Earth (1992) consists of five uninterrupted plotlines, each occurring during the same moments in time and in one of four different time zones. Each of the five simultaneous plotlines involves a taxi driver and his or her fare and the stories take place (in order) in (a, top left) Los Angeles, (b, above left) New York, (c, left) Paris, (d, top right) Rome, and (e, above right) Helsinki. In its use of simultaneous nonintersecting plotlines that are presented successively, the film's structure is rare, perhaps even one-of-a-kind. *Jim Jarmusch, Fine Line Features*

FIGURE 7.11 **Multiple interwoven plotlines**
The Joy Luck Club (1993) tells the stories of four Chinese mothers and the Chinese American daughter of each. The film illustrates how complex the combinations of multiple plotlines may be. In the months before the plot of *The Joy Luck Club* begins, Suyuan (on the left) had died, and Suyuan's middle-aged women friends (seen here) had written to China and located the two women who as babies Suyuan had been forced to abandon during a war in China. The movie begins with a going-away party for Suyuan's daughter June (the second woman from the left), who plans to leave for China the next day to meet her two half-sisters. Most of the movie consists of flashbacks from the going-away party to each middle-aged woman's painful childhood or early adulthood in China, present-tense scenes from the party, and flashbacks to selected events from the lives of the four adult daughters. The film concludes with June's arrival in China and her meeting her two half-sisters. Except for Suyuan, all the other seven major characters meet at one place and time, the going-away party. *Wayne Wang, Amy Tan, Ronald Bass, Patrick Markey; Buena Vista*

Plotlines may even be consecutive yet simultaneous because they occur in different time zones. *Night on Earth* (1992) has five consecutive brief plotlines, each set in one of four different time zones, but each begins at the same moment in time: 7:07 P.M. in Los Angeles, 10:07 P.M. in New York, 4:07 A.M. in Paris and Rome, and 5:07 A.M. in Helsinki (Figure 7.10). As a consequence, viewers are offered the rare opportunity to see what happens at the same moment of time at various places around the world.

Plotlines may be nonchronological and from many time periods yet for all but one of the major characters intersect at one time and place, as in *The Joy Luck Club* (1993), which has eight major plotlines: for four middle-aged women born in China and for the American-born grown daughter of each (Figure 7.11).

TIME

In fictional film there are three tenses: present, future, and past. Also to be considered is the matter of the time it takes to show a film and the time span represented by a story.

Present Time, Flashforwards, and Flashbacks

"Movies should have a beginning, a middle, and an end," harrumphed French Film Maker Georges Franju at a symposium some years back. "Certainly," replied Jean-Luc Godard. "But not necessarily in that order." (Corliss)

Most makers of narrative films agree with Franju and arrange scenes chronologically. But the earliest scenes of a film's story may occur late in the film or even at its ending, and the latest scenes of another story may occur early in the narrative, as in *Heavenly Creatures* (1994). As we will see, these and countless other temporal arrangements of scenes are possible because of flashbacks and flashforwards.

Only a few movies use chronological order with an occasional **flashforward**. *Easy Rider* (1969) is one of them. At one point the Peter Fonda character, Captain America, is in a brothel; he looks up past a small statue toward a plaque that reads "Death only closes a man's reputation and determines it as good or bad." Next we see from a helicopter a split-second shot of something burning off to the side of a country road. In the brothel, Captain America looks down, and the action resumes. Does the shot suggest he vaguely glimpses the future, or are viewers meant to see this as a glimpse of the future, or is the shot meant to make viewers a little uneasy because it doesn't fit in and make sense? Or does the shot function in two or more ways? Viewers cannot even recognize it as a flashforward unless they remember it as they see the end of the film, when Captain America is shot by a passing motorist and his motorcycle explodes into flames off to the side of a country road. Occasionally during the opening credits of a film, a flashforward shows events that are repeated well into the film, as in *The Stilts* (*Los Zancos*, 1984), *My Life as a Dog* (1985), and *GoodFellas* (1990).

Although flashforwards in films are usually mainly visual, they may be auditory. Late in *Medium Cool* the car radio announces a serious car accident that we witness nearly fifty seconds later. According to Marc Vernet, this **technique** was used in Alain Robbe-Grillet's *L'Immortelle* (1962): "We hear the sound of an accident at the beginning of the film even though that crash will occur later in the film" (92).

Flashforwards "can only be recognized retrospectively" (Chatman 64) and are demanding of viewers. They can be confusing and frustrating if the events shown are too far into the future or the flashforwards are frequent or lengthy. Perhaps because flashforwards let viewers glimpse conse-

flashforward: A shot, scene, or sequence that interrupts a narrative to show events that happen in the future.

technique: Any aspect of filmmaking, such as the choices of sets, lighting, and editing.

quences they do not anticipate or are not yet even interested in, they are rarely used.

Flashbacks are much more common than flashforwards. Like flashforwards they are nearly always visual or visual and auditory, but they may be exclusively auditory, as in *The Night Porter* (1974), where the main character has gone fishing with a man, returns home, then remembers and viewers hear the other man's voice seconds before the main character presumably pushed him into the water and let him drown.

Often a flashback briefly interrupts a chronological progression of events to show what influenced a character earlier. A flashback may also be used at the end of a film to reveal causes of previously puzzling events, as in *Exotica* (1994). Near the end of that film viewers are allowed to partially understand how an earlier discovery of a murdered girl affected an enigmatic young woman, and in the film's last two scenes they are shown an even earlier stage in her relationship to the troubled main character. By withholding these revelations until the last scenes, which is what some theorists refer to as a "privileged" placement, the final scenes help clarify the whole. A flashback may also be used within a flashback as when viewers learn who indeed shot Liberty Valance in *The Man Who Shot Liberty Valance* (1962) and as when viewers see scenes that two twelve-year-old characters (Vern and later Gordie) recount or remember in *Stand by Me* (1986).

In some films—such as *8½* (1963) and *Rashomon* (1950)—it is sometimes difficult, sometimes impossible, to know which events happened and which are dreams, fantasies, or lies. In *8½* a director tries to regain his creativity and confidence and finish a costly and complicated film while trying to cope with his wife and his lover. That much of the narrative proceeds chronologically but with frequent scenes of the director's dreams, fantasies, or memories, though sometimes viewers cannot know which is which. In the Japanese classic *Rashomon* viewers cannot know which of the four quite different accounts of a man's death and events leading up to it is the most reliable and which are self-serving lies. Both *8½* and *Rashomon* question "the assumptions on which all conventional (Hollywood-style) film narrative is based, namely that the world is wholly decipherable, that people's motivations can be understood, that all events have clear causes and that the end of a fiction will offer us the chance to fuse all elements of the plot into a single coherent dramatic action" (Armes 103–04).

On rare occasions, a film is basically chronological but includes flashbacks and flashforwards, as in *They Shoot Horses, Don't They?* (1969). That film opens with five brief flashbacks alternating with consecutive short scenes from the present. Later the film uses an occasional brief flashforward revealing the fate of one of the major characters (Figure 7.12). *Don't Look Now* (1973) is also mostly chronological but sometimes uses flashbacks and occasionally flashforwards. One memorable flashforward occurs when the main male character glimpses his wife on a passing boat with two other women,

flashback: A shot or few shots, brief scene, or (rarely) sequence that interrupts a narrative to show earlier events.

```
Past      –  –  –  –  –
          1  2  3  4  5

Present   – – – – ──── ────────── ────────── ──────── ────────── ──
          6 7 8 9 10     11           12          13        14        15

Future              –           –          –          –          –
                    16          17         18         19         20
```

1 The boy Robert and a man chasing a horse.

. . .

6 The adult Robert on a beach outside a dance hall.

. . .

10 Robert in the dance hall.

. . .

15 The dance marathon emcee suggests that Robert and Gloria marry publicly as part of the show. . . . Robert taken off in a police van. The dance marathon continues.

16 Robert in handcuffs being transported inside a police van.

. . .

20 Robert about to be sentenced.

FIGURE 7.12 **The plot and fabula of *They Shoot Horses, Don't They?* (1969)**
The following scenes are arranged chronologically: 1–5, 6–15, and 16–20.
The plot = 1, 6, 2, 7, 3, 8, 4, 9, 5, 10, 16, 11, 17, 12, 18, 13, 19, 14, 20, 15.
The fabula = 1–5 (Robert as boy), 6–15 (adult Robert and dance hall events), and 16–20 (Robert under arrest and tried).

one a blind seer and all three dressed in black. Near the film's ending viewers see some shots related to that earlier scene, but they are from the man's funeral procession in Venice. The flashforward earlier in the film reveals that the man is so psychic he could briefly see beyond his own life although he did not realize what he was seeing then. One movie that jumps around in time extensively is *Slaughterhouse-Five* (1972). It uses many flashforwards and flashbacks, some of which are difficult to place in a chronological ordering of the events, but then the central character has become "unstuck in time."

Chronological Time and Nonchronological Time

Plot is the selection and arrangement of a story's events. **Fabula** is the viewer's or reader's mental reconstruction of a narrative's nonchronological arrangement of events into chronological order. Both a plot and its corresponding fabula contain the same events, but the nonchronological arrangement of events changes focus, mood, and viewer interest—sometimes considerably.

Like many earlier stories including *The Odyssey* by Homer, *Shoot the Piano Player* (Figure 7.13) begins in medias res, in the middle of the story, then flashes back to the main character's earlier life before resuming the story and finishing it. Such a structure has at least two functions in *Shoot the Piano Player*. It allows the filmmakers to begin at an exciting and intriguing point: two men in a car are trying to run down a third man. After the film is well under way and viewers have become interested in the main character, the flashback helps them understand why he is so emotionally guarded.

The plot for *Pulp Fiction* includes many deviations from a straight chronology, and, unlike nearly all fictional films, it also includes repeated action and parallel action. (See pp. 302–03.) In the film, Jules (the Samuel L. Jackson character) is prominent at both the beginning and ending. In the fabula, he does not appear in the last two major sections, though for many viewers he is probably the film's most complex and intriguing character. The nonchronological plot of *Pulp Fiction* makes possible a more exciting, more engaging beginning than a chronological arrangement of all the film's events: the beginning of a robbery versus two guys talking in a car. The nonchronological plot also results in a less upbeat ending: by the ending of the film's plot, we know that for Vincent death lurks around the corner; at the end of the fabula, Butch picks up his girlfriend and they drive off. The plot's last scene also allows viewers to experience the unusual situation of learning what happens before and after the film's first scene. Because of the two viewings of the action in the grill and the revisit to the apartment where men get killed, we can more fully understand the context of actions we saw earlier and see the perspectives of different characters at the same place: for example, the first time in the grill, the film focuses entirely on Ringo and Honey Bunny, the second

The Past   – – – – – – – – – – – – –
                                                         1

The Present   – – – – – – – – – – – –   –
                         2   3

2 Chino, one of Charlie Kohler's brothers, briefly eludes two fellow crooks (Ernest and Momo) and goes to Charlie for help. . . . After Léna and Charlie escape from Ernest and Momo, Léna takes Charlie to her apartment where he sees a poster of himself as Edouard Saroyan, a successful concert pianist.

1 Sometime earlier, Edouard is married to Théresa. Unknown to him, she has reluctantly slept with an impresario so that Edouard could become a famous concert pianist. After she commits suicide, Edouard gives up his career, changes his name, and becomes a piano player in a café.

3 Back in Léna's apartment, Léna and Charlie become lovers. After further complications Léna is killed by Ernest, and Charlie returns to his job playing a piano in the café.

FIGURE 7.13 **The plot and fabula of *Shoot the Piano Player* (1960)**
The plot = 2, 1, 3.
The fabula = 1, 2, 3.

time on them and on Vincent and especially Jules. Compared with the fabula, the plot for *Pulp Fiction* is more demanding of the audience, and for some viewers the film's complex structure is both a challenge and a pleasure, though the plot is so intricate that few viewers could completely reconstruct the fabula after only one showing.

So strong is the human proclivity to try to sort through events and make sense of them (that's one reason most people are endlessly fascinated by narratives) that for most viewers, attempting to construct fabulas is irresistible. But as demonstrated by *Slaughterhouse-Five*, *Jacob's Ladder* (1990), *Lost Highway* (1997), and other movies, constructing the fabula may be problematic because different attentive and thoughtful viewers will disagree if certain actions are present, past, or future events or are only imagined (fantasized or dreamed).

Running and Story Times

Running time is the amount of time it takes to see a film and includes opening and closing credits. Sometimes the credits accompany images of the film's subjects; sometimes they don't. Running times of features vary from one hour to nearly twenty-six hours for a TV series later shown in theaters (*Heimat II*, 1993) or seven hours for a film made for theatrical release (*Sátántangó*, 1993).[2]

Story time is the amount of time covered by the film's fabula. For example, if a film's earliest scene occurs on a Sunday and its latest scene takes place on the following Friday, the story time is six days.

Story time is nearly always *much* longer than running time. The story time of *Independence Day* (1996) is three days; its running time is roughly two hours. The story time of the Chinese film *To Live* (1994) is approximately twenty-five years (from "the 1940s" to "the 1960s" then five or six more years); the running time is 129 minutes. The plot of *Women on the Verge of a Nervous Breakdown* begins one morning and ends approximately 36 hours later, on the evening of the following day; the film's running time is 88 minutes.

In a few movies the story time is approximately the same as the running time. For example, the story time of *High Noon* is about 102 minutes (from about 10:30 to 12:12), and the film's running time is 81½ minutes. The story time of *Nick of Time* (1995) is about 95 minutes (from noon until at least five

---

[2]It is impossible to know which was the longest film for theatrical release because there are no surviving copies for many early films (there are no known copies of more than 70 percent of all feature films made before the 1920s and only about 50 percent of all American films made before 1950) and many films that have survived may be incomplete. Then, too, before the late 1920s, projectors did not run at the same speed. The French film *Travail* (1919) may have run eight hours. The 1925 *Les Misérables* reputedly consisted of thirty-two 35 mm reels (each reel could be from thirteen to sixteen minutes long), so that movie might have run anywhere from seven to eight-and-a-half hours.

The Plot and Fabula of *Pulp Fiction*

THE PLOT OF *PULP FICTION* (1994)

B.2. In a grill, Ringo and Honey Bunny talk about robbery; Ringo calls out "*Garçon*" to the waitress. Ringo and Honey Bunny talk some more; then they decide to rob the grill and its customers, pull out their guns, and shout that it's a holdup.

[Opening Credits]

A.1. Vincent and Jules in car. The two arrive at a building. When they are about to go inside an apartment, it's 7:22 A.M. Inside, they confront two men who had been trying to get away with an attaché case containing something valuable and belonging to the two men's "business partner," Marsellus. Jules and Vincent locate the attaché case and kill the two men.

Title card: "Vincent Vega & Marsellus Wallace's Wife"

C. At Marsellus's business, Marsellus tells Butch that Butch's best times are past and gives him an envelope full of money; after Butch accepts it, Marsellus tells him he's to take a dive in his upcoming boxing match. Vincent and Jules arrive with the attaché case. Marsellus calls to Vincent and embraces him.

D. Vincent buys powerful heroin, shoots up, and (now night) goes to take out Marsellus's wife, Mia, as Marsellus had asked him to do while he is away. Vincent and Mia go out, then return to her and Marsellus's place where she overdoses on drugs and almost dies. . . .

E. Before his fight, Butch dreams about receiving a watch originally acquired by his great-grandfather.

Title card: "The Gold Watch"

Butch wins the fight and escapes. Vincent and Marsellus's bartender (Paul) report about the search for Butch to Marsellus, who is furious at Butch. Butch joins his lover Fabienne then the next morning returns to his apartment, fetches his watch, and kills Vincent. At a nearby stoplight Butch "runs into Marsellus" and tries to kill him; then Marsellus tries to kill Butch. Both enter a pawnshop and are captured and tied up. Marsellus is sexually assaulted;

Butch saves him, takes the motorcycle of one of their captors, and picks up Fabienne.

Title card: "The Bonnie Situation"

A.1. (parallel to part of A.1 at beginning of film) A man in the next room hears Jules speaking immediately before the second of the two murders seen near the film's beginning. Repeating the end of A.1 at the beginning of the film, Jules and Vincent shoot the second man.

A.2. The man from the next room bursts into the room where Jules and Vincent go at the beginning of the film and shoots at them but misses; they kill him. Jules thinks it's a miracle he wasn't killed. In car, Jules says he is going to retire. Vincent accidentally kills their own accomplice (Marvin) thereby splattering blood all over the car and the two men. At Jimmie's, Jules and Vincent seek help (it's 8:00 A.M.). Calls are made, and at 8:50 Mr. Wolf arrives to supervise the cleanup before Jimmie's wife, Bonnie, will arrive home from work at about 9:30. At Monster Joe's Used Auto Parts, Mr. Wolf has presumably made arrangements for the elimination of the car with the accomplice's body in the trunk. Vincent and Jules decide to go for breakfast.

B.1. At a grill, Jules again tells Vincent that he plans to quit the business and "walk the earth."

B.2. (repeat of a line from near the beginning of the film) Ringo calls out "*Garçon*."

B.2. (parallel to the time at the beginning of the film between the time Ringo calls "*Garçon*" and Ringo and Honey Bunny begin the robbery) Jules and Vincent talk some more; then Vincent leaves to go to the restroom.

B.2. (repeat of the end of B.2 at film's beginning) Ringo and Honey Bunny pull their guns and begin the holdup.

B.3. After many complications, Ringo and Honey Bunny complete the robbery and leave; soon afterward Vincent and Jules leave (Jules still has the attaché case he plans to deliver to Marsellus).

THE FABULA OF *PULP FICTION*

A. Vincent and Jules in car. The two arrive at an apartment building. When they are about to go inside an apartment, it's 7:22 A.M. Inside, they confront two men who had been trying to get away with something valuable belonging to Marsellus. Jules and Vincent retrieve an attaché case full of Marsellus's valuables and kill the two men. The man from the next room bursts into the room and shoots at Vincent and Jules but misses; they kill him. Jules thinks it's a miracle he wasn't killed. In car, Jules says he is going to retire. Vincent accidentally kills their own accomplice (Marvin) thereby splattering blood all over the car and the two men. At Jimmie's, Jules and Vincent seek help (it's 8:00 A.M.). Calls are made, and at 8:50 Mr. Wolf arrives to supervise the cleanup before Jimmie's wife, Bonnie, will arrive home from work at about 9:30. At Monster Joe's auto wreckers, the clean car with the assistant's body in the trunk is left. Vincent and Jules decide to go for breakfast.

B. At a grill, Jules again tells Vincent that he plans to quit the business and "walk the earth." Ringo and Honey Bunny talk about robbery; Ringo calls out "*Garçon*" to the waitress. Ringo and Honey Bunny talk some more as Vincent and Jules talk and Vincent leaves to go to the restroom. Ringo and Honey Bunny decide to rob the grill and its customers, pull out their guns, and shout that it's a holdup. After many complications, Ringo and Honey Bunny complete the robbery and leave; soon afterward Vincent and Jules leave (Jules still has Marsellus's valuables in the attaché case).

C. At Marsellus's business, Marsellus is telling Butch that Butch's best times are past and gives him an envelope full of money; after Butch accepts it, Marsellus tells him he's to take a dive in his upcoming boxing match. Vincent and Jules arrive with the attaché case. Marsellus calls to Vincent and embraces him.

D. Vincent buys powerful heroin, shoots up, and (now night) goes to pick up Marsellus's wife, Mia, as Marsellus had asked him to do while he is away. Vincent and Mia go out then return to her and Marsellus's place where she overdoses on drugs and almost dies. . . .

E. Before his fight, Butch dreams about a watch originally acquired by his great-grandfather. Butch wins the fight and escapes. Vincent and Marsellus's bartender (Paul) report about the search for Butch to Marsellus, who is furious at Butch. Butch joins his lover Fabienne then the next morning returns to his apartment, fetches his watch, and kills Vincent. At a nearby stoplight Butch tries to kill Marsellus; then Marsellus tries to kill Butch. Both enter a pawnshop and are captured and tied up. Marsellus is sexually assaulted; Butch saves him, takes the motorcycle of one of their captors, and picks up Fabienne.

minutes after the attempted assassination at 1:30), but the running time, excluding the opening credits, is only about 80 minutes. *Nick of Time* keeps story and running times approximately equal by sometimes condensing story time, sometimes expanding it. For example, the opening events supposedly take 480 seconds, but actually only 143 seconds pass. Conversely, the events shown in the film from precisely 1:28 to exactly 1:30 take not 120 seconds but 327. For both *High Noon* and *Nick of Time* many critics and other viewers have commented that their story times coincide with their running times. Almost.

On rare occasions a film's story time is less than its running time. *Night on Earth* consists of five plotlines set in four time zones, each beginning at the same moment in time and each having a story time of 35 minutes. The film's story time then is 35 minutes; its running time is 125 minutes. Another film with a story time less than its running time is "Occurrence at Owl Creek Bridge" (1962), a story of a civilian facing being hanged from a railroad bridge during the American Civil War. The film's story time is slightly more than 10 minutes; its running time is almost 28 minutes.

Nearly all fictional films are imprecise about how much time supposedly elapses between scenes. "The String Bean" (discussed on p. 275) shows an old woman finding a discarded plant, planting seeds, nurturing the new plant, finding it uprooted, then planting seeds from it, presumably to begin the cycle again. How much time passes between the time the woman first plants the seeds and one sprouts? How much time passes altogether in the film? What is the story time: one month, two months, three? This imprecision is not a weakness of the film but a characteristic of fictional films, which are generally less specific about their story time than fiction or published plays.

Filmmakers can present many actions taken from a brief story time, as in *High Noon*, or relatively few actions taken from a long story time, as in *2001*, which depicts highly selective events from 4 million B.C. to beyond our sense of time. Storytellers may even repeat the same block of story time and segments within it—for example, a twenty-four-hour period and various minutes within it—over and over, though with many variations in the events during each repetition of the time. That was done for parts of a day in *Groundhog Day* (1993).

STYLE

genre: A commonly recognized group of fictional films that share characteristics. Western, science fiction, horror, and comedy are film genres.

Style refers to the manner or way of presenting a subject in a creative work. A style may be used in any type of film. For example, a **parody** (amusing imitation of earlier unamusing behavior, work, or works) may be used in any **genre** or type of film. A western or horror film, for instance, may include a parody, or an entire film may be a parody. There is not space here to introduce all possible film styles, and some film styles, such as parody and **socialist realism**, are discussed elsewhere in the book. What follows will illustrate only two of the most challenging styles for beginning film students: black comedy and magic realism.

Since World War II, many writers, filmmakers, and other weavers of tales in Europe and most of the Americas have tacitly asked viewers to consider the possible humor in subjects previously considered off-limits for comedy, such as warfare, illness, cannibalism, murder, death, and dying. Creative works that treat in an amusing way subjects that were previously avoided are usually called black humor or **black comedy**. Often black comedy is used in **satires**. *Dr. Strangelove* is a satire depicting scientists, military officers, and politicians in completely negative ways, and the film ends with the black comedy scene of an American pilot riding a nuclear bomb toward a Soviet military target as if he were riding a bucking horse followed by a series of exploding nuclear bombs indicating the end of the human race. *Eating Raoul* (1982) shows a married couple, Paul and Mary Bland, luring men swingers into their apartment then killing them for their money. The film ends by implying that Raoul—who had forced the couple into a partnership then had a brief affair with Mary—has met the fate suggested by the film's title. In *I Love You to Death* (1990), a wife and her mother try again and again to kill or have killed the wife's chronically unfaithful husband, and *Serial Mom* (1994) shows the main character killing off a total of seven people who annoy her for one reason or another.

In plot summary black comedies rarely sound amusing because they often involve violence or death. To make them work, their makers must handle timing, **pace**, and mood masterfully. Often black comedies amuse some viewers and shock or offend others. An example is the 1986 version of *Little Shop of Horrors* (Figure 7.14). In *Female Trouble* (1974), the main character has so many problems, some of them outrageous or at least startling, that viewers are offended or amused—or both (Figure 7.15). *The War of the Roses* (1989) also uses heavy doses of humor and pain as it shows a marriage breaking up; some viewers find the film hilarious, others mostly painful. Comedy involves pain—such as embarrassment, confusion, a fall—for someone else. Makers of black comedies dare to include more pain than some viewers are used to seeing in comedies. Depending on the filmmakers' skill in anticipating viewers' responses and on the viewers' backgrounds and tastes, black comedies may amuse or repulse.

Another style used since World War II, mainly in fiction, is **magic realism**, the **symbolic** depiction of improbable or impossible events in a narrative. *Erendira* (1982)—based on a script by a master of literary magic realism, Gabriel García Márquez—has many scenes incorporating magic realism. In one, the cruel grandmother consumes an enormous amount of rat poison mixed into a birthday cake then collapses onto her bed. After she starts to revive, the young man who had poisoned her observes, "Incredible! She's

socialist realism: A Soviet doctrine and style in force from the mid-1930s to the 1980s that decreed that all Soviet creative works, including films, must promote communism and thus the working class and must be "realistic" and thus understandable to working people.

satire: A depiction of behavior through language, visuals, or other means that has as its aim the humorous criticism of individual or group behavior.

pace: A person's sense of a subject (such as narrative developments or factual information) being presented rapidly or slowly.

symbol: Anything perceptible that has significance or meaning beyond its usual meaning or function.

FIGURE 7.14 Black comedy musical
For many viewers and reviewers *Little Shop of Horrors* (1986), a musical black comedy, is often funny until the growing person-eating plant (Audrey II) gets big, ugly, and vicious, and it gets even bigger and uglier and more vicious than the version seen here. *David Geffen; Warner Bros.*

tougher than an elephant! There was enough poison to kill a million rats!" The next morning, the grandmother wakes up, smiles, then says to her granddaughter Erendira, "God bless you, child. I hadn't slept that well since I was fifteen! I had a beautiful dream of love." The only ill effect from her previous night's dessert is that her hair is falling out, which seems to amuse her. The episode is unreal or magical: no person could survive so huge a dosage of poison or would react with amusement as her hair falls out; to many viewers it is also symbolic. The episode might suggest how difficult it is to destroy evil and be free of its influence. Or the two scenes might suggest how actions may not lead to the expected consequences. In this case, an attempt to destroy evil gives pleasure to the evil one.

In the 1991 film *Like Water for Chocolate*, the scrumptious food that Tita prepares causes those who eat it to feel as Tita felt when she prepared it—for example, sad or lustful. A dish Tita prepares so inflames one of Tita's sisters that she quickly loosens the clothing covering her breasts, then moves her hand over them and suggestively to underneath the dining table then rushes outside to take a shower, during which the wooden shack that encloses the shower bursts into flames. Some of the magic realism in the film is unrelated to food. At one point, while riding off in a horse-drawn carriage, Tita trails a shawl nearly half as long as an American football field because of the enormous cold she has been feeling. Magic realism in a film may be less prominent than it is in *Erendira* and *Like Water for Chocolate*. In *Burnt by the Sun* (1994), which is set in the mid-1930s Soviet Union, the menacing and destructive soccer ball–size "sun" that encircles and invades the main character's dacha and flies near the antagonist toward the end of the film can be seen as magic realism, here suggesting the destructive forces let loose by the Stalinist purges.

A film may use one style sporadically, as in *Fargo*, which mixes black comedy with unamusing graphic violence. Or a fictional film may use two or more styles, such as black comedy and parody.

Styles influence how viewers react to a film. If viewers refuse to play along with the magic realism of *Erendira* or *Like Water for Chocolate*, they will miss much of the pleasure of interacting with the film on its own terms. Likewise, if viewers beginning to watch the famous

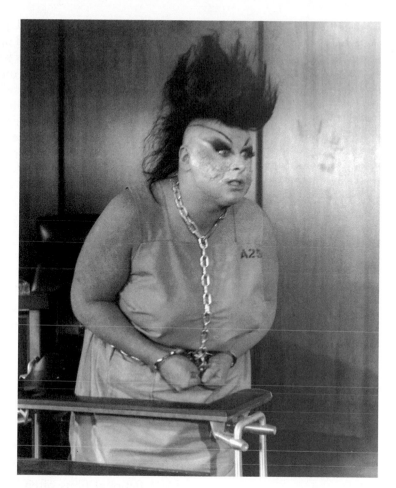

FIGURE 7.15 A black comedy that may amuse or offend
John Water's *Female Trouble* (1974) shows the biography of Dawn Davenport (played by Divine/Dave Lochary), a woman who starts to go wrong in her high school days, especially after her parents fail to give her "cha-cha heels" for Christmas and she attacks them and overturns the Christmas tree on them. Nearly everything that could go wrong in a woman's life goes wrong in Dawn's. For example, she is raped and ends up with an uncontrollable child, who years later in turn is nearly raped by the same man. After many complications, Dawn ends up standing trial for kidnapping and multiple murders. (Her face is scarred because in one of her many unhappy experiences, her former husband's aunt threw acid on it.) For some viewers *Female Trouble* is mostly offensive; to others it is fairly consistently amusing. *Copyright 1974 by New Line Productions, Inc. All rights reserved. Photo by Bruce Moore. Photo appears courtesy of New Line Productions, Inc., New York City*

surrealism: A movement in 1920s and 1930s European art, literature, and film in which an attempt was made to portray or interpret the workings of the subconscious mind as manifested in dreams.

avant-garde film: A film that rejects the conventions of popular movies and explores the possibilities and limitations of the film medium itself.

surrealist avant-garde film "Un Chien Andalou" (1928) expect a film of classical Hollywood cinema and do not quickly recognize that the film consists of a series of discontinuous scenes like the irrationality of dreams, they will fail to interact with the film more or less as was intended. If audiences are watching a film that uses a particular style that they have not previously seen, such as surrealism or magic realism, they need to figure out the film's style quickly and give the film a chance to do what it can do within the parameters it has set out for itself. If viewers know nothing about the film's style and cannot figure it out quickly or if they refuse to play along with a style they know about—for example, decline to be amused by a parody—they will sit glumly and hope for a different style and a different film, in vain.

SUMMARY

Narratives

- A narrative—both in film and elsewhere—may be defined as a series of unified consecutive events (represented actions and happenings) situated in one or more settings. A narrative may be factual or fictional, or a blend of the two.

Structure

- A fictional film is a narrative film that includes at least one character (imaginary person) and largely imaginary events; its settings may be factual or imaginary.

- Usually in fictional films the central character has one or more goals but faces problems in trying to reach them.

- Short fictional films often have only one or two major characters who usually do not change their goals or personalities during a brief story time. The major characters of a short fictional film usually have a goal or goals that are not explained but that viewers can figure out early in the film; have obstacles to overcome; and succeed or fail in reaching the goal.

- Typically, the beginning of a fictional film does not supply much exposition although it establishes where and when the narrative starts. It also attempts to get audiences interested in the story.

- Among other functions, the middle section shows how the central characters deal with problems that impede progress toward their goals and thereby reveal both their nature and the consequences of their actions for them and others.

- The ending of a fictional film shows the consequences of major previous actions. In films with closure, by the end of the narrative the consequences of previous major actions are shown or clearly implied. Most films of classical Hollywood cinema have closure, but many independent films do not.

- A plotline is a brief narrative focused on a few characters or people that could function on its own as a separate (usually very brief) story. Typically, short films have only one plotline, whereas feature films often have multiple plotlines. Many combinations of plotlines are possible. For example, they can be consecutive but with large gaps of time between them; can alternate between different time periods; or can be chronological, simultaneous, and occasionally intersecting.

Time

- Flashforwards are used only occasionally in fictional films, usually to suggest a premonition or inevitability. Flashbacks are often used and can serve many different purposes. On rare occasions fictional films combine present-tense action with flashforwards and flashbacks.

- A fabula is the mental reconstruction in chronological order of all the events in a nonchronological plot. Although a plot contains the same events as its corresponding fabula, a nonchronological plot has different emphases and moods and causes different responses in viewers.

- How much time is represented in a fictional film (story time) is usually unspecified and difficult to determine with any precision, but story time nearly always far exceeds the film's running time.

Style

- A fictional film may be rendered in one or more styles, such as black comedy or surrealism. If viewers know nothing about a film's style and cannot figure it out quickly or if they refuse to accept a style they know about, they will likely fail to become engaged by the film.

WORKS CITED

Armes, Roy. *Action and Image: Dramatic Structure in Cinema.* Manchester, Eng.: Manchester UP, 1994.

Chatman, Seymour. *Story and Discourse: Narrative Structure in Fiction and Film.* Ithaca: Cornell UP, 1978.

Corliss, Richard. Rev. of *Continental Divide,* dir. Michael Apted. *Time* 14 Sept. 1981: 90.

Dunne, John Gregory. *Monster: Living Off the Big Screen*. New York: Random, 1997.

Eidsvik, Charles. *Cineliteracy: Film among the Arts*. New York: Random, 1978.

Rosen, Robert. "Notes on Painting and Film." *Art and Film since 1945: Hall of Mirrors*. Ed. Kerry Brougher. Los Angeles: Museum of Contemporary Art, 1996.

Vernet, Marc. "Cinema and Narration." *Aesthetics of Film*. Trans. and rev. Richard Neupert. Austin: U of Texas P, 1992.

FOR FURTHER READING

Phillips, William H. *Writing Short Scripts*. 2nd ed. Syracuse: Syracuse UP, 1999. Includes three unproduced scripts for short films, detailed descriptions of two award-winning short films, discussion of the short script and short film, and partial credits and brief descriptions for many short films.

Prince, Gerald. *Dictionary of Narratology*. Lincoln: U of Nebraska P, 1987. Although the book focuses on literature and some of its terms and definitions are too specialized and sometimes too precise for beginning film students, many definitions—for example, for *narrative*, *plot*, *sequence*, *surprise*, and *suspense*—are illuminating and thought-provoking.

Stam, Robert, Robert Burgoyne, and Sandy Flitterman-Lewis. "Part III Film-narratology." *New Vocabularies in Film Semiotics: Structuralism, Post-structuralism and Beyond*. London: Routledge, 1992. 69–122. Theoretical issues about narrative for the advanced student.

CHAPTER **8**

Alternatives to Live-Action Fictional Films

I N THE PREVIOUS THREE CHAPTERS we considered the fictional film. This chapter considers documentary, avant-garde, hybrid, and animated films, the four major alternatives to the live-action (nonanimated) fictional film, which has overwhelmingly dominated viewer and critical attention almost since the birth of motion pictures.

DOCUMENTARY FILMS

There's something about the images themselves. It's the way everything seems to shimmer in the light of that particular ordinary Sunday morning, the way everything's in movement, the shadows, the light, the handheld camera, and there's the slight camera shyness of my parents, shyness mixed with happiness and pride, everything sort of quivering with the kind of life that would be very difficult to reenact.

—Ross McElwee's **narration** in *Time Indefinite* (1993), about a home movie made on the day he was baptized

A **documentary film** presents a version of **events** that viewers are intended to accept not primarily as the product of someone's imagination but primarily as fact. Typically, documentary filmmakers do one or more of the following: film what happened, re-create what happened and film it, or film how to make something happen (a how-to film). After they film (and/or gather others' **footage**), they usually determine the presentation of the material through editing and other **techniques**. Documentary filmmakers may be motivated by various goals: "to (1) communicate insights, achieve beauty, and offer understanding . . . , or (2) improve social, political, or economic conditions" (Ellis 7). Documentary films are sometimes referred to as "nonfiction films," but I prefer the older and more widely understood term "documentary films" because "nonfiction films" identifies this group of films not by what they are but

narration: Commentary about some aspect of the film or a subject in the film, often from someone offscreen.

event: Either an action by a character or person (such as Darth Vader and Obi-Wan Kenobi dueling with light sabers) or a happening (such as it raining on the streets in *Blade Runner*).

footage: A length of exposed motion-picture film.

technique: Any aspect of filmmaking, such as the choices of sets, lighting, sound effects, music, and editing.

311

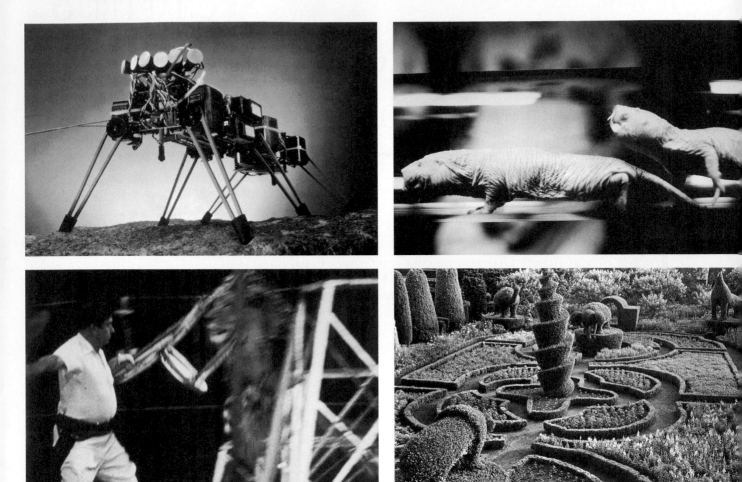

FIGURE 8.1 A nonnarrative documentary film with multiple subjects

Fast, Cheap & Out of Control (1997) alternates between four primary subjects, four occupations and the men who pursue them: (a, top left) making robots shaped approximately as insects, (b, top right) studying mole-rats, (c, above left) taming wild animals, and (d, above right) doing topiary gardening that features plants shaped like large animals. The film presents information about its four major subjects and ideas related to each of them yet implies meanings transcending its parts. Critic Richard Corliss wrote that the film "is a funny, thrilling tribute to people's urge to find play and profundity in the work they do." Chris Chang wrote, "The film amounts to a tremendously moving—not to mention entertaining—evocation of human finitude, and a documentation of various attempts to surmount it." And movie critic Jay Carr wrote that "lurking beneath the surface, with its promise of entertaining eccentricity, are themes of transitoriness, the futility of thinking you can control anything, the poignancy of love and loss, the struggle to invest life and work with meaning and, finally, the trajectory on which youthful dreams move into decay (in two cases) or into an even grander vision (in the other two)." (c) Frame enlargement. *Errol Morris; Sony Picture Classics*

what they are not (they are not fiction) and because "nonfiction film" suggests that this type of film is the opposite of fictional films, whereas these two major film types may have much in common.

Nonnarrative and Narrative

Most documentary films tell no narrative or story. These **nonnarrative documentaries** include most scientific films, many TV documentaries on social conditions, industrial films, training films, promotional films, and many TV advertisements. Most nonnarrative documentary films either present a variety of information organized into categories or make an argument.

An example of a nonnarrative documentary film is *Fast, Cheap & Out of Control* (1997), which conveys a wide variety of information by alternating between four subjects, each pursued by a thoughtful and articulate man devoted to his unusual occupation (Figure 8.1).

Other nonnarrative documentary films make an argument, as in the very brief "Television, the Drug of the Nation" (1992). Like a mantra, "television, the drug of a nation, breeding ignorance and feeding radiation" is heard repeatedly in the film. The rap **narrator** also claims that TV is the reason so few Americans read books and the reason most people think "Central America means Kansas," and the narrator adds, "A child watches fifteen hundred murders [on TV] before he's twelve years old, and then we wonder why we've created a Jason generation." The film's chaotic but mesmerizing visuals suggest that TV is dizzying, fragmented, and highly manipulative yet addictive and dangerous to one's health. "Television, the Drug of the Nation" conveys information but mainly makes an argument: (commercial) TV is detrimental to American life.

Often a nonnarrative documentary film makes an argument by editing; it may **cut** from one **shot** to the next to criticize, as is often done in *Hearts and Minds*, a 1974 film by Peter Davis about U.S. involvement in the Vietnam War. At one point President Lyndon Johnson is undercut coming and going. We see an enraged high school football coach in a locker room shout at and hit some of his players; then part of a football game and an injured player in pain; then President Johnson (whom we may equate with the out-of-control coach) declare that the United States will win (the war in Vietnam). The next footage shows some of the chaos and destruction of the Tet Offensive, a massive surprise counterattack that abruptly cast into doubt when and how the war would finally end. At the conclusion of the film, editing is used to criticize the American contribution to Vietnamese suffering and the militaristic aspects of American society. A shot of countless freshly dug, empty Vietnamese graves accompanied by sounds of moaning and crying is followed by shots in the United States of marching soldiers, a flag-waving spectator, and later marching boys in military uniform, a formation of motorcycle police, and other shots of parades and demonstrations.

narrator: A character, person, or unidentifiable voice that provides commentary before, during, or after the main body of a film, or a combination of these options.

cut: To sever or splice film while editing.

shot: An uninterrupted strip of exposed motion-picture film or videotape made up of at least one frame.

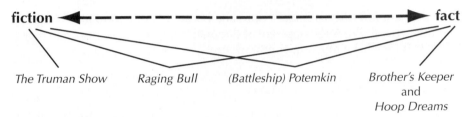

FIGURE 8.2 **The narrative films continuum**
Some narrative films are completely fictional, but many blend fiction and fact. *The Truman Show* (1998) is completely fictional: as we watch it, we recognize no character as being based on a famous person and no actions re-creating real occurrences. But *Raging Bull* (1980) is a fictional film that many viewers will recognize as partially factual: certain aspects of the character Jake are the same as those of the real Jake La Motta, the famous boxer. Some narratives are more difficult to categorize. *(Battleship) Potemkin* (1925) is a blend of fiction and fact, and though scholars usually categorize it as a fictional film, some consider it a narrative documentary. Even narrative documentary films are never entirely factual. For example, significant details might be omitted or the order of some events changed in editing. Narrative films that blend fiction and fact and have as their subjects recent news or history are sometimes called *docudramas*, especially if they were originally made for TV.

A relatively small number of documentary films present a narrative or story. **Narrative documentary films** are largely true narratives: a series of unified factual events. But as Figure 8.2 illustrates, many narratives blend fiction and fact.

Like the fictional film, the narrative documentary often features someone with a goal, as in *Brother's Keeper* (1992), in which the main person has been accused of suffocating a brother suffering from ill health and wants to avoid being convicted (Figure 8.3). In *Hoop Dreams* (1994), two young inner-city men hope to excel in high school and college basketball and eventually play in the National Basketball Association.

Like fictional films, narrative documentaries may not present events chronologically. *The Gate of Heavenly Peace* (1995) focuses on the historical occurrences leading up to the 1989 military crackdown on student demonstrators in Tiananmen Square in China and its aftermath, but from time to time the film also includes historical background footage, some dating as far back as 1919. Viewers watching the film will have little trouble sorting through all the material and arranging it chronologically.

Narrative documentaries are never simply narratives. They also include supporting artifacts and informative language. Consider *Burden of Dreams* (1982), a film by Les Blank, which includes a story about what happened during the filming of the movie *Fitzcarraldo* (1982). Viewers can easily figure out the order of events in *Burden of Dreams* and see how they are connected. The **scenes** are even arranged chronologically, from November 1979 to November 1981. The film focuses on the people filming *Fitzcarraldo*,

scene: A section of a narrative film that gives the impression of continuous action taking place in one continuous time and space.

though occasionally the main story is interrupted for
various details of life in the Amazonian jungle (such as
the size, speed, and dexterity of ants) and, most of all,
details about the lives of the native South Americans
(Figure 8.4). The narrative is also punctuated with frequent interviews, especially with Werner Herzog, the
director of *Fitzcarraldo*. Not that *Burden of Dreams*
lacks unity, but like most narratives, whether fiction or
documentary, it has more going on than a story.

Like nonnarrative documentary films, narrative
documentary films may use editing to criticize or
praise a person or idea. Consider the opening footage
of *Triumph of the Will* (1935). Leni Riefenstahl made
the film to document and celebrate a huge Nazi party

FIGURE 8.5 Multiple plotlines in a narrative documentary *Hoop Dreams* (1994) shows the real stories of two inner-city young men who dream of playing in the National Basketball Association, (a, above right) William Gates and (b, right) Arthur Agee. The film captures parts of their lives from their days in junior high to the beginning of college. Although the two stories occasionally intersect (the two commuted to the same high school for a while and their paths cross occasionally after one of them goes to a different school), basically the film alternates between their two narratives. Frame enlargements. *Fine Line Features*

conference, and it opens with aerial shots of clouds, church spires and the tops of other buildings, an airplane flying above a city, the shadow of the airplane speeding over the ground of the city below, and troops marching in formation; then, on the ground, many alternating shots of excited crowds and the plane landing and pulling to a stop, followed by the emergence of Adolf Hitler, then Joseph Goebbels, the Nazi minister of propaganda. In the next section shots alternate between the large and excited crowds on the sides of the streets and Hitler standing in a moving car and saluting with a stiff arm. Thus in the film's opening shots, Hitler is associated with power, speed, grace, perhaps even spirituality (those churches), and the adoration of the masses.

Narrative documentary films often have only one **plotline**, but like fictional films they may have two or more. *Hoop Dreams* has two plotlines, each about an inner-city youth who hopes to play in the National Basketball Association (Figure 8.5). "The Heck with Hollywood!" (1991) alternates the narratives of three groups of filmmakers trying to market their films outside the Hollywood network: a young man, a young woman, and three young men. Most of *Pumping Iron* (1976) consists of five plotlines: the background and training of two bodybuilders, then their competition for the 1975 Mr. Universe title, followed by the background, training, and competition of three men, including Arnold Schwarzenegger, for the 1975 Mr. Olympia title.

Occasionally it is difficult to categorize a documentary film as narrative or nonnarrative, as is the case with one of the first feature-length documentaries, *Nanook of the North* (1922, restored 1976; Figure 8.6). There is little clear-cut unity to the film's sections (many could be switched without consequences for viewers), yet we get a view of the Eskimos' lives presented more or less

plotline: A brief narrative; a series of related events involving a few characters or people and capable of functioning on its own as a story.

FIGURE 8.6 Narrative or nonnarrative documentary
Nanook of the North (1922), a famous early documentary film, reveals important aspects of Eskimo life, especially getting food and surviving a harsh environment. A title card early in the film indicates that the film's initial actions take place in summer. Later in the film a title card indicates that the following action happened in the winter (presumably the following winter). Through the film's various parts, viewers more or less learn how (a, above left) Nanook, a Canadian Eskimo, and his family could live: for example, by using a kayak, trading, (b, above right) spearing fish on a floe, hunting walrus, traveling, building an igloo, hunting seal, and preparing for a storm. The film's emphasis seems to be as much on presenting different types of information as in telling a story. Frame enlargements. *Revillon Frères; The Museum of Modern Art/Circulating Film Library*

episodic plot: Story structure in which many scenes have no necessary or probable relationship to each other; many scenes could be switched without strongly affecting the overall story or audience responses to the film.

continuity: The editing of a narrative film's visuals and sounds so that viewers can easily understand the relationship of shot to shot and scene to scene.

chronologically (from a summer to a winter). Many critics think of *Nanook* as a narrative, though its story is skimpy and **episodic** and its emphasis at least as much on presenting information as telling a story.

Characteristics of Documentary Films

Whether narrative or not, a documentary film has most or all of the following characteristics: mediated reality, real people instead of actors, location shooting, supporting factual information, and use of a wide range of techniques.

MEDIATED REALITY   Documentary films are one version of mediated reality: they are a selected, perhaps staged, and edited presentation of events. To illustrate: one long scene in Frederick Wiseman's *High School II* (1994) consists of three shots of students sitting around a table talking. In the first two shots we see five students, including a boy in a red cap who says little. Here as elsewhere in the film, the **continuity** of dialogue is so smooth and the editing so unobtrusive that we may not see when the third shot begins and may not notice that the boy in the red cap has disappeared. If we notice the boy's absence from the scene's last shot, we realize that his departure was never filmed or was filmed then excised in editing and that the scene is not complete but selective. Another filmmaker might have chosen to present the scene in one extremely lengthy shot, including the boy's departure. The director and editor (in some films they are the same person) have given viewers a selected version of reality.

Other documentary filmmakers change the subject to be filmed before filming it. While filming *Nanook of the North*, director Robert Flaherty found that the igloos were too small and too dim for him to fit in his bulky 35 mm camera and tripod and to provide enough light to film, so he had the Eskimos build a larger igloo without a top. A similar situation arose in the filming of *Crumb* (1994). An interviewer on the Sundance Channel observed that a large wall cabinet full of 78 rpm records in director Terry Zwigoff's house looked a lot like Crumb's record cabinet in the film. Zwigoff responded, "We actually shot fake scenes in this room where he's [Crumb's] sitting here with, like, a drawing board and we moved this lamp that used to be in his house over here and this [indicating Zwigoff's record cabinet] is the background. We faked it for his house because we didn't want to drive back up there." Near the beginning of cinema, in "The Execution of Mary, Queen of Scots" (1895), the filmmakers substituted a dummy for the person enacting Queen Mary immediately before the beheading (Figure 8.7). Since then, countless documentary filmmakers have staged actions or re-created them or in other ways changed details about the way they were. Like fiction makers, for various reasons—including to save time and money or to show larger truths in an engaging way—documentary makers sometimes fudge the details.

FIGURE 8.7 An early documentary film that re-creates an event
Perhaps "The Execution of Mary, Queen of Scots" (1895) is the earliest example of a documentary
film re-creating events to deceive audiences about what they are seeing. (a, above left) The executioner is beginning to swing his ax downward. The action and shot were stopped, and a dummy
was substituted for "Queen Mary." (b, above right) In the next shot the executioner cuts off the
dummy's head, which remains on the block. Frame enlargements. *The Museum of Modern Art/Film
Stills Archive*

Some filmmakers change the order of presentation through editing. A
title card at the beginning of *Dead Birds* (1963), a film about the lifestyles of
similar warring New Guinea tribes, states that the film

title card: A card or thin sheet
of clear plastic that supplies information in a film.

> is a true story composed from footage of actual events photographed. . . . No
> scene was directed and no role was created. The people in the film merely did
> what they had done before we came and, for those who are not dead, as they do
> now that we have left.

Yet the director Robert Gardner later wrote that the film has "compressions of
time which exclude vast portions of actuality. There are events made parallel
in time which occurred sequentially" (346–47).

PEOPLE, NOT ACTORS When the subject is human behavior, the documentary
film nearly always uses ordinary people, not actors, and certainly not stars.
For example, *Hoop Dreams* is basically about two real young men and their
families. Only rarely do documentaries use actors. Charlie Sheen plays a judge
in Emile De Antonio's *In the King of Prussia* (1983); actors reenact some minor
roles in *The Thin Blue Line* (1988); and actors play all the roles in the many
re-created scenes of *Thirty-Two Short Films about Glenn Gould* (1993).

319

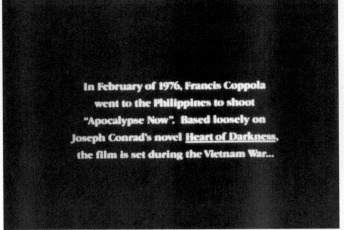

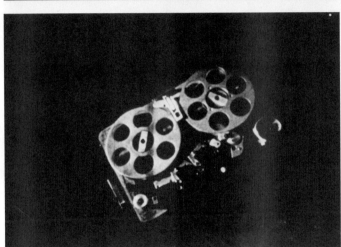

FIGURE 8.8 Varied sources available for documentary films

Hearts of Darkness (1991) is a narrative documentary about the many problems confronted in filming *Apocalypse Now* (1979). The filmmakers used a wide variety of sources, including (from top left to top right) (a) title cards, (b) subtitles, (c) still photographs, (d) clips from rehearsals, and (from above left to above right) (e) audio clips played on a tape player, (f) interviews, (g) newspaper head-

location: Any place other than a constructed setting that is used for filming.

LOCATION SHOOTING   Documentary films are usually filmed on **location**. Location shooting became possible with the development of lighter and more mobile cameras and sound recording equipment in the late 1950s, and recent years have seen the development of equipment that is even more versatile and produces even better quality. Many documentaries are now shot on location with a Hi-8 video camera (see Figure 2.52) or with BetacamSP or a DV cam (digital video camera). More than ever it is possible for one person to go practically anywhere and film and record unobtrusively. Later if the opportunity for a theatrical release arises, the video is transferred to 35 mm film.

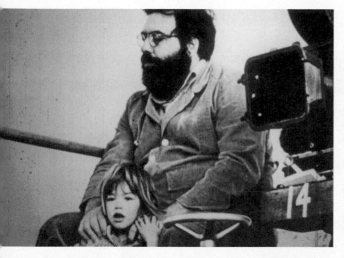

Casting Session, November 1975

Coppola Loses His Beard, 38 Pounds And Star Keitel

By JOSEPH McBRIDE

Harvey Keitel has been fired from the lead role in Francis Ford Coppola's "Apocalypse Now" in what Keitel's agent,

lines, and (h) movie clips from the finished product. The film also alternates between two interviews, and uses audio clips from interviews accompanying visual clips of something else, a phone conversation accompanying visual clips of something else, radio and TV clips, sections of film not included in the final version (outtakes), and drawings made before the filming (storyboards). Frame enlargements. *George Zaloom & Les Mayfield; New Yorker Films*

Occasionally documentary films are not filmed entirely on location. Les Blank told me that his film "Gap-Toothed Women" (1987) was **shot** largely within his own studio instead of in the homes or workplaces of his subjects. Other exceptions: Errol Morris shot parts of *The Thin Blue Line* in New York City, not Texas, and he filmed the interviews for *A Brief History of Time* (1992) and *Fast, Cheap & Out of Control* in a studio.

shot: Filmed, as in "They shot the movie in seven weeks."

SUPPORTING INFORMATION   The documentary film usually presents supporting artifacts and uses informative language (Figure 8.8). Supporting artifacts

FIGURE 8.9 **Supporting artifacts in a documentary film**
"The Match That Started My Fire" (1991) by Cathy Cook consists entirely of supporting documents (various film clips) and informative language (off-camera accounts by women). Here a woman twirls around and around as a woman's voice recounts how as a girl she would sometimes wear a certain type of skirt to school then spin around and around for her pleasure and the boys'. *Photo by Cathy Cook; dancer: Heidi Heistad. Women Make Movies, New York, and Film-makers' Cooperative, New York*

compilation film: A film consisting of edited footage that was filmed by others.

include documents, photographs, objects a person has made or owned, newsreels or clips from movies, home movies, or TV shows. *Brother's Keeper* includes such supporting artifacts as several TV news accounts of Delbert's arrest and footage of events such as a dance. Sometimes only one or a few types of supporting information are used in a documentary film. For example, *The Atomic Café* (1982)—which is about the arrival of nuclear weapons and some of the subsequent U.S. government's responses to their use—consists entirely of excerpts from commercial and government media. Cathy Cook's "The Match That Started My Fire" (1991) consists of found footage and footage she shot for the film (Figure 8.9). *Point of Order* (1963), by Emile De Antonio, is a 97-minute **compilation film** made mostly from 188 hours of TV footage of the 1954 Army-McCarthy hearings.

Supporting information helps persuade viewers of the truthfulness of a film's presentation. It may be incorporated into a film in countless creative ways. In the third part of *Baseball* (1994), we see a photograph of the exterior of a building, presumably where a grand jury is meeting, then a photograph of

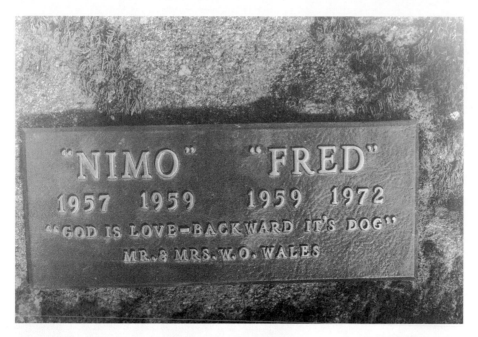

FIGURE 8.10 Informative language in a documentary film
Informative language, which is often used in documentary films, may appear in various forms. Here it is used in a pet cemetery on a headstone honoring departed dogs in Errol Morris's documentary film *Gates of Heaven* (1978). The language helps reveal the owners' feelings for their former pets.
A New Yorker Films Release

a man's face looking toward the camera. As we see these photographs, we hear a gavel banging, the **ambient sounds** of people inside a room, and voices of two actors reenacting a prosecutor posing questions about the throwing of the 1919 World Series and Chicago White Sox player "Shoeless" Joe Jackson responding to them. After the **offscreen** re-created testimony has finished, we are allowed about four seconds to continue to scrutinize the photograph of Joe Jackson in silence.

Often the documentary film includes informative language: narration (or title cards or subtitles), interviews, signs, even headstones (Figure 8.10), or a combination of sources. The words of songs may also function as narration or commentary on the film's subjects, as they do throughout "Chulas Fronteras" (1976). Until the late 1950s, documentary films relied heavily on all-knowing narrators, in part because it was too cumbersome to film and to record synchronous sound on location. In the newsreels shown in movie theaters until the early 1960s, an authoritative narrator was used. Most recent documentary films use interviews more often than narration or use inter-

ambient sound: The usual sounds of a place that people tend not to notice.

offscreen: Area beyond the frame line.

views alone, in part because of the availability of more portable filmmaking equipment and in part because of the widespread belief that no one person or narrator can do justice to a subject's complexity. Some films, such as those directed by Frederick Wiseman, use neither narration nor interviews. And a few—such as *The Times of Harvey Milk* (1984) and *The Wonderful, Horrible Life of Leni Riefenstahl* (1993)—use both.

WIDE RANGE OF TECHNIQUES In the late 1950s and early 1960s, development of 16 mm **fast film**, handheld 16 mm cameras with a **zoom lens**, and portable sound packs gave filmmakers much greater mobility and flexibility (Figure 8.11). In the United States, filmmakers using that equipment developed **direct cinema**, a type of documentary filmmaking in which the film is shot on location with minimal planning. The aim of such films is not so much to prove a point but to explore a subject. An exchange between an inter-

fast film: Film stock that requires relatively little light for re-creation of images.

zoom lens: A camera lens with variable focal lengths; thus it can be adjusted by degrees during a shot so that the size of the subject and the area being filmed seem to change.

FIGURE 8.11 **The portability of direct cinema equipment**
To film the onstage and offstage action of a three-day musical event attended by an estimated 400,000 people, one or two cameras would have been grossly inadequate. Fortunately, by the time of the Woodstock concert in 1969, documentary filmmakers could use portable 16 mm cameras and lightweight, largely unobtrusive magnetic tape recorders. In this photograph can be seen some of the many cameras—some on tripods, some handheld—used in making the documentary *Woodstock* (1970). *A Wadleigh-Maurice, Ltd. Production; Warner Bros.*

viewer for the film journal *Cineaste* and the filmmaker Frederick Wiseman, who is one of the main practitioners of direct cinema, highlights that purpose:

> CINEASTE: And your film [*Welfare*, 1975] doesn't generalize, at all. Nor does it attempt to suggest any possible solutions or answers. That stance characterizes all of your films.
>
> WISEMAN: That's right. I don't know the answers. I'm interested in the complexities and ambiguities of our experience. (Lucia 9)

Makers of direct cinema attempt to minimize interference with their subjects' lives; consequently, they often use the **long take** and the zoom lens so subjects may be seen from afar or close up without the camera distracting them. At about the same time as direct cinema emerged and using the same type of equipment, a similar type of documentary filmmaking, **cinéma vérité**, developed in France, although during filming French filmmakers were likely to ask questions of their subjects and talk with them.

> **long take:** A shot of long duration.

> **cinéma vérité:** A style of documentary filmmaking developed in France during the early 1960s the aim of which was to capture events as they happen.

Two examples of direct cinema are Wiseman's *Titicut Follies* (1967)—which shows some of the activities of the inmates, staff, and volunteers at a Massachusetts mental hospital—and Michael Wadleigh's *Woodstock* (1970), which shows action on- and offstage at a huge open-air rock concert in upstate New York. These and other films of direct cinema often have technical imperfections: the camera operator sometimes does not refocus on a new subject as quickly as viewers are used to seeing in rehearsed, commercial films. The camera work might occasionally be wobbly; the dialogue might be indistinct; and at times the film might be too dark or too light. To some viewers these imperfections only strengthen the film's credibility. Viewers can imagine that the film is not a slick, manipulated presentation—as, for example, *Triumph of the Will* is—but more nearly a presentation of actions as they happened.

At the other extreme, some documentary films look and sound as polished and professionally made as expensive fictional films. In *Brother's Keeper* it's not as if the filmmakers simply recorded one scene after another, cut some dead time, and presented the results. Far from it, as a look at the excerpt in Table 8.1 shows. In scene 1, the man says in effect that Delbert probably put his brother out of his misery as one would a sick cat. In the next scene, viewers see a Ward brother, then a dead cat: the second scene hints at the validity of the point expressed in the first. **Parallel editing** is used to contrast the state police's picture of Delbert with the one viewers see. In scenes 2, 4, 7, and 10, offscreen sound is used, the second and third times from a questioner in the following scene. In the tenth scene, music adds to the mood, as do the many shots of farm life. Throughout the film the cinematography and editing are as accomplished as in many fictional features.

> **parallel editing:** Editing that alternates between two or more subjects or lines of action.

Other documentary films demonstrate yet other possible techniques. Brief sections of *Time Indefinite* include a darkened screen or the tail **leader**

> **leader:** A piece of clear or opaque motion-picture film of any color that usually precedes and concludes a reel of film.

TABLE 8.1
Ten Consecutive Scenes from *Brother's Keeper*

SCENE NO.	LENGTH IN SEC.	DESCRIPTION
1	28	A man in a truck says he now thinks Delbert (the man accused of murdering his brother, Bill) probably did put Bill out of his misery, "like you would a sick cat or something like that."
2	12	Voice of man from previous scene continues as he says of the four Ward brothers, "They've been damn good boys" and we see one of Delbert's brothers lying on the ground. Then we see a cat sniffing a dead cat.
3	24	An official (much earlier a subtitle identified him as Capt. Loszynski of the New York State Police) justifies the use of question and answer in interrogation.
4	7	Long shot of man unloading bales of hay from a conveyor belt as we hear a voice asking the beginning of a question: "Were you befuddled in any way on the 6th of June. . . ."
5	7	Close-up of Delbert as the off-frame voice finishes the question then Delbert answers no; then in response to a follow-up question Delbert admits he doesn't know what "befuddled" means.
6	17	Another official (identified by a subtitle much earlier in the film as Investigator Cosnett) explains in effect that Delbert understood his rights (when he was brought in for questioning).
7	4	Long shot of a man (same as in scene 4) covering bales of hay with a tarp as a voice is heard asking a question.
8	17	Delbert answers the question from the previous scene then upon request demonstrates on the man beside him (much earlier in the film identified in a subtitle as Harry Thurston/Friend) how officials said Delbert suffocated his brother.
9	20	Another official (identified in a subtitle as Investigator Killough) says Delbert has changed his story, but on the night of his interrogation Delbert put his hand over his own mouth to demonstrate "how he did it."
10	65	Shots of foggy farmland and Delbert as we hear the voice of Delbert and presumably the voice of the prosecutor asking whether Delbert understood what he was signing (his confession) and if he had been forced to sign it. Throughout this scene, music is heard, except just before the end when it quickly fades out.

fast cutting: Editing characterized by many brief shots.

swish pan: Effect achieved when a camera pivots horizontally so rapidly that the image is blurred.

of some rolls of film (after the film in the camera had run out) or occasional humorous, deliberately wobbly handheld camera shots. *Unzipped* (1995) also includes frequent wobbly handheld shots plus **fast cutting**, **swish pans**, and even speeded-up motion—all of which contribute to an out-of-control, dizzying effect. *The Thin Blue Line* uses imaginary and repeated re-creations filmed years after the events depicted (Figure 8.12); some extremely **high angles**; **slow motion**; lighting and color that are dramatic rather than strictly functional (note the warm-colored light on and behind David Harris as he is interviewed in prison); parallel editing; unexpected **cutaway shots**; movie clips, some only obliquely related to the subject at hand; and a striking score by Philip Glass. As Errol Morris, the director of *The Thin Blue Line*, acknowledged in an interview, his film style is the polar opposite of Frederick Wiseman's (Bates 17). Yet both strike audiences as credible.

The first and last moving images of Harvey Milk in *The Times of Harvey Milk* are in slow motion. In both cases, viewers see a man who was charismatic and full of energy rendered as graceful yet drained of his vitality. *Dialogues with Madwomen* (1994), which is about the experiences and perspectives of seven northern California women who have suffered from mental illness, consists largely of alternating interviews with the women. During each interview, we see brief clips related to what the speaker is describing. Sometimes these cutaway shots reenact what is being described, for example, children rummaging through trash cans in search of food. Such cutaways are redundant and sometimes even a little insulting to viewers, and they are too literal

high angle: View of a subject from above, taken by the camera pointing downward during the filming.

slow motion: Motion in which the action depicted on the screen is slower than its real-life counterpart.

cutaway (shot): A shot that briefly interrupts the visual presentation of a subject to show something else.

FIGURE 8.12 Re-created scene in *The Thin Blue Line* (1988) Here and elsewhere, the film uses re-creations to show different people's versions of the same event, the killing of a Dallas police officer. As director Errol Morris pointed out in a TV interview with Bill Moyers, it is up to viewers to decide which version of the murder is most probable. *BFI; Third Floor; American Playhouse*

FIGURE 8.13 A negative image and a positive image
Only the concluding shots of Maya Deren's "Ritual in Transfigured Time" (1946) are negative images. (a, right) This frame is from the film's last shot and is of a woman as she sinks deeper and deeper into some water and presumably is dying. (b, below) This image, which does not appear in the finished film, is a positive print of the same negative. Frame enlargements. *The Museum of Modern Art/Circulating Film Library*

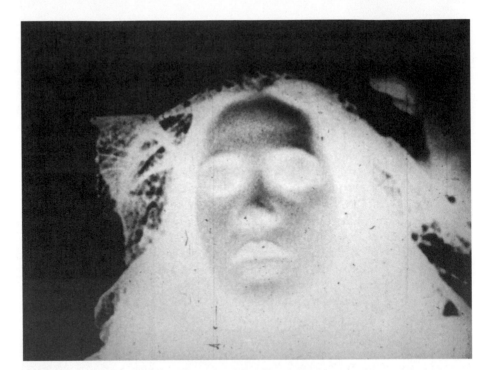

to get at emotional truth. More often, however, the cutaways are **symbolic** and evocative. For example, at one point as we hear a woman explaining what a tyrant her father was, we see a man in a nondescript **setting** gesturing as if directing traffic and walking forward in slow motion. This cutaway is made even more unsettling because it is the **negative** of a black-and-white shot, and the man's face looks light, indistinct, and inscrutable. (For an example of a negative image, see Figure 8.13a.)

Studying documentary films reveals that many share characteristics with fictional films. Often both are filmed and edited versions of human behavior. Like fictional filmmakers, documentary filmmakers have countless options and enormous influence over the films they create (see pp. 330–31). As film scholar Bill Nichols writes, documentary films are

> forms of re-presentation, never clear windows onto "reality"; the film-maker was always a participant-witness and an active fabricator of meaning, a producer of cinematic discourse rather than a neutral or all-knowing reporter of the ways things truly are. ("Voice" 18)

All documentary films purport to be factual. If their makers are scrupulous about details, well informed, and fair-minded (for example, the film clips and interviews are representative of different viewpoints and are not taken out of context), viewers tend to trust them. Unless viewers lose faith in the credibility of the filmmakers or know of contradictory information from other sources, they accept the films as true.

AVANT-GARDE FILMS

> More than 99% of all people do not like films; they like stories. (Mekas)

> The experience [of studying avant-garde films] provides us with the opportunity (an opportunity much of our training has taught us to resist) to come to a clearer, more complete understanding of what the cinematic experience actually can be, and what—for all the pleasure and inspiration it may give us—the conventional movie experience is *not*. (MacDonald 2)

Jonas Mekas writes from the point of view of an avant-garde filmmaker and author who knows that most viewers are slow to embrace films that tell no story. Scott MacDonald is a scholar of the avant-garde film; he and other scholars believe, as I do, that studying avant-garde films deepens one's understanding of the film medium. Indeed, as avant-garde filmmaker and theorist Edward Small demonstrates in his book *Direct Theory: Experimental Film/ Video as Major Genre*, some avant-garde films are correctives to the generalizations of film theorists who focus exclusively on the fictional film.

symbol: Anything perceptible that has significance or meaning beyond its usual meaning or function.

setting: The place where filmed action occurs.

negative: Film that has been exposed and processed; it is normally used to make (positive) prints for projection but is occasionally used in part of a finished film. In black-and-white negatives, the light and dark areas are reversed.

Excerpts from an Interview with Filmmaker Errol Morris

Errol Morris was born in Hewlett, Long Island, New York, in 1948. Thus far, his filmmaking career includes the direction of five feature-length documentary films: *Gates of Heaven* (1978); *Vernon, Florida* (1981); *The Thin Blue Line* (1988); *A Brief History of Time* (1992); and *Fast, Cheap & Out of Control* (1997). The following are excerpts from a telephone interview with Errol Morris conducted on March 20, 1998. For a transcript of the complete interview, see our web page: http://www.bedfordstmartins.com.

PHILLIPS: As a filmmaker, what do you gain from watching other people's films?

MORRIS: I believe this line comes from Godard, but the real university of film is the movie theater. If you want to learn about film, the best place to do it is by going to see movies. I certainly know that's how I have learned about film. When I was a graduate student at Berkeley, there was a specific film archive where I programmed movies and I went to see movies slavishly—two to three to four movies a day—for the good part of a year. I guess it becomes a kind of obsession. You know, I still have this affection for I guess what would be known as art cinema. There are people's work that I try to go and see. I like to be aware of what's going on.

PHILLIPS: Do you still feel strongly that your films should be referred to as nonfiction, rather than documentary?

MORRIS: Well, I still feel that the term "documentary" for many, many, many reasons, is a stigma. I mean, the Academy [of Motion Picture Arts and Sciences, the group of filmmakers that gives the Academy Awards] certainly helps to promote this idea of documentary as a kind of journalism. Documentary is defined by a set of acceptable topics and acceptable formulas and presentation. And if I choose the term "nonfiction feature," it's only to suggest that these constraints are artificial. There really is no reason for them at all, and the documentary can be completely innovative and experimental. . . . It can be something other than what we take to be traditional journalism. . . . I like the fact that in *Fast, Cheap & Out of Control* the four people in the movie are not obvious candidates for documentary material. They're unexpected characters. So, yes, I think the choice of "nonfiction film" is just a way of trying to say that this could be something different from what you expect. Yes, it's based on fact, yes, these are real people in the movie, but it's different from what you'd normally expect.

PHILLIPS: How would you characterize your imprint on the films you have directed?

MORRIS: I think that all of my films reflect my sensibilities and interests. I think that all good filmmaking—documentary and otherwise—incorporates something of the person making it and its relationship to the subject matter and to the film. I like to think that there's a lot of me in *Fast, Cheap & Out of Control* and a lot of me in this current project [tentatively entitled] *Mr. Death*. On the simplest level, the films reflect my concerns or my obsessions. But I like to think that what keeps me going in these films is that there is something that I don't know about these people and about the subject matter of the film itself, that there's some mystery left to be explored. I think one of the ways that *Fast, Cheap* works is that given these four people—the ways in which they describe what they do—unexpectedly connections emerge between these four people, connections that you could never anticipate ahead of time. You could think, well, maybe they'll talk about this or maybe they'll talk about that, but one of the nice things about this kind of filmmaking is this element of surprise, the element of the unexpected.

PHILLIPS: Do you write up any questions before the interviews?

MORRIS: Sometimes I do. I like to think that at least I'm prepared, that I have things in mind that should be covered. But I may write out extensive questions beforehand and then make no use of those questions at all during the interview. It's just a way of preparing yourself, of doing your homework.

PHILLIPS: How do you get your subjects to relax when you interview them in a studio, not in their usual settings?

MORRIS: I'm not sure. I think it's creating a climate where people feel comfortable and willing to talk. Maybe I'm a good listener. I'm certainly a non-threatening listener, or at least I like to think that I am. I am genuinely receptive to what people want to say. I don't go into an interview with some fixed agenda, this is what I need to hear, this is what I expect to hear, what I'm going to get the person to say. I try to avoid that altogether and to let interviews take whatever direction that they take. I like surprises, I like to be surprised in an interview by what I hear. And to the extent that what I hear is what I expect I will hear, the interview actually becomes quite boring.

PHILLIPS: When you were editing *Fast, Cheap & Out of Control*, did you try at any time to use scene cards and arrange them in four columns so you could see—

MORRIS: Yes. I mean, we tried everything.

PHILLIPS: Did that help?

MORRIS: Well, everything helped ultimately. Oddly enough, I think I lost faith in my craft. But it came together, when it came together, relatively quickly. It came together when I started to pay attention to what people were saying. I believe every film I've made has this obsession with language, about how people reveal themselves through how they talk. I lost sight of that in the early attempts to put *Fast, Cheap* together. The cutting was too rapid, it was too disorganized, it was too disjointed, but worst of all, it did not allow people to talk at length. The minute I started putting the movie together in a different way so that the people were talking at greater length, revealing themselves through talk, the movie very quickly started to become a movie. It became about people again. It developed some kind of emotional resonance, some kind of emotional depth.

PHILLIPS: How would you define documentary or nonfiction film?

MORRIS: Well, people have said to me that my films are really not nonfiction because, after all, I have actors and reenactments and so on and so forth. My answer has always been that of course they're documentary, of course they're nonfiction, because these are real people. The drama in the film derives ultimately from the fact that there are real people expressing themselves on camera using their own words, speaking extemporaneously. When you watch *The Thin Blue Line*, this is not an actor portraying Randall Adams. This is Randall Adams. This is not actors portraying the Dallas police. This is the Dallas police. And the drama, in good measure, derives from examining these people and trying to figure out why they're saying what they're saying. Are they telling the truth? What do they really mean by what they're saying? And that's something really quite different from watching a film with actors. In my films, the key difference—well, what makes them documentary films—is this out-of-control element of putting people in front of a camera and allowing them to express themselves without a script. That, I would say, is the documentary essence of my work and what sets it apart from what we would take to be scripted feature filmmaking.

PHILLIPS: Like so many film teachers, I'm trying to get people to appreciate and to enjoy a variety of films for different reasons. I'm wondering what you would say to viewers to persuade them to give documentary or nonfiction films a chance?

MORRIS: It is really exciting to see the unexpected, and so much of Hollywood filmmaking has been boilerplate filmmaking, cookie cutter filmmaking, films which basically look very much alike and work in very similar ways. I'm not sure that this is an argument for everybody, but I think that what's exciting about any art form is seeing people that are really exploring the boundaries, the limits of the medium, rather than doing the same thing as everybody else. Certainly it's what excites me. And I would certainly love to see an audience for that kind of filmmaking as well. Because it's different doesn't mean it can't be dramatic, interesting, exciting. In fact, it could be even more so.

331

Originally **avant-garde** was a French military term meaning "advanced guard," and later, strictly speaking, avant-garde works of art in painting, literature, drama, film, and other creative endeavors are forerunners of subsequent works. But more often, many works called "avant-garde" scarcely influence later works. The enormous variety of films often labeled "avant-garde" makes it difficult to define them. Films like what I am calling "avant-garde" have been referred to as "experimental," "underground," or "independent." All four terms reveal something of the nature of such films, while also hinting at the inadequacy of one term. Whenever you encounter "avant-garde films" in this book, think of films that may have been ahead of their times and were certainly experimental, out of the mainstream, heavy on self-expression, and largely free of the limitations placed on makers of commercial movies.

Avant-Garde Films versus Movies

convention: Technique or content in a film or other creative work that imitates the traditions of preceding examples of the same type of creative work.

Before we examine the avant-garde film in some detail, let's contrast avant-garde films with conventional movies. Avant-garde films experiment with the film medium—for example, the filmmakers may scratch or paint the film itself—and reject the **conventions** of mainstream films. Often a major impulse of avant-garde filmmakers is to rebel against what movies are and what they stand for. Avant-garde filmmaker Stan Brakhage argues:

> Everything we have been taught about art and the world itself separates us from a profound, true vision of the world. We are straitjacketed by myriad conventions that prevent us from really seeing our world. So it is with the filmmakers: the so-called rules of good filmmaking that are so carefully followed by commercial filmmakers prevent them from expressing all but the most trite reformulations of the same boy-meets-girl story. (Peterson 4)

Movies reflect or imply the dominant beliefs of a society, its ideology—for example, its belief that hard work results in success and that one individual can make a difference. Avant-garde films, however, tend to question orthodox beliefs, including a society's political beliefs and sexual mores. Before the American rating system for movies began in 1968, avant-garde films—such as "Scorpio Rising" (1963), "Blow Job" (1963), "Couch" (made in 1964 but unreleased), and "Fuses" (1964–1967, Figure 8.14)—were the most likely outlet in the United States for candid depictions of sexual behavior, including that of gays and lesbians. In "Wedlock House: An Intercourse" (1959), for example, Stan Brakhage includes brief shots of negative film to show and suggest him and his new wife making love. Since 1968 many avant-garde films deal openly with sexuality. Autobiographical films or visual diaries—by Carolee Schneemann, George Kuchar, Robert Huot, Stan Brakhage, and others—show what we never see in mainstream films: the everyday and the intimate. In separate films, George Kuchar and Robert Huot, for example, have

FIGURE 8.14 Avant-garde film defying sexual mores
"Fuses" (1964–67) shows filmmaker Carolee Schneemann and her lover enjoying each other
sexually in ways unimaginable in 1960s commercial movies. In this frame, as elsewhere, the film
uses techniques that momentarily obscure the brief but explicit views of lovemaking: markings from
having been baked, deliberate scratches, out-of-focus shots, superimpositions, unexpected camera
angles, fast cutting, and darkness and ambiguity. Frame enlargement. *Anthology Film Archives*

shown themselves masturbating. Huot's silent film "The Sex Life of an
Artist as a Young Man" (1971) includes the title and later the word *wow*
scratched into the **emulsion**, still photographs and movie clips of nude
women, and clips of Huot mouthing the word *wow* alternating with clips of
him masturbating and ejaculating.

Avant-garde films contrast with movies in other ways. They are often
short—sometimes only a few seconds long and sometimes consisting of only
one shot (so much for editing). Avant-garde films are typically made by one
person or a few people, often friends and neighbors; commercial movies are
the products of large groups of specialists. Avant-garde films can be made on
a low budget with inexpensive equipment, such as super-8 film cameras or
video cameras; commercial movies typically require large budgets and are
often made with the latest equipment.

Avant-garde films deliberately frustrate expectations of viewers brought
up on **classical Hollywood cinema**. They generally do not aim to please

emulsion: A clear gelatin substance containing a thin layer
of tiny light-sensitive particles
(grains) that make up a photographic image.

classical Hollywood cinema:
A type of narrative film dominant throughout most of world
movie history that shows one or
more distinct characters with
clear goals who overcome many
problems in reaching them. Such
films tend to use unobtrusive
filmmaking techniques and to
stress continuity of action.

FIGURE 8.15 **Lack of continuity in a classic avant-garde film** In "Un Chien Andalou" (1928), directed by Luis Buñuel, two frames from consecutive shots illustrate that the film often lacks the usual continuity of movies. (a) A character is about to throw something out an open window at night. (b) In the next shot viewers see what he threw in the previous shot falling toward the ground, but now it is day. Throughout, the film rejects narrative conventions and surprises or shocks viewers. Frame enlargements. *Luis Buñuel; The Museum of Modern Art*

audiences in the usual ways and often aim to startle, if not shock, so they tend to be unpopular. Characteristic of the avant-garde film is "Un Chien Andalou" (1928). In its dreamlike association of scenes, the film avoids the coherence of narrative (Figure 8.15). "Un Chien Andalou" runs only seventeen minutes and is the work mainly of two people, Luis Buñuel and cowriter Salvador Dali, to whom it brought immense notoriety, much to their satisfaction. Buñuel later wrote, "This film has no intention of attracting nor pleasing the spectator; indeed, on the contrary, it attacks him, to the degree that he belongs to a society with which **surrealism** is at war" (30).

Influences, Sources, and Subjects

In the making of avant-garde films, one person tends to carry out all the major functions: scripting (if there is a script), filming, editing (if there is any), and perhaps even distributing.

Avant-garde filmmakers usually work independently of the usual sources for financing and distributing films, and in the United States they are largely unrestricted by censorship or a ratings system; consequently, avant-garde filmmakers tend to be free of outside pressures on the shape and content of their finished films. They are, of course, influenced by films they have seen and inevitably imitate or reject them. Or, as we will see, avant-garde filmmakers may use parts of an existing film or whole films in new ways.

Frequently avant-garde filmmakers use the most recent advances in filmmaking, or they apply advances in other forms of human expression to avant-garde films. For example, once **anamorphic lenses** were developed, some avant-garde filmmakers explored their use. As computer graphics emerged and evolved, some avant-garde filmmakers, such as James Whitney in such films as "Lapis" (1966), explored their uses. Once video became less cumbersome and less costly (and **film stock** and developing film became more expensive), many artists and avant-garde filmmakers rushed to experiment with video's creative possibilities.

Other avant-garde filmmakers take a variety of footage—TV ads and old movie footage, for example—and re-edit it to create compilation films that surprise, entertain, and often "take a critical stance toward the culture that supplies their imagery" (Peterson 11). Bruce Conner's first film, a twelve-minute work entitled "A Movie" (1958), includes disparate footage from "cowboy and Indian" and submarine adventure movies, newsreels, documentaries, so-called girlie movies (which feature nude or scantily dressed young women posing for the camera), various types of leader including black leader, and title cards. The film is the antithesis of classical Hollywood cinema. It tells no story. In its incorporation of leader and its untraditional placement of title cards it is **self-reflexive**. And it continuously thwarts audience expectations: for example, it includes a title card saying "The End" early in the film and more than once but not at the end of the film; the opening title cards are repeated at various points of the film; and it uses rousing music to accompany many images of accidents and disasters (auto, motorcycle, and plane crashes; sinking ships; the dirigible *Hindenburg* on fire; the mushroom cloud of an atomic blast; falling bridges; and the like). (See Figure 8.16.)

surrealism: A movement in 1920s and 1930s European art, drama, literature, and film in which an attempt was made to portray or interpret the workings of the subconscious mind as manifested in dreams.

anamorphic lens: A lens that squeezes a wide image onto film in the camera, making everything look tall and thin. On a projector, an anamorphic lens unsqueezes the image, returning it to its original wide shape.

film stock: Unexposed and unprocessed motion-picture film.

self-reflexive: Characteristic of a creative work, such as a novel or film, that makes reference to or comments on itself.

FIGURE 8.16 Twelve shots from an avant-garde compilation film
Early in Bruce Conner's "A Movie" (1958) occur the following seven brief consecutive shots:
(a–d, top, from left to right) A woman undresses, taking off a nylon stocking. A frame of academy
leader, the numbered piece of opaque film that normally appears at the beginning of a reel to protect the film from damage and to help the projectionist know when the reel is about to begin, but
used here by Conner after his film is under way. The first but not last time the title card "The
End" appears, though it does not appear at the end of the film. Some black frames. (e–g, middle,
from left to near right) Part of the film's title, but here upside down. One of four clear frames,
which when projected results in one-sixth of a second of a bright white screen. An "H," which
is followed by "E," "A," and "D," letters which are also included in academy leaders.

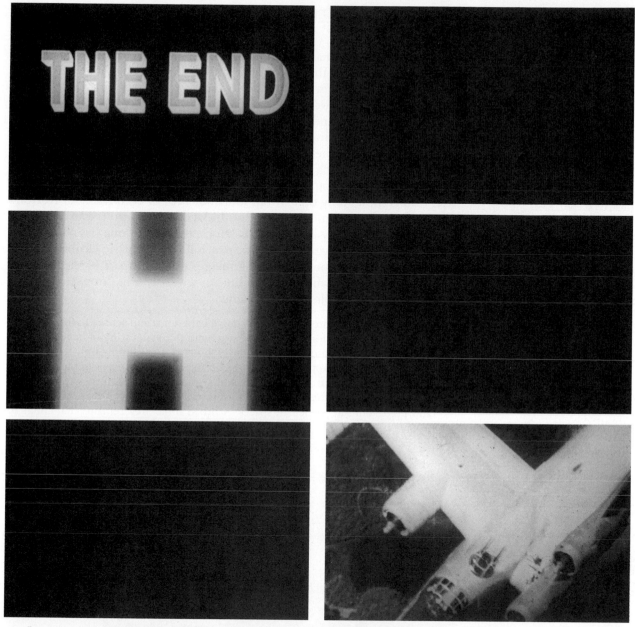

In approximately the middle of the film occur the following five consecutive shots: (h–l, middle, far right, then bottom, from left to right) Some black frames. President Theodore Roosevelt. A suspension bridge waving wildly, pulling apart, and collapsing. Some black frames. A view from above of an airplane breaking up in flight: its wing to the right of the frame is bending upward.

As these frame enlargements illustrate, "A Movie" lacks the usual continuity of "movies" and has no narrative. In fact, except for its violence and sex, fast cutting, and jaunty music, "A Movie" has little in common with the usual entertaining feature fictional films commonly referred to as "movies." The title of Conner's film is tinged with irony. Note, too, that President Roosevelt is satirized by being associated through editing with darkness and disasters: the suggestion is that he causes disasters or is one, or both. *Bruce Conner; Anthology Film Archives*

Avant-garde filmmakers may take not only snippets from various existing films and fashion them into their own film but also whole films, especially films no longer protected by copyright law. For "Intolerance (Abridged)," Stan Lawder took D. W. Griffith's *Intolerance* (1916), which runs over two hours, and copied every twenty-sixth **frame** twice, thus reducing that film's **running time** by a factor of thirteen. In "Intolerance (Abridged)" most of the title cards are unreadable, but so expressive are the film's images that much of its story, structure, **mise en scène**, editing, and camera work flash through the onrush of images. In "Keaton's Cops" (1991), Ken Jacobs shows only the bottom fourth or fifth of each frame of Keaton's classic silent short film "Cops" (1922). In Jacobs's version we can see a subject in its entirety only if it falls or is knocked down. If one has seen Buster Keaton's "Cops," even years earlier, one may follow the story in Jacobs's version; such is the expressiveness of moving images that only part of them evokes what happens in the whole of the film. A viewer who has not seen "Cops" might be more available to Jacobs's aim:

> My intention is to interfere with narrative coherence and sense. To deny it, so as to release the mind for a while from story and the structuring of incident (compelling as it is in Keaton's masterly development). My filming, only showing the bottom fifth of Keaton's black-and-white screen-world, limits us to the periphery of story. Moves us, from the easy reading of an illustrated text, towards active seeing. Reduced information means we now must struggle to identify objects and places and, in particular, spaces. A broad tonal area remains flat, clings to

frame: A separate, individual photograph on a strip of motion-picture film.

running time: The time that elapses when a film is projected.

mise en scène ("meez ahn sen"): An image's setting, subject (usually people or characters), and composition (the arrangement of setting and subjects within the frame).

FIGURE 8.17 Mental states as avant-garde film subject As in many avant-garde films, the main subject of "Nightmare" (1977), an animated avant-garde film from Zagreb, is a man's mental states, in this case nightmares. At this point of the film the man is waking from his most recent nightmare and finds there is no setting. Frame enlargement. *International Film Bureau Inc., Chicago*

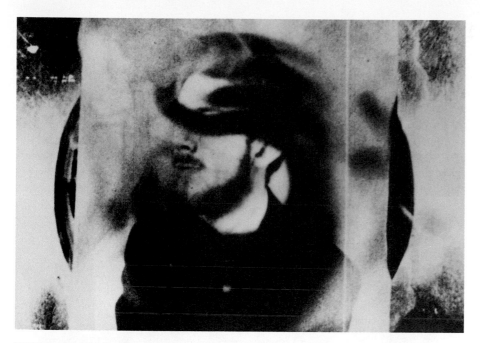

FIGURE 8.18 The limits of memory and other subjects
Hollis Frampton's avant-garde film "(nostalgia)" (1971) is made up of twelve shots, each one of which shows a bird's-eye view of a photograph slowly catch fire on top of a hot plate then completely combust as a narrator describes something about the next photograph viewers will see. After the narration that accompanies each photo ends, in silence viewers are shown ashes slowly twisting on the hot plate. The film's last shot includes narration for a photo we never see (even at the beginning of the film), though the narrator tells us that it is mysterious and even frightening. The film is structured to prevent viewers from experiencing synchronized image and sound. Its structure also suggests the following meanings: the confusion that results when image and sound do not work in tandem throughout a film, the transitory quality of images, the difficulty of linking memory to the appropriate image, and the impossibility of capturing and holding on to the past. Frame enlargement. *Hollis Frampton; Film-makers' Cooperative, New York*

---

the screen, until impacted upon by a recognizable object: Keaton smashes into it, and so it's a wall, diagonal to the screen . . . or a foot steps on it or a wheel rolls across it and it's a road! We become conscious of a painterly screen alive with many shapes in many tones, at the same time that we notice objects and activities (Keaton sets his comedy in some actual street traffic) normally kept from mind by the moviestar-centered moviestory.

Avant-garde films often present dreams and other mental states such as fantasies and hallucinations. Like lyric poems, avant-garde films explore an immense variety of subjects usually avoided in narrative, as in "Un Chien Andalou," "Meshes of the Afternoon" (1943), and "Nightmare" (1977). "Nightmare" is a ten-minute animated film consisting of an introductory scene; six nightmares in which the male dreamer is menaced, after most of which he wakes up; and an epilogue (Figure 8.17). Another subject for avant-garde films is memory, as in Hollis Frampton's "(nostalgia)" (1971, Figure 8.18).

FIGURE 8.19 Making a film without using a camera
Norman McLaren paints on clear 35 mm film in making part of "Begone Dull Care" (1949), an abstract film with music. For a closer view of a frame McLaren painted for this film, see Plate 2 in Chapter 2. *National Film Board of Canada*

lap dissolve: A transition between shots in which one shot begins to fade out as the next shot fades in, overlapping the first shot before replacing it.

saturated color: Intense, vivid, or brilliant color.

Other examples of mental images as subjects in avant-garde films are shifting shapes, colors, and sounds to be experienced for their own sake, as in John Whitney's "Arabesque" (1975) and James Whitney's "Lapis." "Lapis" consists of mostly symmetrical, mostly circular, slowly changing colored shapes made up of multiple parts that often pulsate and occasionally give off a strobe lighting effect. The continuous sitar and drum music and **lap dissolves** contribute to the film's consistent fluidity. With its symmetrical shapes, **saturated colors**, and flowing music, the film seems like what people who have taken LSD report the experience can be like. Shifting colored forms have also been created by painting directly onto clear film, as in Norman McLaren's "Begone Dull Care" (1949, Figure 8.19 and Plate 2 in Chapter 2). In that film the changing abstract forms occasionally correspond to the music; for example, at one point as single double bass notes are played, corresponding vertical white lines are added against the black background.

Yet another subject for avant-garde filmmakers is the scope of human perception and cognition (knowledge), as in J. J. Murphy's "Print Generation" (1974). The film consists of 3,002 shots: 50 generations of 60 shots plus two title cards. A generation is a copy, so the second generation of a shot is not quite as distinct as the first, and the third generation is a copy of a copy and is even a little less clear. Before the fiftieth generation of a shot, its content is unrecognizable. (The same thing happens with a photocopy machine if you make a copy, then a copy of the copy, and so forth for a total of fifty times.) The film begins with the forty-ninth generation of each of sixty shots; these images are a series of abstract patterns of indistinct lights against a reddish background, such as in Figure 8.20a. Gradually viewers see that the film is made up of many brief full-color shots of the same duration (one second each) and can discern more and more of the subjects of other shots until, near the middle of the film, almost all of the subjects are recognizable (Figure 8.20b–h). However, it's impossible to see much of a connection between the sixty shots so, by somewhere near the film's middle, viewers conclude that the sixty shots do not constitute a story.

After a title card, "Print Generation/(A-WIND)/JJ Murphy/© 1973–74," the images begin to degenerate, in fact to return gradually to the abstract patterns seen at the film's beginning. The film ends with the fiftieth generation of each shot then a second title card, "Print Generation/(B-WIND) /JJ Murphy/© 1973–74." Overall as the film progresses from abstract patterns to recognizable subjects then back to abstract patterns, an opposite action is happening on the sound track: sounds of ocean waves gradually become unrecognizable then after the middle title card again gradually become recognizable.

In experiencing "Print Generation," many viewers find themselves constantly watching, listening, and thinking as they try to perceive the film's subjects, then see a unity to the shots, then make some meaning from the film's 3,002 shots. On one level, the film is about the changes that occur to images as more and more generations are made from them: beyond recognizable film images are increasingly abstract patterns; underneath a full-color film image is less and less color until only red remains (the bottom layer of color emulsion). "Print Generation" is also about the limitations of perception, visual and auditory, and cognition: as more and more distortion is introduced into the depiction of the subjects, viewers are limited as to what they can perceive and understand. On the most general level, the film shows that from chaos, signs of life emerge then just as quickly return to chaos. Murphy could have structured the film differently so that it began with recognizable subjects that gradually decompose then regenerate into the original images. Such a structure would have suggested a different, more upbeat meaning: life may decompose into an unrecognizable state then just as quickly regenerate itself.

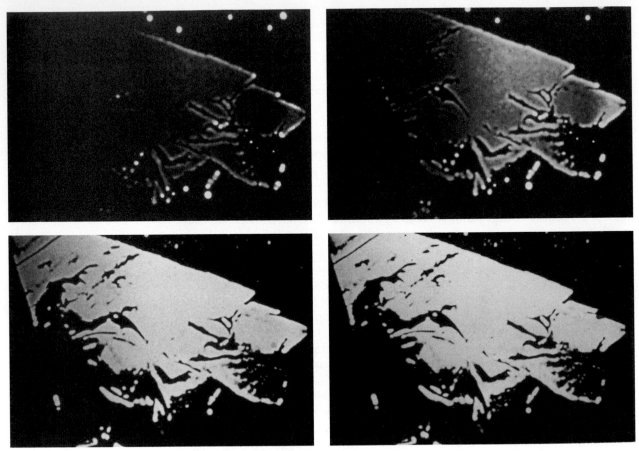

FIGURE 8.20 Perception and cognition as subjects
Eight frame enlargements (top, from left to right, then above, from left to right) from different generations of the same one-second shot illustrate the gradual increased resolution of an image

Filmmaking Techniques

filmic: That which is characteristic of the film medium or appropriate to it.

zoom: To use a zoom lens to cause the image of the subject to either increase in size as the area being filmed seems to decrease (zoom in) or to decrease in size as the area being filmed seems to increase (zoom out).

342

Avant-garde filmmakers tend to use traditional techniques in new ways. As critic Patrick S. Smith points out, Andy Warhol's films from 1963 to 1968 use well-known **filmic** techniques in ways rarely used by mainstream films. During that period, Warhol's films feature an unmoving camera; shots sometimes thirty or more minutes long; strobe cuts (used only in the later films), which result in a few white frames and a loud "bloop" sound at the beginning of each shot; and arbitrary **zooming**. Warhol also welcomed accidents during filming; when one occurred, he would keep filming. Warhol's films "remove the viewer's psychological identification with the performers by means of various interruptions or sustained viewpoints, so that one may notice qualities normally obscured by the perceptions of everyday existence or by the traditional condensations of narrative form" (150).

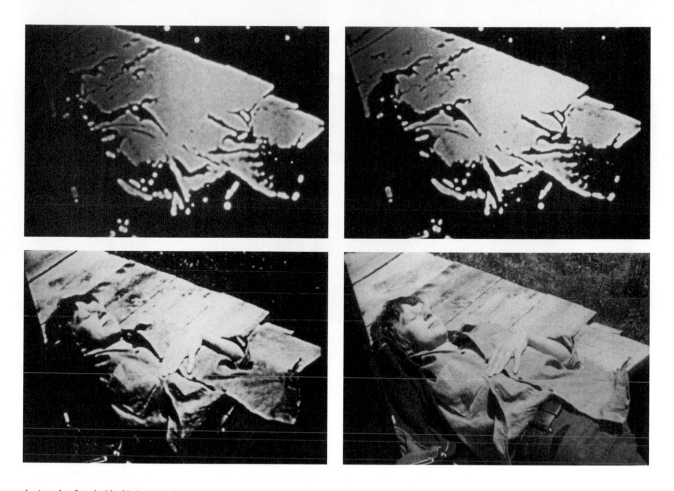

during the first half of J. J. Murphy's "Print Generation" (1974). *J. J. Murphy; Film-makers' Cooperative, New York*

Avant-garde filmmakers tend to experiment with film techniques. They may superimpose a readable text over a moving image, present parts of the film upside down (Figure 8.16e), or use double or triple exposure. Avant-garde filmmakers may alter an exposed and processed film by scratching, painting, dyeing, or baking the film. For example, in some of her films Carolee Schneemann painted over and scratched the film after it had been used to record some action. An entire film may be made without a camera: the film consists of images painted or scratched directly onto film or leader and perhaps a sound track. For part of an untitled black-and-white film made by George Kuchar and a 1970s college film class, Kuchar gave each student actor "white eyebrows, lipstick, etc., on a face that was painted black." Then the footage of the black-faced actors was processed and the processed negative included with the rest of the finished film. "It all worked out OK except that their teeth appeared black whenever they smiled. This made for a rather

 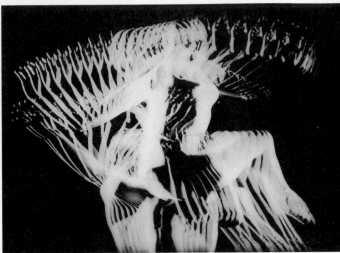

FIGURE 8.21 Untraditional filmmaking techniques, traditional subject
Using an optical printer to make multiple images of two dancers, "Pas de Deux" (1968) combines music with the expressiveness of human movement during the ritual of male and female courtship. The setting is nil; form, movement, and music are all. Frame enlargements. *National Film Board of Canada*

optical printer: A device consisting of a camera and one or more projectors used to reproduce images or parts of images from already processed film.

horrifying and funny effect as we were shooting glamour shots of the rather attractive cast." In "Pas de Deux" (1968), Norman McLaren uses two dancers dressed in white against a black background and on a black floor, opposing lighting from each side of the frame, and frequent flowing multiple images made with an **optical printer** (Figure 8.21). In slow-motion dance the film shows the isolation, courtship, and union of male and female with novelty, grace, and feeling.

Other Characteristics of Avant-Garde Films[1]

Most avant-garde films are less than thirty minutes long; some are only a few minutes or less. Bruce Conner's "Ten Second Film" (1965) is indeed ten seconds. Peter Kubelka's "Schwechater" (1958) is one minute long. Ann Marie Fleming's "New Shoes: (An Interview in Exactly 5 Minutes)" (1990) has precisely the running time it claims to have.

Usually avant-garde films use a minimum of language. This frequent characteristic is in part a consequence of avant-garde filmmakers' affinity for

---

[1] In the following section I have used some of the same phrases as Edward Small did in his book *Direct Theory: Experimental Film/Video as Major Genre*, but I have added, combined, and renamed characteristics and supplied my own examples.

FIGURE 8.22 Film events but no narrative

"Wavelength," a 1967 avant-garde film by Michael Snow, has only four brief events: (1) At the beginning of the film two men carry in a bookcase accompanied by a woman who indicates where to leave it; the men set the bookcase down and all three leave. (2) Later, two women enter the room and go to the far side, where one turns on a radio that plays part of a song and the other closes a window. Soon one woman leaves and the other woman turns off the radio and leaves. (3) After a variety of breaking sounds and footsteps are heard from off-frame, a man slowly walks into the room and collapses. (4) Later a woman enters the frame, looks toward where the man had fallen, goes to the phone, and calls someone. The woman says that she thinks the man is dead, asks what to do, and asks the person on the other end of the phone to come over. She hangs up the phone and leaves. These limited actions are glimpsed during a mostly continuous zoom shot, from wide-angle to close-up of a photograph of waves on the back wall, but, like nearly all events in avant-garde films, they do not add up to a coherent story. *The Museum of Modern Art/Film Stills Archive*

---

mental images. Avant-garde films tend to avoid words in all their manifestations, such as signs, title cards, subtitles, narration, and dialogue. For the most part, avant-garde filmmakers favor imagery over language.

Avant-garde films rarely show stories. If an avant-garde film initially seems to do so, viewers soon realize they cannot find the unity that stories offer. The forty-five-minute film "Wavelength" (1967) initially seems to be a narrative, but viewers eventually realize it is not (Figure 8.22). "The long journey across the loft . . . deliver[s] the audience to the absolute nemesis of the conventional cinema: to a still photograph viewed in silence for several minutes" (MacDonald 36). Like "Un Chien Andalou," at first the classic film "Meshes of the Afternoon" seems to offer a narrative—we see the same character in consecutive scenes—but soon displays lack of continuity (Figure 8.23). Another avant-garde film that is the antithesis of traditional narrative

FIGURE 8.23 Lack of continuity

Maya Deren's "Meshes of the Afternoon" (1943) focuses on one character and various events but lacks narrative continuity and coherence. These nine frame enlargements illustrate five consecutive but discontinuous shots. (a–b, top, far left and near left) Deren looks off-frame; the camera pans left and viewers see what she was seeing: a knife then herself sleeping. (c, top, near right) Now near a window, she looks down, presumably at herself sleeping. (d, top, far right, and e, middle, far left) Outside and below, a woman—whom viewers had seen earlier in the film dressed all in black and with a mirror instead of a face—rushes away carrying a large plastic flower. Later in the shot, Deren runs after her. (f–g, middle, near left and right) The mysterious woman is in the distant background walking rapidly and rounding a corner and going out of sight. Deren is running toward the mysterious woman but is even farther behind her than toward the end of the previous shot; Deren stops and walks off to the left of the frame. (h–i, bottom) Deren is again seen at the window; later in the shot she takes a key from her mouth. Like "Un Chien Andalou" (Figure 8.15), "Meshes" seems dreamlike and sometimes ambiguously symbolic. *Film-makers' Cooperative, New York*

motion pictures is *Blue* (1993), which was directed by Derek Jarman and is not to be confused with another film of the same title directed by Krzysztof Kieslowski. Jarman's film is not pictures in motion that convey a story but seventy-six minutes of unvarying solid blue light and a sound track that includes narration and other voices, sound effects, and music.[2] Andy Warhol's *Empire* (1964), which consists of eight seemingly uninterrupted hours of a view of the Empire State Building from the same camera position, comes close to static images, too, especially in the short term (Figure 8.24).

Finally, avant-garde films often draw attention to themselves as films. As we have seen, both fictional and documentary films may also be self-reflexive, but avant-garde films are much more likely to be so. For example, they may show the camera filming part of what will be included in the final version of the film or include initial leader. They may show the parts of a projector as it is projecting a film. They may make motion-picture film itself the main subject of a film, as Owen Land did in "Film in which there appear sprocket holes, edge lettering, dirt particles, etc." (1965–66).

Film Apparatus and the Avant-Garde Film

As a traditional film or video is made, its components—camera, film, lenses, and so on—are used in conventional ways. For example, since sound was introduced on film in the late 1920s, the speed of the film being exposed is rarely changed during the filming of a shot. When a conventional film or video is projected, its components—projector or video player, film or videotape, screen or monitor—also tend to be used conventionally. For example, traditionally the same lens is used throughout a film showing. Many avant-garde films, though, change one or more of the basic components of making and exhibiting a film or video. For example, a film is normally projected onto a flat, white, reflective, rectangular screen or wall, but

FIGURE 8.24 Avant-garde film as antithesis to movies
Empire (1964)—an eight-hour avant-garde film by Andy Warhol consisting solely of a view of the Empire State Building as seen from the same position—is the antithesis of traditional films. It has no human subject, no perceptible variety in its subject, little noticeable movement from moment to moment, and no variation in filmmaking techniques. And then its pace is *so* slow: it gives viewers extremely little information during its very lengthy duration. Frame enlargement. *Andy Warhol Foundation*

---

[2]For the text of *Blue*, see Derek Jarman, *Blue: Text of a Film* (Woodstock, NY: Overlook Press, 1994).

it need not be so. During the opening night of the 1996 Los Angeles exhibition on the relationship of film and art since 1945, a film was projected onto a woman's bare chest, and throughout the exhibition different films were projected onto objects such as a bucket of milk and a spinning fan. In another part of the exhibit, a video projector suspended above an unmade bed projected a video image of a reclining man onto the bed. Table 8.2 lists the basic components of the film apparatuses and some conventional and unconventional ways in which they may be used.

Categories of Avant-Garde Films

Avant-garde films have been categorized different ways by different scholars. Sometimes they are divided into "representational" and "abstract." In representational avant-garde films, the subjects are recognizable as people and real objects, as in "Un Chien Andalou" (Figure 8.15) and "Nightmare" (Figure 8.17). In abstract avant-garde films, the subjects are unrecognizable, as in "Begone Dull Care" (Figure 8.19). In a more sophisticated classification, film theorist James Peterson divides American avant-garde films since World War II into three "open and flexible grouping[s]": poetic, minimal, and assemblage (especially compilations of footage) (10). Edward Small divides the experimental film and video into five categories: European avant-garde, American avant-garde, American underground, expanded cinema, and minimalist-structuralist (81). So boundless is human imagination, however, that two or three or five categories often prove inadequate, and many avant-garde films elude clear-cut classification.

Avant-Garde Films and Other Arts

Since the 1970s, some films or videos have been combined with other visual objects and arts and have been shown temporarily in museums, usually museums of contemporary art. Such combined artworks are called **installation art**. An example is Jeff Wall's "Eviction Struggle" (1988), which combines a large fluorescent-lit transparency (about 13½ feet wide and 7½ feet tall) on one side of a gallery wall (Figure 8.25a) with nine close-up or medium close-up video excerpts of the same struggle and reactions to it on the other side of the wall (Figure 8.25b). One version of *Bordering on Fiction: Chantal Akerman's "D'Est"* (1995) consists of a showing of *D'Est* (*From the East*, 1993), which is Akerman's feature-length documentary, in one room, video clips from it on multiple monitors in the next room, and a recorded voice from yet another source: "Viewed in its entirety, *Bordering on Fiction: Chantal Akerman's "D'Est"* engages in a deconstructive tour of the production process, working back from the completed feature film to the individual shot segments of which it is constructed and, in the end, back to language itself" (*Bordering* 9).

TABLE 8.2
Film Apparatus and the Avant-Garde Film: A Few of the Visual Possibilities*

APPARATUS	TRADITIONAL USES	AVANT-GARDE USES
PRODUCTION		
CAMERA	Filming at same speed within each shot	Distorting camera lens(es)
		Filming at variable speeds
		Multiple exposure by filming then cranking back and filming again
FILM	Consecutive frames record consecutive fragments of space or time or, most often, both	Mostly clear frames, perhaps resulting in a strobe effect
		Painted
		Scratched
EDITING	Multiple shots, usually continuity editing	One film=one shot=rejection of editing
		Lack of continuity
		Compilation film
EXHIBITION		
PROJECTOR	Projector runs at unvarying speed, usually 24 or 25 frames per second for modern sound film	Film projected upside down, or backward, or both
	No distorting projector lens(es) other than possibly anamorphic	Multiple versions cause multiple images or superimposed images or both
		Film projected through some intervening substance, such as a fish tank
FINISHED FILM	Consecutive frames depict consecutive fragments of time or action or both within each shot	Consecutive frames depict discontinuous fragments of time or action or both within each shot
SCREEN	Screen is flat or concave, white, reflective, rectangular, with a uniform surface	Film projected onto a person's body or an inanimate object, such as a shirt or milk jug
THEATER LAYOUT	Nothing between audience members on the sides	Panels between seats shut off audience members from each other

*A comparable chart could be made for video production and exhibition consisting of video camera, videotape, player, and monitor, or video camera, tape, player-projector, and screen.

FIGURE 8.25 Installation art

Jeff Wall's installation "Eviction Struggle," which was made in British Columbia in 1988, has two sides. (a, top) On one side of an art gallery wall is a large still photograph showing two officers struggling with a man (to the right of the car parked at an angle to the sidewalk), a woman rushing toward them, and various other people in the neighborhood watching the conflict. To make this detailed fluorescent-lit transparency, which is 414 cm (13½ feet) wide and 229 cm (7½ feet) tall, an 8-by-10-inch camera negative was used. (b, above) The other side of "Eviction Struggle" consists of nine 19-inch video monitors showing brief close-up and medium close-up clips enacting some of the situations seen in (a). The three monitors on the left and the two monitors on the right side of the wall show people looking at the struggle. The four central monitors show, from left to right, an officer, the struggling man, another officer, and a woman running toward the men. By looking at the large image in (a) then the nine video monitors (or vice versa), viewers can compare the expressiveness of the still image's mise en scène with the expressiveness of video clips of the same subject. The nine monitors also allow viewers to function as editors in that they will select the order, duration, and repetition, if any, of the clips seen. The installation gives viewers the opportunity to compare and contrast two different representations of the same subject and to consider the potentialities and limitations of still photography and moving images. *Collection: Ydessa Hendeles Art Foundation, Toronto*

Another example of installation art is Bill Viola's five-part "Buried Secrets" (1995). One of the five parts is called "Hall of Whispers," which

> consists of a series of 10 video projections, five each on the long facing walls of a dark corridor. This black and white gauntlet consists of the life-size heads of men and women who have been bound and gagged. Eyes shut, they struggle against tightly-wrapped cloth bandages but their efforts to speak prove futile: only muffled sounds escape into the room. . . .
>
> "Hall of Whispers" announces the underlying concerns of "Buried Secrets": the difficulty, if not impossibility, of communication and the importance of protecting secrets. This can be read on a political level since the figures so clearly conjure images of tortured prisoners in a police state. But so literal an interpretation misses their ambiguity and the wider possibilities of meaning. (Boyle 9)

HYBRID FILMS

Most films are exclusively and unquestionably fiction or documentary or avant-garde. Viewers watching any of the *Star Wars*–related films, for example, never think of them as anything other than fiction. Some films, however, although clearly a member of one of the three types of films, blend aspects from at least one of the other two major types.

On rare occasions, a film may be a **fake documentary**: a film made with documentary techniques that is not factual. Fake documentaries are not necessarily fictional: not all of them show an imaginative story (Figure 8.26). But most fake documentaries are fictional films using documentary techniques, as is the case with *No Lies* (1973), which seems to be a documentary story about a brief part of a documentary filmmaker's life, until the final credits roll and we learn we have been seeing a fictional film all along. In *No Lies*, which was made by Mitchell Block,

> the filmmaker, supposedly a production student working on an assignment, is filming a woman friend in her apartment as she puts on makeup and gets ready to go out to a movie. The woman is understandably at somewhat of a loss for things to say. After a few minutes, she lets it drop that she was raped the previous evening. The filmmaker (who like any good documentarian is quick to exploit a moment of potential drama) proceeds to cajole, challenge, and cross-examine her to get her to elaborate on the incident. Despite the woman's attempts to change the subject, the filmmaker badgers her about it relentlessly . . . until she breaks down. Then, instead of apologizing, he justifies himself. He refuses to turn off the camera, despite her repeated entreaties, until she finally leaves the apartment. (Eitzen 92)

In fact, *No Lies* was made to provoke discussion of feelings about rape, privacy, and media intrusion. The film is fictional and was scripted and re-

FIGURE 8.26 A nonnarrative fake documentary

Slacker (1990) is an example of a fake documentary that tells no story. It was made with a highly mobile camera that records a few subjects briefly (often a one-sided conversation or monologue) then moves on to a new small group of characters, repeating this pattern throughout the film. Richard Linklater—the film's producer, writer, and director—is less interested in understanding individual characters in depth than in presenting a society of mostly youthful outsiders, eccentrics, and loners in Austin, Texas, at the end of the 1980s. The film includes nearly one hundred characters. Here the character on the left, identified in the closing credits as "Been on the moon since the 50s," attaches himself to the young man on the right and walks along with him for five minutes while spouting a continuous stream of unorthodox theories. The character claims, for example, that the United States first got to the moon in the 1950s by using antigravity technology stolen from the Nazis after the end of World War II!

As throughout the film, the episode depicted here looks and sounds like parts of a documentary and is loosely related to the rest of the film (characters largely out of the mainstream, the same twenty-four hours or so, and the same city) but the film lacks the coherence of a story. *Richard Linklater; Orion Classics*

hearsed beforehand and used only actors. Fake documentaries seem factual until viewers learn afterward that they are not.

Mock documentaries are fiction that rely heavily on documentary techniques. *Real Life* (1979) at first seems to be a documentary about trying to make a documentary about a typical American family, but most viewers quickly catch on that *Real Life* is fiction. The documentary filmmaking

FIGURE 8.27 A mock documentary
Fear of a Black Hat (1994) has a fictional rap group as its subject and uses (and sometimes exaggerates) the techniques of cinéma vérité, such as handheld camera work, interviews, and surprising, supposedly even embarrassing developments for the film's subjects. Here the "documentary filmmaker" within *Fear of a Black Hat* (the woman on the right) interviews the straight-faced members of the group, from left to right: Tasty Taste, Tone Def, and Ice Cold. If viewers figure out that the film is fiction in the guise of documentary, they can enjoy its creativity and humor. *ITC Entertainment Group*

independent film: Film made without support or input from the dominant, established film industry.

fast motion: Motion in which the action depicted on the screen occurs more quickly than its real-life counterpart.

characters within *Real Life* announce that they will be objective and unobtrusive, for example by wearing the cameras in a headpiece that fits over their heads, but the filmmaker characters repeatedly intrude into their subjects' lives and contribute to their emotional havoc. In spite of the plans of the filmmakers within the movie, *Real Life* demonstrates that direct cinema may not work out as intended. Another mock documentary is *Fear of a Black Hat* (1994, Figure 8.27).

Combinations of avant-garde and documentary are unheard of in classical Hollywood cinema but appear from time to time in **independent films** from various nations. *Koyaanisqatsi* (1983) is a documentary in subject matter (nature and what humankind does to it) but often avant-garde in its look (extensive use of **fast motion**, for example) (Figure 8.28). In places, *Thirty-Two Short Films about Glenn Gould* is avant-garde documentary, too (Figure 8.29).

"You Take Care Now" (1989) by Ann Marie Fleming is an oblique avant-garde narrative documentary. The film uses a blank screen, a wobbly camera that causes blurred images, repeated close-ups of a live bird's head

FIGURE 8.28 Hybrid film: avant-garde documentary

(a, top) Early in *Koyaanisqatsi* (1983), viewers see many shots of the expanse and wonder of nature untouched by human hands. (b, above) Later the film shows the crowded, rushed, and often polluted world people have made of nature. The speeded-up quality of modern urban life is suggested by the blurred lines of car lights, achieved by time-lapse cinematography. *Godfrey Reggio; New Yorker Films*

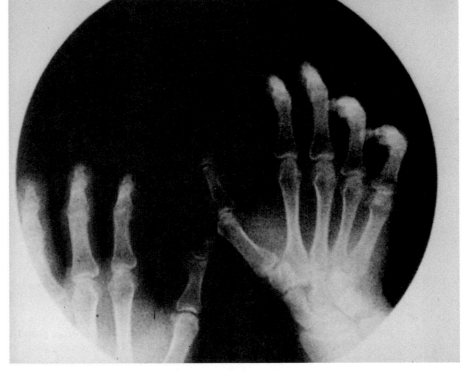

FIGURE 8.29 Occasional avant-garde documentary *Thirty-Two Short Films about Glenn Gould* (1993) is a documentary about the famous pianist, but the film sometimes looks like an avant-garde film. (a, top) One of its thirty-two films is an avant-garde film, an abstract animated film by Norman McLaren accompanied by music played by Gould. (b, right) Another of its short films shows motion-picture X-rays of a person's hands, arms, and head while playing a piano; that brief film is not so much part of a documentary about Gould as it is about human movement rendered in an untraditional, playful, and surprising manner. Frame enlargements. *Samuel Goldwyn*

surrounded by animated lines and patterns, the head of a man jumping up into the frame briefly and repeatedly (the camera is aimed above his head), an extreme close-up of a man's mouth as he presumably shouts curses as viewers hear a dog barking, snow on a TV screen, an out-of-focus night shot, and many other techniques to help convey the disorientation and physical and psychological pain of being raped and on another occasion being hit by one car and run over by another. The film's female narrator recounts two brief, presumably factual stories and provides whatever context and continuity the film has; the visuals show little of the stories and instead create or reinforce moods.

Films, especially independent films, may also combine elements of fiction and avant-garde. *The Cabinet of Dr. Caligari* (1919) is a fictional film with both a mise en scène and a preoccupation with a disturbed mental state more often found in avant-garde films (Figure 8.30). Several films directed by Jean Cocteau, such as *Beauty and the Beast* (1946) and *Orpheus* (1950), can also be labeled avant-garde fiction because of their untraditional cinematic techniques, including a character gliding through space without moving his or her legs or a character seemingly passing through a mirror into another realm. Still another fictional film incorporating avant-garde aspects is *Persona* (1966), much of which is the fictional story of two women. Parts of the film, however,

FIGURE 8.30 Hybrid film: avant-garde and fiction
The expressionistic sets used throughout *The Cabinet of Dr. Caligari* (1919) and the film's preoccupation with mental states are more characteristic of avant-garde films than of fictional films, yet *Cabinet* is fictional. It is a hybrid film. Frame enlargement. *Decla-Bioscop; The Museum of Modern Art/Circulating Film Library*

FIGURE 8.31 A hybrid of fiction, documentary, and avant-garde *David Holzman's Diary* (1968) seems to be a documentary with some avant-garde aspects until the closing credits reveal that the film was scripted and acted. (a, top) This frame enlargement from late in the film illustrates the film's occasional self-reflexiveness by showing most of the filmmaking apparatus used to make it: left to right, the main character's portable reel-to-reel audio tape recorder, rewinds and 16 mm editor/viewer, and above them and reflected in the mirror, a tripod holding a 16 mm camera. Elsewhere in the film, viewers see shots of the zoom lens presumably used in filming *David Holzman's Diary* and the portable tape recorder and the accompanying microphone. (b, bottom) A view through a fisheye lens of the main character seemingly dangling above sidewalks. In this frame he is about to reach up and turn off the camera. This and other shots are characteristic of avant-garde; in fact, it's hard to see how this shot fits into the story of this hybrid film. Frame enlargements. *The Museum of Modern Art/Film Stills Archive*

include material extraneous to the **plot** and repetition rarely found in a fictional film: self-reflexive shots of motion-picture cameras, projectors, and 35 mm film that do not fit into the plot along with accusations by Alma as we see Elisabeth followed by the same accusations by Alma as we see Alma. *Persona* also uses many techniques found in avant-garde films, such as the halves of two faces seemingly fused into one and a lengthy shot that begins badly out of focus then soon comes into focus.

Occasionally a film outside classical Hollywood cinema exhibits characteristics of all three major types of films, as in *David Holzman's Diary* (1968). Examples are the self-reflexive shots of the equipment used during filming and editing (Figure 8.31a); shots of the dark screen accompanied by narration; a galloping succession of shots supposedly representing one frame from each shot of an evening's worth of TV; and a shot viewed through a **fisheye lens** looking down on the top of "David Holzman's" head (Figure 8.31b).

Critics and scholars sometimes disagree about how to classify a film. Some critics see *Female Trouble* (1974) and other early films directed by John Waters as avant-garde fiction whereas others stress that they are fictional films done in a particular style, **black comedy** (see Figure 7.15 on p. 307). Such disagreements are inevitable because they involve judgment calls and sometimes different understanding of terms, and different informed and thoughtful people will categorize certain films differently. Filmmakers' imaginations and creativity often outrun critics' and scholars' classifications.

ANIMATION

> Animation can redefine the everyday, subvert our accepted notions of "reality" and challenge the orthodox understanding of our existence. Animation can defy the laws of gravity, challenge our perceived view of space and time, and endow lifeless things with dynamic and vibrant properties. (Wells 195)

Animation is not a type of film, as are fictional, documentary, and avant-garde. Rather it is a technique for making a film or part of one.

To "animate" means to bring to life. "Animation is based on an animator's knowledge of time and motion. An animator must be able to break down real or actual motion into its component parts so that motion can be artificially constructed out of static images" (Kindem 292). Both flat (two-dimensional) and plastic (three-dimensional) subjects may be animated. Flat subjects include drawings (Figure 8.32); photographs; paper cutouts with hinged and movable body parts; computer graphics images; and drawings, scratchings, or paint applied directly on the film itself (Figure 8.33). Plastic objects that may be animated include clay (Figure 8.34) or plasticine and people in rigid poses. In all cases, the inanimate is brought to life by showing the viewer a rapid succession of changing images of the same subject. If the

plot: The structure (selection and order) of a narrative's events.

fisheye lens: An extreme wide-angle lens that captures nearly 180° of the area before the camera but causes much curvature of the image, especially near the frame's edges.

black comedy: A style used in some narratives since World War II that shows the humorous possibilities in subjects previously considered off-limits to comedy, such as warfare, murder, death, and dying.

FIGURE 8.32 Animation of flat (two-dimensional) subjects
The first Mickey Mouse was seen in "Steamboat Willie" (1928), an example of the animation of flat subjects. *Walt Disney; The Museum of Modern Art/Film Stills Archive*

FIGURE 8.33 Animation done without a camera
Macha is a goddess who takes on human form in the pre-Christian Irish tale "Macha's Curse" ("Mallacht Macha," 1990). This ten-minute film consists of six to seven thousand painted drawings on clear 35 mm film plus original Celtic music, sound effects, and narration. Frame enlargement. *Rose Bond; The Museum of Modern Art/Circulating Film Library*

FIGURE 8.34 Animation using plastic (three-dimensional) subjects
(a, above) On the set for "Sand Castle" (1977), an animated film that has
weather, sand, and an assortment of playful yet constructive clay creatures
as its subjects. Between shots the filmmaker changes the shape of the subjects slightly. Note that here the camera is on the side, not overhead, as it
is while filming most two-dimensional animated subjects. (b, right) In the
finished film, the clay creatures have been brought to life. *National Film
Board of Canada*

subject changes only slightly from frame to frame and many frames are exposed per second, as in the Disney animated features, the projected movement
will seem fluid. Conversely, if the subject is moved appreciably from frame
to frame or is photographed at only six or five or even fewer different images
per second—which is often the case if time or budget is severely limited—
the movement may seem jerky.

Any way animation is done, it is time-consuming and usually expensive. The most basic way is to draw a picture, then draw the next picture and change only slightly the parts that are to move (be animated), then repeat this process many more times. After the drawings and any coloring are finished, each drawing is photographed with a movie camera mounted above it. Jamie Maxfield's 1992 student Academy Award–winning animated film "Above Average" was so made. The six-minute-and-eighteen-second film consists of 2,300 drawings or approximately 6 drawings per second. At the opposite extreme of production, *The Lion King* (1994), with its running time of eighty-seven minutes, required more than a million drawings. Most included one or more painted **cels** (thin plastic sheets) placed on a painted background.

In some computer-assisted animation, penciled drawings are scanned into the computer, then the computer is used to choose and assign colors to areas of the image, ink and paint the images, set the characters against a background, add "camera movements," match the image to the sound track, and transfer the finished product to either film or videotape. Animation without a camera is also an option: subjects are scratched or painted onto the individual frames of film, or, as Stan Brakhage and others have done, small objects are affixed to the film stock then a film copy is made (Figure 8.35).

In the animation of plastic objects, stop-motion cinematography and pixillation are two major techniques. In stop-motion cinematography, which was used in making such films as *Tim Burton's The Nightmare before Christmas* (1993), an object such as a puppet (Figure 8.36) is filmed in a miniature setting, usually from the side, for a frame or two. Then the object's position is changed slightly, and one or two more frames are filmed, and so on. **Pixillation** is jerky stop-motion cinematography that usually uses people in rigid poses as subjects and that makes possible the appearance of new

FIGURE 8.35 Film made with pasted objects
To make "Mothlight" (1963), a four-minute silent film, without a camera, Stan Brakhage pasted pieces of moth wings, grass, leaves, seeds, and flowers on clear 16 mm film then copied the results. Frame enlargements. *Courtesy of Stan Brakhage*

FIGURE 8.36 **Stop-motion animation** (a, left) Producer Tim Burton with some of the puppets used in making *Tim Burton's The Nightmare before Christmas* (1993). Note especially the three small puppets to Burton's left. (b, below) In the movie, each holiday has its own place and own set of characters. The leader of Halloween Town discovers Christmas Town and tells the other Halloween Town residents about it. They are perplexed and do not understand, for example, why children in Christmas Town throw snowballs instead of heads. At first the characters from Halloween Town think that the ruler of Christmas Town is a man like a large red lobster called Sandy Claws. The three masked Halloween Town trick-or-treaters seen here—from left to right, Shock, Barrel, and Lock—announce "trick or treat" then throw a sack over Santa Claus and kidnap him. During filming, the puppets or parts of them were moved slightly between exposures, and twenty-four frames were exposed for each second of finished film. *Tim Burton and Denise Di Novi; Walt Disney; Touchstone*

◄ **FIGURE 8.37 Pixillation**
Five consecutive frames from "Neighbours" (1952) illustrate pixillation. Here two neighbors are maneuvering for possession of a flower that has grown along the property line between them. Pixillation makes possible movements impossible in live action, such as a character sliding around on grass while supported by only one leg. Frame enlargements. *National Film Board of Canada; The Museum of Modern Art/Film Stills Archive*

---

types of movement, such as a person sliding in circles across a lawn while balanced on one foot. It is used in at least three films by Norman McLaren: "A Chairy Tale" (1957), "Opening Speech: McLaren" (1960), and in most of "Neighbours" (1952, Figure 8.37).

Animation may be used throughout fictional films, documentary films (though extended use of animation in documentaries is rare), and avant-garde films (frequently used). Occasionally—as in *Mary Poppins* (1964), *Who Framed Roger Rabbit* (1988, Plate 3 in Chapter 2), *Jurassic Park* (1993), and *Space Jam* (1996)—animation is joined with live action, thereby combining the world viewers know with imaginary worlds.

Animation can allow viewers to see and experience from a new perspective. In "The Fly" (1980), we see the countryside then the inside of a large country home entirely from the point of view of a fly (Figure 8.38). We see and hear and to some extent experience the flying and stopping, flying and stopping. Near the end, we also hear footsteps and the sounds of a person swatting at the fly and finally see through a blur a collection of mounted insects as the fly's life and the film end together. Compared with live-action filming, animation provides filmmakers much greater control of mise en scène. As many scenes in Disney animated movies demonstrate—the death of Bambi's mother in *Bambi* (1942), the terror of the evil witch

FIGURE 8.38 Sustained point-of-view in an animated film ►
"The Fly" (1980) runs two minutes and thirty-seven seconds. Each of the film's nearly two thousand frames was made by drawing with crayon on a cel, and approximately twelve drawings were made for each second of the finished film. (a–d, from top left to middle right) In the first shot the fly flies toward a house, enters it, and gets chased around by someone. (e, bottom left) After a fade-out and fade-in, the film's second and last shot begins. In the film, the drawings for (e–f, bottom right) are hazy on the edges, suggesting that the fly is losing consciousness and dying. *RF Fly Films, Inc., Oakville, Ontario*

in *Sleeping Beauty* (1959), and the death of Mufasa in *The Lion King*—animation can call forth strong emotional viewer responses, both from children and adults. Animation can also create characters as memorable as people: for years throughout the world, Mickey Mouse was as popular as any flesh-and-blood movie star. (Perhaps as computer animation grows more and more powerful and subtle, one day animated stars will rival flesh-and-blood stars and even displace them.) And animation makes possible the impossible, such as a coyote being smashed by a giant boulder yet soon pursuing that elusive roadrunner yet again, or a man metamorphosing (or **morphing**) into a beast then back into a man, or a blossom becoming a nude woman ("Nightmare"). No wonder animation so animates animators: they can play **designer**, casting director, director, and editor; they can show entire narratives from otherwise impossible points of view; they can create life, set it in motion, act out what they wish, and decide the precise moment the life fades out or the image cuts to black.

designer: The person responsible for the visuals of a film, including architecture, locations, sets, costumes, makeup, and hair styles.

SUMMARY

Documentary Films

- Whether narrative or not, a documentary film presents (and occasionally stages) a version of events that viewers are intended to accept primarily as factual, not imaginary.

- Most documentary films present no narrative or story. The information in many nonnarrative documentary films is organized into groups or categories. Other nonnarrative documentary films attempt to change or reinforce a viewpoint—for example, by editing and other techniques—as in *Hearts and Minds*.

- Narrative documentary films present a story that is largely factual, but like fictional films they are never simply a succession of related events: for example, they may also dwell on setting or interrupt the narrative for interviews.

- Documentary films—nonnarrative and narrative—present one version of a mediated reality, but typically they depict occurrences where they happened and use no actors.

- Documentary films usually include supporting artifacts—such as photographs or film clips—and informative language, such as narration or interviews, or both.

- As *Titicut Follies* and *The Thin Blue Line* illustrate, documentary filmmakers use an enormous variety of film techniques: some attempt to use minimal techniques whereas others manipulate the sounds and images in the same limitless ways fictional and avant-garde filmmakers do.

Avant-Garde Films

- Because avant-garde films are so various, no one term—experimental, independent, or avant-garde—entirely captures their complexity and scope.

- Unlike commercial movies, avant-garde films often radically reject the conventions of earlier films and explore the possibilities of the film medium.

- Avant-garde filmmakers often work largely alone and tend to be largely free of censorship.

- Avant-garde filmmakers may explore recent technological advances in communications, use existing films or parts of them in a changed form, or focus on mental states, such as nightmares.

- Often avant-garde films use traditional techniques in new ways, as in "Wavelength," and experiment with filmmaking techniques.

- Avant-garde films are usually brief, highly visual, nonnarrative, and often self-reflexive.

- Often avant-garde filmmakers change one or more components of film-making and film exhibition, for example, by projecting a film onto a hanging shirt.

- Avant-garde films may be divided into representational and abstract, or poetic, minimal, and assemblage, or in other ways. Because of their individuality and enormous variety, however, avant-garde films are especially difficult to define and classify.

- Installation art often combines film or video with other arts or means of expression in new and experimental ways, usually in temporary displays in museums.

Hybrid Films

- Although most films are exclusively fictional, documentary, or avant-garde, some films are hybrids: they exhibit characteristics of more than one type. For example, *The Cabinet of Dr. Caligari*, though mainly fictional, has characteristics of avant-garde films, and *Koyaanisqatsi* is an avant-garde documentary.

Animation

- Animation is not a type of film but a technique that may be used in making any type of film. Animation may be of flat or plastic objects; may be done by various methods, including computer-assisted; and affords film-makers the greatest control over the mise en scène, often making possible the otherwise impossible.

WORKS CITED

Bates, Peter. "Truth Not Guaranteed: An Interview with Errol Morris." *Cineaste* 17, no. 1 (1989): 16–17.

Blank, Les, independent filmmaker. Telephone interview. April 1995.

Bordering on Fiction: Chantal Akerman's "D'Est." Minneapolis: Walker Art Center, 1995.

Boyle, Deirdre. "Post-traumatic Shock: Bill Viola's Recent Work." *Afterimage* Sept./Oct. 1996: 9–11.

Buñuel, Luis. "Notes on the Making of *Un Chien Andalou*." *Art in Cinema*. Ed. Frank Stauffacher. 1947. New York: Arno, 1968. 29–30.

Carr, Jay. "Errol Morris's Dreamscapes." *The Boston Globe*, City Ed. 12 Oct. 1997: N9.

Chang, Chris. "Planet of the Apes." *Film Comment*, 33, no. 5 (Sept./Oct. 1997): 68–71.

Corliss, Richard. "Take this Job and Love It." *Time*, 150, no. 17 (27 Oct. 1997): 111.

Eitzen, Dirk. "When Is a Documentary? Documentary as a Mode of Reception." *Cinema Journal* Fall 1995: 81–102.

Ellis, Jack C. *The Documentary Idea: A Critical History of English-Language Documentary Film and Video*. Englewood Cliffs: Prentice, 1989.

Gardner, Robert. "Chronicles of the Human Experience: *Dead Birds*." *Nonfiction Film Theory and Criticism*. Ed. Richard Meran Barsam. New York: Dutton, 1976. 342–48.

Jacobs, Ken, independent filmmaker. Letter to the author. January 1998.

Kindem, Gorham. *The Moving Image: Production Principles and Practices*. Glenview, IL: Scott, 1987.

Kuchar, George, independent filmmaker and author. Letter to the author. January 1998.

Lucia, Cynthia. "Revisiting *High School*: An Interview with Frederick Wiseman." *Cineaste* 20, no. 4 (Oct. 1994): 5–11.

MacDonald, Scott. *Avant-Garde Film: Motion Studies*. New York: Cambridge UP, 1993.

Mekas, Jonas, independent filmmaker and author. Personal interview. October 1996.

Nichols, Bill. *Ideology and the Image: Social Representation in the Cinema and Other Media*. Bloomington: Indiana UP, 1981.

———. "The Voice of Documentary." *Film Quarterly* Spring 1983: 17–30.

Peterson, James. *Dreams of Chaos, Visions of Order: Understanding the American Avant-Garde Cinema*. Detroit: Wayne State UP, 1994.

Small, Edward S. *Direct Theory: Experimental Film/Video as Major Genre*. Carbondale: Southern Illinois UP, 1994.

Smith, Patrick S. *Andy Warhol's Art and Films*. Ann Arbor: UMI, 1986.

Wells, Paul. "Animation: Forms and Meanings." *An Introduction to Film Studies*. Ed. Jill Nelmes. London: Routledge, 1996. 193–217.

FOR FURTHER READING

Barnouw, Erik. *Documentary: A History of the Non-Fiction Film*. 2nd rev. ed. New York: Oxford UP, 1993. A concise illustrated history plus an extensive bibliography.

Barsam, Richard M. *Nonfiction Film: A Critical History*. Rev. and expanded ed. Bloomington: Indiana UP, 1992. Part One (1820–1933): Foundations of the Nonfiction Film; Part Two (1933–1939): Documentary Films to Change the World; Part Three (1939–1945): Nonfiction Films for World War II; Part Four (1945–1960): Nonfiction Films after World War II; Part Five (1960–1985): Continuing Traditions and New Directions.

Bendazzi, Giannalberto. *Cartoons: One Hundred Years of Cinema Animation*. Bloomington: Indiana UP, 1994. A comprehensive and detailed history and critique of film animation. Includes ninety-five color plates and comprehensive indexes of names and titles.

Borowiec, Piotr. *Animated Short Films: A Critical Index to Theatrical Cartoons*. Lanham, MD: Scarecrow, 1998. Five sections: a brief history of animated short films, reviews of over 1,800 cartoons, director index, chronological index of cartoons from 1906 to 1997, and four- and five-star reviews.

Canyon Cinema Film/Video Catalog No. 7. San Francisco: Canyon Cinema, 1992. Descriptions of available films and videos arranged alphabetically by filmmaker. Especially valuable for information on the avant-garde.

Documenting the Documentary. Ed. Barry Keith Grant and Jeannette Sloniowski. Detroit: Wayne State UP, 1998. Essays by twenty-seven film scholars, each focused on one or two major films.

Film-makers' Cooperative Catalogue No. 7 and *Film-makers' Cooperative Catalogue No. 7 Supplement*. New York: Film-makers' Cooperative, 1989, 1993. Descriptions of films and videos available through the coop, arranged alphabetically by filmmaker. Especially valuable for information on the avant-garde.

James, David E. *Allegories of Cinema: American Film in the Sixties*. Princeton: Princeton UP, 1989. Survey of American avant-garde cinema of the 1960s and its various cultural contexts.

MacDonald, Scott. *A Critical Cinema: Interviews with Independent Filmmakers*. Berkeley: U of California P, 1988. Introductory essay followed by a short essay on the life and films of each of seventeen filmmakers and an interview with each.

———. *A Critical Cinema 2: Interviews with Independent Filmmakers*. Berkeley: U of California P, 1992. Fifteen more interviews plus three interviews each focusing on a film.

———. *A Critical Cinema 3: Interviews with Independent Filmmakers*. Berkeley: U of California P, 1997. Includes an overview for each interviewee, interviews with filmmakers from many nations, film/videographies, and bibliographies.

———. *Screen Writings: Scripts and Texts by Independent Filmmakers*. Berkeley: U of California P, 1995. Includes introduction and a script for or a partial description of a wide variety of avant-garde films. Also includes nearly one hundred stills, most of them frame enlargements; distribution sources; and a bibliography.

Rothman, William. *Documentary Film Classics*. Cambridge: Cambridge UP, 1997. Detailed analyses, supported with many frame enlargements, of some major documentary films.

RESPONSES TO FILMS

W E HAVE CONSIDERED the impact of various filmmaking techniques and the major types of films along with their sources and characteristics. We will now examine how learning about a film's contexts helps viewers understand a film more completely. Then we will consider some of the many complex ways viewers respond to a film. As viewers see a film they form expectations and adjust them as the film progresses. As viewers see a film and think about it afterward, they also usually try to make sense of it—to figure out what in general it is communicating. Viewers often make meanings by explaining the general implications of the story or the significance of a symbol. Part Three examines these issues and how different critical approaches can affect the meanings that viewers perceive. In this part of the book we will also consider some of the ways the formulations of meanings are influenced by the viewer's time, place, and other circumstances. Part Three concludes by applying the book's concepts to one film, *The Player*, thus demonstrating some of the many ways an informed viewer may respond to a particular film.

◀ If a film succeeds in capturing the viewers' interest, viewers react emotionally and mentally, including formulating and reformulating expectations and figuring out the film's general significance or meanings. As illustrated here in a scene from *The Accidental Tourist* (1988), usually film viewing is also communal. *Warner Bros.*

CHAPTER 9

Understanding Films
through Contexts

W E HAVE ALL HEARD OF PEOPLE upset that their statements were "taken out of context" and thus distorted and misunderstood. Conversely, any statement examined within its contexts is more likely to be understood. As this chapter illustrates, knowledge of the conditions that precede and surround the making of a film—its contexts—help viewers understand a film more completely. A film does not begin when the house lights dim and the projector begins to send dancing lights through the darkness or when we turn on the TV and pop a tape into the VCR. What has happened before a film was made and sometimes what is going on while the film is being made may influence how the finished film begins, how it all unwinds, and how viewers respond to it.

Before you are shown a 1920s Soviet film in a course or a film series, someone may stand before the audience and talk about the political climate in the Soviet Union at the time the film was made. As a result, when you watch the film, you understand why it focuses not on a few individuals but on large groups. Imagine that before you see *Fatal Attraction*, you learn that shortly before the film appeared in 1987, the AIDS epidemic had led to mass media warnings about the dangers of unprotected sex. You also learn that in the 1980s, growing numbers of American men felt threatened by successful, financially independent, career-minded, sexually active single women. When you see *Fatal Attraction*, you notice that the film shows horrible consequences after a married man has unprotected sex with a single career woman, and you notice that the movie's career woman is shown unsympathetically. In short, you now understand how societal attitudes at the time of the film's making influenced its content. Finally, imagine that you see *The World of Apu*, a 1958 film from India, and think it curious that the young married couple never kiss, though they are clearly in love. Later you learn that censorship regulations for Indian films of that time prohibited kissing, so the couple's affection had to be conveyed by other means (Figure 9.1). In

FIGURE 9.1 **Showing affection in a 1950s film from India**
Kissing was not allowed in Indian films in the 1950s, so loving feelings had to be conveyed in other ways. In *The World of Apu* (1958) a new wife gives her husband a look that blends love and concern. Frame enlargement. *Edward Harrison*

these and countless other situations, if viewers know something about when and under what conditions a film was made, they can understand the film more completely.

Both makers and exhibitors of movies often consider how much of a film's context their audiences are likely to be aware of. Most filmmakers assume that audiences know something about the context of the film's story. If audiences may not, filmmakers often include background information in the film itself. **Title cards** give tidbits of historical information throughout *Schindler's List* (1993). The opening two title cards in *Das Boot*, or *The Boat* (1981), inform viewers that "the battle for control of the Atlantic is turning against the Germans" as the story begins in the autumn of 1941 and that of the 40,000 German sailors who "served on U-boats during World War II, 30,000 never returned." Channels that focus on old movies, such as Turner Classic Movies, also usually include a brief introduction to each film explaining at least a little of the film's contexts.

Once viewers understand that filmmakers work under forces that influence the shape and content of the finished films, viewers are less likely to misjudge a film for not exploring a political, religious, or sexual subject in greater depth or consistency when that may not have been an option. Viewers who

title card: A card or thin sheet of clear plastic that supplies information in a film.

know when and where a film was made and under what conditions are also more likely to notice when filmmakers follow conventions and when they depart from them. They are more likely to understand how the film's budget precludes certain options and how the available filmmaking technology and the audio and visual presentations of competing media and electronic entertainments may influence the film. The influences at work can be schematized as follows:

contexts ➔ filmmakers ➔ film ➔ viewers

Viewers who see influences behind (and surrounding) filmmakers can more clearly and more fully understand why a film is the way it is.

There are so many possible contexts for a film that it would take a sizable book to begin to explore them fully. This chapter introduces five contexts: society and politics, censorship, artistic conventions, financial constraints, and technological developments. Generally, these contexts are presented from the most abstract to the most concrete—from ideas, such as societal attitudes, to practical realities, such as money and filmmaking equipment.

SOCIETY AND POLITICS

Human freedom is relative: there are always limits to what filmmakers can show. Their freedom to express themselves is strongly affected by dominant attitudes in the society they work in and the society's political climate.

Prevalent societal attitudes may exert powerful influences on filmmakers. For example, dominant attitudes about homosexuality influence whether, when, and how homosexuals are portrayed in films. Because so many people disapproved of homosexuality—some heterosexual males violently so—and because the production code placed restrictions on filmmakers from 1934 into the 1960s (see p. 385), homosexual characters were seldom identified openly in American movies before 1968. In *The Maltese Falcon* (1941), for example, several characters are homosexual though this is not made explicit (Figure 9.2). *Rebel without a Cause* (1955), *Tea and Sympathy* (1956), *Cat on a Hot Tin Roof* (1958), *Suddenly Last Summer* (1959), and many other films refer to homosexuality only obliquely.

FIGURE 9.2 **Advertising for a 1940s movie that hints at a character's homosexuality**
This part of a publicity still for *The Maltese Falcon* (1941) approximates a few brief images from the movie itself and hints at the Peter Lorre character's homosexuality—the cane handle near his mouth—the explicit depiction or mention of which was forbidden by the U.S. production code then in effect. *Warner Bros.– First National*

FIGURE 9.3 Gay stereotypes in a film
The Boys in the Band (1970) includes eight gay or bisexual male characters. It is ambiguous whether the film's one heterosexual character is completely heterosexual. Although the film was the first widely distributed U.S. movie featuring gays, it also perpetuated gay stereotypes, especially the universality of gays' emotional misery. Near the end of the film, one character announces slowly, and in effect twice, "If we [homosexuals] could just learn not to hate ourselves quite so very much." *Leo Productions, Ltd.*

As attitudes in western societies have changed, so has the depiction of homosexuals in films. In his book *The Celluloid Closet: Homosexuality in the Movies*, Vito Russo says that the first positive images of gays in commercial cinema appear in two 1961 British movies, *A Taste of Honey* and *Victim* (126–33). In *A Taste of Honey*, a sensitive homosexual friend cares for the main character, an unwed pregnant teenager. In *Victim*, a British movie star, Dirk Bogarde, plays a man who admits to his desire for another man; some of the film's "character portrayals are relatively sympathetic, given the era and social climate in which the film was made" (Jones 271). After the U.S. film industry abandoned the production code and instituted a rating system in 1968, more adult subjects, including homosexual characters, appeared on the screen. *The Boys in the Band* (1970, Figure 9.3) and *Dog Day Afternoon* (1975) are key films in this regard. In *Dog Day Afternoon* Al Pacino, who up to that point in his career had played only heterosexual characters, credibly acts the role of a bisexual. The film also includes a persuasive performance by Chris Sarandon as the Pacino character's homosexual lover.

In general, as western societies have grown more tolerant of homosexuality, gays have been shown more often and more explicitly in films. Many movies since the late 1960s conform to society's stereotypes of gays and show them as miserable, depressed, and suicidal or as laughable. In the Cuban film *Strawberry and Chocolate* (1993) and in *La Cage aux Folles* (1978), its sequels, and its remake as *The Birdcage* (1996), gay characters have the pivotal roles though they and the situations they end up in are stereotypical, amusing, and nonthreatening to heterosexual audiences. In other films, gay characters are seen in less stereotypical roles, as in *Victor/Victoria* (1982), *Longtime Companion* (1990), and *Philadelphia* (1993). The huge commercial success of *The Crying Game* (1992) is a barometer of changing social attitudes about sexual orientation (Figure 9.4).

FIGURE 9.4 **Tolerance of sexual preference**
The Crying Game (1992), featuring an IRA volunteer (left) and a hairdresser, questions whether sexual preference is the only consideration in a close relationship. The film, which was a critical and popular success, treats its complex characters sympathetically. *Palace; Channel 4; Miramax*

Another example of widespread public attitudes influencing the choice and depiction of subjects occurs in movies about American involvement in the Vietnam War. U.S. military involvement (1963–72) in the Vietnam War (1954–75) was costly, controversial, and divisive (resulting in antiwar speeches and demonstrations in the United States unlike those found during any other war the country has been involved in). In contrast to the situation that prevailed during and after World War II, during American involvement in Vietnam and shortly afterward, there were few American movies about the war. Those that were made, such as *The Green Berets* (1968) with John Wayne, supported American involvement. (The **documentary film** *In the Year of the Pig* [1968] criticized American involvement but was not widely shown.) After American military involvement finally ended in 1972, some of the war's pain began to recede into the dimness of time and American public opinion increasingly questioned the wisdom of U.S. involvement. Then filmmakers with qualms about the war began to make movies critical of it. *Hearts and Minds*, a 1974 documentary film; *Go Tell the Spartans* (1978); *The Deer Hunter* (1978); *Apocalypse Now* (1979); *Platoon* (1986); *Hamburger Hill* (1987); *Full Metal Jacket* (1987); *Born on the Fourth of July* (1989); and others all criticize the American war effort. These films could not have been made during or immediately after the war: they would have been considered unpatriotic during the war and too painful to watch and therefore too uncommercial shortly after it.

Although movies often reflect societal attitudes, **avant-garde** filmmakers are frequently at odds with prevalent attitudes of their time and make their films to protest orthodox beliefs and values. At least one of artist Andy Warhol's films includes explicit heterosexual acts ("Couch," 1964); many of them include cross-dressing (*Screen Test 2*, 1965) and homosexuality (*My Hustler*, 1965). And his films were made unconventionally, for example, sometimes by simply turning on the camera and filming nonstop until the **reel(s)** ran out (*Empire*, 1964). In subject matter and technique, his films defied the mores of 1960s America and traditional moviemaking.

Political developments—especially as reported in the mass media—influence what topics people are concerned about and how they think about them. In turn, political concerns affect the choice of topics depicted in many forms of human expression, including films.

Consider the situation in the United States shortly after the end of World War II, with the Soviet Union's rise in power. With heavy media coverage of those political developments, many Americans began to worry about Communist infiltration of American institutions. As part of its activities, in 1947 the House Committee on Un-American Activities (HUAC, as the committee was often imprecisely called) held hearings in Hollywood to investigate Communist infiltration of the film industry. Some filmmakers who believed that the committee's actions infringed on their constitutional rights (and who in some cases had other reasons) refused to cooperate with

documentary film: A film that presents a version of actions and happenings that viewers are intended to accept not primarily as the product of someone's imagination but primarily as fact.

avant-garde film: A film that rejects the conventions of popular movies and explores the possibilities of the film medium itself.

reel: A spool to hold film.

the committee. Ten filmmakers, mostly screenwriters, the "Hollywood Ten," were eventually sentenced to prison for contempt of Congress. In 1951, HUAC held a second round of hearings on Communist influence in Hollywood, and more than three hundred Hollywood filmmakers either confessed to past membership in the Communist party or were accused by witnesses of having been members. Until well into the 1960s, most of those people were blacklisted and could find no work in the American film industry.

The atmosphere of fear and distrust caused enormous upheaval in the industry. Some filmmakers found other work; some moved abroad to find work; others worked under assumed names. Freedom of expression was curtailed for all who worked in the film industry at the time, not just for those who were accused of being Communists. Filmmakers shied away from controversial projects, especially those with political subjects. Some films commented indirectly on the political climate of the time. For example, some commentators see parallels between those who refused to cooperate with HUAC and the town marshal in the western *High Noon* (1952); both acted on their principles and refused to give in to intimidating forces. Some critics see *The Invasion of the Body Snatchers* (1956) as an oblique commentary on the menace and passivity of the era.

In every era, political climate influences the choice and depiction of subjects. Another example is seen during the cold war period, from the late 1940s to the early 1980s. Such American movies as *Red Dawn* (1984), which shows Soviets and Cubans invading a small Colorado town, and *Rambo: First Blood Part II* (1985) depict Soviets as untrustworthy and treacherous. *Rocky IV* (1985) also reflects the political mood through two boxing matches between representatives of the Soviet Union and the United States, and it's unsurprising which political system the movie champions (Figure 9.5). All these movies exalt Americans and encourage nationalism while denigrating the Soviet system. In contrast, since the increased cooperation between Russia and the United States in the 1990s, few such anti-Russian American movies have been forthcoming.

CENSORSHIP

Censorship is closely related to societal attitudes and political climate. From the beginning of cinema, some people have been concerned about the possible harm of *others* seeing certain behavior, especially sex and violence, or being exposed to certain ideas, particularly religious and political ones. Different societies address those concerns in different ways.

Some societies forbid the making of certain films. Iranian movies, most of which are funded by the government, forbid criticism of the Iranian Islamic government and all religions. In Iranian films women must be shown in head scarf and long coat. Forbidden are close-ups of women, makeup, kissing, hand-

◀ **FIGURE 9.5 The cold war in a boxing ring**
Rocky IV (1985) culminates in a boxing match between Rocky and his Goliath Soviet opponent, Ivan Drago. It's not giving away a surprise ending to reveal that Rocky prevails. He does so for a combination of reasons. In part, Rocky wins because *Rocky IV* is an American movie made during the cold war. Although the film is draped in national flags and the last image before the ending credits is of Rocky with a U.S. flag above him, Rocky's victory is also a victory for the old ways of doing things. (a, left) Rocky trains in nature with nature's objects (rocks, logs, mountains, snow) and simple country tools (saw, sled, ax, block and tackle, rope, yoke, and cart). Here his trainer holds his ankles as he does sit-ups in a barn. (b, below) Drago uses all the most advanced computerized exercise equipment and is injected with chemicals. Rocky is advised by a trainer with years of experience with professional boxing. Drago is trained by a cadre of state-employed scientists and a trainer with no professional experience. Other factors contribute to Rocky's victory. He keeps getting back up and going at Drago, and he is not burdened by arrogance. He also prays and he fights for others, including his late friend Apollo Creed. By the twelfth round, even the initially hostile Soviet crowd begins chanting "Rocky!" "Rocky!" "Rocky!" Of course, Rocky has earned the loving support of his wife and young son. (Are there any emotional buttons this film does not push?) Before the final round, a Soviet official berates Drago, who announces that he fights to win—for himself. Drago is then alone and on the doorstep of defeat. Frame enlargements. *United Artists*

holding, and eye contact between men and women. To assure compliance with these and other guidelines, the government imposes five stages of censorship, beginning with the approval of the script. In China, filmmakers are not supposed to make sexy films, films that criticize the government explicitly or implicitly, or depressing films with sad endings. If filmmakers somehow manage to do so, they probably will not be able to get their films distributed in China. Director Zhang Yimou, for example, has made films such as *Ju Dou* (1990) with equipment and financing from outside China only to see some of the films banned in China. The makers of *Farewell My Concubine* (1993) suffered a similar fate: accolades abroad, censorship in China. The Chinese film *Postman* (1995)—which is not to be confused with the Italian film *Il Postino* (*The Postman*) of the same year or Kevin Costner's *The Postman* (1997)—touches on adultery, prostitution, homosexuality, and drug use. Even before its completion, director He Jianjun was banned from making further films. A society may have a written policy regulating film content, or different people or agencies may enforce standards according to their whim. Some films banned in China, for example, were banned without explanation.

Sometimes government authorities may halt a production, as was the fate of the Soviet filmmaker Sergei Eisenstein, who was forced both to abandon *Bezhin Meadow* in 1937 and to repudiate it publicly. Eisenstein ran into trouble with *Bezhin Meadow* and most of his later films because he did not follow the general guidelines of **socialist realism**. This Soviet doctrine and **style**, which were in force from the mid-1930s to the 1980s (until the Gorbachev era), decreed that all creative works—including music, artworks, and films—must promote socialism, communism, and thus the proletariat

style: The manner of presenting a subject in a creative work.

FIGURE 9.6 Early, local censorship
(a, above left) An 1897 American film, "Fatima's Dance," shows a woman dancing provocatively, at least by the standards of the day. (b, above right) Some exhibitors showed a censored version of "Fatima's Dance" with scratched emulsion obscuring the women's clothed breasts and legs. Frame enlargements. *The Museum of Modern Art/Film Stills Archive*

or working people. Soviet creative works were not to imply approval of western ideas and lifestyles or even ambivalence toward them. Under socialist realism, creative works were supposed to be "realistic" (actually an idealized depiction of the working class) and readily accessible to mass audiences. Styles judged innovative or arty were taboo. Works that were judged to fall short of the standards of socialist realism were labeled "decadent," "bourgeois," "capitalistic," or "formalist"—and sometimes in the 1930s and 1940s Stalin himself made that judgment. At a minimum their makers were publicly rebuked. For fifty years socialist realism severely restricted both the subjects and styles of Soviet artists, not just the filmmakers Sergei Eisenstein and Lev Kuleshov, but also the composers Dmitri Shostakovich and Sergei Prokofiev, writer Isaak Babel, theater director Vsevolod Meyerhold, and many others.

In the United States, early films were sometimes censored by state or city boards (Figure 9.6). By the early 1930s, the American public found many popular American movies offensive. Some viewers seemed especially upset by violence and sex, whereas others swarmed to such popular gangster films as *Little Caesar* (1930), *The Public Enemy* (1931), and *Scarface* (1932) and films featuring unrepentant, sexually assertive women, especially those played by Mae West (Figure 9.7). Of West's impact scholar Ramona Curry writes:

> Unlike most other Hollywood movies of the 1930s, West's films do not suggest that morality or questions of taste dictate female sexual behavior. Instead, West's films and star image present female sexual allure as a commodity that women themselves can control and benefit from. . . . West's movie image exposed contradictions in the well-established American capitalist practice of simultaneously exploiting and repressing female sexuality as a commodity under men's control. (28)

FIGURE 9.7 Mae West as an openly sexual character in pre–production code days
In *She Done Him Wrong* (1933), the first movie Mae West starred in, West wears skintight, low-cut dresses and plays a kept woman who is quick-witted, resourceful, openly mercenary, attractive to many men, and nearly always in control. Though she is skimpy with her displays of affection, she seems to appreciate men's sexuality. For example, more than once in the movie she looks men up and down then hums her approval. To the Cary Grant character (left), who initially resists her encouragement, she says, "You ain't kiddin' me any. You know, I met your kind before. Why don't you come up sometime huh? . . . Don't be afraid. I won't tell. . . . Come up. I'll tell your fortune. Ah, you can be had." Later she sings suggestively, "I'm a fast-moving gal that likes 'em slow. . . . There isn't any fun in gettin' something done if you're rushed when you have to make the grade." Here and in her other early movies, she is sexual, assertive, and unrepentant in ways shocking to many early 1930s U.S. audiences; her movies have been blamed as partially responsible for stricter enforcement of the production code. *Paramount*

FIGURE 9.8 Pre– and post–production code movies (a, right) From the "Pettin' in the Park" musical number in *Gold Diggers of 1933* (1933). After the production code was applied to all movies from 1934 on, such glimpses of sexuality were forbidden on U.S. movie screens. (b, below) A few years after the production code was fully in effect, *Gold Diggers of 1937* (1936) depicts men and women as innocent (dressed in white), childlike (small in comparison to the chairs), and unerotic (covered up and sitting, not uncovered and lying down as in the 1933 film). The language of *Gold Diggers of 1937* is also less suggestive than that of *Gold Diggers of 1933*, and in the later film words such as "pettin'" or "petting" are nowhere to be heard. *(a) Warner Bros.; (b) Warner Bros.– First National*

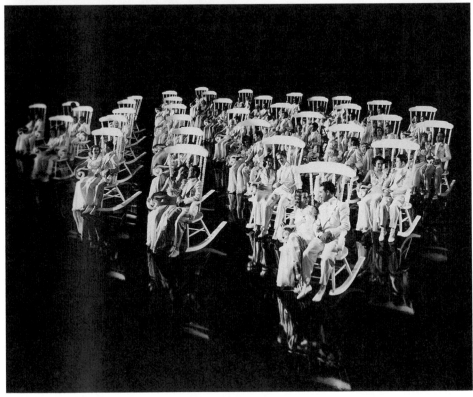

Rather than face government interference, in 1930 American film producers and distributors set up a written production code (see pp. 386–87), a self-regulatory system of acceptable speech and behavior in films. In 1934, the code was revised and from then on more strenuously enforced. Until 1968, all movies to be shown in the United States were supposed to be submitted to the Production Code Administration for a seal of approval. The production code restricted the explicit or attractive depiction of vast areas of human experience—such as illegal drugs, illicit sex (including homosexuality), scenes of passion, prostitution, miscegenation, childbirth, and obscene and profane speech. From 1934 to 1968, to earn the seal of approval American films had to be suitable for audiences of all ages, including young children. Some of the differences between films made before and after the code was enforced are evident in stills for *Gold Diggers of 1933* and *Gold Diggers of 1937* (Figure 9.8).

Enforcement of the code could cause incoherence in movies, as in *The Big Sleep* (1946), a confusing film that omits nearly all references to the sex and drugs so prominent in the source novel by Raymond Chandler. As critic Frank Krutnik shows, enforcement of the code in a romantic scene involving the two main characters in *Out of the Past* (1947) could confuse audiences:

> The couple run through the rain to the beach-house, laughing like carefree young lovers. When they arrive there, Kathie dries his hair, and Jeff does the same for her. He kisses her on the back of the neck and then tosses away the towel, which knocks the lamp over. When the light goes out, there is a swirl of music, and the camera then **tracks** towards the door, which blows open in the wind. There is then a cut to the outside, with the camera continuing its forward-tracking. This leading away from the scene, together with the reprisal of the film's love-theme and the dousing of the light, suggests that Jeff and Kathie are making love. However, the film cuts back to the inside of the beach-house: Jeff closes the door, and Kathie takes a record off the gramophone. There is a marked, seemingly post-coital change in their attitudes. However, although the slow forward-tracking of the camera has implied that intercourse takes place, the cut back to the inside, and the continuity of Jeff shutting the door after it has blown open, suggest that there has been no time-lapse. Sex is thus both firmly suggested and disavowed. (Krutnik 246)

track: To film while the camera is moving.

The code is also responsible for more than one implausible ending, such as in *Detour* (1945). That film was initially refused a seal of approval because it ended with the main character, who had inadvertently killed someone, free and walking along a road. To gain a seal, a short scene was appended: the police drive up, stop, pick up the man, and drive off, as he narrates, ". . . Someday a car will stop to pick me up that I never thumbed. Yes. Fate or some mysterious force can put the finger on you or me for no good reason at all." In this case, the not so "mysterious force" was the production code.

Excerpts from *The Production Code of the Motion Picture Producers and Directors of America, Inc. — 1930–1934*

PREAMBLE

Motion picture producers recognize the high trust and confidence which have been placed in them by the people of the world and which have made motion pictures a universal form of entertainment.

They recognize their responsibility to the public because of this trust and because entertainment and art are important influences in the life of a nation.

Hence, though regarding motion pictures primarily as entertainment without any explicit purpose of teaching or propaganda, they know that the motion picture within its own field of entertainment may be directly responsible for spiritual or moral progress, for higher types of social life, and for much correct thinking. . . .

On their part, they ask from the public and from public leaders a sympathetic understanding of their purposes and problems and a spirit of co-operation that will allow them the freedom and opportunity necessary to bring the motion picture to a still higher level of wholesome entertainment for all the people.

GENERAL PRINCIPLES

1. No picture shall be produced which will lower the moral standards of those who see it. Hence the sympathy of the audience shall never be thrown to the side of crime, wrongdoing, evil or sin. . . .

   I. CRIMES AGAINST THE LAW

   These shall never be presented in such a way as to throw sympathy with the crime as against law and justice or to inspire others with a desire for imitation.

   1. Murder
      a) The technique of murder must be presented in a way that will not inspire imitation.
      b) Brutal killings are not to be presented in detail.
      c) Revenge in modern times shall not be justified. . . .

   II. SEX

   The sanctity of the institution of marriage and the home shall be upheld. Pictures shall not infer that low forms of sex relationship are the accepted or common thing.

   1. Adultery and illicit sex, sometimes necessary plot material, must not be explicitly treated or justified, or presented attractively.
   2. Scenes of passion
      a) These should not be introduced except where they are definitely essential to the plot.
      b) Excessive and lustful kissing, lustful embraces, suggestive postures and gestures are not to be shown.
      c) In general, passion should be treated in such manner as not to stimulate the lower and baser emotions.
   3. Seduction or rape
      a) These should never be more than suggested, and then only when essential for the plot. They must never be shown by explicit method.
      b) They are never the proper subject for comedy. . . .
   6. Miscegenation (sex relationship between the white and black races) is forbidden. . . .

   III. VULGARITY

   The treatment of low, disgusting, unpleasant, though not necessarily evil, subjects should be guided always by the dictates of good taste and a proper regard for the sensibilities of the audience.

IV. OBSCENITY

Obscenity in word, gesture, reference, song, joke, or by suggestion . . . is forbidden.

V. PROFANITY

Pointed profanity and every other profane or vulgar expression, however used, is forbidden.

No approval by the Production Code Administration shall be given to the use of words and phrases in motion pictures including, but not limited to, the following:

. . . broad (applied to a woman); . . . God, Lord, Jesus, Christ (unless used reverently); . . . fanny; fairy (in a vulgar sense); finger (the); . . . hot (applied to a woman); . . . louse; lousy; . . . nerts; nuts (except when meaning crazy); pansy; . . . slut (applied to a woman); S.O.B.; son-of-a; tart; . . . traveling salesman and farmer's daughter jokes; whore; damn. . . .

The Production Code Administration may take cognizance of the fact that the following words and phrases are obviously offensive to the patrons of motion pictures in the United States and more particularly to the patrons of motion pictures in foreign countries: Chink, Dago, Frog, Greaser, Hunkie, Kike, Nigger, Spig, Wop, Yid. . . .

VIII. RELIGION

1. No film or episode may throw ridicule on any religious faith.
2. Ministers of religion in their character as ministers of religion should not be used as comic characters or as villains. . . .

REASONS SUPPORTING PREAMBLE OF CODE

. . . The MORAL IMPORTANCE of entertainment is something which has been universally recognized. It enters intimately into the lives of men and women and affects them closely; it occupies their minds and affections during leisure hours; and ultimately touches the whole of their lives. A man may be judged by his standard of entertainment as easily as by the standard of his work. . . .

3.D. The latitude given to film material cannot, in consequence, be as wide as the latitude given to book material. In addition:

a) A book describes; a film vividly presents. One presents on a cold page; the other by apparently living people.
b) A book reaches the mind through words merely; a film reaches the eyes and ears through the reproduction of actual events.
c) The reaction of a reader to a book depends largely on the keenness of the reader's imagination; the reaction to a film depends on the vividness of presentation.

Hence many things which might be described or presented in a book could not possibly be presented in a film. . . .

In general, the mobility, popularity, accessibility, emotional appeal, vividness, straightforward presentation of fact in the film make for more intimate contact with a larger audience and for greater emotional appeal.

Hence the larger moral responsibilities of the motion pictures.

As more and more films were released without a seal in the 1950s and 1960s, it became harder and harder to enforce the code. As film historian and scholar Robert Sklar explains:

> The tendency in motion-picture production and exhibition had always been to get away with as much risqué and socially disreputable behavior as the vigilance of censors would allow and economic necessity dictated. For nearly two decades after 1934, the Production Code Administration had maintained stringent control over Hollywood productions, and rising box-office figures through 1946 seemed to confirm that clean family entertainment was the road to prosperity. But as families found their clean entertainment on the TV screen, there was a natural impulse in the movie trade to revert to shock and titillation. (294)

In 1953, the American film *The Moon Is Blue* was refused a seal because it treated seduction and adultery comically, and its distributor, United Artists,

FIGURE 9.9 **Sexual frankness in 1960s European films**
Some European films of the 1960s were more candid in their depictions of sexuality than American films and were shown without the production code seal of approval in selected, mostly big-city American theaters. Here one of the two main characters of Ingmar Bergman's *The Silence* (1963) is seen reacting as she masturbates, an act that is not shown. Elsewhere in the film, the other main character sees a couple having sexual intercourse in the back of a movie theater. In both instances, the depictions of sexuality would have been inconceivable in American movies of the time because of the force of the production code. The inclusion of such scenes made these European films more appealing to many American viewers and distributors and probably contributed to the abandonment a few years later of the U.S. production code and adoption of a ratings system that permitted more adult films for adult audiences. Frame enlargement. *Svensk Filmindustri; Embassy*

resigned from the producers association and released the film on its own without a seal. Later in the 1950s and in the 1960s, such European films as the French *And God Created Woman* (1956) were more candid sexually than American films and were shown without a seal of approval in art theaters in large cities throughout the United States (Figure 9.9).

Finally in 1968, the U.S. production code was replaced with a rating system loosely modeled on the British rating system. The American ratings have been modified several times since then. (For an explanation of the current American ratings, see Figure 9.10.) Studios that belong to the Motion Picture Association of America are required to submit finished films for a rating. **Independent film** companies, which operate outside Hollywood control, are not. Advertisements and theaters are to display the rating so viewers will know what to expect, and theaters are supposed to exclude certain age groups from films with certain ratings. Although both the industry and public generally approve of the system, as the *New York Times* reports,

> There are persistent charges that the ratings board is far more critical of films with sexual content than of those with gory violence, that the board allows itself to be bullied by big studios but deals aggressively with less powerful independent companies, and that it seems far more horrified about foul language in films than about foul and murderous behavior. (Weinraub B1)

Because of dissatisfaction with the rating system, from time to time alternatives to it emerge.[1]

In many countries, filmmakers often face pressures, perhaps contractual obligations, to delete parts of a film before its release so that the film can receive a more commercially viable rating (in the United States, an R rating). Commercial interests also impose limits on political views. Few Hollywood movies, for example, focus on Communist characters or ideas. In part because so many American newspapers will not carry ads for NC-17 films and, before them, X-rated movies, American distributors faced with the prospect of that rating sometimes release films as unrated, as was done with two 1995 films, *Kids* and *When Night Is Falling*. American studios that release videotape versions may also face pressure from Blockbuster Video, with the commercial clout of its 6,300 outlets, to re-edit films and omit some of the violence, sex, and obscene language because Blockbuster will not carry films rated NC-17 or X. Even after a film has been rated and released in the U.S. market,

---

[1]Since early September 1995, an agency of the United States Catholic Conference has run a phone service (800-311-4CCC) that provides brief reviews of films currently in theaters and a family video of the week. For six or so films each week, callers can hear explanations for the USCC's classification (A-1 = general audience; A-2 = adults and adolescents; A-3 = adults; A-4 = adults only and with reservations; and O = morally offensive) and the Motion Picture Association of America rating for the same films. Callers also hear a brief description and evaluation of the film. The movie reviews are also available in print on the Web: <http://www.nccbuscc.org/movies/index.htm>.

What Everyone Should Know About The Movie Rating System.

GENERAL AUDIENCES

G

G GENERAL AUDIENCES
All Ages Admitted

Nothing that would offend parents for viewing by children.

PARENTAL GUIDANCE SUGGESTED

PG

PG PARENTAL GUIDANCE SUGGESTED
SOME MATERIAL MAY NOT BE SUITABLE FOR CHILDREN

Parents urged to give "parental guidance." May contain some material parents might not like for their young children.

PARENTS STRONGLY CAUTIONED

PG-13

PG-13 PARENTS STRONGLY CAUTIONED
Some Material May Be Inappropriate for Children Under 13

Parents are urged to be cautious. Some material may be inappropriate for pre-teenagers.

RESTRICTED

R

R RESTRICTED
UNDER 17 REQUIRES ACCOMPANYING
PARENT OR ADULT GUARDIAN

Contains some adult material. Parents are urged to learn more about the film before taking their young children with them.

NO CHILDREN UNDER 17 ADMITTED

NC-17

NC-17 NO CHILDREN
UNDER 17
ADMITTED

Patently adult. Children are not admitted.

◀ FIGURE 9.10 **The current U.S. movie rating classifications**
Before the latest change in the ratings system in 1990, both sexually explicit films and serious films unable to win an R rating were both given an X, which meant that many theaters would not show them, many newspapers would not advertise them, and many video stores would not carry them. The NC-17 rating was devised for films that are not made primarily to stimulate sexual arousal but present their subjects with candor. Since the inception of the NC-17 rating, the Motion Picture Association of America no longer assigns films an X rating. Few sexually explicit films were ever submitted for a rating anyway. © *Motion Picture Association of America, Encino, Cal.*

it may be subjected to inconspicuous forms of censorship. On cable, for example, the people behind Turner Classic Movies may take it upon themselves to edit movies they show. Even such unrated tame films as *L'avventura* (1960) and such PG-rated movies as *Tootsie* (1982) may be preceded with the announcement "This feature has been edited due to content."

Knowing something about the restrictions on filmmakers and film distributors helps viewers understand and judge films more accurately and fairly. Such knowledge may help one understand, for example, why *Detour* stumbles to its conclusion and why two films that share the same general subject and are only a few years apart are so different (see Figure 9.8).

ARTISTIC CONVENTIONS: THE WAYS IT HAS BEEN DONE

In one of his books, film critic Roger Ebert includes examples of movie conventions various viewers sent him:

> All movie bartenders, when first seen, are wiping the inside of a glass with a rag.
> —David W. Smith, Westminster, California

> In an action movie, any car driven by bad guys that crashes will inevitably explode, with flames instantly filling the passenger compartment, just as though they were carrying open cans of gasoline in their laps. This also happens whenever a car occupied by bad guys begins to fall over a cliff, even before the car has hit anything.   —Sam Waas, Houston, Texas

> In scenes set in any kind of laboratory, there are always lots of flasks filled with lots of bright, colorful chemicals—red, blue, green—when in reality virtually everything in most research labs is either clear or some shade of yellow. I can count on one hand the number of organic chemicals that are bright blue or green. The chemicals are invariably in glassware jammed together backward and sideways, in what the set **designer** thought was a neat-looking combination. . . .
> —Derek Lowe, Scotch Plains, New Jersey (Ebert 8, 54, 59–60)

designer: The person responsible for much of what is photographed in a film, including architecture, locations, sets, costumes, makeup, and hairstyles.

© 1992 Universal Press Syndicate

"Bad guy comin' in, Arnie! . . . Minor key!"

FIGURE 9.11 A musical convention in movies
The Far Side © 1992 Farworks, Inc. *Used by permission of Universal Press Syndicate. All rights reserved.*

iris shot: Shot in which part of the frame is masked or obscured.

French new wave: A diverse group of French fictional films made in the late 1950s and early 1960s marked by the independent spirit of their directors and sometimes shot on location with portable, handheld equipment and fast film stock.

And as yet another cowboy dressed in black enters yet another saloon, the music changes from a major to a minor key, but we don't notice the shift because that's the way we've so often heard it being done (Figure 9.11). This use of music in movies is a **convention**—a technique or presentation (like the bartender, the exploding car, and the colorful flasks) that audiences are used to and accept without question. These and many other cinematic conventions are traditional ways of making a film or including traditional content of the type cited in Ebert's book.

Some conventions—such as showdowns and shoot-outs in western films and viewers' being allowed to hear both sides of a telephone conversation although they see only one speaker—endure for decades. If used too often or for too long, some conventions are found to be boring or in other ways ineffective, as in the use of tremolo stringed instruments to accompany suspenseful moments. Conventions may also fall out of favor then be rediscovered. An example is the reintroduction of a variety of techniques, such as **iris shots**, by the directors of **French new wave** films. Another example is the reintroduction into American movies of **wipes**—a transition in which it appears that one image pushes off the preceding image as it replaces it (see Figure 3.10 on p. 135)—with the appearance of *Star Wars* (1977). Yet other conventions—such as the introduction of scenes of memories by an undulation of the image—simply disappear for long stretches of film history (that's not to say they will never be revived).

Often iconoclastic filmmakers draw attention to filmmaking conventions by flouting them. Mel Brooks is one such filmmaker. In *High Anxiety* (1977), for example, the camera moves toward French doors through which viewers can see people sitting at a formal dinner. The camera moves forward and forward until it loudly shatters a glass pane, and the dinner party stares at it; after a brief pause, the camera begins to retreat. In the last scene of the same film, the camera pulls back from its subjects rapidly, and viewers hear a camera operator warn, "We're going too fast. We're going to hit the wall." Almost instantaneously they do, noisily, and make a gaping hole in it. As the camera continues to retreat, the other man says, "Never mind. Keep moving back. Maybe no one will notice." Gliding exploratory camera work is a conventional technique most viewers take for granted. But most viewers have probably neither seen a caméra have accidents nor considered when, how, and why camera movement toward and away from subjects is used.

A film may also be unconventional in its choice of subjects. In the conventional western genre, for example, the protagonist is a European-American male, and his antagonists are American Indians, Mexicans, or European-American male outlaws. In American westerns since World War II, the protagonist may be female (*The Ballad of Little Jo*, 1993; *Bad Girls*, 1994) or African American (*Posse*, 1993) or European-American and Mexican outlaws (*The Wild Bunch*, 1969). The antagonists may be European-American males who are not obvious outlaws, perhaps even a law enforcement officer (*Posse*; *Unforgiven*, 1992). Or the European-American male outlaws may be supported by the inaction of the townspeople (*High Noon*).

Some breaks with conventions—such as having an actor step out of character to speak directly to the audience—never catch on with other filmmakers. Other breaks with conventions seem odd initially but are imitated by other filmmakers and eventually become conventions themselves. One example is the use of **slow motion** to depict violence. When *Bonnie and Clyde* (1967) used it in a violent scene, many viewers commented on its use and found it distracting. But soon other movies, including those directed by Sam Peckinpah, followed the practice. It became widespread and, through repetition, now seems natural to many viewers. As in other arts, the unconventional can become conventional.

slow motion: Motion in which the action depicted on the screen is slower than its real-life counterpart.

Unconventional filmmakers help us see that conventions are arbitrary: they do not have inevitable and unchanging meanings or significance. For instance, a **lap dissolve**—in which one image fades out as the next image fades in and momentarily overlaps it then replaces it—does not have to mean "now the **setting** changes," though it usually does in films of recent decades. In films from the 1920s, lap dissolves are occasionally used within a scene (see Figure 3.9 on p. 134). Filmmaking practices take on widely understood meanings or associations through repeated use in similar contexts. For instance, if enough filmmakers use lap dissolves to suggest that the action now shifts to a new setting, viewers learn that meaning (similarly, we learn the meanings of most words by hearing or reading them in context, not by hearing or reading definitions).

setting: The place where filmed action occurs.

When we examine filmic conventions, we start to see how widespread, expressive, and influential they are. Whether films include them or not, conventions influence how a film is made and in turn how viewers respond. Conventions are like teachers and clergy: they strongly influence succeeding generations.

FINANCIAL CONSTRAINTS

The budget for a film influences the choice of equipment, personnel available, settings, time that can be devoted to making the film, and promotion and distribution. Consider the situation of Terry Zwigoff, the director of the acclaimed documentary *Crumb* (1994), whose lack of money restricted what he could film and influenced how he filmed it.

> I just didn't have any film to use. It was horrible. I'd be in this situation with great stuff happening, and I'd have to allot myself two rolls of film instead of ten. And it was also what forced me to prompt and to stage and to manipulate a lot of things—you just couldn't wait for them to happen naturally with that kind of budget. (Katz 38)

location: Any place other than a constructed setting that is used for filming.

Big feature films are terrifically expensive to make. A movie with stars, special effects, lots of action filmed at foreign **locations**, and widespread advertisements requires a budget in the tens of millions of dollars, perhaps even more than one hundred million dollars. To attract enough viewers to earn back all the expenses and make a profit, such a movie has to be entertaining to huge audiences. In other words, once a big-budget deal is fashioned—as in *Godzilla* (1998)—or the making of the film proves much more costly than it was budgeted for—as with *Titanic* (1997)—the filmmakers are under a lot of pressure to deliver a movie with some proven popular characteristics. Popular components are chases, fights, explosions, spectacular sights, romantic or sexual attraction and interaction, a youthful heart throb, and a happy ending. Filmmakers responsible for making a movie with a big budget are also under pressure to avoid generally unpopular subjects, such as world religions, and unconventional styles, such as **surrealism**.

surrealism: A movement in 1920s and 1930s European art, drama, literature, and film in which an attempt was made to portray or interpret the workings of the subconscious mind as manifested in dreams.

For an independent film without stars, special effects, and exotic locations, the budget will be far less—though raising money to produce it still tends to be very time-consuming and frustrating. With a smaller budget, the return need not be huge to cover all the expenses and turn a profit. Independent filmmakers—such as John Sayles, Jim Jarmusch, Charles Burnett, Ang Lee, Julie Dash, and Robert Rodriguez—are freer to fashion a film more to their liking, such as one with a controversial or offbeat subject or perhaps an ending that does not make clear the consequences of major actions or lacks a happy fate for characters that viewers identify with. As illustrated in *Plan 9 from Outer Space* (1959), budgets may be so restricted, however, as to cause curious results (Figure 9.12).

For a short avant-garde film on video, the budget can be so small that many filmmakers could afford to shoot and edit until they get nearly exactly the results they want. Because such filmmakers do not require a large audience—indeed, they may not require an audience at all—they have enormous freedom to express themselves on film.

Budget Is Destiny?

As the following two hypothetical budgets by a Hollywood producer illustrate, different films result from different budgets. In this case, both planned films originate from the same source story that is set in the 1930s. The big-budget version has stars, a large budget for the script (scenario), a costly (and perhaps famous) director, a lengthy shooting schedule, period sets and costumes, and a sizable music budget. The small-budget version has no stars and a short shooting schedule and is set in the present (lacking the glamour of period sets and costumes). The big-budget version will have a lot of money for advertising (not shown here: the "publicity/stills" entry is for only the unit publicist and still photographer). It will generate attention to itself. The small-budget version will need a shrewd script, creative director, and enthusiastic reviews. Positive word of mouth would be a plus. Recognition at a major film festival and awards would probably help, too. In filmmaking, budget often is destiny.

Source for pp. 396–97: Art Linson, "The $75 Million Difference," *New York Times Magazine* 16 Nov. 1997: 88, 89.

APPOINTMENT IN SAMARRA

START DATE: February 2, 1998
FINISH DATE: May 12, 1998
LOCATION: Albany, NY
TOTAL DAYS: 70
5-day weeks/12-hour shoot/10-hour prep
HOLIDAYS: 2
POST: 22 weeks, Los Angeles

Story rights	$ 300,000
Scenario	1,727,250
Producer	2,740,308
Director	5,305,514
Principal cast costs	32,299,197
Misc. star costs	1,912,747
Julian English	20,000,000
Caroline English	4,000,000
Lute Fliegler	2,000,000
Froggy Ogden	500,000
Harry Reilly	500,000
Dr. English	1,000,000
Al Grecco	2,000,000
Mrs. Walker	250,000
Casting	136,450
Supporting cast	1,939,054
Stunts	317,850
Rehearsals	9,000
ATL travel and living	2,260,112
Total fringes	705,899
TOTAL ABOVE-THE-LINE	**47,604,184**
Extras	1,293,456
Production staff	1,268,019
Art department	925,672
Set construction	2,500,000
Grip/set operations	927,339
Camera	1,216,657
Production sound	262,875
Electrical/set lighting	974,143
Special effects	514,390
Creatures/mechanical FX	0
Set dressing	1,195,882

Animals/handlers	25,000
Wardrobe	2,016,205
Makeup/hair	451,264
Video playback and assist	150,283
Props	249,456
Action props/pic vehicles	929,000
Prod raw stock & lab	600,590
Second unit	250,000
Visual FX (and miniatures)	1,500,000
Tests	50,000
Transportation	1,808,354
Location and office expenses	2,139,335
BTL travel and living	2,085,078
Stage and backlot charges	272,100
Total fringes	3,236,200
TOTAL PRODUCTION EXPENSES	**26,841,298**
Picture editorial	693,221
Sound/music editorial	525,821
Postproduction sound	521,243
Postproduction film/lab	122,380
Stock picture footage	5,000
Music	1,500,000
Visual effects—postproduction	0
Titles/dissolves/wipes	100,000
Projection	45,615
Total fringes	207,966
TOTAL POSTPRODUCTION	**3,721,246**
Miscellaneous charges	194,100
Insurance	727,453
Publicity/stills	114,541
Total fringes	28,765
TOTAL OTHER EXPENSES	1,064,859
TOTAL BELOW-THE-LINE	**31,627,403**
Total above- and below-the-line	79,231,587
Completion bond: 3%	0
Contingency: 10%	0
GRAND TOTAL	**$79,231,587**

APPOINTMENT IN SAMARRA

START DATE: February 2, 1998
FINISH DATE: March 7, 1998
LOCATION: Suburban NYC
TOTAL DAYS: 30
6-day weeks/12-hour shoot/10-hour prep
HOLIDAYS: 0
POST: 18 weeks, NYC

Story rights	$ 50,000
Scenario	54,000
Producer	207,700
Director	116,950
Principal cast costs	239,600
Misc. star costs	1,750
Julian English	50,000
Caroline English	50,000
Lute Fliegler (per week)	5,000
Froggy Ogden (per week)	5,000
Harry Reilly (per week)	5,000
Dr. English (per week)	5,000
Al Grecco (per week)	5,000
Mrs. Walker (per week)	5,000
Casting	32,850
Supporting cast	109,619
Stunts	21,781
Rehearsals	1,000
ATL travel and living	36,880
Total fringes	41,554
TOTAL ABOVE-THE-LINE	**879,084**
Extras	135,637
Production staff	241,950
Art department	76,334
Set construction	15,000
Grip/set operations	126,834
Camera	115,689
Production sound	32,551
Electrical/set lighting	110,708
Special effects	78,086
Creatures/mechanical FX	0
Set dressing	132,673

Animals/handlers	0
Wardrobe	98,469
Makeup/hair	55,470
Video playback and assist	3,740
Props	57,815
Action props/pic vehicles	27,500
Prod raw stock & lab	139,065
Second unit	0
Visual FX (and miniatures)	50,000
Tests	2,500
Transportation	304,430
Location and office expenses	361,296
BTL travel and living	5,000
Stage and backlot charges	0
Total fringes	225,840
TOTAL PRODUCTION EXPENSES	**2,396,587**
Picture editorial	219,042
Sound/music editorial	119,040
Postproduction sound	193,490
Postproduction film/lab	61,550
Stock picture footage	0
Music	125,000
Visual effects—postproduction	0
Titles/dissolves/wipes	33,000
Projection	7,125
Total fringes	49,686
TOTAL POSTPRODUCTION	**807,933**
Miscellaneous charges	83,700
Insurance	63,404
Publicity/stills	25,700
Total fringes	3,432
TOTAL OTHER EXPENSES	176,236
TOTAL BELOW-THE-LINE	**3,380,756**
Total above- and below-the-line	4,259,840
Completion bond: 3%	127,795
Contingency: 10%	425,984
GRAND TOTAL	**$4,813,619**

TECHNOLOGICAL DEVELOPMENTS

New technology makes possible effects that were previously impossible. For example, computers can be used to change parts of images or to combine images. In **morphing**, a transformation of one shape into another, sophisticated software can make one thing seem to transform into something else, as when a pool of liquid forms itself into a man in *Terminator 2: Judgment Day* (1991). Morphing has also been used in movies to show how conspicuous an injured creature might look (Figure 9.13) and to show a person transforming into something else or temporarily changing shape in incredible ways (see Figure 2.55 on p. 117). For parts of *The Lawnmower Man* (1992), computers were

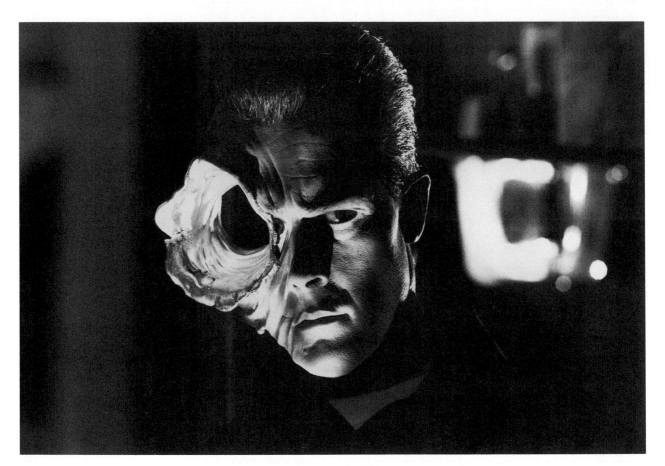

FIGURE 9.13 Computers used to create previously impossible images
This image from *Terminator 2: Judgment Day* (1991) would have been impossible before the use of computers and sophisticated software in the late 1980s. In the movie, the changing shape and distortions of the evil cyborg can be unexpected, threatening, and shocking. *James Cameron; Tri-Star Pictures*

FIGURE 9.14 Computers used to depict virtual reality in movies
For *The Lawnmower Man* (1992) and occasional later movies, computers were used to create scenes of virtual reality, a computer-generated artificial world complete with changing imaginary environment and virtual people who interact with their environment and each other. At one point in the movie a man and a woman in an advanced laboratory don virtual reality headgear then see and seem to experience themselves as is seen here, as virtual people who change shape. Here the cybercouple engage in some affection and demonstrate in a new way the unifying force of love. *New Line Cinema*

used to create virtual realities, computer-generated worlds, complete with changing imaginary environments and virtual people who can interact and continuously change shape (be morphed) (Figure 9.14).

Digital manipulation can be used to eliminate part of an image, such as part of a character's legs in *Forrest Gump* (1994), and to combine images, such as of Forrest Gump meeting and mingling with Presidents Nixon (Figure 9.15) and Kennedy or of the bodies of President and Mrs. Bush with the faces of professional actors in *In the Line of Fire* (1993).[2] With computers, actors

---

[2]"Through the Eyes of Forrest Gump" (1994), a documentary/promotional film, shows how the shot of Forrest meeting President Kennedy was a composite of altered footage of the president meeting with a football team in the White House and a shot of Forrest shaking hands with the air against a blue background. The film also explains how computers were used in the scenes of Lieutenant Dan without his legs, Forrest's championship Ping-Pong match, and that floating feather.

FIGURE 9.15 Computers used to make composites or to combine images
For this shot in *Forrest Gump* (1994), computer specialists and others took film of President Nixon and scanned it into a computer; filmed actor Tom Hanks against a blue screen acting as he will in the final version; modified that footage so that it is as grainy as the earlier footage; scanned the modified shot of Hanks into a computer; then combined the two shots—of President Nixon and the fictional character Forrest Gump. Finally, the finished shot was transferred to film. Frame enlargement. *Paramount Viacomcoei*

can be filmed in front of a blank blue screen and placed in any setting, whether an actual location or a set (the set may be constructed or be created with photographs stored on a computer).

Advances in filmmaking technology are not without their costs and sometimes limitations. In the late 1920s and early 1930s, films began to be made with sound synchronized with the image, but because the microphones picked up the camera noise during filming, the cameras were placed in soundproof rooms and camera movement within dialogue scenes largely came to a halt (Figure 9.16). Such films tended to be unmoving and overwhelmed by dialogue.[3]

---

[3]*Singin' in the Rain*—a 1952 film whose narrative is set in the late 1920s—includes fairly accurate, humorous scenes demonstrating some of the problems of filming while recording on records and later synchronizing the recorded sounds with the projected images.

New technology can also affect the types of movies that get made. The coming of film sound in the late 1920s, for example, brought together vaudeville, which was a type of musical comedy variety stage show, and film.

In the case of Hollywood this produced a new genre—the musical. However, it also put an end to other generic types, such as the gestural, slapstick comedy associated with Chaplin and Keaton. Conversely, it created a new type of comedy: the fast repartee comedy with snappy dialogue (as with the Marx Brothers and W. C. Fields) and screwball comedy—usually based on the "battle between the sexes." (Hayward 322–23)

Competition from other media may also spur the movie industry to develop technology that makes movies more appealing to consumers. For example, when box office revenues began to decline in the United States in the late 1940s with the growth of black-and-white television, the film industry

FIGURE 9.16 Enclosed and immobile cameras
In this unidentified photo, two cameras are enclosed in the type of soundproof rooms used in the late 1920s. Such enclosures prevented the sounds of the operating camera from reaching the recording microphones on the set but also precluded camera movement. (The woman seems to be suggesting that directors will no longer need megaphones to bark directions to actors working in silent movies; the man seems to be holding a wire leading to a microphone off the frame to the right.) *The Museum of Modern Art/Film Stills Archive*

track: A film sound track, a narrow band on one or both sides of the film that contains recorded optical or magnetic sound.

countered with color films and wide screens, most spectacularly with films made in the Cinerama process (1952), which also used seven-**track** stereo sound. Because of the growing popularity of TV, the film industry tried to lure customers into theaters with a few 3-D movies such as *Bwana Devil* (1952), with lions and spears seemingly lunging toward the audience, and *Dial M for Murder* (1954), a suspenseful movie about a man plotting his wife's murder. More recently, in the face of competition from cable and satellite, videotape, laser discs, and CDs, the theatrical part of the business has countered yet again with superior sound systems, such as THX sound, DTS (Digital Theater Systems) six-track digital stereo, and Sony Dynamic Digital Sound.

Competing technological entertainments may even affect how movie stories are conveyed (Figure 9.17).

FIGURE 9.17 **Movie story as computer game**
In *The Game* (1997), Michael Douglas plays a wealthy character who receives as a birthday gift a mysterious game engineered by an enigmatic company. Soon unexpected events begin to disrupt his well-ordered life in major ways: he has become the central character in a dangerous game that he does not understand. What critic Edward Rothstein has written about the Douglas character applies to the large, central section of the story: "It seems as if he were less a film character than a hero of an interactive computer game. . . . Each scene follows another, less because of dramatic logic than because some item or gesture acted as a kind of switch, bringing on another stage of play." For example, in one scene he finds a window crank in his briefcase. Later that item allows him to roll down the window of a sinking taxi he is trapped in and save himself from drowning. Frame enlargement. *PolyGram Films*

FIGURE 9.18 A huge screen in an IMAX theater
Though this screen is not as large as those for 3-D IMAX theaters, which are the equivalent of eight stories high, it extends beyond viewers' peripheral vision. While watching a film in such a theater, viewers looking straight ahead see only the image and are caught up in it. With the marketing of large-scene digital TVs, perhaps Imax will be building more such theaters to keep people coming out of their homes and into theaters. Certainly, history shows that with each improvement in home viewing, the movie industry counters with some technological advance. *Courtesy of Imax Corporation*

It is tempting to speculate that with the arrival of digital TV, more theaters will be built to show the huge-screen 3-D films of the type the Imax Corporation has produced (Figure 9.18). The system's screen can be up to approximately eight stories high and a hundred or so feet wide. Viewers wear special glasses, and a subject in the extreme foreground can appear to be in the viewer's face or to move to the side of the viewer's head. The sense of three dimensionality is so convincing, it's hard not to duck—or at least flinch—as objects seem to hurl toward the audience or as the camera skims over the top of terrain. While viewing "Alaska: Spirit of the Wild" (1997) in the three-dimensional Omnimax, viewers may feel queasy while looking straight down on a vast territory as an airplane flies over it. With no noticeable distortion, the eight-track sound system can vibrate the viewer's feet, armrests, and seat.

Although 3-D IMAX films have proven effective in short documentaries, it is not yet certain how amenable the system is to feature-length narrative films.

> Neither the rapid motion of humans or objects—save for a synesthetic zinger like the hurtle of a subway train in *Sea of Time*—nor the rapid editing of individual shots fits well into IMAX's formal protocols. At times, . . . directing in this format becomes an "engineering feat" instead of a creative endeavor. The IMAX camera weighs over four hundred pounds, takes twenty minutes to reload, and . . . holds only three minutes worth of stock. . . . At least for now, the stipulation to shoot slowfooted aquatic creatures that don't demand retakes hardly seems conducive to our roster of popular story types. Then again. . . . (Arthur 81)

How widespread IMAX theaters become will be determined, as are all technological developments, by economic imperatives: to what extent filmgoers want the product made with the new technology.

Many specific contexts for films are included in a chronology for 1895–1998, which includes columns on major world events, the arts, mass media, and films and videos (pp. 513–54). Now that we have explored some of the factors that shape films and in turn viewer response to them, we will turn our focus in the next chapter to how viewers interact with the films themselves and especially the meanings they find in them.

SUMMARY

Filmmakers are subject to many influences, such as widespread attitudes in a society, censorship, filmic conventions, financing, and technological developments. Viewers who know about these and other contexts of a film can understand the film more completely.

Society and Politics

- Societal attitudes influence how filmmakers depict a subject. For example, before the 1960s, homosexuals were rarely depicted directly and nonstereotypically in American movies, but with greater public tolerance of homosexuality (and the latitude afforded by a ratings system) American movies since the late 1960s more frequently include gays and sometimes show them nonstereotypically.

- The political climate strongly affects how much freedom of expression filmmakers have and what political outlooks are likely to be expounded or implied in films.

Censorship

- Censorship (written or implied) strongly influences the form and content of films.

- In the United States from 1934 into the 1960s, most films were censored by an agency set up by the film producers and distributors to ensure that movies were suitable for viewers of all ages.

- Often governments ban or censor a film as it is being made or after it is completed.

- In many societies a rating system is devised that allows for a wide latitude of subjects but restricts some films to certain age groups.

Artistic Conventions

- Filmic conventions are techniques or content that audiences tend to accept without question.

- Filmmakers either follow conventional practices or reject them, as in many westerns made since World War II.

- Conventions may fall out of favor, and unconventional practices may catch on and become conventional.

- Filmmaking conventions do not have inevitable and fixed meanings; usage, which varies over time, establishes their meanings.

Financial Constraints

- Since the amount of money available to filmmakers helps determine equipment, personnel available, settings, time to film, and distribution, financing is a crucial influence on the making of films and in turn viewer responses to them.

- Generally, the greater the finances needed to make and promote a film, the greater the pressures to make a movie with such popular characteristics as chases, fights, explosions and other spectacular sights, romance or sex, and happy endings.

- In general, the smaller the budget, the greater control filmmakers have over their work and the more individualistic it is likely to be.

Technological Developments

- New filmmaking technology can make new effects possible, but it may also have drawbacks.

- New filmmaking technology may influence the types of films that get made.

- The technology of competing mass media and electronic entertainments, such as television and computer games, may influence the techniques filmmakers use and the ways movie stories unfold.

WORKS CITED

Arthur, Paul. "IMAX 3-D and the Myth of Total Cinema." *Film Comment* Jan./Feb. 1996: 78–81.

Curry, Ramona. *Too Much of a Good Thing: Mae West as Cultural Icon*. Minneapolis: U of Minnesota P, 1996.

Ebert, Roger. *Ebert's Little Movie Glossary: A Compendium of Movie Clichés, Stereotypes, Obligatory Scenes, Hackneyed Formulas, Shopworn Conventions, and Outdated Archetypes*. Kansas City: Andrews and McMeel, 1994.

Hayward, Susan. *Key Concepts in Cinema Studies*. London: Routledge, 1996.

Jones, Chris. "Lesbian and Gay Cinema." *An Introduction to Film Studies*. Ed. Jill Nelmes. London: Routledge, 1996. 257–90.

Katz, Susan Bullington. "A Conversation with Terry Zwigoff." *The Journal* [Writers Guild of America, West] Feb. 1996: 36–40.

Krutnik, Frank. *In a Lonely Street: Film Noir, Genre, Masculinity*. London: Routledge, 1991.

Rothstein, Edward. "Computer Games Capture Filmmakers' Imaginations." *New York Times* 22 Sept. 1997, natl. ed.: B2.

Russo, Vito. *The Celluloid Closet: Homosexuality in the Movies*. Rev. ed. New York: Harper, 1987.

Sklar, Robert. *Movie-Made America: A Cultural History of American Movies*. Rev. and updated. New York: Random, 1994.

Weinraub, Bernard. "Film Ratings Are Raising New Issues of Bias." *New York Times* 6 Sept. 1994, natl. ed.: B1+.

FOR FURTHER READING

Adair, Gilbert. *Hollywood's Vietnam: From* The Green Berets *to* Full Metal Jacket. London: Heinemann, 1989. Analyzes movies about the Vietnam War and shifting public opinion about the war.

Dyer, Richard. *Now You See It*. New York: Routledge, 1990. An examination of gay and lesbian films from 1919 to 1980.

Gomery, Douglas. *Movie History: A Survey*. Belmont, CA: Wadsworth, 1991. In constructing his history, Gomery uses four approaches: aesthetics, technology, economics, and sociology.

History of the American Cinema. Ed. Charles Harpole. Ten volumes are planned; six are so far available:

Balio, Tino. *Grand Design: Hollywood as a Modern Business Enterprise, 1930–1939*. New York: Scribner's, 1993.

Bowser, Eileen. *The Transformation of Cinema, 1907–1915*. New York: Scribner's, 1990.

Crafton, Donald C. *The Talkies: American Cinema's Transition to Sound, 1926–1931*. New York: Scribner's, 1997.

Koszarski, Richard. *An Evening's Entertainment: The Age of the Silent Feature Picture, 1915–1928*. New York: Scribner's, 1990.

Musser, Charles. *The Emergence of Cinema: The American Screen to 1907*. New York: Scribner's, 1990.

Schatz, Thomas. *Boom and Bust: The American Cinema in the 1940s*. New York: Scribner's, 1997.

These volumes are also published in paperback by the University of California Press. Also forthcoming are separate volumes on the 1950s, 1960s, and 1970s.

Koch, Stephen. *Stargazer: The Life, World and Films of Andy Warhol*. Rev. ed. New York: Marion Boyars, 1991. Includes a filmography, organized chronologically, of the films Warhol made between 1963 and 1967.

Sklar, Robert. *Film: An International History of the Medium*. Englewood Cliffs: Prentice; New York: Abrams, 1993. Includes brief chronologies with columns for film, arts and sciences, and world events; bibliography; glossary; filmography; and an extensive assortment of photographs.

Thompson, Kristin, and David Bordwell. *Film History: An Introduction*. New York: McGraw, 1994. A comprehensive, one-volume survey.

Turner, Graeme, *Film as Social Practice*. 2nd ed. London: Routledge, 1993. A textbook that explains how movies can be understood not merely as artistic creations but as "representational forms and social practices of popular culture." To demonstrate the book's approaches, the last chapter, "Applications," explains some possible analyses of two movies.

Wyatt, Justin. *High Concept: Movies and Marketing in Hollywood*. Austin: U of Texas P, 1995. An examination of the historical, institutional, and economic forces that influence the making of popular movies. Includes discussion of the functions of advertising, market research, film structure, and casting.

Viewer and Film

AS WE SEE A FILM AND THINK ABOUT IT AFTERWARD, we respond in many complex ways. This chapter introduces two of the major ways viewers respond to a film: they generate expectations and modify them as the film proceeds, and they formulate meanings.

EXPECTATIONS AND INTERACTIONS

Normally, before we see a film, we know something about it. Usually we know its title and, if it is a movie with popular actors, know something about at least one of them. We may know something about the director and something about the types of films he or she tends to direct. We may have heard or seen a review or talked with a friend who's seen the film. We might even know the **genre**, or basic type of film we are to see, such as western, musical, science fiction, horror, or detective. If so, we will expect the film to conform to the basics of the genre. For example, if we are going to see a 1950s western, we expect to see a lawful man, usually of European descent, challenged by lawless European-American men, Mexicans, or Native Americans. Normally, too, genres set parameters to a narrative: what is possible, what is not. Thus, if we know we are going to see a western, we do not expect alien invaders sixty minutes into the film, nor do we at any time expect the woman who works in the dance hall to dance the lambada or la macarena.

Our expectations may be shaped by other factors. The film's rating may lead us to expect sex and violence. Or we may have seen a **trailer**, which may include material not included in the movie; we may have seen a printed advertisement, visited the film's site on the Internet, seen the film promoted on a cable channel, or seen toy spin-offs or other product tie-ins, all of which created expectations—often false ones. Consider a poster for *High Sierra* (1941) and one for *The Maltese Falcon* (1941, Figure 10.1). Although the poster for *The Maltese Falcon* is misleading, probably it did not hurt the film at the box office; but advertising that creates fundamentally false expectations can hurt a film. Advertising for a movie that is released shortly after an immensely popular

trailer: A brief compilation film shown in motion-picture theaters, before some video-taped movies, or on TV to advertise a movie or a video release.

FIGURE 10.1 Publicity shaping expectations
(a, left) A publicity still for *High Sierra*, a movie that first appeared early in 1941 featuring Humphrey Bogart as a criminal. (b, below) A poster advertising *The Maltese Falcon*, which appeared later in 1941. From the second poster, would-be viewers might expect to see Bogart reprise his role as a criminal because he looks like the criminal character he played in *High Sierra*. Note, for example, that his haircut is the same one he had in the earlier movie and that a vaguely defined shirt has been drawn in beneath his head. Because Bogart holds a smoking gun in the poster for *The Maltese Falcon*, we might expect him to fire a gun in that film (he does not). And we might expect Mary Astor to sport a fancy hairdo and wear glamorous, revealing evening clothing. Wrong again. *Warner Bros.–First National*

film but features the star in a very different role can be especially tricky (Figure 10.2). Often the advertising for a film rouses interest and creates reasonable expectations, as was done by a famous poster for *Persona* suggesting a mystery about the film's dual subjects (1966, Figure 10.3).

FIGURE 10.2 Publicity, expectations, and viewers' responses

(a, above left) In *Four Weddings and a Funeral* (1994), Hugh Grant plays a boyish, reserved, charming, yet nervous and bumbling heterosexual. Frame enlargement. (b, above right) In *An Awfully Big Adventure* (1995), Grant plays a sarcastic gay director of a theatrical group with whom an impressionable sixteen-year-old girl becomes infatuated. Before the film was publicized, its director warned that if *An Awfully Big Adventure* were "marketed as the new film from the star and director of 'Four Weddings and a Funeral' . . . 'they'll kill it stone dead. . . . All the effort this time should go to altering expectations'" (Maslin 11). *(a) Gramercy Pictures; (b) Fine Line Features*

From all these and other sources, we enter the theater or approach the video store rental counter with expectations: to be amused, amazed, mystified, inspired, aroused, or frightened. Once the film begins, it shapes our expectations by its opening credits, initial music, and early images—all of which can suggest, for example, an amusing film or a somber one.

As the film begins, we also begin to interact with it as readers interact with a written text:

> The literary text may be conceived of as a dynamic system of gaps. A reader who wishes . . . to . . . reconstruct . . . the fictive world and action [a work] projects, is necessarily compelled to pose and answer, throughout the reading-process, such questions as, What is happening or has happened, and why? What is the connection between this **event** and the previous ones? What is the motivation of this or that character? To what extent does the logic of cause and effect correspond to that of everyday life? and so on. Most of the answers to these questions, however, are not provided explicitly, fully and authoritatively (let alone immediately) by the text, but must be worked out by the reader himself on the basis of the implicit guidance it affords. . . . Some [gaps] can . . . be filled in almost automatically, while others require conscious and laborious consideration; some can be filled in fully and definitely, others only partially and tentatively; some by a single [hypothesis], others by several (different, conflicting, or even mutually exclusive) hypotheses. (Sternberg 50)

event: In a narrative, either a happening (such as rain falling) or an action.

FIGURE 10.3 Publicity encouraging appropriate expectations
This poster for Ingmar Bergman's *Persona* (1966) nurtures appropriate
viewer expectations and does so almost exclusively by its visuals. On one
level the film is about two women who are as closely linked as the parts
of a puzzle. They are also both puzzling. The film is concerned with the
women's psychology and uses many close-ups of faces, as here and as in
many films directed by Bergman. *United Artists*

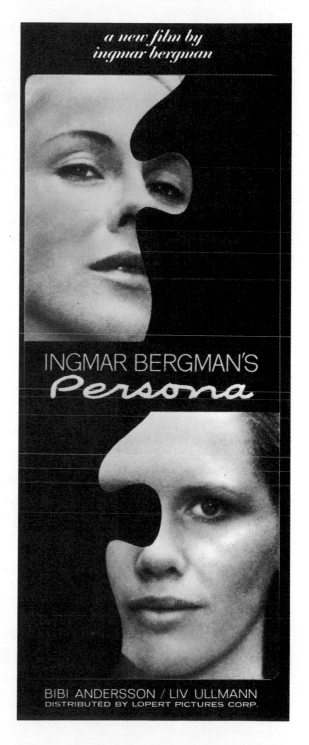

Similarly, throughout a film we interact with its images and sounds: we fill in the gaps with our own inferences and hypotheses. Without the attentive eyes and
ears and active minds of the viewing audience, the film
is incomplete—mere moving images and changing
sounds. Viewers are not mere receptacles of a cascade of
audio and visual information but collaborators and players with a wondrous, elaborate mechanism. The mental
and emotional responses of viewers, which change in
light of viewers' changing expectations and shifting questions and hypotheses, are the focus of viewer-response
criticism.

If the film is to hold our attention, it must arouse
curiosity fairly quickly and from time to time encourage
new curiosities. In narrative films, story developments
encourage us to consider possible consequences. We
will get involved and be satisfied or frustrated in part by
how well the film lives up to our changing expectations.
We like to be manipulated, up to a point. People who
enjoy horror films, for example, want to feel the tiny
hairs on the back of their necks tingle—or at least they
don't mind if they do. But viewers also crave variety,
surprise, suspense, mental challenges. By the film's ending they like to think that they understand the film,
more or less anticipated the major developments, or at
least now see how developments could follow from earlier events, and viewers like to see unity and meaning in it
all. There is much to experience in one viewing; later
viewings of the same film often reveal additional satisfying complexities, subtleties, meanings, and ambiguities.
In analyzing a film, it can be useful to consider many of
the issues relating to expectations and interactions, including consistency, plausibility, predictability, surprise,
and suspense.

TYPES OF MEANINGS

> Cultural artifacts are not containers with immanent meanings, . . . variations among interpretations have historical bases for their differences, and . . . differences and change are . . . due to social, political, and economic conditions, as well as to constructed identities such as gender, sexual preference, race, ethnicity, class, and nationality. (Staiger xi)

We see a film; we think about it afterward; often we discuss it with others. And often we generalize about the film. We may say, for example, that it glorifies violence or shows that wrongdoers end up suffering themselves. When we generalize about a film, we are assigning it meanings; we are explaining in general what we see as significant. In a fictional film, meanings are usually a viewer's generalizations about the characters' situations, personalities, ideas, and behavior. In a **documentary film**, meanings tend to be generalizations about the information presented in the film. In an **avant-garde film**, meanings are typically generalizations viewers make about film **conventions**, the avant-garde film's untraditional depiction of its subjects, or the properties of the film medium itself. The meanings viewers construct may be shaped by many factors, including whatever critical perspectives they use and where and when they live.

Meaning may be divided into three types. **Explicit meanings** are presented directly by the film in some form of language. **Implicit meanings** are generalizations viewers infer from a film. **Symptomatic meanings**, or ideology, are generalizations about how the film is representative of the beliefs or values of many people outside the film.[1]

Explicit Meanings

Explicit **meanings** are general observations given within a work. In silent films, they may be conveyed by a subtitle or a **title card**. A sound film may use these forms of language and many other forms, such as a narrator, dialogue, or a monologue.

In silent films, examples of explicit meaning are commonplace. A title card of the classic American film *Greed* (1925) reads: "First . . . chance had brought them face to face; now . . . mysterious instincts, as ungovernable as the winds of the heavens, were knitting their lives together." Another explicit meaning is found in a title card early in *Sunrise* (1927):

---

[1]For the terms *explicit meaning*, *implicit meaning*, and *symptomatic meaning*, I am indebted to David Bordwell's *Making Meaning*. I define the terms in much the same way Bordwell does but apply the concepts differently. Many scholars use *ideology* rather than *symptomatic meaning*.

documentary film: A film that presents a version of actions and happenings that viewers are intended to accept not primarily as the product of someone's imagination but primarily as fact.

avant-garde film: A film that rejects the conventions of mainstream movies and explores the possibilities of the film medium itself.

convention: In films and other creative works, a frequently used technique or content that audiences tend to accept without question.

meaning: An observation or general statement about a subject.

title card: A card or thin sheet of clear plastic on which information is written or printed.

> For wherever the sun rises and sets . . .
> in the city's turmoil
> or
> under the open sky on the farm,
> life is much the same:
> sometimes bitter, sometimes sweet.

Yet another explicit meaning in a film from the silent era occurs at the end of *Metropolis* (1926): "Without the heart there can be no understanding between the hands and the mind."

Explicit meanings are probably less common in sound films than in silent films. In *Unforgiven* (1992), the Clint Eastwood character, William Munny, sometimes explains an explicit meaning, as when he talks about how wrong it is to kill people. An explicit meaning may be explained less directly. Near the end of the Japanese film *Gate of Hell* (1953), the samurai who has allowed his passion to overrule his conscience says of himself, "What kind of a beast am I? A madman who thought he could take a heart by force." The film is implying that it is insane for people to think they can force someone to love them.

A film's title may also reveal an explicit meaning. An animated film called "Technological Threat" (1988) shows that office workers may be replaced by more efficient anthropomorphic machines. There is also an explicit meaning in the title *Fatal Attraction* (1987). Titles with no verbs or no nouns derived from a verb cannot convey a meaning, only a subject, as in *Intolerance* (1916), *The General* (1926), *The Wind* (1928), *Bend of the River* (1952), and *Schindler's List* (1993). Those titles reveal subjects but say nothing about them.

An explicit meaning is not necessarily comprehensive or persuasive; it is certainly not the final word on any subject. At the end of *King Kong* (1933), for example, one character says of Kong's fate, "It was beauty killed the beast." Many critics find that blame misplaced and that interpretation simplistic. In fictional films, meanings are usually not explicit but implied by **settings**, film **techniques**, actions, or other means. If a fictional film explains meanings too often or if the meanings are already apparent to attentive viewers but they are told what meanings are intended, viewers may be annoyed that they were not allowed to discover the significance for themselves. General statements are commonplace, however, in documentary films, usually in the form of a **narrator**, interviews, subtitles, or title cards.

setting: The place where filmed action occurs.

technique: Any aspect of filmmaking, such as the choices of sets, lighting, sound effects, music, and editing.

narrator: A character, person, or unidentifiable voice that provides commentary before, during, or after the main body of the film.

Implicit Meanings

As Janet Staiger says (p. 412), meanings in cultural artifacts are not fixed and waiting to be discovered once and for all. Different people experiencing the same creative work will construct different meanings, though not all interpretations are based on salient textual details and are persuasively argued.

symbol: Anything perceptible that has significance or meaning beyond its usual meaning or function.

frame: The borders of the projected film or TV set or monitor.

shot: An uninterrupted strip of exposed motion-picture film or videotape. A shot presents a subject, perhaps even a blank screen, during an uninterrupted segment of time.

eye-level angle: A camera angle that creates the effect of the audience being on the same level as the subject.

edit: To select and arrange the processed segments of photographed motion-picture film.

superimposition: Two or more images photographed or printed on top of each other.

fast cutting: Editing characterized by many brief shots, sometimes shots less than a second long.

montage: A series of shots, often joined by lap dissolves, used to condense time and events.

scene: A section of a narrative film that gives the impression of continuous action taking place in one continuous time and space.

lap dissolve: A transition between shots in which one shot begins to fade out as the next shot fades in, overlapping the first shot before replacing it.

Nonetheless, perceptions of different meanings are widespread. A person from one culture or political viewpoint will often see different meanings than someone from a different culture or political outlook. Even the same person experiencing the same work years later—whether it be *King Kong* or *King Lear*—usually sees different meanings. Sometimes a viewer will perceive two or more opposing meanings during the same viewing. In this section, we will see how cinematic techniques, **symbols**, and **narratives** or stories can influence a viewer's interpretation of a film.

CINEMATIC TECHNIQUES   As is explained and illustrated throughout Chapters 1–4, the arrangement of the subjects within the **frame** (**composition**), the lenses, lighting, camera distances and angles, sound mix, and many other aspects of filmmaking may all affect what meanings audiences detect.

Consider a **shot** from *Psycho* (1960, Figure 10.4) that shows a man sitting in a room. Setting, lighting, camera angle, and composition all help suggest that the human subject is strange, if not dangerous. How different the mood and meaning would be if the setting had been a knotty pine back wall with only a large frame containing a print of mountains, the lighting bright and even, the camera angle **eye-level**, and the man in the center of the frame. Then the man would not seem strange and certainly not dangerous.

Editing also influences meanings. As explained in Chapter 3, a shot can develop or undercut the meaning(s) of the preceding shot. **Superimposition** and **fast cutting** can also create meanings. The forty-two-second **montage** of Susan's opera career in *Citizen Kane* (1941) conveys an enormous amount of information, including the consequences of a man forcing a woman to do what she is ill equipped and reluctant to do (pp. 156–57).

Sounds that are selected, modified, and combined can also create or change meaning. During the 1987 Academy Awards ceremony, a clip from *The Sound of Music* (1965) showed Julie Andrews running around in the countryside as viewers heard not the original sound track but sounds of an airplane engine and machine-gun fire. Because of the sounds, viewers incorrectly (and humorously) inferred that she was under attack. In *What's Up, Tiger Lily?* (1966), Woody Allen took a Japanese James Bond–type movie and redubbed it. With the new sound track, the cast of characters now includes Wing Fat and the sisters Terri and Suki Yaki, and the action centers on rivals trying to acquire a famous egg salad recipe. Overlapping dialogue—as in some films directed by Orson Welles and some directed by Robert Altman—suggests how people may talk *at* but not *to* or *with* each other. **Scenes** with this use of sound suggest that people may be together physically but isolated emotionally or spiritually.

Meaning in films, then, is always created or modified by the techniques of cinema, though it is important to remember that a technique's meaning can depend on place and time. As we saw in Chapter 3, in previous years filmmakers tended to use **lap dissolves** to delete insignificant action and

FIGURE 10.4 Mise en scène and cinematography creating meaning
In a scene in *Psycho* (1960), a young woman talks with the motel manager in a room off the motel office. In the shot represented here—one of a dozen taken from the same camera position—setting, lighting, camera angle, and composition help create meaning. The stuffed bird seen above the painting of the nude woman is disquieting on a symbolic level, perhaps especially because that part of the image is balanced visually by the man on the right. The painting behind the man is of a naked woman seemingly menaced by two men. (Soon after this scene, viewers learn that behind that painting is a peephole through which the same young man will see the young woman undress in preparation for a shower.) The setting, shadows, low camera angle, and off-center placement of the human subject all support idea that the setting and the man whose environment it is are strange, perhaps even dangerous. Frame enlargement. *Universal*

time within a scene. Later in the history of cinema, lap dissolves usually mean that the action changes to a different setting and a later time.

Subtlety may be more expressive than an obvious presentation because viewers are forced to imagine what happens and help create meaning (Figures 10.5 and 10.6). Similarly, many viewers believe that horror films and other violent films are more expressive when they use shadows, sounds, and **reaction shots**, not explicit violence.

Many viewers feel that erotic situations are sexier if restraint is used in the presentation. Sometimes a look can carry more erotic charge than caressing

reaction shot: A shot that shows someone or occasionally an animal presumably responding to an event.

FIGURE 10.5 Visual subtlety

Early in *The Third Man* (1949), Holly Martins has arrived in Vienna to visit a friend. As Martins arrives at his friend's building, a car drives by on the left side of the frame and briefly attracts some of the viewer's attention; the ladder is seen in long shot and rather blends with the background—for these and other reasons, viewers may not notice the ladder, let alone consider its possible significance. But walking under a ladder has long been considered bad luck—and indeed Holly Martins is about to undergo a series of mostly unpleasant adventures. Having him walk under a ladder also shows that he is reckless: it can be dangerous to walk under ladders without checking what is above. As the film later shows, Holly Martins rushes into situations where angels would fear to tread. The filmmakers knew what they were doing. They could have moved the ladder or filmed the scene from another angle and thus kept the ladder out of the frame or far off to the side. Or they could have drawn more attention to it, for example by having Martins look at it or hesitate before walking under it. But they filmed and edited the scene as they did, probably hoping most viewers would briefly notice the ladder and appreciate its significance. This scene illustrates one of the paradoxes of western art: less may be more. Frame enlargement. *London Film Productions*

or kissing (Figure 10.7). And often the images that viewers imagine are more erotic than images on a screen. Novelist Leslie Epstein recounts that for her, "Perhaps the most erotic scene in all the sixties occurs in *Persona*. . . . Bibi Andersson tells the half-catatonic Liv Ullmann about the time she and a friend had been lying on a beach [sunbathing nude]. . . . Nothing [much] moves but the one actress's lips and the other's eyes" (289). In the film, the Bibi Andersson character's account begins as follows:

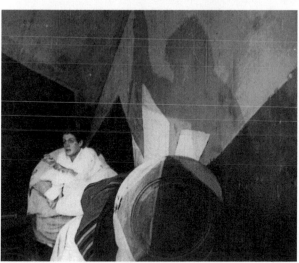

FIGURE 10.6 **Explicit versus implicit representations**
(a, above) A still for *The Cabinet of Dr. Caligari* (1919) shows action that was staged for the benefit of a still photographer. This image was used in publicizing the film but does not appear in it. (b, left) A frame enlargement from the film shows what viewers see of the same murder represented in (a): the victim and shadows. Many people think that an implicit presentation of a subject may be more involving and thus more effective than an explicit version. (*a*) *and* (*b*) *Decla-Bioscop*

Suddenly I saw two figures leaping about on the rocks above us who kept hiding and peeking. "There are two boys looking at us," I said to the girl. Her name was Katarina. "Let them look," she said, turning over on her back. It was such a strange feeling. I just lay there with my bottom in the air not a bit embarrassed. I felt very calm. Wasn't it funny? And Katarina was beside me with her big breasts and thighs. She just lay there giggling to herself. Then I saw that the boys had come closer and were staring at us. They were awfully young. Then

FIGURE 10.7 Expressiveness of looks and gestures
Looks and gestures alone (here as part of a flamenco) may convey romantic attraction or erotic tension or both, sometimes more powerfully than physical contact, as in *Carmen* (1983), directed by Carlos Saura. *Emiliano Piedra Productions; The Museum of Modern Art/Film Stills Archive*

the boldest of the two came over and squatted down beside Katarina and pretended to be busy with his foot and started to poke between his toes. I . . . I felt all funny. Suddenly I heard Katarina say: "Come here a minute." Then she helped him off with his jeans and shirt. Then he was on top of her. She showed him how and held him by his fanny. The other boy sat on the rock watching. I heard Katarina whisper and laugh. The boy's face was close to mine. It was all flushed and puffy.

flashback: A shot or a few shots, a brief scene, or a sequence that interrupts a narrative to show earlier events.

If the film instead showed a **flashback** of what happened, that section of the film would be less erotic for some viewers because instead of hearing once and briefly that the two boys were "awfully young," viewers would continuously see how young they are, and that would be troubling for some viewers who would interpret the scene as being about adults seducing children. For many viewers, then, the restrained presentation in *Persona* is more erotic than a more explicit rendition.

Finally, we can see how less can be more by considering another film that treats an emotionally charged subject with restraint. *Nothing but a Man* (1964) shows an African American man in the 1960s South trying to get and hold a job that allows him some dignity, marrying outside his class (Figure 10.8), attempting to relate to an aloof father, trying to decide whether to take responsibility for a boy who may be his son, and coping with prejudice

FIGURE 10.8 Restraint and understatement
Nothing but a Man (1964) has been much praised for the two main characters' humanity and dignity and for the film's restraint in its presentation of its volatile subjects. The film demonstrates that less may be more. *New Video Group, New York City*

against African Americans. The narrative is involving in part because it shows the situations vividly and believably without explaining them in tiresome detail. For many viewers, it is so off-putting for movies to explain their ideas that writing teachers and writing books implore future scriptwriters to "show, don't tell": don't tell viewers anything that can be shown instead.

Subtle technique is not without risks. If the image or sound is too faint or too fleeting, or both, or if viewers are otherwise engaged, they may miss a significant detail, even on many later re-viewings. An example occurs even in *Citizen Kane*, a film that most critics and scholars revere, in part, for its masterly and often subtle use of filmmaking techniques. As we study *Citizen Kane*, we soon notice that nearly everything in it is deliberate and meaningful and often subtle, so we may start wondering about a second sled that young Charles Foster Kane receives (Figure 10.9). The trouble is, we never see it entirely, and we have a chance to see its logo and part of its name for only a few frames (out of the twenty-four frames projected each second). If you examine the few frames in question, you can discern that the sled is called "The Crusader" and shows a knight's helmet, a more manly symbol than the name and image on Kane's first sled. "The Crusader" also characterizes the type of adult Kane was to become: a young newspaperman criticizing people and groups that benefit from the status quo. In this instance, the filmmakers erred in

FIGURE 10.9 Too subtle to be seen?
This frame enlargement from *Citizen Kane* (1941) is from a shot that is forty-five frames long or less than two seconds. The shot shows Kane's second family and his second sled, "The Crusader." The framing and editing are such that few viewers can ever discern what the sled is called or make out the logo, let alone consider their possible significance. The details are too subtly rendered. Frame enlargement. *RKO General Pictures*

showing us too little for too briefly. Virtually no one can see the sled's name during a film showing. In this case, less is not more meaningful; it's nothing.

Another example of filmmakers being too subtle occurs early in another widely admired film, *The Searchers* (1956). Ethan Edwards hates Comanches because early in the film they kill his brother, Aaron, two of Aaron's three children, and, most important, Aaron's wife, for whom Ethan has more than perfunctory feelings (the film is restrained in suggesting why and how deeply). Understandably, critics seem not to have noticed that Comanches had also killed Ethan's mother. When Comanches are about to attack the Edwardses, Aaron and his wife send their little daughter Debbie to hide by her grandmother's grave. Before Debbie sits in front of the tombstone, for six video frames (out of thirty per second) the following is legible:

Here lies
Mary Jane Edwards
killed by
Comanches
May 12, 1852
A good wife and mother
In her 41st year.

If viewers noticed this detail, they could better understand Ethan's feelings about Comanches and his obsession to retrieve from them his sole surviving relative, Debbie. But how many viewers read the tombstone since they have only a fifth of a second to do so and most will be focused on the endangered little girl soon to appear in front of it?

Like all who hope to communicate effectively, regardless of the medium, filmmakers are challenged to have a clear sense of their audiences and not insult them by being too obvious but not be so subtle that audiences have no chance of getting the point, even during later re-viewings. For those who make creative works, it is a judgment call, sometimes wisely made, sometimes not.

In these examples and elsewhere, the filmmakers may have known how demanding they were being when they used these subtle techniques. Perhaps filmmakers include them for those in the audience who are especially observant. Perhaps they include such subtleties for those who see the film more than once, as rewards for the faithful. Perhaps they include such touches for their own pleasure in being creative and sly. Then, too, possibly the filmmakers were unaware of how demanding they were being and simply goofed, which is possible even in otherwise brilliant films. For example, in the case of Kane's second sled, maybe the filmmakers **framed** the shot carelessly or inadvertently edited out a clear view of the name and logo.

frame: To position the camera in such a way that the subject is kept within the borders of the image.

Sometimes viewers miss the significance of a technique because they watch a videotape version. Release prints of films shown in commercial theaters usually have detailed images. But when films are shown on an analog television monitor, the results are somewhat blurred and **grainy** (since video images have less definition than film images). The lighting is without subtle shades (**high contrast**), and in shadowed areas details tend to get lost because analog TV has far less range of tones than film; thus, many details in dark scenes are especially difficult to see. That is why films with many dark scenes—such as *The Third Man* (1949), the *Godfather* films, some of the *Batman* films since the late 1980s, and most **films noirs**—are frustrating to watch on analog television or videotape. Even in well-lit scenes, on an analog TV monitor viewers are likely to miss such significant details in *Citizen Kane* as the glass paperweight in Susan Alexander's apartment on the night Kane first meets her (Figure 10.10), the whiskey bottle he finds in her room in Xanadu after she leaves him, and, in *Psycho*, the fleeting triple superimposition of the last shot.

graininess: Rough visual texture.

film noir: A type of film characterized by frequent scenes with dark, shadowy lighting; urban settings; characters motivated by selfishness, greed, cruelty, ambition, and lust; and characters willing to lie, frame, double-cross, and kill or have others killed.

SYMBOLS A symbol is anything perceptible that has significance or meaning beyond its usual meaning or function. Every society has certain public symbols: each society invests certain sounds and sights with widely understood meanings. In many societies, for example, a red traffic light symbolizes that people who approach it should stop. Painters, writers, filmmakers, and others

FIGURE 10.10 Subtle visual clue
In *Citizen Kane* (1941), this is a frame from the second of three similar shots in Susan's room: notice the significant glass paperweight on the left side of her dresser. Subtle details such as this can be extremely difficult to see in a videotape or telecast analog version. Frame enlargement. *RKO General Pictures*

who create works of the imagination may also create symbols (not always consciously). Depending on contexts, a sound, word (including a name), color, or representation of an object or action or person may function as a symbol. Viewers (or readers) do not perceive a symbol as merely performing its usual functions; they see it as also representing something general, as conveying meaning.

In *The Godfather* (1972), *The Godfather Part II* (1974), and *The Godfather Part III* (1990), doors or doorways do not always function simply as connections between rooms: they are sometimes symbols. In the last two shots of *The Godfather*, Michael's wife, Kay, sees him through an open door in his office surrounded by three of his men. One of them kisses Michael's hand and says "Don Corleone"—meaning that Michael is now the head of the Corleone family and its criminal business. The second man kisses Michael's hand and, at nearly the same time, the third man goes to the door and closes it. The film's final action obliterates Kay from Michael's and our view and, more important, blocks both Kay and the audience from further views of Michael's criminal life. Here, the door symbolizes how criminal activities must be carried on out of sight. Late in *The Godfather Part II*, Michael finds Kay, who is now estranged from him, sneaking a visit to their two children at the Corleone estate. After a tense, wordless, face-to-face confrontation of about thirty seconds—and many viewers may find that to be an enormous amount of silence in a film with dialogue—Michael shuts the door in Kay's uncertain, then pained face. Late in *The Godfather Part III*, it seems that Kay is about to be reconciled with Michael, and they are holding hands across a table. A man knocks on then opens twin doors leading into the room. In the background a woman weeps. The man backs up into the other room as Michael approaches and asks what's wrong. The man tells Michael that a long-term associate has been shot. As Michael and the man talk, Kay moves sideways to see Michael and the man better then bends slightly sideways then forward to see and hear more clearly. Still with his back to Kay, Michael has put his hand on the man's arm, thereby evidently indicating to him to move sideways; they do so, a little, in effect making it harder for Kay to see and hear. (Probably Michael thinks Kay would be trying to learn what is going on.) We hear Kay's voice saying "It never ends." She watches for a few more moments then turns and walks out of the frame. No reconciliation after all. In all three movies, the door or doorway symbolizes the barrier that has come between Michael and his wife and reinforces an important meaning of the *Godfather* films: involvement in crime separates one from family.

The *Godfather* movies are rich in symbols. Another symbol occurs in *The Godfather* at the beginning and end of the scene where Luca Brasi (Vito's faithful henchman) is strangled to death, and the camera looks into the bar through a glass window with fish etched on it. Later, dead fish wrapped in Brasi's bulletproof vest are delivered to the Corleone compound, and a character explains that it is a Sicilian message that Luca "sleeps with the fishes" (is dead). Then viewers may realize that the etched fish seen briefly in the foreground as Luca is strangled functions as a symbol, not just part of the **mise en scène**.

Because so few viewers of *The Godfather* are likely to know the significance of the Sicilian message of fish, that symbol is explained. However, if we examine how symbols are used in stories, we will notice that like other vehicles of meaning they usually go unexplained and are subject to different interpretations. Objects functioning as symbols are usually shown more than once, are placed in prominent positions, are seen in important scenes, or are used under a combination of these conditions.

Sometimes symbols occur one after another or even one with another. The beginning of *Schindler's List* is in color. Soon we see a Jewish Sabbath candle go out—the film is now in black and white—then we see a wisp of smoke ascend from it. In the next shot, we have been instantly transported

mise en scène: An image's setting, subject (usually people or characters), and composition (the arrangement of setting and subjects within the frame).

match cut: Transition between two shots in which an object or movement at the end of one shot closely resembles an object or movement at the beginning of the next shot.

back in time, and we see a column of smoke then its source, a train engine. The candle's going out, the simultaneous transition from color to black and white, and the **match cut** from candle smoke to train smoke are all symbolic. In countless myths and other narratives—including the Book of Genesis, ancient Greek tragedy, and Shakespearean plays—light is associated with life. Its extinction early in the film, before the story begins, not only suggests death but also compels viewers' attention. Often, draining something of its color suggests weakness and death. And a Sabbath prayer candle, which signifies both religious faith and memory of the departed, goes up in smoke to be replaced by a train, an object used in only one way in the film—to transport Jews to their deaths. Here, as in some poems and music, symbols can summon forth emotion and meaning without being entirely explicable.

Symbols may also be discovered in some avant-garde films and documentaries. The documentary *Crumb* (1994), for example, concludes with a shot of Charles Crumb, the suicidal brother of the film's main subject, slowly lowering a window covering and obliterating the outside light. The title card that follows announces, "Charles Crumb committed suicide the year after he was filmed." The shutting out of light may be seen as a symbol of Charles's killing himself. The 1996 documentary "The Transformation" is primarily about Ricardo, a homeless HIV-positive homosexual transvestite. In the film's brief last two scenes, viewers learn that Ricardo has developed AIDS. The film's last three shots are of a view that includes a receding cemetery in the background, presumably seen from inside the van in which Ricardo rides; a medium **close-up** of a silent, pensive, largely unmoving Ricardo looking out a van window; and a shot of the back of a van as it enters a tunnel and is engulfed by darkness then a concluding **freeze frame**. These carefully chosen and thoughtfully combined images—of a cemetery, a silent and largely unmoving central subject, enveloping darkness, and the cessation of all movement—may symbolize Ricardo's approaching death. Indeed, over the end of the film's last shot is superimposed the following: "In memory of Ricardo/1960–1996."

close-up: An image in which the subject fills most of the frame and shows little of the surroundings.

freeze frame: A projected yet unmoving motion-picture image, which looks like a still photograph.

NARRATIVES: MEANINGS AND UNCERTAIN MEANINGS Viewers also detect meanings in narratives. Sometimes they notice general qualities of settings, such as the beauty but danger of nature in *Never Cry Wolf* (1983), a thoughtful adventure film set in rural Alaska.

More often, viewers detect significance in behavior, the subject of narratives. Consider *The Last Emperor* (1987). Its subject is the life of the last Chinese emperor, from childhood to old age. One plausible meaning of the narrative is that someone who seems to have every comfort and material good may suffer from loneliness. Or consider *Waiting to Exhale* (1995). The main subjects are four single African American women and, secondarily, the men in their lives. Two of the film's narrative meanings are that the friendships of women sustain them and that men tend to disappoint them (Figure

10.11). Viewers also find meanings in narratives about living creatures with human qualities, such as extraterrestrials wanting to go home or the animals in *Homeward Bound: The Incredible Journey* (1993).

Usually a story, even a brief one, has more than one meaning. "The String Bean" was made in France in 1962 and is seventeen minutes long. It has no dialogue, no printed words, no narration. All its scenes take place during daytime in a section of Paris. If you have not seen the film, take a moment to read the plot summary on page 426.

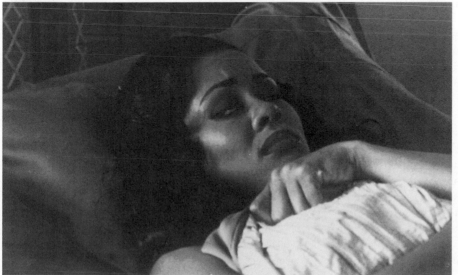

FIGURE 10.11 Women's strengths and men's short-comings with women
Waiting to Exhale (1995) shows four admirable women finding comfort in their friendships with one another as two of the four are treated badly by married men then reject them; one eventually wins the neighborhood Prince Charming; and one is dumped by her husband but eventually wins the respect and love of a sensitive, noble man and a hefty divorce settlement from her husband. (a, above left) Representative of the disappointing treatment by men is the scene where a man carries one of the women to her bed, dumps her on it like a sack of potatoes, then has sex with her selfishly. (b, left) Afterward, he is still oblivious to her feelings, and she pulls the sheet up tight under her chin, looks sideways at him, and gives him the look shown here. Frame enlargements. *Ezra Swerdlow and Deborah Schindler; 20th Century-Fox*

Plot Summary for "The String Bean"

An old woman sews purses in her room. She puts some beans in a pan, adds water, and places the pan on a counter; then she goes out.

The woman walks in a park then sits in the sun on a bench facing flowerbeds. Later she looks at colorful flowers in a shop window.

Near her building she spots a discarded pot with a dead plant in it. She wraps the pot in newspaper and walks away with it.

In her room, the woman pulls the dead plant from the pot and throws the plant away. She plants a bean she had originally taken from a package; then she sets the pot on the windowsill and waters it.

During the following days, she cares for the young bean plant, but it grows to only a certain height.

In a park, she sits on a bench, takes her plant from a tote bag, sets it in the sun, then sews (see figure, top). She gets up and puts the plant under a running sprinkler.

The woman works at the sewing machine again. She looks at the plant on the windowsill. It is still not growing.

The woman plants the bean plant behind a low hedge in the park (see figure, middle) and waters it; then she returns to a nearby bench, sits, and smiles.

The woman works in her room at her sewing machine and at various times visits the plant in the park. It thrives.

One day, the woman sees a gardener pull out her plant and throw it away. She goes to the plant, picks it up, and breaks off some bean pods.

Back in her room, the woman takes several beans from a pod and puts them in the pot she had taken in from the sill. She places the pot back on the sill as a gentle rain begins. She moves the pot so it catches some rain, closes the window, and watches the pot (see figure, bottom).

426

Narrative meanings in a short film
In "The String Bean" (1962), the woman nurtures a plant, sees it uprooted and discarded, then plants fresh seeds in hopes of growing another plant. Although the film is only seventeen minutes long, its plot suggests many meanings, including that an old person may want to stay in touch with nature and nurture young life. Frame enlargements. *Contemporary Films*

A viewer might generalize that the film shows the aged selflessly aiding young life: the woman gives much time and attention to the plant, even after she has planted it in the park. The film shows the continuity of life, from planting to emergence to maturity and death and to the beginning of the next generation from the seeds of the previous one—in other words, from the conception of one generation to the conception of the next. The film also shows concern for more than survival of oneself. The woman not only works at her job but also nurtures young life: she seeks the water and sun needed for the plant to reach full maturity. The woman's fierce persistence and quiet care as she tries to ensure that life flourishes are perhaps the film's most subtle meanings.

The outcome of her attempts is uncertain. Perhaps the fresh beans from the pod will grow more successfully than a bean from a package. But maybe a plant cannot grow to maturity in either confining city quarters or well-ordered parks. If so, the plant that would grow from the seeds the woman plants at the conclusion of the film will end up like the dried-out plant she found early in the film. What is important are the woman's patient efforts to help life begin, grow, and thrive. The film's final images are of rain, and the promise of growth, and of her waiting and watching.

To see how other, very different narratives imply meanings, let's examine fantasy movies, which might be thought of as being of two general types. In one type, viewers perceive the settings and situations as unmistakably fanciful. Examples are *King Kong* (1933) and *Godzilla* (1998).

The second group of fantasy films includes many situations that seem possible and settings that audiences have no trouble believing in, but upon re-flection viewers realize that many of the actions and certainly the resolution of the main characters' problems are more wish fulfillment than plausible.

Examples of cinematic fantasies that have the appearance of being true-to-life are some popular movies showing women achieving their goals in spite of formidable obstacles. Examples are *Nine to Five* (1980), *Sixteen Candles* (1984), and *The First Wives Club* (1996). In *Nine to Five*, three women office workers get revenge against their exploitative, patronizing, harassing, and un-grateful male boss. In *Sixteen Candles* the main character is a rather plain and often awkward sophomore girl who attracts a good-looking senior boy, and they begin a romance (Figure 10.12). *The First Wives Club* shows three women pooling their ideas and skills to get revenge against their middle-aged hus-bands, who are trying to dump them for younger women (see Figure 6.1).

Much more often—both abroad and in the United States—films re-enact popular male fantasies. Several films directed by Alfred Hitchcock—such as *The 39 Steps* (1935), *Saboteur* (1942), and *North by Northwest* (1959)—show a man displaying his resourcefulness, bravery, and appeal to women then eventually clearing himself of the wrongdoing he was falsely accused of early in the story by helping bring the guilty ones to justice. The *Rocky* films show Rocky succeeding athletically, financially, and romantically; to many viewers such films are tidy and reassuring though highly improbable. The *Rambo*

FIGURE 10.12 The ending of *Sixteen Candles* (1984) The Molly Ringwald character gets her birthday wish somewhat improbably but much to the satisfaction of many viewers, especially young heterosexual females. *Channel Productions, Inc.*

FIGURE 10.13 Romantic identification During this scene from *Gone with the Wind* (1939), many women viewers identify with Scarlett O'Hara and enjoy imagining being in Rhett Butler's/Clark Gable's arms and having his full attention. For years, American women viewers voted Clark Gable as the most appealing of all male movie stars. *Metro-Goldwyn-Mayer; Selznick International*

FIGURE 10.14 One woman and the love of two men
In *Jules and Jim* (1961) two men, who are best friends, are in love with the same woman, and she determines the nature of her relationships with them and other men. As in many movies, one person attracts the attention of more than one member of the opposite sex and has power over them. *Films du Carrosse*

movies and such Steven Spielberg movies as *Raiders of the Lost Ark* (1981), *Hook* (1991), and *Jurassic Park* (1993) are all celluloid comic books most often featuring male characters who eventually succeed under difficult conditions. The producers of James Bond and other action movies have raked in truckloads of money by showing heterosexual boys and men what they enjoy imagining themselves doing: dispatching tough guys and attracting an assortment of ravishing women. Most sexually explicit films enact common heterosexual male erotic fantasies: the women are attractive, available, and numerous; the men virile, usually dominant, and eventually sexually satisfied.

Fantasies show life as large audiences wish it to be. These films are not mirrors of life outside theaters but fun-house mirrors that briefly entertain viewers, often by showing them characters and situations that they can identify with and that make them feel heroic, powerful, rich, romantically desirable (Figures 10.13 and 10.14), or sexy (Figures 10.15 and 10.16).

Movies may also draw on viewers' fears and nightmares. Because many people distrust technology and the people who create and monitor it, movies

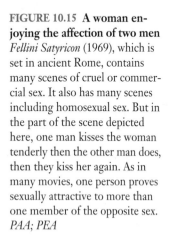

FIGURE 10.15 A woman enjoying the affection of two men *Fellini Satyricon* (1969), which is set in ancient Rome, contains many scenes of cruel or commercial sex. It also has many scenes including homosexual sex. But in the part of the scene depicted here, one man kisses the woman tenderly then the other man does, then they kiss her again. As in many movies, one person proves sexually attractive to more than one member of the opposite sex. *PAA; PEA*

such as *2001: A Space Odyssey* (1968), *Westworld* (1973), and *Jurassic Park* (1993) show technology failing but humans ultimately triumphing, whereas occasional films—such as *The Forbin Project* (1969, a.k.a. *Colossus: The Forbin Project*)—caution that if humans put complete trust in technology, it can become a Frankenstein monster that eventually dominates its creator.

Many movies are not as obviously improbable as the fantasy movies discussed here, but if we examine them, it is difficult to believe their stories and their meanings. An example is *Stand by Me* (1986), a popular film with many teens and young adults (Figure 10.17). The movie's settings look authentic enough and so do many of the main characters' actions, such as their bickering and insulting and bonding. But as in so many movies, more dangerous and exciting events are packed into a short time than most of us ever experience outside movie theaters (Figure 10.17b), as when one of the young boys has to point a gun at the older gang's leader to persuade the gang to leave the boys alone—this in a small town in 1959! Sometimes the boy who tends to act as the leader (on the left in Figure 10.17c) acts like a surrogate father, displaying wisdom and compassion well beyond his years. Most of the film's events considered individually are believable. However, the movie has so many events showing the dangers of adult males and the safety and reassurance of a small gang of young boys in so brief a **story time** (not even forty-eight hours,

story time: The amount of time covered in a film's narrative or story.

excluding the brief scenes of the adult Richard Dreyfuss character) that its story and the meanings implied by the story are not entirely plausible.

Some stories are told in such a way that the stories or parts of them are ambiguous: the meanings are open to two or more interpretations. An example is from a master of ambiguity, playwright and scriptwriter Harold Pinter. In *Betrayal* (1983), Jerry, a friend of a husband and wife who are having a party, confronts the wife in her own bedroom. After his passionate declaration of love, she calmly replies, "My husband is at the other side of that door." Does she mean "I'm not interested and my husband may overhear you and there could be trouble," or "I could be interested but this is a poor time and place," or some other meaning? We cannot be certain. When the husband in *Betrayal* learns that his wife has been having an affair with his friend Jerry, he tells her that he has always rather liked Jerry better than her and that maybe he should have had an affair with Jerry himself. Does the husband mean it, or does he say it to hurt his wife, or both? In the play and film versions of *Betrayal* and many other contemporary creative works, meaning and motive remain unknowable.

Sometimes an ambiguity may be peripheral to a narrative's main concerns. An example is the three brief references to the young girl's father in *The Piano* (1993). The first time, the girl tells two women and her mother that her father was a German composer, but her mother is annoyed with that comment and quickly quiets her. Later, when the mother is not around, one of the two women asks the girl

FIGURE 10.16 A male character enacting a popular male fantasy
In *All That Jazz* (1979), Roy Scheider plays a fast-living, womanizing dancer/choreographer/director who does what many heterosexual males fantasize about: enjoy the attention and physical charms of sexually attractive women. *20th Century-Fox*

FIGURE 10.17 Characters bonding, facing danger together, and nurturing each other *Stand by Me* (1986) is about four boys who are unhappy at home and are united by the indifference or hostility of adults. (a, top) The boys are happy to go off on an adventure together because adults consistently mistreat them. One boy's father, we are told, held the boy's ear "to a stove and almost burned it off." Another boy's father gets drunk and beats his son. A third father, grieving over an older son whom he favored, alternates between indifference and criticism of his surviving son. We learn nothing about the father of the fourth boy (second from left), but by implication perhaps that father has been ineffective, too, because his son is insecure, awkward, and the target of much laughter. Even a woman teacher betrayed one of the boys. After the boy had stolen milk money then turned it over to her, she used the money to buy a new skirt and allowed the boy to suffer expulsion and a blotted reputation. (b, middle) As in many movies, many dangers are packed into the film's brief story time. An example is when the boys are threatened by an onrushing train (presumably driven by an adult male), which doesn't brake and nearly runs down two of the boys on a bridge high above water. (c, bottom) One of the three examples in the movie where a boy cries in front of at least one of the other boys then is comforted by one of the boys. The story of *Stand by Me* suggests that these boys cannot trust the adult world and can find friendship and support only among peers. *Columbia*

where her parents got married; the girl responds with a tale about the wedding ceremony, sees the disbelieving look on her listener's face, admits it was a lie, then names a location where they got married. Soon she also claims her father was killed by lightning (as we see a brief animated drawing of a man catch fire and burn up) and simultaneously her mother struck dumb. The woman seems to accept this last account. In a later scene, the mother nods to her daughter in agreement that the girl's father was a teacher and in reply to the girl's question why they didn't marry she signs, "He became frightened and stopped listening."

What's to be made of all this? Probably the father was a teacher who would not marry the woman. Beyond that, it gets less certain. Perhaps the mother doesn't want the girl talking about the father (less chance of a slip-up about the girl's illegitimacy). Perhaps when the girl is asked about her father, she is afraid of revealing that her father never married her mother, so she tends to lie about him or to kill him off in her accounts so she won't have to talk about him anymore (or perhaps because she is angry at him for not marrying her mother). All the information about the father is presented so fleetingly and obliquely that his status is ambiguous, but audiences will probably not be troubled by the ambiguity, especially because the issue is touched upon only briefly and is peripheral to the story's main concerns.

In other narratives, ambiguity is central. In *Reversal of Fortune* (1990), viewers cannot know whether the main character, Claus von Bulow, attempted to murder his wife or she attempted suicide. Near the end of the narrative, the defense lawyer has come to believe that the wife attempted suicide. His woman assistant concludes that Claus tried to kill his wife. Various scenes focusing on Claus drip with ambiguity, perhaps none more tantalizingly than the one in which he tells the defense lawyer, Dershowitz, the circumstances of finding his wife passed out on the bathroom floor. Next, Dershowitz and Claus arrive at Claus's chauffeur-driven car, and Claus starts to get in.

DERSHOWITZ: Yeah, but is it the truth?

CLAUS (*annoyed*): Of course.

DERSHOWITZ: But not the whole truth.

CLAUS (*more annoyed*): I don't know the whole truth. I don't know what happened to her.

[*Claus finishes getting into the car's backseat.*]

DERSHOWITZ: Wish I didn't believe you. You know it's very hard to trust someone you don't understand.

[*As Dershowitz pauses, Claus, his face now largely obscured by a shadow, turns to look at Dershowitz.*]

DERSHOWITZ (*continuing*): You're a very strange man.

[*Claus's face is still partially covered by a shadow.*]

CLAUS: You have no idea. [*See Figure 10.18.*]

FIGURE 10.18 Ambiguity
At the end of a scene from *Reversal of Fortune* (1990), Claus responds to the observation that he is a very strange man with "You have no idea" then gets into his car and pulls the door closed. His face is quickly obscured by the black car window as almost simultaneously his chauffeur begins to back the car out of the driveway. Here as in other scenes in the film, we cannot know Claus's meaning or nature. Perhaps he has tried to kill his wife. Perhaps he has killed others, as is rumored elsewhere in the film. Maybe he has engaged in deviant sexual behavior, as is also commented on elsewhere in the film. Perhaps Claus means "You'll never get to know me well" or something else. His meaning is elusive, but the shadow on his face and his ambiguous statement are ominous. Frame enlargement. *Warner Bros.*

In *To Sleep with Anger* (1990), ambiguity is also central. We cannot be certain about much of anything related to the visitor (Figure 10.19)—his past actions, his motives, and the full extent of his influence on later developments—but after he comes to visit a family, the host family's problems multiply, as symbolically their well-kept backyard falls into disrepair and disorder.

Ambiguity may result when audiences are uncertain whether a major event occurred. In *Contact* (1997), there is uncertainty whether the main character's vast journey happened. Eyewitnesses and multiple cameras lead viewers to believe that it did not, but her video camera had nearly eighteen hours of elapsed tape, which is impossible for science to account for, and the main skeptic about the trip is untrustworthy (Figure 10.20). In *Reversal of Fortune*, *To Sleep with Anger*, *Contact*, and many other films of recent years, ambiguity is deliberate: key evidence is suggestive but also vague and indecisive.

FIGURE 10.19 The ambiguous main character in *To Sleep with Anger* (1990)
The character played by Danny Glover is ambiguous: he is hard to figure out—what he has done and what he is up to—but his visit to old friends is soon followed by one family problem after another. *SVS Films, Inc.*

FIGURE 10.20 Questionable source creating ambiguity
In *Contact* (1997), James Woods plays a U.S. national security adviser and a prominent member of a presidential investigative committee who is quick to formulate theories and who comes across as anything but fair or scientific. Woods has a history of playing disreputable movie characters; for example, shortly before he acted in *Contact*, he played a racist murderer in *Ghosts of Mississippi* (1996). Encyclopedist Ephraim Katz has written that Woods is "equally able to project villainousness or moral ambiguity" (1486). The skepticism voiced by the Woods character in *Contact* would be more credible to many viewers if the role had been played by someone known for trustworthy characters, such as Tom Hanks. Frame enlargement. *Warner Bros.*

Student Writing

The following essay was written in response to this assignment: Review Chapter 10; then choose either *The Seven Samurai*, *Apocalypse Now*, *Jules and Jim*, or *Local Hero*; next write a 750-to-1,000-word essay on three or four major aspects of its narrative meanings. Be sure to select only a few *major* aspects or meanings, to arrange them in a significant order, and to explain and illustrate each one carefully.

In discussing narrative meanings, it helps to follow three procedures. First, say that a narrative *shows* or *suggests* its meanings—not *says* them—because meanings are usually shown by the narrative, not stated directly. Second, describe each meaning in at least one complete sentence; then write at least one paragraph to explain and illustrate the point. You cannot explain a narrative meaning in a word or phrase. (Chances are, you will identify only a subject.) Third, in your first sentence about a meaning, try to avoid characters' names. If you use them, you may get sidetracked from meanings to the specific characters' personalities.

Three Major Meanings of Jules and Jim

by Cherie L. Miranda

Jules and Jim (France, 1961) deals primarily with the relationships of its three main characters. The relationship of Jules and Jim, the strongest in the film, is a selfless friendship. In contrast, Catherine's relations to both Jules and Jim are unorthodox. Vacillating between the two friends, she constantly wants the man she does not currently possess. Moreover, when she feels that she is losing control of one of her lovers, Catherine becomes desperate, even dangerous. However, the unconventional three-way relationship shared by Jules, Jim, and Catherine shows that the established morality is most appropriate and desirable.

Through the relationship of Jules and Jim, this film reveals that friendship can transcend love. Unlike any of Catherine's relationships, the friendship of Jules and Jim is selfless. In his autobiographical sketch of his friendship with Jules, Jim writes, "Each chose only the best things for the other." Though both are in love with Catherine, Jules and Jim remain the best of friends. Jules is aware of the intimacy between Jim and Catherine, but his feelings for Jim do not change. Conversely, Jim, though planning to marry Catherine at one point, always retains strong feelings of friendship for Jules. For example, when Jules and Catherine return to Paris near the end of the film, Jules and Jim are inadvertently reunited. Though Jim's affair with Catherine was very painful for all of them, the two men are happy to see each other and still seem to share an exceptional rapport. In the scene following the reunion of Jules and Jim, the two men share a gesture of their ongoing friendship: Jim, convinced that Jules's hat is improper in Paris, replaces it with his own. At the cremation of Jim and Catherine, Jules feels relief as well as loss because he had grown tired of the chaos Catherine had brought into his life (Insdorf 33). After Jules ponders his friendship with Jim, however, the narrator states that "the relationship of Jules and Jim had no equivalence in love."

Jules and Jim also demonstrates that people sometimes have the desire to control and possess others, a desire which can result in pain, even tragedy. This aspect of the film is embodied in Catherine's affairs with Jules and Jim--"She controls her relationship with the two men from the very beginning" (Petrie 181). However, her need for control is most evident in her involvement with Jim. Catherine seems to prefer Jim, but she wants to defy traditional morality and keep both Jules and Jim as lovers. Her seduction of Jules is an attempt to establish this situation. The narrator notes that because of Jim's jealousy, Catherine "did not repeat the experiment." Most important, when she feels she is losing control over Jim--even if she has previously renounced him--Catherine again wants him. For example, when the two plan to separate, Catherine tells Jim, "I don't love you and will never love anyone." But almost immediately after Jim's arrival in Paris, Catherine writes to him and tells him to come quickly because she is pregnant. When Jim writes back with indifference, Catherine responds with a letter that begins, "I love you, Jim." Furthermore, Catherine does not threaten Jim's life until she finds out that he is definitely leaving her so that he can marry and have children with Gilberte. In all likelihood, Catherine subsequently kills Jim because he is the man she cannot possess. Indeed, Catherine designates Jules, the man who would not leave her, a spectator rather than a participant in her suicide/murder. She makes certain that she and Jim are the only victims.

Though an untraditional film, Jules and Jim indirectly advocates conventional morality. Because of their three-way relationship, Catherine, Jules, and Jim are thrust inexorably "into a pattern of hurting, humiliating, and finally destroying one another" (Petrie 158). Jules has always been tormented by Catherine's disloyalty, but he would rather tolerate her infidelity with Jim than suffer the even greater pain of losing her altogether. As mentioned above, Jim becomes jealous of Catherine's relations with Jules and is consequently torn between his feelings for her and his feelings for Jules--the narrator states, "In vain did Jim tell himself that he had no right to be jealous."

Similarly, Catherine is hurt by Jim's infidelity, though she causes him pain through unfaithfulness as well. Though not a member of the threesome, Gilberte is inevitably hurt by the confused, vacillating relationship of Jules, Jim, and Catherine. Toward the end of the film, Jim appears to have accepted Gilberte and renounced Catherine. However, the viewer is left with the impression that this interminable, cyclical relationship would have continued indefinitely if the film had not ended with the deaths of Jim and Catherine.

As demonstrated above, Jules and Jim is concerned with human relationships. Though love is a recurring motif throughout the film, the camaraderie of the two men suggests that friendship can be more lasting and powerful. Through Catherine, the film also shows that the desire to possess another human being can be destructive and painful both to oneself and to others. As mentioned in class, Jules and Jim is often criticized as an immoral film, but it actually supports traditional morality. Much of the pain caused by this untraditional, three-way relationship could have been avoided if conventional morality had been observed.

Works Cited

Insdorf, Annette. Francois Truffaut. Boston: Twayne, 1978.

Petrie, Graham. The Cinema of Francois Truffaut. New York: Barnes, 1970.

Symptomatic Meanings or Ideology: World → Film → Viewers

As we saw in Chapter 9, the widespread attitudes or beliefs of a large group may influence how filmmakers depict their subjects. It is not surprising then that a film's meanings, whether explicit or implicit, may be symptomatic of the society out of which the film emerged. In *The Seven Samurai* (1954), the samurais' defense of the farmers depends on coordinated, unified action; thus, when the individualistic Toshiro Mifune character goes off on his own and captures one of the brigands' rifles, the samurai leader reprimands him. The idea reinforced by the film, in unity there is strength, is deeply symptomatic of Japanese society.

Some meanings of *Unforgiven* are unthinkable in earlier westerns but coincide with popular beliefs in early 1990s America, especially the wrongness of many men's violent and unjust treatment of women and the cruel and unlawful behavior of some law enforcement officials. On the latter score, the film shows that upholders of law may themselves lose control: the sheriff is so sadistic that when he becomes violent, the townspeople seem embarrassed by his excesses. It's police brutality, 1880s style. The videotape of part of the Rodney King beating by Los Angeles police officers was shown repeatedly on American TV nearly a year and a half before *Unforgiven* was first released in August 1992. That videotape excerpt increased American public awareness of the potential of police brutality and perhaps influenced some viewers' reactions to the film's sheriff, maybe especially late in *Unforgiven* when the sheriff beats and tortures a black man so mercilessly that he dies.

Viewers aware of the widespread beliefs or values at the time a film was made often detect symptomatic meanings that uninformed viewers will not see. In its depictions of women, 1940s films noirs, which were written and directed by men and largely focus on them, may be symptomatic of the widespread anxiety males felt after enduring the atrocities of war then returning home and finding that women had taken over their jobs and enjoyed greater economic and sexual independence than they had before the war. Some movies—such as the many anti-Japanese films made in the United States during World War II and the anti-Soviet films made in the United States during the cold war (*Red Dawn*, 1984, for example)—transparently reveal widespread fears of a foreign country's beliefs and policies. Often, though, widespread attitudes in a story are reflected obliquely, as in the British film *The Third Man*, which was released four years after the end of World War II. If you have not seen the film, take a moment to read the plot summary on page 440.

As its American coproducer David O. Selznick argued, the film is pro-British and at least partially anti-American in that the main British characters—Calloway and Sergeant Paine—are highly admirable whereas the two major American characters—Martins and Lime—are naive and evil, respectively. (In an earlier draft of the screenplay, a third unsavory character, Tyler, was also American; in the film, that character was renamed Popescu and converted to a Romanian.) In part, the film reflects the ambivalence that some Europeans felt toward Americans after World War II: Americans were widely perceived on the one hand as powerful and generous but on the other hand as deliberately destructive (Lime) or naive, intrusive, and inadvertently destructive (Martins). Viewers who know little about World War II and its aftermath will miss the nationalistic symptomatic meaning in *The Third Man*.

Groups of films may also be symptomatic of the time they were made, as were the Vietnam War films that appeared after the American military involvement in Vietnam ended in 1973. In one of them, *Apocalypse Now* (1979), though no character does so in detail, American military efforts in Vietnam are highly criticized. As has been argued:

> Throughout the film, the U.S. conduct of war is seen as insane, excessive, destructive, futile. . . . Everywhere he goes, Capt. Willard sees signs of drugged stupor, alienation, confusion, lack of purpose. . . . In the film Americans are everywhere, loud, large, yet ineffective, as in the haunting image of the heli-

Plot Summary for *The Third Man*

Holly Martins, an American writer of western fiction, arrives in Vienna to do "publicity work for some kind of charity" that his friend Harry Lime is running. Shortly after Martins arrives, he learns that Lime has recently been accidentally killed and goes to his funeral. Soon Martins is suspicious about the circumstances of Lime's death and stays in Vienna to try to solve the mystery. In three eventful days, Martins meets Lime's lover, Anna, and Lime's three associates. He also keeps meeting up with Major Calloway, who is presumably in charge of the police in the British sector of occupied Vienna, because Calloway is trying to get evidence about Lime's associates, who were involved with Lime in criminal activities. Unexpectedly, Martins sees Lime (see figure, part a). Major Calloway finally convinces Martins that Lime had sold diluted penicillin that caused injury and death for many, including children. To help Anna escape repatriation by Soviet authorities and because Martins is repulsed by what Lime has done, Martins finally agrees to help lure out Lime so authorities may capture him. In the final chase through the sewers of Vienna, Lime kills Calloway's assistant, Sergeant Paine, and Martins himself shoots Lime. After a second funeral for Lime, Anna rejects Martins (see figure, part b).

An evil American and a naive, bumbling one in *The Third Man* (1949)
(a, above left) The first view of Harry Lime. A neighbor has switched on a light and inadvertently revealed Lime, who is hiding in the dark. It may be symbolic that Lime is associated with the dark: he's an inhumane criminal hiding in the dark. (b, above right) In the last shot of *The Third Man*, Anna rejects Holly Martins. Notice the many fallen leaves: it is autumn, the dying time of year. Martins—the intrusive, bumbling American—does not come off at all well in this 1949 British film; neither does his compatriot, Harry Lime. Frame enlargements. *London Film Productions*

copter burning in the tree by the river, and in the huge tail remains of an air-plane whose nose was in the edge of [the] river, and in the colored smoke, flares, and loud music by the bridge near Cambodia. . . . One meaning: an insane war breeds insane behavior. Another meaning: those with will power freed of judg-ment (the VC) will win. A . . . [third] meaning: many men and enormous fire-power are not enough against a devoted enemy that takes the long view. (Phillips 258–60)

The film is symptomatic of the growing doubts after the war about the wis-dom of American military involvement in Vietnam. Many viewers who know nothing about the conduct of the Vietnam War, the massive domestic protests against it, and increasing postwar doubts about the wisdom of American involvement will less likely detect these criticisms of American military efforts and more likely see the film as an exciting adventure with a bizarre ending.

CRITICAL APPROACHES, AND TIMES AND HABITATS OF MEANING

Various factors can influence the meanings a viewer perceives, such as the viewer's age, gender, sexual orientation,[2] religious and political beliefs, expe-rience in general and experience of previous creative works, including films, and critical approaches used to analyze creative works. A **critical approach** (or critical perspective) is a body of related ideas on how to interpret creative works. The ideas constituting a critical approach are sometimes only loosely related and by no means agreed on by all those professing to use the same approach. Not all critics calling themselves feminist, for example, will agree exactly what "feminist criticism" entails. Critical approaches may be thought of as conceptual tools people can use to help build interpretations.

    Many such approaches have been applied to interpreting films and other works of the imagination. New criticism or formalist criticism, neoformalist criticism, and reader-response (or viewer-response) criticism all focus on the work and viewers' responses to qualities perceived in the work. Other ap-proaches focus more on the relationship between the creative work and the world beyond it. Such contextual approaches include myth criticism; psycho-analytic criticism; Marxist criticism; auteur theory, which examines qualities

---

[2]For illustrations of how viewers' sexual orientation may affect their responses to a film, in-cluding interpretations of meanings, see the documentary film *The Celluloid Closet* (1996) and the two essays "Illicit Pleasures: Feminist Spectators and *Personal Best*" by Elizabeth Ellsworth and "Pre-text and Text in *Gentlemen Prefer Blondes*" by Lucie Arbuthnot and Gail Seneca, both of which are reprinted in Erens, *Issues in Feminist Film Criticism*.

of films influenced by one dominant filmmaker; feminist criticism; genre criticism; and reception theory, which examines how historical conditions affect how groups interpret creative works at different times and in different places. Here are introduced three of the most widely used and probably the most accessible critical approaches for the beginning film student: auteurist, Marxist, and feminist.

Auteur Theory

Auteur theory is a set of assumptions about auteurs, or (film) authors, and the films they helped create. The auteur theory is not a **film theory** (a related structure of abstractions about the film medium) but a method of interpreting and assessing films and filmmakers who left a clear imprint on a body of films. After World War II ended and French critics had a chance to see large groups of American films, some critics started to see how certain directors seemed to exhibit their personal vision in the films they directed. Auteur theory evolved from the views of André Bazin, François Truffaut, Jean-Luc Godard, Jacques Rivette, and Eric Rohmer, who published in the French journal *Cahiers du cinéma* during the 1950s and, except for Bazin, later became key directors of **French new wave** films. Initially, "*la politique des auteurs,*" as Truffaut labeled it, hoped to free French directors from traditional script-dominated films. Like the scholars of film noir, the French critics also suggested that many neglected American films—including some by directors who worked entirely within the Hollywood studio system—were worthy of close study, and they spent much time examining the films of such previously neglected directors as Nicholas Ray, Howard Hawks, Samuel Fuller, and Alfred Hitchcock.

As this critical method for interpreting and evaluating films and filmmakers was brought to England and the United States, it was modified and generated controversy. A version of it was first championed in the United States by film critic Andrew Sarris, who gave the method the name "auteur theory." Today, most critics define auteurs as filmmakers, usually directors, who function as the dominant creators of films, and auteurists point out how an auteur's films embody recurrent structures, techniques, and meanings. By examining closely the films directed by Howard Hawks, critic Robin Wood helps his readers understand aspects of one film in the context of other Hawksian movies. Of the main woman character in the western *Rio Bravo* (1959), Wood writes,

> Feathers is the product of the union of her basic "type"—the saloon girl—and the Hawks woman, sturdy and independent yet sensitive and vulnerable, the equal of any man yet not in the least masculine. The tension between background (convention) and foreground (actual character) is nowhere more evident. We are very far here from the brash "entertainer" with a heart of gold who dies

French new wave cinema: A diverse group of French fictional films made in the late 1950s and early 1960s that are marked by the independent spirit of their directors.

(more often than not) stopping a bullet intended for the hero. Angie Dickinson's marvelous performance gives us the perfect embodiment of the Hawksian woman, intelligent, resilient, and responsive. There is a continual sense of a woman who really grasps what is important to her. One is struck by the . . . beauty of a living individual responding spontaneously to every situation from a secure centre of self. It is not so much a matter of characterisation as the communication of a life-quality (a much rarer thing). What one most loves about Hawks, finally, is the aliveness of so many of his people. (42)

During the 1960s and 1970s, the auteur theory was enormously influential in Continental and American criticism, scholarship, and teaching. For example, many film books and college film courses were devoted to one director and the films of that director. Auteur criticism also brought to prominence some previously overlooked directors such as Alfred Hitchcock and John Ford. In addition, it extended film studies beyond a focus on individual films.

The auteur approach works best with directors who exercise strong creative control, such as Hawks, Stanley Kubrick, Alfred Hitchcock, Ingmar Bergman, and Federico Fellini. Many movies, however—especially most American studio movies of the 1930s, 1940s, and 1950s—are more the product of a studio than any individual. Thus Warner Bros. movies were often about current social problems, such as organized urban crime during the prohibition era, and were presented in a way that viewers thought of as true-to-life. MGM movies tended to be lighter, both literally and figuratively, and include the upbeat, big-budget musicals. In recent years, the auteur theory for interpreting films has lost some of its popularity because critics and scholars have come to realize that the qualities shared by films of the same auteur are not always clearly only the auteur's contributions (see the last section of the Introduction, pp. 4–5) nor the only aspects to be considered in interpreting films. Then, too, since the birth of the auteur theory, film theorists have come to emphasize contexts other than additional films directed by the same person. Film theorists now more likely stress the types of contexts discussed in Chapter 9—for example, societal attitudes, political climate, and media technology—as factors shaping a film's content and **style** and downplay the contributions of individual filmmakers.

style: The manner of presenting a subject in a creative work.

Marxist Film Criticism

Marxist film critics draw in varying ways on the writings of the nineteenth-century intellectual Karl Marx and later thinkers. Marxist film critics, such as those who publish essays in the American periodicals *Jump Cut* and *Cineaste*, do not entirely agree with one another as to what Marxist film criticism entails. But all of them agree that the dominant culture largely determines the meanings viewers perceive and that the Marxist film critic should focus on the economic classes of a story's characters and the filmmakers' society—especially the owners of the means of production, the capitalists, and those who create the goods or services, the proletariat or workers. Marxist film critics also stress the political implications of a story. Marxist film critics of recent years tend to think of **classical Hollywood cinema**—whether romantic comedies or horror films or action films or whatever else—as comforting illusions or entertaining distractions from the flaws of a capitalist system yet endorsements of its implied values (ideology), for example, of the importance of individualism, not group effort.

Marxist film critics tend to champion films from socialist countries such as Cuba and from third world countries in Africa, South America, and elsewhere. They may also point out when a mainstream film from a capitalist country is critical of its own society. A Marxist critic, for example, could point out that the popular **satirical** documentary *Roger & Me* (1989) is transparently about the plight of the working class and the indifference of the capitalist masters. Marxist critics could argue that *Unforgiven* shows that a worker (in this case a prostitute) may be attacked and injured while working then be treated by a capitalist as merely damaged, worthless property. A Marxist film critic could point out that it is the capitalist, Skinny, the saloon owner and in effect the "owner" of the prostitutes, who exploits the workers. He and a sheriff who acts as the enforcer of order and the status quo agree that the injury done to the prostitute early in the film can be paid off by a whipping and a fine: new capital to replace damaged capital and little compensation and a bleak future for the injured worker.

Another example of Marxist film criticism is John Hess's essay on *The Godfather Part II*, a film he sees as criticizing capitalism and business and showing the consequent breakup of the family. For Hess, the last shot of the film is especially expressive. In that shot, Michael Corleone is sitting outdoors, presumably at his Lake Tahoe compound. He is wearing dark clothing. He puts his left loose fist up to his mouth and keeps it there for the rest of the shot. Leaves are on the ground. As the camera **dollies** in, it also **tilts** down and we view Michael from a slightly **high angle**. As the camera approaches Michael, the right side of his face falls into darkness; the left side remains in **hard light**. The camera stops with Michael in medium close-up and even more out of the frame on the right. We see Michael for a few moments like this; then the concluding theme music begins as Michael continues to look straight ahead and contemplate. Of the film's last shot, Hess says, "A one-eyed man with his hands over his face (his human expressiveness), being squeezed out of the picture by the ominous, dreary property he struggled and killed to obtain, is the perfect image of this ugly reality of capitalism" (85).

Scriptwriter and critic Lester Cole summarizes much of what Marxist film criticism usually involves:

> The responsibility of a Marxist . . . film critic . . . must be first to understand the society in which . . . [the film] is made and the objective of the producers. . . . It

classical Hollywood cinema: A type of narrative film dominant throughout most of world movie history which shows one or more distinct characters with clear goals who overcome many problems in reaching them. The films tend to use unobtrusive filmmaking techniques and to stress continuity of action.

satire: A depiction of behavior through language, visuals, or other means that has as its aim the humorous criticism of individual or group behavior.

dolly: To film while the camera is mounted on a moving dolly or wheeled platform.

tilting: Effect achieved when a camera on a stationary base pivots vertically, down to up or up to down, during filming.

high angle: View of a subject from above, created by positioning the camera above the subject.

hard light: Light that has not been diffused or reflected before illuminating the subject. On subjects illuminated by hard light, shadows are sharp-edged and surface details are more noticeable than with soft light.

becomes his or her responsibility . . . to help the audience to see . . . the class positions of the characters and to what degree they, as viewers, have been manipulated, lured or distracted from the realities inherent in the film to cunningly directed ways of thinking and feeling callous to human needs, indifferent to political organization for their betterment. (24)

Non-Marxist film critics, in contrast, are likely to stress the psychological implications of stories. For *Unforgiven*, they might stress the psychological consequences of murdering someone. In the case of *The Godfather Part II*, non-Marxists could argue that the film shows the isolation that results when a son who lacks his father's skills with people takes over his father's criminal empire.

Feminist Film Criticism

Feminist critics and feminist theorists may focus on such issues as the representations of women in the arts, often in works largely created by males. Some feminist film critics and theorists point out the types of roles women play in various films, their scarcity in certain films or types of films (such as the war genre), and the typical ways they are depicted, for example, as cunning, duplicitous, and dangerous in films noirs. A feminist critic might point out that in mainstream movies males are much more prominent than females and tend to have power over them and that women are often shown as passive or minor or stereotypical and rarely as complex and entirely believable, and rarely physically plain, let alone unattractive. Some feminist theorists and critics have pointed out that movies usually show women from the male characters' **point of view**, often primarily as someone sexually attractive to heterosexual males. In mainstream movies (and other media), the opposite situation is rarely the case: men are not nearly as often presented as physically attractive and desirable in point-of-view shots. Some feminist theorists and critics contend that traditional movies tend to satisfy, soothe, and reassure male viewers. The worldwide popularity of fantasy films designed for males (discussed earlier in this chapter) supports the contention that most movies of classical Hollywood cinema depict women for the pleasure of heterosexual male viewers. Not insignificantly, the female characters of classical Hollywood cinema have been created and shaped largely by male writers and directors.

Understandably, feminist critics often discover different meanings in a film than do critics who approach films from a different perspective. A feminist critic, for example, is more likely to discuss the gender roles in a film and to notice how the few women in *The Godfather* and other gangster films and the few women in *Unforgiven* and most other westerns are presented only in relation to men and mainly in stereotypical roles, such as the good-hearted prostitute, understanding mother, or long-suffering but forgiving wife. A feminist reading of 1940s and 1950s American westerns might point

point-of-view shot: Camera placement at the approximate position of a character or person (or, occasionally, an animal) that gives a view similar to what that creature would see.

out that in such films as *My Darling Clementine* (1946) and *High Noon* (1952), women are shown either as cultured and emotionally restrained easterners or as emotional, sensual, and slightly disreputable or outright disreputable Mexicans. So stacked is the deck against the Mexican woman in *My Darling Clementine* that she is given the name of a type of dog, Chihuahua, which is a rare if not nonexistent name for a woman in Mexico. (Although Chihuahua is the name of a city and state in Mexico, most American viewers would think of the dog, not the places, when they hear the name.)

Feminist film theorists and critics have not merely made some viewers more aware of certain attitudes and values in the pervasive classical Hollywood cinema. They have also championed both neglected women filmmakers such as Dorothy Arzner and Ida Lupino and overlooked feature films with feminist perspectives, such as *Salt of the Earth* (1954), *The Ballad of Little Jo* (1993), and *Orlando* (1993). Feminist critics have also pointed out the achievements of the many avant-garde films by women—such as "You Take Care Now" (1989, discussed in Chapter 8)—which have long been a much more accessible outlet for feminist images and viewpoints than have documentary or especially fictional films.

In the United States, feminist film theory was much influenced by the women's movement of the 1960s (referred to in the chronology beginning on p. 513); the increased application of semiology, or the linguistical science of "signs" or basic units of communication; and the scrutiny of all modes of communication for their assumptions and built-in meanings and attitudes. Feminist film theory and criticism are part of a much larger examination of communication in the broadest sense, including the exploration of words and idioms for their assumptions and for attitudes that are belittling, demeaning, or condescending in reference to groups.

In recent years, some feminist theorists and critics have cast their nets wider and examined films previously not studied seriously, such as slasher movies and sexually explicit movies. As Patricia Erens writes, feminist scholars and critics are moving on to other issues:

> . . . Many feminist film critics are now investigating the differences between women, especially how race and sexual preference, along with ethnicity and class, establish separate priorities. Focusing on disparate social and cultural heritages and histories, this criticism not only speaks out for new representations, but also for a more diversified theory of female spectatorship [how women, as distinct from men, interact with films]. . . . If the seventies and eighties have been devoted to discovering the pervasive influence of sexual difference (male/female), then perhaps the nineties will be the decade when women will come to a better understanding of the differences between themselves. (xxiii)

In interpreting a film, a critic may be eclectic and use more than one critical approach, such as auteurist-genre, psychoanalytic (or Lacanian)-feminist, or

Marxist-feminist.[3] A Marxist-feminist interpretation of *Unforgiven*, for example, could combine the comments made earlier about the owner and workers with observations about the treatment of women, and journalistic critics who use viewer-response criticism—such as Janet Maslin, Vincent Canby, Pauline Kael, David Denby, and Kenneth Turan—rarely use that approach exclusively in an essay.

Times and Habitats of Meaning

Meanings are not universal and unchanging,[4] a claim confirmed by Barbara Klinger's study of the changing critical reception to films directed by Douglas Sirk—such as *Magnificent Obsession* (1954), *All That Heaven Allows* (1955), *Written on the Wind* (1957), *Tarnished Angels* (1958), and *Imitation of Life* (1959). Klinger studied how Sirk's films have been interpreted by different **habitats of meaning**, groups such as film reviewers or academics that find similar meanings. She discovered that,

> during the 1950s, Universal–International Pictures presented Sirk's melodramas as slick, sexually explicit "adult" films. . . . At the same time, film reviewers decried his melodramas as "soap operas," typical not only of the crass commercialism of the film industry, but also of the frightening mediocrity of a mass culture with fascist tendencies. . . .
>
> In a more contemporary setting, reviewers . . . transformed Sirk's films . . . into "classics," while the revelation of [Rock] Hudson's gay identity in the 1980s made Sirk melodramas into treatises on the artifice of romance and gender roles in the Hollywood cinema. And within the highly self-conscious and **intertextual** climate of today, Sirk's melodramas appear as "camp," as parodic spectacles of excess. (xv)

Klinger's findings are instructive. During the 1950s, the film industry presented Sirk's movies in one light—"slick, sexually explicit 'adult' films"—whereas film reviewers of the time saw them differently: different habitats of meaning operating at the same time produce different meanings. Because of various changes over time, including the revelation of Hudson's homosexuality and his death from AIDS in 1985, more recent reviewers interpret Sirk's movies quite differently than did the reviewers in the 1950s. This illustrates that within the same habitat of meaning, people working at different

habitat of meaning: A group of people with common interests and broadly shared outlook who generate similar sets of meanings.

intertextuality: The relationship that a form of human expression, such as a film, has to other forms of human expression, such as a journalistic article, a play, or another film. Intertextuality can take the form of translation, citation, imitation, or extension.

---

[3]For more information about these and other critical approaches that are widely used in film journals and advanced film courses, see J. Dudley Andrew's *The Major Film Theories: An Introduction*; Tim Bywater and Thomas Sobchack's *An Introduction to Film Criticism: Major Critical Approaches to Narrative Film*; Gerald Mast, Marshall Cohen, and Leo Braudy's *Film Theory and Criticism: Introductory Readings*; Bill Nichols, ed., *Movies and Methods* vols. 1 and 2; R. Barton Palmer's Introduction to *The Cinematic Text: Methods and Approaches*; and Robert Lapsley and Michael Westlake's *Film Theory: An Introduction*.

[4]For seven interpretations of the film *Psycho*, see David Bordwell's *Making Meaning* (224–44).

The Truman Show (1998): Selected Responses

The Truman Show is about Truman Burbank, a young man who is unaware that he has lived his entire life on a gigantic television sound stage as the subject of a long-running, enormously popular TV show. As the story unfolds, Truman begins to question his life and rebel. These passages demonstrate some of the different types of responses possible.

EXPECTATIONS AND INTERACTIONS (VIEWER-RESPONSE CRITICISM)

The film starts out with a burst of information, running the delicious risk of disorienting us by providing more data than we can quite absorb. Its first shot is a tight close-up of a man in a beret who looks directly at the camera and goes to the heart of the matter. "We've become bored with watching actors giving us phony emotions. We're tired of pyrotechnics and special effects. While the world he inhabits is in some respects counterfeit, there is nothing faked about Truman. No script, no cue cards. It isn't always Shakespeare, but it's genuine. It's a life."

The speaker is Christof (Ed Harris), later described as the "televisionary" who created *The Truman Show*. . . .

. . . The film is savvy enough to dole out the ramifications and specifics of Truman's situation in artfully spaced doses. Only in bits and pieces do we find out the true dimension of what has been done to Truman, how it has all been managed.   —Kenneth Turan

EXPLICIT MEANINGS

There are only a few explicit meanings. Christof explains that "we accept the reality of the world with which we're presented," and he explains several explicit meanings near the end of the film, as when he says to Truman, "You were real. That's what made you so good to watch."   —William H. Phillips

IMPLICIT MEANINGS

Cinematic Techniques

From the outset there's something strange about the place: The squeaky-clean tract houses could have been designed by Disney (see figure), the sunsets are so beautiful they're weird, and the town's inhabitants seem larger than life, as if they are characters, even caricatures.

Seahaven is a surreal version of America as America wishes it once was: paradise without the serpent.   —Richard Rayner

Film noir . . . fifty years later . . . looks mannered, and we find no realism worthy of our trust. Every depiction of us needs to be ironic, cool, untouched by conviction or belief. . . . And as we looked for an image that embodied our detachment, our disaffection, we found it in the high-key, undifferentiated gloss of television—a look for those who have given up on the Holy Ghost of believing what they see.

Setting for *The Truman Show* (1998)
Truman Burbank lives out his life in the picture-perfect Seahaven, a gigantic enclosed TV studio. As seen here on a TV screen, Seahaven is incredibly clean, orderly, and light. Frame enlargement. *Paramount*

448

Half a century after the ascendancy of film noir, a new genre may be emerging. Call it film blanc, film lumiere, film fluorescent, film flash, or film deadpan. I like the latter two because they convey the instantaneous oneness of a kind of photography that bombs us with light just to get a picture. It's the kind of light that exists, like climate, on most TV sets and shows: a one-dimensional lighting scheme without depth, shaping, or character; a flood of light that lets you film without having to pause; a light that, with only a little heightening, seems surreal, mad, glaring, and unsettling.

The Truman Show is bathed in such light. What makes this so intriguing is the way it plays off our dependence on and loathing of TV—as if TV had become the base level of visible existence.

—David Thomson

Symbols

In a deft, ironic touch, even Truman Burbank's name simultaneously evokes both reality (true-man) and unreality (Burbank, Calif., of course, home to many a TV and movie studio).   —Michael O'Sullivan

Christof symbolizes a strong-willed TV director-writer with an increasingly unpredictable subject, father figure to a rebellious son, tyrant whose police force helps keep the subject ignorant and in line, and god who restricts his subject's free will, nearly kills him, and finally implores him to continue in his role.

—William H. Phillips

Narrative Meanings

"The Truman Show" is a crowd pleaser that caters to our horror of totalitarianism, our love of personal freedom, our belief—justified or deluded—that knowledge is a powerful tool and that access to information is a God-given right. I'm not sure if the movie is more disturbing because Truman is a prisoner or because he has been lied to.   —Barbara Shulgasser

Pic trades in issues of personal liberty vs. authoritarian control, safe happiness vs. the excitement of chaos, manufactured emotions, the penetration of media to the point where privacy vanishes, and the fascination of fabricated images over plain sight.

—Todd McCarthy

For me, *The Truman Show* was about reality and television, but also about deception and trust, and control and ethics, and voyeurism, and movie-watching, and corporate involvement in our daily lives.

—Lise Carrigg

We're asked to believe that it took Truman 30 years to realize he was being watched—that he hadn't noticed in all that time that everyone else in his life was performing, colluding to protect his innocence.

It's an outrageous conceit, but once we've surrendered disbelief (and what great fable doesn't require such a leap?), "The Truman Show" has a lot to say about the way we live—about voyeurism and lockstep consumerism, about media surveillance and lack of privacy.   —Edward Guthmann

The captive of TV isn't Truman, it's the audience. Us. And our love of that captivity, the gobbling of shows—fictional drama or news or sports or politics, but always shows—engulfs us. We used to go to theaters and films; now . . . TV comes to our homes, entwines us. . . . The shows don't have to be dramatic. . . . They need only be shows, life outside transmitted to the TV screen inside.   —Stanley Kauffmann

Truman is living the universal fantasy, in a disease-, and disaster-, war- and stress-free environment whose minute-to-minute geniality is beamed on Prozac waves into homes around the world, calming the poor, the elderly, the lonely and the working classes with images of a life running its course in paradise.

—Jack Matthews

Its premise is a legitimate one: the shock and violent internal crisis undergone by an individual beginning to see his world for the first time, *really* see it, really see *through* it. A smiling face might suddenly suggest hidden malice, a cozy street complacency and even suffocation. This is not paranoia, but the beginning of knowledge.   —David Walsh

SYMPTOMATIC MEANINGS:
WORLD → FILM → VIEWERS

Would anyone care to guess how many TV shows routinely violate the privacy of ordinary people—often by invitation? Add up the day-time talk tabloids, then factor in all the cops-in-action shows, the seemingly endless supply of the world's funniest home videos. What does this tell us about ourselves, and how we choose to spend our time?

At a certain level, this is the central question in . . . *The Truman Show.* —Stephan Magcosta

The accelerating blurring of news and entertainment, of real and simulated violence, of authentic history and landscape with screen and theme-park fictionalizations: they're all part of Truman's all too eerily familiar world. So is the passivity of an audience that, as Bill Gates has promised, will someday never have to leave its armchairs. —Frank Rich

WORKS CITED

Carrigg, Lise. "Lise reviews *The Truman Show.*" 5 August 1998. <http://www.girlson.com/film/navigation/loader.asp?story -http%3A%2F%2Fwww>.

Guthmann, Edward. "Remote Control Jim Carrey Is a Born TV Star in 'The Truman Show.'" *San Francisco Chronicle* 5 June 1998: C1.

Kauffmann, Stanley. "Caught in the Act." *New Republic* 29 June 1998: 22.

Magcosta, Stephan. "Must-See TV: *The Truman Show.*" 18 July 1998. <http://seattlesquare.com/pandemonium /featurestext/TheTrumanShow.htm>.

Matthews, Jack. "He Doesn't Know His World's a Stage." 18 July 1998. <http://www.newsday.com/movies /rnmxz0d3.htm>.

McCarthy, Todd. "*The Truman Show.*" 18 July 1998. <http://www.variety.com/filmrev/cfralso.asp?recordID =1117477427>.

O'Sullivan, Michael. "'Truman': A Surreally Big Show." *Washington Post* 5 June 1998, Weekend: N58.

Rayner, Richard. "*The Truman Show.*" *Harper's Bazaar* June 1998: 92.

Rich, Frank. "Prime Time Live." *New York Times* 23 May 1998, natl. ed.: A25.

Shulgasser, Barbara. "Carrey Rings True in 'The Truman Show.'" *San Francisco Examiner* 5 June 1998. 18 July 1998. <http://www.sfgate.com/cgi-bin/article.cgi?file =/examiner/archive/1998/06/05/WEEKEND8781.dtl>.

Thomson, David. "*The Truman Show.*" *Esquire* May 1998: 46.

Turan, Kenneth. "His Show of Shows." *Los Angeles Times* Calendar: F1. 5 June 1998.

Walsh, David. "*The Truman Show*: Further Signs of Life in Hollywood." *World Socialist Web Site* 15 June 1998. 18 July 1998. <http://wsws.org/arts/1998/jun1998 /tru-j15.shtml>.

times produce different meanings. A third implication of Klinger's findings: the fact that there have been many and shifting interpretations of meanings of the same films reveals how complex and transitory American society is. It seems likely that in a more homogeneous and less transitory society, the interpretation of meanings would be less varied and less transitory. After examining films directed by Sirk and reactions to them over a nearly forty-year period by different habitats of meaning—such as academics, review journalists, and star publicists—Klinger concludes:

> There has been nothing stable about the meaning of his melodramas; they have been subject at every cultural turn to the particular *use* to which various institutions and social circumstances put them. In this process, meaning itself becomes something we cannot determine "once and for all," but a volatile, essentially *cultural* phenomenon that shifts with the winds of time. (159)

This is not to say that all interpretations of a film are equally convincing. All films establish broad parameters of meanings: a wide variety of meanings is plausible, but some meanings are indefensible. If viewers do not think carefully about their interpretation and support it with examples from the film and perhaps from outside the film (symptomatic meanings), the meanings they see may be merely unpersuasive opinions. In short, what is useful are reasoned and supported arguments, not mere statements of beliefs.

In developing meanings and explaining them to others, viewers, readers, and listeners clarify their own understanding and communicate it, both deep-rooted human needs. Interpretations of meaning may not only illuminate films but also reveal both the interpreters—for example, their assumptions or their critical approach(es)—and the historical time in which the work is being interpreted. Understanding meanings and how they are derived can help viewers realize when a film attempts to unduly manipulate them—as in propagandistic films—or when a film demeans a sex, ethnic group, race, or nation. In societies where citizens need to be informed, critical of orthodoxy, yet tolerant, viewers benefit from training in discovering and questioning meanings in films and other creations of the human imagination.

SUMMARY

Expectations and Interactions

- As viewers watch a film, they interact with it, formulating expectations, responding to clues set forth, guessing, readjusting their expectations, and consequently experiencing puzzlement or clarity and feeling excitement and pleasure or disappointment or boredom.

Types of Meanings

- As used in this book, *meaning* is an observation or generalization about a subject.

- Meanings are not inherent in a creative work, such as a book or film. Mentally active people use the creative work to formulate meanings, but not all interpretations of meaning are equally persuasive.

Explicit Meanings

- Explicit meanings are general observations that are made within a work. They are used more often in documentary films than in fictional films.

- Fictional films that rely heavily on explicit meanings are often thought of as flawed, at least in western societies, because generally modern audiences expect movies to show, not tell or explain, their meanings.

Implicit Meanings

- A viewer may use awareness of cinematic techniques, symbols, and narratives to help discover meanings.

- As Part One of this book shows, mise en scène, cinematography, editing, and sound can influence a viewer's perception of a film's meanings.

- A technique may be used subtly and viewers required to be active participants. However, a technique's significance may not be noticed if the filmmakers are too subtle for the intended audience or if the technique is not noticeable because the film or videotape version being seen and heard obscures important details.

- Filmmakers and other creative artists may create symbols: anything perceptible that has significance beyond its usual meaning or function. Usually symbols go unexplained within the film, and viewers interpret them variously, though not all interpretations are persuasive.

- Narrative itself is a major source of meanings because viewers often infer general implications from it. Fantasy movies, for example, show improbable though usually reassuring stories that suggest that people can overcome overwhelming adversity and achieve their desires.

- A narrative or some aspect of it may be ambiguous: it may withhold information or provide conflicting information. Viewers may be unable to infer its meanings with much certainty, or the narrative or some aspect of it may be subject to two or more plausible interpretations.

Symptomatic Meanings or Ideology: World ➔ Film ➔ Viewers

- A knowledge of the world outside the film sometimes helps viewers discover symptomatic meanings or ideology: explicit or implicit meanings that are the same as a large group's beliefs or values.

Critical Approaches, and Times and Habitats of Meaning

- The meanings one perceives in creative works may be influenced by the critical approaches or perspectives one applies during analysis.

- Auteur critics examine the recurrent meanings and techniques of filmmakers who have left a strong imprint on films they have worked on.

- Marxist film criticism focuses on the economic classes of a story's characters and the filmmakers' society—especially the capitalists and the proletariat or workers.

- Feminist film criticism focuses on such issues as the representations of women in films, the nature and significance of contributions of women filmmakers, and the differing responses to films by different groups of women (female spectatorship).

- People in different habitats of meaning perceive different meanings in the same creative work.

- Perceptions of meanings tend to change as the times change.

- Meanings, then, are to some extent relative, but a film sets parameters to interpretation of meanings, and some interpretations are indefensible.

WORKS CITED

Bordwell, David. *Making Meaning: Inference and Rhetoric in the Interpretation of Cinema*. Cambridge: Harvard UP, 1989.

Cole, Lester. Response to. "Marxist Film Criticism: A Symposium." *Cineaste* Fall 1979: 18–25.

Epstein, Leslie. "The Movie on the Whorehouse Wall/*The Devil in Miss Jones*." *The Movie That Changed My Life*. Ed. David Rosenberg. New York: Viking, 1991.

Erens, Patricia. Introduction. *Issues in Feminist Film Criticism*. Ed. Patricia Erens. Bloomington: Indiana UP, 1990.

Hess, John. "*Godfather II*: A Deal Coppola Couldn't Refuse." *Movies and Methods*. Ed. Bill Nichols. Berkeley: U of California P, 1976. 81–90.

Katz, Ephraim. *The Film Encyclopedia*. 3rd ed. Rev. Fred Klein and Ronald Dean Nolen. New York: HarperCollins, 1998.

Klinger, Barbara. *Melodrama and Meaning: History, Culture, and the Films of Douglas Sirk*. Bloomington: Indiana UP, 1994.

Maslin, Janet. "Is It Unexpected? Is It Strange? It's Here." *New York Times* 28 Jan. 1995, natl. ed.: 11.

Phillips, William H. "Study Guide for *Apocalypse Now*." *Film Studies: Selected Course Outlines and Reading Lists from American Colleges and Universities*. Ed. Erik S. Lunde and Douglas A. Noverr. New York: Markus Wiener, 1989.

Staiger, Janet. *Interpreting Films: Studies in the Historical Reception of American Cinema*. Princeton: Princeton UP, 1992.

Sternberg, Meir. *Expositional Modes and Temporal Ordering in Fiction*. Baltimore: Johns Hopkins UP, 1978.

Wood, Robin. *Howard Hawks*. Garden City, N.Y.: Doubleday, 1968.

FOR FURTHER READING

Although film theory helps us understand the film medium more completely, some recent film theory is frustrating for students to read because of its involved sentence structure and the writers' heavy use of jargon. The theoretical books listed here, however, should prove accessible to many beginning film students.

Andrew, J. Dudley. *The Major Film Theories: An Introduction*. New York: Oxford UP, 1976. Includes an explanation of what film theory entails and a discussion of major film theories: early theorists, realist film theory, and contemporary French film theory.

Approaches to Popular Film. Ed. Joanne Hollows and Mark Janncovich. Manchester, Eng.: Manchester UP, 1995. Eight essays on critical approaches and analyses.

Bazin, André. *What Is Cinema?* Trans. Hugh Gray. 2 vols. Berkeley: U of California P, 1967, 1971. Influential critical and theoretical essays.

Bywater, Tim, and Thomas Sobchack. *Introduction to Film Criticism: Major Critical Approaches to Narrative Film*. New York: Longman, 1989. Includes discussions of major critical approaches; sample student papers; a chronology of film reviewing, criticism, and theory; and a glossary.

Carson, Diane, Linda Dittmar, and Janice R. Welsch, eds. *Multiple Voices in Feminist Film Criticism*. Minneapolis: U of Minnesota P, 1994. A collection of mostly theoretical essays, most for the advanced student.

Close Viewings: An Anthology of New Film Criticism. Ed. Peter Lehman. Tallahassee: Florida State UP, 1990. Part 1 emphasizes formal analysis; Part 2, cultural analysis; Part 3, which consists of one essay, applies many forms of criticism to one film, *The Searchers*.

Columbia Dictionary of Modern Literary and Cultural Criticism. Ed. Joseph Childers and Gary Hentzi. New York: Columbia UP, 1995. Of special usefulness to beginning film students are the entries for *convention, filmic, frame/framing, interpretive community, intertextuality, male gaze, Marxist criticism, master shot, plot, realism,* and *revisionism*.

Film Theory Goes to the Movies: Cultural Analysis of Contemporary Film. Ed. Jim Collins, Hilary Radner, and Ava Preacher Collins. New York: Routledge, 1993. Interpretations of popular American movies in terms of issues in current film theories.

Fischer, Lucy. *Shot/Countershot: Film Tradition and Women's Cinema*. Princeton: Princeton UP, 1989. Each chapter discusses a theme or genre "counterposing two or more [film] works—from the feminist and from the dominant cinema."

Greenberg, Harvey Roy. *Screen Memories: Hollywood Cinema on the Psychoanalytic Couch*. New York: Columbia UP, 1993. Film criticism from a psychoanalytic perspective.

Haskell, Molly. *Holding My Own in No Man's Land: Women and Men and Film and Feminists*. New York: Oxford UP, 1997. Mostly reprints of previously published interviews and essays grouped under the headings "Dames," "Guys," "Literary Heroines," and "The Nineties: Where Do We Go from Here?"

Miles, Margaret R. *Seeing and Believing: Religion and Values in the Movies*. Boston: Beacon, 1996. Examines what popular films of the 1980s and 1990s say and suggest about religion and values. Essays are divided into two parts: "Religion in Popular Film" and "Race, Gender, Sexuality, and Class in Popular Film."

The Political Companion to American Film. Ed. Gary Crowdus. Chicago: Lake View, 1994. Includes essays on filmmakers, genres, racial and ethnic representations, and social characterizations (such as politicians and businessmen). Many essays discuss films' implicit and symptomatic political meanings (broadly defined). Includes a short bibliography after most of the essays.

Powers, Stephen, David J. Rothman, and Stanley Rothman. *Hollywood's America: Social and Political Themes in Motion Pictures*. Boulder: Westview, 1996. The book combines an "extensive systematic content analysis . . . of social and political themes in [popular] motion pictures from 1946 to the present with the most detailed study ever conducted of the political views and personalities of a random sample of leaders in the motion picture industry." Includes many tables presenting the results of the research and an appendix entitled "The Poverty of Film Theory."

Ray, Robert B. *A Certain Tendency of the Hollywood Cinema, 1930–1980*. Princeton: Princeton UP, 1985. In part, by analyzing such classic movies as *Casablanca*, *The Man Who Shot Liberty Valance*, *The Godfather*, and *Taxi Driver*, Ray explains and illustrates "the formal and thematic paradigms that commercially successful films in this country have consistently used."

Salt, Barry. *Film Style and Technology: History and Analysis*. 2nd ed. London: Starword, 1992. Both a critique of much of current film theory and a history of film technology and analysis of its impact on film style.

Tan, Ed S. *Emotion and the Structure of Narrative Film: Film as an Emotion Machine*. Mahwah, NJ: Erlbaum, 1996. A theoretical study of a largely neglected subject with emphasis on the traditional feature film. Sample chapter titles: "The Psychological Functions of Film Viewing," "Thematic Structures and Interest," and "Character Structures, Empathy, and Interest."

Wood, Michael. *America in the Movies*. New York: Dell, 1975. Examines Hollywood movies from the end of the 1930s to the beginning of the 1960s as reassuring fantasies.

CHAPTER 11

Analysis and Synthesis:
The Player

To help you understand some of the scope of the film medium and how individual films can function, this book breaks films down into elements and addresses them one at a time—for example, one chapter on cinematography and one on contexts for films. Of course, when a film is shown, the cinematography and all the other elements function simultaneously and ideally complement one another to produce a unified effect. This final chapter of *Film* applies many of the book's concepts to a single film and serves as a partial summary and review. The goal is to help you appreciate ways to use some of the book's concepts in your own film analyses and in your explorations of the film medium. As with any summary, this section cannot address every aspect of this book or of the film under study, nor for that matter can any one film exemplify all the aspects of cinema. The medium is far too encompassing for any film to serve that function.

The film chosen is *The Player*, which came out in 1992 and was written by Michael Tolkin and directed by Robert Altman. This film was selected because it is often used in introductory film courses; is readily available on videotape, laser disc, and DVD; is fun to watch; and exemplifies many aspects of interest to filmmakers, film critics, and film scholars. Also, *The Player* is a movie about the Hollywood movie industry, filled with references to earlier films and commentary on the Hollywood studio system.

The story focuses on a film studio executive named Griffin Mill whose power resides in his ability to approve story pitches. Mill processes hundreds of pitches a week, but the studio can produce only twelve movies a year. Because he must ultimately reject nearly every pitch he hears, Mill engenders the prayers and the wrath of every writer he meets.

Thanks to Vicki Whitaker of Aztec, New Mexico, for working with me on this chapter.

FIGURE 11.1 Main character, major problem
Almost immediately in *The Player*, viewers see that Griffin
Mill is the main character, that his job for a Hollywood film
studio consists of deciding on the merits of proposed stories,
and that he is being harassed by an anonymous postcard
writer angry with the way Mill treated him. Here Mill looks
at one of the many unsettling postcards. *Fine Line Features*

Viewers quickly learn that an unidentified screenwriter is threatening
Mill (Figure 11.1), and rumor has it that an outsider named Larry Levy will
be brought in to fill Mill's position (Figure 11.6). Mill is also involved romantically with a subordinate, a story editor named Bonnie Sherow (Figure 11.2).

Mill begins to track down David Kahane, a writer who he thinks has been
threatening him. When he calls Kahane's house, Mill is immediately attracted
to the writer's artist girlfriend June Gudmundsdottir (Figure 11.3). Later that
night he finds the writer at a movie theater, has drinks with him, and ends up
in a parking lot with him; tempers flare on both sides, and Mill kills Kahane.
Mill makes the murder look like a botched robbery. The next day, Mill returns
to his job and finds that Larry Levy has come to work at the studio. Later, he
also learns that the writer who had been threatening him is still alive. Mill attends Kahane's funeral and soon begins to pursue his girlfriend romantically.

FIGURE 11.2 Main character's initial love interest
Early in the film, viewers see that Mill is romantically involved with a co-worker, Bonnie Sherow. She is more enthusiastic about him than he about her. Is he preoccupied with the threatening postcard writer or the new hire at the studio, or has the spark gone out of the relationship for Mill? *Fine Line Features*

FIGURE 11.3 Main character's new love interest
Mill sees a luminous vision in the night and is immediately attracted to her, an artist who always dresses in white and works in a shimmering silvery white studio. Soon he is pursuing her as he tries to cope with threatening changes in studio personnel, Sherow's presence, and a persistent and increasingly threatening postcard writer. *Fine Line Features*

Because Mill is a suspect, the police come to Mill's office and interview him about the murder. After a director and producer pitch Mill their plans for *Habeas Corpus*—a story likely to be a huge flop—Mill "allows" Levy to take over championing the story in the hope that the movie will fail and Levy will be discredited.

The police summon Mill to the police station, where he becomes flustered by Detective Avery's questions and methods (Figure 11.4). Later, Mill and Gudmundsdottir slip off to a desert hideaway where at the conclusion of a romantic evening they become lovers. The next day, Mill is called in for a police lineup, but the only eyewitness selects the police officer from among the possible suspects.

A year later, *Habeas Corpus* has been reworked to the point where its director has sold out on every serious issue in its original story line. After a screening at the studio, only Bonnie Sherow points out the sellout the film has become, whereupon Levy fires her. Mill now occupies the former studio head's office and is in charge of the studio. He and Levy are on good working terms.

In the final sequence, Griffin Mill is cruising to his exclusive neighborhood home in a Rolls-Royce convertible while listening to a pitch on his car phone. The speaker obliquely identifies himself as the writer who had been threatening Mill and proposes a story about a movie executive who gets away with murder—in fact, the story of the movie viewers have just seen. Mill's main concern is that the movie executive gets away with the murder and lives happily ever after married to the dead writer's girlfriend. The writer assures him that a green light will guarantee that outcome, and Mill agrees. The writer proposes that the film be called *The Player*.

FIGURE 11.4 Major threat to main character's freedom and happiness
The main impediment to Mill's happiness is a clever police detective, who asks questions that catch Mill off-guard and interrogates him in an unorthodox manner that makes him lose his cool. *Fine Line Features*

MISE EN SCÈNE

In *The Player*, the mise en scène shows selected aspects of contemporary Hollywood and lets viewers mingle with the players, those exercising power, and the trappings of wealth.

Settings

The Player begins in an office interior; then the camera tracks up and back to give an overview of a movie lot in contemporary sunny southern California. The weather is clear yet nondescript, the parking lot tidy and featuring an expensive car; the limited landscaping is well manicured. All players are nattily attired and perfectly coiffed. At once the setting suggests wealth (the clothes), power (the studio itself), and surface orderliness. The opening shot also introduces nearly all the main characters.

Mill's office is crammed with movie posters for *King Kong* (1933), *The Blue Angel* (1930), and six movies dealing with crime, especially murder: *Prison Shadows* (1936), *Hollywood Story* (1951), *Laura* (1944, Figure 11.5a), *Murder in the Big House* (1942, Figure 11.5b), *Prison Break* (1938, Figure 11.5b), and *M* (the 1951 remake). The posters in Mill's office associate Mill with movies about murder. By contrast, the office of the studio head has a poster for *Casablanca* (1942), whose subject is not crime but romance, patriotism, and sacrifice (Figure 11.6).

Another component of the setting used especially expressively is the cars. For most of the film Mill drives a black Range Rover—a status symbol for moneyed Angelenos and a vehicle that can comfortably accommodate actor Tim Robbins's six-foot five-inch frame. The studio head, Joel Levison, drives a black Mercedes, and Mill's rumored rival, Larry Levy, drives a black Mercedes convertible. The cars suggest that Levy has the same tastes as the studio head and is a major player. In the film's last scenes, when Mill is now the studio head, he drives a Rolls-Royce convertible, an obvious symbol of his promotion.

The cars, car phones, car faxes, and clothing so expensive that the cost of a single suit would support a family in a barrio for a month—these are symbols of power within the industry.

Subjects

Except for the writer who is murdered, his girlfriend, and the police, the main characters are all involved in making studio movies. Of them, the central character is Griffin Mill. Because viewers see him in nearly every scene and in a variety of situations that are difficult for him, both professionally and personally, viewers get to know Mill well. He is a complex character: calculating,

FIGURE 11.5 Setting revealing character
Most of the many movie posters in Mill's office are for films involving crime and punishment,
an appropriate backdrop for a man who has committed murder and hopes to evade punishment.
Fine Line Features

FIGURE 11.6 Contrasting setting, contrasting character
Unlike Mill's office, the office of Joel Levison, the head of the studio, has only a few movie posters, the most prominent being *Casablanca*, a commercial and critical success. That image is associated with Levison (off frame), not the images for the mostly low-budget crime films that cover Mill's office walls. *Fine Line Features*

guarded, professionally successful, vulnerable to rage and violence, adept at surviving—and lucky to survive his encounter with the law.

Even to a casual viewer, *The Player* includes an extraordinary number of cameos, mainly of famous actors but also of directors, a film critic, and others. As is typical of cameo performances, none affects the plot in any significant way. One could argue that the sixty-five cameos are part of the densely populated decor, part of the setting rather than subjects in their own right. The cameos also add an element of surprise—whom will viewers notice next?—though there is a danger that the cameos could distract viewers from the story. There are so many cameos, some of them inconspicuous, that attentive viewers may notice even more of them on later re-viewings.

Composition

The film's intended aspect ratio is 1.85:1. That makes it a wide-screen film, but not as wide as it might have been—for example, an anamorphic version with a 2.4:1 aspect ratio. Rarely does *The Player* show subjects isolated from each other on opposite sides of the frame. Occasionally something significant is going on in both the foreground and the background simultaneously, as briefly in the opening shot where a man in a Porsche convertible (an investor's son) flirts with a woman as a group of Japanese investors are being given a tour behind them.

Much more typically the film uses a moving camera or zoom lens to follow a few characters for a while then pick up new characters and follow them. The restless camera and many characters moving rapidly within the frame, and in and out of it, make for frequent changes in composition.

Mise en Scène and the World outside the Film

The most obvious product placement is the Range Rover. It appears in many scenes and is photographed from a variety of distances and angles. Its logo (on both the front and the back of the vehicle) is legible at least four places in the film. Probably the Range Rover is so prominent because the film's producers and the vehicle maker struck a mutually advantageous deal. Among the people and businesses singled out for "Special Thanks" in the end credits is "Range Rover of North America" (see p. 560).

CINEMATOGRAPHY

Aside from the opening shot, which is described on p. 129, the cinematography by Jean Lepine tends to be unobtrusive. It supports the story and helps make the movie easy to follow and pleasurable to watch. Viewers with training in film studies, however, are likely to notice some of the techniques that influence viewers' responses to the actions portrayed on the screen.

Color

The film uses expressive color at various points. One occurs after dark when Griffin Mill drives to David Kahane's house. Mill drives up to a distinctly lit house whose windows glow with an unusual icy, crystalline blue. Unbeknownst to the woman inside, Mill watches the woman as she speaks to him on the phone while working at a canvas surrounded by a clutter of art paraphernalia—all in a variety of blues, whites, and silvers. She claims to have no particular interest in movies as she ranges languidly around in the liquid, shimmering bluish light, which is used to emphasize the icy environment. (Later Kahane will refer to her as the "ice queen.") Throughout the film Gudmundsdottir is associated with white. She even wears white, and a light blue scarf, to Kahane's funeral. Because she has been shown as a disengaged entity, we can understand this radical departure from tradition. Mill, in contrast, dresses in different colors. Initially he wears an off-white suit and generally wears darker and darker suits as the film progresses until he is wearing black in the last sequence.

A second particularly expressive use of color occurs the night Mill kills Kahane. Reddish tones are used to light the karaoke bar where they drink together. When Mill leaves the bar, a splash of red neon colors his footsteps out the door. Just before Kahane mockingly asks to borrow Mill's cellular phone, another red flash originates from behind the camera and is directed onto the back wall. Seconds later, it again flashes against the wall as Kahane makes his imaginary phone call. Eventually, red dominates the scene and is reflected by the shallow pool of water where Mill kills Kahane. As is often the case, the red underscores violence and the loss of blood and life.

Lighting

The Player is not a dark film. It begins in the outdoor morning light and concludes in sunny afternoon light. In between are some night scenes, though they are without deep atmospheric shadows; viewers can still see the subjects distinctly. As might be expected, the light is especially soft during the night scenes of romance between Mill and Gudmundsdottir at the desert resort. There are also numerous interior daytime scenes, many with light shadows from the open venetian blinds. All the daytime interiors are well and evenly illuminated. To accomplish a soft texture in the daytime interiors, cinematographer Jean Lepine used filters that create the feeling of naturally diffused light. Many filters are also used throughout the daytime shots to dampen the glare. The film's lighting supports the film's moods: mostly brightly lit day scenes that have minimal glare and some night scenes for murder, attempted assault with a serpentine weapon, romance, and sex.

The Camera

As is fitting for a satire, the camera is rarely positioned close to the subjects. When the subject is a talking individual, she or he is usually seen in a medium shot or a medium close-up. One exception is when viewers briefly see Mill's face in close-up as he holds Kahane's head under the puddle of water. Another notable exception is when Mill is with Detective Avery in the Pasadena police station. Avery is twirling a tampon and asking difficult questions; her assistant is stalking a fly and swatting it; and the three police personnel are laughing at Mill's desperate responses. Mill's bewildered, frightened reactions are seen in close-up and extreme close-up.

Lepine and Altman often use deep focus to capture group scenes that simultaneously portray the private interactions of famous people (without invading their conversations) and the "busyness" of the larger view. *The Player* also includes deep-focus shots during which the audience is made privy to activities and conversations in the foreground, middle ground, and background. Exemplary among them is a shot of Mill's breakfast meeting with Levison that begins with Burt Reynolds and film critic Charles Champlin at a table in the foreground, bicyclists in the middle ground, and Levison and Mill at a table in the background.

EDITING

The Player is a suspenseful, satirical film in which the main character confronts several problems simultaneously. The editing by Geraldine Peroni[1] unifies the elements of Mill's story and moves the story along at a pace that entertains audiences and keeps them involved.

Continuity Editing

Continuity editing is used throughout *The Player*. An example of effective continuity editing is six consecutive scenes in which Mill tracks down a writer, meets him, and kills him:

1. Tracking the writer—Mill looks through the office date books and at data on a computer, identifies Kahane as his stalker, and gets Kahane's address and phone number.

2. Calling Kahane's house—Mill parks near a house and talks with the woman inside the house on his cell phone while he stands outside.

3. At the Rialto movie theater—Mill sees the end of *The Bicycle Thief*.

4. Mill talks with Kahane in the theater lobby.

5. Karaoke bar—Mill and Kahane drink together and talk some more.

6. The murder—Mill and Kahane confront each other in a parking lot; Mill murders Kahane.

In this nearly sixteen-and-a-half-minute sequence, the film represents approximately two hours of story time. Each shot follows the preceding shot clearly; the characters' emotions and motives emerge; and the content and pace of the scenes are satisfying.

---

[1]Geraldine Peroni is listed as the editor in the film's opening credits, on the laser disc jacket, on the videotape box, and in various printed sources, but inexplicably the concluding credits list Maysie Hoy as editor.

Image on Image and Image after Image

The film includes no lap dissolves or superimpositions. The only transition between scenes other than cuts is a fade-out then the title card "One Year Later" then a fade-in.

Among the most noteworthy cuts is the shift from the murder scene to the next day's executive conference. The image of the murder scene remains on the screen. Viewers subtly become aware that the sound has changed (although the picture hasn't) as background conversation (softly at first) begins to occupy the sound track. Within seconds the discussion assumes a normal volume, and viewers find themselves at a conference in which Larry Levy earnestly proposes making movies without using writers. In other words, the film cuts from a studio executive's murder of a writer to an executive's proposal to eliminate writers from the filmmaking process.

Also expressive is the cut from the lovemaking scene to the mud bath. In the throes of passion Griffin Mill confesses his responsibility for David Kahane's death, but Gudmundsdottir does not want to hear such talk. There is a natural lack of clarity in this erotic exchange as the lovers are more concentrated on their physical arousal than on what is being said. Regardless of Gudmundsdottir's ardor, she has weighty considerations to make concerning the pursuit of an amorous relationship with a murderer. A murky element sullies their liaison. In fact, morally they are up to their necks. And that is what viewers see in the cut from the lovemaking scene to the mud bath scene. The lovers are immersed separately. They do not touch, and they make no eye contact. At this moment it is unclear whether their intimacy will survive.

At least two sets of reaction shots warrant discussion. The first concerns the scene in which Reggie Goldman, a banker's son, is trying to exercise his leverage in his pursuit of various attractive women actors. The scene includes seven reaction shots of the amused and knowing Joel Levison, Walter Stuckel, and Griffin Mill.

The second set of reaction shots occurs during the scene at the Pasadena police station where Mill has been summoned to review mug shots. Detective Avery nonchalantly unwraps a tampon and begins to twirl it while asking Mill whether he had gone out with Gudmundsdottir the night before. Avery wants to know how long Mill has known Gudmundsdottir and whether he has had sex with her. Mill becomes confused and incensed and says he won't answer that question without a lawyer present; then he contends in effect that his rights are being ignored. The camera cuts to Avery, who laughs in reaction to Mill's defensive behavior. Her laughter bubbles over as Detective DeLongpre joins in. Close-up and extreme close-up reaction shots of Mill accompanied by raucous background laughter complete the scene.

The film begins with the highly unusual situation of one shot presenting multiple scenes (see Table 3.1 on p. 129). Most of *The Player*'s scenes, as in most scenes in most movies, consist of multiple shots. Consider the scene in which Mill talks to Gudmundsdottir on his cellular phone. The scene runs

225 seconds and has 26 shots. This scene needs to be long enough to reveal something of Gudmundsdottir's character and allure and to make credible Mill's infatuation with her even though he is preoccupied with locating the threatening writer and dealing with him. The scene also needs to be visually varied and interesting. And it is. The moving subject (Mill) and the moving camera suggest Mill's restlessness and his curiosity about this luminous vision in the night; he wants to view her continually and from various distances and angles. Likewise Gudmundsdottir is usually in motion. It is not only the subjects' movements and the camera movement that inject vitality into the scene. The editing—as well as the varied camera distances and angles it makes possible—also contributes visual variety while excising uneventful time. Although the editing is not fast, its average shot length of 8.65 seconds is short enough to impart some energy to the scene.

Sometimes editing helps vary the pace within scenes. Consider the scene where Mill drives off from the St. James's Club,[2] receives a fax, uncovers a present on the floor of the Range Rover, and reacts to the snake. The first 45 seconds of the scene have an average shot length of 4.5 seconds. The last 54 seconds of the scene, after Mill discovers the rattler, have an even shorter average shot length of 2.7 seconds, with some shots lasting only a second or two. Given the danger to Mill (a crash, bites, or both), the fast cutting reinforces his panicky reaction after he uncovers the snake.

SOUND

Sound in *The Player* contributes to the varied moods. For example, in many scenes in which the characters display nervousness and tension, the music is jangling and edgy, not melodic. The few scenes featuring soothing music and relaxed conversation, such as when Mill and Gudmundsdottir dance at the desert hideaway, offer viewers (and Mill) a welcome break from the tension.

Vocals

Overlapping dialogue (a common experience in everyday life and in most Altman films) is used in group scenes to make some word and phrase recognition possible yet allow other snippets of language to function as ambient sound.

Each restaurant scene in *The Player* includes background din plus fragments of conversation that color the mood or drive the plot. The laser disc version of the film points out that for the scene of Larry Levy's first executive meeting, each actor wore a separately wired microphone that allowed the

---

[2]The spelling is as given on the postcard Mill receives while sitting poolside at the club and talking with the producer and British director.

sound editor to raise and/or lower the volume or shift the focus of dialogue interaction to replicate the flow of sound energy among participants in a high-level business meeting. Because the objective is so well achieved, viewers feel like participants in that meeting. The breakfast meeting scene between Levison and Mill shifts viewers' awareness from foreground to background by combining a zoom-in with a sound track that simultaneously fades out the foreground sound as it fades in the background sounds. The result is a smooth, unobtrusive redirection of viewers' attention.

A vocal is altered for effect when Griffin Mill cries out, "Keep it to yourself" during his rage that results in the murder, and the sound seems amplified by an echo chamber. It is loud enough to get the attention of anyone in the vicinity but does not; however, the distortion helps convey Mill's rage.

While film is not generally a medium in which vocals dominate, *The Player* involves a protagonist who is a professional listener in a busy but never loud environment. Thus, it is appropriate that conversations dominate and surround him.

Music

As in many movies, the sound track consists of previously recorded music and music composed specifically for the film, in this case by Thomas Newman. A major musical theme by Newman is introduced in the opening shot; it does not have a recognizable melody but is strongly rhythmical. What it does have is a certain feeling, busy and visceral at the same time yet light, shimmering, and chiming. As in most movies, including *The Player*, whenever dialogue is important the music fades out to make room for it.

When Mill seats himself by the outdoor pool of the St. James's Club, the music includes a jazzy saxophone reminiscent of film noir. Background sirens and the sounds of a flying helicopter are blended in to enhance the "big city at night" feeling of the music. As Mill is driving home from the St. James's Club and discovers that a rattlesnake has been planted in his car, the music understandably becomes chaotic. It has an accelerated rhythm when Mill uncovers the snake; then it is dominated by loud, rapid bongo drums, horns, and a recurrent sibilant rattling sound.

Music is also a vital component of the lovemaking scene. Visually, there is simply the incontrovertible suggestion of sexual intercourse created by the screen filled with two glistening heads arranged horizontally and facing each other, kissing, moaning, breathing heavily, and speaking intimately. The music takes on complex rhythms while combining rapid chimes, a bongo drum, a snare drum, and various electronic sounds that together enhance the eroticism, simulate orgasm, then fade out. The music helps make the scene erotic.

In *The Player* the music underpins, focuses, and ties together the various film ingredients. Its power is achieved through its versatility—its capacity to include a large number of complementary sounds—and its immediately recognizable feel rather than identifiable melodies.

Sound Effects and Silence

Sound effects are limited in *The Player* because vocals and music play prominent roles and the film does not showcase violence, sexuality, or action (traditional subjects requiring extensive sound effects). Where sound effects are used—as with the faint, distant offscreen barking dog after Kahane's murder—their presence melds so effectively with what is being shown that viewers are unlikely to notice them.

Silence is used briefly after David Kahane is murdered to emphasize that he is dead. Other than that there are conventional split-second slivers of silence to differentiate scenes. Skillful sound editing allows these brief silences to be used as a subtle form of punctuation. Otherwise the silences might become awkward transitions inadvertently left unfilled.

In some scenes, two major types of sound help establish the setting. For example, as Mill arrives at the Pasadena police station, both dialogue and sound effects reveal the strident setting. Two suspects being hauled toward a hallway scream defiantly at the arresting officers as telephones ring and a siren wails.

Transitions

Music is used to connect scenes, as between the end of the opening shot and the next scene, in Mill's secretary's office. Music is used again to connect the ending of that scene to the beginning of the following scene, where Mill and his secretary are outside walking and talking.

Vocals, conversations particularly, are also used to ease the transitions between scenes. An intriguing vocal transition occurs immediately after Mill leaves Kahane for dead. The camera focuses on the murder scene, which is momentarily silent, but viewers' attention is soon diverted by a conversation that gradually assumes a background presence. Briefly, viewers' curiosity is in two places at once: the red pool of water where the body lies and the conversation that is slowly fading in.

SOURCES FOR FICTIONAL FILMS

Michael Tolkin's novel *The Player* was first published in 1988. Tolkin also wrote the screen adaptation and acted the part of one of the two Schecter brothers, writers who are with Mill when Bonnie Sherow comes to his office to ask him if he is involved with someone new.

Novel and Film

In characters and plot, the novel and film have much in common. Both focus on a young Hollywood studio executive, Griffin Mill, who is worried about being displaced by a recent hire and plagued by an anonymous postcard writer. In both, Mill is romantically involved with Bonnie Sherow. In both novel and film, Mill seeks out a writer he thinks is the postcard sender, finds him at a screening of *The Bicycle Thief*, and has drinks with him. Later in a moment of rage Mill kills him and later attends his funeral. Although the names are different, the writer's girlfriend quickly becomes Mill's love interest. In both novel and film, Mill is a suspect, of the studio head of security and the Pasadena police, and in both novel and film he gets away with murder.

One of the most striking differences between the novel and the film is that the novel is driven by Griffin Mill's interior monologues and the film by dialogue and action. Readers have direct and frequent access to Mill's thoughts and feelings. In the opening chapter, for example, in the passage that is analogous to the movie's opening shot, Mill thinks about how much he loves being on the studio lot and how he'll miss this job if he should lose it:

> There would be other work, other studios, but the glow around him was probably lost, and he would never be head of production, not for a major studio, not for this studio or Universal or Disney or Columbia or Paramount or 20th-Century Fox. These were the last studios with property, with soundstages and back lots, where you could point to a building and say, "That was Alan Ladd's dressing room" or "Over there we made *Bringing Up Baby*.". . . Orion and Tri-Star, big companies, were in office buildings, what difference did it make where they were? It just mattered to him, and he couldn't resist the gloom that soon he would have to give up a real studio with a real gate, trade in a parking space with his name painted on a concrete bumper for a pass to an underground garage. He wanted to say, how can you make a movie in an office building? (4–5)

And unlike the novel, the film surrounds the main character with a large, varied group: "Tolkin's novel was chilly, spare and lean: It zeroed right into Griffith's skull. Altman, predictably, has enriched the milieu and built up a huge community around the cipher at the center" (Wilmington 23).

In the book Mill is preoccupied with events that led up to the murder; he works much harder to construct and justify his alibi; and he finds himself musing about the nature of his guilt if he never gets caught. In the novel Mill also details observations about the complex and unstable world of the movie industry. Since the film presents the characters' personalities through action and dialogue, we never see Mill ruminate in the film. Consequently, the celluloid Griffin Mill is less reflective than the conjecture-obsessed creation in the book.

In the novel, Bonnie Sherow works for a different studio and is less prominent than in the film. According to Tolkin, in the novel the Bonnie Sherow character is a bit of a buffoon. But because Cynthia Stevenson is a charming, skilled actor, the filmmakers created the film Sherow in a much more sympathetic light. This is an example of casting influencing characterization, a situation not uncommon in Altman films, which tend to be more collaborative and improvisatory in their making than most films.

Script and Film

The differences between the script and the film are similar to the differences between the novel and the film. In general, the film turned out to be more biting and satirical, and less emotional, than the script and certainly than the novel. For example, at Kahane's funeral the script calls for Kahane's brother to deliver the eulogy:

> 54 INT. CHAPEL—DAY
>
> *We hear Kahane's brother over a p.a. system. Mill takes a black yarmulke from a basket and puts it on.*
>
> BROTHER: Einstein said that God doesn't play dice. I'd like to say that we could console ourselves with the thought that in God's plan, David Kahane's death is necessary for the universe to unfold its majestic design . . .
>
> *He [Mill] opens the door to the chapel.*
>
> 55 INT. CHAPEL—DAY
>
> *The coffin. About thirty mourners. The brother, 25, continues.*
>
> BROTHER: . . . but I can't say that, because David always laughed at mindless faith. Someone in the night killed him, and that person will have to bear his guilt, and he'll never know what he took from David's friends and family.
>
> *Griffin takes a seat in the back row. A few people in the front row turn to see who has come in. June looks at Griffin. She says something to the man sitting next to her, who turns around to see the last man who saw Kahane alive.*
>
> BROTHER: My brother died after seeing a movie, which I guess is sort of fitting. I hope you don't take this the wrong way, but he really loved movies, and I'm glad he didn't die on his way in, you know, before he saw it. That would have hurt me a lot more and this hurts a lot.
>
> *The pressure is too much for Griffin. He goes outside. We hear the Kaddish from inside.*
>
> 56 EXT. HILLSIDE MEMORIAL—DAY
>
> *Mourners shovel earth onto the casket in the open grave. Finished. People walk away.*
> (Tolkin script 44)

In the film a fellow writer delivers Kahane's eulogy:

> The Hollywood system did not murder David Kahane. Not the ninety-eight-million-dollar movie, not the twelve-million-dollar actor, not even the million-dollar deal that David Kahane never landed. No, the most that we can pin on Hollywood is assault with intent to kill because society is responsible for this particular murder. And it is to society that we must look if we are to have any justice for that crime. Because someone in the night killed David Kahane and

that person will have to bear the guilt. And, if David were here right now, I know in my heart that he would have said, "Cut the shit, Phil. What did you learn from all of this? Did you learn anything from this?" I'd say, "Yeah, David, I've learned a lot. We here will, uh, take it from here and the next time we sell a script for a million dollars, the next time we nail some shit-bag producer to the wall we'll say 'That's another one for David Kahane.'"... David was working on something the day he died. I'd like to share it with you. "Blackness. A mangy dog barks. Garbage can lids are lifted as derelicts in the street hunt for food, buzzing as a cheap alarm clock goes off. INT—FLOP HOUSE ROOM— EARLY MORNING. A tracking shot moves through the grimy room. Light streams in through holes in the yellowing window shades. Moths dance in the beams of light. Track down along the floor. The frayed rug. Stop on an old shoe. It's empty." It's as far as he got. That's the last thing he wrote. So long Dave. Fade-out. Thank you.

In the script, the funeral is Jewish, and the eulogy is given by a grieving member of Kahane's family. In the film, the funeral is secular; the eulogy is given by an angry fellow writer; and there is no sign of Kahane's family. In the script, the eulogy and the mourners at the open grave show the devastating impact Kahane's death has had on his family. In the film, the eulogy is more about anger than grief.

The film's eulogy is longer than the one in the script and is supplemented by visual information. Thus, viewers can allow the droning speech to become background noise because they sense the visual information is more important. During the speech, viewers see Griffin Mill arrive silently in his black Range Rover; he approaches the gathering gingerly; he stands differentiated by his clothing (an expensive suit). June Gudmundsdottir, dressed in white, glances back to him. We also see Detective DeLongpre (who has not yet been identified) approach the mourners and stand at the other side of a broad monument next to a tree. Up to this point the audience has been teased with this character. He is curious-looking, suspicious perhaps, and we viewers are wondering whether he is the postcard writer.

The scene illustrates the point that typically films are more expressive visually than is indicated by the script. This combination of sounds and moving images is unique to the film and video media, and the differences between the script and the film allow us to see and hear how the filmmakers have capitalized on this distinctive capability.

Other Films

Films are called intertextual when they evoke or use other films and other forms of human expression. And *The Player* does this throughout. It is, after all, a movie whose main subjects are moviemakers and making movies. Intertextuality in *The Player* runs from the lengthy opening shot and its inclusion of discussions of lengthy shots in other films to the screening of *Habeas Corpus*, a parody of popular movies with serious subjects but distracting stars and last-minute rescues. In between, there are all those movie posters on the walls of Mill's and Levison's offices; the sixty-five cameos, most by famous movie actors but including the film's scriptwriter; the clips from the ending of *The Bicycle Thief*; and all the talk about other films and other filmmakers. *The Player* draws on a wealth of detail not merely from a novel and script but also from other films and a long tradition of moviemaking.

TYPES OF FICTIONAL FILMS

The Player is both classical Hollywood cinema and independent film. It has enough qualities of the former, such as some famous performers and a happy ending, to make it commercially successful and enough of the latter, such as satire of an untraditional subject, to win laudatory reviews and various awards and nominations including Cannes Film Festival awards, National Society of Film Critics' best film award, Independent Spirit award for best film, Golden Globe awards and nominations, British Academy Award nominations, and Academy Award nominations.

Classical Hollywood Cinema

The Player exemplifies all the major features of classical Hollywood cinema: the story is set entirely in a present, external world and is largely seen from outside the action, although point-of-view shots are sometimes included. *The Player* focuses on a character that has an initial goal: to survive in his position of wealth and power. In trying to attain his goal, Griffin Mill confronts two major problems: the anonymous threatening writer and an executive perhaps being groomed for Mill's job. Early in the film Mill develops a second goal: to win June Gudmundsdottir. The film has closure: the plot has no "loose ends" or unresolved issues, other than the identity of the threatening writer. Mill reaches his goals: he gets free of the two threats to his success, gets away with murder, gets promoted, and settles down with the beautiful artist. Like so many popular Hollywood movies, *The Player* shows a male succeeding both professionally and personally. By the end of the film, what happens and why are unambiguous. Finally, the film uses continuity editing and, except for the opening shot, largely unobtrusive filmmaking techniques.

Although *The Player* has a strong mystery component to it and the VHS videotape box categorizes it as a "thriller," it is not an example of the mystery genre: for one thing, much of the story is not devoted to the mystery of who is threatening Mill. The possible Levy threat and Mill's romances with Sherow and Gudmundsdottir also take up much of the plot.

American Independent Film

The Player also exhibits characteristics of the American independent film. Besides a lower budget than typical Hollywood products and freedom from studio creative control, *The Player* has other earmarks of an independent film. Its content has limited appeal, not because it is particularly controversial, but because it requires a certain level of awareness of the film industry; more essentially, *The Player* is a complex and subtle satire that rewards attentive viewing. Finally, its plot is by no means formulaic. The story is surprising and unpredictable.

The movies made by the studio that Mill works for are classical Hollywood cinema of the most commercial stripe. As he explains to Gudmundsdottir, the films his studio makes need "suspense, laughter, violence, hope, heart, nudity, sex, happy endings . . . mainly happy endings." As initially proposed, *Habeas Corpus,* the movie within the movie, is to become an independent film: no stars, mostly true-to-life events, issues outside the mainstream, and a credible unhappy ending. As made by Mill's studio, *Habeas Corpus* is an exaggerated example of crowd-pleasing classical Hollywood cinema, with stars, improbable action, and a happy ending.

CHARACTERISTICS OF FICTIONAL FILMS

As with all narrative films, *The Player* consists of selected and structured events presented over time.

Structure

The Player has two parts: five or six days of selected events; then, one year later, selected events from the day of the screening of the studio's latest offering, *Habeas Corpus.* The two parts are bridged by a title card informing viewers that the following action occurs one year later.

In the first and far more time-consuming part, viewers meet Griffin Mill and learn of his twin problems (the anonymous threatening writer and that rumor that Levy is being groomed for Mill's job) and of his goals (retaining power at work and winning the love of a beautiful artist). To eliminate the first source of anxiety, Mill seeks out his menacing, elusive stalker and ends up killing the person he suspects. Thus, an action designed to help Mill eliminate one of his two major problems thrusts him into an arena where he lacks knowledge or leverage. A misstep or bad luck will unravel his career and plunge him into a legal abyss. He survives his brush with the law only by luck. At about this time, the Levy problem is also solved. Mill is not ousted from the studio; the studio head is. Interwoven with Mill's studio-related problems are scenes of his love life, first with Sherow, for whom he displays no ardor, then with Gudmundsdottir.

By a year later, Mill has assumed the helm of the studio; *Habeas Corpus* has been reworked beyond recognition; the former rival has become an ally; and Mill resumes his life at an even greater degree of prosperity than before. The story ends with Mill approving a story pitch that describes the movie we've just seen. The story promises to be circular.

Time

The story of *The Player* is conveyed chronologically. There are no flashbacks or flashforwards. The first part of the story—from the introduction of Mill and his problems and goals to his winning of Gudmundsdottir and getting away with murder—transpires over five or six days. As in most other films, *The Player* is usually vague about how much time elapses between scenes. If one notes when day scenes give way to night scenes, the first part of the story consumes at least five and a half days. The overall story time is approximately one week plus one year; the film's running time is 124 minutes. As usual in fictional films, the events of *The Player* are highly selective. There is nothing unconventional or even challenging about the film's handling of structure and time, except for the final twist that the anonymous writer's proposed story is the one viewers have just seen.

UNDERSTANDING FILMS THROUGH CONTEXTS

Any work of art is a product of its time and culture. Viewers who know some contexts of *The Player* can understand the film more completely than those who know only the film.

Society and Politics

Historically, the West Coast—Los Angeles specifically—fought for recognition amid aspersions that it was "sleepy," too much a part of the West to be considered a challenge to the East's position as the bastion of intellectual, financial, and social validity. The values that emerged and eventually grew to define Los Angeles are directly related to the emergence and eventual ascension to power of the movie industry. The word *movie* itself depends on the word *image* for its definition. The irony that image is everything and that Los Angeles has little to define itself other than its image is not lost on Angelenos. In fact, there is an air of pride rather than apology surrounding the statement. After all, it is a very large image.

That background lays the foundation for the bravura required to make a film about filmmaking and L.A. *The Player* is L.A. on L.A. Unfiltered water is to be avoided, even though Los Angeles water has long been rated among the best-tasting and safest of all large American cities. Business contacts can be generated at AA meetings; Range Rovers can be equipped with faxes. Success requires that people recognize one another but remain unencumbered by relationships or obligations. These elements help create a pastiche of Los Angeles in the late 1980s and early 1990s.

One side comment: Pasadena, home of the annual Tournament of Roses, has without contest proudly maintained an image of restraint and conservatism. It is doubtful that a character like Detective Avery (played by Whoopi Goldberg) would ever make the roster of the Pasadena police force. Her tampon-twirling distraction is outside the realm of probability for the Pasadena police department. So is her later question "Where the fuck is your mother buried?" to the eyewitness who had sworn on her mother's grave that she had identified the correct suspect in the lineup.

Censorship

The Player was made free of Hollywood studio control; thus the director, writer, and actors enjoyed a wide range of freedom to present the material as they saw fit, including broadly satirizing Hollywood studio filmmaking. The film is rated R—presumably for its partial nudity, a sex scene of heavy breathing and two sweaty, writhing heads, vulgar language, and one scene of murderous violence; the rating also allowed its makers to roam a broad field. Because of one brief scene of partial male frontal nudity, a slightly censored version of the film was shown on cable TV. But the film does not attract audiences because of its sex and violence. In truth, there is little. Its concerns and appeal lie elsewhere—with Hollywood-style deal making and people who make movies.

Artistic Conventions

The Player follows certain conventions. For instance, everyone, from principal characters to studio security to gate attendants, is attractive. Some Angelenos would argue that that is true to life. It is, however, more an adherence to what viewers expect in movies than what is true of the gene pool in Los Angeles. All the "players" are white male. Women are portrayed as competent, coming into their own in a tough, competitive atmosphere, but they are clearly not "players," and the most sympathetic of them gets fired and loses her footing. (That is not only adherence to film convention; it is part of the actual milieu which must be honored if the story is to be accepted.) The trophy woman is a sylph-like beauty dressed in white whose radiance allows her to stand out even among the Beautiful People.

Financial Constraints

By 1991, director Robert Altman had had a relatively successful track record both at the box office and in the reviewers' columns, but in the years before he made *The Player* he had not had a popular or critical success. He also had (and has) the reputation of being a maverick. With its satiric story of Hollywood studio moviemaking, lack of big stars in big roles, and a low quotient of sex and violence, *The Player* had virtually no chance of attracting big audiences. So how did the film get funding? Keeping the satire amusing and good-natured, not vicious, probably helped. Although the concluding credits list a stunt coordinator, special effects, and set medic, the film has no costly special effects and dangerous action scenes, such as a car crash described in the source novel. Certainly, the relatively modest budget of approximately eight million dollars and the willingness of many actors, some of them stars, to be involved in an Altman film at minimal rates also helped make possible the funding and making of the film.

VIEWER AND FILM

The Player has multiple and unexpected story developments and many possible meanings. In this section only a few examples will be pointed out, but other examples are sure to occur to anyone who has seen the film and thought about it.

Expectations and Interactions

Early in *The Player*, viewers read the title card "A Robert Altman Film." Those who have seen other Altman films—such as *M*A*S*H* (1970), *McCabe and Mrs. Miller* (1971), *The Long Goodbye* (1973), *Nashville* (1975), *Short Cuts* (1993), and *Ready to Wear* (1994)—will immediately have certain expectations: satire; insight; complexity in characterizations, plot, and meanings; daring; and a potential for a viewing experience that will linger after leaving the theater.

A film entitled *The Player* may stimulate a viewer's curiosity to see which interpretations of the word will be explored. By denotation, *player* has at least seven meanings about different types of people, including a person who engages in illegal activity. By connotation, the word can evoke shades of artifice, sleight of hand, and imposture. It may also suggest an elevated level of skill and competition.

In the opening shot, viewers discover immediately that they must process visual and verbal information at a demanding pace. We are going to get an insider's simultaneous, multichanneled view of Hollywood filmmakers at work. By reputation we know it to be a treacherous, illusory environment set in luxurious surroundings. The film does not fail us. It is particularly seductive in the way documentaries that recount perilous adventures are: we know we will come out of the experience informed, provoked, vicariously thrilled, and unscathed. By the film's conclusion we understand that Griffin Mill is a player. Larry Levy is a player. Bonnie Sherow is not. Levison was a player—then suddenly and inexplicably was not. The director of *Habeas Corpus* has been converted into one. *The Player* plays on our minds. We are encouraged to interact with it from the point we first encounter the title card "A Robert Altman Film" to the film's final credits and later upon reflection or subsequent re-viewings of the film.

Types of Meanings

There are virtually no explicit statements regarding meaning in *The Player*. In fact, fictional films generally invite viewers to construct their own fabula for nonchronological stories, character attributes and motivations, and meanings. Otherwise, it would be like playing cards with all hands dealt face up.

The Player's portrayal of film industry personnel affirms the industry's reputation: Hollywood engenders an absence of constancy in human relationships. The film suggests only one lasting alliance and that one (between Griffin Mill and June Gudmundsdottir) has the potential for survival only because one of them is completely and contentedly uninvolved in the movie industry.

The film exposes the low esteem in which writers are held. We see this when Larry Levy proposes doing away with writers (expensive and unnecessary appendages) and suggests that the executives can create their own story lines from things as mundane as current newspaper articles. Levy's next idea is to advocate production of *Habeas Corpus*, complete with unknown actors and unhappy ending. As pitched, starting from the title down, it is hard to imagine a less promising story for a commercial film. So after these two false starts, what is Levy's fate? Evidently when Mill assumes control of the studio, Levy gets promoted to Mill's old job. The continuity of mediocre product is assured.

When Bonnie Sherow cries at the end of the film, she violates a cardinal principle of the filmmaking industry: at work, emotional responses are a drawback. Mill refuses to see Sherow and observes icily that she "will land on her feet" as she succumbs to tears, but unless Sherow reinvents herself, it is unlikely she will return to the game. In contrast to Sherow's emotions, recall Mill's largely nonplussed demeanor when Walter Stuckel questions him regarding Kahane's death. Recall Mill's controlled response to each postcard. At one point he dismisses his secretary's suggestion that they involve security to help track down the postcard writer. Mill knows his concern must be muted if he is to remain a player.

The film is wide-ranging in its satiric targets. Writers may be satirized for being so desperate and for wavering when they sense Mill's reluctance. Directors are satirized for selling out the integrity of a story for the sake of money. Studio executives are the most satirized of all. Levy goes to AA meetings, not because he has a drinking problem but because "that's where all the deals are being made these days." Studio executives are shown as concerned only with making a profit. They want to kill writers—literally and symbolically—and get away with it. Of course, the product of all these studio personnel—the studio movie—is parodied and satirized by the distracting presence of stars and the preposterous happy ending of *Habeas Corpus*.

Cinematic techniques that influence meaning include the frequent highly mobile camera and a zoom lens that explore a strange and fascinating world. By moving the camera forward or zooming in, the filmmakers often bring viewers closer to the subjects during a shot. The film also relies heavily on eye-level camera placements; viewers get to see players at an interactive level. Here, as in other films, the filmmakers play to the belief that viewers have a right both to explore the world of people who wield enormous power and to be on an equal footing with them.

The symbolism of the movie posters and cars was discussed under mise en scène. Yet another symbol is the main character's name: Griffin Mill. Hollywood is a griffin mill: a manufacturer of fabled creations. The product includes any number of chimerical masterpieces. But it likewise includes monstrosities. *Mill* has additional relevant meanings, including an institution or business that makes a profit by turning out product without regard to quality, as in "diploma mill," a school that turns out graduates without regard to standards.

Sometimes the expressive aspects of the settings—such as the movie posters—are seen only fleetingly. Another example of subtlety is a book glimpsed in Mill's secretary's desk as Mill begins his search for leads about the threatening writer. For less than a second, viewers have a chance to make out the title of a book, *They Made Me a Criminal*, which is also the title of a 1939 movie. In the Criterion laser disc version of *The Player*, Tolkin says that the actor who plays the eulogizer at Kahane's funeral was used for the telephone voice of the blackmailing writer near the end of the film. Both characters use the phrase "some shit-bag producer." If the two voices belong to the same character, that detail is too subtle for nearly all viewers: the two speeches are brief, far apart, and the second is a telephone voice. Occasionally, though, significant details are not so much glimpsed as thrust into the viewers' faces, as when the camera zooms in on a movie poster or a photograph of the cinematic master of mystery, murder, and suspense, director Alfred Hitchcock.

Critical Approaches

Although *The Player* adheres to the basics of its source novel and screenplay, the film is exemplary of Robert Altman's film work and would be a good candidate for the auteurist approach. Like many Altman films, *The Player* relies heavily on satire without ever becoming venomous, and it is sometimes improvisatory and sprawling in terms of characters and plot. A Marxist critic could point out how *The Player* shows that those in power exploit their workers and that the capitalist producers of images that support the status quo are themselves selfish and self-serving as they busily perpetuate stories of individuality and romance, not stories of collective group efforts for the good of society. A feminist critic could point out how Gudmundsdottir is constructed by males (writer and director), has no credible emotional core, and exists only to be beautiful, alluring, and available to the hero. A feminist reading might also point out how complex and sympathetic Sherow is. Furthermore, a feminist interpretation could point out how the film within the film, *Habeas Corpus*, is typical Hollywood fare created by men and featuring the trite and condescending patriarchal story of a male rescuing an imperiled female.

As with all films, the meanings seen depend in part on the viewer and his or her critical framework(s) for interpreting creative works.

WORKS CITED

The Player. Screenplay by Michael Tolkin. Dir. Robert Altman. Fine Line Features, 1992. (The film's end credits are reprinted on pp. 555–61.)

Tolkin, Michael. *The Player: A Novel*. New York: Atlantic Monthly, 1988.

———. *The Player*. Script, 20 Apr. 1989, first draft. Hollywood: Script City, [1993?]. Photocopy. 124 leaves.

Wilmington, Michael. "Movies; On Location; The Rules of His Game; 'The Player' Marks Altman's Return to Hollywood." *Los Angeles Times* 29 Sept. 1991, home ed., Calendar: 23+.

FOR VIEWING, LISTENING, AND READING

VHS VIDEOTAPE
The Player. New Line Home Video, 1993. 75833. Not in letterbox. Followed by a brief interview with Robert Altman and "never before seen footage."

DVD
The Player. New Line Home Video. 1993. Wide-screen only, 16:9 aspect ratio = 1.777:1. Dolby digital sound. In English or French. Includes trailer, brief cast biographies, director's and writer's commentary, deleted scenes, cameo menu, a seventeen-minute "featurette" on Altman, and scene access. The deleted scenes and trailer are the same as found on the Criterion laser disc, but all the other supplementary material is different.

LASER DISC
The Player. Criterion Collection, 1993. CLV. 2 discs. Catalog: CC1318. Wide-screen. Audio commentary by Robert Altman, Michael Tolkin, and Jean Lepine; video inter-

views with Altman, Tolkin, Lepine, Tim Robbins, Greta Scacchi, and Whoopi Goldberg; interviews with twenty Hollywood screenwriters about their experiences with the film industry; six deleted scenes; "map of the stars" charting the film's sixty-five cameo appearances; annotated photo history of films about Hollywood; and American and Japanese trailers and TV spots.

CD

The Player. Original motion picture sound track. Music by Thomas Newman. Varése Sarabande Digital, [1993?]. VSD-5366. Almost 36 minutes; 19 tracks, not in the order they appear in the film. Instrumentation: piano, electronics, alto saxophone, prepared guitar, winds, percussion, drums, and upright bass.

SCRIPT

Tolkin, Michael. *The Player*. First draft, [date uncertain]. Photocopy. 141 leaves.
———. *The Player, The Rapture, The New Age: Three Screenplays*. New York: Grove, 1995.

REVIEWS AND OTHER ARTICLES

Canby, Vincent. "Inside Hollywood: 'The Player' Tells an Impious Story." *New York Times* 10 Apr. 1992, natl. ed.: B1+. Review.
Film Review Annual 1993. Ed. Jerome S. Ozer. Englewood, NJ: Ozer, 1993. Cast and credits. Reprints thirteen complete reviews, including from *Sight and Sound*, *Film Quarterly*, *Cineaste*, *Village Voice*, *Los Angeles Times*, and *New York*. Citations for eight additional reviews.
"Hollywood's Thirst for Water." *New York Times* 4 May 1992, natl. ed.: B2. A brief article on the eleven brands of bottled water Mill orders in the course of *The Player*.
Rafferty, Terrence. "Killer." *New Yorker* 20 Apr. 1992: 81–82. Review.
Tolkin, Michael. "A Response to 'T. J. Marlowe.'" *The Journal* [of the Writers Guild of America, West] July 1992: 24–25. An informative rebuttal to an article in a previous issue criticizing *The Player*.
Weinraub, Bernard. "Writer of 'The Player' Still Isn't One." *New York Times* 13 May 1992, natl. ed.: B1+. An article about Michael Tolkin; includes photo of him.
Wilmington, Michael. "Laughing and Killing." *Sight and Sound* June 1992: 10–15. Analysis of *The Player*.

CD-ROM   Various CD-ROM's contain information about *The Player*, including Microsoft's *Cinemania*, which includes very brief reviews, a brief plot outline, Academy Award nominations, cast list, credit list, and a photograph and caption.

WEB SITES   Countless Web sites include information and opinion about *The Player*, and many sites have links to other sites. The following are two especially informative sites and the address for the Bedford/St. Martin's Web site, which has many useful links for readers of this book.

The Internet Movie Database: <http://www.imdb.com>. Choose "search."

Movie Review Query Engine at Telerama: <http://www.cinema.pgh.pa.us/movie/reviews>.

Many links to other useful sources on films and the film medium are accessible through <http://www.bedfordstmartins.com/phillips-film>.

APPENDICES

Studying Films: Reading, Thinking, Researching, and Writing

WRITING ABOUT FILMS

> No one ever has been able to give the exact measure of his needs, his concepts, or his sorrows. The human tongue is like a cracked cauldron on which we beat out tunes to set a bear dancing when we would make the stars weep with our melodies. (Flaubert 138)

To try to capture in speech the richness and nuances of human experience can be frustrating. It is no easy task to capture them in writing, either, but writing can bring us closer to that goal than speech can. For understanding and communicating about something as complicated as our experiences of film, writing is indispensable.

Nearly everyone knows about the agony of committing words to paper. After all, the writer's job is to create clear and convincing prose that can be read without interruption, rereading, or puzzlement, often by a stranger, someone who knows nothing about the writer. It is no wonder good writing requires much thinking and concentration and tends to be time-consuming.

Prewriting

Nearly all successful writers divide their work into steps because they know that most writing is too complicated to do well in one sitting or even two. And most writers find they work most efficiently if they don't work too long in a session and alternate periods of work with rest. They also know there's little time to do so the last few days before an assignment is due.

For convenience, I have divided writing into three major parts: prewriting, writing (the first complete draft), and rewriting. I say *for convenience*, because writing is rarely a 1–2–3 process. It defies formulas and predictions. For example, some writers may organize their main points (prewrite), write a first draft, then realize the structure is wrong, reorganize their outline, and redo the draft before moving on to rewriting. Other writers develop an effective structure for their writing by writing draft after draft (no prewriting but it's usually a time-consuming way to discover a useful structure).

Dividing your work into manageable steps and using the strategies explained here will help improve your chances of writing well but do not guarantee it. Also needed are extensive practice in writing (and reading) and much work and persistence in what you now write.

A few people can write well by composing and rewriting one page or paragraph or sentence at a laborious time (they are sometimes called "bleeders"). Probably fewer still compose and revise in their heads, then write and revise slightly. If one of those two approaches works for you, fine, but they probably won't and you will find it useful to divide and conquer your work.

Here is one of my favorite ways of getting some of my responses to a film into writing. As I view the film, I write a few notes. After the viewing, I sometimes write a brief description and always write observations (analysis). Next I reread and revise what I have written so far then the next day rewrite my notes and select the main points and arrange them in a brief outline.

These are the stages I sometimes go through before I write a first draft. Yes, they take time, but they also help me gather my thoughts and arrange them. I'm not saying the first draft is then easy for me. Often it is not. But because of the prewriting, the first draft is always less difficult.

Before you write the first draft, consider the following questions:

- Who is my audience or reader(s)?

- What needs to be explained?

- What does *not* need to be explained?

- How do I want my readers to react to what I write?

Then try one or more of these steps:

- Write and rewrite a thesis statement: a sentence or a few concise sentences that summarize the main and unifying idea of the essay and, ideally, explain the major parts and their arrangement.

- Make an outline.

- Write a "discovery" draft.

THESIS STATEMENT   A thesis statement early in an essay—often at the end of the first paragraph or the beginning of the second—helps both writer and readers. The following thesis statement, for example, reveals the purpose and organization of the essay it helps introduce:

However, despite its reputation for faithfulness, a careful analysis reveals that the film [*The Dead*] is unlike Joyce's novella in three major ways. First, the adaptation expands the scope of the original narrative by adding new scenes. Second, the adaptation deletes important contextual elements from its literary source. Finally, the adaptation modifies significant dramatic elements in the literary source.

Occasionally you can formulate a thesis statement before making an outline or writing a first draft. Sometimes the thesis statement is so well thought out and detailed that you can write a first draft without first making an outline. Often, however, the thesis emerges more clearly as you work on an outline or first or second draft. It usually takes time to figure out what you are trying to say, and often you may start out to make a point and end up saying something else. For the essay to be unified and forceful, though, the thesis statement must eventually step forward and introduce itself or be implied in the introduction and explained in the essay itself. Unlike professional writers, few students can create a focused, clear, and persuasive essay without stating the thesis; without it, readers tend to get lost in a forest of words before emerging from page 2.

OUTLINE   Outlines are useful for most writers most of the time, especially in writing long essays and books or in writing about a new subject, but some successful writers never use them. Instead they think out the major points and their arrangement, jot notes, or write draft after draft. Sometimes a short outline, however, leads to a more detailed one that is a partial first draft.

DISCOVERY DRAFT   Some writers start to organize their material by rapidly writing a draft. Then they look at what they have written and perhaps underline the useful parts, perhaps rearrange its major points. Sometimes they toss out that draft and immediately write another one. For some writers it's a way to get something on paper and to start to discover what they have to say.

In outlines and early drafts, leave wide margins on all four sides of the lines and double-space. Leave room to improve.

Writing

While writing the first draft, most writers find it best to focus on organization (what are the major parts and in what order should they be arranged?) and on examples (how can I illustrate my points to those who may misunderstand or disagree?). While writing the first draft, don't allow yourself to become sidetracked by spelling, punctuation, even sentence structure. Like a sculptor, first rough out the paragraphs; later, do the finishing work on the sentences and words. For most people, fussing over a spelling or a word, or pausing to check a punctuation mark, or looking up a word or passage—any of those halt their momentum and perhaps cause "writer's block," the inability to write anything.

In the first draft, try to see that your main points are arranged in a significant order and that they are explained and illustrated. Do not, as many poor writers do, try to rewrite while you write the first draft. Studies of writers show that few can write *and* rewrite well at the same time.

Rewriting and Rewriting: Some Strategies

"I never write five words but I correct seven." —Attributed to Dorothy Parker

"There are days when the result is so bad that no fewer than five revisions are required. In contrast, when I'm greatly inspired, only four revisions are needed."   —John Kenneth Galbraith

As you rewrite and rewrite, remember three indispensable guidelines:

Studies show that few readers will remember—let alone be impressed by— more than five major points in a speech or essay.

Your goal should be to communicate—not impress. Writers who try to impress their readers often stumble and look silly, waste their readers' time, and puzzle them. Consider, for example, this sentence: "Another major meaning of Orson Welles's film *Citizen Kane* is that Charles Foster Kane has an abiding and persistent hunger to be loved by others" (twenty-five words). The writer misuses one word (*abiding*) and tries too hard to impress, with wordiness, passive voice, and formal words. In contrast, the writer of the following sentence, one of my former students, was more concerned with communicating: "The third trait to note about Kane is his need for love" (twelve words). That sentence is shorter, takes less time to read, and is easy to understand, yet it says much the same as its longer counterpart; indeed, this second sentence is more specific: it indicates that the *third* point is next.

Closely related to the second guideline is the third: *If you focus on only one major point in each paragraph and explain it fully, with detailed examples, you will be understood, probably even appreciated.* If you jump from generalization to unrelated generalization, especially within the same paragraph, you will not be understood by your unfortunate readers. As Samuel Johnson wrote, "What is written without effort is in general read without pleasure."

SOME REWRITING TECHNIQUES   Because it is difficult to spot errors in what *we* write (we are better at spotting errors in what *others* write), we writers need to reread our drafts often and in different ways. Unfortunately, many writers, especially inexperienced ones, reread their drafts once—maybe twice if they want to be thorough!—and they seldom spot what to improve, so they make only a few minor changes, such as in spelling and the use of commas. One or more of the following strategies may help writers see clearly what they have written so that they can rewrite and improve it.

1. After you finish the first or second draft, see if each paragraph explains one important point. Choose a paragraph at random, and read it at least twice; underline the topic sentence or main point. (You may want to use a felt-tip pen so you can quickly spot each topic sentence later.) If a topic sentence is vague or misleading, rewrite it so it accurately explains the main point of the paragraph. If the main point of the paragraph is not stated or clearly implied, write a topic sentence. If you have too many points in a paragraph, eliminate unimportant points and develop what is left, or explain each important point in its own paragraph.

   Next, select a different paragraph at random. See that it has one major point and that it is fully and clearly explained. Proceed in this way until you have an underlined topic sentence for each paragraph. (Study your paragraphs out of order so that you can sneak up on what you wrote and see it for what it is.)

   Now that you have underlined the topic sentence of each paragraph, underline the main ideas of the essay with a double line; then read only the thesis statement and each topic sentence. If any topic sentences do not support the thesis or if the major points do not progress clearly, delete or add or rearrange; then rewrite.

2. a. Reread your essay aloud at different speeds (rapidly one time, slowly the next). For many writers, reading a draft aloud—one time slowly, the next time rapidly—is the best way to spot weaknesses. They hear weaknesses they could not see.

   b. Read your essay aloud at different times (for instance, once after completing the first draft; once after a break; once more the next day).

   c. Reread your essay silently at different times looking for an aspect of writing that has given you trouble in the past—for instance, once for complicated, unclear sentences and once for wordiness. If you tend to write incomplete sentences, reread from the end of the essay to the beginning, a sentence at a time.

   d. Ask someone to read the draft aloud but without interruptions or commentary, perhaps as you close your eyes and listen (not recommended for after lunch or late in the evening).

3. Another way to see what you have indeed written in each sentence is to read each sentence out of order. Pick up the latest draft; choose a sentence

at random; read it twice (once aloud, once silently); then, if necessary, revise it. After you are finished with the sentence, place a check mark at the beginning of it; then repeat the process for every other sentence (out of order). You may be surprised how many weaknesses you can spot and eliminate using this method.

4. Are any sentences still not right? You've thought about them. You've put them aside. But you still frown as you read them. Imagine that you are with a friend, and say aloud what you mean; then write what you just said. Chances are you'll be much closer to writing what you meant all along.

5. Reread your essay and underline every general word; then consider replacing generalities with details from the film. Words like *good*, *great*, *wonderful*, *nice*, *interesting*, and *terrible* can be replaced by specific references to the film. "Vera Miles was great in *The Searchers*" neither communicates much nor convinces a reader who thought she was so-so. Instead, write a paragraph that includes examples from the film. Consider the following: "Vera Miles's Laurie is a complicated character. For example, she is not all patience and sweetness. In the scene where Martin is about to leave for the last time to rescue Debbie, Miles shows vehement and convincing frustration, wrinkling her brow and biting off her words." Although this second description is scarcely a full account of Vera Miles's performance, it is better than the original vague sentence.

While you are checking word choices, make sure that when you describe action in a film, you use present-tense verbs. For instance, "Rambo then blows up a dozen or so men" (not "blew up").

Getting Feedback

Only a few years ago, most college instructors would tell their students to "do all their own work." During recent years, however, research on writing has confirmed that feedback from others can help writers, and increasingly college instructors are encouraging their students to work in groups and otherwise get feedback from others. However, if you do not follow certain procedures, getting feedback can be of little use; it can even be counterproductive.

Find at least one good reader: someone who can read then explain accurately what the reading means. (Unfortunately, such readers may be scarce.) Show the assignment to your readers and ask them to read your paper carefully (and at least twice) and tell you (1) what they understand from it and (2) where the paper is unclear or incomplete, or both. Do not tell your readers beforehand what you intended to convey; let your writing speak for itself.

If your readers evaluate your writing—rate it as excellent, good, or whatever—disregard their evaluations. Your classmates and outside readers are in a weak position to evaluate (or grade) your work: they do not know well the course work out of which the assignment emerged and lack training, experience, and perspective to grade college-level writing (so do you). If you disregard this advice and take the evaluation of your writing by others seriously, you may end up frustrated and in an unnecessary confrontation with your instructor.

Finally, take others' feedback and rewrite your paper to make it fulfill the assignment more successfully. Do not let readers rewrite for you. And do not let them dictate wording either. *You* rewrite (and rewrite) the parts that need improving.

Of course, any rewriting you do will be *your* responsibility. For example, if none of your readers notices an important omission from your paper, do not blame them. *You* failed to include the material. You're responsible.

If misused, feedback can hurt your writing. However, if you follow these guidelines, feedback can help you improve your writing, often considerably.

Most teachers and publishers do not mind a few minor corrections on the final draft, particularly if neatly and consistently made. If you do not write on a computer and you recopy an entire page to eliminate a few minor errors, you may inject new errors that you will not see: by now you are tired, too short of time, too used to what you have written to spot your errors.

Most ineffective writers spend most of their time mired in the first draft, getting exhausted and demoralized by the ordeal. Effective writers, in contrast, tend to prewrite, divide the task into different work sessions, and spend much more time on rewriting than on writing the first draft.

Few writers do all the steps I suggest, nor do writers generally follow the same steps and same order of steps for every writing task. People are different, and writing is usually complicated. Let me repeat, too, that using the writing strategies I suggest will only improve your chances of writing well. Without extensive previous practice in reading critically and writing carefully, you will be limited in how well you can write, no matter what strategies you use. Similarly, even if you know the rules of a sport and follow them when you play it, you cannot play well unless you have worked hard and long at developing your skills. (Skillful coaches help, too.)

To write well about film requires much previous practice in reading and writing, practical strategies (such as some of those discussed in this essay), and patience and persistence. Writing well about anything you care about or enjoy, though, is well worth all the effort, for in writing and rewriting you think and learn, and you can communicate to others with more precision and permanence than you can any other way. When you write about a film or the film medium, you are unlikely to "make the stars weep" with your melodies, but by writing with care, you can capture some of the magic.

The best writers have the satisfaction of knowing that people of distant times and places may learn from and enjoy their writing. What Carl Sagan said about ancient books applies as well to all writings that are preserved and read:

> One glance at . . . [a book] and you're inside the mind of another person, maybe somebody dead for thousands of years. Across the millennia an author is speaking clearly and silently inside your head, directly to you. Writing is perhaps the greatest of human inventions, binding together people who never knew each

other, citizens of distant epochs. Books break the shackles of time. . . . If information were passed on merely by word of mouth, how little we should know of our own past. How slow would be our progress. Everything would depend on what we had been told, on how accurate the account. Ancient learning might be revered, but in successive retellings it would become muddled and then lost. Books permit us to voyage through time, to tap the wisdom of our ancestors.

WRITING DEFINITIONS

An excellent way to gain a deeper understanding of what terms stand for is to write and rewrite definitions of them. To do so, indicate the category that the object or idea being defined belongs to and what differentiates it from other members of the same category. For example:

> **lap dissolve:** A transition between shots in which one shot begins to fade out as the next shot fades in, overlapping the first shot before replacing it.

Notice that a *lap dissolve* is not merely a transition between shots. It is, but so are *wipes*, *fade-outs*, *fade-ins*, and other transitions between shots. What distinguishes a lap dissolve from all the other transitions between shots is that one shot begins to fade out as the next shot fades in, overlapping the first shot before replacing it.

Do not attempt to define a word or phrase by giving only a synonym, especially when dealing with an abstract word. For example, to write that an *evaluation* is an appraisal will not be clear to readers who have only a fuzzy notion about what *appraisal* means. After you indicate the category and what distinguishes the term in question from other members of the same category, you may want to include a synonym—but only after you have *defined* the term in question.

A final pointer: in your definitions use the same part of speech as the word being defined. Do not define *composition* as "arranging settings and subjects (usually people and objects) within the frame," but as "the arrangement of settings and subjects. . . ." "Composition" (a noun) is a matter of "arrangement" (another noun). For more sample definitions, study some entries in the Glossary.

IMPROVING READING COMPREHENSION

Different types of readings make different demands on readers. For example, to read a letter from a friend, most of us simply read it, but to read and sign a contract that affects our emotional and financial well-being for years to come requires more elaborate reading techniques.

Unfortunately, regardless of the reading to be done, many people read and highlight the material, review a little or reread the entire selection largely without marking it, and hope for the best. Many more strategies are possible. You probably won't have time to use all the following techniques, but for each important reading task preread, read, reread, and write. Don't just trust your memory—and hope for the best.

Preread

These steps may take five to ten minutes, but they will help you get much more out of the reading the first time through.

- Learn something about the author and the time period of the writing.
- Consider the significance of the title.
- Consider the section of the book the reading selection is from.
- Try to figure out what the original audience for the reading was like (such as level of education and possible reasons for wanting to read the selection).
- Read the first paragraph (and perhaps the second) and the last paragraph to discover the main point and the conclusion.
- Examine the headings (to find out the major parts).
- Read the summary or abstract (if one is included).
- Read the study questions (if any are included).

Read

In order to discover the structure and purpose of the writing, during the first reading it is crucial that you read without long interruptions and keep your marks, comments, and questions brief.

- Mark important passages.
- Write brief notes in the margins, especially your descriptions of important points and any questions that come to mind.
- Draw lines between related or contrasted points.
- Circle key words (often they are repeated).
- Mark words you don't understand.

Reread

Many readers use far too few rereading strategies. Using them, however, helps them understand and remember the material in ways simply reading and quickly reviewing cannot.

- Reread passages you are still uncertain about, or reread the entire selection.

- Check a dictionary for words you still cannot figure out, and write the definitions in the margins.

- Study all marked passages; study your marginal notes, and rewrite them if necessary.

- Study the summary (if one is included), *or* write a summary of the selection in your own words, *or* make an outline of the selection, *or* write the thesis sentence in your own words.

- Read the study questions and try to answer them, preferably in writing.

EXERCISES AND QUESTIONS

The book's chapters explain and illustrate major information and concepts. By using the following two sections, you can learn more about the film medium by exploring specific aspects.

Exercises

The following exercises may help you become more aware of particular aspects of a film. For example, the sound track or part of it may be studied by listening to it repeatedly with the image turned off. Some of the following exercises may be applied to any film, and many of these exercises may be used with a video disc, videotape, or DVD player. In home or classroom, time and resources limit the number of these exercises that can be used with a film. Probably most readers will want to read the following section quickly to get an idea of the kinds of exercises possible then at various times try out specific exercises. For convenience, the following exercises are divided into four kinds—viewing, listening, reading, and writing—though a number of them unavoidably overlap.

VIEWING

1. Run a scene with the sound off; then discuss what you have learned and how you have learned it. Rerun the same scene and discuss again what the visuals reveal.

2. View a scene with several other people; take notes; then discuss your observations with other viewers and note takers. Watch the next scene again while taking notes. Stop and discuss. Continue for several more scenes.

3. After you have seen a film, view its opening scene again. What moods and meanings does it convey? Next view again the film's concluding

scene. What moods and meanings does it suggest? In what ways are the opening and closing of the film related?

4. Rerun a scene (if possible in slow motion). Where do the filmmakers show more than they might have? Where is less shown than might have been (for instance, by moving the camera back, changing the lighting, using a lens that distorts the image, giving a sound for an object rather than showing it, shortening a shot or omitting shots altogether)? Is the scene characterized by explicitness or restraint? To what effect?

5. Rerun a scene (if possible in slow motion). Explain what the camera angles and distances contribute to the scene.

6. Rerun a scene, probably more than once; pay special attention to the lighting. How hard or soft is it? From what directions does the lighting come? What information is obscured or emphasized by the lighting? What mood is created or reinforced?

7. Rerun a short scene (if possible in slow motion). Explain how the length of each shot, the arrangement of shots, and the transitions or connections between shots all influence the scene's impact. Run the scene yet again; perhaps make an outline of its shots. Review and revise your explanations.

8. View an important scene featuring one of the major characters, once with sound, once without. For the performer playing the major role, explain how face, body build, voice, and gestures all contribute to characterization. What other roles has the performer played that influence your response to this film?

9. View a scene that includes most of the major characters. Compare the scene with the comparable part of the script (preferably a cutting continuity script, which describes the finished film). Run the scene without sound; then run it without the picture but with sound. Discuss what the performers contribute to the scene.

10. Fast-forward through a video version, stopping only to examine the makeup and clothing of one of the major characters. What do they reveal about the character? Do they change significantly during the story? If so, how? What do the makeup and clothing reveal about the time and place of the story?

11. For a subtitled foreign-language film, view several scenes without reading the subtitles. What did you notice that you did not see during earlier viewings? What is the significance of those new details?

12. If you have access to a video player with freeze-frame option, freeze an expressive image; then discuss the importance of what was excluded from the frame and what was included. Next explain the significance of how objects are arranged within the frame.

LISTENING

1. Play a scene with sound only; then play the same scene with the picture only. Finally, play the scene with both sound and picture. *Or* run a scene with picture and sound; discuss the sound; run the scene again with the sound only and discuss.

   a. Discuss what the dialogue (what is said and how), sound effects, music, and silences all contribute to the impact of the scene.

   b. Try to identify as many different sounds as possible within the scene.

   c. Where are sounds faithful to their sources? Where are sounds distorted?

   d. How dense is the sound mix: is it made up of many or few sources blended together? Explain.

2. View a scene without the sound and try to guess what sounds might accompany the images. Replay the scene with the sound, then discuss. Play another scene without the image but with the sound track. Try to guess what images might accompany the sounds. Play sounds and images then discuss.

3. While watching a film, make notes about where music is used. Next play back the scenes where music is used and discuss what the music contributes.

   a. Are any of the melodies or tunes repeated? If so, with or without variations?

   b. Is the music predominantly melodic or rhythmical?

   c. How do instrumentation, volume, tempo, and key affect the music?

   d. What information and mood does the music create during the opening credits?

   e. Is the music sometimes used to cover weaknesses in the film, such as inappropriate acting? If so, where?

4. For a short scene, make up a chart describing its visuals, dialogue, sound effects, and music. See pages 184–85.

READING

1. Read one or more published outlines or synopses of the same film. Where are the descriptions accurate, clear, concise? Where do interpretations intrude? Where are evaluations made or implied? Discuss the usefulness and limitations of each outline or synopsis.

2. Read the fictional or dramatic source of the film, or at least a section of it. View the comparable section of the film. Reread the section of the fiction or play; then consider the following questions:

    a. What are the major differences? In what sense are they "major"?

    b. What are the major similarities? In what sense are they "major"?

    c. What changes were made because of choices made by the filmmakers?

    d. What changes had to be made because of differences between the media of fiction/drama and film?

3. View a scene or two of the film, and compare them to the similar section of the cutting continuity script, which describes the finished, released film. Where is the script accurate? Where is it inaccurate? What kinds of inaccuracies does it contain: interpretation, evaluation, vagueness, wrong facts, or what? In what ways is the script useful?

4. View a scene or two of the film, and compare them to the comparable section of the screenplay or shooting script (versions of the script used before and during the making of the film). In what ways does the finished film differ from the early versions of the script? How important are the changes?

5. Read carefully one or more reviews of the initial showing of the film. Next compare and contrast your responses with those of the reviewers. Where do differences result from different perceptions, assumptions, and emphases?

6. After reading a review or analysis carefully and at least twice, consider the following questions:

    a. Usually certain terms are used repeatedly or prominently in an essay. How clear are they? Are more examples needed to clarify the prominent terms? Are additional definitions necessary?

    b. State the central and unifying idea: describe it as objectively as you can (without passing judgment on it). Is it stated directly (often at the beginning and/or conclusion)? Or is it left for the reader to infer? Finally, how persuasively is the thesis argued?

    c. Is the argument or interpretation amply illustrated with specific, accurate, and relevant examples from the film?

    d. Is the essay clearly organized? What are its major parts? Why are they arranged in the order they are in?

    e. Does the analysis make any generalized statements not subject to proof? If so, what are they? What are some of the assumptions about the nature of the film medium that the writer makes? Are the assumptions (or premises) reasonable? Explain.

    f. What does the analysis suggest about its author's personality and background? How do you know?

WRITING

1. Immediately after seeing a film, jot down a list of the images and sounds that come to mind. From the list select the most important ones; then explain why they are significant.

2. View a short scene with the sound turned up. As objectively as possible, describe the scene in writing: try to avoid making judgments (which reveal your approval or disapproval) and inferences (which show you making certain assumptions, which may not be correct). View the scene a second time, without the sound. Revise your description; perhaps divide it into shots. What aspects of the scene are especially difficult to capture in writing? Why?

3. Make an outline of a sequence or two of a narrative film. Try to describe the action as accurately, objectively, and concisely as possible. Later, formulate headings for the sequence(s) and justify them.

    a. What action is omitted that could have been shown?

    b. What action is shown in detail?

    c. What action is shown only briefly?

    d. What is emphasized by the film's selection and arrangement of scenes?

    Though time-consuming, making an outline has many advantages: it helps you decide what is important in each scene; it helps you see which scenes are merely transitional; it makes you more aware of how individual scenes are connected to form a longer story; it makes you more aware of when you are describing something and when inferences, interpretations, and evaluations slip in; it teaches you that a film is more than its action and that much of the film experience is not easily captured in words.

4. Write and rewrite a one- or two-paragraph plot summary of a narrative film's major actions in the order they occur in the film. Review your draft; make the summary as accurate and clear as you can. (Assume that your reader has not seen the film.)

5. After you see a film, write an interpretation of an important scene; then view the scene again. How accurate was your interpretation?

6. For a film based on a novel or short story, choose a scene from the fiction and adapt it into a scene for a film; then compare your adaptation of the scene with that of the filmmakers. (Satyajit Ray of India did this exercise before he became a film director.)

7. Choose some film terms that you have heard repeatedly but that are not included in the glossary of this book. (You may want to choose some terms you used in one of your essays or in class discussion.) Define each

of the terms as accurately as you can. In your definitions, be sure to explain in what category the term belongs, then what differentiates it from other members of the same category. For example, a projector is a machine (category) that makes possible the presentation of motion pictures on a reflective surface (kind of machine). Before you begin, you may want to review the guidelines for writing definitions (p. 492) and some of the definitions in the book's glossary.

8. Make a set of study questions that apply to a film (and that are not merely adapted from the list of study questions included on pp. 499–505). Try to formulate questions that draw attention to significant details and important issues. Also try to phrase your questions so that they do not encourage a particular answer (leading questions). Try to anticipate how your readers could misunderstand your questions and attempt to reword them to avoid this. Next arrange the questions in a meaningful order.

9. Imagine that you have been asked by someone who has never seen a particular film what it is like. Write an interpretation of the film's major qualities. Before you begin writing, try to organize your thoughts and feelings, and in your interpretation try not to jump from detail to unrelated detail or, worse, generalization to unrelated and unillustrated generalization.

10. Look up a review of a film; photocopy the review; and study it. Write a summary of the review; then explain in writing how accurate and persuasive the review is. Why do you say so?

Questions

The following questions are intended to help viewers understand a film and their responses to it (and eventually the film medium). Not all the questions are appropriate for every film. For those questions most appropriate for the film being examined, please remember: *In thinking out, discussing, and writing responses, be careful to stick with the issues the questions raise, to answer all parts of the questions, to explain the reasons for your answers, and to give specific examples from the film.*

MISE EN SCÈNE

1. Are the settings true-to-life or imaginary? What settings are particularly expressive? What do the settings add to the film?

2. What are the film's major subjects? What actions and appearance are especially revealing?

3. How are the subjects arranged within the frame?

   a. Are significant subjects bunched up within the frame or spread apart? Are they in the center of the frame or off to a side?

   b. Are significant subjects arranged in such a way as to balance out the composition or to create an imbalance?

   c. In what ways do background and foreground subjects relate to each other?

CINEMATOGRAPHY

1. Are the images high grain or low grain? Are both looks used within the same film? What does the degree of graininess contribute to the film?

2. Does the film use "cool" or "warm" colors to achieve certain effects? Is color used in a symbolic way? Is color used to enhance mood? How life-like is the color?

3. Notice any interesting uses of light.

   a. Where is lighting used to support or create a particular mood? What mood?

   b. Where are shadows used to conceal information? To enhance mood? To reveal what a character is like or is feeling?

   c. If a certain kind of lighting is used repeatedly, describe it and explain its effects.

4. For an especially significant part of the film, what camera distances are used? To what effect? Are many close-ups used in the film? Generally, does the camera stay back from the subjects and show much of the setting?

5. For some of the most significant shots in the film, what lens is used: wide-angle, normal, telephoto? With what consequences?

6. In the film, does the subject tend to be filmed in high, eye-level, or low angles? Where are camera angles especially significant or effective?

7. Notice any interesting camera placements.

   a. Where are point-of-view shots used? How often are they used? What effects do they have on your viewing experience?

   b. Where are camera placements used that make you feel like an outsider looking in on the action?

8. Characterize the camera movement.

   a. If the camera tends to remain stationary, what are the advantages and disadvantages of the stationary camera work?

b. If moving camera shots are used, does the camera dolly or truck or move up and down through the air? Are Steadicam shots used? If so, to what effect? What is the effect of the camera movement or lack of movement?

9. Does the camera pan, or tilt? Where and with what consequences?

EDITING

1. Generally, is the film's editing characterized by fast cutting or slow cutting? To what effect?

2. Does the editing tend to be smooth and unobtrusive or disruptive and obvious?

3. Where are shots joined for a particular effect, such as to stress similarities or differences or to create or enhance a mood?

4. Does the film use cross-cutting? If so, where and to what effect?

5. Where is editing used to save time? To make viewers use their imaginations (for example, by use of a cutaway shot)?

SOUND

1. Where and why is offscreen sound used? Where is sound used to suggest the size of a location and the texture of the surfaces?

2. How frequently is dialogue used? Is the dialogue always distinct? Does it sometimes overlap? If so, with what consequences?

3. Where is silence used? What effect does it contribute?

4. Where is volume raised or lowered for effect?

5. Where is sound used between scenes to create a certain effect? What effect is created or supported?

6. Where is sound distorted? What does the distortion contribute?

7. Consider the film's music.

a. Where is music used? For what purposes? Is the music always subordinated to the rest of the film, or does it sometimes intrude?

b. What are the major melodies or tunes? Are they repeated? With or without variation?

c. Is the music a part of the story itself, or is it played as complementary to the story (as in the case where we see characters in a lifeboat while we hear an orchestra)?

d. Where does the music suggest a particular place or time or both?

e. Where is music used to suggest what a character is feeling?

Sources for Fictional Films

1. Is the film based on an original screenplay, or is it an adaptation of fiction or a play? If it is an adaptation, how closely does the film follow its source(s)? In what major ways does it differ from its source(s)? What changes make the film a more effective film?

2. Is the film based on historical accounts? If so, how closely does the film follow the earlier accounts? Where does the film make changes for dramatic effect? Where does it make changes unnecessarily?

3. Is the film based on other films? If so, does the film re-create, parody, or pay an homage to the earlier film(s)?

Types of Fictional Films

1. If the film is fictional, how may it be further classified—as classical Hollywood cinema, Italian neorealism, or some other type? Why do you say so?

2. What major similarities and differences does the film have with earlier fictional films of the same genre or movement?

3. If the film is traditional in some ways but untraditional in others, explain.

Characteristics of Fictional Films

1. Who is the protagonist or main character? Why do you say so? Describe the character's or characters' physical characteristics and personality.

2. What does the main character want? Does he or she succeed? Why or why not?

3. How do characterization and conflict function in the film?

    a. For the major characters, how is characterization revealed: actions, appearance, dialogue, thoughts (ideas, fantasies, dreams, hallucinations)? Which of these four methods of revealing characterization is used most often in the film? Which of the four methods is used least or not at all?

    b. How well do you get to know and understand the major characters? What information about them is revealed? What information about them is withheld?

    c. What are the major conflicts? How are they resolved?

    d. Do any of the characters have internal conflicts (such as uncertainty or guilt)?

    e. Are the film's most important conflicts between sharply distinguished good and evil, or are the most important conflicts more complex and subtle?

4. Consider the film's attitude toward its subjects.

   a. Usually films present their characters and their actions in such a manner that they encourage audience approval or disapproval. If the film presents certain behavior or attitudes in an approving manner, how does it do so?

   b. Which, if any, behavior or attitudes are satirized or made fun of? How strongly felt is the disapproval? How noticeable is the disapproval?

5. Consider the film's structure.

   a. What are the film's sequences (major groups of scenes)?

   b. Does the film have a chronological or nonchronological structure? What are the advantages of the choice?

   c. Does the film have more than one major plotline? If so, how are the different major plotlines related?

6. In what scenes is the story time longer than the running time? Conversely, and much less commonly, in what scenes is the running time longer than the story time?

7. Are any untraditional styles, such as black comedy, being used? If so, what does the film implicitly ask viewers to accept?

ALTERNATIVES TO LIVE-ACTION FICTIONAL FILMS

1. If the film is a documentary, is it narrative or nonnarrative? Why do you say so?

2. What major types of sources are used in the documentary?

3. How accurate is the film? Are excerpts from interviews taken out of context? How do you know? Is editing used to criticize or praise a subject? If so, explain.

4. If the film is avant-garde, in what ways is it unlike classical Hollywood cinema?

5. For avant-garde films, what are the major types of sources (such as earlier films or the filmmaker's imagination)?

6. In what ways does the film surprise or frustrate you, or both?

7. If the film is a hybrid, what major types are combined? What expectations did you have early in the film and how were you surprised as the film progressed?

UNDERSTANDING FILMS THROUGH CONTEXTS

1. When and where was the film made? How do the times and places of its making affect how the film turned out? For example, did the political

climate or widespread societal attitudes of the time preclude certain subjects or treatments?

2. Is the film a big-budget action film aimed at large audiences, a more modestly budgeted independent film, an inexpensive documentary or avant-garde film, or some other type of film? Did limitations in the budget affect the way the film turned out? If so, how so?

3. Does the film follow filmic conventions or is it unconventional in its techniques and choice of subjects?

4. If the film is a genre film, such as a western or horror film, consider the following questions.

   a. If the film is basically a traditional genre film, explain what major features it shares with most films of its genre.

   b. Is the film revisionist? If so, explain in what ways.

   c. Is the film a parody of earlier films of the same genre? In what ways does it imitate earlier films of the same genre? In what ways does it treat the subject(s) humorously? What conventions of the genre does the parody make fun of?

   d. Is the film a combination of genres? If so, explain which genres and which features of them.

5. What does the film convey to you about the history and culture of the society it depicts? How accurate are those impressions? How do you know how trustworthy those impressions are?

VIEWER AND FILM

1. Where do cinematic techniques affect meanings?

2. Does the film sometimes use technique subtly and require attentive viewers and listeners? If so, where and with what consequences?

3. Is the film sometimes subtle? If you were to see the film in a different format or version, what subtle techniques could be difficult to notice?

4. Does the film have any important symbols? What do they mean?

5. What meanings does the narrative itself suggest?

6. If you know the time and place the film was made, do you detect any symptomatic meanings in the film?

7. What are the film's major meanings?

   a. Are the meanings complex or simple? Ambiguous or clear?

b. Do the meanings challenge the status quo or are they reassuring? Why?

c. Do the meanings apply to only a particular culture or time, or are they universal?

d. Are the meanings of the film explicit or implicit, or both?

8. What fantasies does the film reflect? What type of person would enjoy the movie's fantasies?

9. Are any critical approaches particularly useful in analyzing the film? If so, which ones and in what ways are they useful?

10. What meanings might other people (say a different ethnic group, gender, sexual orientation, or nationality) see in the film?

RESOURCES: ANNOTATED BIBLIOGRAPHY AND ELECTRONIC SOURCES

Because Web site addresses change so often, they are not included here but are available through the home page of this book at <http://www .bedfordstmartins.com/phillips-film>.

Film and Video References

BOOKS

Emmens, Carol A. *Short Stories on Film and Video*. 2nd ed. Littleton, CO: Libraries Unlimited, 1985. An alphabetical listing by authors of short stories adapted into films, usually short films. Supplied for each film are the title of short story, title of film, running time or number of reels, black-and-white or color designation, year, director, producer, cast, and a brief description of contents. Also includes indexes.

Enser's Filmed Books and Plays: A List of Books and Plays from Which Films Have Been Made, 1928–1991. Comp. Ellen Baskin and Mandy Hicken. Brookfield, VT: Ashgate, 1993. The main part of the book is an index arranged alphabetically by film titles, with brief information on each film and the name of the author of the source fiction or play. Also includes author and change of title indexes and information on made-for-TV movies and classic British television series.

Film Review Annual, 1981–. Ed. Jerome S. Ozer. Englewood, NJ: Film Review, 1982–. Reprints complete reviews of the feature films released in the United States during a year. Includes full credits, many different indexes, listings of major film awards.

Filmfacts. Los Angeles: Division of Cinema, U of Southern California, 1958–1977, irregular 1969–1977. Contains credits, synopses of films, and reprints of reviews, sometimes in their entirety.

The Focal Encyclopedia of Film and Television Techniques. Ed. Raymond Spottiswoode. New York: Hastings, 1969. Sixteen hundred entries by more than one hundred specialists on film and TV equipment and techniques.

Halliwell's Filmgoer's and Video Viewer's Companion. Ed. John Walker. 11th ed. New York: Harper, 1995. Thousands of entries on scriptwriters, actors, directors, and others; film terms; film movements; recurrent themes (or topics) in films; and some national cinemas. Also includes short quotations from actors, directors, and critics. For most people discussed, a selected list of films she or he worked on is also supplied.

The International Dictionary of Films and Filmmakers. Ed. Nicholas Thomas. 2nd ed. 5 vols. Chicago: St. James. Information and signed critical essays. Vol. 1: *Films* (1990); vol. 2: *Directors* (1991); vol. 3: *Actors and Actresses* (1992); vol. 4: *Writers and Production Artists* (including cinematographers, producers, editors, and designers) (1993); vol. 5: *Title Index* (1994).

Katz, Ephraim. *The Film Encyclopedia.* Revised by Fred Klein and Ronald Dean Nolen. 3rd ed. New York: Harper, 1998. A comprehensive one-volume encyclopedia of world cinema. More than seven thousand entries on individual scriptwriters, producers, directors, and many others; studios and production companies; movements or styles of filmmaking; national cinemas; filmmaking personnel; and jargon and technical terms. For each person discussed, a selected list of films she or he worked on is also supplied.

Konigsberg, Ira. *The Complete Film Dictionary.* 2nd ed. New York: Penguin, 1997. Defines and discusses nearly four thousand terms.

Leff, Leonard J. *Film Plots: Scene-by-Scene Narrative Outlines for Feature Film Study.* Vol. 1. Ann Arbor: Pierian, 1983. Scene-by-scene descriptions of sixty-seven films often studied or written about.

———. Vol. 2. Ann Arbor: Pierian, 1988. Descriptions of fifty more feature films.

Leonard Maltin's Movie and Video Guide. New York: Signet. Appears yearly. Brief description and evaluation of thousands of feature films, theatrical and made-for-TV. Indicates which titles have been released on videotape and which on laser disc. For films made in a wide-screen process, an indication of which process was used. Also an indication of black-and-white titles available in a "computer-colored version."

Magill's Cinema Annual. Ed. Frank N. Magill and Patricia King Hanson. Pasadena: Salem. Published annually, beginning in 1982. For major films of the year, includes selected credits, synopsis of the narrative, essay review, and bibliography of reviews.

Rehrauer, George. *The Macmillan Film Bibliography: A Critical Guide to the Literature of the Motion Picture.* 2 vols. New York: Macmillan, 1982. Vol. 1, *Reviews.* Vol. 2, *Index.*

———. *The Short Film: An Evaluative Selection of 500 Recommended Films.* New York: Macmillan, 1975. For each film, includes title, release date, producer/distributor, running time, black-and-white or color designation, description, audience level suitability, and indication of which books recommended the film. Also included are a list of descriptions of books on the short film and a bibliography of books and film periodicals on the short film.

Sadoul, Georges. *Dictionary of Films.* Translated, edited, and updated by Peter Morris. Berkeley: U of California P, 1972. Brief essays on approximately thirteen hundred films.

Selected Film Criticism. 7 vols. Ed. Anthony Slide. Metuchen, NJ: Scarecrow, 1982–1985. Reprints original reviews of feature-length and short films; one volume includes foreign films.

Subject Guide to Books in Print. New York: Bowker. Under "Moving-picture" and a noun (such as "direction") are listed appropriate books currently in print. Many cross-references. New edition every year.

The Video Source Book. 2 vols. Detroit: Gale. Published annually. Comprehensive information on more than 152,500 programs available on videotape and laser video discs and approximately 2,000 sources for rental or purchase.

Welch, Jeffrey Egan. *Literature and Film: An Annotated Bibliography, 1900–1977*. New York: Garland, 1981.

————. *Literature and Film: An Annotated Bibliography, 1978–1988*. New York: Garland, 1993. Both volumes list and annotate books and articles published in North America and Great Britain having to do with the relation between literature and films.

The Women's Companion to International Film. Ed. Annette Kuhn and Susannah Radstone. London: Virago, 1990. Berkeley: U of California P, 1994. Approximately six hundred alphabetized entries, many including filmographies or bibliographies or both. Also includes an index of films directed, written, or produced by women.

Writers' Program, New York. *The Film Index: A Bibliography*. Vol. 1, *The Film as Art*. New York: Arno Press for the Museum of Modern Art Film Library, 1966. Originally published in 1941, contains 8,600 entries, most of them annotated, on film books, articles, and film reviews or material dealing with a particular film. Part I: History and Technique; Part II: Types of Films. In Part II, synopses are provided for many pre-1915 films and for some post-1915 films.

INDEXES FOR PERIODICALS

Film Literature Index. Albany: Film and Television Documentation Center. Published quarterly beginning in 1973. Indexes articles in more than three hundred international film and nonfilm periodicals. Entries are arranged alphabetically by author and subject (including film titles).

Humanities Index. New York: H. W. Wilson. Published monthly beginning in 1974. At the end of each volume is a section on book reviews.

International Index to Film Periodicals: An Annotated Guide. New York: Bowker. Published annually beginning in 1972. Each volume lists articles and essays on film to appear during the past year in world film magazines. Some entries are annotated. Includes director and author indexes.

Readers' Guide to Periodical Literature. From 1910 to March 1977, film reviews are listed under "Moving Picture Plays"; after March 1977, film reviews are listed under "Motion Picture Reviews." Since March 1976 (vol. 36), book review citations are listed at the end of each volume.

INDEXES FOR NEWSPAPERS

Los Angeles Times Index. Film reviews are listed under "Motion Pictures."
New York Times Index. Film articles and reviews are listed under "Motion Pictures."
The Times Index (London). Film reviews are listed under "Films."

JOURNALS AND MAGAZINES

Afterimage. A wide-ranging publication on the visual arts, including independent film and video, photography, and visual books.

American Cinematographer. Includes many articles on the cinematography used in making particular movies, interviews with major cinematographers, and ads for such equipment as cranes, Steadicams, and cameras. Published monthly.

The American Historical Review. Beginning with vol. 96, no. 4 (Oct. 1991), each October issue includes a section of films reviewed from a historian's perspective.

Big Reel (Dubuque, IA). Includes articles of interest to film and video collectors and hobbyists and ads for films (usually used, 16 mm); film equipment; various collectibles; photos, posters, and lobby cards; videos; and video equipment.

CineAction. Film criticism in terms of race, gender, sexual orientation, and politics. Published three times a year in Toronto since 1984.

Cineaste. Provides coverage of the art and politics of world cinema. Includes film reviews, book reviews, and interviews. A quarterly published without assistance from the film industry or any academic institution.

Cinema Journal. Published four times a year in cooperation with the Society for Cinema Studies, a professional association made up largely of college and university film teachers.

Cinema Technology. "Concerned with all technical aspects of the cinema." Published quarterly in London.

Film & History: An Interdisciplinary Journal of Film and Television Studies. Articles, film reviews, and book reviews. Each issue has a "special focus." Published quarterly.

Film Comment. Published by the Film Society of Lincoln Center (New York). Articles, interviews, and book and film reviews.

Film Criticism. Articles, interviews, festival reports, and book reviews. Published three times a year at Allegheny College.

Film Culture: America's Independent Motion Picture Magazine. Articles on avant-garde films and filmmakers. Published irregularly.

Film History: An International Journal. Each issue includes articles on a special topic. Published quarterly.

Filmmaker: The Magazine of Independent Film. Published four times a year by the Independent Feature Project.

Film Quarterly. Interviews, discussion of film theory and film history, reviews of films and videos, and, especially in each summer issue, book reviews. Published since 1958 by the University of California Press.

Films in Review. Many short film reviews, longer articles on filmmakers, extensive obituaries. Published ten times a year.

The Independent Film & Video Monthly. Published ten times a year by the Foundation for Independent Video and Film (FIVF). Includes profiles of filmmakers, producers, and distributors; festival listings; information on new technology; coverage of political trends and legislation affecting independents; and reports from film festivals and markets.

Journal of Film and Video. Quarterly published by the University Film and Video Association, which consists largely of filmmakers and university film teachers. Earlier known under the title *Journal of the University Film and Video Association*.

The Journal of Popular Film and Television (formerly *Journal of Popular Film*). Published quarterly. Articles on stars, directors, producers, studios, networks, genres, series, and other topics. Includes interviews, filmographies, bibliographies, and book reviews.

Jump Cut. Film reviews, including of third world films, interviews, articles, and critiques. Special emphasis on Marxist, feminist, and gay criticism.

Literature/Film Quarterly. "Articles on individual movies, on different cinematic adaptations of a single literary work, on a director's style of adaptation, on theories of film adaptation, on the 'cinematic' qualities of authors or works, on the reciprocal influences between film and literature, on authors' attitudes toward film and film adaptations, on the role of the screenwriter, and on teaching of film." Also includes interviews, film reviews, and book reviews.

Monthly Film Bulletin. Detailed credits, summary of the story, and review of feature films and short films, contemporary and "retrospective." International coverage. Published from 1934 to April 1991. In May 1991, *Monthly Film Bulletin* merged with *Sight and Sound.*

MovieMaker. Published bimonthly in Seattle. Focuses on independent film and independent filmmakers.

Scenario: The Magazine of Screenwriting Art. Each quarterly issue includes complete (mostly recent) screenplays and interviews with the writers.

Sight and Sound. Published monthly by the British Film Institute. Articles, interviews, book reviews, and film reviews preceded by credits and a plot summary.

Variety. A U.S. trade publication on the entertainment industry, including film reviews and many other types of information.

The Velvet Light Trap: Review of Cinema. Published twice a year by the Department of Radio-Television-Film at the University of Texas. Critical essays on American film and TV.

Wide Angle. Published quarterly. Usually each issue stresses a single topic. Also includes interviews with filmmakers and book reviews.

Widescreen Review. Devoted exclusively to "widescreen digital surround home theatre experience."

Videotapes

Before you go looking for a particular videotape, you want to be certain that the film you seek is available on video. Many people assume that all films are available on video. Not so. To discover which films are available on video, check one of the standard reference works, such as *Leonard Maltin's Movie and Video Guide* (p. 506) or *The Video Source Book* (p. 507).

In addition to the video stores in your area, there are additional sources, especially for older films, foreign films, avant-garde films, and documentaries. Most public libraries, for example, have videotape collections that usually include titles unavailable in local video stores. Another possible local source is a college or university, though you may have to be a student to view the tapes and may be restricted to viewing them in the library. Links for companies that sell or rent videotapes are also available via the home page for this book: <http://www.bedfordstmartins.com/phillips-film>.

Video Discs

Laser video discs are available in two formats: CLV and CAT. CLV can contain up to an hour of film but lacks slow-motion, freeze-frame, and still frames. CAV format has those three options but can store only thirty minutes per side. Some laser titles are available in both formats.

Laser video discs are made by various companies, but the Criterion discs produced by Voyager Company are most useful for film studies: the discs are available only in the original aspect ratio and often include additional material—such as film clips of the production, production photos, screen tests, interviews, costume sketches, storyboards, theatrical trailers, maps, or other ancillary material. More than forty of the Criterion titles—such as *She's Gotta Have It*, *Naked*, *The Silence of the Lambs*, *The Last Picture Show*, *The Player*, *Taxi Driver*, and *Close Encounters of the Third Kind*—are "director approved," meaning that deleted scenes are restored and the film is now as the director intended, not as it was released. Many of the laser discs also contain running audio commentary on one of the two audio tracks.

CD-ROMs

As of this writing, the major film source on CD-ROM is Microsoft's *Cinemania*, which is upgraded yearly and is available for Windows or Macintosh. *Cinemania* includes brief reviews plus information for more than twenty thousand films, directors, actors, and many film topics. Included are black-and-white and color film stills; portraits of actors and directors; film, musical, and dialogue clips; a program to help you decide on a video rental; and a section on recommended sources for mail-order films on video. The CD-ROM may also aid your memory. If you cannot remember the name of a real person connected to filmmaking or something about a film topic or a film genre, you can type in what you know or remember and probably be prompted with the correct information. The CD-ROM contains many links to additional, related information. As in most CD-ROMs, the emphasis throughout is on mainstream films, so third world films, documentaries, and avant-garde films are scarcely represented. Recent reviews can be downloaded from Microsoft's online site and integrated with the *Cinemania* CD-ROM.

Magill's Survey of Cinema, which is also available on CD-ROM but works only with DOS, contains fifteen thousand reviews, five thousand in depth. The in-depth reviews include credits and cast, a plot summary, a review, and a list of additional reviews. Search options allow you to search by such topics as subject, director, and performer.

The Motion Picture Guide for Macintosh and Windows holds all twenty-one volumes of the printed books of the same title and contains information on more than thirty-five thousand films since 1927.

The Mega Movie Guide for Windows contains very brief reviews of forty-five thousand films, including independent, made-for-TV, and sexually explicit features, plus one thousand longer reviews by Rex Reed. Search options include director's name, film title, MPAA rating, and actor's name. Also provided are hypertext links, an indication if the film is available on video, film stills, and two hours of film clips complete with sound.

The Voyager Company has made available on CD-ROM several films, such as *Comic Book Confidential* and *The Day after Trinity* (both documentary films), *It's A Wonderful Life*, *This Is Spinal Tap*, *Salt of the Earth*, and *A Hard Day's Night*. In addition to a film, the CD-ROM includes an enormous amount of information about or related to the film and a search capacity to find out most of what you can imagine to ask. The CD-ROM for *A Hard Day's Night*, for example, includes the complete film, background information on the Beatles, analysis of the film, an original script, all the songs, song profiles, case and crew profiles, movie clips from earlier films directed by Richard Lester, an interview with Lester, and an eleven-minute film Lester directed, "The Running, Jumping and Standing Still Film" (1959). Search options allow you to seek out any scene in the film or any word or phrase in the script. Because the film and songs are programmed on different tracks, you can play the music while you examine other parts of the disc.

Another CD-ROM devoted to a movie was published by Rutgers University Press: *The Rebecca Project*, which includes "QuickTime movie clips, hypertext critical essays, and rarely seen documents" for *Rebecca*, a film directed by Alfred Hitchcock in 1940.

Databases

LIBRARY DATABASES   Various libraries have access to a variety of general databases. Here are a few of them:

InfoTrac has information stored on laser discs; it is updated monthly. The *General Periodicals Index* version of *InfoTrac* includes citations to film reviews. The *National Newspaper Index* allows users to obtain complete texts of film reviews from several major U.S. newspapers, including the *New York Times* and the *Washington Post*.

Newsbank Plus includes citations for films and film articles from regional U.S. newspapers. Since 1993, complete texts are also available.

INTERNET DATABASES

> A caution: some sources included on the Internet include disclaimers that their content may not be entirely accurate. Rightly so. One Internet source, for example, listed the director of the documentary *Black is . . . Black ain't* as Marrion T. Riggs, not Marlon T. Riggs. Most sources included on the Internet are not as accurate as books, which in their making are subject to more levels of review and editing. If you cite a source from the Internet (on such details as a quotation, a date, a name, or a number), you will be wise to double-check its accuracy in at least one other source.

Nexis is a huge database that includes complete texts of articles from a large variety of newspapers and magazines (though almost no film journals), transcripts for selected radio and TV news programs, and powerful searching options. *Nexis* is available to students and faculty in some academic libraries. To begin, select "General News Topics" from the main menu.

For help in sorting through Internet sites for film and video, you may want to consult *Film and Video on the Internet: The Top 500 Sites* (Studio City, CA: M. W. Publications, 1996).

Links to Web sites of interest to film students may be accessed through the home page for this book at <http://www.bedfordstmartins.com/phillips-film>.

WORKS CITED

Flaubert, Gustave. *Madame Bovary*. Trans. Paul de Man. New York: Norton, 1965.
Sagan, Carl. "The Persistence of Memory." Program 11. *Cosmos*. PBS. The wording is from the television program, not the book based on the series.

A Chronology: Film in Context (1895–1998)

Some film history books, such as those by Gerald Mast and Bruce Kawin and by David Cook, are mainly aesthetic histories: they stress the artistic achievements of films that scholars regard as significant or representative. Then there are industrial histories: studies that help us understand films as products of an industry. Other histories focus on film as one of the arts. Social histories emphasize how a society influences the films made, one of the topics discussed in Chapter 9. Sociological history focuses on how films influence viewers. There are many other types of histories of film, and increasingly historians blend different types of histories within the same written accounts because attempting to study films on their own makes for incomplete and misleading history. Dana Polan argues that films "are what they are because of the meanings given them by surrounding situations. A history of films is a history of films in history" (54).

In the last decade or so, scholars have focused much attention on how to study history ("historiography") and have concluded that there is no one history, only various histories. Jack Ellis, for example, entitled his useful book *A History of Film* because he is well aware his is only one selection and interpretation of cinema. Douglas Gomery's *Movie History: A Survey* interweaves four approaches: aesthetics, technology, economics, and sociology. Kristin Thompson and David Bordwell's *Film History: An Introduction* is guided by three main concerns: the uses of the film medium over time; film production, distribution, and exhibition; and international trends in the film medium and the film market. Geoffrey Nowell-Smith coordinated the work of a variety of international film scholars to create *The Oxford History of World Cinema*, which encompasses not just films but "the audience, the industry, and the people who work in it . . . and the mechanisms of regulation and control which determine which films audiences are encouraged to see and which they are not" (xix). The History of American Cinema series, under the general editorship of Charles Harpole, uses four approaches to cinema history: aesthetic, technological, sociological, and economic.

The following chronology supplies information that could be used in constructing a history from four major sources. In the first column, arranged chronologically, are some world events that have affected the lives of many people. The other columns are given over to the arts, including many relationships between film and the other arts (column 2), developments in the mass media (column 3), and varied critically acclaimed films and videos (column 4). Although it's a long and complicated chronology, it is woefully incomplete. Unavoidably, everyone who has studied twentieth-century history will have quarrels with parts of it.

Nevertheless, the chronology can be useful in a number of ways. You can read an entire column to get a sense of the order and in some cases connections between similar types of events (for example, you might notice how conditions in Germany after World War I preceded the Nazis' rise to power). Or you can read all four columns one year at a time to get a sense of what happened in a particular year.

You can also use the chronology to place a film in other contexts. Imagine, for example, you are studying *Casablanca*, which was first shown in November 1942. From the chronology you can learn or be reminded about what else was happening before and during 1942. You might notice, for example, that Europe plunged into World War II in September 1939 and that the United States remained (officially) neutral for over two years (until the Japanese attacked Pearl Harbor in December 1941). On one level, *Casablanca* calls for Americans to put aside any inclination to isolationism and rally behind a major and traditional ally, the French, who at the time of the film's release were under German occupation. Once you consider when *Casablanca* was made, you can better understand its fervor in denouncing the Nazis, extolling the Free French, and criticizing the French government in Vichy that cooperated with the occupying Germans. The chronology can help you understand not only the times when a film was made but also the times a film is set in. For example, the information about events leading up to World War II can help you understand *Saving Private Ryan* (1998) more completely.

The year given for a film is the year it was first shown publicly. Some films do not fit neatly into one of the three distinct categories of films used in this book (fictional, documentary, and avant-garde), but to save space I have usually tried to label the films cited in column 4 by one of those three tags. Sometimes different sources do not agree on a date. Whenever I have become aware of such discrepancies, I have tried to consult at least one additional authoritative source, but occasional inaccuracies may remain.

The chronology is so laid out that there is often space to add notes about what you consider illuminating historical facts or trends. It is hoped that you will not use the chronology as your only source for history but will seek out more complete, coherent, and authoritative accounts, such as those cited following the chronology.

Two notes about film titles: throughout the chronology, as throughout the body of the book, film titles in quotation marks indicate films less than sixty minutes long. Titles in italics indicate films sixty or more minutes long. Parentheses included as part of a film's title indicate that the film is sometimes known by its longer title, sometimes by the shorter one (without the words in parentheses).

	World Events	Arts	Mass Media	Films and Videos
1895	Cuba fights Spain for its independence. First U.S. automobile made for sale on a regular basis. Roentgen discovers X-rays.	*The Red Badge of Courage*, Stephen Crane (fiction). *The Time Machine*, H. G. Wells (fiction). *The Importance of Being Earnest*, Oscar Wilde (play).	Lumière Brothers invent a portable motion-picture camera/projector to film short films and to show them publicly in Paris. First U.S. demonstration of a motion picture shown on a screen, New York City. Marconi sends and receives a radio signal.	Lumière Brothers' first (and very brief) film, "Workers Leaving the Lumière Factory," is also the first documentary film. Other Lumière films: "The Arrival of a Train at the Station" and "Feeding (the) Baby." "The Execution of Mary, Queen of Scots," Thomas Edison.
1896	Olympic Games of ancient Greece are reestablished.		Georges Méliès begins making short films. Some U.S. vaudeville theaters include films in their programs. Some newspapers give synopses of film programs but little criticism of them. Some films are hand-painted with colors.	"The Kiss," Edison. "The Vanishing Lady," Méliès. "The Fairy in the Cabbage Patch," first film by the world's first woman film director, Alice Guy-Blaché.
1897	Discovery of the electron.	*Dracula*, Bram Stoker (fiction).	At a charity film showing in Paris, a fire kills 140 people.	Fitzsimmons-Corbett boxing match is filmed and shown in theaters.

	World Events	Arts	Mass Media	Films and Videos
1898	U.S. wars with Spain. Spain cedes Cuba, Puerto Rico, Guam, and the Philippines.	*The Turn of the Screw*, Henry James (fiction). *The War of the Worlds*, Wells (fiction).	First photograph taken with artificial light.	"Tearing Down the Spanish Flag" (a staged documentary and perhaps the first propaganda film). "Express Train on a Railway Cutting" (documentary), Cecil Hepworth.
1899	Aspirin first marketed, as a prescribed drug.	*McTeague*, Frank Norris (fiction). *Uncle Vanya*, Anton Chekhov (play).	First magnetic recording of sound. Marconi sends a wireless signal across the English Channel.	"The Dreyfus Affair" (a film that re-creates a political scandal), Méliès. "Cinderella," Méliès.
1900	Boxer Rebellion in China, mainly against foreigners. *The Interpretation of Dreams*, book by Sigmund Freud.	*The Wonderful Wizard of Oz*, L. Frank Baum (fiction). *Sister Carrie*, Theodore Dreiser (fiction).	At about this time, Edison uses artificial light in his rooftop film studio in New York City. Lumière Brothers use a 70-by-53-foot translucent screen at the Paris World's Fair so audiences of up to 25,000 on both sides of the screen can see short films.	"One Man Band" (with Méliès himself playing the six band members and the conductor), Méliès.
1901	Queen Victoria of England is succeeded by Edward VII. Nobel Prizes first awarded.	*Three Sisters*, Chekhov (play).	"The Human Figure in Motion," sequential photographs by Eadweard Muybridge. Marconi sends a radio signal from Wales to Newfoundland by tapping out *S* in Morse code.	"Queen Victoria's Funeral" (documentary).

	World Events	Arts	Mass Media	Films and Videos
1902	Boer War ends in South Africa.	*Heart of Darkness*, Joseph Conrad (fiction). *The Wings of the Dove*, Henry James (fiction).	Pathé builds film studio in France. First phonograph recording by Enrico Caruso.	"A Trip to the Moon," Méliès. "Coronation of Edward VII" (documentary re-creation), Méliès.
1903	Wright Brothers fly airplane.	*Man and Superman*, G. B. Shaw (play). Isadora Duncan pioneers modern dance (approx. 1903–1908).	Edwin S. Porter uses matte shots in "The Great Train Robbery." First radio message from U.S. to Britain.	"The Great Train Robbery," "Life of an American Fireman," and "Uncle Tom's Cabin," all by Porter. "La Damnation de Faust," Méliès.
1904	Theodore Roosevelt reelected president.	*Peter Pan*, J. M. Barrie (play). *The Cherry Orchard*, Chekhov (play).	A few nickelodeons— small storefront movie theaters showing programs of short films—in U.S.	"An Impossible Voyage," Méliès.
1905	Police crush demonstration in St. Petersburg; general strike in Russia. Russian sailors mutiny on battleship *Potemkin*. Einstein's theory of relativity.	*The House of Mirth*, Edith Wharton (fiction). *Major Barbara*, Shaw (play).	The first movie theater to show films exclusively and on a regular basis opens in Pittsburgh.	"Rescued by Rover," Hepworth.
1906	Britain launches the first large battleship, *Dreadnought*.		Nearly 1,000 nickelodeons in the U.S. One reel (13–16 minutes for silent films) is the usual length of a movie. Victrola (record player) first marketed.	"Dream of a Rarebit Fiend," Porter. *The Story of the Kelly Gang* (regarded as the first feature-length film), Charles Tait.

	World Events	Arts	Mass Media	Films and Videos
1907	First completely synthetic plastic developed. First blood test for syphilis.	*The Playboy of the Western World*, Synge (play). Picasso's first cubist painting.	Chicago creates its first film censorship board.	"Ben Hur," Sidney Olcott.
1908	Ford Motor Company begins making the Model T.	*A Room with a View*, E. M. Forster (fiction).	From 1908 to 1913, D. W. Griffith directs or supervises hundreds of short films at the Biograph studio.	"The Adventures of Dollie," Griffith. "The Last Days of Pompeii," Luigi Maggi.
1909	Half of U.S. population lives on farms or in small towns.	In art, the Italian book *Futurist Manifesto* exalts the beauty and dynamism of machines.	By approximately this time, 35 mm becomes the standard film gauge throughout the world.	"A Corner in Wheat" and "The Lonely Villa," Griffith.
1910	Mexican civil war begins.	*Howards End*, Forster (fiction). *The Dream*, Henri Rousseau (painting).	10,000 nickelodeons throughout U.S. U.S. actors begin to be identified in film credits. First U.S. motion-picture newsreel exhibited. Max Linder (France) writes, supervises, and performs short comic movies.	"A Child of the Ghetto," Griffith.
1911	Mexican civil war ends. First air flight across U.S.	*Ethan Frome*, Wharton (fiction). *I and My Village*, Marc Chagall (painting).	The standard aspect ratio (4:3) is widely used in film showings.	"The Battle" and "The Lonedale Operator," Griffith.

	World Events	Arts	Mass Media	Films and Videos
1912	The *Titanic* hits an iceberg and sinks on its maiden voyage; more than 1,500 die. Revolution in China and abdication of the last Chinese emperor.	*Death in Venice*, Thomas Mann (fiction).	About 5 million see American movies daily. Most American films now made in Los Angeles. Wireless is useful when the sinking *Titanic* signals for help.	"The Musketeers of Pig Alley," Griffith. *Keystone Kops* (series of short comic films), Mack Sennett. *Quo Vadis?*, Enrico Guazzoni (popular spectacle). "Queen Elizabeth," Louis Mercanton and Henri Desfontaines.
1913	Niels Bohr publishes his model of atomic structure.	First showing of avant-garde European art in U.S.		*Judith of Bethulia*, Griffith. "The Student from Prague," Stellan Rye.
1914	World War I begins in Europe. Panama Canal opens.	*Dubliners*, James Joyce (stories, including "The Dead").	In the U.S. the feature film becomes the norm. The Strand Theater, the first movie palace, opens in New York.	"Gertie," Winsor McCay (first important animated film in U.S.). *Cabiria*, Giovanni Pastrone.
1915	German submarine sinks British liner *Lusitania*; approximately 1,200 die.	*Of Human Bondage*, Somerset Maugham (fiction). New Orleans jazz is popular.		*The Birth of a Nation*, Griffith. *The Cheat*, Cecil B. De Mille. "The Tramp," Charles Chaplin.
1916	Germans use gas against their enemies in the Battle of Verdun, which lasts from February to December.	*A Portrait of the Artist as a Young Man*, Joyce (fiction). Dada (art and literary) movement founded in Zurich.	Camera crane used for filming parts of *Intolerance*. *The Art of the Moving Picture* by Vachel Lindsay and *The Photoplay: A Psychological Study* by Hugo Münsterberg are early and important books on film theory.	*Intolerance*, Griffith. *Civilization*, Thomas Ince. "The Pawn Shop," "The Vagabond," and "The Rink," all by Chaplin.

	World Events	Arts	Mass Media	Films and Videos
1917	Puerto Ricans become U.S. citizens. Revolution in Russia; provisional government is formed; tsar abdicates. U.S. enters World War I. In Russia, Bolsheviks take control; later Lenin becomes chief commissar.		UFA (major German film studio) formed. First jazz recordings.	"The Immigrant" and "Easy Street," Chaplin.
1918	World War I ends.	*The Magnificent Ambersons*, Booth Tarkington (fiction).		"Shoulder Arms," Chaplin. *The Sinking of the* Lusitania, McCay (perhaps the first feature-length animated film). *Carmen*, Ernst Lubitsch.
1919	Prohibition amendment ratified in the U.S. (goes into effect in 1920), making the manufacture or consumption of alcohol illegal. Civil war in Russia. League of Nations founded. Versailles peace treaty marks the end of World War I.	*Winesburg, Ohio*, Sherwood Anderson (fiction). Jazz arrives in Europe.	United Artists (distribution company) formed by Chaplin, Griffith, Mary Pickford, and Douglas Fairbanks. RCA founded.	*Broken Blossoms*, Griffith. *Blind Husbands*, Erich von Stroheim. *The Homesteader*, Oscar Micheaux (first feature film about U.S. blacks written and directed by an African American). *The Cabinet of Dr. Caligari*, Robert Wiene. *J'Accuse*, Abel Gance (the "Griffith of Europe").
1920	Gandhi leads India's struggle for independence from Britain. U.S. women get the vote. Russian civil war ends.	*Main Street*, Sinclair Lewis (fiction). *The Age of Innocence*, Wharton (fiction).	Lev Kuleshov founds film workshop in Moscow and begins experimenting with editing. U.S. films popular throughout much of the world. KDKA in Pittsburgh offers regularly scheduled radio programs.	*Way Down East*, Griffith. *The Golem*, Paul Wegener and Henrik Galeen.

	World Events	Arts	Mass Media	Films and Videos
1921	Major inflation in Germany. Hitler's storm troopers in Germany and Fascist Blackshirts in Italy terrorize political opponents.	*Six Characters in Search of an Author*, Luigi Pirandello (play). *The Dream*, Max Beckmann (painting).	British Broadcasting Corporation (BBC) begins. For the first time, a U.S. president (Harding) speaks to the U.S. populace over the radio.	*The Kid*, Chaplin's first feature. *The Orphans of the Storm*, Griffith. *The Weary Death*, Fritz Lang. "Rhythmus 21" (avant-garde), Hans Richter.
1922	Mussolini forms Fascist government in Italy. USSR formed by various Soviet states.	*Ulysses*, Joyce (fiction). Beginnings of surrealist movement. *Twittering Machine*, watercolor and pen and ink by Paul Klee.	New York Philharmonic concert aired on radio.	*Foolish Wives*, von Stroheim. *Nosferatu*, F. W. Murnau. *La Roue*, Gance. *Nanook of the North* (early documentary), Robert Flaherty. *Witchcraft through the Ages* (avant-garde documentary), Benjamin Christensen. *Kino-Pravda* (until 1925): creatively edited newsreels by Dziga Vertov.
1923	In Germany, Hitler's attempted coup fails.	*St. Joan*, Shaw (play).	Warner Bros. film studio founded. Kodak produces first 16 mm movie film (black-and-white). Vladimir Zworykin develops television camera tube. *Time* magazine begins.	*Safety Last*, Sam Taylor and Fred Newmeyer. *Our Hospitality*, Buster Keaton and Jack Blystone. *The Ten Commandments*, De Mille. "Retour à la raison" (avant-garde), Man Ray.
1924	Lenin dies; struggle for succession begins. American Indians given full citizenship by an act of Congress.	*A Passage to India*, Forster (fiction). *Juno and the Paycock*, Sean O'Casey (play). "Surrealist Manifesto," André Breton (essay).	MGM film studio formed. 1.25 million radios in use in U.S. Introduction of the Moviola editing machine.	*Greed*, von Stroheim. *The Last Laugh*, Murnau. *Die Nibelungen*, Lang. (*The Story of*) *Gösta Berling*, Stiller. *Strike*, Sergei Eisenstein.

	World Events	Arts	Mass Media	Films and Videos
1924 (cont.)				"Entr'acte" (avant-garde), René Clair. "Le Ballet Mécanique" (avant-garde), Fernand Léger.
1925	Scopes trial, about teaching Darwinian theory, takes place in Tennessee. Hitler publishes part of *Mein Kampf* (*My Struggle*).	*The Great Gatsby*, F. Scott Fitzgerald (fiction). *The Trial*, Franz Kafka (posthumous fiction).	Cinematographer Karl Struss uses colored makeup and color filters to depict the healing of lepers.	*The Gold Rush*, Chaplin. *Ben Hur*, Fred Niblo. *Body and Soul* (film debut of singer and actor Paul Robeson), Micheaux. *The Joyless Street*, G. W. Pabst. *Variety*, E. A. Dupont. (*Battleship*) *Potemkin*, Eisenstein.
1926	New York–London telephone service begins. Rocket launched by R. H. Goddard (U.S.).	*The Sun Also Rises*, Ernest Hemingway (fiction). *Orphée*, Jean Cocteau (play). *The Seven Pillars of Wisdom*, T. E. Lawrence (nonfiction book).	*Don Juan* with Vitaphone: film plus synchronized music from disks. *The Black Pirate*: one of the first films to use the two-color Technicolor process.	*The General*, Keaton. *Metropolis*, Lang. *Mother*, V. I. Pudovkin. *Faust*, Murnau.
1927	Charles Lindbergh flies alone nonstop from New York to Paris. German economy collapses.	*To the Lighthouse*, Virginia Woolf (fiction). *Show Boat*, Jerome Kern and Oscar Hammerstein II (stage musical). *Bird in Space*, Constantin Brancusi (sculpture). *Manhattan Bridge*, Edward Hopper (painting).	Warner Bros. releases *The Jazz Singer* using the Vitaphone sound system. *Napoléon* (Gance) includes triptychs: a wide-screen image made up of three synchronized standard images. "To Build a Fire," avant-garde fiction by Claude Autant-Lara,	*Underworld* (early gangster film), Josef Von Sternberg. *Sunrise*, Murnau. *Napoléon*, Gance. "The Italian Straw Hat," Clair. *Bed and Sofa*, Abram Room, USSR. *Berlin, Symphony of a Great City* (avant-garde documentary), Walter Ruttmann.

	World Events	**Arts**	**Mass Media**	**Films and Videos**
1927 (cont.)			is the first film to use anamorphic lenses developed by Henri Chrétien. AM radio band created. Sales of radio sets increase dramatically in U.S.	
1928	German dirigible *Graf Zeppelin* makes first transatlantic crossing. Penicillin, first antibiotic, discovered.	*Lady Chatterley's Lover*, Lawrence (fiction). *Orlando*, Woolf (fiction). *Greta Garbo*, Edward Steichen (photograph). *Three-penny Opera*, Kurt Weill (stage musical).	First all-talking film: *The Lights of New York*, uses the Vitaphone sound system. Feature films released on two rival sound-on-film systems, Movietone and Photophone. Kodak introduces 16 mm color movie film. First scheduled TV broadcast, in Schenectady, NY.	*The Circus*, Chaplin. *The Crowd*, King Vidor. *The Wind*, Sjöström. "Steamboat Willie," first Mickey Mouse film released. *October*, a.k.a. *Ten Days That Shook the World*, Eisenstein. *The Passion of Joan of Arc*, Carl Theodor Dreyer. "Un Chien Andalou" (avant-garde), Luis Buñuel.
1929	U.S. stock prices fall precipitously. European economic crisis begins. Stalin becomes absolute ruler of USSR.	*A Farewell to Arms*, Hemingway (fiction). *All Quiet on the Western Front*, Erich Maria Remarque (fiction). Museum of Modern Art opens in New York City.	Sound film projector speed is standardized in U.S. at 24 frames per second. Postdubbing first used: sound added after filming. First Academy Awards ceremony held, for films for 1927–28. *Amos 'n' Andy* radio show debuts and quickly proves popular.	*Applause*, Rouben Mamoulian. *Hallelujah!* (first sound feature with all-black cast), Vidor. *Blackmail* (first British sound film), Alfred Hitchcock. *Pandora's Box*, Pabst. "Drifters" (documentary), John Grierson. *Man with a Movie Camera* (avant-garde documentary), Vertov.
1930	Discovery of the planet Pluto. Black Muslims founded.	*The Maltese Falcon*, Dashiell Hammett (fiction).	U.S. production code for certifying movies is instituted	*All Quiet on the Western Front*, Lewis Milestone.

	World Events	Arts	Mass Media	Films and Videos
1930 (cont.)		*Composition in Red, Yellow, and Blue*, Piet Mondrian (painting).	but only loosely enforced. Rear projection developed. Worldwide, approximately 250 million people attend movies weekly.	*The Blue Angel*, von Sternberg. "The Blood of a Poet" (avant-garde), Jean Cocteau.
1931	Cyclotron invented by Ernest Lawrence. U.S. unemployment is 16% and more than 800 banks close.	*The Persistence of Memory*, Salvador Dali (painting).	*Dick Tracy* comic strip begins.	*City Lights* (includes sound effects and music but no dialogue), Chaplin. *Frankenstein*, James Whale. *Dracula*, Tod Browning. *M*, Lang.
1932	First nuclear reaction. U.S. unemployment: 24%. Franklin D. Roosevelt elected U.S. president.	First mobiles, mobile sculptures, by Alexander Calder.	First international film festival: Venice Film Festival. Technicolor three-color process first used, in a Disney cartoon, "Flowers and Trees." Radio City Music Hall, a huge and opulent movie palace, opens in New York City.	*Scarface*, Howard Hawks. *I Am a Fugitive from a Chain Gang*, Mervyn LeRoy. *Trouble in Paradise*, Lubitsch. *Dr. Jekyll and Mr. Hyde*, Mamoulian. *À nous la liberté (Freedom for Us)*, Clair.
1933	Hitler appointed German chancellor. Nazis erect their first concentration camp, and boycott of Jews begins in Germany. First round-the-world airplane flight, by Wiley Post. Prohibition ends in U.S.	*The Shape of Things to Come*, Wells (fiction). *Blood Wedding*, Federico García Lorca (play). *Man at the Crossroads*, Diego Rivera's fresco for Rockefeller Center.	British Film Institute founded. Nazis control German film industry. World's first drive-in movie theater opens in Camden, NJ. President Roosevelt uses radio for the first of his "Fireside Chats" to the nation. *The Lone Ranger* debuts on radio.	*King Kong*, Ernest Schroedsack and Merian C. Cooper. *Duck Soup*, Leo McCarey. *Gold Diggers of 1933* (with choreography by Busby Berkeley), LeRoy. "Lot in Sodom" (avant-garde), James Watson and Melville Webber. "Zero for Conduct" (avant-garde), Jean Vigo.

	World Events	Arts	Mass Media	Films and Videos
1934	Radar developed. Stalin's purge of Communist Party begins.	*The Postman Always Rings Twice*, James M. Cain (fiction). *The Children's Hour*, Lillian Hellman (play).	Henceforth (until 1968) all films to be shown publicly in the U.S. were supposed to be first submitted to the Production Code Administration for a seal of approval.	*It Happened One Night*, Frank Capra. *L'Atalante*, Vigo. *Man of Aran* (documentary), Flaherty. "Composition in Blue" (avant-garde), Oskar Fischinger.
1935	Germany begins massive military build-up. Italy invades Ethiopia.	*The Treasure of the Sierra Madre*, B. Traven (fiction). *Porgy and Bess*, George Gershwin (stage musical). Popular songs: all five Irving Berlin songs from the film *Top Hat*.	Museum of Modern Art Film Library opens. First three-color Technicolor feature film: *Becky Sharp*, directed by Mamoulian. *The March of Time* newsreels appear monthly in the nation's theaters, until 1951. FM radio developed.	*Mutiny on the Bounty*, Lloyd. *The Informer*, John Ford. *Top Hat*, Mark Sandrich. *The 39 Steps*, Hitchcock. *Triumph of the Will* (Nazi-sponsored propaganda), Leni Riefenstahl.
1936	Spanish civil war begins. Mussolini and Hitler agree to Rome-Berlin Axis.	Frank Lloyd Wright's Kaufmann House, Pennsylvania (architecture). Popular song: "A Fine Romance" (from the movie *Swing Time*).	La Cinémathèque Française (France's film archive) founded. *Life* magazine begins.	*Modern Times*, Chaplin. *Fury*, Lang. "A Day in the Country," Jean Renoir. "The Plow That Broke the Plains" (documentary), Pare Lorentz. *Olympia* (documentary), Riefenstahl.
1937	Stalin's purges result in millions of deaths and imprisonment in slave labor camps (in 1937 and 1938). Japan invades China.	*Of Mice and Men*, John Steinbeck (fiction). *The Hobbit*, J. R. R. Tolkien (fiction). *Guernica*, mural by Picasso that depicts the results of aerial bombardment.	Chrétien links two cameras with an anamorphic lens to produce an image 200 feet wide by 33 feet high for a Paris exhibition. The crash of the dirigible *Hindenburg* is broadcast live on transcontinental radio.	*A Star Is Born*, William Wellman. *Snow White and the Seven Dwarfs* (first Disney animated feature). *Grand Illusion*, Renoir.

	World Events	Arts	Mass Media	Films and Videos
1938	Germany annexes Austria. House Committee on Un-American Activities (HUAC) formed. U.S. and Germany sever diplomatic relations.	*Les Parents Terribles*, Cocteau (play). *Recumbent Figure*, Henry Moore (stone sculpture).	Orson Welles's radio broadcast of *The War of the Worlds* causes panic nationwide on Halloween. Superman first appears, in Action Comics.	*Bringing Up Baby*, Hawks. *The Lady Vanishes*, Hitchcock. *Alexander Nevsky*, Eisenstein.
1939	Spanish civil war ends with Franco's forces victorious. Pan-American Airlines begins scheduled flights between U.S. and Europe. World War II begins when Germany invades Poland.	*The Big Sleep*, Raymond Chandler (fiction). *The Grapes of Wrath*, Steinbeck (fiction). *Alexander Nevsky*, cantata by Prokofiev based on his film score. Popular song: "Over the Rainbow" (from *The Wizard of Oz*).	Hollywood studios produce 400 movies during the year. National Film Board of Canada founded. RCA demonstrates TV at New York World's Fair. First FM radio station begins operation, Alpine, NJ. Batman first appears, in Detective Comics.	*The Wizard of Oz*, Victor Fleming. *Stagecoach*, Ford. *Mr. Smith Goes to Washington*, Capra. *Gone with the Wind*, Fleming (the last director to work on the film). *The Rules of the Game*, Renoir.
1940	Churchill becomes prime minister of Britain. Germans enter Paris. All-night air raids by Germans against London begin.	*Farewell, My Lovely*, Chandler (fiction). *The Ox-Bow Incident*, Walter van Tilburg Clark (fiction). Popular song: "When You Wish upon a Star" from the movie *Pinocchio*.	28.5 million American homes have a radio. Edward R. Murrow's radio broadcasts from London during German air raids. Republican and Democratic National Conventions are broadcast on radio.	*The Grapes of Wrath*, Ford. *The Great Dictator*, Chaplin. *His Girl Friday*, Hawks. *The Bank Dick*, Eddie Cline. *Fantasia* and *Pinocchio* (Disney animated features). *Jud Süss* (anti-Semitic film), Veidt Harlan.
1941	First jet airplane flies. Germany invades Russia. Japan bombs Pearl Harbor. U.S. and Britain declare war on Japan. Germany and Italy declare war on U.S.	*What Makes Sammy Run?*, Budd Schulberg (fiction). *Moonrise, Hernandez, New Mexico*, Ansel Adams (photograph).	NBC and CBS granted commercial TV licenses.	*Citizen Kane*, first film directed by Orson Welles. *The Maltese Falcon*, first film directed by John Huston. "Target for Tonight" (documentary), Harry Watt.

	World Events	Arts	Mass Media	Films and Videos
1942	Germany begins killing Jews in gas chambers. Japan invades the Philippines. Heavy German air raids on London.	*The Stranger*, Albert Camus (fiction). *Nighthawks*, Edward Hopper (painting).	In U.S., radio is the main source of information about the war.	*Casablanca*, Michael Curtiz. *The Magnificent Ambersons*, Welles. *To Be or Not to Be*, Lubitsch. "The Battle of Midway" (documentary), Ford. "Why We Fight" (series of seven wartime documentaries, 1942–45), produced by Capra.
1943	Allied forces land in Sicily. Mussolini dismissed as Italian premier. Italy surrenders then declares war on Germany.	*Oklahoma!*, Rodgers and Hammerstein (stage musical).	*Perry Mason* radio series begins with Raymond Burr, later a TV series.	*Shadow of a Doubt*, Hitchcock. *The Ox-Bow Incident*, Wellman. "Report from the Aleutians" (documentary), Huston. *Fires Were Started* (documentary), Humphrey Jennings. "Meshes of the Afternoon" (avant-garde), Maya Deren and Alexander Hammid.
1944	Allies D-Day landing in northern France. German V-2 rockets used against Britain. Roosevelt elected U.S. president for fourth term.	*The Glass Menagerie*, Tennessee Williams (play).		*Hail the Conquering Hero* and *The Miracle of Morgan's Creek*, Preston Sturges. *Double Indemnity*, Billy Wilder. *Murder, My Sweet*, Edward Dmytryk. *Henry V*, Laurence Olivier. "Memphis Belle" (documentary), William Wyler.

	World Events	Arts	Mass Media	Films and Videos
1945	President Roosevelt dies unexpectedly. United Nations charter signed in San Francisco. War ends in Europe, 35 million killed, 6 million of whom were Jews. U.S. drops two atomic bombs on Japan. Japan surrenders. Independent republic of Vietnam formed. Nuremberg trials of Nazi war criminals begin.	*Animal Farm*, George Orwell (satirical fable). *Carousel*, Rodgers and Hammerstein (stage musical). Beginnings of abstract expressionist movement in painting.	*Meet the Press* debuts on radio.	*The Lost Weekend*, Wilder. *Detour*, Edgar G. Ulmer. *Open City* (a.k.a. *Rome, Open City*), Roberto Rossellini. *Brief Encounter*, David Lean. *Ivan the Terrible*, Eisenstein. *Children of Paradise* (made in France during German occupation), Marcel Carné. "The Battle of San Pietro" (documentary), Huston.
1946	Cold war between USSR and its allies and U.S. and its allies begins. Juan Perón elected president of Argentina. Philippine independence from the U.S., July 4. Nuremberg trials end. French women get the vote.	*Zorba, the Greek*, Nikos Kazantzakis (fiction). *All the King's Men*, Robert Penn Warren (fiction). *Annie Get Your Gun*, Irving Berlin (stage musical).	Each week about 90 million Americans go to the movies, a record. Cannes (France) Film Festival founded. U.S. television begins broadcasting and TV sets go on sale.	*My Darling Clementine*, Ford. *The Killers*, Robert Siodmak. *The Best Years of Our Lives*, Wyler. *It's a Wonderful Life*, Capra. *Beauty and the Beast*, Cocteau. *Great Expectations*, Lean. *Shoeshine*, Vittorio De Sica. "Let There Be Light" (documentary made but not released), Huston.
1947	India becomes independent of Britain. Jackie Robinson becomes first African American to play major league baseball.	*A Streetcar Named Desire*, Williams (play). The Actors Studio, which teaches Method acting, founded.	HUAC investigates possible Communist influence in Hollywood. Regular TV news broadcasts begin.	*Out of the Past*, Jacques Tourner. *Crossfire*, Dmytryk. *Monsieur Verdoux*, Chaplin. "Fireworks" (avant-garde), Kenneth Anger.

	World Events	Arts	Mass Media	Films and Videos
1947 (cont.)	India is divided into India and Pakistan. U.S. plane flies faster than sound.		Zoom lens developed, at first for use in TV.	
1948	Gandhi assassinated in India. U.S. Congress passes Marshall Plan: economic assistance for rebuilding Europe. Israel proclaimed a country. Apartheid becomes government policy of South Africa. USSR blocks all traffic between Berlin and the West; a few days later western countries begin to airlift supplies into Berlin.	*The Naked and the Dead,* Norman Mailer (fiction). *Cry, the Beloved Country,* Alan Paton (fiction). *The Loved One,* Evelyn Waugh ("black comedy" fiction). *Christina's World,* Andrew Wyeth (painting). *City Square,* Alberto Giacometti (bronze sculpture).	Drive-in theaters increase in popularity. Hollywood Ten found guilty of contempt of Congress. In the *Paramount* case, the U.S. Supreme Court rules that the major Hollywood studios' control of production, distribution, and exhibition violates antitrust laws. TV is becoming a threat to the film industry. Long-playing phonograph record introduced. Transistor developed. 135 million paperback books sold in U.S. during the year.	*The Treasure of the Sierra Madre,* Huston. *The Naked City,* Jules Dassin. *Force of Evil,* Abraham Polonsky. *The Lady from Shanghai,* Welles. *The Red Shoes,* Powell. *Oliver Twist,* Lean. *The Fallen Idol,* Carol Reed. *The Bicycle Thief* (a.k.a. *Bicycle Thieves*), De Sica. *Les Parents Terribles* (film version of his own play of the same title), Cocteau.
1949	NATO created, a collective defense alliance initially of twelve nations. Berlin airlift ends. USSR tests its first atomic bomb. Chinese Communists come to power. Republic of India begins.	*1984,* Orwell (fiction). *Death of a Salesman,* Arthur Miller (play). *South Pacific,* Rodgers and Hammerstein (stage musical). Popular music: zither music from the film *The Third Man.*	1 million TV sets in U.S. 45 rpm record introduced.	*Gun Crazy,* Joseph H. Lewis. *Pinky,* Elia Kazan. *All the King's Men,* Robert Rossen. *The Third Man,* Reed. *Kind Hearts and Coronets,* Robert Hamer. *Late Spring,* Yasujiro Ozu. *The Quiet One* (documentary), Sidney Meyers.

	World Events	Arts	Mass Media	Films and Videos
1949 (cont.)				"Begone Dull Care" (avant-garde), Norman McLaren.
1950	Sen. Joseph McCarthy claims U.S. State Department is full of Communists. North Korea invades South Korea and Korean War begins.	*The Third Man*, Graham Greene (novel published after the film). *Guys and Dolls*, Swerling, Burrows, and Loesser (stage musical).	Live TV comedy show *Your Show of Shows* with Sid Caesar and Imogene Coca begins and runs until 1954. *The Jack Benny Show* begins on TV. *Peanuts* comic strip begins.	*Sunset Boulevard*, Wilder. *All About Eve*, Joseph L. Mankiewicz. *Rashomon*, Akira Kurosawa. *Los Olvidados* (literally *The Forgotten Ones*, but sometimes known as *The Young and the Damned*), Buñuel. *Diary of a Country Priest*, Robert Bresson.
1951	Japanese women get the vote. Organization of American States founded.	*The Caine Mutiny*, Herman Wouk (fiction). *From Here to Eternity*, James Jones (fiction).	Second congressional hearing on possible Communist influence in Hollywood (1951–52). Nitrate-base film, used for most professional 35 mm movies, replaced with safety-base films. Color TV introduced in the U.S. TV shows *I Love Lucy* and *Today* begin.	*The African Queen*, Huston. *A Streetcar Named Desire*, Kazan. *Strangers on a Train*, Hitchcock. *The Lavender Hill Mob*, Charles Crichton.
1952	Juan Batista seizes power in Cuba. Coup in Egypt deposes king and leads to the establishment of Egyptian Republic.	*Invisible Man*, Ralph Ellison (fiction). *The Old Man and the Sea*, Hemingway (fiction). *Waiting for Godot*, Samuel Beckett (play).	A three-projector version of Cinerama is introduced with the travelogue *This Is Cinerama*. *Bwana Devil* starts a brief craze for 3-D movies.	*High Noon*, Fred Zinnemann. *Singin' in the Rain*, Gene Kelly and Stanley Donen. *Limelight*, Chaplin. *Ikiru* (*To Live*), Kurosawa.

	World Events	Arts	Mass Media	Films and Videos
1952 (cont.)	Puerto Rico becomes a U.S. commonwealth. U.S. explodes first hydrogen bomb. General Dwight D. Eisenhower elected president.	Popular song: "Do Not Forsake Me," from the film *High Noon*.	Eastman color film, which is easier to process and cheaper than Technicolor, gains in acceptance and results in increased use of color in Hollywood films. Handheld transistor radios marketed in U.S. *Mad* magazine debuts.	*Umberto D*, De Sica. "Neighbours" (symbolic fictional film), McLaren.
1953	Stalin dies. Publication that DNA's double-helix structure can be deciphered. Elizabeth crowned Queen Elizabeth II of England. Korean War ends.	*Fahrenheit 451*, Ray Bradbury (fiction). *Picnic*, William Inge (play).	U.S. theaters begin to show anamorphic movies. Academy Awards ceremony first telecast. *The Moon Is Blue* released without a Motion Picture Association of America seal. Eisenhower's inauguration broadcast live on TV. *Playboy* begins publication.	*Shane*, George Stevens. *Peter Pan* (Disney animated feature). *Mr. Hulot's Holiday*, Jacques Tati. *Ugetsu* (*Monogatari*), Kenji Mizoguchi. *Tokyo Story*, Ozu. *Gate of Hell*, Teinosuke Kinugasa.
1954	Discovery of polio vaccine announced. U.S. Supreme Court rules that school segregation is unconstitutional. French defeated in Vietnam; Vietnam divided into North and South. Joseph McCarthy discredited and censured by his U.S. Senate colleagues.	*Invasion of the Body Snatchers*, Jack Finney (fiction). *Lord of the Flies*, William Golding (fiction). First volume of *The Lord of the Rings*, J. R. R. Tolkien (fantasy novels).	*White Christmas* filmed in VistaVision, a nonanamorphic widescreen system. Approximately half of American homes have a TV. Army–McCarthy hearings carried live on TV. First U.S. TV color telecast, Rose Bowl parade. *The Tonight Show* (with Steve Allen) debuts on TV.	*On the Waterfront*, Kazan. *Rear Window*, Hitchcock. *La Strada*, Federico Fellini. *The Seven Samurai*, Kurosawa. *Late Chrysanthemums*, Mikio Naruse. *Godzilla*, Inoshiro Honda.

	World Events	Arts	Mass Media	Films and Videos
1955	Civil war begins between North and South Vietnam. Warsaw Pact signed by Eastern European countries. Blacks boycott segregated city buses in Montgomery, Alabama.	*Lolita*, Vladimir Nabokov (fiction). *The Diary of Anne Frank*, Albert Hackett and Frances Goodrich (play). *The Family of Man*, photographic exhibit organized by Edward Steichen.	Filming from helicopters becomes more practicable. Todd-AO (a nonanamorphic wide-screen) process used in film version of *Oklahoma!* Disneyland opens in California. Highest rated TV show (1955–56): the quiz show *The $64,000 Question*. *Alfred Hitchcock Presents* TV show airs until 1962.	*Rebel Without a Cause*, Nicholas Ray. *Night of the Hunter*, Charles Laughton. *Smiles of a Summer Night*, Ingmar Bergman. *Pather Panchali* (the first of three Apu films), Satyajit Ray.
1956	Soviets crush Hungarian revolt. Israel invades Sinai Peninsula.	*Long Day's Journey into Night*, O'Neill (play). *Look Back in Anger*, John Osborne (play). *My Fair Lady*, Lerner and Loewe (stage musical).	Elvis Presley appears on *The Ed Sullivan Show* on TV. TV westerns are popular. Singer Nat King Cole becomes the first African American to host a network TV show. *Huntley-Brinkley Report*, a TV news program, debuts.	*The Searchers*, Ford. *The Killing*, Stanley Kubrick. *The Seventh Seal*, Bergman. *A Man Escaped*, Bresson. "The Red Balloon," Albert Lamorisse. "Night and Fog" (avant-garde documentary), Alain Resnais.
1957	Martin Luther King Jr. and others found the Southern Christian Leadership Conference. President Eisenhower sends troops to help desegregate the University of Arkansas. Soviets launch *Sputnik*, the first satellite to circle earth.	*Doctor Zhivago*, Boris Pasternak (fiction). *On the Road*, Jack Kerouac (fiction). *West Side Story*, Leonard Bernstein and Jerome Robbins (stage musical).	*Raintree County*, first film released in Ultra-Panavision 70. *Perry Mason* begins its nine-season run on TV. *American Bandstand* (with Dick Clark) is first shown on national TV.	*Paths of Glory*, Kubrick. *The Sweet Smell of Success*, Alexander Mackendrick. *The Nights of Cabiria*, Fellini. *Wild Strawberries*, Bergman. *Throne of Blood*, Kurosawa. "Two Men and a Wardrobe" (avant-garde), Roman Polanski.

	World Events	Arts	Mass Media	Films and Videos
1957 (cont.)				"A Chairy Tale" (avant-garde), McLaren and Claude Jutra.
1958	European Common Market formed. First successful launch of a U.S. satellite. U.S. troops sent to intervene in Lebanese civil war.	*The Birthday Party*, Harold Pinter (play).	More than 4,000 U.S. drive-in movie screens in operation. Stereophonic LP's and phonographs come into use. Most popular TV show (1958–59): the western *Gunsmoke*.	*Touch of Evil*, Welles. *Vertigo*, Hitchcock. *Ashes and Diamonds*, Andrzej Wajda. *Ivan, the Terrible, Part Two*, Eisenstein (completed in 1946). *Room at the Top*, Jack Clayton. *The World of Apu*, Satyajit Ray. "A Movie" (avant-garde), Bruce Conner.
1959	Approximately a month after leading a successful revolution against the Cuban president, Fidel Castro becomes premier of Cuba. Yasir Arafat and others found Palestine Liberation Organization.	*The Tin Drum*, Günter Grass (fiction). *Naked Lunch*, William Burroughs (fiction). *A Raisin in the Sun*, Lorraine Hansberry (play). "Happenings," multimedia events, first staged in New York City.	TV quiz show scandal. *Adventures in Good Music*, classical music radio program by Karl Haas, begins on a Detroit station.	*Ben-Hur*, Wyler. *North by Northwest*, Hitchcock. *Some Like It Hot*, Wilder. *The 400 Blows*, François Truffaut's first feature. *Breathless*, Jean-Luc Godard's first feature. *Hiroshima, mon amour*, Resnais. *Look Back in Anger*, Tony Richardson. *Floating Weeds*, Ozu. "Window Water Baby Moving" (avant-garde), Stan Brakhage.
1960	FDA approves use of birth control pill. Nigeria becomes independent nation. Laser invented.	*To Kill a Mockingbird*, Harper Lee (fiction). *Camelot*, Lerner and Loewe (stage musical).	*Echo 1*, the first communications satellite, launched. Historic TV debate between presidential	*Psycho*, Hitchcock. *Saturday Night and Sunday Morning*, Karel Reisz. *The Entertainer*, Richardson.

	World Events	Arts	Mass Media	Films and Videos
1960 (cont.)		Minimalist style in painting, sculpture, and music. Albums by John Coltrane: *Coltrane Plays the Blues* and *My Favorite Things*.	candidates John Kennedy and Richard Nixon. *Harvest of Shame*, TV documentary film on migrant farm workers, Edward R. Murrow, commentator. Approximately 100 million TV sets in Europe and U.S.	*L'avventura*, Michelangelo Antonioni. *La dolce vita*, Fellini. *Shoot the Piano Player*, Truffaut.
1961	U.S. establishes Peace Corps. USSR begins manned space flights. U.S.-sponsored Bay of Pigs invasion of Cuba fails. Communists build Berlin Wall to deter East Germans from fleeing to the West.	*Catch-22*, Joseph Heller (fiction). *The Moviegoer*, Walker Percy (fiction). Comic-strip and comic-frame paintings, Roy Lichtenstein.	First live TV coverage of a presidential news conference. *The Dick Van Dyke Show* begins and runs five years on TV.	*Shadows*, John Cassavetes's first film as director. *West Side Story*, Robert Wise. *Jules and Jim*, Truffaut. *Last Year at Marienbad* (avant-garde fiction), Resnais. *Viridiana*, Buñuel. *Chronicle of a Summer* (cinéma vérité), Jean Rouch. "Prelude to Dog Star Man" (avant-garde), Brakhage.
1962	John Glenn is first American to orbit earth in a spacecraft. Algeria wins independence from France. U.S. and USSR in tense confrontation over Soviet missiles in Cuba.	*A Clockwork Orange*, Anthony Burgess (satirical fiction). *The Death of Artemio Cruz*, Carlos Fuentes (fiction). *One Flew over the Cuckoo's Nest*, Ken Kesey (fiction). *Who's Afraid of Virginia Woolf?*, Edward Albee (play). First public awareness of pop art.	*The Alfred Hitchcock Hour* TV show airs until 1965. Johnny Carson becomes host of *The Tonight Show*, NBC's late-night TV talk show and remains so until 1992. Walter Cronkite becomes anchor (until 1981) of *CBS Evening News*. *Telstar* satellite (for TV and telephone relays) launched.	*The Man Who Shot Liberty Valance*, Ford. *Vivre sa vie* (*My Life to Live*), Godard. *Knife in the Water*, Polanski. *8½*, Fellini. *Lawrence of Arabia*, Lean. *The Loneliness of the Long Distance Runner*, Richardson. "An Occurrence at Owl Creek Bridge" (avant-garde), Robert Enrico.

	World Events	Arts	Mass Media	Films and Videos
1962 (cont.)			Most popular TV show (1962–64): *The Beverly Hillbillies*.	"La Jetée" (avant-garde), Chris Marker. "Cosmic Ray" (avant-garde), Conner.
1963	Alabama civil rights march results in beatings of blacks, arrest of Dr. Martin Luther King Jr., and the sending of federal troops. Four black girls killed in bombing of Birmingham, Alabama, church. President Kennedy assassinated. By year's end, the U.S. has sent economic aid and 16,000 "advisers" to South Vietnam.	*Cinema*, George Segal (life-size sculpture). *Mona Lisa*, Andy Warhol's painted version.	New York Film Festival established. *Movietone News* last presented in U.S. movie theaters. Poll reveals TV now the major source of news for most Americans. TV networks expand evening news programs from 15 to 30 minutes. Martin Luther King Jr.'s "I Have a Dream" speech in DC is televised. Unprecedented four-day TV coverage of President Kennedy's assassination and burial. Audiocassettes used to record and play back music.	*The Birds*, Hitchcock. *Tom Jones*, Richardson. *Dr. Strangelove: Or, How I Learned to Stop Worrying and Love the Bomb*, Kubrick. *Lord of the Flies*, Peter Brook. *Dead Birds* (documentary), Robert Gardner. *Point of Order* (documentary), Emile De Antonio. *Sleep* (avant-garde documentary), Andy Warhol. "Scorpio Rising" (avant-garde), Anger. "Mothlight" (avant-garde), Brakhage.
1964	Martin Luther King Jr. wins Nobel Peace Prize. Zambia (formerly Rhodesia) becomes an independent nation.	*The Woman in the Dunes*, Kobo Abe (fiction). *Little Big Man*, Thomas Berger (fiction). *Fiddler on the Roof*, Bock and Harnick (stage musical). *Jackie*, Andy Warhol (painting of Jacqueline Kennedy).	Sports telecasts begin to use videotaped instant replay. The Beatles appear on *The Ed Sullivan Show* on TV.	*Nothing but a Man*, Michael Roemer. *A Hard Day's Night*, Richard Lester. *The Gospel according to St. Matthew*, Pier Paolo Pasolini. *Woman in the Dunes*, Hiroshi Teshigahara. *A Married Woman*, Godard.

	World Events	Arts	Mass Media	Films and Videos
1964 (cont.)		First Moog (electronic) synthesizer. Popular song: "Raindrops Keep Falling on My Head," from the film *Butch Cassidy and the Sundance Kid*.		*The Red Desert*, Antonioni. *A Stravinsky Portrait* (documentary), Richard Leacock. "Fuses," 1964–67 (avant-garde), Carolee Schneemann. "Dog Star Man" (avant-garde), Brakhage.
1965	Malcolm X, a Black Muslim leader, murdered in New York. In U.S., growing demonstrations against U.S. involvement in Vietnam.	*The Autobiography of Malcolm X*, Alex Haley (nonfiction). Luis Valdez founds Teatro Campesino in California. *Campbell's Soup Can*, Andy Warhol (painting).	Super-8 film introduced. TV coverage of Vietnam War expands. Eight-track tape players (forerunners of cassette tape players) introduced.	*The Pawnbroker*, Sidney Lumet. *Pierrot le fou*, Godard. *Juliet of the Spirits*, Fellini. *The Shop on Main Street*, Jan Kadár and Elmar Klos. *To Die in Madrid* (documentary), Frédéric Rossif. "The War Game" (fake documentary), Peter Watkins. "The Sins of the Fleshpoids" (avant-garde), Mike Kuchar.
1966	Cultural Revolution—led by Mao Zedong—begins in China (ends in 1971), resulting in terrorism, purges, destroyed artworks, and restructuring of the education system. Black Panther Party founded in Oakland, California. National Organization for Women formed.	*The Last Picture Show*, Larry McMurtry (fiction). *In Cold Blood*, Truman Capote (nonfiction). *Cabaret*, Ebb and Kander (stage musical). *Sweet Charity*, Simon, Fields, and Coleman (stage musical based on Fellini's film *The Nights of Cabiria*).	Color TV becomes popular in U.S. *Star Trek* begins its three-season run on TV. *Mission: Impossible* adventure series on TV until 1973. *Amos 'n' Andy* reruns dropped from TV because of protests against the show's racial stereotypes.	*Who's Afraid of Virginia Woolf?*, Mike Nichols. *Blowup*, Antonioni. *Persona*, Bergman. *Closely Watched Trains*, Jiri Menzel. *The Battle of Algiers*, Gillo Pontecorvo. *La Guerre est finie*, Resnais. *Black Girl*, Ousmane Sembène. *The Chelsea Girls* (avant-garde), Warhol.

	World Events	Arts	Mass Media	Films and Videos
1966 (cont.)	By year's end, 389,000 U.S. troops are in Vietnam.	*The State Hospital*, Edward Kienholz (mixed media). *Witness to Our Time*, Alfred Eisenstaedt (photographic collection).	*Sixteen in Webster Groves*, TV documentary.	"No. 4 (Bottoms)" (avant-garde documentary), Yoko Ono. "Film in Which There Appear to Be Sprocket Holes, Edge Lettering, Dirt Particles, Etc." (avant-garde), George Landow (a.k.a. Owen Land). "The Flicker" (avant-garde), Tony Conrad. "Lapis" (avant-garde), James Whitney.
1967	Six-day war between Arab nations and Israel results in Israeli victory and acquisition of territory. Thurgood Marshall becomes first African American Supreme Court justice. First human heart transplant, in South Africa. By year's end, more than 500,000 U.S. troops in Vietnam.	*100 Years of Solitude*, García Márquez (fiction). *Rosencrantz and Guildenstern Are Dead*, Tom Stoppard (play). *Hair*, Ragni and Rado (rock musical). First major rock festival, Monterey, California.	American Film Institute founded. *Rolling Stone* magazine founded. Smothers Brothers (satirists) are popular on TV. *Ironsides* with Raymond Burr on TV until 1975. *The Carol Burnett Show*, on TV until 1979.	*Bonnie and Clyde*, Arthur Penn. *The Graduate*, Nichols. *Weekend*, Godard. *Playtime*, Tati. *Belle de Jour*, Buñuel. *Accident*, Joseph Losey. *Don't Look Back* (documentary), Donn Pennebaker. *Portrait of Jason* (documentary), Shirley Clarke. *Titicut Follies* (documentary), Frederick Wiseman. "Quixote" (revised version; avant-garde documentary), Bruce Baillie. "Wavelength" (avant-garde), Michael Snow.

	World Events	Arts	Mass Media	Films and Videos
1968	Successes of surprise Tet Offensive demoralize U.S. and South Vietnamese forces. Martin Luther King Jr. assassinated. Senator Robert Kennedy assassinated. Soviets invade Czechoslovakia and end its liberal policies. Outside Democratic Convention in Chicago: rioting and police brutality.	*2001: A Space Odyssey*, Arthur C. Clarke (fiction). *Black Rain*, Masuji Ibuse (fiction). *I Never Sang for My Father*, Robert Anderson (play). *The Great White Hope*, Howard Sackler (play).	Motion Picture Association of America institutes four-part rating system for films. Czech film movement ended by Soviet invasion of Czechoslovakia. *60 Minutes* TV show begins. *Rowan and Martin's Laugh-In*, featuring very short satiric pieces, is popular on TV until 1973.	*Faces*, Cassavetes. *Night of the Living Dead*, George Romero. *David Holzman's Diary* (fake documentary), Jim McBride. *2001: A Space Odyssey*, Kubrick. *Shame*, Bergman. *Memories of Underdevelopment*, Tomás Gutiérrez Alea. *High School* (documentary), Wiseman. "Pas de Deux" (avant-garde), McLaren.
1969	Yasir Arafat becomes head of Palestine Liberation Organization. U.S. astronauts land on moon for the first time and return. Woodstock, NY, musical festival draws an estimated 500,000. Large U.S. demonstrations against Vietnam War continue. My Lai (Vietnam) massacre of villagers by U.S. soldiers revealed. American gay liberation movement begins.	*Fat City*, Leonard Gardner (fiction). *The Godfather* by Mario Puzo becomes the best-selling U.S. novel of the 1970s. *Portnoy's Complaint*, Philip Roth (fiction). *Slaughterhouse-Five*, Kurt Vonnegut Jr. (fiction).	Live TV broadcast from moon captivates the world's attention. PBS begins broadcasting TV programs, including *Sesame Street*, which uses techniques of TV commercials to teach children basic language skills. Most popular TV show (1969–70): *Rowan and Martin's Laugh-In*.	*Midnight Cowboy*, John Schlesinger. *Medium Cool*, Haskell Wexler. *The Wild Bunch*, Sam Peckinpah. *I Am Joaquin*, possibly the first film written, produced, and directed by Latinos in the U.S. *My Night at Maud's*, Eric Rohmer. *If . . .*, Lindsay Anderson. *Boy*, Nagisa Oshima. *Monterey Pop* (early rock documentary), Pennebaker. *Salesman* (documentary), Maysles Brothers. *In the Year of the Pig* (documentary), De Antonio. *Tom, Tom, the Piper's Son* (avant-garde), Ken Jacobs. "Back and Forth" (avant-garde), Snow.

	World Events	**Arts**	**Mass Media**	**Films and Videos**
1970	U.S. Supreme Court approves school busing to achieve integration. U.S. and South Vietnamese troops enter Cambodia. At Kent State University, Ohio National Guard shoot at demonstrating students and kill four. Massive student demonstrations against the Vietnam War close hundreds of U.S. colleges and universities.	*Deliverance*, James Dickey (fiction). *Spiral Jetty*, 1,500-foot jetty, Great Salt Lake, Utah, Robert Smithson.	Rapid growth of film studies in U.S. colleges and universities. IMAX ("image maximum"), extremely large-screen film format, introduced at World's Fair. National Public Radio begins broadcasting. *The Phil Donahue Show* is first seen nationally on TV and runs until 1996. About 231 million TV sets used throughout the world. *The Mary Tyler Moore Show* (sit-com) begins on TV. *Doonesbury* (satirical) comic strip begins.	*M*A*S*H*, Robert Altman. *Patton*, Franklin Schaffner. *The Wild Child*, François Truffaut. *Even Dwarfs Started Small*, Werner Herzog. *Woodstock* (documentary), Michael Wadleigh. *The Sorrow and the Pity* (cinéma vérité), Marcel Ophüls. *Gimme Shelter* (documentary), Maysles Brothers. *Zorns Lemma* (avant-garde), Hollis Frampton. "Remedial Reading Comprehension" (avant-garde), Landow/Land. "Runs Good" (avant-garde), Pat O'Neill.
1971	Soviets put the world's first space station into orbit. Saddam Hussein seizes power in Iraq. Pakistan attacks India but is defeated in two-week war. Bangladesh established as independent nation.	*Maurice*, Forster (posthumous fiction). *Being There*, Jerzy Kosinski (fiction). *. . . And the Earth Did Not Devour Him*, Tomás Rivera (fiction).	Movie theater receipts are down sharply. *Ms.* magazine founded to promote women's movement. Cable TV is growing. Ban on TV cigarette advertising goes into effect. *Masterpiece Theatre* begins on PBS, with Alistair Cooke as host. Top U.S. TV show (1971–76): *All in the Family* with Carroll O'Connor as Archie Bunker.	*McCabe and Mrs. Miller*, Altman. *The Last Picture Show*, Peter Bogdanovich. *Sweet Sweetback's Badass Song*, Melvin Van Peebles. *A Clockwork Orange*, Kubrick. *Claire's Knee*, Rohmer. *Walkabout*, Nicolas Roeg. *The Conformist*, Bernardo Bertolucci. "(nostalgia)" (avant-garde), Frampton. "Kiri" (avant-garde), Sakumi Hagiwara.

	World Events	Arts	Mass Media	Films and Videos
1972	White House announces the last U.S. ground combat units have left Vietnam. Men working for the Republican Party caught in the DC Watergate Hotel trying to break into Democratic National Headquarters.	*Bless Me, Ultima*, Rudolfo A. Anaya (fiction). *Story Show*, Laurie Anderson (multimedia performance). *Grease!*, Jim Jacobs and Warren Casey (stage musical). Christo wraps large section of Australian coastline in plastic sheeting.	*M*A*S*H* TV series begins and runs for 11 seasons. Home Box Office is available through cable TV. *Deep Throat*, first sexually explicit feature to gain U.S. national audience.	*The Godfather*, Francis Ford Coppola. *Cabaret*, Bob Fosse. *Fat City*, Huston. *Frenzy*, Hitchcock. *The Discreet Charm of the Bourgeoisie*, Buñuel. *Last Tango in Paris*, Bertolucci. *Aguirre, the Wrath of God*, Herzog. *Cries and Whispers*, Bergman. "Near the Big Chakra" (avant-garde documentary), Anne Severson.
1973	U.S. Supreme Court rules abortion is constitutional. Vietnam cease-fire agreement signed; U.S. combat deaths: 47,000+. Salvador Allende, Marxist president of Chile, is overthrown and reportedly commits suicide. Amid scandal, Spiro T. Agnew resigns as U.S. vice president.	*Fear of Flying*, Erica Jong (fiction). *The Gulag Archipelago*, Solzhenitsyn (first volume of three-volume fiction). *Equus*, Peter Shaffer (play). Scott Joplin's ragtime music is popular after its frequent use in the movie *The Sting*.	Omnimax, huge dome screen for use with IMAX, developed. Senate Watergate hearings broadcast on TV. *An American Family*, 12-hour TV documentary series, Alan and Susan Raymond.	*Mean Streets*, Martin Scorsese. *American Graffiti*, George Lucas. *Payday*, Daryl Duke. *No Lies*, Mitchell Block. *The Harder They Come*, Perry Henzell. *Don't Look Now*, Roeg. *Day for Night*, Truffaut. *Fantastic Planet* (animated), Rene Laloux. *Spirit of the Beehive*, Victor Erice. *Distant Thunder*, Satyajit Ray. *Touki Bouki* (*The Journey of the Hyena*), Djibril Diop Mambety. "Three Transitions" (avant-garde videos), Peter Campus.

	World Events	Arts	Mass Media	Films and Videos
1974	Nixon resigns presidency; Gerald Ford becomes president. President Ford grants Nixon a pardon for possible criminal offenses while in office. OPEC oil embargo causes oil shortages and serious economic problems in U.S. and elsewhere.	*Jaws*, Peter Benchley (fiction). *Carrie*, Stephen King (fiction).	*Little House on the Prairie* runs on TV until 1983. *The Rockford Files* runs on TV until 1980. *Happy Days* runs on TV until 1984. *Prairie Home Companion* radio program with Garrison Keillor as host begins.	*The Godfather Part II*, Coppola. *Chinatown*, Polanski. *A Woman under the Influence*, Cassavetes. *Amarcord*, Fellini. *Scenes from a Marriage*, Bergman. *Xala* (*Impotence*), Sembène. *Antonia: A Portrait of the Woman* (documentary), Jill Godmilow. *Film about a woman who . . .* (avant-garde), Yvonne Rainer. "Print Generation" (avant-garde), J. J. Murphy. "8½ x 11" (avant-garde fiction), James Benning.
1975	Personal computers introduced in the U.S. U.S. ends all involvement in Vietnam. Soviet space probes transmit first pictures of Venus's surface. Generalíssimo Franco of Spain dies; Juan Carlos sworn in as king. Khmer Rouge kill at least one million Cambodians, 1975–79.	*Ragtime*, E. L. Doctorow (fiction). *American Buffalo*, David Mamet (play). *A Chorus Line*, Kirkwood, Dante, and Hamlisch (stage musical), opens in New York and runs 15 years.	Dolby film noise reduction system introduced. *Saturday Night Live* debuts on TV. Sony introduces Beta home videotape format.	*Nashville*, Altman. *One Flew over the Cuckoo's Nest*, Milos Forman. *Barry Lyndon*, Kubrick. *The Rocky Horror Picture Show*, Jim Sharman. *The Mystery of Kaspar Hauser*, Herzog. *The Story of Adele H.*, Truffaut. *Jeanne Dielman* (avant-garde documentary), Chantal Akerman.
1976	Argentine military government begins "dirty war" against dissidents; tens of thousands of citizens	*The Woman Warrior*, Maxine Hong Kingston (fiction). *The Shining*, King (fiction).	Steadicam, a lightweight, portable mount for holding a motion-picture camera, first used in	*Taxi Driver*, Scorsese. *Network*, Lumet. *Face to Face*, Bergman. *Seven Beauties*, Lina Wertmuller.

	World Events	Arts	Mass Media	Films and Videos
1976 (cont.)	disappear or are murdered, or both. Apple Computer Company founded. Two U.S. spacecraft land on Mars, run tests, but find no signs of life.	*The Kiss of the Spider Woman*, Manuel Puig (fiction). *Roots*, Alex Haley (nonfiction).	making a feature film (*Bound for Glory*). Louma (lightweight, modular, 25-foot) camera crane with remote-control camera head first used in filming a feature (*The Tenant*). U.S. broadcasts views from Mars worldwide. *The McNeil-Lehrer Report* begins on PBS (TV).	*In the Realm of the Senses*, Oshima. *Harlan County USA* (documentary), Barbara Kopple. *Word Is Out* (documentary), Robert Epstein and Peter Adair. "Chulas Fronteras" (documentary), Les Blank. "Projection Instructions" (avant-garde), Morgan Fisher.
1977	American space probes *Voyager 1* and *2* are launched; two years later they send back extensive data and many photographs of Jupiter.	Pompidou Center, Richard Rogers and Renzo Pieno, Paris (architecture).	8-part TV dramatization of Haley's book *Roots* is a popular and critical success. *The Lou Grant Show* runs on TV until 1982.	*Annie Hall*, Woody Allen. *Star Wars*, Lucas. *Equus*, Lumet. *Close Encounters of the Third Kind*, Steven Spielberg. *Providence*, Resnais. *1900*, Bertolucci. *Ceddo*, Sembène. "Video Weavings" (avant-garde video), Stephen Beck. "Turn to Your ~~Gods~~ Dogs" (avant-garde), Richard Beveridge.
1978	In Nicaragua, Sandinista guerrilla war develops into a civil war (until 1988). The Vietnamese occupy Cambodia and end Khmer Rouge slaughter of Cambodians. First "test-tube" baby born, in England.	*Zoot Suit*, Luis Valdez (play). *Ain't Misbehavin'*, jazz musical celebrating the music of Fats Waller. The sound track albums for the movies *Saturday Night Fever* and *Grease* are popular.	120 million people see U.S. TV movie *Holocaust*. *Dallas* runs on TV until 1991. Laser video disc players and video discs first marketed in U.S.	*The Deer Hunter*, Michael Cimino. *Grease*, Randal Kleiser. *Girlfriends*, Claudia Weill. *Get Out Your Handkerchiefs*, Bertrand Blier. *Autumn Sonata*, Bergman. *The Marriage of Maria Braun*, Fassbinder.

	World Events	Arts	Mass Media	Films and Videos
1978 (cont.)				*Gates of Heaven* (documentary), Errol Morris. "Daughter Rite" (documentary), Michelle Citron.
1979	Shah of Iran forced into exile; Ayatollah Khomeini becomes new leader. Nuclear disaster almost occurs at Three Mile Island, Pennsylvania. Sandinistas overthrow Nicaragua's President Somoza and establish a Marxist government. About 100 U.S. embassy personnel taken hostage in Teheran. Smallpox declared eradicated worldwide.	*Sophie's Choice*, William Styron (fiction). Spalding Gray begins to write and perform mostly autobiographical monologues. *The Right Stuff*, Tom Wolfe (nonfiction). *Evita*, Andrew Lloyd Webber and Tim Rice (stage musical).	Sony Walkman (portable audiocassette player) introduced in U.S. *The Far Side* comic strip begins. *I Know Why the Caged Bird Sings*, TV adaptation of Maya Angelou's autobiography.	*Apocalypse Now*, Coppola. *All That Jazz*, Bob Fosse. *Breaking Away*, Peter Yates. *Breaker Morant*, Bruce Beresford. *My Brilliant Career*, Gillian Armstrong. *Best Boy* (documentary), Ira Wohl. "Peliculas" (avant-garde), Patrick Clancy. "Thriller" (avant-garde), Sally Potter. "Hearts" (avant-garde video), Barbara Buckner. "A Portrait of Light and Heat" (avant-garde video), Bill Viola.
1980	USSR continues its invasion of Afghanistan. Rhodesia gains independence and becomes the new republic of Zimbabwe. In Poland, Lech Walesa becomes leader of new trade union, Solidarity. Iraq invades Iran, starting a war that lasts until 1988 and kills more than a million.	*Amadeus*, Shaffer (play).	*Cosmos* series with Carl Sagan, on PBS (TV). Home dish antennas to receive TV signals from satellites begin to gain in popularity. Cable News Network begins. U.S. TV networks begin to offer some closed captioning for hearing-impaired viewers.	*Raging Bull*, Scorsese. *Atlantic City*, Louis Malle. *Melvin and Howard*, Jonathan Demme. *The Empire Strikes Back*, Irvin Kershner. *The Shining*, Kubrick. *Berlin Alexanderplatz* (TV miniseries, shown in some theaters), Fassbinder. *Moscow Does Not Believe in Tears*, Vladimir Menshev.

	World Events	Arts	Mass Media	Films and Videos
1980 (cont.)	Ronald Reagan elected president.		First interactive video disc: *How to Watch Pro Football*.	*Kagemusha*, Kurosawa. *Model* (documentary), Wiseman. (*The Life and Times of*) *Rosie the Riveter* (documentary), Connie Field.
1981	Iran releases remaining U.S. hostages. First U.S. space shuttle successfully flown. Scientists first identify AIDS. Sandra Day O'Connor becomes first female U.S. Supreme Court justice. Egyptian soldiers assassinate Egyptian President Anwar Sadat.	*The Name of the Rose*, Umberto Eco (fiction). *A Soldier's Play*, Charles Fuller (play).	Walter Cronkite retires from regular TV broadcasting. *Hill Street Blues* runs on TV until 1987. Highest rated TV show (1981–82): *Dallas*. MTV, a 24-hour-a-day music video channel, begins.	*Zoot Suit* (first Chicano Hollywood film), Valdez. *Gallipoli*, Peter Weir. *Pixote*, Hector Babenco. *Das Boot* (*The Boat*), Wolfgang Petersen. *Céleste*, Percy Adlon. *Mephisto*, Istvan Szabo. "Ancient of Days" (avant-garde videos from 1979 to 1981), Viola.
1982	Argentina invades Falkland Islands, resulting in a war won by Britain. Maya Lin's *Vietnam Veterans War Memorial* with its 58,000 etched American names dedicated in Washington, DC. First permanent implant of a mechanical heart in a human.	*The Color Purple*, Alice Walker (fiction). *Cats*, Webber and Nunn (stage musical), opens on Broadway. Popular songs: "Eye of the Tiger," from the film *Rocky III* and the "Chariots of Fire" melody from the film of the same title.	28 million U.S. homes have cable TV. *Cagney and Lacey*, TV series about two women police partners, runs on TV until 1988. *Cheers* runs on TV until 1993. *USA Today*, a newspaper available nationwide, begins publication. Computer technology used to make images of settings and props for the film *Tron*. Digital audio CDs first marketed.	*Tootsie*, Sydney Pollack. *E.T., the Extraterrestrial*, Spielberg. *Fanny and Alexander*, Bergman. *Night of the Shooting Stars*, Paola and Vittorio Taviani. *Fitzcarraldo*, Herzog. *Lola*, Fassbinder. *Wend Kuuni* (*God's Gift*), Gaston Kaboré. *Burden of Dreams* (documentary), Blank. "Reassemblage" (avant-garde documentary), Trinh T. Minh-ha.

	World Events	Arts	Mass Media	Films and Videos
1983	President Reagan backs Contra rebels in their war with Marxist Nicaraguan government.	American Telephone & Telegraph Building in New York City, designed by Philip Johnson and John Burgee, is regarded as an important post-modernist structure.	*The Day After*, a TV movie about nuclear war, is seen by half of U.S. adults. Popular TV series *M*A*S*H* ends; final episode seen by an estimated 50 million. HBO begins producing feature films.	*El Norte*, Gregory Nava. *Betrayal*, David Jones. *Local Hero*, Bill Forsyth. *Entre Nous*, Diane Kurys. *Erendira*, Ruy Guerra. *Koyaanisqatsi* (avant-garde documentary), Godfrey Reggio.
1984	Apple Macintosh computer first sold. Indian army troops invade Sikh temple and kill 1,000 Sikh fundamentalists using the temple as a haven and headquarters. Indian Prime Minister Indira Gandhi assassinated. Ethiopian-Eritrean war, disease, and famine kill one million.	*The Lover*, Marguerite Duras (fiction). *Love in the Time of Cholera*, García Márquez (fiction). *The Unbearable Lightness of Being*, Milan Kundera (fiction). *The House on Mango Street*, Sandra Cisneros (novella of vignettes).	PG-13 film rating begins. *The Cosby Show* runs on TV until 1992. *Murder, She Wrote* runs on TV until 1996. U.S. Supreme Court rules that noncommercial private home videotaping of off-the-air programs is legal. Michael Jackson's "Thriller" video is a huge hit.	*Stranger than Paradise*, Jim Jarmusch. *Amadeus*, Forman. *Blood Simple*, Joel Coen. *Frida*, Paul Leduc. *Paris, Texas*, Wim Wenders. *Yellow Earth*, Chen Kaige. *The Times of Harvey Milk* (documentary), Robert Epstein. *Burroughs* (documentary), Howard Brookner. "In Heaven There Is No Beer?" (documentary), Blank. "The Ties That Bind" (avant-garde documentary), Su Friedrich.
1985	Gorbachev becomes Soviet general secretary. Rock Hudson, movie star, dies of AIDS—first known famous person to do so. Gorbachev and Reagan meet for a summit in Geneva.	*The Handmaid's Tale*, Margaret Atwood (fiction). *Old Gringo*, Fuentes (fiction). *The Accidental Tourist*, Anne Tyler (fiction). *Les Liaisons Dangereuses*, Christopher Hampton (play). *Fences*, Wilson (play).	For the first time, home movie video revenues exceed those of theatrical revenues. Sundance Film Festival founded by Robert Redford to promote independent films. First laser video disc players and video discs with digital sound.	*Prizzi's Honor*, Huston. *The Purple Rose of Cairo*, Allen. *My Life as a Dog*, Lasse Hallström. *Vagabond*, Agnès Varda. *The Official Story*, Luis Puenzo. *Ran*, Kurosawa. *Shoah* (documentary), Claude Lanzmann.

	World Events	Arts	Mass Media	Films and Videos
1985 (cont.)				*George Stevens: A Film Maker's Journey* (documentary), George Stevens Jr. *The Man Who Envied Women* (avant-garde), Rainer. *Naked Spaces—Living Is Round* (avant-garde documentary), Minh-ha. "Standard Gauge" (avant-garde), Morgan Fisher. "Roulement de Billes" ("Rolling Balls"; avant-garde video), Richard Barbeau.
1986	U.S. space shuttle *Challenger* explodes shortly after lift-off, killing entire crew. Haitian dictator Jean-Claude Duvalier ousted by revolution; flees the country. Corazon Aquino declared the winner of Philippine presidential election and President Ferdinand Marcos flees into exile. Soviets orbit first permanent space station. Nuclear accident at Chernobyl, Ukraine, pollutes Europe. President Reagan admits that subordinates sold weapons illegally to Iran to raise money for Nicaraguan rebels.	*Phantom of the Opera*, Webber and Charles Hart (stage musical).	Colorization of videos of older black-and-white films is controversial. *L.A. Law*, TV series set in an L.A. law firm, begins. *The Oprah Winfrey Show*, popular TV talk show, begins. Highest rated TV show (1986–89): *The Cosby Show*. *Calvin and Hobbes* comic strip begins.	*Platoon*, Oliver Stone. *True Stories*, David Byrne. *Blue Velvet*, David Lynch. *Mona Lisa*, Neil Jordan. *Tampopo*, Juzo Itami. *Sherman's March* (documentary), Ross McElwee. *Mother Teresa* (documentary), Ann and Jeanette Petrie. *Rate It X* (documentary), Lucy Winer and Paula De Koenigsberg. *Private Practices: The Story of a Sex Surrogate* (documentary), Kirby Dick. *Home of the Brave* (avant-garde), Laurie Anderson.

		World Events	Arts	Mass Media	Films and Videos
1986 (cont.)		25,000 AIDS cases diagnosed in U.S.			
1987		World population: 5 billion. Gorbachev and Reagan sign a treaty banning all short- and medium-range nuclear weapons in Europe.	*The Bonfire of the Vanities*, Wolfe (fiction). *Beloved*, Toni Morrison (fiction). *Driving Miss Daisy*, Alfred Uhry (play).	Home videotape rentals in U.S. continue to grow. *Eyes on the Prize*, film series on the civil rights movement, is shown on PBS.	*The Dead*, Huston. *Full Metal Jacket*, Kubrick. *The Last Emperor*, Bertolucci. *Red Sorghum*, Zhang Yimou. *A Taxing Woman*, Itami. *Yeelen* (*Brightness*), Souleymane Cissé. "Damned If You Don't" (avant-garde fiction), Friedrich.
1988		Soviet troops begin to retreat from Afghanistan. UN mediates ceasefire between Iran and Iraq; Iraq then takes military action against rebelling Kurds. Uprising by Palestinians in West Bank and Gaza Strip begins. Crack cocaine increasingly used in U.S. cities.	*The Satanic Verses*, novel by Salman Rushdie, condemned by Muslim fundamentalists and its author forced into hiding. *The Player*, Michael Tolkin (fiction). *The Heidi Chronicles*, Wendy Wasserstein (play).	Morphing first used in making parts of a feature film (*Willow*). Iran/Contra congressional hearings televised live. *Roseanne* TV series begins. *Oxford English Dictionary* becomes available on CD-ROM. Apple MacIntosh with CD-ROM player can play music CDs.	*The Unbearable Lightness of Being*, Philip Kaufman. *The Last Temptation of Christ*, Scorsese. *Dangerous Liaisons*, Stephen Frears. *Little Vera*, Vasily Pichul. *Saaraba* (*Utopia*), Amadou Seck. *The Thin Blue Line* (documentary), Morris. *Comic Book Confidential* (documentary), Ron Mann. *Hotel Terminus: The Life and Time of Klaus Barbie* (documentary), Ophüls.
1989		In Czechoslovakia, large peaceful opposition to Soviet dominance. Prodemocracy students occupy Tiananmen Square in Beijing;	*The Mambo Kings Play Songs of Love*, Oscar Hijuelos (fiction). *The General in His Labyrinth*, García Márquez (fiction).	U.S. National Film Registry established to recognize significant American films; the first group announced includes	*Drugstore Cowboy*, Gus Van Sant Jr. *Mystery Train*, Jarmusch. *Do the Right Thing*, Spike Lee.

	World Events	Arts	Mass Media	Films and Videos
1989 (cont.)	approximately two months later, the government uses tanks to disperse them; thousands believed killed. Berlin Wall torn down. Playwright Vaclav Havel becomes president of Czechoslovakia.	*The Joy Luck Club*, Amy Tan (fiction). *When Harry Met Sally*, popular film sound track album.	*Citizen Kane* and *Casablanca*. Time, Inc. buys Warner Communications, creating the world's largest entertainment group. Most popular TV shows (1989–90): *Roseanne* and *The Cosby Show*.	*sex, lies, and videotape*, Steven Soderbergh. *The Little Mermaid* (Disney animation). *Lawrence of Arabia*, re-released in revised and restored version. *My Left Foot*, Jim Sheridan. *Yaaba*, Idrissa Ouedraogo. *Roger & Me* (satirical documentary), Michael Moore. "You Take Care Now" (avant-garde), Ann Marie Fleming.
1990	Nelson Mandela freed from prison in South Africa. Yugoslavia moving toward split-up. Boris Yeltsin resigns from Communist Party. Iraq invades Kuwait; various diplomatic solutions sought. Germany reunited. Lech Walesa elected Poland's president.	*Orphée*, opera with music by Philip Glass and libretto by Jean Cocteau (the screenplay for his film of the same title). Music from the film *Mo' Better Blues*, album by Branford Marsalis.	NC-17 rating instituted. First film so rated: *Henry and June*. *The Civil War*, 11-hour documentary film series shown on PBS, Ken Burns. *Twin Peaks*, TV series directed by David Lynch. *Billboard* announces that home video revenue is now twice that of theatrical box offices.	*GoodFellas*, Scorsese. *Reversal of Fortune*, Barbet Schroeder. *To Sleep with Anger*, Charles Burnett. *The Grifters*, Stephen Frears. *Ju Dou*, Zhang. *Tilaï*, Ouedraogo. *Finzan: A Dance for the Heroes*, Cheick Oumar Sissoko. *Berkeley in the 60's* (documentary), Mark Kitchell. *Paris Is Burning* (documentary), Jennie Livingston. *Privilege* (avant-garde fiction), Rainer.
1991	U.S. and its UN allies defeat Iraq in 100-hour battle and free Kuwait.	*The Sweet Hereafter*, Banks (fiction).	Morphing used in parts of *Terminator 2* to show the transformation of an android	*Life Is Sweet*, Mike Leigh. *Europa, Europa*, Agnieszka.

	World Events	Arts	Mass Media	Films and Videos
1991 (cont.)	Rajiv Gandhi, prime minister of India, assassinated. Boris Yeltsin elected president of Russia. Part of former Yugoslavia, Bosnia-Herzegovena, deep into civil war. After a coup against Gorbachev fails, Communist rule ends in the USSR and the cold war ends.		into various other characters. Highest rated TV show (1990–91): *Cheers*.	*Sango Malo* (*The Village Teacher*), Bassek ba Kobhio. *Hearts of Darkness: A Filmmaker's Apocalypse* (documentary), Fax Bahr and George Hickenlooper. "First Comes Love" (avant-garde documentary), Friedrich.
1992	After a California jury in the Rodney King trial finds the police defendants not guilty, people in parts of L.A. riot. 58 die; hundreds of millions of dollars in property damage. The USSR divides into 15 nations, including Russia.	*Angels in America*, Tony Kushner (two-part play). "I Will Always Love You," popular song written and earlier sung by Dolly Parton is sung by Whitney Houston in the film *The Bodyguard*.	Johnny Carson retires as host of *The Tonight Show* (TV) and is replaced by Jay Leno.	*Unforgiven*, Clint Eastwood. *The Player*, Altman. *Reservoir Dogs*, Quentin Tarantino. *Like Water for Chocolate*, Alfonso Arau. *The Crying Game*, Jordan. *Quartier Mozart*, Jean-Pierre Bekolo. *Guelwaar*, Sembène. *A Brief History of Time* (documentary), Morris. *Brother's Keeper* (documentary), Joe Berlinger and Bruce Sinofsky. *Visions of Light: The Art of Cinematography* (documentary), Arnold Glassman, Todd McCarthy, and Stuart Samuels.

	World Events	Arts	Mass Media	Films and Videos
1993	Israel and PLO formally recognize each other. Outside diplomatic pressures have little impact on the warring parties in the former Yugoslavia.	*Arcadia*, Tom Stoppard (play set in 1809 and the present). *Marilyn*, opera about Marilyn Monroe by Ezra Laderman.	Last original *Cheers* episode draws record TV audience.	*Schindler's List*, Spielberg. *Short Cuts*, Altman. *The Ballad of Little Jo*, Maggie Greenwald. *Orlando*, Sally Potter. *Naked*, Leigh. *The Piano*, Jane Campion. *Farewell My Concubine*, Chen. *Thirty-Two Short Films about Glenn Gould* (documentary), François Girard. *The Wonderful, Horrible Life of Leni Riefenstahl* (documentary), Ray Müller. *Blue* (avant-garde), Derek Jarman.
1994	Civil wars in Yemen, Georgia (part of former USSR), and Rwanda. In its first multiracial election, South Africa elects Nelson Mandela president. Uprising by Chechens wanting their independence (in southern Russian republic) leads to protracted guerrilla warfare. U.S.-led occupation of Haiti results in reinstatement of its democratically elected president.	*The Hour We Knew Nothing of Each Other* (100-minute wordless play with sound effects), Peter Handke. *La Belle et la Bête* ("an opera for ensemble and film") combines a showing of Cocteau's film without its sound track but with supertitles and live music composed by Philip Glass. *The Dangerous Liaisons*, Conrad Susa and Philip Littell (opera). The Andy Warhol Museum opens in Pittsburgh.	Spielberg, Jeffrey Katzenberg, and David Geffen form Dreamworks SKG to produce theatrical films, animation, television programs, records, and interactive media. Independent Film Channel offered on some cable systems. (Short) IMAX 3-D films shown in U.S. (previously shown in Japan and Europe). More than 80% of all U.S. households have at least one VCR. Marketing films first in video and perhaps later to theaters is a small trend.	*Pulp Fiction*, Tarantino. *Vanya on 42nd Street*, Malle. *Ed Wood*, Tim Burton. *The Lion King*, Disney animation. *Exotica*, Atom Egoyan. *Il Postino* (*The Postman*), Michael Radford. *Red*, Krzysztof Kieslowski. *Burnt by the Sun*, Nikita Mikhalkov. *To Live*, Zhang. *Eat Drink Man Woman*, Ang Lee. *High School II* (documentary), Wiseman. *Crumb* (documentary), Terry Zwigoff. *The Troubles We've Seen* (documentary), Ophüls.

	World Events	Arts	Mass Media	Films and Videos
1994 (cont.)			DirectTV, Digital TV, offers multiple channels from satellites. Kodak introduces a digital imaging system in many U.S. stores, allowing customers to scan a photograph into the system, then alter the image and print out new copies.	*Hoop Dreams* (documentary), Steve James. *Carmen Miranda: Bananas Is My Business* (documentary), Helena Solberg. *A Great Day in Harlem* (documentary), Jean Bach.
1995	American space shuttle docks with Russian space station and astronauts from the two countries work together. In Japan and the U.S., domestic terrorists attack and kill civilians, using gas in Japan and a bomb that kills 168 in Oklahoma City. U.S.-brokered peace plan for Bosnia-Herzegovina agreed to by presidents of Serbia, Bosnia, and Croatia. Yitzhak Rabin, Israeli prime minister, assassinated by right-wing Israeli radical.	*Seven Guitars*, Wilson (play). *Rent*, Jonathan Larson (stage musical). Untitled 8½-by-11-inch film stills made by Cindy Sherman, Washington, DC. *24 Frames per Second*, dance homage to the Lumière Brothers, Bill T. Jones and Lyons Opera Ballet.	*Toy Story* is first feature film made entirely with computer animation. Percentage of Americans reading a newspaper daily continues its decades-long decline. Two studies show that the average American continues to spend more on books each year than on recorded music or home videos. *Puppet Motel*, CD-ROM with Laurie Anderson. Disney and Capital Cities/ABC merge and form the world's largest media company. *Calvin and Hobbes* comic strip ends.	*A Little Princess*, Alfonso Cuarón. *To Die For*, Van Sant. *Hate*, Mathieu Kassovitz. *Babe*, Chris Noonan. *Black Is . . . Black Ain't* (documentary), Marlon T. Riggs. *Orson Welles: The One-Man Band* (documentary), Vassili Silovic. *Theremin: An Electronic Odyssey* (documentary), Steven M. Martin. "A Cinema of Unease" (documentary on cinema of New Zealand), Sam Neill and Judy Rymer. "Buried Secrets" (avant-garde video and audio), Viola.
1996	Boris Yeltsin reelected president of Russia over his Communist rival. Uprising by Chechens (in southern Russian	*In the Beauty of the Lilies*, Updike (fiction).	Sundance (Independent) Channel offered on some cable and satellite systems. The Federal Communications Commission	*Fargo*, Coen. *The English Patient*, Anthony Minghella. *Breaking the Waves*, Lars von Trier. *Shine*, Scott Hicks.

	World Events	Arts	Mass Media	Films and Videos
1996 (cont.)	republic) ends with peace agreement. War and famine in eastern Zaire kills massive numbers of people. Suicide bombings by militant Muslims kill 61 in Israel, hamper peace talks, and contribute to election defeat of Israel's ruling party.		approves standards for digital TV, which is to have wider screens and sharper pictures than previous TVs and will gradually replace analog TV.	*Trainspotting*, Danny Boyle. *Secrets & Lies*, Leigh. *Prisoner of the Mountains*, Sergei Bodrov. *Shall We Dance?*, Masayuki Suo. *The Celluloid Closet* (documentary), Rob Epstein and Jeffrey Friedman. *A Personal Journey with Martin Scorsese through American Movies* (documentary). *Lumière and Company* (documentary), Sarah Moon.
1997	China's top leader, Deng Xiaoping, dies. Announcement that Scottish embryologist cloned a sheep. In Britain the Labor Party comes to power ending 18 years of Conservative control, and Tony Blair becomes prime minister. Rebel forces capture the rest of Zaire; longtime dictator Mobutu Sese Seko flees into exile; the country is renamed Democratic Republic of Congo. Britain returns control of Hong Kong to China, ending 156 years of British rule.	*How I Learned to Drive*, Paula Vogel (play). *The Lion King*, a Disney musical based on the film, opens on Broadway.	*Star Wars* is revised slightly, rereleased to theaters, and passes *E.T.* as the highest grossing movie in history, until *Titanic* appears the following year. For the year, 413 movies were released in the U.S., 125 more than ten years earlier. U.S. movie attendance is up over the previous year and box office receipts set a U.S. record. Broadcast and cable networks begin using a four-part age-based rating system for most of their programs.	*L.A. Confidential*, Curtis Hanson. *The Ice Storm*, Ang Lee. *Eve's Bayou*, Kasi Lemmons. *The Apostle*, Robert Duvall. *The Sweet Hereafter*, Atom Egoyan. *Will It Snow for Christmas?*, Sandrine Veysset. *The Full Monty*, Peter Cattaneo. *The Wings of the Dove*, Iain Softley. *Taste of Cherry*, Abbas Kiarostami. *Fast, Cheap & Out of Control* (documentary), Morris. *Public Housing* (documentary), Wiseman.

	World Events	Arts	Mass Media	Films and Videos
1997 (cont.)	*Pathfinder*, an unmanned craft, lands on Mars; from *Pathfinder* the first mobile explorer of another planet emerges and sends data and photographs to earth. Mother Teresa dies at age 87. In Algeria, Islamic extremists continue to massacre civilians; more than 60,000 killed since 1992.		First digital video discs (DVDs) and DVD players marketed in the U.S., but not all studios agree to market their films on them. The discs hold movies up to 133 minutes on one side. Most models also play music CDs. NASA reports 45 million per day visit its computer sites for information about the *Pathfinder* exploration of Mars. Compaq introduces the PC theater: a combination of a computer and large-screen TV.	*Waco: The Rules of Engagement* (documentary), William Gazecki. "Bill Viola: Trilogy (Fire, Water, Breath)," avant-garde installations.
1998	Ireland, Britain, and the U.S. broker a peace settlement for Northern Ireland, which Irish voters later accept. President Suharto of Indonesia is forced to step down after 32 years in power. Asian economic crisis continues to worsen and to hurt economies elsewhere. Terrorist bombs near U.S. embassies in Kenya and Tanzania kill 258. President Clinton faces possible impeachment for perjury and obstruction of justice.		*Titanic* passes *Star Wars* as the highest-grossing movie in history, but *Gone with the Wind* has sold more tickets. *Seinfeld* airs its last TV show in an hour-long finale. A survey reveals that Internet use is up; TV and VCR watching and reading are all down. Total ticket sales for summer movies set a U.S. record. Four interactive movies released on DVD allow viewers to periodically choose plot developments.	*The Truman Show*, Weir. *Saving Private Ryan*, Spielberg. *Men with Guns*, Sayles. *Smoke Signals*, Chris Eyre. *Touch of Evil* (1958) is rereleased in a revised and restored version. *The Butcher Boy*, Jordan. *Un Air de Famille*, Cédric Klapisch. *Leila*, Dariush Mehrjui. *Best Man* (documentary sequel), Wohl. *Moon over Broadway* (documentary), Pennebaker and Chris Hegedus. *Wild Man Blues* (documentary), Kopple. "Everest," a narrative documentary, is the most commercially successful film in IMAX history.

SOURCES

Barnouw, Erik. *Tube of Plenty: The Evolution of American Television*. 2nd rev. ed. New York: Oxford UP, 1990.

Beaver, Frank E. "An Outline of Film History." *Dictionary of Film Terms*. New York: McGraw-Hill, 1983.

———. *Dictionary of Film Terms: The Aesthetic Companion to Film Analysis*. Rev. ed. New York: Twayne, 1994.

Benét's Reader's Encyclopedia. Ed. Katherine Baker Siepmann. 3rd ed. New York: Harper, 1987.

Bohn, Thomas W., and Richard L. Stromgren. "A Film Chronology." *Light and Shadows: A History of Motion Pictures*. 3rd ed. Palo Alto: Mayfield, 1987. xiv–xlv.

Brownstone, David M., and Irene M. Franck. *Timelines of the Arts and Literature*. New York: Harper, 1994.

Bywater, Tim, and Thomas Sobchack. *Introduction to Film Criticism: Major Critical Approaches to Narrative Film*. New York: Longman, 1989.

Chronicle of the 20th Century. Ed. Clifton Daniel. New York: Dorling, 1995.

Cook, David. *A History of Narrative Film*. 3rd ed. New York: Norton, 1996.

Ellis, Jack C. *The Documentary Idea: A Critical History of English-Language Documentary Film and Video*. Englewood Cliffs: Prentice, 1989.

———. *A History of Film*. 4th ed. Boston: Allyn, 1995.

Gomery, Douglas. *Movie History: A Survey*. Belmont, CA: Wadsworth, 1991.

Greenspan, Karen. *The Timetables of Women's History: A Chronology of the Most Important People and Events in Women's History*. New York: Simon, 1994.

Grun, Bernard. *The Timetables of History: A Horizontal Linkage of People and Events*. 3rd ed. New York: Simon, 1991.

Hilliard, Robert L., and Michael C. Keith. *The Broadcast Century: A Biography of American Broadcasting*. Boston: Focal, 1992.

Kane, Joseph Nathan. *Famous First Facts: A Record of First Happenings, Discoveries, and Inventions in American History*. 4th ed. New York: Wilson, 1981.

Katz, Ephraim. *The Film Encyclopedia*. 3rd ed. Rev. Fred Klein and Ronald Dean Nolen. New York: Harper, 1998.

Monaco, James. *How to Read a Film: Movies, Media, Multimedia*. 3rd ed. New York: Oxford UP, 1997.

Nowell-Smith, Geoffrey, general ed. *The Oxford History of World Cinema*. Oxford: Oxford UP, 1996.

Ochoa, George, and Melinda Corey. *The Timeline Book of the Arts*. New York: Ballantine, 1995.

Polan, Dana. "History of the American Cinema." *Film Quarterly* 45 (Spring 1992): 54–57.

Rood, Karen L. *American Culture after World War II*. Detroit: Gale, 1994. Pages xix–xxx consist of two timelines, works and events.

Samuelson, D. "Equipment Inventions That Have Changed the Way Films Are Made." *American Cinematographer* 75, no. 8 (1994): 74, 76.

Sklar, Robert. *Film: An International History of the Medium*. Englewood Cliffs: Prentice; New York: Abrams, 1993.

Strauss, William, and Neil Howe. *Generations: The History of America's Future, 1584–2069*. New York: Morrow, 1991.

Winston, Brian. "Z for Zoetrope." *Sight and Sound* July 1998: 28–30.

Various issues of *Billboard*, the *New York Times*, and the *World Almanac*, and many publications accessed via Nexis.

How to Read Film Credits

Most movies now run a long list of credits at the end identifying the many people who worked on the film. But did you ever wonder what a gaffer does, or a best boy, or a grip? To help you appreciate all the work involved in making a typical movie, the closing credits from *The Player* are reprinted here along with brief explanations of the terms that a typical viewer might not know.

The chapters of this book explain the roles of the professionals with the high-profile jobs: producers, directors, cinematographers, editors, writers, composers, designers, and actors. In *The Player*, these people are identified in the opening credits. (In many older films, the entire crew is listed in the opening credits, but that is now rare.) The closing credits, listed here, identify all the actors and everyone else associated with the production but not listed at the film's beginning.

A caution: Film credits do not always indicate accurately who did what. Some job titles are largely ceremonial, favors to friends, supporters, or movie executives with a lot of clout. Two films may use a different term to indicate the same type of work. Then, too, some job titles are simply vague, and others (such as *construction coordinator* and *construction foreman* and *promotion* and *publicity*) are synonymous or overlapping. All these caveats aside, most of the titles and descriptions here accurately describe who did what. Although you cannot always know what certain producers do, you can be certain what a Foley artist and a dolly grip do.

CLOSING CREDITS FOR *THE PLAYER*

Cast

Griffin Mill	TIM ROBBINS
June Gudmundsdottir	GRETA SCACCHI
Walter Stuckel	FRED WARD
Detective Avery	WHOOPI GOLDBERG
Larry Levy	PETER GALLAGHER
Joel Levison	BRION JAMES
Bonnie Sherow	CYNTHIA STEVENSON
David Kahane	VINCENT D'ONOFRIO
Andy Civella	DEAN STOCKWELL
Tom Oakley	RICHARD E. GRANT
Dick Mellen	SYDNEY POLLACK
Detective DeLongpre	LYLE LOVETT
Celia	DINA MERRILL
Jan	ANGELA HALL
Sandy	LEAH AYRES
Jimmy Chase	PAUL HEWITT
Reg Goldman	RANDALL BATINKOFF
Steve Reeves	JEREMY PIVEN
Whitney Gersh	GINA GERSHON
Frank Murphy	FRANK BARHYDT
Marty Grossman	MIKE E. KAPLAN
Gar Girard	KEVIN SCANNELL
Witness	MARGERY BOND
Detective Broom	SUSAN EMSHWILLER
Phil	BRIAN BROPHY
Eric Schecter	MICHAEL TOLKIN
Carl Schecter	STEPHEN TOLKIN
Natalie	NATALIE STRONG
Waiter	PETE KOCH
Trixie	PAMELA BOWEN
Rocco	JEFF WESTON

These actors have major roles and appear in several scenes. Except for Sydney Pollack's name, their names also appear in the opening credits.

These actors have minor roles. Most of them appear in only one scene.

As Themselves

STEVE ALLEN	MAXINE JOHN-JAMES
RICHARD ANDERSON	SALLY KELLERMAN
RENE AUBERJONOIS	SALLY KIRKLAND
HARRY BELAFONTE	JACK LEMMON
SHARI BELAFONTE	MARLEE MATLIN
KAREN BLACK	ANDIE MacDOWELL
MICHAEL BOWEN	MALCOLM McDOWELL
GARY BUSEY	JAYNE MEADOWS
ROBERT CARRADINE	MARTIN MULL

These are all of the sixty-five cameos—brief roles played by well-known people.

These are all of the sixty-five cameos— brief roles played by well-known people.

CHARLES CHAMPLIN
CHER
JAMES COBURN
CATHY LEE CROSBY
JOHN CUSACK
BRAD DAVIS
PAUL DOOLEY
THEREZA ELLIS
PETER FALK
FELICIA FARR
KASIA FIGURA
LOUISE FLETCHER
DENNIS FRANZ
TERI GARR
LEEZA GIBBONS
SCOTT GLENN
JEFF GOLDBLUM
ELLIOTT GOULD
JOEL GREY
DAVID ALAN GRIER
BUCK HENRY
ANJELICA HUSTON
KATHY IRELAND
STEVE JAMES

JENNIFER NASH
NICK NOLTE
ALEXANDRA POWERS
BERT REMSEN
GUY REMSEN
PATRICIA RESNICK
BURT REYNOLDS
JACK RILEY
JULIA ROBERTS
MIMI ROGERS
ANNIE ROSS
ALAN RUDOLPH
JILL ST. JOHN
SUSAN SARANDON
ADAM SIMON
ROD STEIGER
JOAN TEWKESBURY
BRIAN TOCHI
LILY TOMLIN
ROBERT WAGNER
RAY WALSTON
BRUCE WILLIS
MARVIN YOUNG

Works closely with the producer(s) on artistic and financial matters. Unlike some "producers," the associate producer has day-to-day involvement with the making of the film.

Manages the production crew and the business arrangements for each day's shooting, such as housing, meals, transportation, and payroll.

The director's assistants; typically they keep track of scheduling, manage crowd scenes, supervise rehearsals, and prepare call sheets and production reports.

Often the film editor is listed only in the opening credits. For *The Player*, the opening credits list Geraldine Peroni as the editor; thus, this listing is a puzzle. Perhaps the credit here should have read "Assistant Film Editor." Or perhaps Maysie Hoy edited only the clip from *Habeas Corpus*, the film-within-the-film in *The Player*.

Creates the look of the film and runs the art department; ultimately responsible for all the visuals in the film, including architecture, locations, sets, decor, props, costumes, and makeup.

In *The Player*, one scene occurs in a karaoke bar, where videos are playing in the background. This person made those videos.

Associate Producer
Unit Production Manager
First Assistant Director
Second Assistant Director

DAVID LEVY
TOM UDELL
ALLAN NICHOLS
CC BARNES

Film Editor

MAYSIE HOY

Production Executives

CLAUDIA LEWIS
PAMELA HEDLEY
JIM CHESNEY

Production Supervisor

Art Director
Set Decorator
Leadman
Location Manager

JERRY FLEMING
SUSAN EMSHWILLER
PETER BORCK
JACK KNEY

First Assistant Camera
Second Assistant Camera
Third Assistant Camera
Karaoke Videos

ROBERT REED ALTMAN
CARY McKRYSTAL
CRAIG FINETTI
LARRY "DOC" KARMAN

Responsible for the business and administrative aspects of making a film; assisted by the associate producer.

A.k.a. Production Manager. Supervises and coordinates all business and technical matters.

Decides how to decorate the indoor sets with furniture, props, art, and so on.

Finds locations for shooting and negotiates for their use.

The camera crew; they maintain the equipment, load the film, and use a clapboard or comparable electronic device to mark the beginning of each take.

The editor's assistants; they splice the film, maintain the editing equipment, and keep records. ⎫ Assistant Editor / Second Assistant Editor / Apprentice Editor — A. MICHELLE PAGE / ALISA HALE / DYLAN TICHENOR

Supervising Sound Editor / Dialogue Editors — MICHAEL REDBOURN ← Responsible for the final sound track; supervises the mixer, ADR (automated dialogue replacement) editor, dialogue editor, sound effects editor, music editor, and assistant sound editor.

JOSEPH HOLSEN / ED LACHMANN

Sound Effects Editor / Assistant Sound Editor — KEN BURTON / BILL WARD

Edits the music to make sure it complements the film's action and the other elements of the sound track. → Music Editor — BILL BERNSTEIN

Music Scoring Mixer — JOHN VIGRAN ← Blends and balances the tracks of the various film scores.

Orchestration By — THOMAS PASATIERI ← Arranges the score for the parts of the orchestra.

Postproduction technicians who mix vocals, sound effects, music, and silence to produce the master sound track. → Re-Recording Mixers — MATTHEW IADAROLA / STANLEY KASTNER / RICH GOOCH

Records sound during shooting; reports to the production sound mixer. → Recordist

Foley Artists — JOHN POST / PAUL HOLTZBORN / BOB DESCHAINE / DAVID JOBE ⎱ Sound specialists who use various objects to simulate and record sound effects while synchronizing them with their corresponding movie images.

Foley Mixer / Foley Recordist

Mixes the sound produced during shooting to get the desired combination of vocals, sound effects, and ambient sound. → Production Sound Mixer — JOHN PRITCHETT, C.A.S.

Boom Operator — JOEL SHRYACK ← Sound technician who operates the boom, a pole with a microphone at one end.

Cable Puller — EMILY SMITH-BAKER

Protects the cables and wires of the sound equipment from damage and the production crew from injuries from the cables and wires. ↑

Gaffer — DON MUCHOW ← The head electrician, assisted by the best boy electric. Supervises the electricians, who are responsible for supplying current and lights on the set.

Best Boy Electric / Electricians — ANDREW DAY / ROBERT BRUCE / VAL DE SALVO / TOM McGRATH / CHRIS REDDISH / ANTHONY T. MARRA II / MICHAEL J. FAHEY

Manages the grips, or stagehands, who set up and move equipment and props. Assisted by the best boy grip. → Key Grip

Best Boy Grip

Dolly Grip — WAYNE STROUD ← Moves the dolly during shooting.

Stagehands or crew workers. → Grips — KEVIN FAHEY / SCOTT "EL GATO" HOLLANDER / TIM NASH

Obtains the costumes and takes care of them during filming. Assisted by the wardrobe assistants. → Wardrobe Supervisor / Wardrobe Assistants — LYDIA TANJI / ANGELA BILLOWS / VICKI BRINKKORD / DEBORAH LARSEN

Runs the makeup department; applies the makeup to the actors. → Make-Up Artist

Hairdresser — SCOTT WILLIAMS ← Arranges the actors' hair.

June's Artwork — SYDNEY COOPER ← In *The Player*, the character June is an artist, and her artworks are seen in her house. This person created that art.

Description (left)	Job Title	Name	Description (right)
Oversees acquisition and maintenance of all props. →	Property Master	JAMES MONROE	
	Assistant Property Master	JULIE HEUER	
Get the set ready for filming and disassemble it after filming.	Set Dressers	MATTHEW ALTMAN	
		JOHN BUCKLIN	
		DAVID RONAN	
		JIM SAMSON	
	Swing Gang	DANIEL ROTHENBERG	
		MARIO PEREZ	
	Assistant Location Manager	PAUL BOYDSTON	
The member of the construction crew who paints the sets. →	Scenic Painter	JOHN BEAUVAIS	
	Painter	RICKY RIGGS	
	Construction Coordinator	LOREN CORNEY	Supervise the construction crew, who make the sets.
Build the sets, furniture, props, and camera tracks. →	Construction Foreman	PAT MAURER	
	Carpenters	CHRIS MARNEUS	
		DARRYL LEE	
		KENNETH FUNK	
		THOMAS CALLOWAY	An administrator in charge of communication, correspondence, travel, accommodations, and bill paying. Assisted by the assistant coordinator and the production secretary.
Responsible for coordinating the visual elements of the film (other than the camera work). →		JOHN EVANS	
		JUSTIN KRITZER	
	Art Department Coordinator	MICHELE GUASTELLO	
Keeps track of all expenditures during production and supervises payment of salaries and bills. Assisted by the assistant accountant. →	Production Coordinator	CYNTHIA HILL ←	
	Assistant Coordinator	BETSY CHASSE	
	Production Secretary	STACY COHEN	
	Production Accountant	KIMBERLY EDWARDS SHAPIRO	
	Assistant Accountant	CHERYL KURK	
	Avenue Financial Representative	SHERI HALFON ←	Avenue Pictures was a small film production company. Its chairman at the time *The Player* was produced was Carey Brokaw, who served as executive producer of *The Player*.
	Additional Accounting Service	JUDY GELETKO	
	Post-Production Accountant	CATHERINE WEBB	
Personal assistants, who help the director and producers.	Assistant to Robert Altman	JIM McLINDON	
	Assistants to Cary Brokaw	ROBIN HAGE	
		DANIELLE KNIGHT	
Sandcastle 5 Productions, Inc., is a small film and TV production company closely associated with Robert Altman. →	Assistant to Nick Wechsler	ALISON BALIAN	
	Sandcastle 5 Representative	CELIA CONVERSE	
	Production Assistants	ANGIE BONNER	Run errands for the director and assist him or her in various other small ways.
		JOHN BROWN III	
		SIGNE CORRIERE	
		STEVE DAY	
		KELLY HOUSEHOLDER	
Keeps a log of the details in each shot to make sure continuity is maintained from shot to shot. →	Script Supervisor	CAROLE STARKES	Plans, arranges, and supervises the stunts.
	Stunt Coordinator	GREG WALKER ←	The department responsible for the shots unobtainable by live-action cinematography.
	Special Effects	JOHN HARTIGAN ←	
Handles the animals on the set; in *The Player*, a rattlesnake appears twice. →	Animal Trainer	JIM BROCKETT	
	Still Photographer	LOREY SEBASTIAN ←	Takes photographs for publicity and advertising.
	Set Medic	TOM MOORE	

Responsible for maintaining and operating all vehicles.

Drive the vehicles that transport equipment and personnel.

Perform odd jobs, such as getting coffee and snacks for the cast and crew.

Hires the actors who speak no lines and do not stand out as individuals.

Lab person who adjusts the color of the negative as needed, often in coordination with the cinematographer.

Designs the words that appear on the screen (such as the credits).

This organization, here a Japanese-based bank, lent the producers money to produce the film.

Publicizes the film through advertising and other publicity.

Arranges publicity events, such as interviews and appearances.

Transportation Coordinator	DEREK RASER
Transport Captain	"J.T." THAYER
Drivers	CHRISTOPHER ARMSTRONG
	RON CHESNEY
	STEVE EARLE
	DON FEENEY
	D.J. GARDINER
	GREG WILLIS
Caterer	RICK BRAININ CATERING
Craft Service	STUART McCAULEY
	ANDREA BERTY
Extras Casting	MAGIC CASTING
Location Security	ARTIS SECURITY
Negative Cutter	BOB HART
Color By	DELUXE ®
Color Timer	MICHAEL STANWICK
Titles & Opticals By	MERCER TITLE & OPTICAL
Title Design	DAN PERRI
Legal Services	SINCLAIR TENNENBAUM & Co.
	WYMAN & ISAACS
Financing Provided By	THE DAIWA BANK LTD.
Completion Bond	FILM FINANCES, INC.
Promotions Arranged By	ANDREW VARELA
Publicity By	CLEIN + WHITE INC.
Title Painting By	CHARLES BRAGG

Maintains security for scenes shot on location.

Cuts and splices the negative to make it match the final edited version of the film.

Uses an optical printer or perhaps a computer to create the words that appear on the screen.

The company responsible for drawing up the contract between the producers and the financiers that guarantees the film will be completed at a set time and within a set budget.

SPECIAL THANKS TO

PATRICK MURRAY	SUZANNE GOLDMAN	MIMI RABINOWITZ
RANDY HONAKER	TOYOKO NEZU	MORGAN ENTREKIN
LUIS ESTEVEZ	REEBOK	GEOWORKS
BASELINE	MARK EISEN	BALLY

These people or companies donated products or services or allowed the filmmakers to use certain locations. For *The Player*, companies such as Reebok, Bally, and Range Rover may have paid a fee for product placement.

GERALD GREENBACH & TWO BUNCH PALMS
BOB FLICK & ENTERTAINMENT TONIGHT
STEVE TROMBATORE & ALL PAYMENTS
RANGE ROVER OF NORTH AMERICA
MARCHON/MARCOLIN EYE WEAR
SPINNEYBECK/DESIGN AMERICA
HARRY WINSTON JEWELERS
L. A. MARATHON

These people or companies donated products or services or allowed the filmmakers to use certain locations. For *The Player*, companies such as Reebok, Bally, and Range Rover may have paid a fee for product placement.

THE LOS ANGELES COUNTY MUSEUM OF ART
JANIS DINWIDDIE
JULIE JOHNSTON
RON HAVER
THE LES HOOPER ORCHESTRA

THE BICYCLE THIEF
© RICHARD FEINER & CO., INC.

These are copyright acknowledgments, required whenever a film uses material that someone else claims copyright to.

"SNAKE" & "DRUMS OF KYOTO"
© Lia-Mann Music
Written & Performed By
KURT NEUMANN

"TEMA PARA JOBIM"
© Mulligan Publishing Co., Inc.
Music by GERRY MULLIGAN
Lyrics by JOYCE
Performed by JOYCE
MILTON NASCIMENTO
Courtesy of Estudio Pointer Ltda.
& RCA Electronica Ltda.

"PRECIOUS"
Written by LES HOOPER
© Chesford Music Publications

ENTERTAINMENT TONIGHT
Theme by
MICHAEL MARK
Published by ADDAX MUSIC CO. INC.

Re-Recording Facilities
SKYWALKER SOUND
A division of LucasArts Entertainment Company

This film recorded digitally in a THX Sound System Theatre.

RECORDED IN
ULTRA-STEREO

SOURCES

IMDb Film Glossary (Internet Movie Database Web site): <http://us.imdb.com/Glossary>. Accessed 29 July 1998.

Katz, Ephraim. *The Film Encyclopedia*. Revised by Fred Klein and Ronald Dean Nolen. Third edition. New York: Harper, 1998.

Konigsberg, Ira. *The Complete Film Dictionary*. 2nd ed. New York: Penguin, 1997.

Law, Jonathan, et al., eds. *Cassell Companion to Cinema*. Rev. ed. London: Cassell, 1997.

Oakey, Virginia. *Dictionary of Film and Television Terms*. New York: Barnes, 1983.

Singleton, Ralph S. *Filmmaker's Dictionary*. Beverly Hills: Lone Eagle, 1990.

Illustrated Glossary

I<small>N THIS GLOSSARY I HAVE TRIED TO DEFINE</small> and explain key terms used in the book. The number in parentheses at the end of an entry indicates where that term is discussed extensively in the text. For additional terms explained in more depth, see Ira Konigsberg's *The Complete Film Dictionary*, 2nd ed. (New York: Penguin, 1997); Frank Beaver's *Dictionary of Film Terms: The Aesthetic Companion to Film Analysis*, rev. ed. (New York: Twayne, 1994); Susan Hayward's *Key Concepts in Cinema Studies* (London: Routledge, 1996); and Kevin Jackson's *The Language of Cinema* (New York: Routledge, 1998).

ADR (automated dialogue replacement): A postproduction process in which an actor rerecords dialogue by means of a projector interlocked with a magnetic film recorder or computer that permits playback of sound. Used to correct or supplement sound recorded during filming.

ambient sound: The usual sounds of a place that people tend not to notice. In a woods, for example, the ambient sound may consist mainly of trees moving in the breeze and insects heard at very low volume.

anamorphic lens: A lens that squeezes a wide image onto a film frame in the camera, making everything look tall and thin. On a projector, an anamorphic lens unsqueezes the image, returning it to its original wide shape (usually approximately 2½ times wider than its height). Many movies from the 1950s to the 1980s and some from the 1990s were filmed and projected with anamorphic lenses. Sometimes called a *scope lens*. See also **CinemaScope**. (39)

animation: Motion-picture film technique that seems to impart motion to drawings or other stationary objects by presenting a rapid succession of single-frame images. (358)

animatronic: A puppet likeness of a human, creature, or animal whose movements are directed by electronic, mechanical, or radio-controlled devices.

aperture: (1) The adjustable opening in the camera lens that permits the operator to regulate how much light passes through the lens to the film. The size of the aperture helps determine depth of field and whether deep focus or shallow focus will result. (2) The rectangular opening in a motion-picture projector that helps determine the size and shape of light sent from the projector to the screen; the size and shape may be changed by the use of an aperture plate in front of the aperture.

aperture plate: (1) A small metal plate with a rectangular opening that is used in cameras to determine the shape and area of light reaching the film. (2) A small plate with a rectangular opening used in projectors to determine the shape and area of the light reaching the screen from the projector.

aspect ratio: The proportion of the width to the height of the image on a TV or movie screen or on the individual frames of the film. The most common aspect ratio for nontheatrical film showings is 1.33:1 (4:3); that is also the approximate aspect ratio of analog TV screens. Currently, most movies shown in theaters have an aspect ratio of 1.85:1. The aspect ratio has nothing to do with the *size* of the image; rather it indicates the *shape* (width in proportion to height) of film images. (37)

1.85:1
The aspect ratio used for
most U.S. theatrical showings
since the 1960s

---

asynchronous sound: A sound from a source on-screen that precedes or follows its source, such as words that are not synchronized with lip movements. (193)

auteur ("oh TOUR") theory: Not a film theory, but a critical approach for analyzing certain films and their makers. Auteur (French for "author") critics usually examine the recurrent meanings and techniques of filmmakers who have left a strong imprint on a group of films they helped create. Auteur critics assume that the major creative decisions of a film are the responsibility of one person, normally the director, though sometimes a producer, writer, or actor. (442)

automated dialogue replacement: See **ADR**.

avant-garde film: Literally "advanced guard film." A film that rejects the conventions of mainstream movies and explores the possibilities of the film medium itself. Probably the best-known avant-garde film is "Un Chien Andalou," a surrealist effort by director Luis Buñuel and the artist Salvador Dali. Sometimes called *experimental film, underground film,* or *independent film.* (329)

backlight or **backlighting:** Lighting from behind the subject. If used alone or if the backlighting is the strongest light used, the subject's identity may be obscured. Used in combination with other lighting, backlighting may help set the subject off from the background. (78, 85)

bird's-eye view: Camera angle achieved when the camera films the subject from directly overhead. (100)

black comedy: A style used in some narratives since World War II that shows the humorous possibilities in subjects previously considered off-limits to comedy, such as warfare, murder, death, and dying. Black comedies are often also satiric. Examples of films using black comedy are *The Ladykillers* (especially the five deaths and disposal of the five bodies that are treated comically toward the end of the film); *Kind Hearts and Coronets*; *Dr. Strangelove: Or, How I Learned to Stop Worrying and Love the Bomb*; *Catch-22*; *Monty Python and the Holy Grail*; *Life of Brian*; and *To Die For.* (305)

boom: See **crane**.

bridge (music): Music used to link two or more scenes. Often used to enhance continuity. Sometimes called *sound bridge.*

cameo: A brief role in a narrative entertainment—such as a TV show or film (fictional or documentary)—performed by a well-known person, usually a famous actor, whose name is often not included in the credits or publicity. (32)

canted framing: See **Dutch angle**.

catchlight: Light from one or more sources that is visible in the pupils of a subject's eyes. By examining the catchlight, one can often discover the number and direction of some or all of the light sources.

cel: A thin sheet of clear plastic on which images are painted for use in making some animated films. To produce such films a series of cels is superimposed on a painted background and photographed one by one.

celluloid: (1) Short for cellulose nitrate, film stock used until the early 1950s. The nitrate-based films could produce high-quality images but were subject to decomposition and combustion (illustrated by the projection room fire in the film *Cinema Paradiso*). (2) Any transparent material used as the base for motion-picture film. (3) Synonym for movie, as in "celluloid heroes."

character actor: An actor who specializes in well-defined secondary roles. Dennis Hopper, for example, is a character actor who has made a career of playing unstable and dangerous secondary characters. (30)

cinéma noir: See **film noir.**

CinemaScope: A wide-screen process introduced in 1953 made possible by filming and projecting with an anamorphic lens.

cinematic: See **filmic.**

cinematographer: Person responsible for the photography during the making of a film. Often called *director of photography* (DP).

cinematography: Motion-picture photography, including technical and artistic concern with such matters as choice of film stock, camera distance and angle, camera movement, and choice and use of lenses. (Chapter 2)

cinéma vérité: Literally "film truth." A style of documentary filmmaking developed in France during the early 1960s the aim of which was to capture events as they happened. To this end, cinéma vérité filmmakers used unobtrusive lightweight equip-ment to film and to record sound on location. Similar to the direct cinema arising at about the same time in the United States, although the French filmmakers were likely to question their subjects. Practitioners of cinéma vérité include Jean Rouch, Chris Marker, and Marcel Ophüls (as in his monumental *The Sorrow and the Pity*).

Cinerama: A wide-screen process involving the use of three synchronized projectors showing three contiguous images on a wide, curved screen. Cinerama was first used commercially in the early 1950s and was available only in selected theaters in large cities.

classical Hollywood cinema: A term used by some film scholars to describe the type of narrative film dominant throughout most of world movie history. Classical Hollywood cinema shows one or more distinct characters with clear goals who overcome many problems in reaching them. The films tend to use unobtrusive filmmaking techniques and to stress continuity of action. (235)

close-up: An image in which the subject fills most of the frame and little of the surroundings is shown. When the subject is someone's upper body, the close-up normally reveals all of the head and perhaps some of the shoulders. Close-ups are used to direct viewers' attention to texture or a detail or, probably most often, the expressions on a person's face. (95)

closure: The degree to which a story's ending supplies information about the consequences of previous major actions. A film that has closure leaves viewers with no major unanswered questions about the fate of the major characters or the consequences of their actions. (289)

colorization: The process of using computers to replace the black, white, and grays of films on videotape with color. Usually the process is done without input from the original filmmakers. (77)

compilation film: A film made by editing footage shot by others. Sometimes used in creating a documentary film—as in *Point of Order, To Die in Madrid,* and *The Atomic Café*—or an avant-garde film, as in Stan Lawder's "Intolerance (Abridged)" and Bruce Conner's "A Movie."

composition: The arrangement of settings and subjects (usually people and objects) within the frame. Like editing, composition can be an extremely expressive aspect of filmmaking. (37)

continuity (editing): Film editing that maintains a sense of uninterrupted action and continuous setting within each scene of a narrative film. (138)

contrast: In photography and cinematography, the difference between the brightest and darkest parts of an image. Low-contrast images show little difference between the intensity of the brightest part of the image and that of the darkest part. In high-contrast images, the dark parts are very dark and the bright parts very bright.

convention: In films and other creative works, a frequently used technique or content that audiences tend to accept without question. For example, it is a convention that movie audiences are allowed to hear both sides of a telephone conversation even if we see only one of the conversationalists; it is also a convention that westerns include showdowns and shoot-outs.

crane: A mechanical device used to move a camera through space above the ground or to position it at a place in the air. A shot taken from a crane gives

the camera operator many options: different distances and angles from the subject, different heights from the surface, and fluid changes in distance and angle from the subject. Sometimes called a *boom*. (112)

critical approach: A body of related ideas on how to interpret creative works. The ideas constituting a critical approach are sometimes only loosely connected and by no means agreed on by all those professing to use the same approach. Examples of critical approaches are Marxist criticism, auteur theory, feminist criticism, viewer-response criticism, reception theory, and genre criticism. (441)

criticism: Description and analysis of a work of art. Film critics describe and analyze the film experience, perhaps compare it with other film experiences and the experiences offered by other creative works, and possibly relate it to a critical approach or film theory or both. Critics also evaluate the quality of the work, explicitly or implicitly.

cross-cut: In editing, to alternate between events at different settings and often presumably transpiring at the same time. Sometimes called *intercut*. See **parallel editing**. (150)

cut: (1) The most common transition between shots, made by splicing or joining the end of one shot to the beginning of the following shot. When the two shots are projected, the transition from the first shot to the next appears to be instantaneous. (2) Version of an edited film, as in "director's cut," meaning the version the director intended. (3) To edit, as in "They cut the movie in four months." (4) To sever or splice film while editing. (130)

cutaway (shot): A shot that briefly interrupts the visual presentation of a subject to show something else. Used in many ways, such as, to reveal what a character is thinking, show reactions, maintain continuity, avoid showing sex or violence, or allow a passage of time. In *The Dead*, for example, viewers see the beginning of a dinner, a cutaway to the street outside, then back to the dinner table where the guests have finished eating.

cutting continuity (script): A written description of a finished film. Often contains detailed technical information, such as shot and scene divisions, descriptions of settings and events, dialogue, camera angles and distances, sometimes even the duration of shots and transitions between them. Extremely useful for studying a film, especially a foreign-language film, because any dialogue is usually translated more completely and more accurately than in the film's subtitles. See also **screenplay** and **shooting script**.

dailies: The positive prints usually made from a day's filming (exposed negatives). The director, cinematographer, and perhaps editor usually check the dailies to see if the recently filmed shots are satisfactory and if additional takes or shots are needed. Also called *rushes*.

deep focus: A term used widely by film critics to indicate photography in which subjects near the camera, those in the distant background, and those in between are all in sharp focus. Achieved in photography by use of wide-angle lenses or small lens aperture or both. In low illumination, fast lenses and fast film stock also help create deep focus. Filmmakers are likely to use the phrase "great depth of field" rather than "deep focus." Opposite of **shallow focus**. (90)

depth of field: The distances in front of the camera in which all objects are in focus.

desaturated color: Drained, subdued color approaching a neutral gray. Often used to create or enhance an effect, as throughout *Nosferatu the Vampyre* and the dust bowl section of *Bound for Glory*. Opposite of **saturated color**. (See Plate 2 in Chapter 2.)

designer or production designer: The person responsible for much of what is photographed in a film, including architecture, locations, sets, costumes, makeup, and hairstyles.

diffuser: (1) Material such as spun glass, granulated or grooved glass, or a silk or thin nylon stocking placed in front of the camera lens to soften the image's resolution. (2) Translucent material such as silk or spun glass placed in front of a light source to create soft light. (91)

direct cinema: A type of documentary film developed in the United States during the 1960s in which actions are recorded as they happen, without rehearsal, using a portable 16 mm camera with a zoom lens and portable magnetic sound recording equipment. Editing is minimal, and usually narration is avoided. Similar to cinéma vérité, which developed in France at about the same time, though direct cinema attempted to be less directive and intrusive. Used by such American documentary filmmakers as Robert Drew and Richard Leacock, Albert and David Maysles, Donn Pennebaker, and Frederick Wiseman and an influence on some fictional filmmakers, such as John Cassavetes. (324)

director of photography (DP): See **cinematographer**.

dissolve: See **lap dissolve**.

docudrama: A film that dramatizes occurrences from recent history by blending fact and fiction. Usually applied to TV movies that purport to be factual accounts of newsworthy people or occurrences.

documentary film: A film that presents a version of events that viewers are intended to accept not as the product of someone's imagination but primarily as fact. A documentary film may present a story (be a narrative film), or it may not. Sometimes called *nonfiction film*. (311)

Dolby sound: Trade name for a system that reduces noise on optical and magnetic sound tracks.

dolly: (1) A wheeled platform most often used to move a motion-picture camera and its operator around while filming. (2) To film while the camera is mounted on a moving dolly or wheeled platform. See **track**, definition 1. (111)

dominant cinema: See **classical Hollywood cinema**.

dub: (1) To add sound after the film has been shot. Sometimes used to supplement sounds that were recorded during filming. (2) To replace certain sounds, for example, to substitute native speaking voices for the original voices of a foreign-language film.

Dutch angle: Camera angle in which the vertical and horizontal lines of the motion-picture image are in an oblique relation to the vertical and horizontal lines of the film's frame. For example, in a Dutch angle shot, the vertical lines of a door frame will appear slanted. Often used to suggest disorientation by the subjects filmed or to disorient the viewers or both. (103)

edit: To select and arrange the processed segments of photographed motion-picture film. Editors, often in collaboration with directors, determine which shots to include, what is the most effective take (version) of each shot, the arrangement and duration of shots, and transitions between them. To edit a film is sometimes called "to cut a film." (Chapter 3)

editing table: A table with equipment used for editing or assembling a film. Advanced models allow the editor to arrange and compare different versions quickly. (123)

effects: (1) A shortened form of **sound effects**. (2) A shortened form of **special effects**. In both cases, "effects" is often represented by the abbreviation FX.

emulsion: A clear gelatin substance containing a thin layer of tiny light-sensitive particles (grains) that make up a photographic image. The emulsion and a clear, flexible base are the two main components of a piece of film. (69)

episodic plot: Story structure in which some scenes have no necessary or probable relation to each other; many scenes could be switched without strongly affecting the overall story or audience response. Episodic plots are used in *Nashville*, *Clerks*, and occasional other films. Such stories may be unified by means other than character and action, such as setting.

establishing shot: A shot, usually a long shot or extreme long shot, used at the beginning of a scene to "establish" or show where and sometimes when the action that is to follow takes place.

event: As defined by some narrative theorists, either an action by a character or person (such as Darth Vader and Obi-Wan Kenobi dueling with light sabers) or a happening (such as rain falling on the streets in *Blade Runner*). Settings, subjects, and events are the basic components of a narrative.

experimental film: See **avant-garde film**.

explicit meaning: General observation that is made within a work. In films, explicit meanings may be revealed, for example, by a narrator, a character's monologue or dialogue, a title card, a subtitle, a sign, or a newspaper headline. See also **implicit meaning** and **meaning**. (412)

exposition: Information supplied within a narrative about characters (or people) and about events that supposedly transpired before the earliest event in the plot. Exposition is intended to help the audience better understand the characters or people and make sense of the plot. (287)

expressionism: A style of art, literature, drama, and film sometimes used early in the twentieth century, especially in Germany. The primary goal of expressionism is not to depict external realities but to convey the artists' imaginations and their feelings about themselves and their subjects or to convey the characters' states of mind. As Ira Konigsberg says, in film this goal "was accomplished through distorted and exaggerated settings, heavy and dramatic shadows, unnatural space in composition, oblique angles, curved or nonparallel lines, a mobile and subjective camera, unnatural costumes and makeup, and stylized acting" (126). One of the first and most widely known examples of film expressionism is *The Cabinet of Dr. Caligari*. (17)

exterior: A scene filmed outdoors.

extreme close-up: Image in which part of the subject completely fills the frame and the background is largely or completely excluded. If the subject is someone's face, only part of it is visible. (95)

extreme long shot: Image in which the subject appears to be far from the camera. If a person is the subject, the entire body will be visible (if not obstructed by some intervening object) but very small in the frame, and much of the surroundings will be visible. Usually used only in the outdoors, often to establish the setting of the following action. (93)

eye-level angle: A camera angle that creates the effect of the audience being on the same level as the subject. (102)

eyeline match: A transition between shots in which the first shot shows a person or animal looking at something offscreen, and the following shot shows what was being looked at from the approximate angle suggested by the previous shot. (139)

fabula: A term used by the Russian Formalist school of literary theory and some later film theorists to mean the mental chronological reconstruction of the events of a nonchronological narrative. See also **plot**. (299)

fade-in: Optical effect in which the image changes by degrees from darkness (usually black) to illumination. Frequently used at the beginning of a film and sometimes at the beginning of a new sequence.

fade-out: Optical effect in which the image changes by degrees from illumination to darkness (usually black). In old movies frequently used at the conclusion of a sequence and at the end of a film as a gradual exit from its world.

fade-out, fade-in: A transition between shots in which a shot changes by degrees from illumination to darkness (usually to black); then, after a pause, the image changes from darkness to illumination. Sometimes used to indicate the passage of time. (132)

fake documentary: A film that purports to be a documentary film and seems to be so until viewers learn otherwise after the film has ended. Examples are "The War Game," supposedly a documentary about the aftermath of a nuclear attack, and *David Holzman's Diary*, which seems to be a documentary about a filmmaker's life until the final credits roll and viewers learn that the film is fictional after all. Also called *staged documentary* or *simulated documentary*. See **mock documentary**. (352)

fast cutting: Editing characterized by many brief shots, sometimes shots less than a second long. Most recent American action movies, music videos, and trailers have extensive fast cutting. Opposite of **slow cutting**. (154)

fast film (stock): Film stock that requires relatively little light for re-creation of images. Fast film, especially before the last decade or so, tends to produce grainy images. Opposite of **slow film (stock)**.

fast lens: A lens that is efficient at transmitting light and thus transmits more light than a slow lens used in the same circumstances.

fast motion: Motion in which the action depicted on the screen occurs more quickly than its real-life counterpart, as when cowboys in the early 1920s films seem to ride horses faster than any yet seen by people outside movie theaters. Achieved whenever the projector runs significantly faster than the speed at which the camera filmed, for example when the projector runs at 24 frames per second and the camera filmed at 14 frames per second. Opposite of **slow motion**.

feature (film): A film usually regarded as being at least sixty minutes long.

fill light: A soft light used to fill in unlit areas of the subject or to soften any shadows or lines made by other, brighter lights. (80)

film continuity: See **cutting continuity (script)**.

filmic: (1) That which is characteristic of the film medium or appropriate to it, such as parallel editing or the combination of editing and a full range of vocals, silence, and music. (2) Characteristics of the film medium used prominently elsewhere, as in literature, drama, or artworks. For example, a novel or play with many shifts between two locales (similar to parallel editing in a film) may be called filmic. Sometimes called *cinematic*.

film noir ("film nwahr"): Literally, "black film." A type of film first made in the United States during and after World War II, characterized by frequent scenes with dark, shadowy (low-key) lighting; (usually) urban settings; characters motivated by selfishness, greed, cruelty, ambition, and lust; and characters willing to lie, frame, double-cross, and kill or have others killed. The moods of such films tend to be embittered, depressed, cynical, or fatalistic and their plots compressed and convoluted. Examples are *Murder, My Sweet*; *Out of the Past*; and *Touch of Evil* (below). Sometimes called *cinéma noir*. (248)

film stock: Unexposed and unprocessed motion-picture film. Sometimes called *raw stock*. (68)

film theory: A related structure of abstractions about the film medium. As Dudley Andrew has pointed out in his *Major Film Theories*, a film theory often includes considerations of the properties of the medium, its techniques, its forms, and its purposes and value. See also **criticism**.

filter: A sheet of transparent plastic or glass either in a color or a shade of gray placed before or behind the camera lens to change the quality of light reaching the film.

final cut: The last version of an edited film.

fine cut: A late version of an edited film, though perhaps not yet the final cut. See **rough cut**.

fisheye lens: An extreme wide-angle lens that captures nearly 180 degrees of the area before the camera and causes much curvature of the image, especially near the edges. (89)

flashback: A shot or few shots, a brief scene, or (rarely) a sequence that interrupts a narrative to show earlier events. (297)

flashforward: A shot, scene, or sequence—though usually only a shot or two—that interrupts a narrative to show events that happen in the future. For example, *GoodFellas* begins with a few scenes that occur again late in an otherwise chronological narrative. Flashforwards are rarely used, though examples are found in *Don't Look Now* and *Heavenly Creatures*. (296)

Foley artist: Sound specialist who uses various objects such as different types of floor surfaces (usually in a Foley studio) to simulate sound effects and synchronize them with their corresponding movie images. (176)

footage: A length of exposed motion-picture film, as in "How much footage did they shoot yesterday?" and "Additional footage of Winston Churchill was recently found."

form: See **structure**.

form cut: See **match cut**.

frame: (1) A separate, individual photograph on a strip of motion-picture film. (2) The borders of the projected film or TV set or monitor. (3) To position the camera in such a way that the subject is kept within the borders of the image. (128)

frame enlargement: A photograph of an individual frame from a motion picture, blown up (enlarged) to reveal its details. Used in some publications, including this one, to illustrate certain features of a film or the film medium. Not to be confused with *publicity still*, which usually refers to a photograph taken for promotional purposes with a still camera during the making of a film. (84 top)

freeze frame: A projected yet unmoving motion-picture image, which looks like a still photograph, achieved by having the film laboratory reprint the same frame or two repeatedly. Sometimes used at the end of a film; often used at the conclusion of TV sitcoms. Used, for example, in films directed by Truffaut and in *Tom Jones* and *GoodFellas*. Many videodisc, videotape, and DVD players also make it possible to freeze a frame.

French new wave (cinema): See **new wave (cinema)**.

gauge: In filmmaking and film studies, the width of a film, as in "The gauge of most theatrical films is 35 mm." (69)

genre ("ZHAHN ruh"): A commonly recognized group of fictional films that share characteristics and conventions. Western, science fiction, horror, gangster, musical, and comedy are film genres. (236)

grain: One of the many tiny light-sensitive particles embedded in gelatin that is attached to a clear, flexible film base (celluloid). After the film is exposed to light and developed, the many grains make up a film's finished images. (68)

graininess: Rough visual texture caused when individual particles clump together in the film emulsion. Graininess also results if a film is magnified excessively during projection, as when a 16 mm print is used to fill up a large screen intended for 35 mm films. (69)

habitat of meaning: A group of people with common interests and broadly shared outlook who generate similar sets of meanings. Examples of habitats of meaning are academic film scholars, film reviewers for newspapers and magazines, and publicists for films. (447)

happening: As defined by some narrative theorists, a change brought about by a force other than a person or character, for example the rain in *Blade Runner*. In narratives, happenings and actions by characters or persons constitute events.

hard light: Light that has not been diffused or reflected before illuminating the subject. On subjects illuminated by hard light, shadows are sharp-edged and surface details are more noticeable than with soft light. Examples: midday sunlight on a clear day or unreflected and focused light from a spotlight. Opposite of *soft light*. (78)

high angle: View of a subject from above, created by positioning the camera above the subject. (101)

high contrast: Photographic image with few gradations between darkest and lightest parts of the image. Black-and-white high-contrast photos are made up mostly of blacks and whites with few shades of gray. Opposite of **low contrast**. (58 top)

high-key lighting: High level of illumination on the subject. With high-key lighting, the bright frontal key lighting on the subject prevents dark shadows. Often used to create or enhance a cheerful mood, as in many stage and movie musicals. Opposite of **low-key lighting**. (82)

homage (in French and in film studies, pronounced "oh MAZH"): A tribute to an earlier film or part of one, for example by including part of the original film or re-creating parts of it or respectfully imitating aspects of it. French new wave films often contain homages, especially to American movies. An homage may also be to a film director's distinctive style; for example, sometimes entire films, such as some directed by Brian De Palma, are seen as homages to Alfred Hitchcock. (227)

hybrid film: A film that is not exclusively fictional or documentary or avant-garde but instead shares characteristics of two or all three of the major types of films. An example is Andy Warhol's *Sleep*, which can be characterized as avant-garde documentary. (352)

ideology: See **symptomatic meaning**.

implicit meaning: A generalization a viewer makes about a film or other creative work, for example about the implications of a narrative or the significance of a symbol. See also **meaning**. (413)

independent film: (1) Film made without support or input from the dominant, established film industry. Usually an independent film is made without costly stars, director, and writer(s) and thus has a budget far below the big studio-backed movies. Sometimes called an *indie*. (2) In some publications, the phrase is used as an alternative to *avant-garde film*. (266, 269)

installation art: A temporary art exhibit, usually shown in a museum, integrating two or more arts—such as video and one of the performing arts or sculpture—into an ensemble or environment. (349)

intercut: See **cross-cut**.

intercutting: See **parallel editing**.

interior: A scene filmed indoors.

intertextuality: The relation that a form of human expression, such as a film, has to other forms of human expression, such as a journalistic article, play, or another film. Intertextuality can take the form of translation, citation, imitation, and extension. For films, intertextuality includes allusion, homage, parody, remake, prequel, sequel, and compilation film. (222)

intertitle (card): See **title card**.

iris-in: An optical effect usually functioning as a transition between shots in which the image is initially dark, then a widening opening—often a circle or an oval—reveals more and more of the next image, usually until it is fully revealed. (137)

iris-out: An optical effect usually functioning as a transition between shots in which the image is closed out as a constricting opening—usually a circle or an oval—closes down on it. Normally the iris-out ends with the image fully obliterated.

iris shot: Shot in which part of the frame is masked or obscured, often leaving the remaining

image in a circular or an oval shape. The iris shot was widely used in films directed by D. W. Griffith, Sergei Eisenstein, and Abel Gance and in many other early films but is rarely used today except as an homage. (40)

Italian neorealism: See **neorealism.**

jump cut: A discontinuous transition between shots, used to shorten the depiction of an event or to disorient viewers or both. It sometimes results unintentionally from careless editing or missing footage. Opposite of **continuity editing.** (131, 142)

key light: (1) The main light in a shot. (2) The lighting instrument used to create the main and brightest light falling on the subject. (80)

lap dissolve: A transition between shots in which one shot begins to fade out as the next shot fades in, overlapping the first shot before replacing it. Usually used between scenes or sequences to suggest a change of setting or a later time or both. Also frequently known as a *dissolve,* but *lap dissolve* conveys what happens: (over)lapping (by the second shot) and dissolving (of the first). (133)

leader: A piece of clear or opaque motion-picture film of any color that usually precedes and concludes a reel of film. It is used to decrease damage to the film print, to contain information about the reel of film, and to thread a projector. It has even been included in some avant-garde films. (336)

letterbox format: Videotape, videodisc, and DVD format that retains the film's original theatrical aspect ratio by not using a portion of the top and bottom of the analog TV or monitor screen. (42)

limbo: An indistinct setting that seems to extend to infinity. In such a setting, the background may be all black or all white, as in most shots in *THX 1138,* or all the same color. Also called *limbo background* or *limbo set.* (15)

location: Any place other than a constructed setting that is used for filming. For example, the Monument Valley region in Utah and Arizona was a location for the 1939 *Stagecoach* and other westerns, and

Schindler's List was filmed on location in Poland, not on a studio set built to resemble Poland. See **set.** (10)

long lens: See **telephoto lens.**

long shot: Shot in which the subject is seen in its entirety, and much of its surroundings are visible. See also **long take.** (93)

long take: A shot of long duration, as in the opening of *Touch of Evil, Halloween, The Player, Boogie Nights,* and *Snake Eyes.* See also **long shot.**

loose framing: Techniques in which the subject is far from the edges of the frame. Such framing can be used to give a sense of the subject's freedom of movement or of the subject being lost in or engulfed by a large environment. Opposite of **tight framing.** (45)

loose shot: See **loose framing.**

low angle: View of the subject as seen from below eye level. (103)

low contrast: Photographic image with many gradations between darkest and lightest parts of the image. In black-and-white film, low-contrast images have many shades of gray. Opposite of **high contrast.** (144)

low-key lighting: Lighting with predominant dark tones, often deep dark tones. By using little frontal fill lighting, the filmmakers can immerse parts of the image in shadows. Often used to con-

tribute to a dramatic or mysterious effect, as in many detective and crime films and in many horror films. Opposite of **high-key lighting**. (248)

magic realism: A style in a narrative in which highly improbable or impossible events are used symbolically. Probably the best-known film using magic realism is *Like Water for Chocolate*. (305)

masking: Technique used to block out part of the image (usually) temporarily. Normally used to block out extraneous details and focus viewer attention, to elongate or widen the viewed image, or to censor certain details. Used more often in early films—such as those directed by D. W. Griffith or Sergei Eisenstein—than in sound films. (40)

master-scene format: A screenplay format that describes and often numbers scenes but does not break them down into shots. A film script in the master-scene format includes descriptions of setting and action and all the dialogue but usually excludes most instructions about the actual making of the film, such as indications about the camera setups. (201)

master shot: A shot, usually made with an unmoving camera, that records an entire scene. Parts of the master shot plus other shots of the same scene may be used as the final version of the scene, or the entire master shot may be used.

match cut: Transition between two shots in which an object or movement (or both) at the end

of one shot closely resembles (or is identical to) an object or movement (or both) at the beginning of the next shot. Also known as a *form cut*. (130)

matte: A partial covering placed in front of a camera lens so that another image (usually a matte painting) can be added to the unexposed area of the image. A matte shot is made by using one or more mattes in front of the camera lens and later by filling in the unexposed areas with images from other sources. Today, matte shots are usually made entirely in a film laboratory. (13)

meaning: An observation or general statement about a subject. Meaning in films may be explicit, a generalization made within a film; implicit, a generalization a viewer makes about a film; or symptomatic, an explicit or implicit meaning that coincides with the belief of a large group of people at a particular time and place. (412)

medium close-up: Image in which the subject fills most of the frame, though not as much as in a close-up. When the subject is a person, the medium close-up usually reveals the head and shoulders. As with the close-up, medium close-ups are used to direct viewer attention to a part of something or to show facial expressions in detail. (94)

medium shot: Shot in which the subject and surroundings are given about equal importance. When the subject is a person, he or she is usually seen from the knees or waist up. (94)

Method acting: Acting in which the performer studies the background of a character in depth, immerses himself or herself in the role, and creates emotion in part by thinking of emotional situations from his or her own life that resemble those of the character. (29)

mise en scène ("meez ahn sen," with a nasalized second syllable): French for "staging." An image's setting, subject (usually people or characters), and composition (the arrangement of setting and subjects within the frame). (Chapter 1)

mix: (1) To select sound tracks of music, dialogue, and sound effects; adjust their volumes; and combine them into a composite sound track. (2) A final composite sound track consisting of a blend of other sound tracks. (168)

mock documentary: A fictional film that parodies or amusingly imitates documentary films. Because mock documentaries use some of the techniques of many documentary films — such as interviews, handheld cameras, and the absence of stars — at first viewers may think they are seeing a documentary. Examples of mock documentaries are *This Is Spinal Tap*, purportedly a documentary about an inept, aging heavy metal band, and *Fear of a Black Hat*, supposedly a documentary film about the endless problems confronted by a rap group. See also **fake documentary**. (227)

montage ("mon TAZH"): From the French *monter*, to assemble. (1) A series of brief shots used to present a condensation of time and events. In *The Godfather*, for example, the gang warfare set off after Michael kills the rival gang leader and the police captain is presented in a montage. (2) A type of editing used in some 1920s Soviet films (as in [*Battleship*] *Potemkin* and *Ten Days That Shook the World*) and advocated by some Soviet film theorists, such as the director Sergei Eisenstein. In films using this type of editing, the aim is not so much to promote the invisible continuity of a narrative favored in classical Hollywood cinema, as to suggest meanings from the dynamic juxtaposition of many carefully selected details. (3) Editing, especially in European usage. (158)

morphing: (1) Alteration of a film image by degrees by use of sophisticated computer software and multiple advanced computers. As Kevin Jackson has written, "Thanks to morphing, the director of live-action films can now achieve the kind of wild images previously reserved for the animator" (161). Used increasingly since 1988 in TV commercials and feature films, as in *Men in Black*. (2) Changing the shape of a subject. (117)

narration: Commentary about some aspect of the film or a subject in the film, usually from someone offscreen. Occasionally the narration comes from a person on-screen, as in *Zoot Suit*, where the action often freezes briefly as the character played by Edward James Olmos steps out of character and comments on some aspect of the story or the times of the story. Narration may be used in documentary films and TV commercials, fictional films, and avant-garde films. Also called *voice-over*.

narrative: A series of unified consecutive events situated in one or more settings. A narrative may be fictional or factual or a blend of the two. (275)

narrative closure: See **closure**.

narrative documentary: A film that presents mainly a factual narrative or story. Examples are *Roger & Me*, *Hearts of Darkness*, and *Hoop Dreams*. See also **docudrama**. (314)

narrator: A character, person, or unidentifiable voice that provides commentary before, during, or after the main body of a film, or a combination of these options.

negative: (1) Unexposed film stock used to record negative images. (2) Film (other than reversal film) that has been exposed but not yet processed or developed. (3) Excluding reversal film, film that has been exposed and processed; it is normally used to make (positive) prints for projection but is occasionally used in part of a finished film. In such films, negative footage may be used to suggest death, as in Cocteau's *Orpheus*, where a negative image represents the world of the dead outside a limousine. In black-and-white negatives, the light and dark areas are reversed. In color photography and cinematography, the colors of the negative image are complementary to those of the subject photographed. (229)

neorealism: A film movement in Italy at the end of and after World War II whose films are a mixture of imaginary and factual occurrences usually located in real settings and showing ordinary and believable characters caught up in difficult social and economic conditions. Other characteristics of this "new realism" are a heavy but not exclusive reliance on nonprofessional actors, available lighting,

chronological narratives, few close-ups, straight-forward camera angles and other unobtrusive film-making techniques, and natural dialogue that includes a range of dialects. Probably the best-known example of a neorealist film is *The Bicycle Thief*. (261)

new wave (cinema): A diverse group of French fictional films made in the late 1950s and early 1960s marked by the independent spirit of their directors. Like cinéma vérité, some new wave films were shot on location with portable, handheld equipment and fast film stock. Often new wave films include unconventional editing, homages, and surprising or whimsical moments. Examples of new wave cinema are the early feature films of Truffaut (such as *The 400 Blows* and, more so, *Shoot the Piano Player*), Godard (*Breathless*), and Claude Chabrol (*Handsome Serge*). (263)

nickelodeon: Literally, "five-cents theater." Small storefront movie theater popular in the United States from 1905 to roughly 1915. The successor to one-person peephole machines and the forerunner of large, elaborate movie theaters that were sometimes called "movie palaces."

nitrate: See **celluloid**, definition 1.

nonfiction film: See **documentary film**.

nonnarrative documentary: A film that presents primarily factual information without using a narrative or story. Examples abound, such as Wiseman's *High School II* and *Public Housing*, many TV commercials, and many industrial and training films. Often called simply *documentary film*. (313)

normal lens: Of all camera lenses, this one provides the least distortion of images and movements. The normal lens—50 mm on a 35 mm camera—comes closest to approximating the perceptions of the human eye. (99)

nouvelle vague: See **new wave (cinema)**.

objective camera: Camera placement that allows the viewer to see the subject approximately as an outsider would, not as someone in the film sees it. Opposite of **point-of-view shot**.

offscreen: Area beyond the frame line, which has many possible uses. For example, someone may look offscreen at something else; a shadow may be cast into the frame by something offscreen; or a sound may be heard from offscreen. See **offscreen sound**.

offscreen sound: Sound that does not derive from any on-screen source, such as an unseen dog barking or music that is not played by anyone within the frame. (190)

on-screen sound: Sound that derives from an on-screen source, such as a character viewers see and hear sneezing. (190)

optical effect: Special effect usually made with an optical printer. Examples are lap dissolves, wipes, and freeze frames.

optical printer: A device consisting of a camera and one or more projectors used to reproduce images or parts of images from already processed film. It can be used to make a matte shot, lap dissolve, wipe, and many other optical effects.

outtake: A take or shot not included in a film's final version, although occasionally outtakes are included during the ending credits, especially in a comedy, as in *The Nutty Professor* (1996). Often shots or even whole scenes or whole sequences are deleted during editing, frequently because the film's running time is too long and the excised material is judged to be expendable.

pace: A viewer's sense of a subject (such as narrative developments or factual information) being presented rapidly or slowly. A highly subjective experience that is influenced by many aspects in a film, such as the film's editing (fast cutting or slow cutting) and the frequency of new and significant subjects. (154)

panning: Effect achieved when a motion-picture camera on a stationary base pivots horizontally during filming. Used frequently to show the vastness of a setting, such as a sea, plain, mountain range, outer space, or the inside of an immense hangar. The term derives from the word *panoramic*, because with this movement the camera shows an extensive area. When the camera pans too rapidly, the resultant blurred image is called a *swish pan*. (109)

parallel editing: Editing that alternates between two or more subjects or lines of action, often suggesting that different actions are occurring simultaneously or are related to each other, but sometimes depicting subjects or events from different times. Sometimes called *cross-cutting* or *intercutting*. (150)

parody: (1) An amusing imitation of unamusing human behavior, often in the form of a creative work, part of a work, or works. For example, a parody may be of a famous narrative, part of a narrative, or genre. Examples of film parodies are *Rocky Horror Picture Show*, a musical parody of horror movies, and

Spaceballs, a parody of sci-fi movies, especially of *Star Wars*. Sometimes called a *spoof*. (2) To imitate a serious work in an amusing way. (223)

perspective: As used by painters, photographers, and cinematographers, the relative size and apparent distances between objects in a photographic image. (98)

pixillation: Animation that shows discontinuous or jerky movements. One way to create pixillation is to film a subject, usually people, for only one or a few frames; stop the camera; and change the subject's position more so than would be done for fluid animation. The same process is repeated many times until the shot is complete. (362)

plot: The structure (selection and order) of a narrative's events. (299)

plotline: A narrative or series of related events usually involving only a few characters or people and capable of functioning on its own as an entire story. Short films tend to have one plotline, but many feature films combine two or more. (291)

point-of-view shot: Camera placement at the approximate position of a character or person (or occasionally an animal) that gives a view similar to what that creature would see. It is almost as if someone in the film had a camera strapped on. Sometimes called *p.o.v. shot* or *subjective camera*. Opposite of **objective camera**. (103)

pop art: An art movement begun in the United States and Britain in the 1950s and extending into the 1960s whose subjects were everyday objects—such as soup cans, clothespins, comic strips, or celebrity images—that were presented archetypically, whimsically, or ironically.

p.o.v. shot: See **point-of-view shot**.

prequel: A narrative film made after the original film that tells a story that happens before the original. For example, *Butch Cassidy and the Sundance Kid* came out in 1969; ten years later the prequel *Butch and Sundance: The Early Days* was made. Opposite of **sequel**. (229)

preview (of a coming attraction): See **trailer**.

producer: A person in charge of the business and administrative aspects of making a film. The producer's job typically includes acquiring rights to the script and hiring the personnel to make the film. Sometimes producers influence the filmmaking process by insisting on changes at various stages of production. Producers are known under a wide variety of titles, such as executive producer and assistant producer; their actual involvement (if any) remains obscure to those outside the production.

production: The making of a film or video, which typically involves three stages: preproduction (which may include planning, budgeting, scripting, designing and building sets, and casting); production (filming or taping); and postproduction (which includes editing and mixing sound).

production still: See **publicity still**.

product placement: The practice of including commercial products, such as Coca-Cola cans or bottles, in films so that viewers can notice them. Used to promote the product and to help finance the making of the film. (61)

product plug: See **product placement**.

publicity still: A photograph taken, usually during production, to help publicize a film. (84 bottom)

pull focus: See **rack focus**.

rack focus: Changing the sharpness of focus during a shot from foreground to background or vice versa. Also known as *pull focus*. (53)

reaction shot: A shot, usually of a face, that shows someone or occasionally an animal presumably reacting to an event. Used frequently in fictional films to intensify a situation and to cue viewers how they should react. (146)

rear(-screen) projection: The process of projecting (usually moving) images on a screen behind actors seen in the foreground. Often used to create the illusion of characters in a moving vehicle.

reel: (1) A metal or plastic spool to hold film. (2) One thousand feet of 35 mm motion-picture film stored on a spool. Since the speed of projection was not standardized before the late 1920s, early films were measured in terms of the number of reels. For example, the 1925 version of *Les Misérables* reputedly consisted of thirty-two reels (each reel could take from thirteen to sixteen minutes to project). Today, a 35 mm reel of sound film takes approximately eleven minutes to project if the film has leader attached to it or ten minutes if it has no leader.

reflexive: See **self-reflexive**.

revisionist: Referring to a new interpretation or representation of a traditional subject (such as history, a narrative, or genre). *Unforgiven* is a revisionist western, for example, in that most of the film is critical of violence and killing. Opposite of **conventional**.

rough cut: An early version (usually the first complete or nearly complete version) of an edited film. See **fine cut**.

running time: The time that elapses when a film is projected. The running time of most feature films is 80–120 minutes. (301)

rushes: See **dailies**.

satire: A depiction of behavior through language, visuals, or other means that has as its aim the humorous criticism of individual or group behavior. In attempting to reach this goal, satirists often use irony or other styles, such as parody, black comedy, or surrealism. The tone of a satire may be tolerant amusement or bitter indignation or something in between.

saturated color: Intense, vivid, or brilliant color. Opposite of **desaturated color**. (See Plate 1 in Chapter 2.)

scene: A section of a narrative film that gives the impression of continuous action taking place in continuous time and space. Most fictional films are made up of many scenes—often one hundred or more—as are narrative documentary films, such as *Hearts of Darkness* and *Hoop Dreams*. (128)

scope lens: See **anamorphic lens**.

screenplay: In this book and elsewhere, the earliest version of a script, a script written before filming begins. Usually a finished film varies considerably from the original screenplay. See **shooting script** and **cutting continuity**.

self-reflexive: Characteristic of a creative work, such as a novel or film, that makes reference to or comments on itself. In self-reflexive works, one subject is the same type of creative work (for example a film about film or filmmaking) or a creative work that interrupts itself to draw attention to some aspect of itself. Examples are Luigi Pirandello's play *Six Characters in Search of an Author*, John Fowles's novel *The French Lieutenant's Woman*, and the films *Man with a Movie Camera*, *Tom Jones*, *Persona*, and various movies directed by Mel Brooks, such as *Silent Movie*. Many avant-garde films are also self-reflexive, as are occasional documentary films. (268)

sequence: A series of related consecutive scenes, perceived as a major unit of a film that conveys a story, such as the Sicilian sequence in *The Godfather*. A sequence is analogous to a chapter in a novel or an act in a play. (128)

serial: From the 1910s until the early 1950s, an action film divided into chapters or installments, one of which was shown each week in movie theaters. Typically, each chapter or installment ended with an unresolved problem; in action and adventure serials, for example, one or more of the main characters was placed in mortal danger (that's why they were often called "cliff hangers"). The *Star Wars* trilogy, the series of *Raiders* films, and other action movies have been influenced by serials. (xxiii)

set: Constructed setting where action is filmed; it can be indoors or outdoors. See also **location**. (10)

setting: The place where filmed action occurs. It is either a set, which has been built for use in a film, or a location, which is any place other than one built for use in a movie. Setting is often used to imply a time period and to reveal or enhance style, character, mood, and meanings. (10)

shallow focus: A term used widely by film critics to indicate photography with sharp focus in only a

short distance between the foreground and the background, for example, between ten and fifteen feet from the camera. Achieved in photography by using a long or telephoto lens or a large lens aperture, or both. The technique is often used to de-emphasize the background and focus attention on the subject in the foreground. Opposite of **deep focus**. Filmmakers often use the terms *restricted depth of field* or *shallow depth of field* rather than *shallow focus*, the term favored by film critics. (91)

shooting script: The version of the script used by the director and other filmmakers during filming. Because of frequent changes during filming and editing, the finished film usually varies considerably from the shooting script. See **screenplay** and **cutting continuity**.

short film: Variously defined, but usually regarded as a film of less than sixty minutes. (282)

short lens: See **wide-angle lens**.

short subject: See **short film**.

shot: (1) An uninterrupted strip of exposed motion-picture film or videotape. A shot presents a subject, perhaps even a blank screen, during an uninterrupted segment of time. (2) Filmed, as in "They shot the movie in seven weeks." (128)

simulated documentary: See **fake documentary**.

slow cutting: Edited film characterized by frequent lengthy shots. Most of the early films directed by Michelangelo Antonioni and *2001: A Space Odyssey*, for example, have much slow cutting. Opposite of **fast cutting**. (154)

slow film (stock): Film stock that requires a large camera aperture or bright light for appropriate re-creation of images. Slow film produces images with fine grain and sharp detail. Opposite of **fast film (stock)**. (71)

slow motion: Motion in which the action depicted on the screen is slower than its real-life counterpart, as when people are seen running slowly. Achieved whenever the projector runs at a slower speed than the speed at which the camera filmed. Opposite of **fast motion**.

socialist realism: A Soviet doctrine and style in force from the mid-1930s to the 1980s that decreed that all Soviet creative works, including films, must promote communism and thus the working class and must be "realistic" and thus understandable to working people. (381)

soft light: (1) Light that has been reflected before illuminating the subject. On subjects illuminated by soft light, shadows are soft-edged and surface details are less noticeable than with hard light. Soft light is available during the so-called magic hour, the time after sunset but before dark or the time of increasing light before sunrise. Another source of soft light is the light emitted through a frosted lightbulb then reflected off a cloth lamp shade. Opposite of **hard light**. (2) A type of open-faced lamp that creates soft or diffused light. (78)

sound bridge: See **bridge**.

sound dissolve: A transition in which the first sound begins to fade out as the next sound fades in and overlaps the first sound before replacing it. (188)

sound effect: A sound in film other than vocals or music that is usually added after filming is completed. Three examples of sound effects are a door slamming, a dog barking, and thunder. (172)

sound stage: A permanent enclosed area for shooting film and recording sound, especially useful be-cause its controlled environment allows for filming and sound recording without unwanted sights and sounds.

Soviet montage: See **montage**, definition 2.

special effect: Shot unobtainable by live-action cinematography. Includes split screen (one subject in part of the image, another subject in another part of the image); most superimpositions; freeze frame; and many others.

spoof: See **parody**.

staged documentary: See **fake documentary**.

standard aspect ratio: Until the 1950s, the usual shape of motion-picture screens throughout the world and still the usual shape of analog TV screens. In the standard aspect ratio, the width to height ratio is 4:3 or 1.33:1. (38)

Steadicam: A lightweight and portable mount for holding a motion-picture camera that provides for relatively steady camera movements during hand-held shots. Especially useful for filming in rugged terrain or tight quarters. (112)

still: See **publicity still**.

stock footage: Footage stored for possible duplication and use in other films. Often stock footage is of subjects and locations difficult, impossible, or costly to film anew, such as warfare or the Paris background in the flashback section of *Casablanca*.

stop-motion cinematography: The process of filming a subject for only one or a few frames, stopping

the camera and changing something in the mise en scène, then filming again, and repeating this process many times. May be used to create a continuous movement, as in most animated films made with stop-motion cinematography, or discontinuous or jumpy movement, as in pixillation. See **time-lapse cinematography**.

story: See **narrative**.

storyboard: A series of drawings of each shot of a planned film or video narrative, usually accompanied by brief descriptions.

story time: The amount of time covered in a film's narrative or story. For example, if a film's earliest scene occurs on a Sunday and its latest scene takes place on the following Friday, then the story time is six days. Nearly always the story time for a movie is much longer than its running time. (301)

straight cut: See **cut**, definition 1.

structure: The selection and arrangement of the parts of a whole. In a film that conveys a story, "structure" can be thought of as the selection and arrangement of scenes or sequences. In other films, structure refers to the selection and arrangement of discernible parts. In a documentary film, for example, the structure might consist of the selection and arrangement of interviews and film clips. Sometimes called *form*. (276)

style: The manner of presenting a subject in a creative work. Possible styles for fictional films are irony, farce, fantasy, surrealism, magic realism, and parody. In film studies, style also includes a consideration of the filmmakers' techniques. The style of many films directed by Alfred Hitchcock, for example, includes flashes of black comedy, frequent point-of-view shots, occasional unconventional camera angles, considerable camera movement (especially tracking shots), experimentation with filmmaking techniques, and frequent use of surprise and suspense. Style is sometimes contrasted with content, though most theorists argue that the two are not exclusive but symbiotic. (304)

subjective camera: See **point-of-view shot**.

superimposition: Two or more images photographed or printed on top of each other. Can be achieved in the camera during filming or, more often, by using an optical printer. At the beginning of many movies, the credits are superimposed on the opening action. During a lap dissolve, one image is momentarily superimposed on another. Sometimes, as in several scenes in *Drugstore Cowboy*, two or more shots may be superimposed to suggest a character's emotional or physical instability. The technique is often used in avant-garde films but rarely in documentary films. (140)

surrealism: A movement in 1920s and 1930s European art, drama, literature, and film in which an attempt was made to portray or interpret the workings of the subconscious mind as manifested in dreams. Surrealism is characterized by an irrational, noncontextual arrangement of material. The surrealist movement has been especially influential on some avant-garde filmmakers, such as Luis Buñuel ("Un Chien Andalou" and *L'Age d'Or*) and Jean Cocteau, especially his "The Blood of a Poet." It has also had an impact on some music videos.

swish pan: Effect achieved when a motion-picture camera (usually on a stationary base) pivots horizontally during filming so rapidly that the resultant image is blurred. Occasionally used within a shot; sometimes used as a transition between shots. Sometimes called *zip pan*. (267)

symbol: Anything perceptible that has significance or meaning beyond its usual meaning or function. Thus, depending on the contexts, a sound, object, person, word (including a name), color, action, or something else perceived by the senses may all function as symbols. In *Citizen Kane*, for example, many viewers believe that the glass paperweight Kane drops at the beginning of the film and his two sleds not only are objects serving their usual functions but also suggest meanings. (421)

symptomatic meaning: Meaning stated or, much more often, suggested by a film that is the same as a society's belief or value. For example, *Fatal Attraction*, which first appeared in 1987, suggests that casual sex can be dangerous, even deadly, and that belief is symptomatic of the growing concerns in late 1980s America about casual sex and the spread of AIDS and other sexually transmitted diseases. Sometimes called *ideology*. See also **meaning**. (438)

take: A version of a shot. More than one take of each shot is usually made because of some mistake or to improve on the previous take(s). Different takes of each shot are usually made in shooting theatrical films, though often not TV movies. One of the major jobs of the editor is to select the most effective take of each shot to be used in the finished film.

technique: Any aspect of filmmaking, such as the choices of sets, lighting, sound effects, music, and editing. How well techniques are selected and used is a strong determinant of a film's style, impact, and success.

telephoto lens: A lens that makes subjects appear closer and larger than a normal lens does. With its long barrel, a telephoto lens resembles a telescope. Not to be confused with a **zoom lens**, which is capable of varying by degrees from telephoto range to normal, sometimes even to wide-angle range, while the camera is filming. (99 bottom)

theme: See **meaning**.

THX sound: A multispeaker sound system developed by Lucasfilm and used in selected motion-picture theaters to increase frequency range, audience coverage, and dialogue intelligibility while decreasing low bass distortion.

tight framing: A shot in which the subject is close to the edges of the frame. Uses for such framing include giving a sense of the subject's confinement or lack of mobility. Opposite of **loose framing**. (16)

tilting: Effect achieved when a camera on a stationary base pivots vertically during filming. Often used as a way of slowly revealing information, as when we first see someone's shoes, then the camera tilts to reveal the wearer, as is done memorably near the beginning of *Strangers on a Train*. See also **panning**.

time-lapse cinematography: The process of filming the same subject one frame at a time at regularly spaced intervals, for example one frame every thirty minutes or one frame every twenty-four hours. When the processed film is projected at normal speed, any movement that was photographed is much accelerated, perhaps even blurred. Can be used to show the basics of a long process in a brief time, such as the building of a house or the budding of a flower, or for some other purpose, as in *Koyaanisqatsi*, in which time-lapse cinematography was used to convey the speeded-up quality of modern urban life. See **stop-motion cinematography**. (355 bottom)

tinting: The process of dyeing a film with color. Sometimes used before the adoption of color film stock in the late 1930s. In such movies, often each scene or sequence would be tinted one color. For example, blue was often used for night scenes or scenes set in the cold, and red for scenes of violence, danger, or passion or for scenes set in hot settings. (74)

title card: A card or thin sheet of clear plastic on which is written or printed information in a film. Before the late 1920s, title cards were used to give credits, exposition, dialogue, thoughts, descriptions of actions not shown, the numbered parts of a movie, and other types of information. Since the late 1920s, they have been used less often but they can be seen, for example, in *The Shining* and *Raging Bull*; in some documentary films, such as *The Thin Blue Line*, *Hearts of Darkness*, and *Hoop Dreams*; and in occasional avant-garde films.

track: (1) To film while the camera is moving. Sometimes the camera is mounted on a cart set on tracks; sometimes it is handheld and the camera operator moves or is moved about in a wheelchair or on roller skates or by some other means. In some publications, *to track* and *to dolly* are used interchangeably. (2) A film sound track, a narrow band on the film that contains recorded optical or magnetic sound. (112)

trailer: A brief compilation film shown in motion-picture theaters, before some videotaped movies, or on TV to advertise a movie or a video release. Sometimes called a *preview* or a *preview of a coming attraction*.

treatment: A condensed written description of the content of a proposed film, often written in paragraphs and without dialogue.

underground film: See **avant-garde film**.

vocal: Any sound made with the human voice, including speech, grunts, whimpers, screams, and countless other sounds. Along with silence, music, and sound effects, one of the components of the typical film sound track. (170)

voice-over: See **narration**.

wide-angle lens: A camera lens (significantly shorter than 50 mm on a 35 mm camera) used, for example, to photograph more of the sides of a setting than is possible with a normal lens. (99)

wide-screen film: Any film with an aspect ratio noticeably greater than 1.33:1 (a shape wider than that of an analog TV screen). Most current films shown in U.S. commercial theaters have a wide-screen aspect ratio of 1.85:1. Wide-screen film formats have been tried out since nearly the beginning of cinema but have been used in most theaters only since the 1950s. (38)

wipe: A transition between shots, usually between scenes, in which it appears that a shot is pushed off the screen by the next shot. Many kinds of wipes are possible; perhaps the most common is a vertical line (sharp or blurred) that moves across the frame from one side to the other, seemingly "wiping away" a shot and replacing it with the next one. (134)

zip pan: See **swish pan**.

zoom: To use a zoom lens to cause the image of the subject to either increase in size as the area being filmed seems to decrease (zoom in) or to decrease in size as the area being filmed seems to increase (zoom out).

zoom lens: A camera lens with variable focal lengths; thus it can be adjusted by degrees during a shot so that the size of the subject and the area being filmed seem to change. If the zooming continues long enough, the lens assumes the properties of a telephoto lens or normal lens or wide-angle lens. Zooming in or zooming out from the subject approximates tracking or dollying toward or away from it, though the trained eye will notice differences. In zooming, the camera appears to move in or away from a flat surface and the depth of field changes, whereas in tracking or dollying, viewers get a sense of contour and depth and the depth of field remains unchanged. The zoom lens is often used in direct cinema and cinéma vérité but has also been used in many other films since the 1960s. Throughout nearly all of the avant-garde film "Wavelength," the camera imperceptibly zooms in on a photograph on the background wall.

Acknowledgments (continued from p. iv)

Jacobs, Ken. Excerpt from letter to William H. Phillips, May 7, 1998. Reprinted by permission of Ken Jacobs.

Kuchar, George. Excerpt from letter to William H. Phillips, January 8, 1998. Reprinted by permission of George Kuchar.

Linson, Art. "The $75 Million Dollar Difference" from *The New York Times Magazine*, November 16, 1997. Copyright © 1975 by The New York Times. Reprinted by permission.

The Motion Picture Association of America. Excerpts from "The Production Code of the Motion Picture Producers and Directors of America, 1930–1934." Reprinted by permission of the Motion Picture Association of America.

Phillips, William. "Excerpts from an Interview with Errol Morris." Reprinted by permission of Errol Morris, Fourth Floor Productions.

Index